The Encyclopedia of Crafts

A to E
VOLUME 1

The Encyclopedia of Crafts

LAURA TORBET, Editor

Gary Tong, Illustrator

CHARLES SCRIBNER'S SONS • NEW YORK

Library of Congress Cataloging in Publication Data
Main entry under title:

The encyclopedia of crafts.

    1. Handicraft—Dictionaries. I. Torbet, Laura.
TT9.S37   745'.03'21   80-13431
ISBN 0-684-16409-4   Set
ISBN 0-684-16661-5   Volume 1
ISBN 0-684-16662-3   Volume 2
ISBN 0-684-16663-1   Volume 3

1 3 5 7 9 11 13 15 17 19 C/V 20 18 16 14 12 10 8 6 4 2

Printed in the United States of America

81-1738

staff

Editor: Laura Torbet

Illustrator: Gary Tong

Associate Editors: Luthera Stone, Adele Hudson

Copy Supervisors: Jane Robbins, Michael Harkavy

Illustration Supervisors: Diane Tong, Mark Sahim

Assistant Editors: E. M. Hatton, Paul L. Hecht

Editorial Staff: Demetre Bove, E. M. Hatton,
                            Donna Rothchild, Paul Hecht,
                            Patricia Holtz, Kay Hutton,
                            Christina Birrer, Kalia Lulow,
                            Glenn Robbins

contributors

ROBERT ADZEMA
Basketry, Woodworking

JOHN CROSS
*Candlemaking, Kites,
Mosaics, Tincraft*

LINDA CROSS
*Beadwork, Block Printing, Découpage,
Fabric Printing, Leather, Papercraft,
Papier Mâché, Stenciling, Miscellaneous*

THOMAS GENTILLE
Jewelry

ENID HOFSTED
Stained Glass

JOLYON HOFSTED
Ceramics

MABLEN JONES
Metalworking, Plastics

DAVID KARLIN
Enameling, Gemcutting

JEAN RAY LAURY
*Batik and Tie Dye, Quilts, Stitchery
(including Appliqué and Patchwork),
Toys (including Dollmaking)*

MARY WALKER PHILLIPS
Crochet, Knitting, Macramé

RICHARD SCHMITZ
*General Art and Design, Glass,
Silkscreen*

LUTHERA STONE
*Bookbinding, Amber,
Bone, Coral, Horn, Ivory, Jet,
Shell Carving*

LYDIA VAN GELDER
Lacemaking, Tatting

ERICA WILSON
Crewelwork, Embroidery, Needlepoint

NELL ZNAMIEROWSKI
*Rugmaking, Spinning and
Dyeing, Weaving*

introduction

A number of years ago people started making things by hand again. What started out slowly, as a way to get back to nature or to avoid the sameness (and often the shoddiness) of mass-produced goods, soon mushroomed into a major crafts boom that had just about everyone making something—tie-dyed T-shirts, beaded necklaces, needlepoint pillows, leather belts, plastic-dipped flowers. An inundation of craft fairs, hobby shops, craft schools, kits, workshops, lectures, magazines, galleries, and exotic new tools and supplies followed in swift pursuit.

A decade later the dust has settled somewhat; the faddishness of the crafts movement has passed. What remains seems to be hundreds of thousands of people who choose to spend their increased leisure time making things by hand for the pure pleasure of it. Some of these people pursue a single craft at the hobbyist level. Others have learned new trades and earn their living at their craft. Still others have found that their interest has escalated into more complex areas or crafts such as glassblowing, glaze chemistry, or weaving. Today crafts are often combined in a mixed-media approach and are fast attaining the status of fine art. Combine the growing legions of craftspeople with the proliferation of new tools, techniques, and materials and you get a tremendous need for information.

This is where the *Encyclopedia of Crafts* comes in. It will fulfill a long-standing need for a single source reference, an adjunct to single-craft books for the contemporary craftsperson, a jumping-off point for further research into individual crafts, an aid to the mixed-media craftsperson. These volumes will enable the reader to put a name to an old family quilt pattern, identify a stitch in a sampler, a toy from one's childhood, or the brand name of a special dye.

The *Encyclopedia of Crafts* covers nearly fifty crafts. There are over 12,000 extensively cross-referenced entries and 2,500 original illustrations. It is hoped that this encyclopedia will find its place in the library of everyone who has ever so much as made a paper airplane, and prove a valuable basic tool to professional and amateur alike.

guide to the use of the encyclopedia

1. *Entry word or phrase.* The entry word or phrase is printed in boldface sans serif type.

▼

> **mold.** Candlemaking. Any container or receptacle that will not melt or break when subjected to the relatively high

2. *Craft classification.* The craft or crafts to which the entry pertains is printed in sans serif type, in alphabetical order immediately following the entry word or phrase.

▼

> **machine appliqué.** Quilts. Stitchery. The attaching or applying of one fabric to another with sewing machine

3. *Synonyms, variations, abbreviations.* This information will be found enclosed in parentheses immediately following the craft classification(s).

▼

> **machine satin stitch.** Quilts. Stitchery. (Also called closed satin stitch, closed zigzag stitch, machine appliqué stitch).

4. *The entry.* The text of the entry is printed in roman type.

▼

> **mosaic stitch.** Needlepoint. The mosaic stitch worked horizontally consists of three small diagonal stitches, one short, one long, one short, forming a square unit. It has a firm backing and resembles small mosaic tiles when worked up. It is very effective when worked in geometric

5. *Main entry.* The main entry for each craft is printed in sans serif capital letters with a ruled line above and below. This entry is often broken down into subheadings and contains general information about the craft.

Metalworking includes **bench work,** sheet-metal work, art work, **forging, heat treatment,** metal **casting, welding,** and the use of tools and machines for metal construction. The

6. *Cross-reference system.* A word or phrase printed in boldface roman type has a separate entry under the same craft classification.

   a. "See." An entry may consist of no more than a direct cross-reference to another entry.

▼

machine direction. Bookbinding. See **grain.**

   b. "Also see." At the end of many entries, cross-references to other entries that contain supplementary or related information are listed alphabetically. Those cross-references that refer to the main entry of a craft are capitalized and appear at the end of such a list.

Apply bleach only in a well-ventilated room. Discard any unused solution immediately. Also see **finish** and **Woodworking: Finishing.**

▲

   c. A boldface word or phrase within the text of an entry indicates that this word appears as a separate entry.

mold. Glasswork. The metal or wooden form used to shape blown **glasswork.** Often the mold has two hinged sections

▲

7. *Illustrations.*

   a. The fact that there is an illustration relating to an entry is indicated by the phrase "See ill." This phrase follows the body of the relevant entry immediately before any "Also see" references or occurs at the end of a subhead within a main entry.

▼

should be kept oiled and greased. See ill. Also see **faceting unit, point carver, slabbing saw,** and **Gemcutting: Safety Precautions.**

   or

frequently with tallow, soap, a soap-and-oil mixture, or a commercially prepared compound for lubricating. See ill.

▲

   b. Boldface lower-case letters in parentheses within the body of an entry correspond to captioning in an accompanying illustration.

The piece (or split) mold is made in two or more sections **(d.).** A carefully planned piece mold permits making cast-

The
Encyclopedia
of Crafts

A axis. Gemcutting. See **C axis.**

abaca. Toys. See **manila rope.**

abalone. Jewelry. A seashell with a layered iridescent interior that can be carved or cut and used for **inlay.**

abalone. Shell Carving. A large, ear-shaped edible marine gastropod, genus Haliotis, with a pink and blue-green iridescent shell that is used for carving, **inlay,** and jewelry. Also see **cowrie, helmet, nacre** and **Shell Carving: Shell.**

abbreviations. Tatting. See **Tatting: Abbreviations.**

Abcite. Plastics. See **acrylic.**

abrading tools. Woodworking. See **woodcarving tools.**

abrasive. Amber Carving. See **Amber Carving: Finishing.**

abrasive. Enameling. See **cleaning metal, polishing, stoning.**

abrasive. Gemcutting. A natural or synthesized material used to wear away the surface of gems. Abrasives are usually ground to a powdery form and used wet. Their strength depends on the size and **hardness** of the abrasive particles. Size is measured in **microns,** or it is graded by the number of openings per square inch in the finest screen through which the particles will pass; this number represents the grit (also called mesh or sieve size). Roughly, a 10 grit abrasive has particles averaging 2,000 microns in size. Thus, 100 grit converts to 149 microns; 400 grit to 37 microns. Hardness is measured from one to ten on the **Mohs' scale of hardness.** The finest abrasives are called polishing compounds. They are used on **laps,** or on leather, felt, and canvas buffs.

Silicon carbide, accidentally discovered at the beginning of the century by a chemist experimenting on the production of artificial diamonds, has hardness of 9½. It is used in loose powder form for **tumbling,** lapping, carving, and drilling. Grits ranging from coarse (46, 60, 80 and 100) to medium (180 and 220) are used for rough shaping; 320, 400, and 600 are used for smoothing the work; and grits rated F, FF, FFF, FFFF, and XF (equivalent to 1,000, 1,200, 1,600, 2,000, and 3,200 grits) are used for **polishing.** Silicon carbide is bonded into **grinding wheels, sanding cloths,** and **carving points.** Carborundum is a brand name for silicon carbide.

Alumina (also called levigated alumina, ruby powder, sapphire power) is a synthetic **corundum** with hardness of 9. It is available in grits similar to silicon carbide and used specifically for polishing and fine grinding.

Boron carbide (a synthetic abrasive) is slightly harder than silicon carbide and can be used for lapping very hard gems.

Emery (a natural abrasive) is a derivative of black corundum with hardness of 9. Emery is used as an abrasive and polishing agent in loose grits, bonded into grinding wheels, or glued to paper. Emery is seldom used in its sandpaper form in gemcutting because the paper is not waterproof.

Garnet is a natural gem material with hardness of 7½. It may be crushed and used in sandpaper. Sometimes it is used for lapping gems.

Diamond is the best abrasive because it is the hardest material, has sharp-edged particles and **fractures,** and can be pressed into soft metals. Flawed crystals (called borts and carbonados) are cryptocrystalline diamond and very similar to synthetic products; these are crushed and graded in a variety of sizes. Whole carbonados are used in drill bits and **wheel dressers.** Coarse grits (16–80) are used for **slabbing saw** blades and diamond grinding wheels; finer grits (80–400) are used for smaller saw blades, **tube drills,** and carving points. Diamond powders are used on laps for grinding and polishing **facets** on gems; they are carefully graded from 30 to ¼ microns (equivalent to 600–100,000 grit) and are available in oil and paste compounds.

Linde A (synthetic alumina, hardness 9) has an approximate micron size of .3 (64,000 grit). It is an excellent polishing agent and is sometimes added to other compounds to improve their efficiency.

Tripoli (natural abrasive, hardness 5½) is derived from the **opal**ized skeletons of fossilized sea creatures (diatoms). Tripoli is used as a preliminary polishing agent.

Tin oxide (synthetic abrasive, hardness 6½; also called putty powder) is a pure white polishing compound widely used for polishing faceted stones, as well as most gem material, on a tin lap.

Cerium oxide is used to polish optical glass and is very effective on **quartz** gems on an acrylic lap. Cerium oxide is more expensive than tin oxide.

Chrome oxide (hardness 5½) is a green powder available dry in 15 micron grade, and in a water solution in 1–½ micron grades (equivalent to 1,200–60,000 grit). Chrome oxide readily penetrates crevices in gem material and is hard to remove.

Rouge is iron oxide ranging in color from crocus black to reddish rouge. It is similar to **hematite** and is used for polishing metals and some softer gem material.

abrasive. Jet Carving. The abrasives used to smooth and polish **jet** are emery powder, **rottenstone**, jeweler's rouge, **crocus** powder, **tin oxide,** and **charcoal** powder. Also see **Jet Carving: Polishing.**

abrasive. Jewelry. Materials of natural or synthetic origin used to wear away metal to refine forms, sharpen tools, remove file marks and other imperfections in preparation for **buffing,** or produce scratched **matte** finishes on jewelry. Abrasives come in a variety of grades; in powder, sheet, strip, belt, or drum form; mounted on cloth or paper backings; bonded into variously shaped **grinding wheels** and on to assorted implements to aid in **hand polishing;** and impregnated into **buffing compounds, cutting compounds, greaseless compounds,** and **bobbing compounds.** The various abrasives used in jewelry making may be referred to by the name of the abrasive followed by the method of application; i.e., **emery stick, crocus cloth, carborundum paper, steel wool.** Also see **Arkansas oilstone, lapping.**

abrasive blasting. Metalworking. See **sandblasting.**

abrasive compounds. Jewelry. See **bobbing compound, buffing compound, cutting compound, greaseless compound.**

abrasive paper. Découpage. See **sandpaper.**

abrasive paper. Stained Glass. Wet or dry sandpaper used for removing the rough edges from cut pieces of **glass** rods. Wet the paper and rub the glass edge with it. After using the paper let it dry; it can be used again. Using this paper dry shortens its life.

abrasives. Metalworking. Plastics. Woodworking. A material used in **grinding** and **polishing.**

In metalworking there are two classes of abrasives: natural and synthetic. Most abrasives are manufactured or mined in chunk form and crushed into particles in sizes to pass through screens with different size openings. The size of the opening determines the mesh number: 36 holes per inch in the screen gives an abrasive grit of 36. This number may go up to 400. The smaller the grain size, the higher the number on the abrasive. The abrasives may be sold in particle form or bonded to a piece of paper or sanding belt, or embedded in a grinding wheel.

There are eight natural abrasives. Corundum (also called natural emery) is a mined mineral containing 75–95% aluminum oxide used for polishing metals. It may be purchased in 9″ × 11″ sheets, rolls 3″ wide, and on discs.

Emery is a black mineral containing corundum, iron oxide, and aluminum oxide. It is named for Cape Emeri on the Greek island of Naxos, where it was mined in ancient times. It is better used for polishing metal rather than for cutting or grinding. Avoid using emery on **pewter** because the particles may become embedded in the fiber **mallet** and ruin the metal surface. Use it only for leveling bottom edges when using it on pewter objects.

Flint, a form of quartz, is one of the oldest common abrasives. It is used on common sandpaper for abrading both metals and wood, but is not very durable.

Garnet, a natural mineral usually purchased bonded to paper or cloth, is used for polishing and sanding metals and wood. The particles fracture when used so that new points are exposed, keeping the paper sharp for longer work periods than flint.

Pumice is a fine porous volcanic glass purchased in powder or lump form used for cleaning and polishing metals and finishing or smoothing wood. On wood pumice is used with oil or water (and used to remove imperfections and produce a gloss). It comes in grits ranging from #2 and #1 coarse to #2-0 fine and FF very fine. A medium-fine 2-0 pumice stone is recommended for average **rubbing.** Scotch stone (also called Water-of-Ayr stone) is finer than pumice and is used for cleaning and finishing metals. The solid form of this mineral is used as a **sharpening stone.**

Tripoli is a form of amorphous silica used for polishing metals. It is the only abrasive recommended for polishing the outside surface of **pewter.**

Whiting is a powdered chalk, or calcium carbonate, used for the final hand polishing of metals, especially soft ones such as pewter, and also after **antiquing** metals so as not to remove their **patina.**

The first synthetic abrasives were invented in the late nineteenth century. Aluminum oxide (also called aloxite) is composed of fused bauxite (an aluminous clay), coke, and iron filings. It was compounded in 1897 and is considered the toughest and most durable, although not the hardest, abrasive. It is usually sold glued to various backings such as paper, cloth, fiber, and combinations of these materials. Use it on both wood and metals. Use corundum aloxite for smoothing edges only, not the surfaces of metals. A flexible abrasive file used only with aloxite can be used for filing outside seams of joined sheet-metal objects. Aluminum oxide cloth or paper is recommended for pewter finishing because the particles do not become embedded in the soft metal. Grade #320 medium-fine is useful for pewterwork.

Use grade 000 **carborundum** for polishing nonferrous metal. It will not remove deep scratches. Crocus cloth is a fine abrasive cloth containing red iron oxide often used for final polishing of metals by hand. Rouge (also called jeweler's rouge) is an abrasive chemically prepared from iron oxide.

Silicon carbide (also called wet-or-dry sandpaper) was the first synthetic abrasive made and is still one of the hardest and sharpest. It is composed of coke, sand, salt, and sawdust heated to a high temperature, and is used to grind **cast iron, bronze,** and both tough and soft nonferrous metals. It fractures during use, creating new cutting points. Silicon carbide is most frequently available on cloth and paper backings. It may be used with water or dry on woods, metals, and plastics. It comes in grades from fine (220) to extra fine (600).

Steel wool is woolly shavings of steel compacted together in a pad or mass, used to clean metal before **soldering.** It comes in seven grades from 4-0, the finest, to three, the coarsest. In woodworking, steel wool is used to remove small surface imperfections during finishing. Use 2-0 or 3-0 for a satin smooth finish. Use greaseless steel wool when possible because the grease or oil in some types of steel wool affects the flow of solder on the metal seam. In plastics the abrasives used in **finishing** include **pumice,** wet-or-dry or garnet sandpapers, **jeweler's rouge, tripoli,** or any of the various brands of **polishing compounds** that wear away or cut the surface.

In woodworking, sandpaper is used for the smoothing and **finishing** of wood and wood finishes. It may be obtained in four types of abrasive coatings: flint, garnet, aluminum oxide, and silicon carbide. Sandpaper, besides coming in different materials and grades, comes in rectangular sheet form for hand sanding; sanding belts for **belt sanders;** and circular discs for **disc sanders.**

Aluminum oxide sandpaper, sometimes known as production sandpaper, is coated electrically with aluminum oxide. It is extra long-lasting, cuts quickly and is grayish in color. It makes excellent finishing sandpaper for surfaces of **shellac, varnish,** or **lacquer.** It comes in grits from medium coarse (100) to very fine (320A).

Flint sandpaper is of quartz of silica and is recognized by its yellowish color. Because it wears quickly, and is inexpensive, it is used best for removing old finishes that clog sandpaper easily.

Garnet sandpaper is an economical, strong, durable paper that uses garnet as its abrasive coating. It is reddish-brown in color and comes in a wide grit range from #2, very coarse, to #7-10, very fine. It can be used for rough sanding or **finishing.**

Carborundum is a silica carbide-type abrasive used in **grinding wheels, sharpening stones,** and sandpaper.

Rottenstone is a very fine slate powder used with oil or water and rubbed on a finished surface to produce a very high gloss.

Rubbing compound is an abrasive paste containing wax and pumice or other abrasives. It is available in a number of grades from coarse to fine. Although it produces a grime that is relatively difficult to remove, it is excellent for rubbing down a lacquer finish.

Also see **sanding tools** and **Metalworking: Finishing, Plastics: Finishing, Woodworking: Finishing.**

absorption. Ceramics. The ability of materials such as clay and plaster to take up liquid. Also see **adsorption.**

abstract. (Also called nonrepresentational, nonobjective.) A term to describe designs or paintings that tend less to represent features of the physical world than to stylize all form as closer to geometrical shapes and straight lines.

acacia gum. See **gum arabic.**

acanthus. Quilts. A semistylized leaf motif common in quilts based on the flowing lines of the acanthus leaf. The motif is used in both **appliqué** and **quilting,** particularly in traditional work. Also see **Quilts: Quilting.**

accelerator. Plastics. (Also called activator, promotor.) A chemical added to **resin** to increase the speed of **curing,** or to promote curing at lower than ideal temperatures. It works only in the presence of a **catalyst.** Never mix an accelerator and a catalyst together directly; an explosion may result. Use only recommended accelerators and catalysts for each specific resin. Also see **Plastics: Casting.**

accordion folding. Papercrafts. See **accordion pleating.**

accordion pleat. Batik and Tie-dye. A series of equal folds in **fabric.** The surface of the material makes an up-and-down **zigzag.** The accordion pleat is an excellent **folding** method in **tie-dye** to make **chevrons, diamonds,** and zigzag patterns.

Small parallel folds of equal size are made beginning at one end of the fabric and flipping the fabric after each fold. (**a.**). Folding is continued until all fabric is pleated (**b.**). See ill.

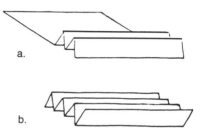

a.

b.

accordion pleating. Papercrafts. (Also called accordion folding.) The folding of paper at regular intervals into zigzag folds to give stability to the form and to provide regular patterns of light and shadow. The depth of the folds is a function both of the distance between folding lines and the degree to which the folds are extended, or pulled open. To form an accordion pleat, draw lines across a sheet of paper at regular intervals, then fold on the lines, turning the paper over on alternate folds. Heavy paper will require **scoring** before folding. For best results, rule and score alternate lines on one side, then turn the sheet over and rule and score lines between the lines already scored on the other side. The folds also may be done freehand by folding the paper at various angles and widths. See ill.

Accordion pleating

accumulating bar. Macramé. A smooth, solid row of **double half hitch**es, often made at the end of a piece.

Over the knot-bearing cord, tie a double half hitch, using the first **cord.** Pick up the second cord and tie a double half hitch, incorporating the first cord with the knot-bearing cord. Continue across the row in this manner. See ill. Also see **finishing.**

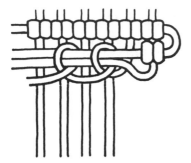

Accumulating bar

acetate. Batik and Tie-dye. Stitchery. Toys. A **manmade fiber** similar to **rayon.** Acetate is partly **cellulose fiber** and partly chemical fiber. Acetate accepts only its own dyes. Acetate is also produced in forms other than **fiber**s or strands; among these are clear and colored **acetate sheet**s.

acetate. Plastics. See **cellulose acetate.**

acetate. Stained Glass. A transparent sheet of plastic used for the preliminary design for a stained-glass window. The design is painted on acetate with special plastic paints to create an exact replica of the proposed stained-glass window. This design method is very time consuming.

acetate glue. Toys. A clear, fast-drying, waterproof cement or household **glue,** sometimes sold as **airplane glue.** It is used on a great variety of materials. The **solvent** for acetate glue is **acetone,** or nail polish remover. Acetate glue has an unpleasant odor and is toxic, so care must be taken to read and follow directions on the containers and to avoid breathing the vapors. It is available at art and hobby shops, and at hardware or variety stores. Also see **household cement.**

acetate rayon. Stitchery. See **rayon.**

acetate sheet. Puppets. Quilts. Stitchery. Toys. (Also called clear acetate.) A sheet of clear plastic available in art and stationery stores. The sheets are produced in various sizes and gauges. **Acetate**s are sometimes used to create transparent areas in **stitchery.** It is a good safe material sometimes used to simulate glass in **toy** cars or toy buildings. Acetate sheets are also available in clear colors. Also see **acrylic plastic sheet.**

acetic acid. Batik and Tie-dye. Dyeing. Stained Glass. A colorless liquid chemical compound added to the **dyebath** as the **assistant** in dyeing silks and woolens. Photographers' **glacial acetic acid** may be used. White vinegar is 5% acetic acid dilute solution. About one-half cup of white vinegar equals 2 tablespoons of acetic acid.

In dyeing, acetic acid is used to soften or neutralize alkaline water and is also used as a solvent for **dyestuff**s. Acetic acid can aid in **mordanting** by acidifying a **dyebath** or it can act as the mordant when used in conjunction with salt.

In stained glass work, acetic acid is used in a mixture of **gum arabic,** water, and glass paint that fixes the layer of paint so that other washes of paint may be applied over it without smearing. Also see **firing, painting on glass.**

acetone. Batik and Tye-dye. Plastics. Stained Glass. Toys. A clear, colorless, volatile, flammable liquid. It dissolves various substances, including gums, oils, resins, and fats, including **wax.** The chemical is used commercially in paint and varnish removers and in some polishes and **lacquer**s. Both nail polish and nail polish remover contain a large percentage of acetone. Some rayon materials will dissolve if touched by it. Caution should be used to avoid any prolonged breathing of the vapors.

When working with plastics, do not use acetone on your skin to remove resin. The acetone will dilute the resin, causing it to further penetrate into the pores.

Acetone is used in **dalle de verre** for cleaning glass thoroughly before setting it into **epoxy resin** or **concrete.** Acetone is spontaneously combustible with polyester resins and should be stored separately. Also see **polyester resin technique** and **Plastics: Casting, Safety Precautions and First Aid, Stained Glass: Safety Precautions.**

acetylene. Metalworking. A synthetic gas formed from carbon and hydrogen that is burned in combination with air or commercially pure oxygen as fuel to generate high temperatures for **welding** and hard **soldering.** Acetylene was first discovered in 1835, but an inexpensive method of manufacturing the gas was not found until 1892, when a Canadian inventor, Thomas L. Wilson, heated limestone and coke and cooled them with water. When limestone and coke fuse they produce calcium carbide, a compound that releases acetylene when it comes in contact with water. Today acetylene is purchased in tanks or cylinders which should be handled carefully because the gas is highly flammable. It should not be used at working pressures of more than 15 pounds per square inch, or there is danger of an explosion. Never point a lighted welding or soldering torch at the acetylene tank. The gas is also mildly toxic, causing nausea and headaches if inhaled for long periods of time. Also see **oxyacetylene welding equipment.**

achroite. Gemcutting. See **tourmaline.**

acid. Enameling. See **cleaning metal, etching** and **Enameling: Safety Precautions.**

acid. Jewelry. See **aqua regia, etching, pickle, Sparex #2** and **Jewelry: Safety Precautions.**

acid brush. Stained Glass. A stiff-bristled brush that is only slightly affected by the acid of **flux.** The stiff bristles work the flux through any remaining oxides coating the **lead came** and into its surface, increasing its receptivity to the **solder.** Select an inexpensive brush from your local hardware or art supply store for this job.

acid burns. Jewelry. Stained Glass. See **Jewelry: Safety Precautions, Stained Glass: Safety Precautions.**

acid dye. Batik and Tie-dye. A synthetic or **aniline dye** that requires an acid liquid as the **assistant** in the **dyebath**. The most common assistant in home dyeing is **acetic acid,** although some brands of acid dye may also call for common **salt**. This class of **dyestuff** produces a wide range of bright, intense colors that are generally fast to light and washing, although this varies. They have a special affinity for **animal fibers**, such as silk and wool, but are also used on nylon, acrylic, and a few **polyester** fabrics. They are not usually used by the home dyer on **cellulosic fibers** (or **vegetable fibers**) because they require a **mordant** (usually tannic acid).

Acid dyes give best results when used at hot temperatures, but can be used cool for **batik**. The **dye** is boiled (140–212° F) in the dyeing process for **tie-dye**, but for batik a cool dye (90° F) is used. Fabrics must be left in the dyebath for 15–60 minutes. The dyed fabrics may be finished by **steaming** or **ironing** to **set** the color.

To prepare the dye for use, a small amount of the dyestuff is **pasted** with a little hot water. For each ½ teaspoon of dyestuff used, add 1 pint hot water, 2 tablespoons salt, and 1 teaspoon 30% acetic acid solution and stir well.

To make a 30% acetic acid solution from **glacial acetic acid,** add 1 part acid to 2 parts water and shake. It will have a strong, vinegary smell. Keep the 100% glacial acid away from children and observe precautions.

If using white vinegar, a 5% acetic acid liquid is used; ½ cup vinegar equals 2 tablespoons glacial acetic acid.

For cold dyeing the dyebath should first be brought to a boil, then cooled. Mixed leftover acid dyes will keep for several weeks in airtight containers.

Acid dyes vary in **colorfast**ness, although most fabrics dyed this way retain color well during dry cleaning and on exposure to light. They are not fast to washing. If they are washed at home they should be given a quick warm wash.

Some brand names or distributors of acid dyes are Aljo, Craftool (black label), Fezan, Keco-Aid (Keystone), Kriegrocene, 7-K, and Miyako.

acid dye. Dyeing. Water soluble dye that utilizes an acid in the **dyebath**. The acid used is usually sulphuric acid. The dyes are noted for their brightness, but they vary in fastness to light and washing. They are used on wool, silk, nylon and acrylics. They are popular because of the relative low cost and the good easy results.

acid etching. China and Glass Painting. The technique of etching on china or glass in which all parts of the design not to be etched are covered with **turpentine asphaltum,** an acid-resistant, thick, brown liquid. When **hydrofluoric acid** is brushed on, all uncovered areas are etched. The etching process takes approximately one hour. Repeat the process four or five times, rinsing under running water between applications to wash away acid. Etching on glass requires fewer applications than on china. Do the final cleaning with turpentine, naphtha, or kerosene. All materials are available in hardware or drugstores. The acid is extremely strong; wash all exposed skin immediately in ammonia and water, using ½ tsp. ammonia per cup of water.

A variation of acid etching, sponge acid etching, is done with a sponge for textured backgrounds. Dip a rubber sponge in asphaltum and dab on the areas intended to resist the etched designs. The holes in the sponge leave holes of varied sizes that will take the acid, thus etching the background in an allover texture of random spotting.

acid-free tissue paper. Embroidery. Specially treated tissue paper, usually black, used for wrapping real-metal **metallic thread**s for storage. The absence of acid in the paper prevents tarnishing.

acid mordant. Batik and Tie-dye. The **mordant** used on viscose rayon or **cotton fabric** in **tie-dye** to prepare it to accept **basic dye**. The mordant consists of 2 oz tannic acid mixed with 5 pints cold water until dissolved. The material is soaked in this for 24 hours. The mordant solution with fabric immersed can be gradually heated to 140° F, then left to cool for two hours. The material is squeezed to remove excess liquid and dried without rinsing. The mordant must then be **fix**ed by dipping the fabric for 3 minutes in a bath made up of 1 oz tartar emetic (antimony potassium tartrate) dissolved in 5 pints cold water to which ½ oz chalk (calcium carbonate) has been added. Rinse in cold water, dry, and the fabric is ready for **dyeing**.

acid polishing. Glasswork. See **etching**.

acid resist. Stained Glass. See **stopping-out agent**.

acid resistance. Ceramics. The degree to which ceramic **ware** can resist acid corrosion. This resistance varies according to the clay and **glaze**s used. Some glaze ingredients, especially **white lead,** tend to dissolve in acidic solutions, rendering them poisonous. Containers for storing acidic solutions, such as wine or vinegar, are made of vitrified ware and are often **salt-glaze**d for protection. Also see **vitreous**.

aciding. Stained Glass. A technique used on **flashed glass** to remove the thin, colored flash from selected areas, etching a portion of the glass and leaving two colors showing on one piece of glass. In aciding, **hydrofluoric acid** is used to remove the flash from areas not painted with a **stopping-out** agent. The glass can then be used as is, painted, stained, or plated.

The tools for stained glass include a plastic developing tray—a large one to hold water, several smaller ones to hold acid set on a table—and a plastic bucket of water on the floor.

The equipment for stopping out includes a hot plate, a double boiler to melt **beeswax** mixture (melting wax over water helps prevent it from catching fire); brushes (once used for wax, they will harden and must be placed in hot water to remelt them for reuse); and water to clean glass after aciding.

The materials for stained glass are hydrofluoric acid and stopping-out agents (a mixture of 1-3 paraffin wax, 1-3 brown sculpture wax, and 1-3 beeswax). Alcohol-based block paint, bitumen paint, or stove polish—used with alcohol solvent base—are other stopping agents. Its disadvantage is that it is more difficult to remove after aciding. Turpentine and rags are required. It has the advantage that, for thick flashes, it can remain in the acid for 24 hours or more. Rubber latex glue can be used but is not considered as reliable as the other stopping-out agents.

To dispose of acid, dilute it by adding five parts water. Then add bicarbonate of soda a spoonful at a time until the solution stops bubbling. The solution is too hot for glass but can be emptied into a plastic bottle. Fill the bottle only halfway, to prevent its boiling over. To cool the solution, place the bottle in a sink filled with cold water. It can then be poured into the ground (not near any valuable wildlife).

To neutralize the solution for pouring down home plumbing, add still more bicarbonate of soda at a ratio of about one part soda to 10 parts acid solution. If the mixture becomes too thick to pour, add water. It doesn't hurt to add too much bicarbonate of soda.

TECHNIQUE   a. Fill aciding trays with water to a depth of ½" above the ribs in the bottom. Add acid in proportion of one part acid to two parts water. Always add acid to water, not the other way around.

b. Cut small H-sections of **lead came** about ¼" long and place them in the acid bath. The lead sections support the glass, allowing a free flow of acid solution around it. They also make it easier to pick up the glass. You may use as many pieces of lead as necessary, depending on the size of the piece of glass; they gradually disintegrate and have to be replaced. See ill.

c. Stop out areas of the glass by painting on it with the hot wax mixture. The acid will eat away areas without the wax. Also stop out the edges of the glass.

d. Place the glass on the lead pieces so that the side of the glass to be acided is suspended in the solution while the other side is above the top of the liquid.

e. As soon as the flash is acided off—you will see when through the back—place the glass in the large tray of water to stop the action of the acid. It is advisable to keep the acid trays covered with pieces of **plate glass** between uses to keep the solution clean. After a few days, the acid bath should be cleaned and discarded. Also see **painting on glass, plating, staining** and **Stained Glass: Safety Precautions.**

Aciding

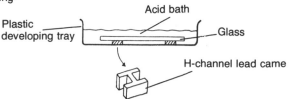

Small pieces of H-channel lead came supporting glass in acid bath

acrobats. Puppets. Toys. (Also called pyramid figure, stacking figure.) Cutout figures that have interlocking hands and feet so that they can be stacked. Many variations of these acrobats have been made, both by hand and manufactured. They function similarly to **blocks** but require more dexterity to fit and lock into pyramid forms. Also see **athlete.**

acrobat. Toys. See **jumping jack.**

acrobat-on-a-stick. Toys. See **monkey-on-a-stick.**

"across the grain." Batik and Tie-dye. Quilts. Stitchery. See **cross-grain.**

Acryl. Plastics. See **acrylic.**

acrylic. Batik and Tie-dye. Puppets. Quilts. Stitchery. Toys. See **acrylic fabric, acrylic paint.**

acrylic. Découpage. Plastic-base tempera paints or varnishes that are water-soluble when wet but permanent and water-resistant when dry. Also see **acrylic gesso, polymer medium.**

acrylic. Plastics. (Also called polymethyl methacrylate.) A popular **thermoplastic** manufactured in many stock forms suitable for craft and commercial use: paints, pastes, sheets, rods, tubes and solid forms. It is light-weight and easily machined, cemented, and heat-formed. It is available in a wide variety of colors in a range from transparent to opaque. Acrylic is more shatter-resistant than glass but scratches easily. It is attached by some chemicals and its colors deteriorate in sunlight. Some brand names for sheet and solid acrylics are Acryl (ICI, Europe), Altuglas (France), Acrylite (American Cyanamid), Lucite (Du Pont), Perspex and Abcite (ICI, Europe and U.K.), Plexiglas (Rohm and Haas, USA), Resartglas (Germany), and Shinkolite (Mitsubishi, Japan). Also see **acrylic cement, acrylic paint, acrylic solvent, gesso, polymer emulsion** and **Plastics: Carving.**

acrylic brush. Toys. A nylon bristle brush made especially to be used with acrylic and **acrylic polymer emulsion** paints. Because the **acrylic paint**s dry fast, the brushes are often kept in water. The bristles of the nylon brush are not affected by long soaking.

acrylic canvas. Stitchery. Toys. A sturdy **awning fabric** made of **synthetic** polymer **fiber**s, especially good where materials are to be used outdoors, since it does not mildew, fade or rot. **Banner**s, outdoor **panel**s, decorative **canvas** furniture covers and canvas swings can all take advantage of the special qualities of acrylic canvas.

acrylic cement. Plastics. Acrylic cements are not true **adhesive**s, but **solvent**s that soften and dissolve the surface of **acrylic** pieces to be joined so that the molecules of one piece fuse with those of the other. The most common acrylic cements are MDC (methylene dichloride) and EDC (ethylene dichloride). Both are clear water-white, transparent liquids, but MDC is less toxic, less flammable, and faster-drying than EDC.

acrylic emulsion. Découpage. See **polymer medium.**

acrylic emulsion. Plastics. See **polymer emulsion.**

acrylic fabric. Batik and Tie-dye. Quilts. Stitchery. Toys. A generic term for **fabrics** made from acrylic resin. Many furlike **pile** fabrics are made from this **synthetic fiber**, as are **stuffings** used in **dolls**, **pillows**, and **quilts**.

acrylic fabric. Crewel. Embroidery. See **background fabric**.

acrylic finishing. Plastics. See **Plastics: Finishing**.

acrylic gesso. Découpage. Papercrafts. A white, pasty, plastic-base **gesso** used to seal wood or canvas, available from art and paint supply stores. It can be tinted with water-base paints, such as watercolor or tempera, for pastel coloring, or, when applied to a surface and allowed to dry, can be painted with any type of paint, Two coats of gesso provide a very smooth surface, ideal for découpage.

In papercrafts gesso is often used in **papier mâché** to give the completed dry piece a smooth, durable surface before painting. The gesso should be absolutely dry before paint is applied.

acrylic gesso. Plastics. See **gesso**.

acrylic paint. Plastics. A paint with an **acrylic polymer emulsion** vehicle to carry the pigment. Acrylic paints mix and thin with water and are fast-drying, nontoxic, and nonflammable. Do not mix acrylic paint with oil paint. Popular brand names include Liquite, Aquatec, Shiva Acrylic, Politec (Mexico), and Cryla (England).

In needlepoint acrylic paint should be tested for permanence before painting a design onto a needlework **canvas**. Also see **Needlepoint: Preparation and Layout**.

acrylic paint. Puppets. Quilts. Stitchery. Toys. **Pigments** in a base of acrylic resin; usually with plasticizers. It is an excellent **paint** for the craftsperson because it may be thinned or cleaned with water but becomes insoluble upon hardening. Many kinds are available in tubes, jars, or by the quart or gallon; directions should be read for each. Acrylics are fast-drying, nontoxic, come in a full range of colors, and do not yellow. They will adhere to almost any surface. Also see **acrylic brush, baker's clay recipe, water-base paint**.

acrylic plastic sheet. Puppets. A hard, thin layer of transparent or opaque plastic. Plexiglas is a commonly known brand of acrylic plastic. It can be purchased by the square inch in hobby shops, in full sheets from plastic, glass, or sign companies, and sometimes from hardware or surplus stores in precut sizes. It is made in a range of thicknesses, with ⅛−¼″ most commonly available. When purchased it usually has sticky-backed paper applied to each side. Because Plexiglas scratches readily, the paper should not be removed until all cutting, sanding, etc., is finished. It can be cut with any saw, although a coarse blade will shatter the edges. A fine blade on a small electric jigsaw or a larger power saw will cut a smooth line. Acrylic **solvents** are available for use in joining pieces of Plexiglas, as in making boxes. Acrylic plastic is also avail-

able in rods or tubes. Also see **shadow play, shadow puppet, silhouette puppet**.

acrylic polymer medium. Plastics. See **polymer emulsion**.

acrylic solvent. Plastics. Any chemical that will dissolve **acrylic. Acrylic cements** are **solvents** used for cementing and bonding. There are **hydrocarbon** solvents contained in household cleaning compounds, spray paints, synthetic varnishes, printing inks, and contact **adhesives** that may dissolve and cause **crazing** of the surface of acrylic (e.g., **acetone**, lacquer thinner, fire-extinguisher fluid, benzene, carbon tetrachloride, dry-cleaning fluid, and window spray).

acrylic spray. Toys. A spray coating used as a **sealer** on bread dough figures, **papier mâché**, wood, or **water-base paints**. Also see **baker's clay, baker's clay glaze**.

acrylic yarn. Crewel. Embroidery. Needlepoint. A synthetic yarn fashioned from a silklike fiber that is twisted and brushed up to give the appearance of wool. It is brilliant of colors, strong, economical, and may be machine washed. Also see **Needlepoint: Yarn**.

Acrylite. Plastics. See **acrylic**.

actinolite. Gemcutting. A mineral of the amphibole group having the same chemical composition, **hardness, specific gravity,** and **cleavage** as the nephrite **jade**. It often occurs in long thin **crystals** of the monoclinic system in an intense green color. Also see **pyroxene**.

action toy, activity toy. Toys. A plaything that involves activity, exertion, or manipulation on the part of the person playing with the **toy**. A **hoop roll** or stick horse involves running action; the gee-haw **whimmydiddle** and **ring-and-pin** require a more limited or controlled action. Both **flipperdinger** and **whirligig** use only a blowing action. Action toys include toy tools and appliances. Also see **Toys: Construction Toys**.

activator. Plastics. See **accelerator**.

active cords. Tatting. A term sometimes used to describe the two **threads** used when **working with two shuttles**.

active element. Basketry. A name for the more flexible woven material or strand that is used to tie or secure a less flexible structural material in place when making a basket. It is called "active" because it is easily bent or tied. Also see **passive element, weft**.

adamantine luster. Gemcutting. See **luster**.

adding beads. Macramé. Plastic, glass, wood, or ceramic beads can be added to macramé work quite easily by threading them through the cords being knotted. The knots made over and beneath each bead hold the bead securely in place.

If the cord is too large to be threaded through the hole in the bead the hole can be enlarged slightly by gently filing it with a rattail file. Threading can also be simplified by applying a lacquer or varnish, such as nail polish, to the tip end of the cord, letting it dry to form a stiff point, and then threading the cord through the hole. See ill.

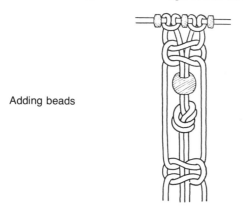

Adding beads

Square knots with bead and overhand knot

additive. Candlemaking. Plastics. Any material added to plastics to change their basic characteristics—for example, to increase strength, flame retardance, flexibility, color retention, or **shelflife** and **pot life**. Additives may be chemicals, inert **fillers**, **thixotropic** agents, or **colorants**.

In candlemaking, additives are used to modify the quality, color, texture, and odor of the basic wax candle. **Stearic acid** is dissolved in the melted wax to add strength to the candle and make it burn better; dye is added for limitless color variations, **mottling oil** for surface variations, and scents for the way the candle smells as it burns. Also see **antioxidant, Krystalline, texturing**.

additive process. Stitchery. Toys. A way of working in which shapes are built up or gradually developed through the addition of one piece of material on top of another. **Papier mâché,** laminated wood, and **appliqué** are all additive processes. The additive way of working is the direct opposite of the **subtractive process.**

adherer. Silkscreen. A lacquer solvent used to soften the top layer of **cut-film stencil** materials like Profilm so that the **stencil** sticks to the screen. In practice, the film stencil is placed on the printing surface and the screen is lowered into position until it contacts the film stencil evenly. Adherer is applied to the top surface of the screen with a soft rag in the smallest quantity necessary to join the stencil to the screen; too much adherer will curl the stencil or destroy the edges, resulting in a blurred or out-of-**register** print. After the stencil is firmly adhered to the screen, the backing film, or paper, of the stencil medium is stripped off the back of the screen, opening the stencil-and-screen combination.

adhesive. Bookbinding. Kites. Mosaics. Plastics. Bookbinder and library supply sources sell prepared bookbinding adhesives in **paste, glue,** powder, pearl, and block forms. The solid forms require melting in a **gluepot** or the addition of a solvent. Adhesives are used frequently in binding processes but should be applied with care; a book is usually pressed after the application of glue or paste (to help shape it or to help it keep its shape) and any excess adhesive is likely to be squeezed out, possibly gluing the pages together or seeping through to the surface of the **board**s where it could ruin a cloth or paper finish. Adhesives are used to paste down endpapers and for attaching cloth, leather, and paper to the cover boards. They can also be used to soften old adhesive materials so they may be easily scraped off in preparation for rebinding.

Adhesives are used in kite construction to bond the kite joints or the **covering** material to the kite framework or guideline. Common white glue is most often used.

The development of superior **epoxy resin** and **plastic adhesive** has greatly increased the use of adhesives as a bond for mosaics.

Contact cement may be used for bonding dissimilar porous and nonporous materials, but may deteriorate the surface of some plastics. **Polyester** is best joined to itself by making an adhesive from catalyzed polyester resin. Epoxy will adhere to metal but polyester will not. Rubber cement may be used for joining **polystyrene** or **polyurethane foams.** Also see **Mosaics: Setting the Material, Tools and Materials.**

adhesive. Découpage. See **glue.**

adhesive. Puppets. Quilts. Stitchery. Toys. Any substance used to join one surface to another. There is a great range of adhesives available, including specific ones for specific materials. The adhesive used may also be determined by scale and conditions of use, such as indoors or outdoors. Among the more common adhesives are **white glue, airplane glue, epoxy glue, rubber cement, contact cement, wood glue,** and **mucilage.** They are made from a variety of sources to fill a wide range of needs.

Adhesives are sometimes preapplied to paper or fabric to make them easy to use. **Iron-on tape** is coated on one side; some interfacings are coated on both sides. Decorative **tape**s may come on rolls, as do surgical adhesive tape or masking tape. Still other adhesives are available in pressurized spray cans or special applications such as the **hot melt glue gun.** Also see **alcohol, animal glue, sawdust** and **Stitchery: Gluing.**

adhesive. Tincrafting. See **Tincrafting: Joining the Tin.**

adhesive. Woodworking. Animal (or hide) glue. Made from gelatin of bones and hide and traditionally used in woodworking, it has largely been replaced by synthetics. The contemporary animal hide glue is strong and excellent for general woodworking and on all porous materials, such as cork and leather. It is light brown or amber in color and highly resistant to heat and mold, although not waterproof. It may have to be heated to facilitate spreading at temperatures below 70° F. Apply full clamp pressure while setting.

CASEIN GLUE A water-resistant wood glue made from milk curd. It is used where extra strength is required, as on joints, gluing beams, sashes, doors, and other heavy-duty work. It comes in a powder form and is mixed with water at all temperatures above freezing. It is particularly good for gluing oily woods like **teak,** limewood, or other fruitwoods, but it may stain some dark or acid woods.

PLASTIC RESIN (OR WHITE) GLUE   A very strong, white, water-resistant wood glue made from a **polyvinyl alcohol** base. It is used on all furniture and interior woodworking, and works best when the joints fit accurately. Apply at 70°F or warmer. White glue is resistant to mold and rot, is chemically neutral, and will not stain or mar woods. Firm clamping pressure is needed.

RESORCINOL GLUE   A very strong, waterproof, two-part wood glue used on outdoor furniture, boats, etc. It consists of a powder resin and a catalyst that are mixed together at temperatures over 70°F. It demands accurate jointing and must be firmly clamped for up to 10 hours at the mixing temperature.

CONTACT CEMENT   A bonding cement that is best used on nonporous surfaces: one common use is for gluing thin plastic laminates such as **Formica** to **particle board.** It is not a strong wood glue and is generally highly flammable. The cement is applied to both surfaces to be glued; when dry, the surfaces must be pressed together accurately because the cement bonds instantly. Also see **Woodworking: Gluing and Clamping.**

adhesive tape. Crewel. Embroidery. Needlepoint. Adhesive tape is useful for holding paper or **fabric** in place. Also see **Crewel: Preparation and Layout, Needlepoint: Preparation and Layout.**

adhesive tape. Stitchery. Any of a variety of plastic or cloth tapes which have an **adhesive** substance on one surface. Some, such as **iron-on tape,** must be applied with heat. Others may be used on paper or wood but will not last through a machine washing when used on fabric. Most are plastic-coated and waterproof, and are covered with a self-sticking adhesive. Among some of the commonly available brands are Contact tape and **Mystik tape.**

adire. Batik and Tie-dye. The term for the **tie-dye** produced by the Yoruba women of West Nigeria. The patterns are formed on **fabric** by using the clump, **folding,** and **tritik** methods and then dyed with **indigo.** The tritik, or sewn technique, employs **raffia** or **bast** for the sewing and **binding.** This Nigerian tie-dye work is sometimes referred to as "adire alabere" or "adire ido."

adjective dye. Dyeing. Those dyes needing a **mordant** in order to be affixed to the fiber. Without the mordant, the fiber will not "take" the dyestuff. Also see **dye.**

adjustable draw gauge. Leather. See **draw gauge.**

adjustable gouge. Leather. (Also called adjustable groover.) A tool with U-shaped gouge blade which can be adjusted for the depth of the groove. It is used to cut ³/₃₂″ grooves for recessed stitching or to aid folding or creasing.

Push the gouge along a marked line, holding it at the same angle for the length of the groove. See ill.

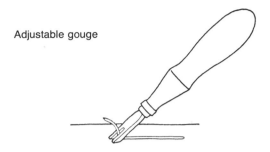

Adjustable gouge

adjustable groover. Leather. See **adjustable gouge.**

adjustable-screw hoop. Crewel. Embroidery. Needlepoint. See **embroidery frame.**

adjustable V-gouge. Leather. (Also called **V-gouge.**) A leather tool similar to a carpenter's plane which can be adjusted to cut various sized V-grooves in heavy leather. Also used for scoring fold lines in heavy leather in preparation for folding. See ill. Also see **gouge** and **Leatherwork: Creasing, Scoring and Folding Leather.**

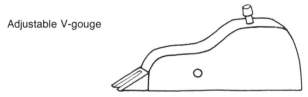

Adjustable V-gouge

adjustable wrench. Woodworking. See **wrench.**

adobe clay. Ceramics. See **Ceramics: Clay.**

adsorption. Ceramics. The result of a solid surface taking up a liquid vapor or gas. Adsorption causes expansion of the clay body even after it is fired and causes **crazing** of the glaze. Also see **absorption, moisture crazing.**

adularescence. Gemcutting. See **luster.**

adularia. Gemcutting. See **feldspar.**

adult toy. Toys. Any **toy** made for the amusement and delight of an adult. Many adult toys are witty, make use of elaborate devices and designs, or are social comments; others are **miniatures.** Often there is little distinction between adult toys and children's toys, especially in the areas of **optical toys** and **mechanical toys.**

Souvenirs may be regarded as adult toys because they are usually purchased by and for adults. **Scale models** and miniatures are similarly of interest to adults or collectors. Adult toys are more often intended to be kept, whereas children's toys tend to be short-lived. Also see **Toys.**

advancing the warp. Weaving. See **Weaving.**

adz. Woodworking. (Also spelled adze.) An axlike tool the cutting blade of which is at right angles to the handle (as on a hoe), used for **roughing out** or **dressing** wood or timbers. The cooper's adz, the most commonly used today, has a curved, **gouge**-type blade often balanced by another gouge blade or by a straight **chisel** blade. Generally, adzes come in two sizes or weights: those for use in one hand have a handle the size of a **hammer**'s, and those for use with two hands have a large ax-size handle. See ill.

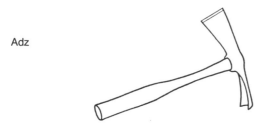

Adz

Aeolian figure. Toys. See **balance toy.**

Aeolian toy. Toys. See **balance toy.**

aerial toy. Toys. See **airplane.**

aerodynamics. Kites. The science dealing with the forces exerted by air and other gases in motion. The basic tenet as it applies to kite flying is that air resists any object that attempts to move through it. Kites are designed and rigged with a **bridle** to make the forces work to send the kites skyward. With proper angling of the kite's surface, the leading edge can divide the resistance so that some air passes above and some below. When wind blows past the winglike edges of the kite, the angle allows the air moving over to travel faster than the air passing beneath. The faster-moving air flowing over the top of the kite creates a partial vacuum immediately next to the upper surface that, when coupled with the higher air pressure on the underside, results in what is known as **lift.** If the lift is sufficient to counteract gravity and the kite's **drag,** or frictional resistance to the wind, the kite should fly.

aeroplane control. Puppets. See **horizontal control.**

affinity for dye. Batik and Tie-dye. A degree of receptivity on the part of a **fiber** for **dye** particles. An **animal fiber** or **cellulose fiber** has a natural affinity for dye, whereas a **synthetic fiber** or **man-made fiber** has little affinity for the colorant. **Fabrics** with special **finish**es must be treated with any of various **finish removal** processes to make them receptive to dye. Various processes such as mordanting and "wetting out" may also increase a fabric's receptivity to dye. Also see **Batik and Tie-dye: Fabrics for Dyeing.**

afghan hook. Crochet. A special **crochet hook** used to crochet the **afghan stitch.** It is 9″ or 14″ long; the shank is uniformly thick and has a knob at one end and a hook at the other. The additional length is necessary because the hook is used to work an entire row of stitches at a time. Also see **Crochet: Tools and Materials.**

afghan stitch. Crochet. (Also called Tunisian crochet, Victorian crochet.) A stitch that produces a flat surfaced fabric with distinct sides; this stitch resembles knitting more than any other type of crochet. The afghan stitch is used in the making of afghans, but can also be used to work **tapestry crochet,** or any other type of crochet requiring a tightly worked finished surface.

The afghan stitch is worked from one side only, and therefore cannot be worked in the round or turned while being worked. The afghan stitch requires a special hook because all the stitches remain on the hook throughout the first row; on the second row, the loops are all worked off. The many variations of the afghan stitch follow the same basic pattern. Remember, it takes two rows to complete one row of afghan stitch.

Using an **afghan hook,** begin by making a **foundation chain** of **chain stitch**es the required length.

Row 1: Draw a loop up through the second chain from the hook (working in the top of the stitch); keep this loop on the hook. *Insert hook in the top of the next chain, draw up one loop, keep loop on the hook * . Repeat * to * until you have drawn loops through each stitch (a.).

Row 2: Yarn over the hook, draw yarn back through first loop. * yo, draw through two loops *. Repeat * to * until one loop is left on the hook (b.). This last loop will count as the first stitch of the next row (c.). For row 3 and all odd numbered rows, repeat row 1, drawing up a loop in each upright bar, starting with the second bar, and retaining all loops on the hook (d.). Pick up last loop, repeat row 2. See ill.

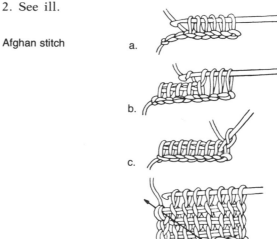

Afghan stitch   a.

                       b.

                       c.

                       d.

African beadwork. Bradunk. See **Beadwork: African Beadwork.**

African Mahogany. Woodworking. See **mahogany.**

afterbath. Dyeing. A final **dyebath** coming after the fiber has already been dyed to the desired color and rinsed in water. This last bath, which contains ordinary salt, is used to deepen or set the color.

afterimage. The image left for a short time on the retina of the eye after fixating or staring at a particular spot for some time. Thirty seconds is usually enough to tire the rods and cones on the retina enough, so that on looking away, a reverse of the fixated color or image appears when the eye's field is shifted to a blank piece of paper or other neutral field. Closing the eyes is often enough to make an afterimage apparent. Also see **complementary colors.**

against the grain. Bookbinding. The direction across the lengthwise fibers that compose the **grain** of **paper, boards,** or **cloth.** A paper folded at right angles to its grain is said to be folded against the grain. In bookbinding all materials are used with the grain running from the **head** of the book to the **tail.**

agate. Gemcutting. See **quartz.**

agate burnisher. China and Glass Painting. A tool with a wooden handle and a smooth tip of agate used for **burnishing gold** to a high luster on plate rims and **raised paste** lines. It is also used for tracing designs on matte **gold.** See ill.

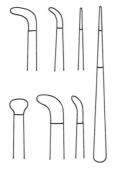

Agate burnishers

agate burnisher. Découpage. See **burnishing tool.**

agate ware. Ceramics. A ceramic **body** that resembles the marbled appearance of agate stone. This effect is produced by the layering of different colored clay bodies with the same rate of **shrinkage.**

age of dolls. Toys. It is difficult to age-date **dolls** precisely, but there are many clues to aid in estimating age. Catalogs and advertisements offer one of the best sources of information. Many dolls were manufactured over a long period of time, however, so catalogs do not always offer precise information. Patents or copyrights provide further data, although often dolls were produced for a year or more before they were patented, and certainly long after. Molded hair, hairstyles, and shoes offer clues because they can be dated. There was, however, a lag in doll fashions, with clothes or hairdos appearing on dolls long after they were in popular use. Certain dolls may have been manufactured for only a short period of time, giving assurance of fairly accurate dates on those dolls.

As many clues as possible should be gathered. If written histories are available they will certainly help in dating, but they are by no means always infallible. Accurately dating dolls requires knowledge of not only the manufacture of dolls, but also of styles in clothes and hair, trademarks, and materials. Many reference books are available to assist in the identification process.

aggregate. Stained Glass. See **ballast.**

aggri. Beadwork. Brightly colored **glass** or porcelaneous **beads** that were probably imported to Africa in ancient times from Egypt or Mesopotamia. Their origin is considered a mystery by the natives. According to legend, their presence was announced in the night by flames rising from the ground and if one were to dig in that spot, aggri beads would be discovered. European traders introduced an imitation aggri bead for trading, but the older natives were always able to distinguish the genuine aggri beads from the copies. Aggri beads were valued so highly that a bride might receive a single bead on her wedding day. Also see **trade bead**s, and **Beadwork: African Beadwork.**

aging of clay. Ceramics. See **Ceramics: Clay.**

air bubbles. Candlemaking. See **bubbling.**

air cool. Jewelry. See **air quench.**

air-drying. Woodworking. See **wood.**

air-floating. Ceramics. See **Ceramics: Clay.**

air-gas torch. Jewelry. See **gas-air torch.**

air hole. Jewelry. When making a completely closed **hollow construction** such as a bead, it is necessary to leave a small hole somewhere in the construction or the construction will implode or explode.

airplane. Toys. An **aerial toy** that has been popular since the first airplane flight in 1903. Early ones were simple metal and wood. Within a few years biplanes, zeppelins, and clockwork airplanes were popular.

Model airplanes comprise a large part of the toy industry, mostly in the form of kits. The early ones were constructed from **balsa wood** and tissue paper; many were accurate **scale models** and were based on the principles of aerodynamics. Current model airplane kits consist of numerous finely detailed parts to be assembled, usually of plastic.

Simple **paper airplane**s made of folded paper and cardboard are schoolroom favorites. Also see **airplane glue, wind toy.**

airplane glue. Toys. An **adhesive** available in tube form commonly used in the construction of model **airplane**s. It is sometimes available as **acetate glue,** although airplane glue is the common hobby shop name. It dries hard and clear. Precautions must be taken to avoid breathing concentrated fumes. The glue is flammable and directions and warnings should be carefully read. **Duco cement** and Testor's glue are common brands of airplane glue.

air quench. Jewelry. To allow metal to cool in the air at a natural rate after **annealing.** Brass, for example, should be air cooled instead of receiving the normal liquid **quenching** which is immediate, because the zinc content may cause it to **fracture** from sudden thermal stress.

"air rolled in wool." Spinning. See **rolag.**

air-setting mortar. Ceramics. A type of mortar used for building and repairing **kiln**s. Clay **grog** mortar hardens when the kiln is fired, while air-setting mortar hardens at air temperature. Also see **kiln wash.**

air shield. Plastics. A covering that shields the surface of **curing** resin against air. Some resins contain a **wax** that rises to the surface of the **catalyzed** liquid, providing the air shield; with others, one may have to place an overlay sheet of **cellulose acetate, cellophane, Mylar,** or other **sheeting** on top of the surface.

akabar. Coral Carving. See **coral.**

alabaster. Gemcutting. See **gypsum.**

à la cathédrale. Bookbinding. A decorative bookbinding style with a geometric central motif suggestive of a cathedral window.

alae. Bookbinding. A decorative motif used on book bindings. The term is from an Arabic word meaning "wings."

à la fanfare. Bookbinding. See **fanfare.**

Albanian knitting. Knitting. A historical type of **color knitting** that originated in Albania; it includes the use of the **Tunisian horizontal stitch.**

Albany slip clay. Ceramics. See **slip glaze.**

albite. Gemcutting. See **feldspar.**

album quilt. Quilts. A quilt made up of a number of **block**s, usually **appliqué,** each of a different design. Two distinct kinds of quilts are referred to by this name, one made by an individual, the other by a group.

The first is a collection of appliqué blocks **set** into a quilt, all sewn by one person. The blocks record the favorite flowers, birds, trees, **wreath**s, etc., of the quiltmaker. There is usually some continuity of color, pattern, or design, because only one person's work is used.

The second is made up of a series of elaborately designed blocks, usually appliqué, each sewn by a different woman. The blocks are identical in size and each bears the name of its creator. The blocks are joined (or set) and then quilted. These were often made as gifts, or tokens of appreciation. Also see **autograph quilt, friendship quilt, presentation quilt.**

alcohol. Batik and Tie-dye. Toys. (Also called ethanol, ethyl alcohol, rubbing alcohol.) A class of colorless liquids that have unusual powers to dissolve. Alcohol looks like water but has a slight odor; it is used as a **solvent** for shellac, natural or synthetic resins, **lacquer,** and oils. It is also an ingredient used in making ditto dye and is used as rubbing alcohol.

There are other types of alcohol that are chemically related but have distinct properties. One is methyl alcohol (also called methanol or wood alcohol), which is used to turn ethyl alcohol into denatured alcohol, and used primarily in lacquers. Isopropyl alcohol is essential to the manufacture of **acetone** and acetone derivatives and is important as a solvent and in lotions. Butyl alcohol is a solvent for resins, lacquers, **adhesive**s, and varnishes. Ethylene alcohol is used in making many inks, stains, and **dye**s. Glycerine, or glycerol, is also an alcohol.

alcohol. Stained Glass. A mild solvent used for cleaning grease and dirt from stained glass. Also see **dalle-de-verre, mosaic** and **Stained Glass: Safety Precautions.**

alcohol. Woodworking. See **solvent.**

alcohol-base black paint. Stained Glass. See **aciding.**

alcohol lamp. Gemcutting. See **dopping.**

alcohol lamp. Jewelry. A small glass or metal lamp with a wick that burns **denatured alcohol** to produce a continuous, nonsmoking flame. It is used with a **blowpipe** for **soldering** and to soften wax to be used for **casting;** it also provides a flame for the heating of tools. See ill.

Alcohol lamp

alcohol spirit stain. Woodworking. See **wood stain.**

alder. Woodworking. A small tree or shrub of the **birch** family. Its wood is a pinkish-brown and is of medium weight. Only the larger red and white alders of the Pacific Coast are used for **lumber.** They grow by streams and swamps and are often used for bridges and piles because they resist underwater rot.

Alexander Mosaic. Mosaics. A mosaic of superior quality uncovered in Pompeii. The work, created in 90 B.C., is based on a Greek painting of the Battle of Issus done during the fourth century B.C. An incredible illusion of three-dimensionality is created by the approximately one million red, white, yellow, brown, and black **tesserae.** Also see **Mosaics.**

alexandrite. Gemcutting. See **chrysoberyl, corundum.**

Algerian eyelet stitch. Needlepoint. This stitch is worked in a perfect square (Algerian eyelet) (**a.**) or a diamond (diamond eyelet) (**b.**) with an open hole or eyelet in the center. It can be worked over any number of threads, depending upon the desired effect. To make eyelet holes, work satin stitches over the threads of the canvas into one central hole. The effectiveness of the stitch relies on the clear open hole in the center and the evenness of the stitches. Insert scissors into the hole that will be the center of the eyelet and twist so as to enlarge it, taking care not to break any of the threads (c.). Always go down in the center, rotating the needle in the hole as you take each stitch, to force it open. Draw the thread tight. Take care to place stitches side by side; do not allow them to overlap, or the hole will close up and the stitches will not be smooth. You may find the outside threads separated as a result of pulling tightly. For a finished effect, cover this with **back stitch.** See ill.

Algerian eyelet stitch

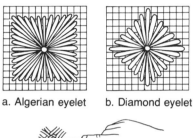

a. Algerian eyelet   b. Diamond eyelet

c. Algerian eyelet (1)

alginate thickener. Batik and Tie-dye. A thickening agent containing sodium alginate. It is used to give a more workable consistency to **fiber-reactive dye**s in **direct-dye painting.** Halltex is a trade name of alginate thickener.

Algonquin Trail. Quilts. See **Drunkard's Path.**

Alhadi doll. Toys. A folk **doll** made in Bengal. It is distinctive in that it emphasizes primary sexual characteristics in the figures.

alizari. Dyeing. See **madder.**

alizarin. Dyeing. See **madder.**

Aljo. Batik and Tie-dye. See **acid dye, direct dye.**

alkalinizing. Enameling. See **cleaning metal.**

alkali test. Batik and Tie-dye. A test for determining whether **fabric** is made up of **animal fiber**s or **vegetable fiber**s. Animal fibers will disintegrate in alkalis. Also see **washing soda** and **Batik and Tie-dye: Identifying Fibers.**

alkyd. Plastics. A type of **polyester** modified with fatty acids and vegetable oils. Alkyds are used in **enamel** paints, **adhesive**s, printing inks, **sheeting,** and table coverings. It is also an ingredient in **lacquer** paints, adding durability, flexibility, and nonyellowing traits. It may cause skin irritation either as a resin or in a finished product, if not modified by **additive**s.

all-along stitching. Bookbinding. Stitching that runs through each **section** from one **kettlestitch** to the other.

all-bisque. Toys. A term used to refer to any **doll** made entirely of **bisque,** whether in one piece, like the **Frozen Charlotte**s, or **joint**ed. Sometimes the term "all-bisque" is used to refer to any unglazed ceramic ware, such as **earthenware, clay,** or **Parian.**

allen wrench. Metalworking. Woodworking. See **wrench.**

alligator skin. Leather. Skins from alligators, crocodiles, or other reptiles of the same family, having a distinctive pattern. Alligator skin is used for various leatherwork projects. Imitation alligator grain is available embossed on other skins, such as horsehide, calf, or cowhide.

all-in-one doll. Toys. See **Frozen Charlotte.**

allochromatic. Gemcutting. See **color.**

all-over appliqué. Quilts. An **appliqué** design that covers an entire quilt, in contrast to one in which **block**s are **appliqué**d and then **set** to make the quilt **top.** The all-over quilt is usually one large-scale design—for example, a landscape or a floral arrangement and may be symmetrical or patterned. It is sewn to a large bed-size piece of material. Also see **"whole-cloth" quilt.**

all-over batik. Batik and Tie-dye. A design for **batik** in which the pattern is spread equally over the entire area of the fabric. This is in contrast to a **medallion** type of design that has a strong central **motif** or single repeat design. **Tjap printing** is often employed to produce all-over batik designs.

all-over design. Bookbinding. A design planned to cover the entire side of a binding as opposed to a corner, center, or border design. It can be made up of a single **motif,** different motifs, or a repeated motif.

all-over pattern. Quilts. Stitchery. Those patterns that use a unit or **patch join**ed so that each is adjacent to others. There are no **band**s of fabric separating the units of an all-over pattern, nor are there alternating **block**s of prints or solids. **Baby Block**s and **hexagon quilt** are examples of all-over patterns. In direct contrast to the all-over pattern is a still-life or landscape, which uses an **overall** arrangement.

Elements within the composition of a wall hanging may be covered with all-over patterns of **appliqué** or stitching. Fabrics that are printed in all-over patterns have an even sprinkling of design, giving the effect of texture. Also see **quilting motifs.**

alloy. Jewelry. A homogeneous mixture of two or more metals. Also see **eutectic.**

alloy. Metalworking. A combination of two or more pure metals, usually melted and mixed, in the molten state, although some may be fused by beating the metals to-gether until they form a single uniform mass. Some alloys are fusions of a metal and nonmetal, such as **steel** made from **iron** and carbon, "cermets," made from ceramic ma-terial and metal. An alloy has properties not available in the pure **base metal** itself—for example, added **toughness,** durability, or **ductility.** The name of the alloy is often given according to which metal is in the largest amount in the compound. Also see **steel.**

alloy steel. Metalworking. See **steel.**

all-white quilt. Quilts. (Also called white quilt, whitework quilt.) A quilt or counterpane of white or off-white fabric that relies only on the use of **quilting** for its decorative effect. It is neither **pieced** nor **appliquéd.** Sometimes a **trapunto** quilt is called an all-white quilt because it has a relief surface pattern of **quilting stitch**es and **stuffing.** An all-white quilt may also be made with **flat-quilting.** Also see **Quilts: Quilting.**

almandine. Gemcutting. See **garnet.**

almond oil. Ivory and Bone Carving. A yellowish oily fluid pressed from almond kernels. It is almost odorless and nondrying. Also see **Ivory and Bone Carving: Finishing, Care and Maintenance.**

alouette. Toys. (Also called flying propeller.) One of the first flying toys. It is probably developed from the **moulinet,** which has propellers at the top in a similar ar-rangement. The propeller device (three propeller arms set into a rim) is set in motion by pulling a string wrapped at a point that extends at the base. The twirling of the arms or vanes will lift the toy into the air. Also see **propeller toy.**

aloxite. Metalworking. See **abrasive.**

alpaca. Knitting. The wool spun from the fleece of the al-paca, a domesticated South American camel. Alpaca yarn is silky, heat-retentive, and has good tensile strength. The natural colors are white, black, fawn, and gray. Also see **Knitting: Materials.**

alpaca. Spinning. Weaving. A South American cameloid animal noted for its **fleece.** It is smaller than its relative, the **llama,** and more nearly resembles another relative, the **vicuña.** It is found in the Andes Mountains south of the equator, where it is kept in semidomesticated flocks by the Indians who weave warm and fine cloth from its wool. The alpaca's coat consists of a thick growth of woolly hair, which in color can be black, dark or reddish brown, light brown, gray, fawn, cream or white. The **staple** length of its hair usually measures from 5" to 12" and can be even longer. The **fiber** is fine, but strong, elastic, lustrous and

silky to touch. The name "alpaca" is given to both the yarn and the resulting fabric.

alphabet blocks. Toys. Small cubes used for children's building **blocks** that have letters of the alphabet added to one or more surfaces by any of a variety of ways. In hand-made wood blocks the letters may be painted, inked, in-cised, carved, or silk-screened. Printed paper **cutouts** can be glued to the wood and sealed. In **stuffed fabric block**s lettering may be accomplished by using needlepoint, **appliqué, felt** appliqué, embroidery, or **marking pens.** The letters are often accompanied by pictures.

Antique, or just old, alphabet blocks were not always cubes. Some were cubes that were halved, others were rectangular. Many had embossed letters and intricate de-signs on two opposing sides. The letters stood out in **bas-relief,** and were often painted. The remaining four sides of the block had printed designs or were left blank. Also see **constructional toy, learning toy** and **Toys: Construction Toys.**

alpha brass. Jewelry. See **brass.**

alternately. Tatting. (abbr. alt.) A pattern term used when **working with two shuttles,** each wound with a different color **thread.** They are used alternately to produce a change in color. For contemporary tatting, different-textured cords or threads may be used, i.e., dull and shiny or smooth and textured.

alternating double square knots. Macramé. A knotting series employing the **double square knot** (worked with four **cord**s).

To begin, work a row of double square knots, using four cords. Work the second row of double square knots on the four cords made up from the two innermost cords from the previous knots. The knots in the second row will be cen-tered underneath adjoining knots in the row above. See ill. Also see **square knot.**

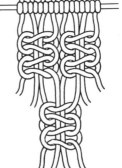

Alternating double square knots

alternating half hitch. Macramé. (Also called alternating single chain.) The **half hitch** worked alternately from left and right, forming a .chain (a.). The half hitch can be worked with two or four **cord**s. To work the alternating half hitch with two core ends (**b.**) use four cords, working half hitches with the outer cords. The two inner cords are the **core ends**. See ill. Also see **chain knot, single chain.**

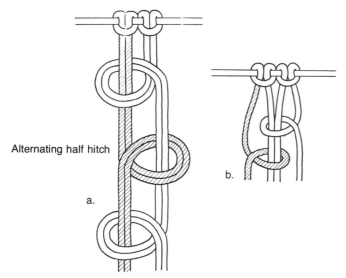

Alternating half hitch

a.

b.

alternating half hitch with two core ends. Macramé. See **alternating half hitch.**

alternating reverse double half hitch. Macramé. Work **reverse half hitch**es alternatingly over a center **cord** or cords. Repeated to form a **sennit**. See ill.

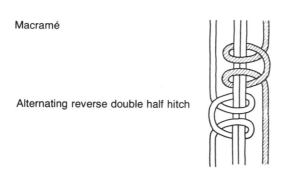

Macramé

Alternating reverse double half hitch

alternating shell stitch. Crochet. See **Crochet: Basic Stitches.**

alternating single chain. Macramé. See **alternating half hitch.**

alternating square knot. Macramé. Alternating square knots form a recurring macramé motif and are worked very simply.

First form a row of **square knots**, using four cords at a time across the row. To alternate knots in the second row, work a square knot using the four inner cords (**a.**). Repeat row 1 and 2 for a pattern.

The alternating square knot can also be worked with three cords (**b.**). See ill.

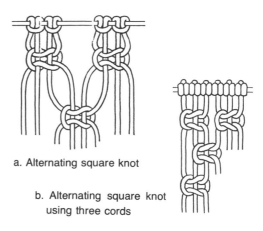

a. Alternating square knot

b. Alternating square knot using three cords

alternating wefts. Weaving. See **pick-and-pick.**

alto-relief. Stitchery. Toys. An almost three-dimensional sculptured surface area which stands out in **relief** from a flat **background**. The use of **stuff**ed **nylon stocking doll** figures are sometimes used to add alto-relief to **wall hangings.** Body coverings sometimes make similar use of **stuffed figures** or forms. Bread dough figures are often used on flat wood panels in alto-relief.

Altuglas. Plastics. See **acrylic.**

alum. Basketry. Batik and Tie-dye. Dyeing. An astringent mineral salt used as a **mordant** or fixing agent when dyeing **reed** or other basketry materials with vegetable colors. Alum can be used in either hot or cold water; it is mixed sparingly with cream of tartar in **mordanting** wool to keep the wool from getting sticky. Alum is available at drugstores and in some grocery stores. Also see **mordant formula, paste-resist batik** and **Basketry: Dyeing and Coloring.**

alumina. Ceramics. The chief oxide in the neutral group. It imparts more strength and higher firing temperatures to the body and glaze. When alumina is added to a **glaze** it forms a matte texture, inhibits devitrification, and increases the **viscosity** of the glaze during firing.

alumina. Gemcutting. See **abrasive.**

aluminum. Enameling. See **metal, metal foil.**

aluminum. Metalworking. A lightweight bluish-white metal that may be shaped by most common methods—**casting, spinning, raising, welding, brazing,** and **soldering.** There are two types of sheet aluminum: pure aluminum and aluminum **alloys,** which are sold in 24″ x 72″ sheets or by the linear foot on rolls.

Pure aluminum has a low melting point, becomes weak

when heated, and may collapse suddenly. It conducts heat three times faster than iron, and has a shrinkage rate 50% greater than that of iron. Support your aluminum sheet when welding it and take precautions to prevent **distortion** from shrinkage. Hammering aluminum sheets is difficult because they require **annealing.** Annealing is complicated because the metal does not change color when heated and may easily melt if an accurate pyrometer or a temperature-controlled oven is not used.

The two basic groups of aluminum alloys commonly used are those for casting and those called "wrought," used for hammering and welding. Heat-treated alloys are not recommended for welding because the heat will eliminate the effects of earlier **heat treatment.** Aluminum alloys with large amounts of magnesium are difficult to solder but are better for casting than pure aluminum. Aluminum bronze, an alloy of **copper** with no more than 10% aluminum, is stronger than ordinary bronze but is also more difficult to finish because it is harder. Ask your metals distributor to recommend an alloy to suit your specific working requirements.

Muriatic (hydrochloric) acid will etch the surface, and water-staining may result when sheets of the bare metal are stacked in the presence of moisture, which will be drawn between the sheets by capillary action. Separate aluminum sheets before storing them outdoors. Sheets and plates with fine surfaces may be protected from scratches by sheets of specially designed protective paper that will not absorb moisture. Clean the surface with mild soap, detergent, nonetching household cleaner, or **polishing compound.** Do not mix cleaners or apply them on sun-heated metal or on cold days; streaking may result. Do not permit the cleaner to remain on the metal longer than the time specified in the instructions, and remove it with clear water. Do not leave traces of the cleaner in the cracks or corners, or it will dull the metal. Prevent weathering and darkening of the surface if the metal is placed outdoors by coating it with a clear coat of lacquer. Coat it for indoor use with a paste wax. Although aluminum will not corrode, it will acquire a coat of oxide when placed outdoors that dulls and darkens the surface.

aluminum anodizing. Metalworking. A hard protective coating of **oxide** produced on **aluminum** by a commercial electrochemical process. The coating may be clear or colored by a variety of dyes, or inorganic pigments may be applied into the pores of the oxide coating. Although anodizing is most commonly used on commercial products, it is also used on large aluminum sculptures or constructions where the natural weathering effects (loss of shine and luster, and possible darkening or waterstaining of the surface) of aluminum may be undesirable.

aluminum bronze. Metalworking. See **aluminum.**

aluminum foil. Papercrafts. Household aluminum foil, foil wrappers from food, and colored foil papers are useful in papercrafts. They can easily be modeled, crumpled, or folded to stay in desired shapes. Foil sheets may also be incised with designs as described under **foil embossing.**

Aluminum foil is an excellent material for use in **papier mâché.** It can be modeled into shapes, then covered by the **paper-strip method** or with **paper mash.** Foil can be shaped into three-dimensional or **relief** forms, such as masks. Occasionally other materials will be needed to add strength to large foil sculptures. **Found objects,** wire, or wood may be used for added **support.**

aluminum oxide. Jewelry. An abrasive occurring naturally in corundum used to reshape and grind tools, and to shape, texture, and refine jewelry forms. It is available in forms suitable for hand and machine use.

aluminum oxide. Metalworking. See **abrasives.**

aluminum oxide sandpaper. Woodworking. See **abrasives.**

aluminum pencil. Gemcutting. A stout aluminum wire sharpened to a point for marking outlines on gem material which won't wash off when sawing and grinding. Bronze wire about ⅛" thick or an aluminum knitting needle sharpened to a point may be used instead. Also see **cabochon** and **Gemcutting: Orientation, Tools and Materials.**

Amacote. Enameling. See **firescale.**

amalgam. Enameling. See **mercury gilding.**

amalgam. Jewelry. Any mercury-based **alloy.**

amazonite. Gemcutting. See **feldspar.**

amazon stone. Gemcutting. See **feldspar.**

amber. Amber Carving. Beadwork. Amber is the fossilized resin of coniferous trees. It has a **hardness** of 2½, a refractive index of 1.54, and a **specific gravity of 1.05−1.10.**

Millions of years ago, huge forests, probably diseased or injured, began issuing abnormal amounts of resin. Layer after sticky layer oozed from the trees, engulfing in their waves insects, fragments of plant life, and water. These masses of resin, buried beneath water and earth and swept over by glaciers, fossilized into amber. Amber displays no crystalline structure but it is related to the mineral world because it occurs in beds in the earth's strata.

Amber is principally mined from the Baltic seashore, but it also occurs in the U.S., Great Britain, Poland, Germany, France, Sicily, Siberia, and Burma. The largest recorded piece of amber found weighed 18 lbs.

Amber is warm to the touch and emits the fragrance of a forest when sawn or heated. The fumes of burning amber are aromatic as well, but are irritating due to the presence of succinic acid. Amber softens at 380° F and melts at 518−707° F. When the surface is tested with a blade it chips rather than peels, and scratches to a white powder. Amber is flammable, it fluoresces green under ultraviolet light; it is decomposed by acid; it dissolves in alcohol; it will float in salt-saturated water; and when briskly rubbed it produces a strong charge of electricity, enabling it to attract small bits of paper and straw. Plastic, **copal,** and kauri gum are a few of the substances used to imitate amber; the identifying characteristics above are used to discern an imitation from the authentic material.

Shell amber is a mass of thin layers; it is transparent, or "clear," as it is called in the trade. It is usually in the clear amber that **inclusions** are found; these may be ants, moths, spiders, snails, small animals, flowers, pine needles or other bits of vegetation, and crystals of iron pyrite. Clear amber is more desirable than opaque amber and also more expensive, which will sometimes encourage the owner or dealer to **clarify** an opaque specimen.

The other main structural classification of amber is massive amber, which is usually cloudy and as compact as if it were cast. There are specimens representing all the grades between the extremes of perfect transparency and total opacity.

A warm golden color is the most common, from pale yellow through brown. Although more rare, amber is also found in red, green, and blue varieties; Sicily mines a rainbow-colored amber, and there is an opaque amber ranging from white to brown, known as osseous amber, that resembles ivory or bone.

When mined from amber-bearing strata beneath the sea or culled from the seashore, amber bears the name of sea amber or "sea stone." When dug from the shore or inland it is called pit amber.

Apart from its ornamental associations, amber produces **amber varnish,** is available as **pressed amber,** is used as an incense, and at one time was used extensively in the manufacture of cigar and cigarette holders and pipe stems. Also see **amber oil.**

AMBER CARVING

Amber was the most important gem in the ancient world. It has been considered both valuable and powerful since prehistoric times. Remnants of amber were found in the cave dwellings of Switzerland, in prehistoric Assyrian and Egyptian ruins, and in Mycenae in prehistoric Greek graves. Homer makes the first recorded reference to amber. The Greek name for amber was elektron, from which we get our word electricity, because of its ability to produce an electrical charge when rubbed. Greek legend says the tears wept by the sun god, Apollo, when he was expelled from Olympus became amber as they fell. Not all Greeks believed this, however; some thought amber to be crystallized urine of the male lynx, and yet others believed it to be the tears of enchanted birds. It is thought that the pungent perfume of burning amber was one of the four incenses Moses commanded to be used in the tabernacle. The Chinese believed it to be burned honey. Amber was worn for protection and ingested to prevent and cure many diseases, particularly those associated with the throat.

In free cities in medieval Germany, the Guild of Amber Workers was formed as craftsmanship in this most precious material rose. Amber was considered so valuable that unauthorized collectors were classed with the worst of criminals and hung.

TOOLS AND MATERIALS   Amber must be worked delicately, with hand tools. Although it is soft, amber is also brittle and will chip, crack, or splinter if treated brusquely. It is therefore not advisable to hold amber in a vise; instead, nail a wood block to the top of the workbench and brace the amber against it while carving or cutting. Another excellent holding device is a **carpet underlay;** small pieces of amber may be held by **beeswax** to a surface. More specialized holders are a **lapstick** and a **bead-holding jig.**

Form and slice amber with a fine-toothed jeweler's saw. Shaping and incising can be done with a variety of tools: steel carving tools, gravers, needle files, **Eskimo style**s, X-acto knives, and **pumice pencils.**

Drilling is done with a hand drill, brace and bit, **browdrill,** or **needle drill.**

Polishing may be done with a variety of fine abrasives: sandpaper (600 or finer), **putty powder, pumice powder, rottenstone,** tripoli powder (lapidary compound rather than jeweler's), **tin oxide,** powdered gypsum **crocus, whiting,** and **rouge.** A board with a piece of chamois tacked to it, called a lapboard, is used to hold the abrasive powders while polishing, with olive oil used as a medium for the powders; a **bead-polishing board** may be used for beads.

Canada balsam glue is the best glue for amber repair, and for attaching findings. Shellac is used to fill holes in amber.

Silver or gold foil can be used under amber in settings to enhance its beauty.

CARVING   Carve the design into the amber with an **Eskimo style;** it will leave white, easy-to-follow lines.

It is not advisable to attach amber to a dop stick, as it would adhere too firmly and be difficult to remove. Use a **carpet underlay** or wood block attached to the bench (to lean the amber against), or cradle it in the palm of the hand to work it.

As amber cannot be secured in a vise without danger of smashing or cracking it, it is sometimes better to secure the tool itself (such as a drill) and feed the amber onto the bit or blade. Clamp the handle of the brace or hand drill into the vise or C-clamp with the bit pointed upward. Turn the handle with one hand while feeding the amber with the other hand. Do not force the amber down on to the bit, but drill it lightly and slowly, cleaning the bit regularly to prevent it from being gripped in the amber. Should this occur, a few drops of oil should liberate it. When drilling the hole through a bead, drill halfway through from one side, then drill the rest of the way through from the other side. Drilling the channel this way prevents the bead from splitting, but you have to be careful to line up the second hole with the first. **Needle drills** are useful for small pieces. Secure small beads in a **bead-holding jig** for drilling.

Because amber is a resin, the heat of friction will cause it to become sticky. Therefore, when sawing, move the blade slowly, and if the material grows warm, lubricate and cool the blade with water. If the teeth become clogged, the amber may seize the sawblade and crack, so keep the blade cool and clean.

Use files and **pumice pencils** for forming. If using an X-acto blade use only the point to slowly eat material away in a pecking fashion.

With all carving tools, work slowly; they will move easily through the amber. If there is an **inclusion** in the piece, work around this area very carefully, as it is likely to have a weaker structure. Faceting is done as for gems—the amber is moved while keeping the lap stationary.

Also see **bead-polishing board, beeswax, bowdrill, lapsticks.**

FINISHING   Use sandpaper to remove file marks, beginning with grade number 12 to #1-0 to #2-0. Rolling the paper can facilitate reaching crevices. **Pumice powder** on a Q-tip moistened with water also makes small areas accessible to polishing.

The first **abrasive** used is ground **pumice,** or pumice powder, then lapidary polishing tripoli compound, and finally **whiting.** The classical amber carver used powdered gypsum for the final polish, but it is difficult to find gypsum in powdered form so you would have to pulverize it yourself with a rolling pin. It is applied with wet leather.

Apply the abrasives to the **polishing** board. Use a clean covering of leather for each different abrasive. For the final polishing, flannel may be used. Rinse the amber thoroughly of each previous abrasive.

Spread the abrasive on the board and dampen it with water; move the amber in wide swiping movements (to prevent it from overheating) over the abrasive. Hold the amber carefully so as not to round edges that were meant to stay sharp. The abrasive whiting is used with olive oil instead of water.

The final polish is with a clean soft rag and olive oil. Although hand tools have been recommended throughout all operations, it is possible to buff amber on a power wheel. As usual, take care not to let it get overheated.

The cement or glue used with amber must be clear, as the material is transparent. Canada balsam cement used for balsa wood is an excellent gluing agent for amber. Another harmonious substance that is used with first-rate results is shellac. When attaching findings, fill the drill hole with glue or shellac, heat the post of the finding, and insert it into the hole. It will melt the glue or shellac around it and then be fastened securely when it rehardens.

If repairing a piece of amber that has been previously glued, do not attempt to remove the old glue with solvents, as they could attack the surface of the amber and soften it. Instead, very carefully scrape the old glue away with a sharp blade or X-acto knife. Be careful near the edges, so as not to chip them. Do not rub the broken surfaces against each other. Coat each surface with cement, allow it to become tacky, and press the two sides together and hold until the glue sets (rubber bands are useful for holding the pieces together). Allow to dry for two days.

Gold and silver foil are sometimes glued to the underside of amber to make it appear more brilliant.

Bicarbonate of soda is used for cleaning amber; follow it with a polish of olive oil on a soft rag.

Also see **bead-holding jig, bead-polishing board, beeswax, bowdrill, lapstick.**

amber lac. Amber Carving. See **amber varnish.**

amber oil. Amber Carving. Oil obtained from the dry distillation of **amber.** It possesses the characteristic amber odor and acrid taste and is colorless to yellowish-brown.

amber varnish. Amber Carving. (Also called amber lac.) A varnish made up of the colophony of **amber** (the nonvolatile residue of melted, partially decomposed amber, representing approximately 70% of the weight of the original specimen) in solution with linseed oil or oil of turpentine. The advantage of this varnish is its hardness when dry; its drawback is its dark color.

ambroid. Amber Carving. See **pressed amber.**

American Crafts Council. The Research and Education Department of the American Crafts Council is one of the best facilities of its type in the United States. It has a small but excellent library, and the best research files on American craftspeople in the world. For information write: American Crafts Council, Research and Education Department, 44 West 53rd Street, N. Y., N. Y. 10019.

American folk toy. Toys. Those **folk toys** that developed in America and are especially associated with it. One of the areas that was particularly rich in folk toys, perhaps due in part to its poverty and isolation, was middle and southern Appalachia. Toys are still produced there that are similar to the ones handed down through many generations. Cornhusk dolls and **whimmydiddles** are among the many American folk toys. Also see **flipperdinger, peashooter, whiplash, whirligig** and **Toys: Folk Toys.**

American Indian beadwork. Beadwork. See **Beadwork: American Indian Beadwork.**

American oak. Woodworking. See **oak.**

American Pewter Guild. Metalworking. An organization of pewterers that sets standards for the manufacture of lead-free American **pewter.** The guild was founded in Columbus, Ohio, in 1958 to develop metal standards, provide information about pewter, and stimulate high-quality production.

American run system. Spinning. Weaving. See **yarn count.**

American Standard Gauge. Jewelry. See **gauge.**

American Standard Wire Gauge. Metalworking. See **sheet metal gauge.**

American stitch. Crewel. Embroidery. See **Roumanian stitch.**

American Wire Gauge. Jewelry. See **gauge.**

amethyst. Gemcutting. See **quartz.**

amide catalyst. Plastics. See **epoxy.**

amine hardener. Plastics. See **epoxy.**

Amish quilt. Quilts. A **pieced quilt** made by the Amish women in Pennsylvania, usually identifiable by characteristic color and design. Amish quilts are very simple and vigorous, often incorporating a large diamond or **block** in the center surrounded by one or two wide **border**s. The colors are startlingly brilliant and intense, and in unusual and stunning combinations. Although a traditional people, the Amish quilters often use sewing machines to piece fabrics together. Among the favorite patterns of these highly skilled quiltmakers are the **geometric** designs of **Ninepatch, Log Cabin, Streak of Lightning, Sawtooth,** and **Sunshine and Shadows.** The hand **quilting** of Amish work is intricate and exquisitely done. Other variations of Amish quilts are **bar quilt**s, **border quilt**s, and **diamond quilt**s.

The works of some modern painters, such as Albers, Noland, and Vasarely, seem remarkably similar to the Amish quilts, with which they are often compared. Also see **Trip Around the World.**

ammeter. Enameling. See **electroplating.**

ammonia. Jewelry. Household ammonia, usually with some detergent added to it, is used to remove grease or wax from a piece between applications of different **buffing compound**s, and for the final cleaning of a piece. Ammonia can also be used to produce a **patina** on **brass** and **bronze.**

amorphous. Gemcutting. See **crystal.**

ampere. Jewelry. The amount of electric current sent by one volt through a resistance of one ohm.

amphibole. Gemcutting. See **pyroxene.**

amphora. Ceramics. See **Ceramics: Form.**

amphoterics. Ceramics. Oxides which play the balancing role in a **glaze** recipe. They make the glaze adhere to the **ware** and not run off when fired. **Alumina** is the basic amphoteric. Also see **binder, chemistry of pottery, flux, refractory.**

analysis of fabrics. Weaving. See **fabric analysis.**

anchoring. Bookbinding. The method of fastening a **tail** or **head band** to a book by drawing a thread from the front to the back of a **section.**

anchoring. Macramé. **Pinning** the work to the knotting surface with T-pins to hold it securely in place. It is important to move the **pins** down the work as the design pro-

gresses. This maintains an equal and firm tension on all the cords and prevents the knotting from becoming irregular. Also see **Macramé: Tools and Materials, Basic Procedures.**

anchor pour. Plastics. A small pouring of **catalyzed polyester resin** on top of or around an object to be embedded in **casting.** This will hold it in place on top of the **base pour** before pouring the remainder of the resin into the **mold.** Also see **Plastics: Embedment.**

andalusite. Gemcutting. A mineral composed of elongated aluminum silicate **crystals** of the orthorhombic system. Andalusite has **hardness** of 7.5, **specific gravity** of 3.15, and refractive indices of 1.634 and 1.644 with some dichroism. It has distinct **cleavage** parallel to the **C axis** and a vitreous luster. Andalusite occurs in green, brown, or yellow color in various degrees of transparency to opacity. It is cut and **facet**ed with main crown facets at 43–45° and main pavillion facets at 39–41°; it is usually polished on a tin **lap** with tin oxide.

Chiastolite (also called cross stone) is an unusual occurrence of andalusite in which an elongated crystal is penetrated and quartered diagonally by an **inclusion** of slate parallel to the C axis. When cross cut, the dark slate forms a cross against the lighter colored crystal. Also see **faceting, polishing, refraction.**

andradite. Gemcutting. See **garnet.**

angle blade. Leather. See **swivel knife.**

angle grinder. Metalworking. See **grinding tools.**

angle iron. Stained Glass. Metal braces with right angles used to support kiln shelves. Also see **kiln tray.**

angle raising. Metalworking. See **raising technique** and **Metalworking: Raising.**

angling. Macramé. Angling can be worked in one or two colors with the vertical and **horizontal double half hitch**es. The ends to be used are secured by **pins** (or the work can be mounted on a **mounting bar** by **reverse double half hitch**es) to the knotting surface. Angling can be done from left to right, right to left, or in numerous other variations.

For left to right angling, take the left-hand cord (insert a pin slanting to the left before pulling the cord to the right) and hold it in the right hand. Work **horizontal double half hitch**es across the row with the remaining cords (**a.**). Repeat from the left to complete rows of double half hitches (**b.**). Insert a pin at the right before beginning to tie **vertical double half hitch**es with what were the **holding cord**s for the horizontal knots (**c.**). By repeating these two steps, a biaslike fabric is constructed (**d.**).

The piece can be continued to form a right-left angle (**e.**). See ill.

Angling

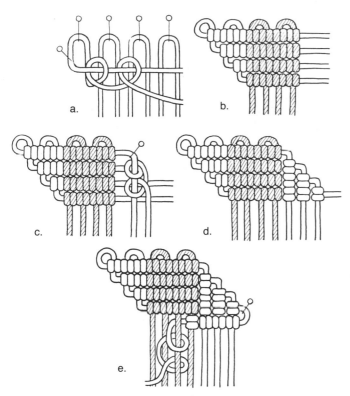

a.

b.

c.

d.

e.

Angora. Crewel. Embroidery. Knitting. Needlepoint. Spinning. Weaving. The name usually refers to a goat known for its long, silky, fine hair, but it can also refer to very lightweight but warm rabbit hair, or to the fabric or yarn resulting from either of these animals. Very often the yarn is a mixture and is combined with wool to facilitate handling or to lower the price. The fleece from the Angora goat is called **mohair.** The chief characteristics of mohair yarn are tensile strength, luster (which determines the value), felting qualities, and resiliency. When mohair is dyed, the colors have a very high luster. The Angora goat originates in central Turkey and was introduced in South Africa and the southwestern United States.

anhydride hardener. Plastics. See **epoxy.**

aniline. Dyeing. See **aniline dye.**

aniline dye. Crewel. Dyeing. Embroidery. Needlepoint. Dyes produced from aniline, a colorless, poisonous, oily liquid, originally formed from **indigo** and used as a permanent color base. In the nineteenth century similar substances were synthetically produced from coal-tar products, making it possible to inexpensively provide a great variety of strong colors that became especially fashionable for use in **Berlin wool work.** Aniline dyes are not used in all forms of needlework.

In dyeing aniline dyes, or basic dyes, were the first of the many groups of synthetic dyes that followed. The early anilines were harsh in tone, faded easily, and ran when wet. These tendencies were somewhat corrected and the dye became desirable for dyeing yarn, fabric made of animal and vegetable fibers, and fur and paper. Aniline dyes

feature prominently in **Navajo weaving** replacing the natural indigo blue that the Indians used. Also see **batik, fiber, natural dye, tie-dye.**

animal dye. Dyeing. See **natural dye.**

animal fiber. Batik and Tie-dye. Quilts. Stitchery. The **natural fiber** that comes from animals. Animal fibers include wool (from sheep), silk (from the cocoon of a silkworm), and hair (such as alpaca, llama, vicuna, angora, and cashmere). Also see **alkali test, burn test** and **Batik and Tie-Dye: Identifying Fibers.**

animal fiber. Spinning. Weaving. See **fiber.**

animal glue. Toys. An **adhesive** obtained by boiling hoofs, bones, skins, etc., of animals to a gelatinous state. The gelatin material is heated with water until it is of a spreading consistency. It was at one time the most common **glue,** especially as a **wood glue.** For household use it has largely been replaced with **white glue,** epoxy, etc.

animal glue. Woodworking. See **adhesive.**

animal ring. Toys. See **turned-wood animal.**

animated booklet. Toys. (Also called cartoon booklet, flicker book.) A small paper book made up of a series of drawings in slightly varied progressive movements. When flipped through rapidly, animation results. Animated booklets are based on the principle of the **chromatrope.**

animated figure. Puppets. Any **puppet** that can be moved or manipulated to suggest changing positions of the figure or figure parts.

The term "animated figure" also refers to a specific small cardboard figure that is **joint**ed. It is made in the manner of the Halloween skeletons that "dance" into various positions. The parts of the figure are cut separately and then overlapped and held together with brass paper clasps. The parts can then be moved to suggest different poses. Some **shadow puppet**s and paper dolls are made with joints so that they can assume different positions. Also see **articulated puppet.**

animated toy. Toys. Any **toy** that moves in a lively way to suggest a living thing. An animated figure will make movements similar to those made by a human, although the figure is not necessarily articulated. A **clothespin wrestler** is animated because it makes very lively movements when wound up tight, even though the parts are not articulated. A **jack-in-the-box** is animated, as are **balance toys.** Sometimes an animated toy is also an **articulated toy.** Also see **athlete axle.**

anisotropic. Gemcutting. See **refraction.**

annealed temper. Jewelry. The softened condition of metal after heat treatment. Also see **annealing.**

annealing. Enameling. See **metal.**

annealing. Glasswork. Stained Glass. The process by which glass is slowly cooled in an oven to prevent cracking and **devitrification.** If glasswork is allowed to cool too quickly, the surfaces exposed to air harden and contract before the interior, setting up a state of compression in the surface and a state of tension in the interior. This force can be of sufficient strength—as much as tons per square inch—to break the cooling piece forcefully. A **Prince Rupert's Drop** illustrates the forces built up in an abruptly cooled globule of glass.

To prevent the buildup of such force, glasswork is allowed to **soak** at the **annealing point,** the temperature at which glass will not quite deform in response to gravity but is viscous enough to allow stresses to be relieved. The oven in which annealing is carried out is called a **lehr,** or annealing oven. A pottery oven, easily obtainable, can be used as an annealing oven.

After pieces are formed in glassblowing and cracked off from the iron they must immediately be placed in the lehr because glass can fracture within a minute or two of cooling from its molten state. In glassforming, the annealing cycle can be carried out in the same oven used for fusing the glass. **Lampwork** annealing is somewhat simpler, both because the **borosilicate glasses** frequently used for lampwork are resistant to **thermal shock** and because the finished pieces are thinner. An annealing oven for lampwork can be simply fashioned from metal or other heat-resistant material and heated on a kitchen gas burner. Because lampwork pieces are already partially cooled when they are finished, the annealing procedure calls for the slow reheating of the piece to the annealing point, a soak period at that temperature, very slow cooling by about 75° C, and then somewhat more rapid cooling to room temperature. It is common practice in glassblowing to keep the lehr at the annealing temperature continuously while pieces are being fashioned and hurried into it. At the end of the day's work, the oven is turned off and allowed to cool for the 8 to 12 hours it takes to return to room temperature. Also see **annealing chamber, antique glass, firing, glass stress, kiln.**

annealing. Jewelry. A process of heat treating metal to relieve the stresses caused by working it. As metal is worked, in **forging** or **drawing wire,** for example, it becomes work hardened due to **compression.** This stress, if not relieved by annealing, will cause the metal to crack.

Most metal is available pre-annealed; re-anneal the metal if a great deal of work is going to be done on it. It takes a little practice to determine when a metal should be annealed, but there are several indications. Metal becomes more and more resistant as it is worked; when it reaches a point where working it is difficult, it is ready for annealing. When forging, the first blows with the **forging hammer** will sound dull; as the metal becomes work hardened the pitch will rise. If the metal cracks, the annealing point has been passed. To determine when a metal should be annealed, forge test pieces of different metals (heavy **gauge** wire is best for this purpose) until the metal cracks. Note the resistance of the metal prior to cracking. Most metals do not need to be heated to a red color for annealing as their annealing temperature is below that point. In fact, some of the workable qualities of metal can be destroyed by overheating, although this is not as serious as overheating the metal to its melting point. This can be avoided by keeping the heating area dimly lit to be able to see the metal glow or use a paste **flux** as a temperature indicator. It becomes glasslike just prior to the temperature at which easy **solder** melts; heat the metal beyond this point to anneal it.

Each metal requires a different temperature for properly annealing; however, the above information can be used as a general guide on **silver, gold, brass, copper,** and **bronze.** Heavy gauge metals may require more than one annealing to soften them enough for further work. Metal which is worked again will harden again. Consequently annealing should be repeated as it becomes necessary.

To anneal sheet metal: cover all surfaces with paste flux. Place the metal in an annealing pan filled with lump pumice or carborundum grains, which will help retain and distribute the heat. Use a large soft flame with a slightly yellow tip. A simulated reducing flame atmosphere is created by covering the metal with flux to prevent **fire scale. Quench** or **air quench,** depending on the type of metal.

To anneal wire: follow the same procedure as for sheet metals, except that the wire should be wound into a loose coil to avoid getting kinks in the wire. The ends of the wire can be wrapped around the coil to hold it in position during annealing, which will make it easier to handle. Be careful with the **torch** because the wire melts easily and heats much more unevenly than sheet metal.

A **kiln** can be used to anneal wire. The kiln heats the coil of wire far more equally than a torch. If the kiln is equipped with a **pyrometer,** the exact annealing temperature can be determined.

Well annealed wire can be pulled through the **drawplate** at least three times (thereby reducing it three gauges) and sometimes as many as six or more times. Also see **temper, work hardening.**

annealing. Metalworking. Plastics. A **heat treatment** process in which a metal is heated to a specific temperature and then cooled to soften it by relieving internal stresses caused by work-hardening and by aligning the metal grain. Annealing makes the metal easier to shape and cut. If raised metals are not annealed they may warp or crack during the forming or shaping. Mill manufacturing can also create stresses, and therefore many metals are annealed after they are rolled or cast. **Pewter** and **gold** do not **work-harden** during forming, and so do not require annealing. However, most other metals need to be annealed frequently during shaping.

In plastics annealing gives the plastic object greater **dimensional stability** and greater resistance to **crazing,** and strengthens cemented joints. Heat the object for five to seven hours to below forming temperature (120–175° F) before the parts are cemented and again after all finishing processes and assembly have been completed. Let it cool gradually. If the object is large, anneal parts assembly only before. Anneal machined parts to reduce stresses in the machined area. Also see **metal, raising techniques** and **Metalworking: Heat Treatment, Plastics: Cementing.**

annealing chamber. Stained Glass. The chamber in which a piece of glass is slowly cooled to avoid cracking and to temper the glass. Also see **annealing, antique glass, kiln.**

annealing pan. Jewelry. See **annealing, carborundum pan.**

annealing point. Glasswork. The temperature at which glasswork is held in **soak** to reduce the internal stresses developed by uneven cooling. The annealing point for a typical **soda-lime glass** is 500° C. A piece with no part thicker than about one inch would be heated to 500° C for an interval of 40 minutes, held at the annealing point for 20 minutes, cooled to 425° C for an interval of 70 minutes, and then cooled to room temperature for another 45 minutes. This typical annealing cycle takes about 3 hours. So-called "hard" **borosilicate glasses** require higher temperatures for proper annealing but can be cooled somewhat more quickly. Actually there is no one annealing point for a variety of glass but rather a range of temperatures at which a glass is sufficiently soft to reduce internal stresses without untoward deformation. Theoretically, glass can anneal at room temperature by **cold flow,** although it would probably take several million centuries! Also see **annealing.**

annual ring. Woodworking. See **wood.**

annular. Ceramics. An aid to centering which involves making a doughnut shape or a disk with a hole in it out of the clay ball that is to be centered. Some potters find it easier to center large unwieldy masses of clay with the help of this technique. See ill. Also see **Ceramics: Throwing.**

Annular

anode. Enameling. The positive pole of a battery or other source of direct current. In **electroplating** and **electroforming,** the anode supplies the metal that is deposited onto the **cathode,** or negative pole. In **electroetching,** the piece to be etched is attached to the anode. Also see **cathode.**

anodizing. Metalworking. See **aluminum anodizing.**

anta. Ivory and Bone Carving. See **vegetable ivory.**

antimacassar. Stitchery. A doily or small lacy form, usually circular or oval, originally used on the backs of Victorian easy chairs or sofas. Its specific function was to protect the furniture from Macassar oil, a nineteenth-century hairdressing for men which left a spot where a man's head touched the furniture. Long after the hair dressing outran its popularity, the antimacassar continued to be produced in profusion, now in sets, with matching doilies for the arms of chairs. Eventually it became the means by which women displayed their lacemaking arts. The antimacassar could be made by any of various methods, including crochet, knitting, drawn-thread work, tatting, or various lacemaking techniques. The doily remained popular for years and it developed into a series of **geometric** patterns of incredible variety. It is used in contemporary **wall hanging**s for texture as well as in **lace appliqué.**

antimonial tin solder. Metalworking. See **solder.**

antimony. Metalworking. A brittle, hard, silver-white metal used only in **alloy**s to increase their hardness and resistance to corrosion. Two alloys containing antimony are **pewter** and antimonial tin **solder.** Antimony is also mixed with **lead** for casting to increase its durability. It is toxic and when burned gives off fumes of **oxide** of antimony.

antioxidant. Plastics. (Also called light stabilizer, ultraviolet stabilizer.) An **additive** used to prevent brittleness, discoloration, and surface **cracking** caused by the ultraviolet rays of the sun. **Polyester** is one plastic that requires an antioxidant for outdoor use. Some antioxidants are opaque, some, such as Tinuvin and Uvinual, are transparent, and others are also **filler**s and **pigment**s that contribute strength and color, respectively.

antique amber. Amber Carving. See **pressed amber.**

antique finish. Toys. See **antiquing, baker's clay glazes.**

antique glass. Stained Glass. A form of hand-blown **glass** invented during the nineteenth century. Antique glass is made by blowing molten glass into a large bubble, piercing it at the end, and slowly spinning it into a cylindrical form that is firm enough to stand by itself. It measures about 3′ long and 14″ in diameter. The ends are snipped off and the cylinder is split lengthwise. It is placed in an **annealing chamber,** where gentle heat flattens the cylinder and tempers the glass so that it can be handled. Because it is a handmade glass it is more expensive than **rolled glass.** The varied textures and roughnesses of antique glass are an attempt to imitate the irregularities of the glass of the Middle Ages. Also see **annealing, cathedral glass, crackle glass, crown glass, English antique glass, flashed glass, French antique glass, fused glass technique, German antique glass, pot metal glass, reamy glass, rondels, streaky glass** and **Stained Glass: Tools and Materials.**

antique glass colorants. Stained Glass. Antique glass is colored with metallic oxides. It is the factory chemist who determines the exact proportion of oxides to use, and it is his sensitivity that determines the quality of the colors produced. The following is a basic list of colors and of the colorants used to obtain them:
Blue—cobalt oxide and combinations of cobalt and chromium.
Red—selenium in combination with copper and cadmium salts.
Red-pink (Gold-pink)—manganese oxide, gold oxide; colors vary between deep cherry red and light camellia pink; extremely expensive glass

Purple—manganese used with cobalt blue
Yellow—selenium and chromium used with cadmium salts
Sulphur Yellow—sodium
Black—concentrated copper salts
Green—copper and chromium salts
Also see **flashed glass.**

antique lace. Lacemaking. **Knotted lace filet** embellished with an overlay of loosely attached fancy stitches and **filling stitches** to complement the **design.**

antique stitch. Crewel. Embroidery. See **Roumanian stitch.**

antiquing. Bookbinding. See **blind tooling.**

antiquing. Découpage. Toys. A technique used to make a subtle, textured surface imitative of eighteenth-century **finish**es. The antiqued surface is achieved with various layers of glazes—such as **varnish** to which some color has been added—that are wiped over the base color. It should be remembered that varnish itself has a mellowing effect on colors, making them slightly yellow. A white base, for example, will turn a cream color after a découpage finish of many coats of varnish is completed.

Many paint companies have put out antiquing kits, complete with the undercoat paint, the color glaze, **brush**es, **sandpaper,** and cheesecloth for applying the glaze.

You may make your own antique glaze by combining varnish with oil paint or **bronze powder.** Another traditional glaze is made by mixing one part varnish, three parts turpentine, a few drops of linseed oil, and about one inch of color from a tube of oil tinting color. Brush the antiquing glaze on over the dried, painted surface and wipe with a clean, soft cloth to desired tone.

To antique a **print** on paper by applying random "age spots," moisten the print on both sides, and then drip brown watercolor, coffee, or tea on the surface. Dry the print flat, and then proceed with cutting. Also see **gesso, gold metal leaf, gold sizing, metallic spray paint, papier mâché.**

antiquing. Jewelry. An antique finish, or a **patina,** can be given to metals by **coloring** or **heat oxidation.**

antiquing. Leather. A finishing process that gives leather a lustrous appearance with highlights and shadows. Rub in a liberal amount of antiquing paste quickly with a soft cloth, then remove excess, according to how dark a finish is desired; mottled, streaked, and textured effects are easily obtained with the motion of the cloth. Antiquing paste is available in jars and comes in many colors. Antique finishes are especially good over dyed, tooled, or stamped leather, over felt-tip pen designs, and on edges of belts and straps. Antiqued leather must be lacquered to be waterproof. Also see **Leatherwork: Dyeing and Coloring.**

antistatic treatment. Plastics. The application of a specially designed coating to retard accumulation of **electrostatic charge** that attracts dust and other particles. The coating is good for several months unless worn off by frequent dry-wiping. Some brands of antistatic coatings are Anstac ZM, Dextrol Lektrostat C, Like Magic, and Nudela 1306. Also see **Plastics: Care, Cleaning, and Maintenance.**

anvil. Jewelry. Metalworking. An iron or steel form over which metal objects are shaped by hammering. Although the terms "anvil" and "stake" are used interchangeably when referring to **raising** or forming blocks, the stake usually fits into a hole on an anvil, workbench, wood stump, or a stake holder attached to the workbench. The bench anvil and the blacksmith's anvil are usually much heavier and larger, and have holes or depressions to receive accessory equipment.

A blacksmith's anvil (also called a forging anvil or large anvil) may weigh from 25 to 800 lbs, but a weight between 100 and 200 lbs is common for **blacksmithing (a.).** The horn, or curved, pointed end, is used for shaping curves; the flat face is the main working surface and has the hardie (or hardy) hole, which holds the **anvil tools.** The pritchel hole is used for punching holes and to hold round tools. The anvil should be firmly anchored to its base so it cannot be knocked off.

A **bench anvil** is a small anvil, usually with a base about 4" x 5" and a horn 3" long; it is used for small metalwork and jewelry (**b.**).

A stake is an iron, steel, or hardwood form that fits into a hardie hole, bench hole, or workbench vise, upon which metal objects are hammered into shape while raising and **forging.** There are several basic stakes for raising metal shapes: the T-stake (or straight and round-end anvil stake) is 12" long and used for beginning a piece and general raising processes (**c.**); the domed-head (or mushroom) stake is used for **bouging** and **planishing (d.)**; the bottoming (or circular flat-head) stake is used to square the bottom of an object (**e.**); the crimping stake is used to crimp or put depressions into a metal sheet (**f.**); and the anvil stake with pointed ends is used to form narrow pointed shapes. Assorted hardwood shapes are used for **pewterworking** because metal ones will mar the soft **pewter** surface (**g.**). See ill. Also see **steel block.**

Anvil

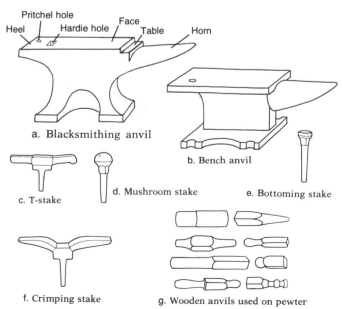

a. Blacksmithing anvil

b. Bench anvil

c. T-stake

d. Mushroom stake

e. Bottoming stake

f. Crimping stake

g. Wooden anvils used on pewter

Anvil. Quilts. A **pieced block** design consisting of triangles and squares joined to make strong diagonal lines. It is one of many quilt patterns named for trades and occupations. See ill.

Anvil

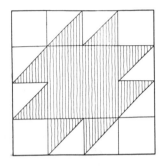

anvil bick. Metalworking. See **blacksmithing tools.**

anvil tool. Metalworking. See **blacksmithing tools.**

apatite. Gemcutting. A mineral composed of calcium phosphate with chlorine and fluorine in **crystals** of the hexagonal system. Apatite has a **hardness** of 5 and **specific gravity** of 3.2; it possesses no **cleavage** planes. It occurs in colorless, violet, green, yellow, blue, and red varieties with slight dichroism. Its refractive indices are 1.637 and 1.640. This material is cut and faceted carefully with allowance for its softness, brittleness, and tendency to crack from overheating. Main crown **facets** are cut at 43° and pavillion mains at 39°; it is polished on a wax **lap** with Linde A, or on a lead lap with 14,000 grit diamond. Its name derives from a Greek word meaning "to deceive," because apatite gems imitate the colors of more precious gems. Also see **faceting, fluorite, polishing, refraction.**

à petits fers. Bookbinding. A term used to describe **tooling** a design with various small **tools.**

apple doll. Toys. See **apple-head doll.**

apple-head. Puppets. Toys. A puppet or **doll head** made from an apple that has been carved and dried. A firm, hard apple is essential, avoiding an overripe or mealy one. Rome Beauties or Pippins are excellent, although some dollmakers use a red or golden delicious. The apple must be peeled so that at least 2/3 of the surface is exposed to air. That allows it to dry rather than to soften or rot. The face area is usually completely peeled, and features are carved with a paring knife or **jackknife** before drying.

The apples dry best and fastest in low-humidity warm air. A pilot light in a gas oven offers just about the right conditions. Anything warmer may just bake the apples. They may be left at room temperature to dry.

To make an **apple-head doll** or an **apple-head puppet,** various means have been devised by which the head can be held erect. This usually involves inserting a wire, a wood stick, or a tube into the apple-head before it dries.

Apple-heads dry and shrivel to produce faces full of character and line. The carver does not usually have complete control over the features that the carved head will assume; they change as they dry, so that the work is partly controlled and partly "happens."

Grains of rice, small pearl beads, white beans, wood beads, and other similar materials may be embedded in the apple faces to suggest teeth or eyes before they dry. The drying holds them firmly in position. Experience will aid in size and placement, although sometimes the most amusing results are achieved by chance.

A **fixative** may be applied to the surface of the apple after it has thoroughly dried. There are some commercially available coatings especially for use on apple-heads.

apple-head doll. Toys. (Also called apple doll.) A **doll** the head of which is a carved and dried apple. The costume, made of various fabrics, is usually attached over an armature made of wire, wood, or cornhusks.

The body of the doll may be attached to the **apple-head** in any of several ways. One method is to use an **armature** of wire. The wire can be inserted either before or after the apple is dried. Arms, body, and legs are all fashioned of wire, then padded and dressed.

Another way of forming the body is to insert a wood **tongue depressor** or popsicle stick into the apple-head before it dries. This supplies a handle to which a body can later be attached. Then the stick can be inserted into a cone of cardboard, made by rolling railroad board or shirt cardboard, into a teepee shape; or the stick can be stuck into a styrofoam cone, or a **pulp mâché** core from commercial yarn cones. Sometimes the tongue depressors must be shaped or sharpened to slide easily into the apple. They are much wider than **craft stick**s or popsicle sticks, but also offer more wood surface to which other wood pieces may be attached.

Cornhusks, shaped and trimmed level at the bottom, also make a good base. A stick (protruding from the apple-head like a neck) is held up (head pointing down), and a number of damp cornhusks are wrapped around the stick with the lengths of the husks hanging down over the apple-head. Then the doll is turned upright. Arms can be made of an extra section slid in crosswise and tied in place; then a waistline can be tied. The bottom is then trimmed off to make a flat base. The cornhusks must dry and stiffen before the doll can be dressed. Also see **bead.**

apple-head puppet. Puppets. A **hand puppet** made by using a carved and dried apple for the head. The process for making this **puppet** is the same as that used for the **apple-head** doll.

The apple head must have firmly attached a stick or handle at its **base.** A popsicle stick or tongue depressor will work very well. By inserting the stick before the apple dries, the flesh of the apple is allowed to shrink and contract around the wood, making a tight fit. The apple head of the hand puppet is held upright by holding the stick in one hand. That means the fingers are not free to move the arms, so the entire hand puppet is moved at one time. Another tongue depressor, glued at right angles to the first one, will form the arms. If a tunnel or sleeve of fabric is attached to the wood stick so that one finger can be inserted, the head can be controlled by that finger, leaving the thumb and third finger free to become the puppet's arms.

Another means of freeing the fingers requires that a tube be inserted into the apple. This will allow one or two fingers to fit into it so that the arms of the hand puppet can be **manipulate**d. It will require some experimenting to find a tube that will work. Sometimes a cardboard cylinder slipped into an opening cut into the apple will work, although it may simply absorb the moisture from the apple and disintegrate. A plastic tube, such as a short section of plastic pipe or hose, works better.

If the apple is not too hard it will be possible to take stitches into it to attach clothes directly. Otherwise, the wood stick can be tightly wrapped with strips of cloth, and the clothes can be sewn directly to the cloth.

apple mill. Toys. A **momentum toy** similar to the **moulinet** but easily made from household objects. Slices of apple are placed at one end of a vertical **dowel** rod. An empty nut shell provides the hollow sphere or ball added at the center of the rod, through which a string emerges. The string is wound on the dowel, inside the ball, then pulled sharply. This sets the toy in motion; it is kept running by a yo-yolike manipulation of the string. See ill.

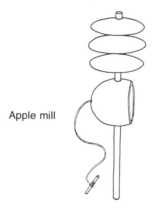

Apple mill

Appleton crewel wool. Crewel. Embroidery. Needlepoint. (Also called English crewel yarn.) A trade name for a two-ply, slightly twisted **yarn** made in England. There is an excellent range of colors in close shadings of both clear and muted colors dyed to match the colors used in antique English embroideries. This fine wool may be used in one, two, or more strands, depending on the desired effect. It is strong, wears well, and is colorfast. Also see **Crewel: Yarns.**

applied decoration. Ceramics. Texture or three-dimensional decoration applied to soft or **leather-hard** clay to create a design. Also see **brushwork, calligraphy, combing, crackle, crater glaze, cullet, engraving, firecord, fluting, gilding, impressing, luster, painting on pottery, resist method, silkscreen, silver luster, sgraffito, stamp.**

applied fringe. Rugmaking. Weaving. See **fringe.**

applied top. Quilts. A **quilt top** to which a design has been applied. It starts out as a large piece of fabric that covers the bed—a sheet, a **cotton** spread, or lengths of fabric sewn

together. The design is applied in any of several ways. It may be embroidered by hand or machine, or it may be painted on the fabric. Small pieces of cloth may be sewn to it, as in a collage. It is not formed from **blocks,** as most **pieced quilts** and **appliquéd quilts** are. Also see **"whole-cloth" quilt.**

appliqué. Beadwork. See **spot stitch.**

appliqué. Jewelry. The technique of **soldering** separate decorative units onto a metal **baseplate.** Also see **damascene, encrustation.**

appliqué. Knitting. Lacemaking. From the Latin "applicar," to join or attach, and the French "appliquér," to put on. The "appliqué" means to sew a fabric or **motif,** onto a foundation of a different fabric. This technique was used from the thirteenth century to the sixteenth century in making very fine laces with handmade net grounds.

In lace appliqué, individual floral motifs are first made on the **pillow** or otherwise worked, as in **needle lace,** then placed on the **net** and sewn down. To do this cut out a piece of **blue paper** the size of the lace **pattern.** Lay the motifs in the design desired, right-side down on the paper, and tack with a **running stitch** to hold. Place the net over this; pin down, taking care not to stretch the net. Sew with a small **overcast stitch** around all the outlines of the motifs. Cut away the net where there are open areas in the lace pieces. Overcast the net edges in the cut areas to prevent the net from fraying, and turn in and sew the net firmly at the outside edge of the lace. Cut the running stitches at the back of the blue paper and remove the lace carefully. Press on the wrong side with a pressing cloth between the lace and iron, if desired.

In knitting, appliqué refers to a motif or motifs sewn onto the finished knitting as trim or decoration.

appliqué, Leather. (Also called mosaic work.) The technique of applying patterns cut from thin leather (one or more colors) which are arranged and glued or sewn on another leather surface. Leather appliqué may also be applied to cloth or wood backgrounds. Cut the shapes with a knife or **scissors,** then apply glue to the back side with a brush, working over scrap paper or blotting paper, taking care not to use too much glue. Place shapes on the background surface, and when nearly dry, press gently down to secure with clean blotting paper placed over the design. The edges may be flattened with a wheel or tracer. Also see **stuffing** and **Leatherwork: Gluing and Bonding.**

appliqué. Quilts. Stitchery. Toys. To sew or apply one piece of **fabric** on top of another. The term may refer to the sewing of small decorative shapes to a **block,** to the sewing of blocks to a larger background, or to the sewing of shapes directly to a **background** fabric. The pieces of fabric are cut out, pinned in place, sometimes **baste**d, and finally sewn with any of a variety of **appliqué stitches.** It includes both **hand appliqué** and **machine appliqué.** Some of the materials which can most easily be hand appliquéd are **gingham, percale, calico,** shirting, and **broadcloth.** Any **cotton** or **cotton blend** is easier to turn under and sew than is a **synthetic fabric**, which tends to be springy. In machine appliqué, materials which have greater **body** or stiffness are easier to handle. There are many variations of basic appliqué, including blind appliqué **cut-through appliqué, double appliqué, felt appliqué,** and **lace appliqué.**

In **appliqué quilts** the sewing usually attaches designs identical or similar in size, color, or pattern to a series of blocks all cut to the same size. On some appliqué quilts, however, a single design may be sewn over the entire top of the bed cover. The most common way of sewing the appliqué designs is by hand appliqué, though many contemporary quilters have made excellent use of machine appliqué.

When appliqué is used for **wall hangings** or **banners** the choice of using hand appliqué or machine appliqué is often one that is determined by the weight of the fabric being used and the scale of the work. A fine fabric more appropriately uses fine hand stitching for the appliqué, whereas the heavier textured fabrics and **upholstery materials** are in scale with the wide **machine satin stitch.** A straight machine stitch is also used for appliqué for a completely different effect.

Toys, dolls, and soft sculpture frequently incorporate the use of appliqué on **stuffed fingers** or forms. In these, the appliqué pieces may incorporate India ink drawings, **batik, direct-dye painting,** and many other techniques. Also see **Stitchery: Hand Appliqué, Machine Appliqué.**

appliqué border. Quilts. See **border.**

appliquéd rug. Rugmaking. A combination of embroidery and cloth in which pieces of material have been cut into patterns or shapes, are laid over a foundation material, and are sewn on using stitches that may or may not contribute to the decoration. The foundation or ground material may be left exposed in areas if it is part of the design. The techniques of appliqué most often found in rugs are superimposing materials; inlaying of patterns into the ground fabric in which both patterns and ground are cut into shapes and then sewn together; patchwork; working indented stitches which in effect quilt the rug; or any combination of these techniques. Denim, **burlap,** or plain awning canvas make good ground fabric. In choosing the pattern fabrics and yarns, care must be taken to pick materials that are tightly woven and that will stand up well under normal rug usage. If the rug is to be washable, prewashing of all pattern fabric pieces is recommended to prevent puckering of the finished rug and to test for **color fastness.** Any embroidery **stitch** may be used to attach the fabric pieces by hand, or by a sewing machine which makes fancy stitches. There are also available special fabric adhering solutions which will glue pattern pieces to the foundation material. Also see **shirred rug.**

appliqué patterns. Quilts. The **block** designs from which **appliqué quilts** are made.

Appliqué quilts are not made as frequently as **pieced quilts,** so there are fewer patterns. However, because this method lends itself so readily to variation, there are many designs, and each variation seems to require a new name, even though it may be similar to another. There are also general categories based on the dominant element of the design, such as **basket patterns, flower designs,** or **star patterns,** and **quilt types,** such as **bride's quilts, presentation quilts,** and **storytelling quilts.**

Following is a list of many of the best-known appliqué patterns and a list of those that use **appliqué** in combination with **piecing.**

APPLIQUÉ PATTERNS

Ben Hur's Chariot Wheel
Bird of Paradise
Breadfruit
Bridal Wreath
California Rose
Charter Oak
Cherry Basket
Combination Rose
Coxcomb
Dahlia Wreath
Democrat Rose
Double Hearts
Eternal Flame
Feather Crown
Fern
Flowers in a Pot
Garden Island
Garden Wreath
Garfield Monument
Golden Glow
Grapevine
Harrison Rose
Iris Leaf
Japanese Fan
Ke Kahi O Kaiulani
Kentucky Flowerpot
Koomi Malie
Lafayette Orange Peel
Laurel Leaves
Little Red Schoolhouse
Lobster
Log Cabin
Lotus Flower
Love Apple
Maidenhair Fern
Martha Washington's Wreath
Mexican Rose
Missouri Rose
North Carolina Rose
Nosegay
Oak Leaf
Oak Leaf and Reel
Oak Leaves and Cherries
Ohio Rose
Orange Peel
Orange Slices
Original Rose
Ostrich Plume
Overall Bill
Pine Tree

Pomegranate
Prairie Flower
Prairie Rose
Press Gently
Pride-of-the-Forest
Prince's Feather
Princess Feather
Princess Feather and Tulip
Radical Rose
Rebecca's Fan
Reel, The
Rising Sun and Princess Feather
Rose and Buds
Rose in Bud
Rose of Sharon
Rose of Tennessee
Rose of the Field
Rose Tree
Rose Wreath
St. Valentine's Patch
Schoolhouse
Spice Pink
Star and Plumes
Star Flower
Sunbonnet Girl
Sunbonnet Sue
Tree of Life
Wandering Foot
Whig Rose
Winding Ways
Wreath of Pansies

COMBINATIONS OF APPLIQUÉ AND PIECING

Aster
Cactus Flower
Cactus Rose
Cleveland Lilies
Cleveland Tulip
Colonial Tulip
Conventional Tulip
Cornucopia
Cottage Tulip
Dresden Plate
fan quilt
Fire Lily
Friendship Ring
Japanese Fan
Lily
Little Red Schoolhouse
Log Cabin

Maple Leaf
Mariposa Lily
Meadow Lily
Melon Patch
Mountain Lily
Mrs. Ewer's Tulip
Noonday
Noonday Lily
North Carolina Lily
Old Homestead

Oriental Poppy
Peony
Pine Tree
Prairie Lily
Tiger Lily
Tulip
Tulip Tree
Virginia Lily
Wood Lily

appliqué quilt. Quilts. Any quilt that has as its basic design motif areas or shapes that are **appliqué**d. These may be **block**s or **square**s, or they may be appliqués that cover the entire quilt, making a single **overall** design.

appliqué stitches. Quilts. Stitchery. Any of a variety of stitches commonly used to join one piece of fabric onto the surface of another, usually for decorative effect. Among the most common appliqué stitches are the **running stitch**, **blind stitch**, and **whip stitch**. The **blanket stitch, buttonhole stitch**, and **overcast stitch** are sometimes used, although they are not as common in contemporary stitchery. Each stitch gives a different appearance to the edge of the fabric.

appliqué work. Beadwork. See **overlay stitch.**

applying finished needlepoint to fabric. Embroidery. A **stumpwork** technique that is an excellent means of adding a dimensional effect to needlework.

To apply finished needlepoint to fabric, first unravel your raw edges around your finished needlepoint so that single threads appear on all four sides. Then pin and baste the needlepoint in position on the background material. With a large-eyed needle take each thread through to the reverse side of the fabric (**a.**). Turn to the reverse side and knot the needlepoint threads together in pairs, pulling snugly so that the canvas is held firmly in place on the front (**b.**). Now turn to the right side again and outline the canvas with any edging stitch you prefer (**c.**). **Stemstitch** is shown at A, **couching** at B, and a couched cord at C. D shows the needlepoint canvas left plain without an edging, which is also equally effective if desired. See ill.

Applying finished needlepoint to fabric

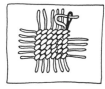

applying the design. Crewel. Embroidery. See **Crewel: Transferring a Design.**

applying the design. Needlepoint. See **Bargello Preparation and Layout** and **Needlepoint: Preparation and Layout.**

apprentice. A novice at a craft or trade; a student, especially one who studies a craft while working for a **master** of that craft. Under the medieval **guild** system, apprentices were often legally bound for a period of several years to a particular master, in the manner of an indentured servant. At the end of the apprenticeship, the learner became a **journeyman** and could work for the same or another master for a wage.

apron. Weaving. A piece of strong fabric (usually **canvas**) nailed or stapled to the **warp beam** of a **harness loom.** Another such piece is similarly attached to the **cloth beam.** The width of the fabric is slightly narrower than the beam and the length is such that it reaches close to either the first or last harness. The free end of an apron is hemmed and a steel rod is inserted in this hem. A second rod is laced to the first with a strong cord. This is the **apron bar** which attaches the **warp** to the loom so that it can be rolled backward onto the warp beam or forward onto the cloth beam. In some types of harness looms, canvas tapes or very long cords are used in place of the canvas fabric. Also see **beaming, dressing the loom, harness loom, warping.**

apron bar. Weaving. (Also called apron rod.) This is the steel bar, or rod, by which the **warp** is attached to a **harness loom.** The bar attached to the **warp beam** is known as the back apron bar and the one attached to the **cloth beam** is known as the front apron bar. The bar can also be of wood of a thickness that does not interfere with the smooth winding of the warp. Also see **apron, beaming, dressing the loom, warping.**

apron cord. Weaving. The cord lacing the **apron bar** to the rod inside the **apron** hem. Also see **dressing the loom.**

apron rod. Weaving. See **apron bar.**

aquamarine. Gemcutting. See **beryl.**

aqua regia. Jewelry. (Also called king's water, royal water.) A combination of nitric and hydrochloric acids that will etch **precious metals** such as gold and platinum. The above metals are insoluble in either of the acids alone. The formula is 1 part nitric acid to 3 parts hydrochloric acid. This formula can be diluted with water to as much as half strength, but the action will be slower. Sulfuric acid can be used in place of the hydrochloric acid. Add one acid to the other very slowly and with caution as the combinations of acids will generate great heat. Aqua regia has poisonous fumes and is highly corrosive. Always pour acid into water, **never** the reverse. Also see **Jewelry: Safety Precautions.**

Aquatec. Plastics. See **acrylic paint.**

arabesque. Bookbinding. Fanciful book cover decoration, perfected by Arabian bookbinders. It combines foliage, fruits, flowers, curves, and figures.

arabesque. Quilts. Flowing, curvilinear designs formed of interlacing lines, sometimes using fruit and flower motifs.

Arabesques are often used in **quilting patterns**. Also see **Quilts: Quilting.**

Arabian color knitting. Knitting. One of the earliest means of varying the look of knitted fabrics, by using colored yarns to form simple geometric patterns. (Often these forms took the shape of a cross or a diamond.) The earliest extant example dates back to the fifth or sixth century A.D. and was found on the site of the ancient Coptic town of Antinoe. Also see **color knitting** and **knitting.**

Arabian Star. Quilts. See **Dutch Tile.**

Arabic Lattice. Quilts. A **pieced quilt** of a **geometric overall** design that is cut in such a way that no scrap of fabric is ever wasted. It is difficult to piece the interlocking parts.

aragonite. Gemcutting. See **calcite.**

Araldite. Plastics. See **epoxy.**

Aran Island design. Knitting. See **Aran knitting.**

Aran knitting. Knitting. A knitting style particular to the Aran Islands. Aran Island-designs are a heavily embossed combination of **bobbles, cables,** and the **one-over-one principle.** These designs are often used in **fisherman's knit** sweaters and caps.

arbor. Gemcutting. See **machinery.**

arbor. Woodworking. The shaft of a rotating tool, such as a **power saw,** onto which a blade or bit is fastened.

arbor saw. Woodworking. See **power saw.**

arced. Weaving. See **tapestry.**

arches. Tatting. See **chain.**

archetypal toy. Toy. A **toy** on which many variations are based. Toy authorities disagree over the existence of archetypal toys, some maintaining that the basic forms kept emerging in different parts of the world at different times, while others insist that the toy forms are invented or developed spontaneously in varying cultures.

The **ball** is one common example of an archetypal toy. The **chicken and egg,** animal forms, and figures are others. Also see **emergent toy.**

Archibald Ormsby Gore. Toys. See **Archie.**

Archie. Toys. (Also called Archibald Ormsby Gore.) The much-loved and well-known **teddy bear** that belonged to John Betjeman, the poet. The bear, which was covered with patches, was immortalized in verse.

arching. Rugmaking. Weaving. See **bubbling.**

architect's linen. Stenciling. (Also called tracing cloth.) A cloth, available in sheets, used as **stencil paper.** The cloth

sticks to tacky varnish, holding the cut designs in place while the **paint** is applied. For this reason it is particularly useful for **stenciling furniture.**

architectural playthings. Toys. **Toys** or **models** of houses and buildings. Early ones, made of paper, were produced in the 1700s and were **cutouts,** joined or assembled by the model-makers. Elaborate castles and churches were later printed in color. The most recent ones are of the punch-out variety so that the tedious and time-consuming task of cutting is eliminated.

Architectural playthings were made entirely from wood or paper until the early 1900s when metal ones were first manufactured. Paper buildings have maintained varying popularity over 200 years. Small wood buildings, with patterns of applied printed paper or painted designs, are also considered to be architectural toys. Some are designed so that parts of specific buildings can be assembled. Others are **blocks** that can be assembled according to the wishes of the builder. Also see **Toys: Construction Toys.**

arch punch. Leather. A variety of **drive punch** so named because of the arch over the punch barrel. Arch punch sizes range from $3/16''$ to a $2''$ hole diameter; they are stronger, generally punch larger holes than standard drive punches, and are most useful on heavy leather. Use an arch punch as you would any drive punch. Place the opening of the punch, straight up and down over the leather, right side up, on the spot where you want the hole. Strike the punch head with the **mallet** solidly, holding the punch firmly in place, until you have completely and cleanly pierced the leather. See ill.

Arch punch

arch-shaped doll. Toys. A basic **doll** form so easy to construct that no pattern is required. The primary advantage to this form is that the head and body are one piece. Arms and legs can be stuffed or left unstuffed, although the body is usually filled with **dacron polyester batting.** The doll consists of two rectangles of identical size, rounded or arched at the top. These provide the front and back of the doll. Arms and legs are cut and sewn separately and inserted in the **seams** when the body pieces are joined.

When made from **felt** the stitching can be done on the top or the outside. When woven materials are used, pieces

Arch-shaped doll

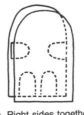

a. Right sides together

b.

are stitched on the wrong side, then turned right-side out and stuffed.

The beginning **dollmaker** finds this type of doll easy and satisfying to make. However, the possibilities for variation in the form and in animation are so great that even the most advanced stitchers enjoy this method. See ill. Also see **single-shape doll.**

arcing. Rugmaking. Weaving. See **bubbling.**

arc welder. Metalworking. See **arc welding equipment.**

arc welding. Metalworking. See **welding** and **Metalworking: Welding.**

arc-welding equipment. Metalworking. The equipment necessary to do basic arc **welding** that makes up the arc-welding circuit (**a.**).

The main tool is the arc welder, or arc welding machine, which transforms electric current from outside power lines by stepping down the voltage into usable welding current. This machine has controls for regulating the amount of heat for welding different thicknesses of metal. Two cables from the arc welder carry and complete the circuit of current to the work, and then back to the welder. One cable ends with the insulated electrode holder, which holds the electrode (see below), and the other terminates in the ground clamp, which attaches to the work piece or to a metal workbench. There are two basic types of machine: the transformer type, and the direct current (DC) type. The transformer machine, which uses alternating current (AC), is cheaper, easy to maintain, and can be used for home and school shops.

Wear gloves with long gauntlets (usually of leather), a high-necked shirt with long sleeves, and long trousers that overlap leather shoes or boots. Do not use leather gloves to pick up hot metal; this will burn and stiffen the leather. They are only for protection from the arc rays.

A helmet made expressly for arc welding is necessary to screen out dangerous ultraviolet and infrared rays. Sunglasses or ordinary goggles for gas or oxyacetylene **welding** should not be used.

a. Arc-welding circuit

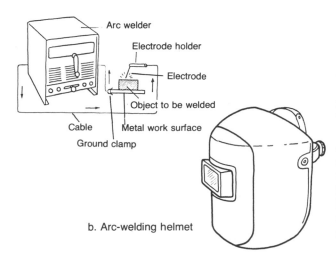

Arc welder
Electrode holder
Electrode
Object to be welded
Cable
Metal work surface
Ground clamp

b. Arc-welding helmet

The electrode is a wire or rod coated with a baked chemical **flux** that is held by the electrode holder. When the electrode coating burns, it forms a gas shield around the molten metal, preventing oxygen and nitrogen from creating impurities in the weld. The wire or rod inside provides **filler metal** for the seam. The flux mixes with the molten weld metal and floats impurities to the weld surface, creating **slag.** The size and type of electrode varies with the thickness and type of metal to be welded and the type of arc welding machine to be used. Many manufacturers use their own systems of identification. Some use names and others use numbers, colors, or coding. The manufacturer's package usually states the maximum and minimum amount of power to be used with the electrode.

See ill. Also see **Metalworking: Welding.**

argatch. Rugmaking. Weaving. An extra **filling** reinforcement of the **selvadge** threads in a **knotted pile** rug. Usually the pile does not extend to the selvadges at either side of the rug since the edges then would tend to curl under. The pile knots take up space on the rest of the warp ends that here at the selvadges is left empty. Extra **picks** are woven across or wrapped around the selvadge threads taking up the empty space and providing a stronger edge. The addition of these picks can also provide a decorative edge.

The amount of extra filling is determined by the thickness of the knots and the warp space they use. Too much filling at the selvadges and the rug will buckle, as will also happen if the extra filling is pulled tighter than the **ground weave.** The extra filling can be of the same yarn as the ground weave or in a thicker weight.

There are several ways of adding the extra filling. In one method two supplementary butterflies of yarn weave back and forth in a **plain weave** across each selvadge. The ground weave filling weaves in addition to these butterflies or just around the first selvadge thread.

In another method the same **shuttle** that is used to weave the ground weaves back and forth across first one set of selvadge threads and then goes across and weaves back and forth on the second set of selvadge threads before resuming the remainder of the ground weave.

Yet another variation extends the weaving of the butterflies past the selvadge threads into the ground weave. This is done as a triangular insert by moving over neighboring warp ends. In this case the ground weave does not reach over any of the selvadge threads.

As opposed to weaving on the selvadge threads the butterflies of argatch can wrap around these ends—either simply as if overcasting or in a pattern such as figure-of-eight.

Argatch is a Persian word and the technique is often found in Persian rugs. The term "bound" edge is sometimes used to denote the same reinforcement of selvadges.

Argyle knitting. Knitting. A basic knitting **motif** based on an overall pattern of diamond shapes, usually worked in two or three colors in the **stocking stitch.** The name comes from the district of Argyle in the West Highlands of Scotland. Tartan socks, which are knit in the colors of the clan tartans and are worn by the highland regiments, are made this way. Also see **geometric knitting.**

ariscuro. Coral Carving. See **coral.**

"aristocrat of fibers." Spinning. Weaving. See **vicuña.**

Arkansas oilstone. Jewelry. A natural abrasive stone quarried in the Ozark Mountains used to produce a fine cutting edge on steel tools, such as **engraving** tools. A light oil is used for lubrication and a rotating movement is used in sharpening. Also see **engraver's sharpener, graver, India oilstone.**

Arkansas oilstone. Woodworking. See **sharpening stone.**

Arkansas stone. Block Printing. See **sharpening stone.**

Arkansas Traveler. Quilts. (Also called Cowboy Star, Travel Star.) A **pieced block pattern** of four diamond shapes that point to the corners of the **block.** See ill. Also see **Kaleidoscope, star patterns.**

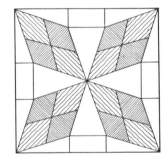

Arkansas Traveler

armature. Papercrafts. See **support.**

armature. Puppets. Toys. The rigid framework which is built to support another form, such as a **doll** or a soft sculpture. Wire and wood are the most common forms. Sometimes ready-made objects, such as chairs, hall-trees, or sawhorses can be used for the armature of large soft sculptures. Wood armatures are sometimes made so that part of the armature shows and can be utilized visually. Smaller forms, **toys** or dolls, may require only a wire or cardboard tubes or cones.

armature. Stained Glass. A structural reinforcement system used as a support. Armatures can be made of strips or wires of mild steel, galvanized iron, and copper. The internal armature can be tack-welded together, reinforcing vertically and horizontally at 2' intervals. It is placed in the mold before the concrete is added. There is also an armature that extends around the inside perimeter of the panel, set about 1–2" from the edge.

Fiberglass **roving** may be used for added tensile strength in **epoxy resin.** In very large panels there should be one continuous strip of reinforcement extending from the panel top to the bottom of the panel, and another from side to side. Also see **dalle-de-verre, polyester resin technique, wire hangers.**

arm bar. Puppets. The **cross bar** to which the **arm strings** or **hand strings** are attached on the **horizontal control.** In the **vertical control,** the wooden arm bar is replaced by a length of **galvanized wire,** which is run through the **vertical rod.** This wire swings free so that it can be lifted or dropped. The arm strings are attached to the wire arm bar. Also see **Puppets: Stringing the Marionette.**

arm puppet. Puppets. A variation of the **hand puppet** in which the figure is made to reach to the elbow. It is especially suitable for representing dragons, snakes, and alligators.

The puppet is made in either of two ways. The simplest method is to use a long cotton stocking, placing the fingers into the toe of the sock. Eyes, teeth, legs, etc. may be glued or sewn on. A second method uses two long strips of **felt,** each a little wider than the arm. These are rounded at the end to suggest an animal head. A circle can then be folded in half and set at the seam of the rounded end, with the folded center to the inside. That suggests a mouth, which can be opened and closed with the fingers. Details are added by gluing or sewing.

arm's length. Stitchery. See **yard.**

arm string. Puppets. A term applied to either the **hand strings** or the **elbow strings** of the **marionette.** The hand strings are most often used; they are attached to the **arm bar** in the **horizontal control.** Usually, one **string** is used; it runs from one hand up to a **screw eye** on one end of the arm bar, to another screw eye at the opposite end of the arm bar, and down to the other hand. In this way the arms can be controlled simultaneously. If a **vertical control** is used, there are two hand strings, which are attached to a wire shape. The wire, which goes through the vertical bar, can be lifted or dropped to move the arms. If elbow strings are used, they require an additional pair of strings and a separate attachment.

Also see **Puppets: Stringing the Marionette.**

around-the-post stitch. Crochet. See **Crochet: Basic Stitches.**

Around the World. Quilts. See **Drunkard's Path.**

arras. Weaving. See **tapestry.**

arrow. Rugmaking. Weaving. See **soumak.**

Arrowhead. Quilts. See **Tree Everlasting.**

arrowhead fold. Papercrafts. A paper construction variation in which triangular shapes are formed. Fold a piece of paper with **accordion pleating,** and before unfolding, fold the entire folded piece diagonally from two of the corners. Press the fold for a sharp crease. Then unfold the sheet and shape so that the folds face alternate directions. See ill.

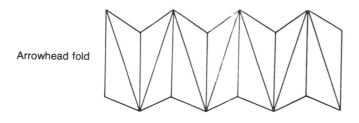

Arrowhead fold

Arrowhead Star. Quilts. See **star pattern.**

art canvas. Rugmaking. See **canvas.**

arte povero. Découpage. (Also called lacche povero, or poor person's lacquer.) A term from the Italian, meaning "poor person's art," used to describe the art of découpage. The term originated in eighteenth-century Venice, where hand-painted furniture made by the guilds was in such demand that designs were printed up in great quantities for hand-tinting, cutting, and adhering to furniture. The finished products of these treatments closely resembled the hand-painted pieces. The master painters of fine furniture considered this type of mass-produced furniture decoration a cheap imitation and called it "arte povero" in derision.

art fabric doll. Toys. A figure printed on **fabric** that was cut out, sewn, and stuffed to make a **doll.** These were popular in the early 1900s and are again being made by silk-screen printing and other fabric printing processes. Also see **cutout printed doll.**

Art Foam. Plastics. See **foam.**

art glass. Stained Glass. A name given to the enamel painted **opalescent glass** of the Art Nouveau era. The term now refers to any glass that is used for its beauty rather than strictly utilitarian purposes. Also see **Stained Glass.**

articulated. Puppets. **Joint**ed or segmented according to body structure. In figures used on the **puppet stage** or in a **puppet play,** the articulated joints are those that allow for movement between rigid body parts—for example, at the knee or the neck.

articulated puppet. Puppets. (Also called jointed figure.) A **puppet** figure with movable **joints.** The fully articulated figure is a **marionette** with numerous **strings** to control all parts of the body. Some simple figures, such as **animated figure**s or **shadow puppet**s, may be partially articulated, with joints made flexible through the use of clasps or tabs that allow parts to slide and change. Also see **card marionette** and **Puppets: Making the Marionette Skeleton.**

articulated toy. Toy. Any **toy,** especially that of a figure or an animal that is **joint**ed or segmented. The **jumping jack, dancing man,** and **whirligig figure** are all articulated toys with joints placed and attached to suggest a lifelike action. The articulated toy is usually also an **animated toy** and an **action toy.**

artificial dye. Dyeing. See **synthetic dye.**

artificial grain. Leather. A surface texture which has been artificially produced in the **tanning** and finishing process; for example, leather which has been embossed to resemble alligator or pigskin. Also see **Leatherwork: Finishing, Leather Tanning.**

artificial silk. Embroidery. Needlepoint. See **cotton embroidery floss.**

artist's resin. Plastics. See **polyester.**

Art Nouveau. Mosaics. A turn-of-the-century arts-and-crafts movement that was strongly decorative in character and usually used forms from nature as basic motifs. Artists associated with Art Nouveau, such as Antonio **Gaudí,** found **mosaics** a stimulating medium and did much to revitalize the craft as a creative art form. In stitchery Art Nouveau refers to a style that is characterized by expressive lines of flowing, swelling reverse curves. Patterns were crossed and interlaced, and often employed a whiplash curve. Also see **Mosaics.**

Art Nouveau. Stained Glass. See **art glass** and **Stained Glass.**

asbestos. Jewelry. A fire-resistant, fibrous mineral that is processed and manufactured into **powdered asbestos,** asbestos pads, **asbestos gloves,** asbestos soldering blocks, **coiled asbestos, asbestos ring sticks,** etc. Avoid inhaling asbestos, as it is carcinogenic.

asbestos. Stained Glass. A natural fibrous material that is resistant to heat and acid, used as insulation in **kiln** materials. Also see **kiln tray** and **Stained Glass: Safety Precautions.**

asbestos gloves. Enameling. See **firing** and **Enameling: Safety Precautions.**

asbestos gloves. Jewelry. Gloves made of woven asbestos, available singly or in pairs, and usually about 14" long to provide length enough to protect the hand, wrist, and lower arm from heat while removing or turning **flask**s during **burnout** in preparation for **casting.** They are also used when transferring flasks to the **centrifugal casting machine.** Also see **flask tongs.**

asbestos pad. Jewelry. (Also called soldering pad.) A firm but not hard **asbestos** pad used to protect working areas while **soldering.** Soldering is done directly on the asbestos pad. If the heat still travels through the board, two or more ½" thicknesses may be required, depending upon the degree of heat used to solder. The work can be pinned to the pad. CAUTION: The fibers from asbestos are dangerous to breathe, as they are carcinogenic. Consequently, when handling asbestos, do so carefully, so as not to get the fibers airborne. Also see **carborundum pan, charcoal block, magnesium block, transite board.**

asbestos ring stick. Jewelry. A round, tapered stick of **asbestos** used to hold rings during **soldering.** Also see **carborundum pan, carbon ring stick.**

asbestos rope. Stained Glass. See **firing** and **Stained Glass: Safety Precautions.**

asbolite. Ceramics. An impure form of cobalt oxide used by Chinese potters in making blue stoneware **glaze**s.

as-drawn-in. Weaving. See **treading-as-drawn-in.**

ash. Woodworking. A heavy brown **hardwood** that is quite strong and elastic. The three most common varieties are the red, white, and black ash. It is commonly used for tool handles and baseball bats. Because black ash is less strong but is more elastic than other ashes, it makes good **splint**s for baskets.

ash glaze. Ceramics. A glaze that contains about 40% ash, used as a **flux** when firing at high temperatures.

ashing. Plastics. A finishing process used for smoothing rough areas and removing scratches, sometimes done instead of sanding. Also see **Plastics: Finishing.**

aspen. Woodworking. See **poplar.**

asphaltum. A black semisolid pitch obtained from the distillation of coal. It is acid resistant and waterproof; its melting point is 302° F. It dissolves in all petroleum distillates (gasoline, lighter fluid, and benzene).

asphaltum. Enameling. (Also called asphaltum varnish.) A black varnish used as a **resist** with nitric and sulfuric acids.

asphaltum. Tincrafting. The dark brown solution of asphalt in oil or turpentine used as a coloring agent with **lacquer** or **varnish** in **japanning.** Also see **Tincraft: Finishing the Tin.**

asphaltum varnish. Enameling. See **asphaltum.**

asphaltum varnish. Jewelry. A thick, black tarlike substance the consistency of molasses used as a **resist** in **etching.**

assaying. Jewelry. The chemical testing or analysis of a metal to determine the amount of precious metal it contains.

assemblage. Mosaics. A form of art involving the arrangement or assembly of diverse materials or objects into a **mosaic**like collage.

assemble. Quilts. To join the parts of a **quilt top.** On a **block quilt** this would include the set and any **border**s or dividing **bands.** In a **pillow quilt** or **yo-yo quilt,** or in **quilt-as-you-go,** "to assemble" means to join the prefinished sections. Also see **Quilts: Hand Quilting.**

Assisi work. Embroidery. A type of **cross stitch** embroidery on linen, generally monochromatic. The design is outlined in **double running stitch** and the background of the design is filled in with cross stitch. This style of needlework originated in Assisi, Italy.

assistant. Batik and Tie-dye. A chemical mixer, usually **salt, acetic acid,** or **glacial acetic acid,** used in the **dyebath** to help the **dye** combine with the **fiber.** The particular assistant used depends on the fiber being dyed. Salt is essential in the formula of a **cotton** or **linen** dye, as it serves as an ionic conductor, or electrolyte, to help drive the dye molecule into the fiber. If salt is omitted the dye will rest on the surface of the fibers and will easily wash out. Common uniodized salt, available at grocery stores, is used.

Acetic acid is essential in a dye formula for **silk** or **wool.** If purchased at a pharmacy, chemical, or photo supply shop, it is designated **glacial acetic acid.** It is available from grocery stores as white vinegar in a 5% acetic acid solution.

Occasionally a **dyestuff** requires **alcohol** to **paste** the dye and serve as assistant. Wood alcohol (from a paint store), not rubbing alcohol, should be used.

assistant. Fabric Printing. A chemical that is added to the **dye bath** to help bend the **dye** or the **mordant** to the fiber.

Assumption sash. Weaving. A plaited sash made by Canadian Indians in the mid-nineteenth century for the Hudson Bay Trading Company. It was named after a parish in Canada. The typical design was composed of an arrowhead motif in many colors with red as the predominant color. The technique includes interlocking the **warp** threads by looping them around each other at the point of reversing direction while **plaiting.** Also see **ceinture flechée.**

Aster. Quilts. See **Dresden Plate.**

asterisk. Tatting. (abbr. *). An asterisk indicates to repeat all instruction from one * to the other *.

asterism. Gemcutting. See **cabochon, corundum, luster.**

astrogalus. Toys. See **knucklebones.**

asymmetry. Unbalance or unequal proportions. Designs using asymmetrical elements tend to seem active or in movement, whereas symmetrical designs are likely to seem at rest or static. Asymmetrical designs can be irritating to look at unless the apparent unbalance is compensated in some way. For example, if two squares of unequal size are in symmetrical positions on a background, the visual effect will be unbalanced. To compensate, the larger square could be colored lighter than the smaller square, the reduced "weight" of color making up for the difference in size. Also see **figure and ground, golden section, proportion.**

athlete. Toys. An **animated toy** similar to the **acrobat**s, but in which the figure's hands are attached to a rod instead of to strings. Usually two figures are used and they are moved by means of a handle that turns the rod and activates the figures.

atomizer. Enameling. A tool used for spraying water-soluble **binder.** It can be a manually operated bottle with a rubber bulb and nozzle, although larger setups with a spray gun and compressor are also available. Another type consists of an aerosol unit screwed on top of a bottle. Atomizers can also be used for spraying liquid **enamel** if it is fine enough. Also see **Enameling: Tools and Materials.**

attach. Tatting. (abbr. att) (Also called joining.) A tatter might join a **ring** to another ring by attaching one **picot** from a previous ring to the ring in process. When using one **shuttle,** a **single thread** could be a joining from one **motif** to another. See ill.

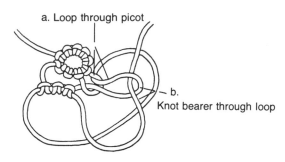

Attach

a. Loop through picot

b. Knot bearer through loop

attached buttonhole stitch. Crewel. Embroidery. See **buttonhole stitch.**

attached fly stitch. Crewel. Embroidery. See **fishbone stitch.**

Attic Windows. Quilts. A small **pieced block** composed of a square and two trapezoids. These are joined in a manner similar to the **Box Quilt** or **Baby Blocks.** In this pattern, however, the square is black and the trapezoids are colored, which makes the square appear to recede, suggesting windows or grillwork.

Aúbusson bobbin. Weaving. See **flute.**

Aubusson loom. Weaving. See **low-warp, tapestry loom.**

Aubusson stitch. Needlepoint. A flat tapestry weave named after a town in the department of LaCreuse, France. Also see **rep stitch.**

Aubusson tapestry. Weaving. A **tapestry** originating from Aubusson. **Low-warp** tapestry has been practiced here for centuries. With certainty it goes back to the fourteenth century and according to tradition it dates back to the thirteenth century. Also see **interlocking, slit tapestry.**

auger bit. Woodworking. See **drill bit.**

Aunt Eliza's Star. Quilts. See **star patterns, Texas Lone Star.**

Aunt Sukey's Choice. Quilts. A **block** design for a **pieced quilt** using diamonds, triangles, and squares. The finished block has a central cross and corner squares.

Austrian knitting. Knitting. A type of **Swiss darning** used to create patterns on knit fabric. This can be done in place of **color knitting** to create a multicolored effect in what was originally solid color knitting.

autoclave. Batik and Tie-dye. A piece of equipment designed for sterilizing which utilizes superheated steam under pressure. It is essentially a large pressure cooker. It is an expensive appliance, used primarily in hospitals and laboratories, but is a tremendous aid to anyone wishing to steam set or **heat set** a dyed fabric. Also see **steamer.**

autograph quilt. Quilts. (Also called friendship quilt, Friendship Medley, presentation quilt.) Any of various quilts that include the names of the quilters on the particular **blocks** that they contributed. The signatures are embroidered or sometimes written in India ink. Some **album quilts** included autographs, but not all. Also see **tithing quilt.**

automatic awl. Leather. (Also called lock stitch awl.) An aid for sewing heavy leather which combines awl, needle, and thread in the same tool, therefore punching and stitching in one operation. The threaded needle is pushed through the leather, then pulled back to form a loop, which locks automatically when tightened. The stitch has the same effect as a lock stitch on a sewing machine. See ill.

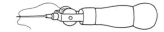

Automatic awl

automatic center punch. Jewelry. An automatic, adjustable, spring-driven tool used to punch dents in metal preparatory to drilling holes. The spring-driven mechanism is tightened or loosened by turning the cap at the top of the tool. Because punching too hard can bend metal in the surrounding areas, a test should be made on a piece of scrap metal and the tension of the spring should be adjusted accordingly. The punch should be held in a position perpendicular to the metal, and pressure applied with the palm of the hand for accurate control. See ill. Also see **center punch.**

Automatic center punch

automatic engraving tool. Jewelry. See **electric engraving tool.**

automatic let-off. Weaving. See **friction brake.**

automatic screwdriver. Woodworking. See **screwdriver.**

automatic toys. Toys. Mechanical toys. There are literary references to automatic toys that date back several thousand years. In the "Iliad" there is a mention of mechanical toys, and they were known in Alexandria and Asia Minor before the birth of Christ.

The French were making superb automatic toys by the eighteenth century, following the toymakers of Nuremberg who produced toys of incredible variety during the 1700s. The first known **clockwork toy** in Germany was recorded as having been made in 1672. The earliest musical accompaniments for automatic toys were made by the Swiss, but there seems to be little question that the German toymakers were the leaders. They remained in the lead for years, producing inventive, delightful, and intriguing toys.

Most of the museum examples of automata, as mechanical toys are called, are from the eighteenth and nineteenth centuries, when interest in these toys was at its peak. They were operated in any of a number of ways, including **clockwork**s, sand motors, and music boxes. Monkey automata became very popular in the middle nineteenth century when they were made to perform such tasks as playing in orchestras and puffing on cigarettes. Other automatic toys included running ducks, hopping frogs, and running mice. Also see **autoperipatetikos, bell** and **Toys: Mechanical Toys and Moving Toys.**

autoperipatetikos. Toys. **Toys** or **doll**s operated by a **clockwork** mechanism. The system was patented about 1860 when toys of this kind were popular and highly prized. Also see **automatic toys.**

Autumn Leaf. Quilts. See **Yankee Pride.**

avanturescence. Gemcutting. See **luster.**

aventurine. Gemcutting. See **quartz.**

aventurine glaze. Ceramics. A normally high firing temperature glaze combined with soda or **boric oxide** as a **flux.** It also contains excessive amounts of **zinc oxide** and **iron oxide** (more than 6%). The excessive amounts of zinc oxide and iron oxide form small crystals during cooling that reflect light.

aviation snips. Jewelry. A form of **universal shears.** Also see **shears, snips.**

aviation snips. Metalworking. See **snips.**

awl. Basketry. See **bodkin.**

awl. Bookbinding. Embroidery. Tincrafting. A tool used to perforate holes in the sections of books to facilitate sewing. It can be used for all operations requiring holes in the absence of a **hand brace.**

In embroidery an awl is used to pierce small holes in background fabric. It is useful in metallic thread embroidery where it is necessary to make openings in the **fabric** in order to end off the metallic thread.

In tincrafting an awl is attached securely to a hardwood handle that is used for punching holes and scratching or **scoring** lines on **tinplate.** Also see **Tincraft: Cutting the Tin, Folding the Tin.**

awl. Leather. See **awl and haft.**

awl. Woodworking. A small, sharp-pointed hand tool used primarily for making holes in wood. It may be used to make the entire screwhole in softer wood or a starting hole for **drilling** harder woods. An awl is sometimes used to **scribe** lines where a pencil would prove ineffective. Also see **marking tools.**

awl and haft. Leather. (Also called awl tracer.) A two-pieced pointed metal tool consisting of a handle, or haft, and an awl blade. This tool is used to punch and enlarge slits and holes for **lacing** and sewing, and to etch or trace guidelines and patterns. There are two types of hafts, the sewing haft and the peg awl haft which are used with interchangeable awl blades. Awls come in different sizes and point shapes. See ill. Also see **fid, harness awl, space marker** and **Leatherwork: Care and Maintenance of Tools, Creasing, Scoring and Folding Leather.**

Awl and haft

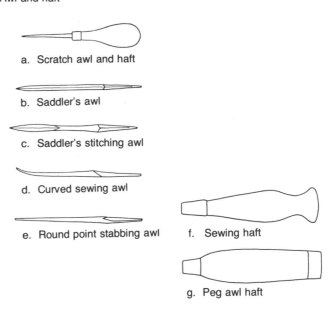

a. Scratch awl and haft

b. Saddler's awl

c. Saddler's stitching awl

d. Curved sewing awl

e. Round point stabbing awl   f. Sewing haft

g. Peg awl haft

awl tracer. Leather. See **awl and haft.**

awning fabric. Stitchery. Toys. A **plain weave** sturdy **fabric,** usually **cotton,** drill or **duck** in various weights. It is sometimes available with a vinyl coating for use outdoors. For **banners** which must withstand weathering, a vinyl-coated awning fabric or **acrylic canvas** may be used.

axinite. Gemcutting. A mineral composed of aluminum and calcium silicate with water and boric acid in **crystals** of the triclinic system. Axinite has **hardness** of 6½–7 and **specific gravity** of 3.3; it has granular **fracture.** Translucent to transparent material, it occurs in **color**s of clove-brown tinged with violet, honey-colored, and yellow-gray.

It has moderate dichroism and a vitreous **luster.** Its refractive indices are 1.679 and 1.690. This material is faceted to display color and is polished with tin oxide on a tin **lap.** Also see **faceting, polishing, refraction.**

axle. Spinning. The piece joining the wheel to the **upright** support (or supports) on a **spinning wheel.** The wheel revolves around the axle during spinning. Also see **treadle wheel, wool wheel.**

axle. Toys. A shaft to which wheels are attached in many **wheeled toy**s. Sometimes the axle and wheel are firmly joined and they rotate together; in other toys the wheel revolves on the axle.

An eccentric axle is often used in **animated toy**s, especially wheeled toys. In these a portion of the axle is set off-center, or a U-shaped jog in the axle may be connected to some moving part. When the wheel moves, the axle turns, and any part connected to the axle moves with it.

In most handmade toys the axles are made of wood **dowel,** although any cylindrical form to which a wheel can be attached is usable. Also see **Toys: Wheeled Toys.**

Ayrshire work. Embroidery. White-on-white embroidery developed into a cottage industry in Ayreshire, Scotland, in the early 1900s. The work consisted of fine **chain stitching** on sheer lawn or **batiste** and was used to decorate aprons, baby bonnets, shawls, and similar articles. Cottagers paid their children one penny a day to keep their needles threaded. Also see **Whitework.**

azoic. Batik and Tie-dye. See **naphthol dye.**

azured tool. Bookbinding. A **finding tool** with close, diagonal, parallel lines.

azurite. Gemcutting. This mineral is also called chessylite; composed of copper carbonate in different proportions than **malachite.** It is dark blue, has **hardness** of 3¾, **specific gravity** of 3.8, and vitreous **luster.** Its refractive indices are 1.73 and 1.83 and when transparent **crystals** of sufficient size occur, they are faceted despite their softness.

After preparation on a worn 600 grit **sanding** cloth, azurite is polished on leather with chrome oxide and moderate pressure.

Burnite is a variety of azurite discovered by Frank Burnham in 1952 in Nevada.

Also see **faceting, polishing, refraction.**

Baby Blocks. Quilts. (Also called Block Patterns, Cubework, English T-Box, Steps to the Altar, Tumbling Blocks.) A pattern for a **pieced quilt** made entirely from diamonds of one size. Joined, the diamonds give an optical illusion of stars, blocks, compasses, or cubes. Similar patterns are **Box Quilt** and **Attic Windows**. Also see **diamond patchwork**.

baby doll. Toys. A **doll** made to resemble a baby. Until about 1820 dolls were made in the form of adults. Children until then were generally regarded as small adults and were dressed as such—as were their dolls. Baby dolls are among the favorite dolls of small children of all times.

baby flannel. Quilts. (Also called flannelette.) A soft **cotton** flannel of a **plain weave**. It is usually white or a pastel blue, pink, or yellow. Also see **cotton flannel, flannel.**

baby toy. Toys. See **cradle toy, nursery toy.**

Bachelor's Puzzle. Quilts. A **block pattern** used in **piece quilt**s that gives a lattice effect of diagonal, horizontal, and vertical lines with squares where the lines intersect.

back. Basketry. The convex surface of a **willow** rod.

back. Bookbinding. The edge of the book that is bound.

back. Leather. A term used to describe the top part of the hide, or **side** (the section along the center back of the animal), which is the choicest part of the leather skin. Also see **bend.**

back. Stitchery. To line or cover the back or reverse side of a fabric **panel,** as with a **backing** material.

Also, the underside of a **fabric.** In some fabrics there is no difference between back and front. On others, like **corduroy, velveteen,** or **flannel,** the **pile** is on the front or **face** and the back is plain. The patterns of some weaves vary from front to back, as in **pique, waffle-weave** or **brocade.**

back apron bar. Weaving. See **apron bar.**

back beam. Weaving. The flat, horizontal, wooden beam located in the back over the **warp beam** in a **harness loom.** The warp passes from the warp beam over the back beam and is guided to the harnesses. It corresponds to the **breast beam** in the front of the loom. In many old looms, the back beam is omitted and the warp travels directly from a raised warp beam to the harnesses. Also see **beaming, jack type loom, table loom, warping.**

backbone. Bookbinding. See **spine.**

back bridge. Puppets. See **rear bridge.**

backcloth. Puppets. See **backdrop.**

back curtain. Puppets. The curtain hung behind a **backdrop,** especially important when the backdrop is rigid and has doorways cut into it. Without a back curtain, the openings in the backdrop would allow the audience to see through to **backstage**. Also see **flat** and **Puppets: The Puppet Stage.**

backdrop. Puppets. (Also called backcloth.) The material used to cover the back of the stage as viewed by the audience. Sometimes it is a **flat** and has a **set** painted on it. If there are doorways, a **back curtain** is used behind the backdrop so that the audience does not see all the way through. The backdrop may be a plain black curtain, which provides the background for the play, or it may be an elaborately painted scene. Also see **bridge, drop, top drop** and **Puppets: The Puppet Stage.**

back edge. Bookbinding. The edges of the **sections, boards,** and leaves that face the binding. Also see **spine.**

backed material. Puppets. Stitchery. Toys. (Also called foamed-backed, latex-coated material.) Either those **fabrics** which have a layer of another material affixed to them, such as **bonded fabric**s and **laminated fabric**s, or material with a **synthetic,** latex or rubber backing. The synthetic and other similar backings are usually applied to upholstery fabrics to prevent them from skidding or slipping when used as furniture covering. **Upholstery materials** are often used in stitchery, but only those materials which can readily be sewn should be used. Some backing substances are too thick, causing friction, which heats the sewing machine needle and leads to eventual jamming. Heavily backed materials are equally difficult to sew by hand. A very lightly backed fabric will not interfere with stitching, but it would be helpful to test the fabric to determine any difficulty in sewing by drawing the needle through it.

backfire. Metalworking. A loud popping sound in the lit **welding** torch. It may result from any of these causes:

a. welding with a dirty torch tip

b. welding with a loose or overheated torch tip

c. touching the welded work with the torch tip while welding

d. welding with too low an **acetylene** working pressure (called starving the tip)

e. turning off the acetylene valve too quickly when turning off the torch

Also see **oxyacetylene welding equipment.**

background. Quilts. The base material for the **block** of an **appliqué quilt** or for an **overall** appliqué design. It is usually chosen to contrast in color and value with the appliqué fabrics.

background. Stitchery. The main body of **fabric** to which **embroidery, appliqué, stitchery** etc., are sewn for **wall hangings.** A finished **panel** is usually hung or **mount**ed in such a way that the background carries the weight of all the **needlework.** The background itself may be **fold**ed and **hem**med to provide a **channel** for a **rod,** or the background may be stretched over a **wood panel.** Also see **relief.**

background fabric. Crewel. Embroidery. Needlepoint. (Also called base material.) A term used to describe the fabric upon which any form of needlework is done. The choice of a background fabric depends upon the type of needlework, the yarn, and the use of the finished product. Also see **batiste, Belgian linen, binca cotton, brocade, burlap, canvas, coarse weave linen, cotton canvas, felt, fine weave linen, Glenshea linen, hardanger fabric, Hessian fabric, Irish linen, linen canvas, linen fabric, Maltese silk, pegboard, perforated cardboard, silk canvas, window screen, worsted yarn** and **Bargello: Materials; Crewel: Materials; Needlepoint: Materials.**

background laying. China and Glass Painting. See **ground laying.**

background tool. Leather. A tool used to mat down background areas when **tooling** leather. Also see **stamp.**

background weave. Weaving. See **ground weave.**

backing. Bookbinding. Backing is the operation that accomplishes the final distribution of the **swell.** It produces the **groove** that the cover **board**s will fit into and helps ensure that the **back** will retain its rounded shape and that the leaves will lay flat when the book is opened. It is executed by delivering light glancing blows to the back of the joined sections with a **backing hammer,** alternating from one side to the other.

Mark both **endpapers** at the **head** and **tail** ⅛–³/₁₆″ from the back edge, or a distance twice the thickness of the cover board. Set the book between **backing boards** with the back and the backing marks perfectly parallel to the edges of the boards. If the book slips while you are trying to adjust it between the boards, moisten the insides of the

boards with a damp sponge. To prevent damaging the **tape**s they should remain outside the boards. Backing must be done before the glue sets.

Lower the boards and the book into the **lying press** and adjust them so that they are square. The importance of proper positioning cannot be overemphasized as this operation will permanently fix the shape of the book; there must be even pressure exerted along the length of the book. Screw the press up as tightly as possible.

Hammer the back gently with glancing blows to fan out sections as evenly as possible. First use the face of the backing hammer and then the toe, slowly hammering toward you and then on the other side, away from you. Repeat this procedure until the back has an even, rounded shape. The sides should be hammered down against the backing boards to create a neat, sharp groove for the cover. Take care not to damage the **threads.** The height of the arc, or the degree of roundness of the back, is a matter of taste; the important element is the even distribution of the sections to prevent a lopsided shape. When finished, rub down with the **bone folder.** See ill. Also see **French groove.**

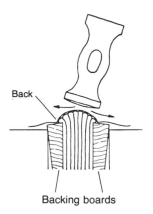

Back

Backing boards

backing. Enameling. See **counterenamel.**

backing. Mosaics. (Also called base, support.) The surface or object to which **mosaic** materials are fixed. All mosaics require some kind of backing or base, whether it be an existing wall, floor, or object, or a surface specifically constructed for the purpose. Traditionally, mosaics were almost always constructed directly on an existing **cement** wall or floor with a fresh layer of cement **mortar** as the bond. A **concrete backing** is still preferred by many professional craftspeople because of its strength, rigidity, durability, and capacity to resist damage from the elements. However, cement surfaces can be difficult to construct and cement-backed pieces of any size are very heavy and cannot be hung. Because of these disadvantages, waterproof plywood or masonite backings are frequently used. For smaller mosaics, masonite or ½″ plywood is usually adequate; for larger pieces, ¾″ plywood is recommended. If the mosaic is to be very large, some type of cross-bracing behind the backing is advisable. In all projects where wood is to be used as a backing or base, every surface, including fresh-cut ends, must be sealed against moisture with wood sealer. The effect of translucent mosaic materials can be heightened by using plate glass or Plexiglas as a backing. Also see **Mosaics: Tools and Materials; Setting the Material.**

backing. Quilts. Stitchery. The fabric used on the reverse side of a **quilt, panel,** or **banner,** as a **lining.** Occasionally, the term "backing" is used to refer to the **background.** Actually, it is the lining of the background fabric. A backing fabric hides loose threads and **stitch**es and **finish**es the reverse side of a work. Also see **quilt back.**

backing. Rugmaking. See **rug backing.**

backing boards. Bookbinding. Wedge-shaped boards usually made from beech with top edges sloped at an angle of 80°. The book is placed between them and inserted in the **lying press** during **backing** to help form the **joint** or **groove** for the **cover boards.** Also see **backing.**

backing for pillows. Crewel. Embroidery. Needlepoint. See **Crewel: Finishing; Needlepoint: Finishing.**

backing hammer. Bookbinding. A hammer with a convex face and a broad toe used for the **backing** and **rounding** processes in bookbinding. It is also used for **knocking down swell.** See ill.

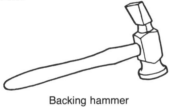

Backing hammer

backing the rug. Rugmaking. A process of finishing the rug by putting on a protective cover either to insure that the stitches or **pile** will not be pulled out, or to lengthen the wear of the rug. The protective covers are put on after the rug surface and the hem, or other edge finishing, are done. They can be used with every kind of rug backing or technique but are not often found on woven, crocheted or knit rugs, or rugs using a **Scandinavian rug backing.**

One type of protective cover is a rug lining which protects the back of the rug from dirt, lessens the wear and acts as a cushioning agent. It gives more body to the rug and helps prevent the surface knots, loops or stitches from pulling out. Linings are usually of heavy **burlap,** heavy-duty denim, serge, cotton **rep** or any other closely woven strong fabric. The lining fabric is cut to the size of the rug plus 1½″ for the lining hem. The fabric is then pinned to the back of the rug and adjusted so that it fits perfectly and does not show at the edges of the rug. It is sewn to the rug hem with a strong, matching color thread. There is also a special hessian cloth with an adhesive backing that is simply ironed on to the back of the rug.

The finished rug may also be backed with latex, a liquid rubber adhesive which makes the rug skidproof and anchors the loops in a **hooked rug.** Latex is not necessary if the rug is made of very tightly packed cut loops or in a knotted pile rug, but with the continuous rows of uncut loops that hooked rugs are made of, there is always the possibility that a heel could catch in one loop and pull out the whole row. Liquid latex is available at rug supply and needlework stores. Proper ventilation is absolutely necessary when applying the latex coating. Care must be taken that the rug is lying flat on the floor before the latex is applied or the latex may harden into uneven ripples. If the rug has been worked on a **frame,** it is best to apply the adhesive while it is still stretched in the frame. Latexing will dissolve a little each time a rug is washed, nevertheless, it will give years of service. It is possible to skid-proof a rug by latexing only the edges or corners of the rug. The same effect is achieved by attaching to the corners large rubber triangles cut out of a carpet pad or rubber jar rings. Corners that turn up can be backed with lead drapery weights.

backlight. Puppets. A light that comes from behind. In **puppetry** the **shadow play** utilizes a backlighted **screen** against which the shadows of **silhouette puppets** or figures or **shadow puppets** perform. The front of the screen faces the audience. The light source is directed toward the audience but strikes the screen that separates them. The shadow puppets must be placed next to the screen, between it and the light source. Care must be taken to block out any backlight except for the area of the screen, or the audience will have light shining in its eyes.

backlighting. Stained Glass. The method by which stained-glass panels are lighted from behind when exhibited indoors. The best method is to place a sheet of transluscent white plastic behind the panel, with the lighting in back of it, so that the bulbs and their glare are invisible. The most effective way of achieving a professional-looking exhibit is to make a portable light box for each piece. Another alternative is to direct a white light at a plain white wall behind the stained-glass exhibit, which will illuminate the exhibit by reflection.

back lining. Bookbinding. The process and the material of reinforcement of the **back** of a book. After **rounding** the back, cut a strip of **crash** ⅛–½″ shorter and 2½″ wider than the **spine;** glue it to the back and rub down (do not glue overlap). Cut a piece of **kraft paper** to the exact width of the back but longer at the **head** and **tail;** glue and rub down and cut the kraft paper flush with the head and tail.

back mark. Bookbinding. A short black stripe printed on the fold of the back of each **section,** positioned to form a series of steps when the text is in the correct order. It is used as an aid to positioning and collating the sections of a book. It is visually more apparent if an error has occurred with back marks than with **signature**s, as a misplaced section is obviously indicated by a break in the series.

back of knitting. Knitting. This is the side of knitting not intended to be seen; the back of knitting in many cases is formed by the even-numbered rows (i.e., rows 2,4,6, etc.).

back of stranding. Knitting. The **back of knitting** side of a piece of **color knitting.** All the colors used in the knitting are stranded along this side of the work whenever they are not being used in the knitting stitches (i.e., the various colored balls of yarn are not cut each time the color changes, but are "carried" along). Also see **stranding.**

back rest. Gemcutting. See **faceting unit.**

back rest. Weaving. See **back beam.**

back saw. Bookbinding. A saw commonly used to make saw cuts across the **back** of the book to facilitate sewing the **section**s together and to cut kerfs for **cord**s. A dull hacksaw or coping saw may be used as well. Also see **sawing-in.**

backsaw. Woodworking. See **hand saw.**

backstage. Puppets. Behind the stage proper. The **controller** in the **marionette theater** stands backstage. Also see **back curtain, puppet play, wing.**

backstitch. Crewel. Embroidery. Needlepoint. One of the most basic and simple stitches. When worked correctly, it can be highly decorative. It can be worked either in the hand or on an **embroidery frame.** The stitch is most effective when kept regular and uniform in size, and is therefore worked easily on an **evenweave fabric.** It is an extremely important stitch in **backwork** and **counted-thread embroidery,** excellent for lines and outlines, and particularly recommended for stitching initials or a name on a completed piece. It is the foundation for **backstitch threaded.** Worked on **canvas,** it is extremely useful for covering threads exposed by stitches being pulled too tightly.

Come up at A, go down at B, then up ahead at C and back down at A. Repeat going back into the first hole of the previous stitch. Keep all the stitches the same size. See ill. Also see **line stitch.**

backstitch. Leather. A commonly used stitch which fills in the spaces between the needle holes and thus reinforces the seam.

back stitch. Quilts. Stitchery. A hand **stitch** used for lines or outlines. It is a tight sturdy stitch, worked from right to left. The thread is brought up thru the **fabric** on the line to be sewn. The **needle** goes to the right of the thread for a short distance, into the fabric and under. It emerges at an equal distance to the left of the thread and is pulled through. The needle goes back to the right, touching the last stitch, into the fabric, under and emerges at the left. See ill.

The machine-made back stitch is the reverse **straight** stitch which reinforces the seam and avoids the necessity of tying the thread ends.

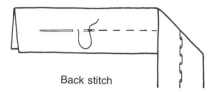

Back stitch

back stitch, threaded. Crewel. Embroidery. (Also called interlaced back stitch.) A **line stitch** used for borders, outlines, and open fillings worked on a foundation of **back stitch.** Work a line of back stitch, and using a **tapestry needle** and contrasting color, thread it through. The needle passes under the first back stitch from right to left (not into the material), through the second back stitch from left to right, and so on. Do not draw the interlacing thread too tightly, as it will destroy the soft flow of the finished stitch. See ill. Also see **threaded.**

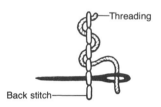

Threading

Back stitch

backstrap loom. Weaving. (Also called body loom, girdle-back loom, stick loom, strap loom, waist loom.) A simple, economical, portable, and lightweight **primitive loom** that has one end attached to a tree or other stationary support, and the other end attached to the weaver's waist or hips. Although called a **horizontal loom** the **warp** is actually at an oblique angle between the support and the weaver. The warp runs between two sticks or rods that correspond to the **warp beam** and either the **cloth** or **breast beam** of a **harness loom.** At one end, attached to the support by a rope, is the warp stick. At the opposite end, at the front of the loom, is the cloth stick to which is attached a band of fiber, cloth or leather that goes around the weaver. As the weaver pulls against the support with her body, **warp tension** is achieved and controlled, and she is able to weave.

The backstrap loom was the loom of the pre-Columbian weavers of Peru and Mexico as well as of early people in India, Tibet, the Philippines and the Far East. It is still used in Peru and Mexico, Ecuador, Bolivia, Guatemala and in remote areas of southeast Asia and Africa. The North American Indians have used a backstrap loom in conjunction with a **rigid heddle.** That version and the simple stick version have become popular with contemporary handweavers in the states.

A **shed stick** or shed roll and a **heddle bar** achieve the **sheds,** although at one time in some cultures, the fingers alone picked up the sheds. A **batten** is used to beat down the **filling.** In cases of pattern weaving, when the pattern is not picked up by the fingers or a **pick-up stick,** extra pattern heddle bars are put in. These are normally placed ahead of the usual heddle bar. The shuttle used is either a **bobbin** or **stick shuttle.** A second cloth roll or bar is often found next to and above the cloth stick, around which the finished fabric is wound as the weaving progresses. The second bar goes on top of the fabric to prevent it from slipping around the cloth bar. The weaver, as she rolls up the fabric, moves constantly closer to the warp stick. When not in use, the loom with the weaving and empty warp is simply rolled up and put away.

The warp is measured out beforehand on either a **warping board** or **reel** or on pegs in the ground as the ancient Peruvians did. The **cross** or lease is secured with **lease sticks** or a **lease cord.** A long cord is slipped into the loop at each end of the warp. This cord is then used to transfer the warp to the warp and cloth sticks, or it becomes the cord by which the warp is attached to the sticks. In the latter method, the cord must be long enough so that the warp can be spread to its full width along the sticks. The cord is tied at each end of each stick and a lacing cord is added that lashes the transfer cord to the sticks. In yet another method, the primitive warp pegs stuck into the ground serve as the warp and cloth sticks so that no transfer of the warp is needed. The **heddle cord** and heddle bar are put in to be able to raise one shed, and the shed stick is inserted for the **countershed.** Weaving can then begin.

When using a rigid heddle, the warp is cut at the looped end opposite the cross. The cut ends are then threaded through the rigid heddle and tied to the cloth stick with a **tie-on knot** as in a **harness loom.** The looped end near the

cross is slipped over the warp stick. The backstrap or band must be attached to the cloth stick and around the weaver, and the warp stick must be attached to the support prior to tying the ends onto the cloth stick, so that the tension can be adjusted as the ends are tied.

The width of the loom is determined by what the weaver can handle, which is usually no wider than 30″ and very often much narrower. On these looms are woven beautiful ponchos, mats, bags, blankets, wraps, waistbands, and fabrics for skirts, jackets, and blouses. There are also backstrap **belt loom**s for the weaving of belts, ties, narrow bands, and ribbons. There is no limit to the type of cloth or pattern that can be woven on a backstrap loom as evidenced by the Peruvian weavers who wove **double cloth,** intricate **gauze weave**s, and highly detailed **laid-in** and **tapestry** work. See ill.

back string. Puppets. (Also called bowing string.) The cord or **string** that connects a point on the **marionette**'s back to a **screw eye** on the end of the **control bar.** Most marionettes **manipulate**d by a **vertical control** bar have a back string. A different arrangement is used on the **horizontal control** bar, where **hip string**s are usually substituted for the back string. Also see **Puppets: Stringing the Marionette.**

back-trac. Basketry. See **border.**

badger brush. Stained Glass. See **brush**es.

badgering. Stained Glass. See **matting.**

baffle. Ceramics. See **bag wall.**

baffle. Stained Glass. A spare tray used in **firing** in an open **kiln.** It is made of metal instead of **asbestos** and is not covered with plaster. It is placed in the higher position in the firing chamber and functions to moderate the direct heat of the electric elements above and protect the glass below.

bag punch. Leather. See **oblong punch.**

bag swing. Toys. A single **rope swing** that is a bag filled with **sawdust,** sand, rags, or similar material and tied at the top and hung from a rope. Also see **swing** and **Toys: Rope and Swing Toys.**

baguette. Gemcutting. See **facet.**

bag wall. Ceramics. (Also called baffle.) A wall between the flame and the **ware** in a **kiln.** This wall deflects heat upward and prevents the flame from directly hitting the ware. See ill. Also see **flashing, muffle.**

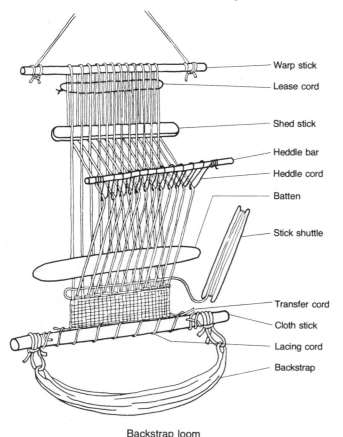

Warp stick
Lease cord
Shed stick
Heddle bar
Heddle cord
Batten
Stick shuttle
Transfer cord
Cloth stick
Lacing cord
Backstrap

Backstrap loom

Bag wall

baize. Weaving. See **Navajo weaving.**

baker's art. Toys. An ancient art form in which doughs of various kinds are shaped and baked. Some are **edible doughs** and others are **inedible doughs,** purely to decorate and delight. Recently, baker's art has come to include the use of inedible **baker's clay** for modeling dough sculpture. **Cookie art** includes the decorative work applied to the cookie, or the way in which the cookie is formed. **Bread dough sculpture** is made from yeasted bread dough or from a **salt dough.**

Various kitchen tools and devices lend themselves particularly well for use in baker's art. The dough can be forced through a garlic press or ricer to make curls for hair or fur; a pastry wheel gives a decorative edge; a melon ball cutter is an aid in making round shapes; and toothpicks, nut picks, and other kitchen utensils can be used to add details. Also see **bread clay, bread doll** and **Toys: Ephemeral Toys.**

baker's clay. Dough Sculpture. Toys. An inedible, claylike mixture of flour, salt, and water that can be formed into shapes and baked in a household oven to harden.

Mix 4 cups all-purpose flour with 1 cup salt in a bowl. Add 1½ cups water, mixing thoroughly with hands. The amount of water added may vary with the humidity of the weather. The dough should be quite stiff. Remove the dough from the bowl and knead for about 10 minutes. Dough may be stored in a tightly closed plastic bag. However, because fresh dough yields better results, a fresh batch should be made each time. The dough can be rolled flat with a rolling pin for cutting into shapes, or it can be formed like clay. When joining one piece of dough to another, use small dabs of water for better adhesion. When completed, bake the pieces on a cookie sheet in a preheated over 350° F oven until hard and golden brown. Baking time varies, depending on the size and thickness of the pieces (from about half an hour for small pieces up to 2 hours for large pieces). Cool the pieces on a rack. When thoroughly cooled, and painted if desired, pieces should be given one of the clear, protective finishes, such as spray acrylic gloss, that are readily available.

There are a few variations to the basic method. When making the dough, liquid household dye (the type purchased at a dime store) or **food coloring** may be added to the water before adding it to the salt and flour. Experiment to determine the correct amount of dye to add, because the color changes during baking. Spices, vegetable juices, cocoa, or **water base paints** will also add color. Be-

fore baking, designs and patterns can be incised in the pieces with kitchen implements such as forks, straws, and small sharp knives. Materials such as beads, seeds, and shells may be imbedded, mosaic-style, in the clay, provided they will withstand the heat of baking. If the piece is to hang, a wire hook should be inserted or a hole for a string pierced with a straw or toothpick before baking. Baker's clay may be formed over a mold and left on the mold during baking. Strips of clay, interwoven over a bread pan and baked in place, make a nice bread basket. Remember that the pan must be heat resistant. Allow the piece to cool on the pan before removing.

For the rich appearance of baked bread, rather than a painted surface, the piece may be given a glaze before or after baking. Also see **baker's clay glazes.**

baker's clay glazes. Toys. (Also called dough art glaze.) Various glazes can be used on **baker's clay,** applied before, during, or after baking. Following is a list of common glazes.

Canned milk glaze. Brush canned milk onto the dough before baking; it provides a **glossy** brown surface.

Egg-yolk glaze. Paint on the shaped dough before baking. The egg yolk makes a thick, dark glaze. **Food coloring** can be added to egg yolk to give bright, glossy colors.

Mayonnaise glaze. Paint onto the shaped dough before baking, then again during baking; it gives a yellowish glaze.

Sugar-water glaze. Paint on before baking. It gives a sparkly glaze that is satisfactory for edible foods but not good for anything that is to be preserved.

Shoe-polish glaze. Rub a dye-and-shine or wax-type shoe polish onto partially baked dough. It will finish glazing as it bakes.

Acrylic paint glaze. Apply **acrylic paint** to shaped dough after baking. An additional color or **antiquing** glaze can be added.

Antique glaze. After baking, coat the dough sculpture with an **acrylic spray** or acrylic paint. Then wipe an ordinary wood finish stain (such as walnut, oak, etc.) over the piece so that the stain settles in creases and grooves.

Spice glaze. Colored spices can be pasted or diluted with water and rubbed over the dough sculpture with the fingers after baking. Saffron, nutmeg, or curry powder can all be used to add a color glaze.

All baker's clay objects should be protected with a glaze or a spray coating of some kind. Because of the high salt content, the pieces will absorb moisture in damp weather if the seal is not complete.

baking soda. Batik and Tie-dye. See **sodium bicarbonate.**

baking soda. Candlemaking. Because hot melted wax is highly flammable, it is advisable that powdered baking soda be kept readily available to extinguish any fire that might accidentally occur. Never use water on a wax fire because it will spread the flame. Also see **Candlemaking: Safety Precautions.**

baking soda. Jewelry. Sodium bicarbonate, used to remove tarnish from silver. Immerse the silver in an aluminum pot containing a dilute solution of baking soda, table salt, and some soap; bring it to a boil and allow it to stand for several minutes. Remove the silver, rinse it in clear water, and dry.

balance. Kites. See **Kites: Construction.**

balanced cloth. Weaving. A fabric that uses the same size yarn in both **warp** and **filling** and has the same number of **pick**s per inch as **ends** per inch. Checks and plaids could be examples of balanced cloth since there is only a color change here that would not affect the other conditions. An unbalanced cloth is the opposite of the above and results in the woven structure being either predominantly **warp-faced** or **filling-faced. Tapestry** is an example of an unbalanced fabric with a **balanced weave (plain weave).** The warp in this case is totally covered and the fabric is filling-faced.

balanced plaid. Weaving. See **plaid.**

balanced tie-up. Weaving. A **tie-up** that has the same number of **harness**es tied to each **treadle** as are left untied. In a **four-harness loom** this would mean that each treadle has two harnesses tied to it and two left untied. When the tie-up is unbalanced in **counterbalanced loom**s, the sheds open with difficulty and not on the same level. This can be corrected with a **shed regulator.**

balanced twill. Weaving. See **twill weave.**

balanced weaves. Weaving. (Also called even-sided weave, 50-50 weave.) Weaves that have as many **warp ends** rising as sinking in one repeat of the weave pattern. **Plain weave** (1:1), **twill weave** (2:2) and **overshot** are examples of balanced weaves. To weave a **balanced cloth** from a balanced weave, the number of ends per inch and **pick**s per inch must be equal and the yarn size must be the same for both warp and **filling.** Unbalanced weaves are those like a **warp-faced** twill (3:1) and a **filling-faced** twill (1:3) that raise either more or less warp ends than the total in one repeat.

balance scale. Plastics. A scale that operates by balancing quantities of materials against standardized weights. A scale is necessary for precise measurement of **resin**s and **additives** in plastics formulas. It can usually be purchased from chemical laboratory supply companies. An excellent model is the triple-beam balance scale, which contains three measurement beams: a front beam balance scale, which contains three measurement beams; a front beam divided into tenths of a gram and single grams, a center beam marked into 100-gram units up to 500 grams, and a back beam divided into 10-gram units up to 100 grams. Weights to suspend on the beam tracks and additional weights to be hung at the ends of the beams are supplied with the scale.

Keep handy a pencil and a sheet of paper so that you can subtract the weight of the weighing container from the total amount weighed to find the weight of the resin alone. Set out your formula and write down the desired weights of each of your ingredients.

Set the balance of the scale at zero by turning the adjustment screw under the weighing platform balance pan. The pointer at the ends of the beams should line up with the white line on the end of the scale. Weigh your resin container and a clean mixing stick. Place them on the balance pan and rebalance the scale by moving the weights on the bars. Weights must be placed exactly in the notches on the bars for the scale to be accurate.

Start by pushing the 500-gram weight on the middle bar until the beam dips down to the overweight position. Then move it back one notch until the bar rises. Next move the 100-gram weight on the rear bar until the beam tilts down again. Back up the 100-gram weight one notch, also letting the bars rise again. Push the small weight on the front bar along its beam until the scale exactly balances and the pointer is lined up with the white zero mark on the right end.

Read the middle bar first to find the 100-gram weight figure, then read the back bar to find the 10-gram figure, and then read the front bar to find the individual grams to the tenth of a gram. Write this weight down. Remember to take the weight of the container into account when calculating the weight of the chemicals.

Set the balance at the desired number of grams and slowly pour the resin into the mixing container on the balance pan until you get close to the balance point. You may use an eye dropper or measuring spoon to measure out the last few grams.

Repeat the weighing procedure with any other additives, and then finally with the **catalyst.** See ill.

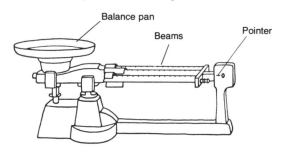

Triple-beam balance scale

balance toy. Toys. (Also called gravity toy, rocking toy.) Any of several varieties of **toys** that are weighted or counterweighted in such a way that they will rock and move without tipping or falling. Some simple balance toys have rounded bases, weighted with rocks or something similar secured in position inside the toy. The figures are usually **papier mâché,** but sometimes wood. Some are called Aelian figures, with the name (a fairly recent one) from a story in Claudius Aelianus (third century A.D.) about a man so lightweight that his feet had to be leaded to keep him from being blown away. A balance toy is sometimes called an aeolian toy, from aeolus, meaning wind-borne, or moved by the wind.

The Japanese **folk toy** of this type is called the **Daruma doll.** Its origin may have been Chinese; the French name for the toy, Poussah, comes from Pou-sa, meaning "Buddha." Easterners associate the toy with Buddha and the Eternal Truth. The toy is called a tombola in England, and roly poly or kelly in the United States.

The counterbalance toy is probably also Oriental in origin. It was not known in Europe until the sixteenth century. It usually uses two equivalent weights that balance (or counterweight) one another. The weights are added below the balancing part of the toy. For example, a figure resting on a single point could hold two weights at the ends of long curving handles or arms. The weights hang below the level of the point on which the figure rests. This point is set on some object or post, usually a part of the toy and having a slightly indented area. The toy cannot be tipped when it is set in motion because the weights control the motion so that balance is retained.

Weighted balance toys have been made in tremendous variety from materials of all kinds. The Burmese made them of wood, and in Dahomey and India they were cast in brass. Contemporary toymakers prefer wood, usually brightly decorated and painted, with leaded weights.

Some balance toys were weighted with mercury or quicksilver. Mercury-loaded tumblers such as the **tumbling men** could move down short flights of stairs; lead-weighted toys of Japan waddled down slopes. Both were operated by weights that shifted in position. The Slinky, a coiled spring that appears to walk intentionally down stairs, is probably the simplest and most intriguing of all shifting-weight toys. Also see **animated toy.**

baleen. Ivory and Bone Carving. The fibrous black bone from the upper jaws of the right whale and other toothless whales that is most often used for inlay. Also see **scrimshaw** and **Ivory and Bone Carving: Carving.**

ball. Toys. An **archetypal toy** that is a small sphere. In the British Museum there is a five-thousand-year-old stone ball. Ancient leather balls were filled with bran, hair, husks, feathers, or fig seed. Early Egyptian balls of ivory, bronze, clay, wood, or **composition** have been dated at 1400 B.C. Deerhide balls and bladder-type balls have been found from other cultures. Early Greek balls were made of skin stuffed with wool.

The discovery of rubber assured the lasting popularity of balls. **Celluloid,** rubber, and metal have all been used for balls in countless games, and today plastic has been added to the list of materials used. **Fabric balls** have remained as popular as **India rubber** balls.

ball-and-cup. Toys. See **cup-and-ball.**

ball-and-socket joint. Toys. See **ball joint.**

ballast. Stained Glass. Any inert granular material used in filling out **epoxy resin.** Although the epoxy hardener mixture expands at a different rate from **glass,** the addition of a ballast causes the rate of expansion of the epoxy to balance that of the glass. Use of a ballast also makes the epoxy go further, and thus reduces the expense.

Ballast is also called aggregate when it is used with **cement** to make **concrete** for casting. Examples of ballast

include mixtures of different grades of **sand,** marble dust, quartz dust, and **micro-ballons.** Also see **dalle-de-verre.**

ball clay. Ceramics. See **Ceramics: Clay.**

ball cutter. Puppets. Toys. (Also called watermelon ball cutter.) A small kitchen tool designed to cut spheres of melon or other fruit. It consists of a hollow half sphere mounted on the end of a handle. It is a convenient tool for digging out soft materials. **Clay** or **Plasticene** can be removed from a **papier-mâché** form with this tool. Also see **Puppets: Making the Puppet Head.**

ball-end modeler. Leather. See **modeler.**

ball fringe. Stitchery. Toys. A trimming material which consists of a woven band with **pompon**s attached. Commonly available in **cotton,** it comes in a wide range of sizes and colors.

ball joint. Toys. (Also called ball-and-socket joint.) A **joint** for dolls in which a ball is fitted with two adjacent sockets strung together with elastic, making a smooth movable joint. Ball joints were commonly used on **composition** dolls and sometimes on dolls made of wood, metal, **bisque,** and **celluloid.** Also see **Toys: Dolls.**

ball mill. Ceramics. A device used to blend and grind **glaze** and **body** ingredients. Usually, a porcelain jar is filled with flint pebbles and rotated with either a wet or dry charge of chemicals to achieve the desired results. Also see **pebble mill.**

balloon. Ceramics. The balloon is used as a **former** in the building of **slab** forms. The natural shrinkage of **clay** does not cause the balloon to crack, since it is compressed as the clay shrinks. The balloon may be pierced with a pin and removed after the clay has dried sufficiently. Also see **Ceramics: Form.**

balloon. Papercrafts. A balloon of desired shape provides a suitable **support** for any **paper-strip method** sculpture requiring a smooth, round volume as its basic shape. Additional sculptural details or appendages, made from **aluminum foil,** newspaper, or **found objects,** can be taped directly onto the balloon or attached after the initial layer of **papier mâché** has been applied and allowed to dry. Once covered, the balloon may deflate without affecting the final form.

ball-peen hammer. Jewelry. Tincrafting. (Also called machinist's hammer.) A steel hammer with one flat face and one domed or rounded end, used as an all-purpose hammer for striking such things as **punch**es in conjunction with the **dapping die** and the **center punch.** Other hammers in jewelry are specialized and their surfaces can be easily marred if used indiscriminately for hammering. Ball-peen hammers are available in weights ranging from a couple of ounces up to four pounds.

In tincrafting, a ball-peen hammer is used to beat sheet metal, such as **tinplate,** into rounded forms. Care should be taken to avoid damaging the smooth surface of the ball because any mar on the hammer will show up on the metal. See ill. Also see **Tincrafting: Preparing the Tin can.**

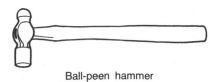

Ball-peen hammer

ball-peen hammer. Metalworking. See **hammer.**

ball-point needle. Stitchery. See **needle.**

ball thread. Tatting. When **working with two shuttles,** the **loop thread** is sometimes called the ball thread. If a change of color is not indicated, but the tatting **pattern** says that the **single thread,** which occurs when one **shuttle** is used, should be covered, then a ball thread is used. This would be for single-color tatting. The ball thread would always remain as the loop thread, and therefore it would not be necessary to wind this thread on a shuttle; i.e., it can remain on the original wound ball.

ball tool. Leather. A kind of **stamp.**

ball vise. Jewelry. See **engraver's block.**

ball winder. Spinning. Weaving. A small implement clamped to a table edge that quickly winds yarn into a neat ball. The ball, which can be from 4 to 8 ounces in weight, unwinds from the center. The ball winder is used to wind yarn from **spinning wheel**s, **skein**s or very large **cones.** See ill.

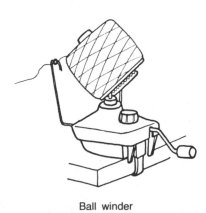

Ball winder

ball winding. Knitting. The winding of yarn from a skein or **hank** into a ball prior to beginning to knit.

To wind yarn, have someone hold the skein of yarn over his or her outstretched hands or put on a yarn swift. Holding one loose end of the yarn between two fingers of one of your hands, use your free hand to wind the yarn from the skein loosely around your fingers in such a way that it forms a ball. Also see **winding.**

balsa. Kites. Puppets. Toys. Woodworking. An extremely soft, lightweight wood that is excellent for **whittling** and for making model boats, airplanes, and kite structures. Because it is soft and fibrous, it tears easily unless worked with extremely sharp tools. Consequently, it is suitable only for the construction of very small, light-wind kites. Also see **airplane, model, puppet heads, soft wood** and **Kites: Tools and Materials.**

bamboo. Basketry. Kites. A treelike, tropical grass with a long, hollow, jointed stem. It is native to southern and eastern Asia and can attain a height of 120'. As a basketry material it is quite versatile. The strong, glossy stems may be used whole for structural elements or split for strong, light fibers.

Bamboo is also the traditional wood-framing material for kites because it is light in weight and extremely flexible. Also see **Kites: Tools and Materials.**

bamboo. Beadwork. See **found object bead.**

band. Bookbinding. The ridge across the **spine** of a book caused by the **cord** showing through the leather. Also, the cord on which a book is sewn.

band. Quilts. Stitchery. (Also called divider, dividing band, strip.) A strip of fabric cut on the straight of the material. Bands are sometimes used in **edging panel**s or **banner**s, to **assemble** or to **set** a quilt, or to add **binding** or edging to any fabric. Also see **Quilts: Binding.**

band clamp. Woodworking. See **clamping tools.**

banded alloy. Jewelry. See **mokumé.**

bandhana work. Batik and Tie-dye. The traditional **tie-dye** work of India. The name is descriptive of designs of small spots, usually white, arranged into patterns on a fabric dipped in **dye.** This type of design was copied in fabric prints in the nineteenth century in which **synthetic dyes** replaced the **vegetable dye**s common in the Indian work. The girls who produced the work were called "bandhani"; the term "bandhana work" was derived from that name. The bandhani grew the nails of their thumbs and forefingers very long to enable them to deftly lift the tiny points of fabric for tying. The name for the bandana, a red handkerchief print, is derived from "bandhana."

bandilure. Toys. See **yo-yo.**

B & I machine. Gemcutting. See **machinery.**

banding. Ceramics. China and Glass Painting. A technique of decorating china, glass, or ceramic ware with a line or band, generally around the rims and edges. Make the line in a single, steady stroke. Ceramic ware is banded on a **banding wheel** rather than manually. To band china or glass by hand slowly turn the cup or plate around with one hand while holding the brush between the thumb and forefinger of the other hand, steadied by the little finger placed on the edge of the china or glass as a guide. Keep the hand with the brush steady, the elbow resting on the table. Hold the brush gently but firmly on the revolving china until a complete circle is made. Then lift the brush gradually to avoid a darkening of color caused by overlapping at the joining. A banding wheel can be used to turn the piece to be decorated.

Various styles of banding have been used traditionally. Solid bands or stripes that are clearly defined are called clear banding. When the bands of color are joined with strokes added in another color, the lines are blended together in interesting color effects, called diffuse banding. For spiral banding, place a brush at the center point of the plate or bowl as it is revolving on the banding wheel. As the plate revolves, draw the brush to the outer edge in a straight line. The revolutions of the wheel create the desired spiral effect.

For **gold** rims, apply gold paint along the edge of the revolving plate with a brush or fingertip. Cups are difficult to manage on a banding wheel because the handle interrupts the flow of the brush. With care, this problem can be solved by beginning and ending at the handle, with the cup revolving slowly enough so that you can lift the brush at the required moment.

banding. Stained Glass. (Also called barring, wiring.) The process by which bands of lead, copper, or zinc are attached to either the inside or the outside of a completed stained-glass window for reinforcement. These bands are wrapped around the **saddle bars** placed across the inside or outside of the window. The bands are twisted around themselves on the outside of the bar, securing the bar and stained glass to each other. Also see **copper ties**, **fitting**, **rebate.**

banding wheel. Ceramics. China and Glass Painting. (Also called turntable, whirler.) A revolving wheel used to turn china or glass to facilitate **banding** or other decorating. Start the wheel spinning with one hand while the other hand holds the brush against the piece to be decorated. In this way a line or band can be painted around a plate or bowl in a continuous stroke, without having to touch the piece. Both manual and electric wheels are available. See ill.

a. Manual banding wheel   b. Electric banding wheel

bandloom. Weaving. A narrow-width loom popular during Colonial times for the weaving of braid, tape, belts, suspenders, garters, and ties and loops for clothing and household items. Wicks for oil lamps were woven on the bandloom. Among early settlers, the Shakers were noted for their bandweaving. The lap loom was the simplest type of loom used to weave these narrow strips. It was actually a narrow **rigid heddle** paddle suspended on the **warp**, which was attached to support, or perhaps the front ends

were tied to the weaver's waist. The **filling** was beaten into place with the fingers or with a small knife-like **beater** (**a.**). Eventually the paddle was set into a box frame with a **warp beam** at one end that could hold considerably more warp than that possible with the suspended rigid heddle. This was called a bandloom or tape loom and came in various models (**b.**). Some types were miniatures of a large **floor loom.** They had two small and narrow **harnesses** mounted in the middle of a stand and an equally small **reed,** warp, and **cloth beam**s. See ill.

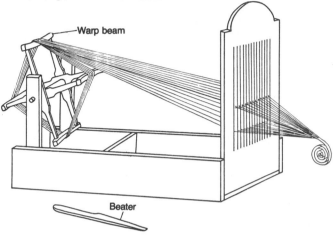

Bandloom, rigid heddle model

band nippers. Bookbinding. Nickel-plated pincers with flat jaws used for straightening **band**s, or "nipping up" the leather that covers the **spine.**

bandoleer. Toys. See **yo-yo.**

bandsander. Jewelry. A motor-driven vertical belt sander that uses **abrasive**-coated cloth or paper belts for shaping and contouring metal.

band saw. Metalworking. Plastics. Woodworking. See **power saw.**

bandstrip. Bookbinding. The strip of material that forms the basis of a **head band** or tail band.

band tying. Batik and Tie-dye. Close, solid **binding** over the fabric to produce a complete **resist** in **tie-dye.** The bands can be tied at regular intervals to give an even resist (**a.**), or they can be tied in an irregular pattern (**b.**). See ill. Also see **Batik and Tie-dye: Tie-dye.**

Band tying

bank kiln. Ceramics. A crude **kiln** cut into the side of a hill where the earth supplies insulation. The Japanese **climbing kilns** are based on this principle. See ill. Also see **chambered kiln.**

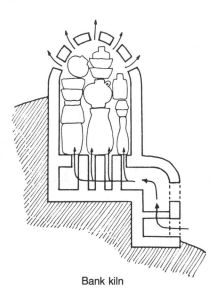

Bank kiln

banner. Stitchery. A decorative **panel** of **fabric** usually vertical in proportion and hung from above. Banners are often symbolic in design and of a somewhat ceremonial nature. Traditionally, banners were carried in pageants or parades and along with **flags** and **pennants** served to identify the carrier. Also see **standard** and **Stitchery: Stitchery Forms.**

bar. Lacemaking. In **bobbin lace** and **needle lace,** the joining between two sections of lace.

Bobbin lace bars can be made in braid or cloth stitch with two pairs of bobbins. The braids may or may not have picots on the edges. Many terms are given these joinings: braid, braided bar, bride, half stitch plait, leg, plaited bar, and strap. Braid and bride are the most commonly used terms.

Another joining bar is done with one pair of **bobbins,** giving the bobbins of that pair a multiple number of **twists** sufficient to close the space.

Needle lace bars are made in a **buttonhole stitch,** and also may or may not have picots. Secure a foundation thread across the joining space. Place one, two, or three threads across, according to the thickness of the bar desired, and work a buttonhole stitch back over this foundation thread. These bars are called **buttonhole bars.** The **wheels** made in needle lace are worked on foundation threads called bars also.

bar. Puppets. See **cross bar.**

bar. Quilts. See **rail.**

bar clamp. Woodworking. See **clamping tools.**

BARGELLO (Needlepoint)

Bargello is a type of needlework in which a background of **evenly woven canvas** or fabric is entirely covered by long, vertical stitches forming geometric designs. Because chairs covered with this **brick stitch** needlework were found in the Bargello Palace in Florence, Italy, this name has been given to the technique in America.

In the Benedictine abbey at Engelberg, Switzerland, there is a cope that dates from the fourteenth century. It is said to have been donated by the great benefactor of the convent at Engelberg, Queen Agnes of Hungary. It is worked entirely in silk brick stitch on linen, and is probably one of the ancestors of bargello or Florentine embroidery as we know it today. Many similar embroideries done in Saxony, Germany, and Switzerland in the thirteenth or fourteenth centuries were patterns in silk floss, counted on the linen. They may well have been inspired by the earlier copes and chasubles stitched in England with couched gold threads, known as **Opus Anglicanum.**

There is a legend that a Hungarian noblewoman, on her marriage to one of the Medici, brought the stitch to Italy on articles in her trousseau. Seven chairs are still kept in the Bargello in Florence, from the time when the museum was a great patrician dwelling in the seventeenth century. By the eighteenth century, the fashion for bargello had spread from Europe and England to America, where a wide range of articles were decorated with it—purses, bench covers, pockets, shoes, boxes, hand fire screens, bed hangings, and table carpets in beautiful combinations of home-dyed colors. In Victorian times, more elaborate geometrics and raised designs in **Turkey work** somewhat superseded the simpler bargello patterns. Newly developed **aniline dyes** were inclined to make color contrasts harsh and somewhat jarring.

Today's revival of bargello is producing some novel effects that are perhaps closer in feeling to the beautiful European vestments of the fourteenth century. Although not as hard wearing as needlepoint, bargello is quick, easy, and effective.

PATTERNS **Brick stitch** is the basic bargello stitch **(a.).** In England, bargello is more generally known as Florentine, **Hungarian point,** or flame stitch. Flame stitch refers to one of the most popular patterns, in which horizontal bands of chevrons are worked across the canvas, often with softly shaded colors or rainbow effects **(b.).**

Today, all kinds of contemporary applications have been found for the colorful and versatile patterns of this technique. Garments such as skirts, vests, or jackets may be worked in bargello patterns on interlocked canvas. When complete, the garment is washed in cold water so that it becomes as soft and supple as any tweed or wool fabric.

Another interesting variation is kaleidoscope bargello. A square canvas is divided diagonally from corner to corner in both directions, forming four pie-shaped pieces. The flame stitch design, with its interesting variety of curves, points, and chevrons, is worked horizontally across one of these four shapes. At the corner, where the diagonal line intersects, the work is turned, and the line is repeated exactly across the next pie-piece, and so on until the four sides of a square have been formed. The design is then filled, following this basic line around and around (**c.**). The juxtaposition of harmonious or contrasting colors can give beautiful effects to these designs. Sometimes the outside of a kaleidoscope pattern may be worked with **trompe l'oeil** ribbons, while the center is filled with such representational objects as fruits or flowers. See ill.

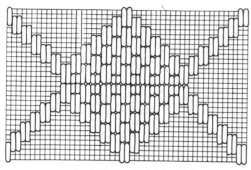

a. Basic bargello brick stitch

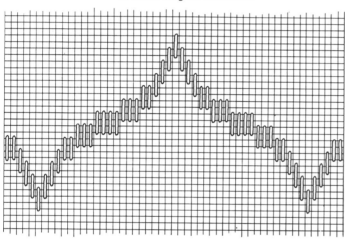

b. Flame stitch

c. Kaleidoscope bargello

MATERIALS The **background fabrics,** wool, and needles for bargello are the same as those used in needlepoint.

PREPARATION AND LAYOUT Because all bargello patterns are geometric, each design must be counted onto the canvas, following a graph or embroidered pattern. It is helpful to mark the outline of the finished design first with a pencil or permanent marker so that you can work easily within a framework. Leave at least four inches of canvas all around for turnbacks. Once you have marked the outside line of your pattern, fold the canvas in half and half again, crease the folds firmly, open it up, and mark these center lines horizontally and vertically with a pencil. (Run the pencil lightly between the threads of the canvas, allowing them to guide you in keeping the lines straight.) After you have established the center point in this way you can start stitching the pattern. Begin in the middle so that your design will be equally balanced on all four sides. Although you may hold the work in your hand, you will find it much easier to count threads and work with even tension if you stretch the work taut in an **embroidery frame.**

The essence of bargello is its smooth, flat effect. To keep this, always work with the shortest stitch possible on the reverse side. For instance, if you pass over four threads on the front, pick up only two in the back. This may seem confusing to those taught to use as much thread as possible for better wear, when working **tent stitch** (continental or basketweave); however, the stitches on the reverse side of bargello would become so long they would wear **less** well, and the long, exposed threads, double the length of those on the front, would also tend to make the needlework thick and bulky. Also see **Needlepoint: Materials, Finishing.**

bargello stitch. Rugmaking. Weaving. See **Hungarian stitch.**

bar increase. Knitting. See **Knitting: Increasing.**

barium. Ceramics. A mineral often used to give hardness and brilliance to a **glaze. Barium carbonate** is used with other fluxes to produce **matte** textures in low-fire glazes. At high temperatures it is a strong **flux.** Barium chromate is used as a **pigment oxide** to produce pale yellow to light green **overglaze** decoration.

barium carbonate. Ceramics. See **barium.**

barium chromate. Ceramics. See **barium.**

bark. Woodworking. See **wood.**

bark slip. Ivory and Bone Carving. The remainder of ivory left after the manufacture of piano keys. The outside is dark, curved, and patterned with lines, and the inside surface is flat and white. Bark slip is an inexpensive source of ivory for small carvings.

bark tanning. Leather. See **vegetable tanning.**

Barley-corn. Weaving. See **Bronson weaves.**

Barn Raising. Quilts. A name given to a specific **set** for **block**s, as well as the name by which quilts of that set are known. In this arrangement, **band**s of dark and light colors form squares around the central block. The Barn Raising arrangement can be used on **split nine-patch, Log Cabin,** and **Courthouse Steps** blocks, and any of these quilts can be identified by either or both names.

baroque. Gemcutting. (Also called tumble.) A smooth, rounded, irregular-shaped gem made by **tumbling** stones in a barrel with **abrasive**s.

bar quilt. Quilts. A simple quilt of Amish origin consisting of a series of seven bars, or wide stripes. These are **pieced** together, and then plain, solid-color **border**s are added. The quilts are stunning in their use of rich color, minimal pattern, and exceedingly detailed and skillful **quilting.** Also see **Amish quilt, band.**

barring. Stained Glass. See **banding.**

Barrister's Block. Quilts. A variation of the pieced **block** design of **Kansas Troubles.**

Bartholomew baby. Toys. A **doll,** similar to the **penny wooden doll,** made in Holland and sold primarily at the Bartholomew Fairs in England. The doll was made of wood, with movable arms and legs.

base. Basketry. The bottom of a basket. It is the most important area in determining the kind of basket woven and its finished size. One must choose the number, length, and size of base **rod**s and determine how they will be joined.

There are three distinct types of base or basket structures: woven, plaited, and coiled. In addition, each basic base structure has a round, square, and oval shape variation. Also see **Basketry: Woven Basket Construction, Plaited Basket Construction, Coiled Basket Construction.**

base. Mosaics. See **backing.**

base. Puppets. The bottom or lower surface of a **puppet head** or **marionette head.** In the **hand puppet,** the base is always open so that a finger, or fingers, can be inserted. The base of the marionette head is solid so that a **screw eye** can be attached. Also see **apple-head puppet, finger hole, flange** and **Puppets: Making the Puppet Head.**

baseball stitch. Leather. See **cross stitch.**

base board. Basketry. A flat board sometimes used in place of a woven base. The board is first cut to the desired shape and holes are drilled on the outer perimeter board. Then **stake**s are inserted partway through these holes so that the shorter ends can be tied or secured with a simple

trac or **foot border.** Also see **Basketry: Woven Basket Construction.**

base border. Basketry. See **border.**

base cloth. Rugmaking. Weaving. See **ground cloth.**

base material. Crewel. Embroidery. Needlepoint. See background fabric.

base metal. Jewelry. Metalworking. One of the three main divisions of nonferrous metals (precious metals, alloys, and base metals), which includes **copper, aluminum, lead, tin, nickel,** and **zinc.** Base metals are often used to make the alloys: **brass, bronze, pewter, nickel silver, solder, sterling silver,** and karat gold.

As a term in **welding,** base metal (also called parent metal) is opposed to the **filler metal** (usually contained in the **welding rod**).

base number. Weaving. See **satin weave.**

baseplate. Jewelry. The piece of metal upon which **sweat soldering, appliqué,** or any other three-dimensional additive is applied.

base pour. Plastics. The first pouring of resin into a **mold** when making an **embedment.** The base pour never has objects embedded in it, but serves only as a base for the **inclusion**s. Also see **Plastics: Embedment.**

basic. Beadwork. See **basic row.**

basic count. Beadwork. See **basic row.**

basic dye. Batik and Tie-dye. A synthetic **dyestuff** used in **tie-dye** and sometimes in **batik.** Basic dyes were the first synthetic dyestuffs to use salts of colored organic bases. They are sometimes called cationic dyes because the dye molecule is positively charged.

Basic dyes give brilliant and rich colors; however, they are **fugitive color**s and therefore limited in use. They are often preferred for theatrical costumes because of their intensities. They do not fade in artificial light, so costume designers especially enjoy working with them. They fade readily in sunlight.

Basic dyes can be used on cotton, viscose rayon, silk, and wool. They are fairly **colorfast** on **acrylic fabric**s. Cotton and viscose rayon require an **acid mordant** and **fixer,** but wool and silk can be dyed directly. In dyeing the **cellulose fiber** fabrics, test samples for the desired color. The dyeing time required varies. In dyeing silk or wool, allow a longer time for soaking in the **dyebath.** If the water is hard, a little **acetic acid** may be added to the dyebath. The colors are brilliant on silk, but the **acid dye**s are better for wool.

Fabrics dyed with basic dyes can be treated by **discharge dyeing,** as the colors can readily be removed.

basic dye. Dyeing. Coal-tar dyes that will color silk and wool directly in a slightly acid bath. On vegetable fibers, such as cotton, the basic dyes require a tannic acid **mordant** to provide the necessary chemical affinity so that an insoluble color base will be produced. Basic dyes are usually brilliant colors but have very poor **color fastness** as to washing, light or **crocking.** They are also used on certain synthetic fibers such as nylon and modacrylic. Also see **aniline dye, tannin.**

basic four-patch. Quilts. See **four-patch.**

basic loop. Beadwork. A technique of wiring **glass beads** in rounded or pointed oval shapes for making flower petals or leaves in **bead flowermaking.** Work from fine **spool wire** threaded with beads, with the end crimped to keep the beads from spilling. (Bead rows are spaced far apart in diagrams for clarity.)

a. Form a wire loop with beads at either side.
b. Flower patterns give the required number of beads for the **basic row.** Twist wires together to crimp. Beads on the spool side of the wire (called the feed wire), will form the basic row (also called basic, or top basic wire). The loop at the bottom is called bottom basic loop, or stem.

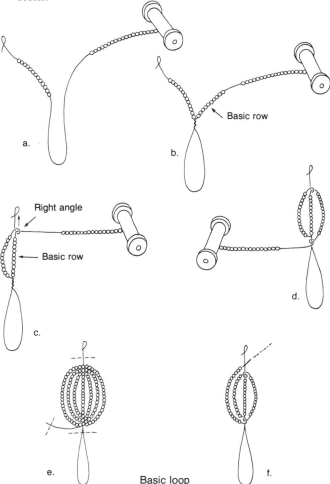

Basic loop

c. Bring beads on the loose side up on the left side of the basic row. Twist the wire together at the top, crossing it in front of the spool wire. Then pull the spool wire at right angles to the basic row.
d. Bring down the beaded feed wire from the spool on the right side, wrapping the bare wire around the twisted loop wire at the bottom. The bare beading wire crosses in front of the loop wire, twists around back, and is pulled around to the front again. Now symmetrical curves are on either side of the basic row.
e. Continue wrapping the beaded spool wire around the basic row, twisting the wires over the unit wires at the top and bottom in the same way until the desired shape is completed. Keep beads close together in neat rows. Allow 4″ of bare spool wire at the bottom and cut from the spool. Cut the other wires, leaving ¼″ at the top and bottom. Bend the ¼″ of wire at the top down the back, tucking it in neatly. Twist loop ends together at the bottom.
f. To make more pointed ends, add two beads beyond the top of the basic row before wrapping it at the top, and change the angle of the wire to a 45° angle in relation to the basic row. Push beads into a point and shape it with fingers. The point can be elongated by raising the spool wire to increase the elongation of the top and by adding more beads. See ill. Also see **Bead Flowering: Basic Techniques.**

basic nine-patch. Quilts. See **nine-patch.**

basic row. Beadwork. The center row of wired **beads** in petals or leaves in **bead flowermaking,** around which additional rows of beads are formed. It is also referred to in patterns as basic, basic count, stem or top basic wire. Also see **basic loop.**

basic weave. Weaving. A **weave** is considered basic if it cannot be reduced or traced to some simpler structure and if it has its own variations or derivatives. Generally, it is acknowledged there are three basic weaves: **plain weave, twill weave,** and **satin weave.** All other **loom-controlled** weaves are variations of one of these three or derivatives or combinations of them.

basket. Basketry. A receptacle made of woven **cane,** grass, wood, or other material.

A basket may be one of three types: woven, coiled, or plaited. Its shape might be round, square, or oval, depending on the beginning formation of the **slath** in the **base** of the basket. In order for a basket to cease being a flat plate and to begin to have sides, it must be worked upward in a process called the **upsetting.** In addition, a basket usually has a finished edge or **border** that terminates the weaving as well as a **foot** on which it sits. Baskets may differ depending on the function, design, materials, and the kinds of **strokes** or **weaves** used. Depending on the design and the use, a basket may or may not have a handle or lid. See ill. Also see **Basketry.**

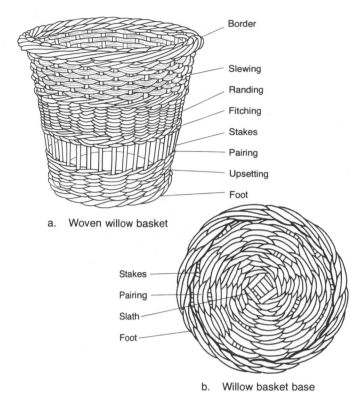

a.   Woven willow basket

- Border
- Slewing
- Randing
- Fitching
- Stakes
- Pairing
- Upsetting
- Foot

- Stakes
- Pairing
- Slath
- Foot

b.   Willow basket base

basketmaking. Basketry. The theory, art, and process of making basketware articles. Also see **Basketry.**

basket patterns. Quilts. Basket patterns have always been a favorite in both **appliqué** and **piecing.** They exist in countless combinations and variations, all depicting baskets containing flowers or fruits, sometimes with a bird or ribbon.

Piecing lends itself to the depicting of a somewhat **geometric** basket. These are often planned so that the **block** is used on the diagonal. Geometric flowers blossom from triangles and squares in arrangements that require painstaking piecing.

The appliqué basket designs allow for a little more flexibility in shaping. Flowers or fruit might vary from one block to the next, or a ribbon might take on another hue. Rarely is an **appliqué quilt** repeated exactly. So variable are these baskets that almost every change brings on a new name, often derived from the fruits or flowers the basket contains. The daisies, sunflowers, or lilies identify the design, and quilts called Basket of Oranges, Basket of Tulips, Cherry Basket, Rose Basket, and Garden Basket abound.

Many of the designs simply show a basket shape with no contents. Dozens of quilt designs are known using the basket as a central motif.

BASKETRY

Basketry is a form of weaving that utilizes stiff, usually natural materials instead of fibers or threads. These basketry materials include **cane, willow** rods, thin sticks, and **raffia.** They are woven together in a variety of techniques to produce not only the common basket but also hats, mats, belts, furniture, and numerous other articles.

Historically, basketry is the oldest and most universal of textile crafts. Because vegetable fibers are highly perishable, the exact beginning of basketry is difficult to date accurately. However, because of certain conductive environmental conditions, such as dry sand, many early samples have survived. Prehistoric examples have been uncovered in Nevada and Utah from about the year 5000 B.C. Additional evidence has been found in Neolithic China, where the impressions of basket weaves were found on pottery; from this, it is deduced that the baskets were lined with clay and fired to make them waterproof. This also suggests that basketry predates the development of pottery. Numerous examples of highly sophisticated basketry have appeared in civilizations once considered remote and backward, indicating its early and widespread development. The Pueblo Indians of the southwestern U.S. were called "the Basketmaker People" because of their great skill in this field.

By the time of the Industrial Revolution baskets no longer had to be made for utilitarian purposes, and the symbolic meaning once given to the making of baskets by all early cultures had disappeared. Nevertheless, since the nineteenth century, basketry has had numerous revivals, both as a craft and as a subject of study. Its history and complex tradition have been fairly well documented by archeologists and today it is a highly regarded craft. Paradoxically, many underdeveloped nations today continue to practice and develop the art of basketry both as a craft necessary to their society's needs and as an item of export to countries where it is appreciated as an art.

TOOLS AND MATERIALS   The importance of materials to the development of basketry cannot be overemphasized. Each of the three basic types of basket were developed using the natural materials available to the weavers of a specific region. **Coil basketry,** utilizing sparse twigs and pine and cactus needles, evolved in desert regions. **Woven basketry** developed in temperate zones where there is an abundance of **willow;** the tropics capitalized on large amounts of palm for **plaited basketry.**

Both natural and synthetic materials are available to the basket weaver today. Characteristics of good basketry material are long length, flexibility, strength, adaptability, and availability. Natural materials such as reed (**cane**), **bamboo, willow,** and **raffia** can be bought in a variety of sizes and shapes or handpicked from the wild. For instance, reed may be bought from craft stores in round and flat shapes in numerous sizes, and in coils or **hanks** 300–1000' long. Handpicked materials, such as wild grasses, pine needles, twigs, splints, hedgerow stuff, cattail, and rushes, must be carefully cut, prepared, and graded before use. Synthetic reed and raffia are also commercially available.

The basic basketry tools include a sharp **knife** for cutting and trimming, a pair of **round-nose pliers** for crimping reed, a **bodkin** or awl for making spaces in woven material, and a **bucket** to soak the material in.

Some more specialized tools are a **rapping iron** to tighten the **weave,** a **side cutter** for cutting **cane, shears** for cutting heavier material, a **screwblock** to hold **rods** in **squarework,** a cleave for splitting willow rods, and a **singe-**

ing lamp to singe off loose fibers. Miscellaneous items are a **lapboard,** a **tapestry needle** for **coil basketry,** a measuring tape, and clothespins.

Of these tools, the metal ones should be kept sharp and should occasionally be lightly coated with machine oil to prevent rusting. Wooden tools, such as the screwblock and lapboard, should be coated with lacquer or shellac to prevent checking or warping.

PLANNING A BASKET The first step is to decide the kind of basket wanted: woven, plaited, or coiled, and the type of materials to be used. To determine the amount of material, you will need to know the types of weaves you will use and the approximate size and shape of the basket. For instance, on a round woven basket you must divide the circumference of the basket by the distance between the **stakes** in order to determine the total number of stakes. If there is an odd number of stakes it will require specific weaves different from weaves used on an even number of stakes. For example, randing or checked weave may be done with an odd number of stakes, **chasing** with an even number, and the **pairing** weave with either an odd or even number.

To determine the length of each stake you must decide on the type of **border** you want, the height of the **siding,** and the distance across the **base.** The size and amount of the **weaver** will depend totally on the size, shape, and design of the basket. You can roughly estimate the amount needed by counting the **rounds** per inch in a basket similar to the one you are planning and multiplying by the circumference and then by the height of the proposed basket.

PREPARING THE MATERIALS Each material picked from nature demands specific operations before it can be used. Bark may have to be removed. Take out the soft and spongy **pith** from fibrous materials and split them into uniform thicknesses.

Evaluate each **rod** and separate it according to its size and use. For example, the bottom **stakes,** sometimes called rods, are the thickest, and the **weavers** for the base are the finest. The **siding** is usually made of medium-grade weavers. This sorting process is called grading, cutting out, or drafting.

Most natural materials must be soaked in water anywhere from a few minutes to many hours to become pliable so that the fibers can be more easily worked without cracking.

WOVEN BASKET CONSTRUCTION Woven baskets consist of upright **rods** interwoven by a more flexible binding element.

To begin this **base,** with a **cross** start, take eight rods of equal length and divide them into two groups of four. Cross the two groups in the middle perpendicular to each other. If the basket will use a **checked weave,** add an extra **rod** half as long as the others by wedging its end into the center and keeping it with one of the groups of four. The odd number will permit the **weaver** to **stagger** on each successive **round.**

Wrap a long weaver around the groups securely, weaving behind the bottom group and across the top group for a few turns (**a.**). Next, **open out,** or separate, the spokes so

that they radiate from the center and begin to **rand,** working the weaver over one spoke and under the next (**b.**). Continue to the desired diameter.

To begin a round base with a woven start, weave four pairs of rods through a second group of four pairs perpendicular to the first; this will form the openwork for the bottom.

To weave on this even number of stakes, take two weavers, inserting them in adjoining spaces, and begin **chasing** (**c.**). After a round or two, open out the pairs so that they radiate evenly and continue weaving.

Woven starts are also convenient for both square and oval baskets. For a long oval, add more pairs of rods to one group; the number of additional pairs depends on the relative length and width of the proposed basket.

So as not to crack the **willow** or **reed** rods, **upsetting** is necessary. Squeeze each **stake** with **round-nose pliers** (**pricking** for willow) close to the edge of the weaving and bend it up to the desired angle of the side. A **hoop** may be used to hold this angle (**d.**). Next weave a four-rod wale at this juncture by **waling** to secure the angle and to give a **foot** to the basket.

There are several basic weaves in woven basket construction. For checked weave (randing), begin with one weaver and an odd number of stakes. Work the weaver in front of one stake and behind the next (**e.**).

Begin the **pairing** weave with two weavers in two consecutive openings. The total number of stakes may be odd or even. Take one weaver, cross over the other weaver, and behind the next stake, and out to the front. Repeat with alternate weavers (**f.**).

Slewing is begun for a two-rod slew with two willow weavers and an odd number of stakes. Place the butt end of one weaver between two stakes and rand with it until it is half used up. At this point take the second weaver, place it between two stakes and on top of the first weaver, and rand with these two as if they were one (**g.**). Whenever the lower weaver runs out take another willow weaver, again place it on top of the upper rod, and continue weaving as before (**h.**).

For **fitching,** bend your weaver in the middle and loop it around a stake at the desired distance above the previous rounds. This distance will be the opening in the **siding.** With both ends coming out to the front and on both sides of the first stake, take the furthest **right-hand weaver** and cross it over the left-hand one. Then take hold of both weavers near this cross-over and twist them one full turn toward you so that the weaver to the front of the first stake is again out to the front of the second stake and the weaver coming from behind the first stake is behind the second stake.

Repeat by always taking the furthest right-hand weaver, crossing it over the left-hand weaver, and then adding the full twist. Continue around the basket until the **spokes** or stakes are secure.

Fitching is often necessary after leaving a gap in the weaving. Sometimes an extra second twist is used if the stakes are wide apart; the direction of the twist may be reversed if desired. Added **bye-stakes** are not only decorative but also help to separate the rows of fitching (**j.**).

Wrapped weave is done with a very flexible weaver or

binding element tied to a stake. Insert it down into the weaving of the previous rounds, pass it one complete turn around the next stake in a counterclockwise motion, and continue on around each stake in the same manner (**k.**).

Joining in can be done with round reed or winding reed.

With round reed when your weaver runs out, place the new end over the old at the back of the weaving, leaving the ends long enough to rest behind the adjacent stakes (**m.**). Trim or **pick off** the excess ends when finished with **side cutter**s.

With winding reed, simply weave in or overlap the new end in front of the old for the minimum distance of two stakes (**n.**).

A variety of **border**s can be used to finish woven baskets. A **handle liner** must be inserted before the border is begun if the basket is to have a **handle.**

Simple trac or base border may be used as a regular finishing **border** at the top of the basket or as a simple base border or **foot border.** Begin by **pricking** or squeezing all the stakes just above the siding with round-nose pliers, or, if it is to be a base border, just beyond the **base board.**

Bend the first stake down, pass it behind the next stake, and in front of the second stake facing away, leaving it on the inside of the basket behind the third stake away (**p.**). Continue this stroke around the basket and finish by tucking in the last rod to follow the pattern. Pick off the loose ends inside with side cutters.

For a three-rod plain border, soak the stakes at the top of the weaving with water to make them pliable. If the stakes are extra thick, crimp them with round-nose pliers so they will not crack.

Bend the first three rods down—1 behind 2, 2 behind 3, and 3 behind 4 (**q.**). Pass 1 over 2 and 3, in front of 4, behind 5, and out to the front. Bend down 4 around 5 so that it lies beside 1. Repeat with 2 and 3 as for 1, turning down 5 and 6 as for 4. Pass 1 over 2 and 3, in front of 4, behind 5, and out to the front. Bend down 4 around 5 so that it lies beside 1. Repeat with 2 and 3 as for 1, turning down 5 and 6 as for 4 (**r.**).

With three pairs projecting, continue around the basket, always taking the second stake from the left over two pairs in front of the first upright, in back of the second upright, and out to the front. The left-hand reed of each pair is always left projecting to the front. Continue this until one stake is left standing. Then take the second reed from the left of the normal 3 pairs in front of the upright stake and thread it under the very first reed you started with so that it projects out to the front. Bend down the upright stake beside it.

Finish off by threading each right-hand reed of the remaining pairs through to the front to follow the pattern. With a knife or side cutter, pick off all ends close to the border.

For a **three-stroke braid,** or plaited border, use a reed the same thickness as your stakes; cut two 3″ lengths and three 8″ lengths. Bend down stake 1 over one of the short lengths and place one 8″ piece alongside it so that about 2½″ of it projects to the inside of the basket (**s.**). Repeat this operation on the second stake using another short and long reed.

Take the first pair (the first stake and the first long piece) under the second 3″ piece, over the second pair, and in front of the number 3 stake, leaving the ends to the back behind the number 4 stake (**t.**). Bend 3 down over the first pair and lay the third 8″ piece alongside it. Take the left-hand pair of stakes (the number 2 stake and the second long piece) and pass it over the third pair and in front of 4, leaving them to the rear.

Bend down 4 over this second pair and bring the first pair alongside it so that all three lie side by side (**u.**).

Take the furthest left-hand pair in front of this last group of three, in front of number 5 stake, and to the inside of the basket.

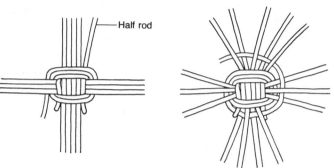

a. Cross start   b. Opening out

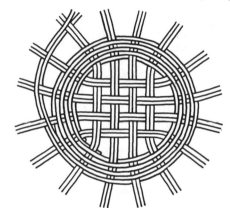

c. Woven start (showing chasing)

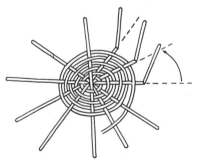

d. Upsetting

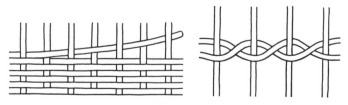

e. Checked weave (randing)   f. Pairing

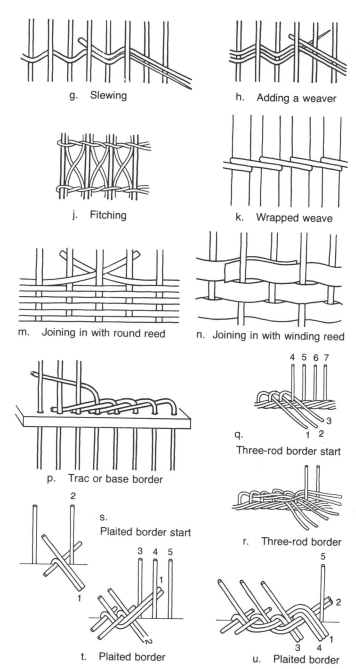

g. Slewing

h. Adding a weaver

j. Fitching

k. Wrapped weave

m. Joining in with round reed

n. Joining in with winding reed

p. Trac or base border

q. Three-rod border start

r. Three-rod border

s. Plaited border start

t. Plaited border

u. Plaited border

length. You will now have 3 pairs of rods to the inside, with the right-hand one of each pair the longest, and three ends from the first 8" pieces. To complete this border, weave in these long ends where the 8" substitute ends are, keeping the order and pattern consistent.

A handle may be added after the **border** is finished, but before the border is started, cut a handle liner and insert it in the weaving where the handle bow is expected to go.

For a wrapped handle, after the border is finished cut a handle bow to the length required, allowing a few inches for the ends to be pushed down into the siding, and **slype** each end. Having soaked and bent the handle bow into the desired shape, remove the handle liner and insert the bow down into the **bow mark**s. To the right of the handle bow and a few inches below the border, pull a long piece of wrapping cane through the siding and to the inside of the basket a few inches. Take this shorter end straight up and over the border and then down diagonally across the handle bow. Again pull it through the siding to the inside of the basket and up alongside the handle bow (**v.**). Pull the other end up diagonally and across to the left side of the handle bow and begin wrapping the short end to the handle (**w.**). Continue wrapping across the handle and tie in the other side in the same manner.

For a small **single-rod roped handle**, cut a rod long enough to pass over the handle arch three times plus some. Slype one end and insert it down into the weaving.

Bend the rod into the desired arch and thread it from the outside to the inside of the basket a few inches below the border (**x.**). Take this long end and wrap it 3 or 4 times around the arch back toward the slyped end. There, the same distance down as on the other side, thread it through to the inside of the basket and up, wrapping it around the handle arch in a rope effect (**y.**) Slype this end also and pass it down into the weaving (**z.**) See ill.

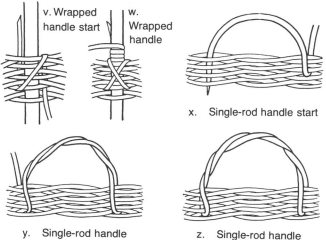

v. Wrapped handle start

w. Wrapped handle

x. Single-rod handle start

y. Single-rod handle

z. Single-rod handle

As before, bend down 5 and bring the second pair alongside it to the front so that you have 2 groups of 3 to the front and one pair to the rear. Take the two furthest left-hand reeds of the left group of three, pass them over the second group of three to the back and between the first two uprights. Leave the furthest reed of the first group of three projecting out to the front by itself.

Bend the first upright over these last two and bring the pair to the rear out to the front alongside it so you again have 2 groups of three out front. Continue this all around the border.

To finish, take the two furthest left-hand reeds and pass them over the second group of three and underneath the very first stake—in place of the first short 3" reed. Take the next two furthest left-hand reeds and pass these to the back in the same way under and in place of the second 3"

PLAITED BASKET CONSTRUCTION Plaited basketry forms a matlike surface by interweaving flat elements from two or more directions.

For **checked plaiting** a square base, start with an even number of **splint**s of equal length and weave them in a standard over-one, under-one pattern to the desired size (**a.**). Rectangular bases can be made in the same way as square bases by using unequal numbers of splints in the two perpendicular groups. The group with the greater number would use proportionately shorter splints. For variations, any basic plaiting weave can be used on the base.

To upset a plaited base, cut a board with slightly rounded corners to the square or rectangular shape of the base and center it on top of the work. Nail it to the **lapboard** with one nail near the center.

With the flat splints quite wet, split a middle rib to make an odd number of ribs for the sides so that the succeeding **round**s weave and do not stack; bend up the splints sharply around this wooden template. Hold or tie the splints in this position and weave two or three rows of horizontal splints to secure (**b.**).

a. Checked plaiting, square base

b. Plaited upsetting

BASIC WEAVES To do a **checked plaiting** weave, lay out a series of parallel splints on a flat surface. Take an equal number of them and, perpendicular to the first group, weave them in one at a time in a simple over-one, under-one pattern (**c.**). After the **upsetting** has been completed, use one long splint to weave each horizontal row. If the basket is large, join in an extra length by overlapping the new end over the old and concealing it behind a vertical stake. Continue weaving each row separately until the desired height for the border is reached.

For a **twilled plaiting** weave, lay out a series of parallel splints on a flat surface. With an equal number of them placed perpendicular to the first group, weave the first one in, **float**ing it over two or more and under one or more. **Stagger** the second perpendicular element by weaving it under the first vertical splint (the one the previous horizontal splint floated over), then over two or more and under one or more splints. Continue in this pattern, staggering the successive rows to produce the twilled effect (**d.**).

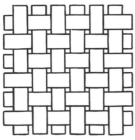

c. Checked plaiting

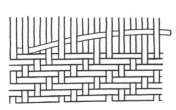

d. Twilled plaiting

e. Inverted border (inside view)

Numerous variations on twilled plaiting can be worked out. A **herringbone** pattern is produced by weaving under, then over, equal numbers of splints—e.g., over two, under two—staggering each row one splint. More complicated patterns can be plotted on graph paper.

To join in flat material used in plaited baskets, weave or overlap the new end over the old and conceal the ends under the transverse splints.

To make an inverted border, with the splints or winding reed quite wet and **slype**d, place or bring the last (top) row of horizontal plaiting to the inside of the basket without weaving it in. Carefully crease or fold the splints over the top and down into the weaving on the inside of the basket for at least 3 horizontal rows (**e.**) See ill.

COIL BASKET CONSTRUCTION To make a round reed **foundation** coil **base**, first trim the reed to a gradually sloping point with a sharp **knife** (**a.**). With this end well soaked, preshape it into a small **coil**. With a **tapestry needle** threaded with **raffia**, wind it a few inches from the end toward the tapered end (**b.**). Roll the end into the smallest possible coil and sew the raffia from the outside of the coil up through the center (**c.**). Proceed to coil the reed around the center, sewing the outer row of reed to the coil beneath. Use a figure-eight stitch or other basic coil stitch.

After the desired size of coiled bottom is reached, begin **upsetting** by gradually binding the successive rows of coil above each other instead of beside. Continue weaving as before; no change of stroke or weave is necessary.

The figure-eight stitch is a basic stitch used in **coil basketry**. It is a good stitch when strength is required and is often used to introduce color and occasionally to finish a border. Thread the **tapestry needle** with raffia and start the basic coil. Take the raffia around the back of the outer reed and under it to the inside of the basket. Keeping the raffia flat, take it down between the adjacent rows beneath and back up to the inside of the outermost reed (**d.**).

The **lazy squaw stitch** can be used in coil basketry; it consists of a long and a short stitch. The long stitch goes under the row beneath and the short stitch goes around the **foundation** only.

After a round reed **foundation coil** has been started, wind the raffia from the outside in and around the outermost reed (foundation) and back out for a short stitch. Take the raffia back in, but this time take it under and up between the previous row and out back for a long stitch. When starting the first row, the long stitch will have to pass through the center hole of the coil.

Continue around by alternating a long and a short stitch, being careful that the long stitch always wraps around the short stitch of the previous row (**e.**).

As the weaving gets larger it will be necessary to add two or more stitches into each space (.nstead of one) so that all the stitching looks as if it radiates from the center.

Another stitch is the **lace stitch**. After the basic **coil** is started, hold the reed the desired distance away from the previous coil. Wrap it with raffia in a series of short stitches the desired distance between knots. Pass the raffia down around the adjacent coil in a long stitch, still keeping the rows apart. Bring it over the upper coil and back in and around the middle of the long stitch. To knot, wrap this long stitch a few turns between the coils being joined and continue weaving (**f.**). See ill.

To join in round reed, **slype** both ends so that when placed together they form the uniform size of reed being used. Tie or wrap these ends with a fine thread and continue weaving.

To join in raffia, hold the reed in the left hand and press with the forefinger and thumb over both the old and new ends of raffia. Wrap the new raffia around the old a few turns and proceed to weave as before.

To make a simple **border**, cut or gradually taper the reed or foundation material to a point. This will insure that the last row of coil will blend in. Bind the last row with raffia with the same stitch as you did the others. Finish by carefully tying or wrapping the tapered end to the coil beneath with a figure-eight stitch. Cut off the loose end on the inside of the basket.

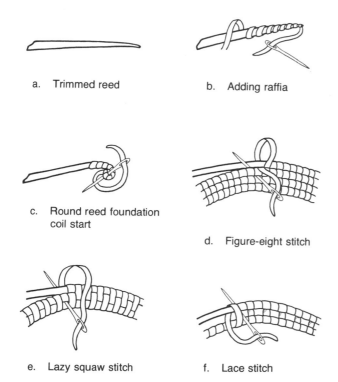

a. Trimmed reed

b. Adding raffia

c. Round reed foundation coil start

d. Figure-eight stitch

e. Lazy squaw stitch

f. Lace stitch

DYEING AND COLORING   The most common means of coloring basketry materials is with vegetable dyes. They are not as messy or time-consuming to work with as aniline dyes and they produce softer and more natural colors. Vegetable dyes are commercially available and come in a powdered form. Colors include red, yellow, blue, green, orange, brown, purple, scarlet, and black.

In soft water, or in hard water treated with vinegar, dissolve the mordant **alum** in a ratio of three ounces per quart of water for a fixing solution. Soak the **stuff**, whether **cane** (reed), **raffia**, or other material in this solution overnight. In an enamel container, prepare the color bath by dissolving the chosen vegetable dye in a ratio of two ounces of dry powder per gallon of water. Bring it to a gentle boil, and then let simmer. While the material is still damp from the fixing solution, transfer it to the color bath for about a half-hour, turning the material over and occasionally testing for color intensity. When the desired color is obtained, remove and let dry.

FINISHING   For a common polished finish of a reed or rattan basket, mix 2 parts turpentine to 1 part varnish. Apply with a fine paint brush or spray gun. Shellac also may be used and thinned in the same proportions with denatured alcohol for a slightly yellow-tan, glossy finish. When dry, lightly buff with steel wool.

CARE, CLEANING, AND STORAGE   Improper or rough handling causes the most damage to a basket. Care for a basket as you would any fabric, being careful to replace or repair broken pieces. Reweave or glue in ends that become loose.

Clean a basket by first dusting thoroughly. Damp-wash it with a cloth that has been treated with a mild detergent. Damp-rinse and let dry.

Keep all baskets in a cool, dry place. If stored for extended periods, poison the basket with a weak solution of arsenic dissolved in alcohol. This will prevent rodents and insects from attacking it. Be sure to damp-wash the basket thoroughly before using after bringing it out of storage.

basketry. Lacemaking. Some baskets have a very open and lacy look. Baskets of Italy, Spain, Colombia, and Mexico, worked over a wire structure with **raffia** or like material in the open areas of the frame, are examples. The open areas of the base of these baskets are filled in with a simple weaving of the fiber, widely spaced, with **filling stitch**es similar to a **darning stitch**. In the side of the basket in the open spaces between the wire frame, the fillings are also worked in the darning stitch, but with a more open design effect. The wire frames of the baskets from Italy have a padding and are covered with a simple wrapping technique, whereas the frames of the baskets from Spain, Colombia, and Mexico are covered with a **buttonhole stitch**. The Papago and Pima Indians of the southwestern United States construct a carrying frame, similar to a knapsack, which they call a kiaha. It is made of two-ply fiber cord, prepared from the leaves of the agave and maguey (a species of agave). The technique is called lace coil, but is in fact a simple looping (**a.**). A twisted looping, in combination with the simple **looping**, creates elaborate designs (**b.**). See ill.

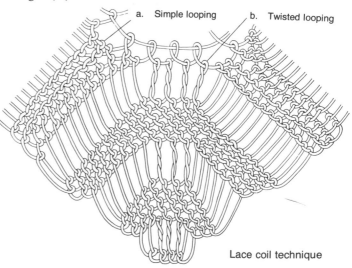

a. Simple looping   b. Twisted looping

Lace coil technique

basketware. Basketry. The finished product or products made by using basketry techniques, including baskets, bedding, hat, mats, furniture, fish traps, bags, and cages. Basketware may be articles roughly woven for temporary use and discarded after they wear out, or highly finished or decorated articles carefully made to last. Also see **Basketry.**

basket weave. Quilts. Stitchery. A variation of **plain weave** in which two or more **warp** or **lengthwise threads** cross over two or more **weft** or **crosswise threads. Hopsacking** and **monk's cloth** are examples of basket weave materials.

basket weave. Weaving. A derivative of **plain weave.** Two or more parallel **warp** threads interlace with two or more parallel **weft** threads to form various size squares or rectangles that look like enlarged plain weave. Basket weave fabrics are loose in structure and difficult to work with, but they form interesting surface effects. **Monk's cloth** is an example of basket weave. See ill. Also see **grouped threads.**

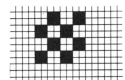
Basket weave

basketweave stitch. Needlepoint. (Also called bias tent stitch, diagonal basketweave stitch, diagonal tent stitch.) From the front this stitch has the appearance of a **continental stitch** and a **half cross stitch,** but the reverse side has the appearance of a woven basket, hence its name.

Although it uses a lot of yarn, this stitch is particularly

Basketweave stitch

a.

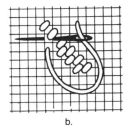
b.

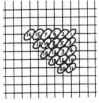
c. Front of work, showing order of working stitches

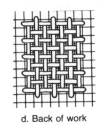
d. Back of work

useful for needlepoint backgrounds in the **tent stitch** for several reasons: the needle always goes down into the previous row of stitches, never splitting the yarn and giving a smooth, clear effect; working back and forth diagonally across the background does not distort the canvas as much as other stitches; the interlocked mesh formed on the reverse side (basketweave) is extremely strong and wears well; and working diagonally eliminates the need to turn the canvas at the end of each row, as is necessary when working straight rows of tent stitch (this makes the work quicker and more even).

Begin in the top right-hand corner, and always work the rows alternately—first from top to bottom, and then from bottom to top, starting with one stitch and increasing each row. Always leave a thread hanging in the middle of the row if you have to leave the canvas so that when you pick it up again you can tell whether you were working up or down. When two rows are worked in the same direction the basketweave on the back is interrupted; this makes an undesirable break that shows on the front. See ill.

basketwork. Basketry. The techniques or stitches used in the making of **basketware.** These weaves and the basic structure vary according to the type of basket being woven, its shape, and the material used to weave it. Also see **Basketry.**

bas-relief. Stitchery. Toys. (Also called low relief.) A sculptured surface in which areas of design stand out in **relief** only slightly from the **background.** Some **padded stitchery** and **quilt**ed **panels** have bas-relief surfaces. Many **fabric dolls** which use **stitch**es to delineate the features employ bas-relief.

basse-lisse. Weaving. See **low-warp, tapestry loom.**

basse-taille. Enameling. A term derived from a French word meaning "low-cut." This is a technique of enameling in which the surface of the **metal** is first etched, engraved, hammered, carved, stamped, or scratched, and then transparent enamels are fired over the texture metal. This produces brilliant reflection through the **enamel,** contrast between the smooth enamel surface and the rough metal below, and an exaggerated feeling of depth. Also see **repoussé** and **Enameling: Tools and Materials.**

basswood. Woodworking. A soft, lightweight wood that grows from Canada to the lowlands of the Mississippi. It is easily carved, warps very little, and has a close, fine, straight grain and an even texture. Negatively, it has little resistance to decay. The color of the wood ranges from a creamy white, the **sapwood,** to a medium reddish brown, the **heartwood.** It is used for crates and boxes, sashes, doors, and general **millwork,** and as **core** material for **plywood veneer.**

bast. Batik and Tie-dye. A **fiber** used as the **binding material** in **tie-dye,** particularly where more primitive methods are in use. The bast is a strong, woody plant fiber used to make cord and rope. Either bast or **raffia** are used in the Nigerian **adire** work.

bastard cut file. Metalworking. See **file.**

bast fiber. Knitting. (Also called stem fiber.) Bast fiber is the fibrous section in the inner bark of the stems of dicotyledenous plants. Also see **jute, ramie.**

bast fiber. Rugmaking. Spinning. Weaving. See **fiber.**

basting. Crewel. Embroidery. Needlepoint. The making of large **running stitch**es wherever necessary to temporarily hold two pieces of **fabric** together, as when backing stretchy fabrics such as knits while they are being embroidered, or holding a hem in place. Also used in transferring a design when **dressmaker's carbon,** ink, or paint are impractical, and to prevent raw edges of a **background fabric** from raveling while a design is being worked. Also see **Crewel: Preparation and Layout, Transferring a Design, Needlepoint: Preparation and Layout.**

basting stitch. Stitchery. An exaggerated **running stitch** used to temporarily hold two pieces of **fabric** together.

bastite. Gemcutting. See **hypersthene.**

bat. Ceramics. A disk or slab of **plaster of paris** used for forming, transporting, or drying pottery. **Pots** are thrown on a removable wheel bat so that they can be moved at any stage without touching or possibly damaging the object.

bat head. Spinning. See **spinning head.**

bath toy. Toys. Any toy designed specifically for use in water or in the bath. **Stuffed toy**s are sometimes made for the water by using sponge or **foam rubber** as the **filler** with a washcloth or terrycloth covering. Squeezing the toy removes the water so that it can dry. Floating toys, carved soap toys, and some **magnetic toy**s are suitable for the bath. The **water lens** and **bubble blower**s can be used as bath toys. Painted surfaces that will peel or soak off, **glues** that will soften in water, or materials that will warp or rot must be avoided. Also see **beach toy, boat, soap carving** and **Toys: Ephemeral Toys.**

batik. Batik and Tie-dye. Puppets. Quilts. Stitchery. Toys. A method of **resist** dyeing that employs the technique of protecting designed portions of **fabric** with **wax,** then dyeing the fabric. It is an ancient Javanese process still in use today.

Hot **batiking wax** is applied to the fabric so that it will penetrate the **fibers. Natural fabric**s work best, having the greatest affinity to **dyes. Cold-water dye**s are used in batik because heating during the dyeing process would melt the wax design. **Waxing** and dyeing are continued alternately through a series of colors, depending upon the complexity of the design being executed. Many traditional designs use only one color applied to a colored fabric.

When all dyeing has been completed the wax must be taken out of the fabric. **Removing wax** is accomplished in any of several ways, including **ironing, boiling,** scraping, or flaking, and the use of cleaning **solvent**s. Also see **Batik and Tie-dye.**

BATIK AND TIE-DYE

The ancient arts of **batik** and **tie-dye** are essentially **resist-dye** processes. While each utilizes different techniques, both involve treating fabric so that areas will resist color when the fabric is dyed. Each has characteristics by which it may be identified.

There is a great current interest in both of these traditional arts. The involvement in them is part of the larger craft renaissance and they are being explored in many imaginative and innovative ways. Newly developed dyes and readily available fabrics of all kinds have expanded the potentials of these processes.

The term "batik" applies to both the process of **wax-resist dyeing** and to the finished fabric treated by this method. The word is Indonesian and means, literally, "wax writing."

The batik process employs the technique of protecting selected areas of fabric without wax, then dyeing the fabric. After the dye process the wax is removed, revealing the original color of the fabric. This process can be continued through several wax and dye treatments so that the pattern and colors become very complex. Some waxes may be removed and new designs applied before additional **dyebath**s.

Tie-dye, or "tie-and-dye," refers to the **resist** process as well as to the finished fabric embellished by this **dye** method. The material is literally **tied,** or bound, and then dyed in a dyebath.

The technique of tie-dye involves the use of a series of **binding methods** in which fabric is so tightly tied that dye cannot penetrate the bound areas. These areas of resist then retain the original color of the fabric. Tie-dye is usually accomplished by using an alternating series of bindings and dyeings. Some bindings may remain through an entire series of dyeings. Others may be united and retied for overlapping color effects.

Discharge dyeing is considered a tie-dye technique, although the process used in the tie-dye reverses the usual one. In it, bindings are used to make some parts of the fabric resistant. A colored fabric is always used—one previously tie-dyed, one treated by contrast dyeing, or a solid-color material. Instead of dipping the tied material into a dye, it is dipped into a **bleach** solution, or **color remover.** The bound areas retain color and the loose portions of the fabric are bleached to a lighter color or white.

The origins of batik are lost in history, but evidence has been uncovered to suggest that the Persians and Egyptians wore garments decorated by batik over 2,000 years ago. Some authorities on the history of textiles suggest that batik began in the Indian archipelago and spread out from there; others maintain that Asia was its birthplace, and that only later did it move as far as the Malaysian area.

What is certain is that the art was highly developed in Java and Bali by the 1200s. The art was without doubt widely practiced in Asia, particularly in Japan, China, and India, and was also known in Africa. It was in Java, however, that batik became a significant art form.

The history of the island of Java in the Indonesian archipelago has become a part of the **Javanese batik** designs. Religious and mystic symbolism predominates and the various designs are important for specific occasions. Certain designs have been devised for use on **fabric**s for the newborn infant; others are made especially for marriage ceremonies or religious offerings. The influence of nature is seen in all the Javanese designs, which are rich in depictions of birds, plants, fish, vines, and flowers. The influence of the Islamic religion in Javanese work after the fifteenth century is seen in the stylization of animals and birds. Because, according to religious tenets, no man or creature could be represented, intricate patterns were developed so that the birds and animals became part of an abstract intertwining of shapes.

The batik designs of Java were so developed stylistically that people could be identified as to rank or social status by the designs they wore. Sometimes a design would identify a family or a village. Dyes, indigenous to certain areas, also served to identify the locale from which a person came.

The different parts of Asia developed not only their own dyes, but also their own methods and tools. In the Celebes Islands, wax was applied with bamboo strips. In Java in the middle of the eighteenth century the **wax** was applied through the use of the newly developed **tjanting.** The **tjap,** or stamp print, was also in use. Various areas developed **paste**s to replace wax as a resist, and in some localities pastes were deftly applied with the tips of the fingers.

Eventually, traders and exporters on the early trade routes took batik fabrics and the process to Holland. The Dutch then introduced the technique to Europe.

By the seventeenth century batik had been introduced throughout the Western world. There were many attempts to reproduce batik on a large scale, particularly later when fabric printing became more common. **Vegetable dyes** were used in the early copies, but after the 1860s, when **aniline dye**s were developed, the process found greater success. Reproducing the **crackle** effect of batik was the most difficult part of the printing.

Art Nouveau greatly influenced European batik design; batiks were popular during the early 1900s and remained so for some years. Germany produced batik and a variety of glass and metal tjantings and an electric wax-writing pencil. The pencil was designed to make possible a change in the wax flow, allowing for variation in the width of lines.

After the 1920s, commercial batiks were no longer produced in Europe. When the Republic of Indonesia was established after World War II, the production of Javanese batiks resumed. They retained many of their traditional patterns, such as the **parang** and **kawang**, and these are being produced today. In the same way, the batik produced in Nigeria is often based on the traditional **adire** pattern.

Today, textile artists find in batik an extremely versatile medium. Many artists use it as a painting medium, doing **freehand batik. Tjap printing** methods are also being revitalized. Batik is used in wall hangings and panels and for clothing, home furnishings, and stuffed soft sculpture.

Tie-dye also is known to be an ancient art. Remnants of tie-dyed fabrics suggest that it developed in Asia and spread to India, Malaya, and across Africa. Burial grounds have yielded relics of tie-dyed textiles from along the caravan and silk routes through China and Persia.

Some early records of this art date from the Chinese T'ang dynasty in the late seventh century. From there it moved to Japan, where tie-dye was used on the beautiful silk fabrics of nobility. India developed the art about the same time as or earlier than Japan, and examples of it are depicted in fresco paintings in the caves of Ajanta, Hyderbad. These paintings show people wearing fabrics with circular white patterns called **plangi** as early as the sixth and seventh centuries.

Other examples of tie-dye came from Cambodia, Thailand, and Indonesia. The process is still used in both Java and Bali. The Peruvian Incas were familiar with tie-dyeing, and examples from tombs predate the arrival of the Spaniards in that country in the sixteenth century.

African tie-dye is noted for the boldness of its design, as Indonesian is known for its complexity and symbolism. As individual countries or geographic areas developed dyes that distinguished their work, they also developed styles by which their work is recognized.

Tie-dye is currently a very popular craft, particularly for clothing, wall hangings, and accessories of all kinds.

BASIC PROCEDURES FOR BATIK   The most commonly used **resist agent** in batik is **batiking wax.** It is usually a combination of **beeswax** and **paraffin,** with each of the ingredients contributing specific characteristics. The flexibility of the beeswax leaves the **resist**-treated fabric so supple that the wax does not crack under ordinary conditions. The paraffin, by contrast, is brittle and will crack readily to allow dye to penetrate those lines. Either of these waxes may be used, depending upon the desired effect, although a combination of the two is most common. The **crackle,** or breaking of the wax, produces the characteristic **fracture** that usually identifies the batik process.

Melting the wax involves certain hazards. Because the hot wax is always a potential danger for small children, other wax methods have been devised for their use. **Oil resist** is probably one of the simplest and it avoids the necessity of any heating. **Wax resist drawing**s can be done with wax pencils or crayons. Various other methods, such as **crayon batik** or **candle-drip bàtik,** simplify the process, although they may offer other limitations. **Paste-resist** methods have been used for hundreds of years. When the **paste** is dry, dyes are painted over the material, and the paste resists **dye penetration.** The fabric is usually steamed to **set** the dye before the paste is removed. There are numerous **paste resist recipe**s; almost all use some combination of flour or **starch** and water. **Paper batik** and **rub-off batik** offer ways of working with resist agents on paper. The effect is distinctive and hot waxes are not used. Colored waxes provide not only areas of resist, but also color, as the **colorant** can be set into the fabric.

A fairly new resist agent now on the market is the **cold resin resist.** It is available in liquid form, and its primary advantage is that fabric painted with it can be immersed in hot water. The use of most waxes limits batik to **cold water dye**s. Cold resin resists are removed after the dyeing process with cold water, in contrast to waxes, which must be removed with **solvent**s or by heating.

Most beginning batikers select one class of dyes and work with it in various ways and on assorted materials. As the potentials and limitations of that combination become clear the batiker may wish to add another dye, or the selection of another fabric may require a change of dyes.

The batik process basically remains the same for all fabrics and dyes. Some batik artists stretch their fabrics over a frame. This keeps the material taut and makes it easy to draw brushstrokes of the hot melted wax over the material. Thumbtacks and a wooden frame are essentially all that are needed. A simple **batiking frame** can be made by tacking the fabric over an empty cardboard box. Frames made especially for batiking are available at batik supply shops. Simple ones can be devised at home from picture frames, canvas stretchers, or from four pieces of wood grooved to fit together at the corners. Some batikers prefer to leave their fabric lying flat on a table so that they can paint directly onto the loose material. It is helpful to first place a padding of newspapers on the table. Wax paper or other nonabsorbent paper placed on top of the newspapers and under the fabric will keep the wax from soaking through to the newspaper, or the fabric can be held taut off the surface of the table with one hand while it is painted with the other. However the fabric is placed, it is helpful if the fabric is secured in some way.

After the fabric is prepared the design is applied. Sketches are lightly made on the fabric with chalk or charcoal. If only an occasional guideline is needed, a pencil dot can be used. The drawing should not be penciled in completely because the pencil line cannot always be removed in washing.

If a drawing is to be transferred to the fabric, a sheet of dressmaker's carbon is placed on the flat piece of material, carbon side facing the fabric, with the drawing on top. A **tracing wheel** is then used to outline the drawing, leaving a dotted line of carbon marks on the fabric.

There are also **marking pen**s and dressmaker's chalks for drawing directly on the fabric. Wax or paste is applied directly over these, or the lines are brushed off or blown off as the work progresses. If a **freehand batik** is being produced, the **resist** may be applied directly, with no sketch lines at all. When the design sketch is finished (if one is used), the resist agent is applied.

The **batiking wax** must be sufficiently hot to penetrate the fabric thoroughly. **Melting the wax** demands careful attention, as there is potential hazard if the wax is overheated. Wax must never be placed in a container over direct heat. A **double boiler** is the best arrangement, although one can readily be improvised with an electric frying pan or a hot plate. Baking soda should always be kept on hand to extinguish fires. Water should not be used on a wax fire.

Insufficiently heated wax will appear milky when used because it starts to harden before it is absorbed by the fibers. If wax is overheated, it will begin to smoke. Overheated wax has a greater tendency to run or bleed on the fabric. The bleeding will blur the line between the wax and the resist areas. It is important that the wax thoroughly penetrate the threads. The fabric should be checked from both sides to be sure wax has completely penetrated before dyeing. If necessary, some areas may have additional wax added from the reverse side of the material in what is called a **double-waxing** process. This is often done when heavy fabrics are used.

Wax can be applied in any of several ways to the fabric. A batiking **brush** can be set into the hot wax; a wire strainer set into the wax container keeps the bristles from resting on the bottom and becoming permanently bent. The **tjanting** is a tool often used to apply wax. It has a small container for the hot liquid that allows a more continuous, flowing drawn line. Several varieties of the traditional tjanting, the tool used in the Javanese **tulis** balik, are now available. Wax can also be applied with stamps. The traditional Javanese stamp was the **tjap,** and many variations of the stamp method are possible. **Tjap printing** can be done by dipping any of various tools into the hot wax and then setting them onto the material. The tjap or stamp can be used to make an all-over batik print if the blocks are printed side by side.

To produce medallion designs, border prints, or large single scenes, **direct-wax painting** is most often employed. Any areas painted with wax can be incised with a sharp, pointed tool so that when the material is dyed the color will penetrate the incised lines to make a fine linear pattern.

After the **waxing** is finished and cooled the fabric can be deliberately **crackle**d for a strong pattern of fractures. If the waxed material is placed in a freezer or refrigerator for a few minutes, it will fracture readily. If it remains warm or at room temperature, it will retain some flexibility, bending rather than crackling. The composition of the batiking wax or resist agent will also have an effect on the crackle; the more paraffin, the more brittle the wax. Cold-water dyes must be used when wax is the resist.

When **cold resin resist** is used the fabric may be immersed in a hot dyebath. If **paste** is the **resist,** the dye is usually brushed onto the fabric, and cold dyes are used. The dye is then **set** by **steaming,** or whatever is required by the dye.

The waxing process is usually alternated with the dyeing process when a number of colors are used. With a single-color batik, there is one wax, or resist, application and one dyebath. This results in at least two colors, as there is the original color of the fabric, the dyed color, and those areas where some color bleeds to make an area of middle value. For a two-color batik, there are two waxings and two dyebaths, though there are more than two colors.

The procedure in dyeing is always to start with the lightest color and progress to the darkest. Every color to remain must be coated with wax to protect it during consequent dyebaths. After each dyeing, the fabric must be thoroughly dried before painting on the next layer of wax because moisture would interfere with wax absorption into the fibers. Avoid drying the fabric directly over any heat, such as a radiator, which could melt the wax. Avoid direct sun if the dyes are not completely **colorfast.**

When all dyebaths have been completed the dyes must be set according to the directions given for each dye. The wax is removed by any of various methods. Some wax can be shaken loose or scraped off with a table knife or with the fingers; if the wax is cold, it will shake off more easily. After the largest chunks of wax have been removed, the fabric may be sent to a commercial dry cleaner. This, of course, means waiting to see the final results; the fabric may be dipped in a home dry cleaning agent such as carbon tetrachloride. Precautions must be taken in using any **solvent**s, and directions on containers must be carefully read. Some are toxic, volatile, and flammable.

A safer method for removing wax is **ironing** it out between blotter papers or layers of newspaper. If permanent **cold-water dye**s have been used the fabric can be dipped in simmering water to melt out the wax. As the wax floats to the top of the water, it can be skimmed off. When the water is cool the hardened layer of wax can be lifted off the top and reused. Steam cabinets offer another means of removing wax and **heat set**ting the dyes. A steam cabinet may have to be specifically built, or a steamer can be adapted to this use.

Direct-dye painting is sometimes combined with the use of resist agents to create variations on the batik process. In this, dyes are painted directly onto the fabric. A number of colors can be applied at one time because the fabric is not immersed in the dyebath. **Procion** dyes and **Versatex** are often used for direct-dye painting. They allow for the use of a specific color in a specific area without subjecting the entire wax fabric to the dye. When **fiber-reactive dye**s are used, an **alginate thickener** is added to give the dye a more workable consistency.

BASIC PROCEDURES FOR TIE-DYE   The tie-dye process does not require the ability to draw, so many people who hesitate to work in batik feel more comfortable with the tie-dye process. It involves a complex use of color and design composition, but it can be approached very simply for very effective results. Most beginners in tie-dye limit themselves initially to a single kind of dye and a single fabric. When some control is gained over the use of these, new fabrics and dyes are tried.

Any of a variety of **binding material**s can be used in the **resist** process. **Cord for tie-dye** includes linen thread, cotton thread, string, **carpet thread,** and clothesline. Other **bindings** commonly used are rubber bands, twine, clothespins, nylon stockings, flexible plastic, wire, and masking tape.

When fabrics are tied with previously **dyed binding thread** some flecks of dye will transfer to the fabric, adding rich color detail. The thread or string can be immersed in strong **dye liquor** and left unrinsed to intensify this effect although it should be dry before tying. Strings of a number of different colors will give a variegated effect.

The fabric must be **gather**ed or collected in some way so that it can be tied. One of the most versatile ways of working with lengths of fabric is **folding.** The fabric can be folded lengthwise or crosswise, at a diagonal or in **accordion pleats.** Folding can be continued to make **bundles,** or it can be started at the center with folds going out, umbrellalike. The folded pieces can then be tied with any of the tying methods to produce an unending variety of stripes, diagonals, and **zigzag**s.

Fabrics can also be bunched or wadded, as in **bundle**

tie-dye, or twisted or coiled as in **knotted tie-dye.** The **pin-pivot method** offers another way of gathering the material for binding.

Other ways of collecting the material are those in which the fabric is wrapped around an object. **Clump tying** can be done over pebbles, corks, or wood chunks. **Wood block tie-dye** sometimes sandwiches fabric between clamped blocks of wood. **Clamps,** clothespins, and **bulldog clips** can be used as clamping devices. The fabrics can be **pleat**ed, gathered, rolled, tied over gadgets, or hemmed over boards. The **ruching** method of tie-dye offers a means of making very small gathers. Safety pins can be used to sew through the gathered fabric.

The greatest degree of control is in **tritik,** or sewn tie-dye. Hand or machine **stitch**es can be made very tight to produce tiny patterns in the fabric. **Sewn spiral**s and **sewn tuck**s are both accomplished by tritik. Oversewing is a variation of tritik.

Binding is accomplished by first tying the cord to the fabric in a step known as **fastening-on.** This secures the end of the binding cord so that tying or wrapping can continue. Sometimes a slip knot is used to fasten on. The way in which the binding materials are tied onto the fabric has an obvious effect on the finished pattern.

There are endless possible variations in the ways binding can be done. Spiral binding, crisscross binding (or lattice binding), line binding, and band tying are among those most frequently used. When the binding material is pulled tight it should give a complete resist to the area, rejecting all dye.

In **spiral binding** the pattern moves in one direction to form a spiral line over the cloth. The first string may be followed by a second placed precisely on top of the first to widen or strengthen it.

The **crisscross binding,** or lattice method, uses a string that crosses back and forth diagonally, going over itself and offering a partial resist. The lines thus tied over the gathered fabric will appear somewhat broken after the dyeing is completed.

The **line binding** method uses string wrapped around and around in one spot and then knotted. This method does not give large areas of resist but will make a linear pattern. The tightness or looseness of the binding determines how much dye will penetrate the cloth.

The **band tying** method of binding covers areas of the fabric with one or two solid layers of string or cord.

The **spot technique** of binding produces a pattern of tiny dots and is achieved by tying very small portions of fabric. Ovals, circles, and diamonds can all be formed by this method of binding.

Binding or tying is sometimes hard on the hands, and the constant pulling of fibers over the skin may cause blisters. To avoid this, cotton or leather gloves may be worn, or the areas subject to rubbing can be covered with plastic bandables or Band-aids. A spool or pencil wrapped onto the cord makes it possible to grasp the tool to draw the cord tight, or cord can be secured to a stationary object so that tension can be put on the cord to wrap and tie it tightly.

When binding or tying is finished, the cord must be secured with a step called **fastening-off.** This must be carefully done to prevent the ties from loosening and allowing dye into the resist areas.

When the fastening-off is complete, the bound areas can be made further resistant to dye by covering them with a **flour paste** or by tying **polyethylene binding** over them.

The tied fabric is then ready for the wetting out, which prepares it for the **dip dyeing.** The length of time the fabric is left in the **dyebath** and the temperature of the water are determined by the kind of **dye** used. Unlike **batik,** tie-dye can be simmered or boiled because there is no wax to melt away.

After dyeing, the fabric is removed from the dyebath, squeezed, and rinsed until the water is clear. It is best to rinse by totally immersing the material in water.

In some cases, the ties or bindings are removed and the fabric is hung to dry. In others, the fabric is left to dry while still tied. The timing for removing the bindings is determined by the effect desired in the fabric and by the dye used. Sometimes the dyes are **set** by **ironing, steaming,** or autoclaving before a second tie-and-dye process, although when **hot dyeing** is used, ironing may be left until the very last step.

FABRICS FOR DYEING   The selection of an appropriate **fabric** is essential for successful batik or tie-dye. The best dye results are usually obtained when fabrics made from **natural fiber**s, as opposed to **synthetic fiber**s, are used. The natural fibers include the vegetable or **cellulose fiber**s as well as the animal or **protein fiber**s. Of these, the **vegetable fiber**s are easier to work with because there is less problem of shrinkage if **hot dyeing** methods are used. In the vegetable or cellulose group are cotton, **flax, hemp, jute,** and **ramie.** Among the animal or protein fibers are silk, wool, and hair.

Synthetic or **man-made fiber**s do not take dye well, with the exception of viscose rayon, which is a **cellulosic fiber.** While some **household dye**s are made for use on synthetics, the results are not usually **colorfast,** and the colors are not intense. There are, however, some dyes designed especially to be effective on synthetics.

Among the most common synthetic fibers are **acetate,** acrylic, Dacron, nylon, polyester, rayon, and glass. They are often used in blends, combining synthetic with natural fibers.

When the dyed product must be colorfast, vegetable fibers such as cotton and linen are recommended. They have a great **affinity for dye**s and can be subjected to heat in the tie-dye process.

When buying fabrics it is important to note the fiber content. The description can be stapled to a small sample of the fabric and kept as a record, or a number and corresponding information can be inked into a corner of a fabric scrap and the scrap filed. The label on the bolt is the best source for accurate information. While many craftspeople who work with fabrics can identify a fiber by texture, it is very difficult to determine the identity of blends. Because knowledge of the fiber content is essential in dyeing, it is sometimes necessary to test a fabric of unknown origin.

A good fabric for use by the beginner in batik or tie-dye is sheeting from well-washed sheets or pillow cases. The soft material absorbs the dye readily and it is an inexpensive source for experimental work. All cottons work well. Among those most commonly used are batiste, calico, cambric, casement, corduroy, cotton satin, cotton velvet, flannel, lawn, lightweight muslin, poplin, sateen, toweling, velveteen, and voile. Linens, silks, and wools offer a great range of fabrics, but they are more expensive than cottons. A less expensive material is burlap, or sacking, made from jute and hemp; it takes dye nicely, although it is sometimes hard to find light colors and has limited applications.

Some **blend**s of cotton with synthetic fiber may use one **fiber** for **warp** and a different one for **weft.** In this case, the warp and weft absorb the dyes differently, offering color variations that may or may not be desirable. A few **household dye**s contain several kinds of **dyestuff** so that blends can be dyed evenly.

Woolens can be used for cold or warm water, but care must be taken to avoid shrinkage if hot **dyebath**s are required. Cotton, viscose rayon, linen, and silk remain the best fabrics. Any viscose rayons can be used if they are absorbent.

The silks used for dyeing include voile, silk chiffon, and raw silk. The silk chiffon is favored by many tie-dye artists because it takes dye beautifully and has the added effects of semitransparency and flowing movement. Satin dyes well; it should not be boiled first, as this affects the smoothness of the weave. It should be washed in the same way that all new fabrics are prepared.

Coarser, heavier fabrics that have excess bulk, or those with raised weaves, are more difficult to use in tie-dye or batik, although they may offer specific desirable characteristics. While the heavier fabrics can be used, they may require **waxing** on both the front and reverse sides, as in a **double-waxing** technique. They are more difficult to tie into small patterns of folds and gathers. Closely woven thin cottons and those woven of fine spun threads will absorb the dye most readily, and will **fold** or **gather** into the tiniest patterns for tie-dye.

It is not necessary to work only on white fabrics; pale colors or pastels are also suitable. Bright colors can be used, especially in the simpler single-color batiks or single-color tie-dye, but the dyed fabric will never be lighter than the original fabric. As dyes are continued, the fabric colors grow darker. (**Discharge dyeing,** a **bleaching** process, is the one exception to this.)

It should be remembered that dye does not obliterate the original fabric color, but blends with it. If you are working on a yellow cotton it will be almost impossible to obtain light blue, as the blue over yellow will produce green; a very intense blue would be required to overpower the yellow. Dyes are transparencies, laid one over another on the base color of fabric.

PREPARATION OF FABRIC   Almost all new fabric has had some **finish** applied to it that should be removed before the tying or **waxing** begins. **Calendering,** sizing, and starching are common finishes that can be removed easily by washing. Mercerizing is a finish that gives the material a greater **affinity for dye.**

Wash-and-wear and **drip dry** fabric finishes will inhibit the fabric's receptivity to **dye.** Remove dye resistant finishes by soaking fabric for one-half hour in 190° F water to which ½ oz muriatic acid for every two gallons of water has been added. If that is not done the dye will not be effective. Perma-press is one finish that cannot be removed, as it is a permanent resin coating. Fabrics treated with that finish should not be used for **tie-dye** or **batik.**

All new fabric, with the exception of wool, is first washed in hot water with detergent or soap. Wool should be immersed in warm sudsy water, under 100° F and handled carefully to prevent matting the fibers. Always avoid sudden temperature changes in handling woolens to avoid shrinkage.

Many fabrics will require two or three washings, depending upon how heavy a layer of size of starch was added. When a fabric readily retains **crease**s made by the fingernail, this indicates a probably high degree of starch. It is best to agitate the fabric in an automatic washer. If that isn't possible, immerse the fabric completely, agitate and wring it, then rinse. Mercerized cotton need not be washed. Washing the fabric removes not only the starch or size, but also any dust or **grease.** If special washing instructions are given with any fabric, they should, of course, be followed.

Add a water softener, such as **Calgon,** to the wash water of the fabric to enhance dye receptivity.

All chemicals must be handled carefully and all precautions on the containers must be observed. Always rinse fabrics thoroughly after washing or after **removing size** or fabric finish. A simple way to remove a **drip-dry finish** is to boil the fabric for 15 minutes in a 1% **acetic acid** solution. This is the equivalent of about 1 part white vinegar to 4 parts water, or a quart of vinegar to a gallon of water.

The final step in preparing the selected fabric for dyeing is **ironing.** The smooth finish will make it easier to control the folds in **tie-dye** and will aid in the even application of **wax** in **batik.** Sometimes the wrinkled and unironed fabric can be used to textural advantage, but under most circumstances pressing is recommended.

Fabrics for tie-dye can be **mordant**ed, another process to increase receptivity to dye. This process involves dipping the **tied** fabric into a solution made up from a **mordant formula.** The fabric goes directly from the mordant bath to the **dyebath.** Fabrics for batik are never mordanted.

IDENTIFYING FIBERS   It is essential to identify correctly the fiber content of a fabric so that the appropriate dye can be selected. One simple test that can be used at home is the **burn test.** The test involves burning a small piece of the fabric and observing the way the fibers burn, how they smell, and what the residue looks like. These reactions offer indications or clues that assist in determining the makeup of the material.

To conduct the burn test, cut a small piece of fabric about 1″ wide by 2″ or 3″ long. Hold it over some nonburnable area, such as in a fireplace, a sink, or over dirt or concrete. It is helpful to hold the fabric with tongs or to hang the material over the end of a metal tool or gardening trowel or fork. Light one end of the strip and observe the

way it burns. Cotton and linen flare up quickly, burn rapidly, and smell like burned wood or paper. They leave a residue of light, soft ashes. Rayon (viscose rayon) burns quickly, flares, and smells like burned paper. It leaves very little ash. Acetate rayon appears to melt or drop rather than burn. The edges curl and pucker, and it has an acrid odor, smelling like burned sugar. Wool burns slowly and smells like burned hair or feathers. When the flame is removed the wool stops burning. The ash is crisp and bead-like. Silk burns and smolders slowly, leaving as residue a crisp, black ball. It smells similar to burning wool but the odor is less strong. Nylon melts as it burns and leaves a residual bead that is hard, round, and light brown. It smells like burning wax.

The tests for cotton and linen give similar responses, but as the two fabrics usually react similarly to dyes, it may not be essential to distinguish between them. If it is important, the **oil test** can be used. A drop of oil placed on each will give different results. The linen will develop a translucent spot that can be seen when it is held up to light. Cotton remains opaque when oil is added. Another simple test to distinguish between cotton and linen is to place a sample in water. Linen will absorb water quickly, evenly, and thoroughly. Cotton absorbs it slowly and unevenly.

Another very simple test to identify fiber is the **alkali test,** which can be made to distinguish the protein or **animal fiber**s (wool, silk, mohair, etc.) from the vegetable or **cellulose fiber**s (cotton, linen). This test involves treating the fibers with an alkali such as ammonia, **washing soda, lye,** or Clorox. Animal fibers will disintegrate in the alkali; **vegetable fiber**s will remain intact. Nylon can be dissolved in formic acid; acetate rayon dissolves in **acetone.**

The best means of identifying any fabric is to retain information from the bolt when the fabric is purchased; the burn test, oil test, and alkali test are for use when fabrics are of unknown origin. Through careful observation and practice it is possible to become sensitive to visual and textural changes in fibers and to be able to identify many by sight and touch. However, some **synthetic fiber**s are deceptively similar to **natural fiber**s and are spun or woven to resemble them. A few tests will be less costly than dye failures in terms of time, energy, and expense.

DYES AND DYEING   The search for permanent, easy-to-use, safe, and **colorfast** dyes is continuous; even industrially dyed material will **fade** eventually.

Dyestuffs can usually be kept without deteriorating as long as they remain unmixed, but once they are added to water they should be used. Freshly mixed dyes give the best results, although some dyes last for many hours. The manufacturer's directions that accompany a dye should be consulted. Experimentation will determine how best to preserve the dyes.

If an algae forms over the surface of a stored dyebath the dye should be discarded, as should any liquid from which dye particles have settled out. To store the mixed dyes, pour them into large glass or plastic containers and keep them labeled and tightly closed. A small test piece of fabric can later be used to determine whether or not the dye is still sufficiently effective.

Dyestuff is dissolved according to the individual dye directions and mixed with the assistant and water to make the dyebath. To determine how much dyestuff to use the fabric should be weighed. The amounts of the dyestuffs used are given in proportion to weight. About 3 yards of 36″ wide medium-weight material weighs approximately a pound.

For direct dye, acid dye, or household dyes use the following amounts of dyestuff for each pound of fabric to be dyed: ½−1½ teaspoons dyestuff for light intensity (1.5−4.5 grams); 1½−4 teaspoons dyestuff for medium intensity (4.5−12 grams); 4−6 teaspoons dyestuff for deep intensity (12−18 grams). The dyestuff is added to the **dye liquor** to make the dyebath. There should be ample liquid to easily cover the fabric. A more intense solution will produce color in a shorter time than a weaker solution.

Assistants also are measured per pound of fabric, using 3 tablespoons **salt** (90 grams) or 4 teaspoons **acetic acid** (12 grams) per pound. A higher water temperature hastens the dye process; a lower temperature retards it. The amount of time the material is left in the dyebath will also affect the intensity.

If particular colors are to be duplicated, all the variables must be noted. These include the fabric weight; amount of dyestuff, assistant and water; extent of agitation; temperature of water; and duration of dyeing.

The fabric to be dyed should be wet before being dipped into the dyebath. This is called **wetting out** and it insures a thorough saturation and **level dyeing.** There must be a large enough **dye vessel** to hold adequate dyebath to make penetration of all fibers possible.

In dyeing, the treated fabric should be totally immersed in the dyebath to move freely over and around the material. In batik, to avoid excess **crackle,** the dye may be scooped up in a cup or pitcher and poured over any fabric exposed at the top; this also serves to continuously mix the dyebath. Fabric is left in the dyebath for the recommended length of time and assistants or fixers are added as needed. When the material is removed from the dyebath it must be carefully dried to maintain the even level of dye. Spreading fabrics out flat on plastic or wax paper keeps dye from running to lower ends, as it may if the fabric is hung on a line. Clothesline rope may absorb dye from the fabric and leave a light streak across the dyed fabric. The **fiber-reactive dye**s require slow, thorough drying; other dyes are sometimes best ironed while still damp to help **set** the color.

The chemical contents of dyes vary, and there is a wide variety available for both hot and cold dyeing.

Acid dyes, usually available in the form of salts, are used with the addition of acetic acid in the acid dyebath. Formic acid or sulfuric acid is sometimes used commercially, but for **home dyeing** acetic acid is safer. It is available as **glacial** acetic acid, or diluted as white vinegar. Acid dyes are used primarily on silk and wool, although nylon, acrylic, and some polyesters can be dyed with it. **Cellulose fibers** cannot be dyed with acid dyes unless a **mordant** that has an affinity for both fiber and **dyestuff** and thereby serves as a bridge between the two is used. Some acid dyes also call for the use of salt as an assistant. They may be used on silk, wool, and nylon without a mordant. Acid dyes vary in colorfastness; most are **fast** to **dry cleaning,** but not to washing.

Basic dyes (cationic dyes) render bright, striking color; their name is derived from their molecular character, which is an alkaline base. They have an affinity for wool, silk, nylon, acrylic fibers, and **jute.** They are not satisfactory for other materials unless a mordant is used. Cotton and viscose rayon require an **acid mordant** and a fixing agent. The directions and instructions supplied with basic dyes should be carefully followed.

Direct dyes (substantive dye) are generally best for cellulose fibers, including cotton, linen, and rayon. They are salts of color acids and require no mordant. They are not usually recommended for wool or silk, although some brands state that they are prepared for use on those fabrics. Direct dyes can be used hot, simmered at 140° F for tie-dye. They are also adaptable to **cold dyeing** at 90−100° F. Fabrics should remain in the **dyebath** for 20−60 minutes. Direct dyes can be used over most other dyes as a final color. Their fastness varies and dry cleaning is recommended; they fade from light or from washing. The bulk of packaged dyes are direct dyes.

Dispersed dyes were developed for use on cellulose acetate and are also used to dye polyester, nylon, and acetate rayon. Heat is required in dyeing, so it is not satisfactory for use in batik. The dyes are "dispersed" in the sense that the coloring matter, which is sometimes water soluble, is held in a water suspension. These finely divided particles of color are dispersed and transferred to the fiber during the **hot dyeing.**

Fiber-reactive dyes (**cold water dye**s, **Procion dye**s) are very popular with batik artists. They work most efficiently at 90°−100° F, which does not melt **wax,** and the colors are fast to light and washing. When used in tie-dyeing the fabrics should always be dried thoroughly before the **binding** is removed. With these dyes the fibers are coupled with the **colorant** through a reaction with hydroxide (OH) in the cellulose molecule. The dye molecule becomes a part of the **cellulose;** it is therefore colorfast on cellulose fibers. The dye usually requires an alkali as a catalyst, which promotes the transfer of electrons and causes the integration of color and fiber. Common alkalis (electrolytes) are sodium carbonate, sodium bicarbonate, and **caustic soda.** Fiber-reactive dyes always require salt for the assistant and **washing soda** as the **fix**er. In dyeing wool, acetic acid is used as the assistant. Fiber-reactive dyes work best on cotton, but are also used on linen and viscose rayon. When used on silk, **Glauber's salt** replaces regular salt as the assistant. The directions for fiber-reactive dyes vary from one brand to another. Generally, any dye that requires salt as the assistant and soda as the fixer is of this class. The fiber-reactive dyes are more colorfast than direct dyes, brighter than vat dyes, and offer a better range of color than acid dyes. The most popular fiber-reactive dye among those who do tie-dye and batik is Procion M. Others are Color Fast, Dylon, Fabdec, Fibrec, Hi-dye, Putnam, and Pylam.

Household dyes (union dye) are packaged in either liquid or powder form and contain a mixture of various dyestuffs (basic, acid, direct, etc.). Because of this variety they can be used to **dye blend**s, as each fiber will absorb the appropriate dyestuff. The directions that accompany each package must be read, as requirements and assistants vary according to the different fibers being dyed.

Mordant dyes are used on the same fabrics as acid dyes; the fabric must be mordanted before being immersed in the dyebath. They have little or no affinity for fibers, but when metallic salts, particularly salts of chromium, are used in the mordant, the colors can be fixed. The fixing is a reaction of the dyes with the mordant salts. Chrome dyes are mordant dyes, but are less frequently used in tie-dye and batik than some of the other dye classes. Chrome dyes take their name from the fact that chromium is used as the mordant. The dyes are not fast to washing. Some mordant dyes are used essentially as **pigment**s, meaning that they coat fibers rather than penetrate to unite chemically with the fibers. Many **vegetable dye**s are applied to mordanted fibers.

Naphthol dyes (azoic) are not recommended for general home dyeing, but are preferred by some experienced batik and tie-dye artists because of their colorfastness. The naphthol dyes are used primarily on cotton and linen. They can be dyed in an 85° F cold water bath. They are really acid dyes and take their permanence from the chemical reaction that binds them to the fibers. Naphthol dye takes its name from the naphthol that is required as an assistant in this dye.

Vat dyes got their name from originally having to steep in the **vat** for so many days. Vat dyes are good in terms of fastness to washing and light, and are particularly fast on cottons. The dyestuff must first be put through a **vatting** process. The vat can then be mixed with the **dyebath**. A vatting operation is one in which an insoluble color is made soluble by a chemical reduction of the chromophore. It goes from a cationic compound to a **leuco** compound. In the presence of an alkali the pigment will bond. When **oxidize**d it goes back to its original color as a pigment. Caledon vat dye is one that must be vatted by the dyer. Precautions must be observed because vatting involves handling **caustic soda** and sometimes **lye**. Inkodye is a vat dye that has already been made up into a leuco base. In this state the pigments can combine with fibers rather than only coat them, as most pigments do. **Indigo** can be vatted to make a blue dye, and **potassium permanganate** to make a brown. The colors of vat dyes develop only after they have been applied to fabric and exposed to heat. They are used on cotton, linen, silk, wool, and viscose rayon.

Pigment dyes are dispersed in a bonding agent. The color does not penetrate the fiber but rests on the surface and can be removed by rubbing or abrasion. The pigments are insoluble colorants, so they are not absorbed as are true dyes. The process of using them may be similar to dyeing, as the fabric can be immersed in a solution containing the pigments. They can be used on cotton, acetate, rayon, and blends of cellulose or polyester. Synthetic pigments in synthetic resins are most often used in the pigment dyes. The pigments have little affinity for the fibers, but the resins bind the colors to the fabric. This kind of color on fabric is subject to **crocking,** but it is reasonably **lightfast** and colorfast. Pigment dyes are usually opaque.

Almost all classes of dyes must be set or fixed; this may be accomplished in any of several ways. Some, such as vat dyes, achieve their final color and are set on exposure to heat, such as by **ironing** or exposure to sun. Others are **heat set** by **steaming.** Dispersed dyes are ironed while still damp, but fiber-reactive dyes must dry slowly, as the dyes continue to set as they dry. The way in which the dye is set depends upon the class of dye and the fabric used.

Along with all the commercially available dyes, there is tremendous interest in **natural dye**s and **vegetable dye**s, particularly among weavers. Materials such as **dye wood, cochineal, madder, henna,** and **brazilwood** are well-known sources of natural dyes. Lichens produce beautiful vegetable dyes. Most of these require the use of mordants, often in the form of metallic oxides.

Various common household products can also be used as dyes, but they are not necessarily permanent. Laundry markers, India ink, permanent inks, and **marking pen**s can be used to add small areas of color to the tie-dye or batik. Wine, beet juice, tea, coffee, and chocolate are remarkably permanent. A **ditto dye** can be made from used ditto papers, and **leather dye** or dry-and-shine liquids can also be used to add color.

batik dye. Batik and Tie-dye. The **dye** selected for **batik** must be one that can be used for **cold dyeing**—that is, in water not over 100° F. **Hot dyeing** would melt and thus remove the wax resist. Procion M, a **fiber-reactive dye,** is one of the dyes most used by batik artists.

Household dyes are among the easiest and safest to use but they lack **colorfast**ness, fading in light or from washing. **Acid dye** and **direct dye** are both used for batik. The bright-colored **basic dye**s can be used but are not colorfast. **Naphthol dye**s are not recommended for home use, and **dispersed dye**s cannot be used because they require heat. Also see **Batik and Tie-dye: Dyes.**

batik egg. Batik and Tie-dye. See **pysansky egg.**

batiking frame. Batik and Tie-dye. (Also called wax frame.) A wood frame made to hold the **fabric** taut for **waxing** in the **batik** process. Shops that specialize in batik products usually have readymade frames. These consist of four notched boards that fit together to produce a frame that can vary in size and proportion.

An empty cardboard box can be used as a batiking frame, with fabric stretched over the open area and tacked at the edges. A picture frame can be used with the fabric tacked over it in the same way. Stretcher bars or canvas stretchers will provide a suitable frame, as will any wooden box. Also see **Batik and Tie-dye: Basic Procedures for Batik.**

batiking wax. Batik and Tie-dye. Any **wax** or wax mixture used in the **batik** process. It may be **beeswax, paraffin,** candle wax, or crayons. Beeswax lends flexibility to any mixture because it remains pliant after being applied to the **fabric.** Paraffin hardens and will shatter or **fracture** to give the characteristic **crackle** effect to batik.

Batik wax is premixed beeswax and paraffin available commercially from craft shops. Batiking wax may be all paraffin, one-half paraffin and one-half beeswax, all beeswax, or a combination of any waxes, including candles or crayons. Candle wax is usually a pure, hard paraffin. Crayons and colored candle waxes can be used for **colored-wax batiks**. The wax recipes of traditional batik artists were closely guarded secrets. Most, however, were combinations of paraffin, beeswax, resin, varnish gums, and tallow.

Care must always be taken in heating wax because it is flammable. It is safely heated by placing the wax in a can or container set into water, never directly over heat or flame. If it smokes, it is too hot. Also see **Batik and Tie-dye.**

batik printing. Batik and Tie-dye. See **stamp printing.**

batik puppet. Puppets. A **hand puppet** made up of **batik**ed fabrics. The features, hair, and costumes may all be suggested in the batik painting, so that the shape of the puppet is very simple. One piece, for the front, includes head, body, and arms, with ample room allowed for the head to be inserted. A second piece, identical in shape, makes up the back. A **stiffening** fabric, such as iron-on interfacing, iron-on fabric, or **felt**, can be cut identical in size and shape to the front and back pieces to be used as a lining. In joining front, back, and lining, all four layers are sewed through at once. That gives the puppet enough body or stiffness so that no stuffing is needed. If the batik is on heavy fabric, no lining or stiffening may be required. Sometimes stiffening is needed on the head portion only.

batik quilt. Quilts. A quilt that uses batik as the decorative element. A large piece of **fabric** may be decorated by the batik process and then quilted, or **block**s may be cut from batik and sewn together, as in a **pieced quilt.** One can also **appliqué** batik shapes to the material of the **quilt top.**

bating. Leather. In processing leather, after **curing,** soaking, and **fleshing,** the hides are given a two-part bating treatment. First the skins are treated with a chemical compound to neutralize the lime, then washed in water. Next, bates (enzymes) are added to destroy any remaining nonleather substances, such as hair roots. Then the skins are again washed in water and given a pickling treatment. Also see **Leatherwork: Tanning and Manufacture.**

batiste. Crewel. Embroidery. A finely woven cotton used in **white work** embroidery as a **background fabric.** It is similar to **muslin** but slightly more opaque. Its use in crewel embroidery is limited to transferring a design with **basting stitch**es. The design is drawn onto the batiste, and this is basted on the background fabric. Also see **Crewel: Transferring a Design.**

batiste. Stitchery. A **cotton fabric** that is a sheer, combed, **mercerized muslin.** It is usually plain, though sometimes printed, and may be made of **cotton** and **polyester blend**s. It is used for baby clothes, handkerchiefs, and in some stitchery **appliqué.**

batt. Quilts. Stitchery. Toys. A single roll of **batting** or **filler,** packaged by weight or (if in sheet form) by the quilt size it will fill. Also see **cotton batting, Dacron polyester batting, glazed polyester filler, padding.**

batt. Spinning. The layer of carded **wool** or **cotton fiber** prepared by hand **carders** or on a **carding machine.** The layer is removed and prepared for spinning by either pulling it off into long strips or elongating the entire batt by slowly stretching it into a narrow strip. Yarn spun from a batt is spun as if it were combed **worsted,** since the fibers are arranged parallel to each other the way they would be in combing. Also see **carding, combing.**

batten. Weaving. A flat, long, wooden sword used to beat the **filling** down in place in **backstrap, frame,** and other **primitive loom**s. It is smooth with at least one thin, knife-like edge. Also see **backstrap loom, beater, Navajo loom.**

batting. Puppets. Quilts. The **stuffing** or **padding** material for a quilt. It is sometimes called wadding. **Wool** or **cotton batting** is traditional, although now **Dacron polyester batting** is preferred by most quilters. Some batting comes with a glazed surface, which is an advantage for a tied **comforter** or quilt because the glazing prevents the batting from shifting or sliding out of place during laundering. The disadvantage in **quilting** with it is that the layer of batting cannot be split or separated when a thinner filler is preferred. The **glazed polyester filler** is very resilient and makes a quilt too puffy for many quilters' tastes. Also see **filler, wadding.**

Battle Ax of Thor. Quilts. See **Swastika.**

battlement fold. Papercrafts. A variation of **accordion pleating** in which the paper is folded at regular intervals with the direction reversed every two folds. See ill.

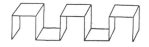

Battlement fold

bat wash. Ceramics. A **silica** and **china clay** mixture applied to kiln furniture in a thin coat to prevent pots from sticking in the event the **glaze** runs during the firing. Also see **kiln wash.**

bauxite clay. Ceramics. See **Ceramics: Clay.**

bayberry candle. Candlemaking. Settlers in New England discovered that native bayberries could be boiled down to provide a pleasantly scented, waxy candlemaking substance. The traditional bayberry candle recipe for the production of one **taper** requires a quart and a half of bayberries picked in the fall and boiled for 6 minutes. The boiled berries are allowed to sit until a waxlike substance rises to the top. The skimmed wax can then be formed by either **dipping** or **molding** to produce a bayberry candle. For best results it is suggested that the bayberries be boiled in small quantities and that the wax be formed into candles as soon as possible. If any delay is involved, the wax should be stored in sealed jars to preserve the bayberry **scent.**

bayeta. Weaving. See **Navajo weaving.**

Bayeux Tapestry. Crewel. The Bayeux tapestry is actually not a tapestry at all but a long panel worked in crewel wool on linen. It depicts the Norman conquest of England by William the Conqueror in 1066. It measures 20″ by 230′ and is worked in rich earth colors of gold, rust, brown, and blue. The techniques used are **stem stitch, chain stitch,** and **laidwork** tied with crossbars.

There are many versions of the history of this hanging. One is that it was commissioned by Bishop Odo of Bayeux, half-brother of William, and worked by William's wife, Queen Matilda, and her ladies. These ladies may have been assisted by men and women in the needlework schools in operation in England from 1070. Remarkably, this hanging is still colorful and in good condition. It can be viewed at the Cathedral of Bayeux in northwestern France.

bayonet saw. Woodworking. See **power saw.**

beach toy. Toys. Any **toy** used at the beach and usually, therefore, impervious to water. **Sand toy**s of metal have been the most common although plastics have replaced most. Rubber balls, often large, are common beach toys. Wood is often used, but if the **finish** or painted surface is broken water will soak into the wood. Most **bath toy**s and **boat**s are suitable for beach toys. Also see **ball.**

Bead. Beadwork. A small object that has been pierced for stringing. Beads are commercially available in a wide variety of materials, shapes, and colors. Bead sizes are gauged by the millimeter. Beads are sold loose or in clusters of 10 or 12 strings; generally, clusters contain 18″ to 20″ of strung beads.

The word "bead" comes from an Anglo-Saxon word, **"bede,"** meaning a prayer. It was the custom for bedesmen or bedeswomen to offer prayers for those whose names were recorded on the bede-rolls of the churches. In time, the word "bede" became associated with the beads on which the prayers were counted rather than with the prayers. Also see **amber, beadmaking, bugle beads, ceramic beads, coral, crow beads, crystal beads, cultured pearls, donkey beads, embroidery beads, eye beads, found object beads, gesso beads, glass beads, gold beads, jade, lined beads, millefiori, molded beads, paper beads, papier mâché beads, pearls, perfumed beads, pony beads, seed beads, seed pearls, seeds, sequins, shell, stem beads, turquoise, wood.**

bead. Bookbinding. The twisted stitch formed in **head band**ing.

bead. Ceramics. Beads for necklaces and other jewelry can be made of ceramic materials. **Egyptian paste,** a self-glazing material, is easy to work with, because the beads do not tend to stick together in firing. However, glazed beads must be strung together on heat-resistant nichrome wire while firing to keep the beads separate and the holes open.

bead. Embroidery. Macramé. Any type of bead which may easily be incorporated into a macramé design, provided the holes through the center of the beads are large enough to be strung through 1 or 2 **cord**s.

Cylindrical tile beads and rounded crow beads are often used in macramé work; they can usually be found at hobby and craft stores. Wooden beads are also suitable for macramé work, as are small pieces of hardware with center holes (such as nuts, washers, and rings). Also see **beadwork, adding beads.**

bead. Lacemaking. Beads are sometimes attached to the butt of the **bobbin** shaft for use in **bobbin lace.** Also see **spangle.**

bead. Metalworking. The deposit of melted metal in overlapping drops during **welding.** The heat of the torch **puddles** either the base metal alone, or both the **base metal** and a **welding rod.**

bead. Papercrafts. See **paper bead.**

bead. Stitchery. Toys. Very tiny glass beads of the kind used in Indian beadwork are sometimes used to suggest the teeth or eyes in dried **apple-head doll**s. Larger glass beads are used for eyes in **stuffed animal**s and **doll**s.

Large wooden beads are easily attached by nails to wood toys to suggest knobs or wheels and to provide handles for **pull string**s. The wooden beads can be stained or painted, but if they are to be used by small children, care must be taken to fasten them carefully, to paint them with a nontoxic paint, and to avoid procedures that would allow paints to chip or peel.

beaded edging. Beadwork. Among the oldest forms of **bead embroidery** are the simple techniques used by the American Indians for stitching rows of beads to a folded edge, a hem or a pleat of fabric or animal skin. A large area can easily be covered with an all-over pattern by creasing or pleating the material in close rows and beading the edges. Though any number of beads could be stitched to an edge, single- and two-beaded edgings were most common.

For single-beaded edging, the needle is pushed through the fabric, the bead is threaded on to hang between the stitches, and then the needle is again stitched through the edge (**a.**).

For two-beaded edging, the needle is inserted through the bead as it enters and leaves the fabric; the second bead is then threaded and hung as in the single-beaded edging (**b.**). See ill.

a.   Single-beaded edging   b.   Two-beaded edging

beaded knitting. Knitting. See **bead knitting.**

beaded stem. Beadwork. In **bead flowermaking**, the **wire** stem is finished by adding large green **stem beads** directly onto the stem wire, or by winding small wired beads around the stem. Stem ends should first be finished off with **floral tape.**

To make a beaded stem, string small green beads directly onto 30 or 32 gauge **spool wire.** Wrap the end of the wire around the stem at the base of the flower, twisting tightly to secure. Push the beads on the spool wire tightly up to the flower head. Slowly turn the flower while the beads on the taut wire are wrapped around the stem with the rows close together and with no spaces between the beads. Continue wrapping until the place where the leaves are to be added is reached. Leaf stems may be attached with fine **wire** or floral tape, or just held in place while the wrapping is continued. Then secure the wire at the stem end, cut the wire from the spool, wind it around the stem twice, and push the end up under the beading.

bead embroidery. Beadwork. Various types of **beads**, from **glass** and **pearl** to beads made from natural materials, are available for stitching onto cloth or leather. Beads have been used since ancient times to decorate clothing and objects of daily use. The North American Indians stitched **quills** and beads to buckskin, using the **lazy stitch** and **overlay stitch** to secure rows of beads in elaborate geometric patterns accented with **rosettes.**

During the Middle Ages in Europe, beads were incorporated in embroidery—perhaps as a substitute for pearls or precious gems—to decorate church vestments, wall hangings, and clothing. In Victorian England, beadwork was lavishly used on dresses and household decorations.

Once again, beadwork is increasing in popularity and being used in combination with embroidery stitches. Rows of threaded beads can be secured by a simple couching stitch, such as the **overlay stitch,** or the beads can be slipped onto the needle and stitched in place as you work. The combining of beadwork with embroidery produces an effect even more lustrous than the beauty of the two crafts by themselves. Also see **Beadwork.**

beader. Jewelry. See **beading tool.**

bead flower. Beadwork. Decorative flowers, the petals, stems, and leaves of which are formed completely of beads by various beadwork techniques. Varicolored **glass beads** are first strung on fine **spool wire,** so that the work can be done directly from the spool of beads. Each petal or leaf is completely shaped from the prebeaded wire before cutting the wire from the spool. Loose wire ends should be crimped to prevent spilling beads. Completed flower sections are then wired together and combined to form bead flower bouquets. Also see **Bead flowermaking: Basic techniques.**

bead flower bouquet. Beadwork. Bead flowers are mounted on **stem wires** covered with **floral tape** or **stem beads,** and arranged in a container filled with modeling clay for a bead flower bouquet. The clay can be covered with florist's **sheet moss** or small stone chips. Also see **bead flowermaking.**

bead flowermaking. Beadwork. A **beadwork** technique in which small colored **glass beads** are strung on fine **spool wire,** shaped into flower petals and leaves, and twisted together to form bead flowers. The first bead flowers were made during the Middle Ages by the church **bede** men and women who recited prayers. These flowers were strung on horsehair or human hair, and used for church decoration.

Bead flowermaking, which reached a peak during the Victorian era, is again becoming popular. Instructions are available for making many species of flowers. Accurate botanical details are limited with the tiny wired beads, forming each stamen, petal, and leaf separately with delicate accuracy. The flowers may then be wired together and combined in a **bead flower bouquet,** using a basket or vase as a container.

TOOLS AND MATERIALS Small, colored **glass beads,** such as **seed beads,** are generally used for bead flowers. Bead sizes 11-0 or 1-9 mm are easy to use because the wire passes readily through the holes. Beads are counted out for small designs and they are measured in inches of beaded wire for large designs. Fine **wire** for beading, around 30 or 32 gauge, is available as **spool wire,** like sewing thread, and used for constructing flowers and petals, for **lacing,** and for assembly.

For **stem wire,** heavier gauges are used, such as 12 or 13 gauge. When each flower is completed, the exposed wire is covered with **floral tape, stem beads,** or, for **silk stems,** embroidery floss.

An inexpensive **wire cutter** can be used, but sharp needlenose **pliers** are recommended. Thumbtacks and a small ruler are needed. Leather gloves may be worn to protect the hands when pulling or twisting the wire.

SETTING UP A WORKSHOP It is helpful to have the work area covered with a piece of cloth, such as felt, to catch any spilled beads. Each kind of bead should be stored in a separate container or compartment of a storage box.

BASIC TECHNIQUES Books and pamphlets of instructions are available for an endless number of floral species. Fortunately for the beginner, most patterns are based on a few simple techniques. The **basic row** of beads corresponds to the center vein of the petal or leaf, and additional rows of beads are formed around this central row to form most designs. This basic petal, or leaf, technique is called the **basic loop,** and is the basis for most bead flower instructions. The ends of the basic loop can be round or pointed.

Most patterns for bead flower designs are written in abbreviated lists, with materials given first, for each section of the plant (petals, leaves, etc.). Each piece is made individually, and the flower is assembled when all pieces are complete. Generally, glass **seed beads** are used for flowers, and **crystal beads** are used for foliage, so some instructions may list only the color of the beads to be used. Next, the gauge of the wire will be listed, and then the general procedures. For example, instructions for making petals might read as follows:

#28 silver (indicating the gauge and color of **wire**)
Basic 6   (indicating that 6 beads will be used to make the basic row)
Rows 12   (indicating that there will be 12 rows across the petal)
Pointed top (indicating the shaping of the petal ends), round bottom
Make 6   (indicating the number of petals required)

In some patterns, the beads of the basic row are listed in inches, rather than number. Specific methods are indicated in the pattern as they are required. The right side of the petals and leaves are referred to as "front," the wrong side as "back."

For efficient work, the beads should be transferred to the **spool wire;** more beads should be strung than will be needed. For easy handling, push a thumbtack into the top of the spool of wire. The wire can be hooked around the tack to prevent beads from spilling. All flower parts are worked directly from the beaded wire on the spool. The connecting twists are made with the bare wire by pushing the beads aside momentarily, then back to fill up the strands snugly after each twist is completed.

To begin the basic loop, slip the required number of beads down from the spool wire to form the basic row. Read the pattern the number of rows across the petal, and pull the beaded wire around and around the basic row, twisting the wires together at each end. Rotate the petal in a clockwise motion as you work with the same side facing you at all times, to establish a front and a back to the petal. The basic loop forms a petal with rounded ends (**a.**).

The basic loop can also be tapered to a pointed end by varying the angle at which the spool wire is wrapped around the basic row. The procedure is the same as for a round petal until the second row. When the second row is nearly completed and is positioned parallel to the basic row, two extra beads are added before crossing the basic row. The feed wire is then pulled across the basic row at an angle, bringing the feed wire to a higher point than the previous row. The angle of the feed wire should be pulled at a 45° angle to the point where the feed wire would normally cross for the rounded basic loop. To maintain this pointed shape, extra beads must be added every time the feed wire reaches the pointed end of the petal (**b.**).

For a more elongated point the feed wire can be pulled to a higher point, at about a 70° angle (**c.**).

Once you have mastered these basic loop variations, other techniques can be used to obtain a wider variety of shapes. The **continuous single loop** makes repeated loops for a daisy shape. Extra rows of beads can be added around these loops with the **continuous single loop** technique. More elaborate petal arrangements with symmetrical loops on either side of the basic row are made with the **continuous loopback** technique. The **crossover loop** is used to fill in petals solidly with rows of beads. Detailed instructions of the more complicated methods are usually included with the patterns in flower beading booklets.

To add firmness and strength to large petals or leaves, wire **lacing** is worked across the center of the shape, or skip-lacing is worked over the ends of the petal loops, joining two strands at a time. Tonal changes of color within a petal can be achieved by **shading** with darker beads around the outer rows. See ill. Also see **continuous loopback, continuous single loop, continuous wraparound loop, crossover loop.**

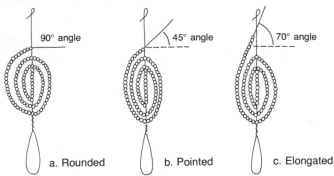

a. Rounded   b. Pointed   c. Elongated

Leaf and petal shapes

Assembly   When all the pieces are completed, they are wound tightly to the **stem wire** with **spool wire.** Place the leaf stems downward, close to the stem. Each leaf or petal is attached with the same piece of binding wire, beginning at the top leaf and winding down the stem. When all the pieces have been joined to the stem, go around the stem two more turns and cut the wire. The bare wire stems of completed bead flowers are covered by wrapping with **floral tape,** embroidery floss (for **silk stem**s), or tiny wired beads (for **beaded stem**s); they may also be strung with **stem bead**s (**d.**). See ill.

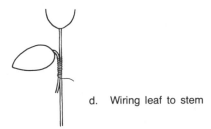

d.   Wiring leaf to stem

Care and maintenance   Bead flowers are completely washable. Gently wash in mild soap and warm water, then rinse in cool water and allow to dry on absorbent toweling.

bead-holding jig. Amber Carving. Coral Carving. Ivory and Bone Carving. A device that holds a bead stationary during forming and drilling operations. It can hold materials that are too brittle or soft to be held in a vise. It also aids in keeping a set of beads uniform when shaping.

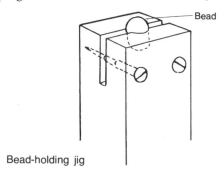

Bead-holding jig

Saw a 2 × 2″ or 2 × 4″ across the end to a depth of about twice the length of the bead. Drill a hole in the center of the line of the saw kerf that will accept only half of the bead. The diameter should be slightly smaller, so that the bead must be forced into the hole. Additional pressure can be applied by squeezing the end of the jig with one hand; by inserting two screws and tightening them as required; or by using a C clamp or string tied around the jig. Secure the bead jig in a vise for drilling operations.

beading. Stained Glass. See **floated solder seam.**

beading. Weaving. See **stippling.**

beading needle. Beadwork. Embroidery. A long fine **needle** with a sharp point suitable for threading **beads** in beadwork.

beading needle. Stitchery. A long **needle** with a very thin shaft, used for bead embroidery and bead stringing. It has a long slender eye. Because it is fine and slips through material so readily, many stitchers use this needle for other kinds of sewing.

beading tool. Jewelry. (Also called beader.) A tool used in **bead setting** for simultaneously forming and **burnishing** the bead that holds the stone in position. The concave end, used with a rotating, rocking motion, smooths the sharpness of the curl of metal formed during the setting process. Also see **perloir, punch.**

bead knit. Macramé. See **bobble.**

bead knitting. Knitting. (Also called purse knitting.) In bead knitting, the beads are actually on the stitches; in beaded knitting, the beads are in between the stitches on alternate rows. The pattern is charted on graph paper; each square represents one bead and the color of that bead is indicated in the square. The beads are then strung onto a fine strong thread. Thread beads starting from the top left-hand row if the pattern ends on the odd number row; if the pattern ends on the even row, begin threading from the right-hand corner of the graph. The last bead on the thread will represent the first square at the bottom right corner. Bead knitting uses the crossed Eastern knit and purl stitches with a bead of the charted color knit into every stitch. The knitting is only a means of securing the beads in place and does not show on the front of the work. Bead knitting was at its peak during the eighteenth and nineteenth centuries. The work was so fine that it was possible to create pictures of flowers, animals, and anything else that could be charted on graph paper. Bead knitting was also used to embellish children's clothing, scarves, dresses, gloves, and lace.

Beaded knitting differs from bead knitting in that the beads are threaded onto the yarn selected, and are often one color. The beads are added on alternate garter-stitch rows for best results. After a stitch has been knitted, a bead is moved into place before the next stitch is knitted. This method of doing beaded work gives more flexibility to the work because the beads can be used according to the desire of the knitter.

For creative bead knitting, remove the stitch before or after working it, thread the loop through the hole of the bead, return the stitch to the needle, and continue knitting. See ill.

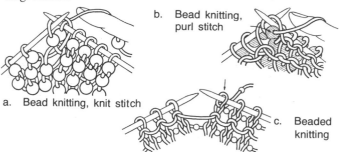

a. Bead knitting, knit stitch
b. Bead knitting, purl stitch
c. Beaded knitting

bead leno. Weaving. A **cross weave** technique that uses tubular beads in place of **doup**s to accomplish the twist in a cross weave. The bead leno method can be used for **gauze weave**s and **leno** and can be a hand method or a mechanical one. In the hand method the beads, about ½″ long, are not tied to a **harness** as doups are, but are free hanging and are placed between the **beater** and the harness. Two **warp** yarns, working as a pair, are threaded through holes in the opposite ends of the beads. When weaving the fabric, the beads are turned individually one complete revolution toward the right or the left. The **filling** is inserted through the **shed** and a counter-revolution with the yarns going back to their original position is made. The second shed of **plain weave** is woven.

If the beads are to be used in a mechanical way, as the doups are, whereby the lifting of a harness can provide the twist, then either tubular beads or short plastic tubes can be used and a frame must be built and added behind the harnesses that will act as a tension release for the warp yarns that will be twisting around other warp yarns. The frame should be lightweight and consist of two narrow wooden bars kept apart at a distance of about 2″. Those warp ends that are the acting or twisting warp ends go over and under the release bars, through separate harnesses, but through the same bead. They act as a pair and between them is a third (and, perhaps, a fourth) **warp end** that runs over the release bars and is not threaded through a bead. When the harness attached to one of the two threads in a bead is lifted, the release bar is also lifted. This slackens the warp end that is also threaded through the same bead, but not the same harness, so that this end comes up either to the right or left of the third (or fourth) warp end. Lifting the other harness with the end through the bead will cause the twisting end to come up in the reverse position (i.e., if the previous lifting was to the right of the third [or fourth] warp end, then this lifting will be to the left). A suggested **threading** (given by Mary M. Atwater) is: 4, 1, 2, 3, repeat. The warp ends on harnesses 4 and 3 are threaded through the same bead and those on 1 and 2 remain free.

bead loom. Beadwork. See **loom.**

BEADMAKING/BEADWORK

As early as prehistoric times, man picked up small objects (bone, **shell**, teeth, **seeds,** or **wood**), pierced holes for stringing, and used these primitive **bead**s for ornamentation, magic, and medicine. Simple disks were chipped from shell, soapstone, or carnelian, drilled and strung. Clay was rolled and pierced for beads that were then hardened by fire and painted. Later on, clay beads were glazed with designs similar to those used on bowls. With the perfection of glaze techniques, **faience** was developed. Faience beads are made of powdered, sandy quartz coated with a vitreous glaze to which copper has been added. After firing, the beads range in color from blue to green, with occasional darker or lighter tones. During the Twelfth Dynasty of Egypt, a brilliant turquoise blue was introduced, the color generally associated with Egyptian beadwork. These beads were preserved on mummies and became known as mummy beads.

At some point faience craftspeople experimenting with glazes discovered how to make **glass bead**s. Some authorities attribute this discovery to Egypt during the Eighteenth Dynasty (1500–1450 B.C.); glassworks were in operation at Thebes, and at Tell el Amarna. Since Egypt and Mesopotamia were closely linked by trade routes, faience and glass techniques developed at about the same time in both areas. Beads were produced at Ur in a great variety of color and material. Some of the earliest magical **eye beads** with simple spot decoration were made at this time. Glass, prized for its translucent color, became the leading material in bead production.

The first **millefiori** beads were developed when the Phoenicians made cane glass. Canes or rods of glass were heated and dipped into molten glass of another color, then sliced into small disks that were inserted into the viscous glass bead matrix. Millefiori glasswork was perfected during the Roman Empire.

During the Middle Ages, various glass beads were manufactured in Venice and Murano: cristallai, **crystal beads;** conterie, ordinary **trade beads,** and tiny beads for embroidery. By 1492 the Venetian glass industry was booming, meeting the demands of merchant explorers. Venetian craftspeople had set up a glass house in London by 1549 and one in Amsterdam by 1608. Shortly thereafter Germany, Holland, and France were also producing beads.

One of the early glass beadmaking techniques was the winding of molten glass around a center. A lump of molten glass was pulled out into a long, thin, solid rod. The cooled rod was then broken into short lengths, which were softened and wrapped around a small copper or iron wire. The wire was heated to fuse the ends of the glass pieces. During cooling, the metal would shrink more than the glass, so the wire could be easily withdrawn, leaving a hole for stringing. Wound beads are large, with the layers of glass slightly visible.

A more efficient technique was developed using a tube of glass, so that sections cut from the tube contained holes for stringing. This process of "drawing" beads was used in Venice for manufacturing large quantities of glass beads. The glass tube is formed by blowing a hollow bubble of molten glass of the desired color on the end of a blowing iron, into which a metal rod is introduced so that the bubble closes around it. This glob of glass is then pulled through a long, very fine tube, sometimes over 100 ft. long. The rod is cut into manageable lengths, which are later cut into bead-size pieces. Each tiny piece still has the perforation left from the original tube for a center hole. Cylindrical beads, called **bugle beads,** are made this way.

Most beads are further processed to round off the edges. They are tumbled in a drum with a pulverized mixture of sand and ashes, or clay. The drum is kept hot while it is rotating to soften the glass slightly. When cooled and rinsed, the beads are smooth and spherical. Beads may be colored at this time, if colored glass was not used, with aniline dyes or lustered with enamels, and then polished.

Today, though beads of many materials are manufactured, glass beads are still widely used for beadwork and jewelry. For the craftsperson working in the studio, beadmaking processes vary depending on the type of materials and equipment available; glass and ceramics require a more elaborate set-up. However, there are unlimited possibilities for making beads by hand using simple materials and **found objects** that can be cut, pierced, and strung with very little equipment required.

TOOLS AND MATERIALS A small **saw** such as a junior hacksaw or tension saw (back saw) will be needed for sawing hard materials such as **wood,** bone, or bamboo into bead lengths.

To make holes for stringing, a **drill** such as a Yankee ratchet drill is recommended. The size of the bit for the drill is determined by the diameter of the material being used.

Depending on the materials used, finishing materials such as sandpaper, **dye,** or paint may be needed—and, of course, **thread,** or **wire** for stringing the beads.

SETTING UP A WORKSHOP Bead materials should be stored in separate containers for easy handling. A fishing tackle box is helpful for organizing materials.

For working with wood and other hard materials, a workbench is necessary for cutting and drilling. To facilitate sawing, a bench stop can be made with strips of wood nailed to the workbench to support strips of beadmaking material. A vise or a lump of **plasticine** on the workbench will prevent slipping while drilling.

CUTTING AND DRILLING Hard materials such as **wood** can be sawed into small lengths, straight across at an angle, or in a V-shape. Holes must then be drilled through the center. To finish, wooden beads need to be sandpapered, and may then be dyed.

COLORING AND FINISHING To make a dye bath, cover the beads with warm water plus a few drops of vinegar or acetic acid and enough ink or household fabric dye to produce the desired color. Wood beads should soak in a dye bath, with occasional stirring, until the correct intensity of color is reached. Remove the beads from the dye and allow them to dry on absorbent toweling. When dry, rub them with furniture oil. Also see **ceramic beads, gesso beads, molded beads, paper beads, papier mâché beads.**

bead mosaic work. Beadwork. A style of **lace beading,** popular in England around 1855, in which large, colored **glass beads** were strung with needle and thread in geometrical open mesh patterns to make decorative lamp shades, baskets, and mats that were often finished with beaded fringes. Also see **bead weaving with needle and thread.**

bead-polishing board. Amber Carving. Coral Carving. Ivory and Bone Carving. Jet Carving. A felt-covered board with a groove running the length of it that holds strung beads to facilitate polishing them. Secure the cord the beads are strung on at both ends. See ill.

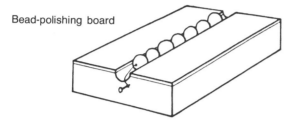

Bead-polishing board

bead setting. Jewelry. A technique generally reserved for the setting of faceted, transparent gem stones. A series of small curls of metal are formed, pointing inward toward the stone, which is set just below the surface of the metal. With a **beading tool** the curls of metal are then formed into a bead which will hold the stone in position. The method does not work well with silver because it is too soft, but does work well with platinum and **karat** golds.

bead stitch. Crewel. Embroidery. See **coral knot.**

bead weaving. Beadwork. A technique of weaving **beads** onto the weft threads on a simple **loom.** A design is prepared on bead **graph paper**; beads of uniform size should be selected. The loom should be as wide, and 6″ longer than, the designed piece. The loom is strung with nylon or cotton **thread,** which is then waxed with **beeswax.**

a. Draw the warp threads back and forth until there is one more thread than beads in the width of the pattern; double the outside threads for added strength. Tie the warp threads to the loom securely.
b. Begin beading in the middle of the loom. Tie the weft thread to the outer double thread at left, using an ample amount of thread.
c. Pick up beads on the needle and pass under the warp threads from left to right, pushing the beads up between the warp threads from below with the left hand.
d. To secure the beads in position, bring the needle above the warp and run it back through the bead holes from right to left, on top of the warp threads. For the second row, repeat from **c.** Continue beadwork in this way until that half of the design is finished. To end the weft thread, weave back a ways through the preceding bead rows to prevent raveling. To begin the new weft thread, tie a knot at the end of the thread and pull it through a few preceding rows of beads; the knot will catch inside. Then work as before from **c.** until the design is completed. See ill.

To finish a design that is to be stitched to a leather or other backing, wrap a piece of adhesive tape around the warp threads immediately next to the beadwork before cutting it from the loom. The tape is then turned underneath and hidden when the beadwork is stitched to backing.

If the design is not to be backed or lined, the cut thread ends may be fringed or knotted. To make beaded fringe, split the warp threads into strands a few beads wide and bead each strand, or thread the warp threads with a needle and bead, knotting at the end. Another method of finishing is to tie the warp threads in knots, in groups of 3 to 5 threads, close to the beaded edge.

a. Warp threads on loom with double threads at outer edges

b. Weft thread tied to double warp thread at left

c. Weft thread under warp, with beads pushed up between warp threads

d. Needle run back through beads from right to left on top of warp

bead weaving with needle and thread. Beadwork. An ancient technique of weaving beadwork in the hand without a **loom,** using only needle and thread. The following simple brickwork pattern can be made by using two needles with doubled thread ends tied together, or one thread threaded with a needle at both ends.

a. Each needle passes through a bead (1 and 2), then both needles pass through the hole in the 3rd bead (3). Each needle now goes through separate beads (4 and 5), then both needles again pass through the same bead (6). This pattern of alternating two and one beads is continued for the desired length.
b. To widen the design, another row of beads can be added at one side by threading one needle from bead (10) through the hole in the adjacent bead (11) and through a new bead (12) and then back onto the bead above it (8).

Bead weaving with needle and thread

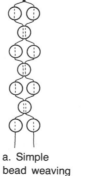

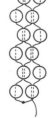

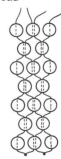

a. Simple bead weaving

b. Adding row

c. Extending pattern

c. To continue, another new bead is strung (13) and the thread goes into another old bead (5) and so on, alternating needles for each new row. See ill.

BEADWORK

In the course of history, **bead**s have been used as adornment, as money, as prayer beads, as a show of wealth, and as a record of history. They have been regarded as a source of mystical powers, and have been used to conduct magic. Beads have been strung since prehistoric times, and **beadmaking** has been practiced in every civilization. Beads have been knotted, stitched, woven, and knitted into fabric.

Since early times, small **shell**s, beads, and lucky stones have been used as charms to prevent sickness and misfortune. Certain materials or stones were attributed with mystical powers, and beads and amulets were made of materials believed to have specific effects. **Turquoise**, for example, protected the traveler and his beasts from falling; serpentine, which is usually green with light streaks and associated with snakes, was worn to prevent snakebites; **amber** was attributed healing power. The Greeks and Romans used red **coral** as a protection against shipwrecks and other travel mishaps. Sky blue beads were used as a general protection against danger and evil. Perhaps the most visually symbolic design was the **eye bead**, the eye itself as a protection against the evil eye.

Piles of stones, knots, tally sticks, and beads were used as counting devices. The abacus is a development of this practice. Strung beads carried on the hand and passed through the fingers have always had a reassuring effect on man; in Greece and Turkey, short strands of beads, called **worry beads**, are still carried. Beads were counted out for the number of prayers said, leading to the development of the **rosary.** Shell beads were used as a record of historic events and as currency in **wampum** belts. Stone beads also were occasionally used as money, and until the market became flooded, **glass beads** were widely used as currency on trade routes in Africa, India, Polynesia, and North America. Explorers and traders set out with shipfuls of beads from Europe and the Mediterranean. These **trade beads** were exchanged all over the world for spices, ivory, animal hides, and precious metals.

AFRICAN BEADWORK   Beadwork has ancient roots in Africa. The traditional **aggri** bead was valued so highly that traders were eager to produce an acceptable facsimile to exchange for gold, ivory, and slaves. European imitations, made of multicolored glass, were widely used as trade beads. African craftspeople utilized these in rich decorations, stringing them in dazzling combinations of color and pattern. Color was of utmost importance, and in some areas so symbolic that particular meanings were ascribed to each bead color. By stringing beads of the desired symbolic colors, the Zulus sent **talking beads** as messages.

Besides imports from Europe, various beads were available from Limadura, near Cambay on the eastern coast of Africa, where carnelian was plentiful.

AMERICAN INDIAN BEADWORK   At the time America was discovered, **bead**s made of seeds, shell, stones, claws, and bones were used. Tribes that had access to shell made **wampum** disk beads, which were woven into wampum belts. Dyed **quills** were used by most plains and woodland Indians for decorating clothing. Traders soon found that porcelain, metal, and glass beads were accepted as trade for furs, and such beads became widely used by the Indians. Beads soon either replaced or were combined with quills.

Beads were traded by the Spanish in the Southwest as early as 1540. In eastern North America they were introduced by the English, Dutch, and French traders around 1880. The first bead to be widely distributed was the **pony bead,** but the most popular beads were small, opaque white beads and round, colored (preferably blue) glass **seed bead**s from Venice and Czechoslovakia. Although beadwork is associated with the American Indians, only the Hidatsa of the plains learned the craft of glass **beadmaking,** and that only to the extent of melting and reshaping the **trade bead**s.

Indian beadwork is noted for its strong geometrical design, with occasional animal and thunderbird motifs. When the missionaries introduced floral-embroidered vestments, the lake Indians, and later other tribes, adapted these floral motifs for their rich beadwork designs. Long before white men arrived, the Indians had developed techniques of stitching hair and quill to buckskin. Indian women had developed ingenious methods of attaching the dyed quills in brilliant designs against the natural background of skins to decorate clothing. Later, when European beads were included in quillwork, these same methods were used, and continued to be used for **bead embroidery.** Most of this work was done with two basic stitches, the **lazy stitch** and the **overlay stitch.** The overlay stitch, the most commonly used, was useful both for covering large surfaces and for intricate motifs such as rosettes. The lazy stitch was faster, but only suitable for allover patterns. A variation of bead embroidery was decorating with rows of **beaded edgings.**

The Indians developed several weaving techniques. Bands of **bead weaving** were worked on a simple **bow loom.** Red, yellow, blue, green, and opaque white seed beads were worked into decorations to be stitched to a background of cloth or skin. Some designs were done in black and white, similar to the geometric wampum patterns. Strips of hand beadwork were made by a process of bead weaving with needle and thread. Some variations of hand weaving were **lace beading,** a delicate, loose work, and peyote beadwork, a brickwork patterning of beaded rows.

VICTORIAN BEADWORK   Beadwork has gone in and out of fashion. During the mid-Victorian era beadwork was extremely popular, embellishing clothing and home furnishings. The Venetian glass manufacture was booming, and not all of the beads were shipped off as trade beads. **Bugle bead**s, widely distributed for embroidery, were worked with fine, waxed sewing silk into elaborate patterns on garments and tapestries. Women's weekly magazines carried instructions for fancy beadwork and **bead flowermaking. Tambour work,** beads incorporated into embroidery, was popular around 1881. Later, various designs were made, ranging from geometric to floral, on backings of cloth, velvet, and leather. Openwork without a backing, such as **bead mosaic work** in which beads were strung to make lacy, household decorations was done ca. 1885. **Beaded edgings** and fringes were combined with gimp and braid for further embellishment.

As beadwork became widely popular on clothing, manufacturers tried to produce imitations of handwork, and a machine to attach beads to fabric was invented in 1891. Most beads of the day were either too uneven in shape or too large to be reproduced by machine, so metal beads of uniform size were made. However, the garments produced were too heavy to be worn comfortably. Finally, a method was developed in which threaded beads on bobbins were fed into a machine, producing long linear patterns, using designs that were already in use for machine embroidery. Braidwork patterns, such as elaborately revolving scrolls, were also copied in machine beadwork.

Today innumerable types of beads are available to supply the increasing demands of craftspeople; the addition of plastics to the traditional materials allows for great diversity in beadwork.

Although beadwork has had a rich and varied history, the basic techniques are universal. Whether working with simple materials or commercially processed beads, and whether stringing or weaving, the basic processes are simple. The resulting design is determined by the creativity in selection and placement of bead color, size, and texture.

TOOLS AND MATERIALS   Different beads should be stored in separate containers. Various background materials are available on which to stitch beadwork—felt, velvet, wool, or soft, tanned leather such as deerskin or cowhide. The leather should be easy to pierce with a needle.

For certain beadwork techniques, special equipment will be needed as described under the specific technique (e.g., **bead embroidery, bead flowermaking, bead weaving**). In general, the following tools will be needed: **thread, wire, needles, beeswax,** and **wire cutters.** Needlenose pliers are useful for breaking unwanted beads off strings when necessary, instead of unstringing. Embroidery hoops may be used for beading small items on leather or cloth. **Graph paper** is used for planning intricate patterns. A piece of fabric on the work surface to catch any beads that spill is helpful also.

BEADING TECHNIQUES   Beads have unlimited applications. They can be worked by stringing, weaving, or wiring. They can be applied to fabric, leather, or other materials. Information on methods is listed under specific headings. Also see **bead embroidery, bead flowermaking, bead mosaic work, bead weaving, bead weaving with needle and thread, beaded edgings, buglework, crocheting with beads, knitting with beads, lace beading, passementerie, Stuart beadwork, stumpwork, tambour work, tatting with beads,** and **Beadmaking.**

beadwork. Embroidery. Needlework in which tiny beads form the pattern. The final result has an enamel-like sheen. The beads may be sewn to **canvas** or any **background fabric** individually, or they may be put onto a thread in the correct order and couched down. Sometimes the entire surface of the article is covered with beads; sometimes the pattern is formed by leaving spaces where fabric shows between the beads.

Beads have been found in prehistoric caves in North America and have been used by the American Indian since ancient times. Later, European settlers coming to the New World brought trade beads with them. Christopher Columbus, landing on Watling Island in 1492, became friendly with the Indians by giving them "red caps and some glass beads."

Danish travelers brought glass beads to the Eskimos, and Russians used beads for fur trading in Alaska. Beadwork in the Mississippi Valley, beautifully done on velvet, was said to have been influenced by the Spanish. The Ojibways were prolific producers of beadwork that has greatly influenced contemporary designers. Coats, waistcoats, pants, and moccasins were all decorated with beadwork by Indians all over North America. The most usual background was leather or deerskin. Feathers, shells, and fur were often incorporated with the bead embroidery. Sometimes, when beads were hard to obtain other materials such as horn, bone, teeth, and claws were dyed with juices of natural plants and used instead of or combined with the beads.

Beads have traditionally been used in Europe to enrich ecclesiastical embroidery. For instance, seed pearls were sewn down as an edging, to heighten the effects of gleaming gold threads in church robes.

In the Victorian era, beadwork, combined with needlepoint and **cross stitch** on canvas, was very popular, presumably because it was felt the sheen of the beads contrasted with the matte appearances of the wool. Also see **couching, porcupine quill embroidery, stumpwork.**

beaker. Ceramics. See **Ceramics: Form.**

beam. Weaving. A beam refers to any one of many parts of a **harness loom** that guide the cloth while weaving. A beam is either a large cylindrical roller or a heavy flat wooden piece. Also see **back beam, breast beam, cloth beam, sectional warp beam, warp beam.**

beaming. Weaving. That part of **dressing the loom** that deals with winding the unwoven **warp** on the **warp beam** so that it is stored there until it is rolled forward to be woven. Various methods of beaming can be employed, but they fall mainly in one of two categories: either, the warp is all beamed or wound first and then threaded through the **heddles** and **reed,** or it is threaded first through the reed, then the heddles, and finally attached to the back **apron bar** to be wound around the warp beam. Basic to all methods is that the beaming is done under even tension by **spreading the warp, padding,** and combing the warp to insure that the warp **ends** go on evenly and in a straight line from beginning to end. The combing can be done by pulling the **lease stick**s forward constantly or by pulling by hand. Tugging, shaking, or snapping the warp aid in straightening out tangled spots and in picking up slack ends. It also helps keep the hand combing to a minimum, since it is best to handle the warp threads as little as possible. Success in weaving is often dependent on the care taken in beaming so that the warp goes on as perfectly as possible.

In the first method mentioned above, the weaver is working from the back of the loom to the front. The lease sticks are inserted through the **cross** and attached to the loom in back of the **castle** so that they are in a taut position but are movable. The rest of the **warp chain** lies in front of the castle. The back apron bar goes through the loop of the warp nearest the cross, the **lease cord** is cut, and the warp is spread with the aid of a **raddle** if desired. The warp beam is revolved by the handle at the back **ratchet** and the warp is wound around using padding so that each layer of warp rests on a smooth surface. **Chokes** are removed as they are reached. The warp is entirely wound around the warp beam until only about 10"–12" remain in front of the castle. The ends are cut and **drawing-in** and **sleying** take place. A helper can be used to hold the warp under tension as it is being beamed, but most weavers today have devised their own methods of tension control so that they do not have to depend on having help.

In the second method, the lease sticks are inserted in the cross and attached to the loom in front of the **beater.** The end loop facing the beater is cut, the reed sleyed, and the heddles threaded from front to back. The warp chain is either wound around or tied to the **breast beam,** so that when the warp ends are pulled through the **dent**s and the heddles, the pulling is done against tension and all ends are pulled an equal length. No spreading is necessary. The warp ends after threading are tied to the back apron bar in small bundles and the winding then proceeds as in the first method. The lease sticks can be removed when beaming is completed or reinserted in back of the castle.

These two methods are the primary ones used in beaming, with slight variations according to innovations made by individual weavers as they feel necessary. There are other methods not so widely used. One of these includes a back to front technique where the warp chain is placed behind the loom with lease sticks in the cross between the castle and the **back beam.** The last loop of the warp chain faces the castle. It is cut, threaded, and sleyed, then tied on to the front apron bar. It is beamed on to the **cloth beam** until the other end of the warp is reached. This is then cut, tied to the back apron bar, and the warp is rewound onto the warp beam. In some cases, this is excessive wear and tear on fragile or clinging warp yarns, but some weavers claim that the double winding gives a warp that is more smoothly beamed and with better control over the tension. A variation on this method is to start as above, but to put the lease sticks between the breast beam and beater and not to thread or sley. Instead, only a raddle is put on at the front of the loom and the warp spread and then wound around the cloth beam. The warp is then sleyed and threaded, tied to the back apron bar and rebeamed.

Another method is related to industrial practices of beaming in that the warp is never chained, but comes directly from the **warping reel.** The warping reel must be of the horizontal variety and have a brake on it in order to control the speed at which the warp is wound off the reel. The warping reel is placed in front of the loom, the warp passed through a raddle and laced to the back apron bar and the tension equalized. The warp is then wound on. Lease sticks are an asset, but they usually are not used and only inserted when the warp is fully beamed and ready for threading. Also see **Berian Method, chaining, lacing on.**

bean bag. Toys. A small cloth bag filled with beans or any similar material. Bean bags are often made in the form of animals or familiar objects and are used in many children's **toss game**s.

bean doll. Toys. See **Daruma doll.**

Bear's Paw. Quilts. (Also called Bear's Track.) A very popular **block** pattern for **pieced quilt**s made up of squares and triangles joined in such a way as to suggest tracks. Bear's Paw was a common pattern in Pennsylvania and Ohio in the 1950s. The same pattern was known in Long Island as Duck's-Foot-in-the-Mud, while to the Quakers of Philadelphia it was known as Hand of Friendship. Other variations of the block are Cross and Crown, Crowned Cross, Duck Puddle, Goose Tracks, and Premium Star. See ill.

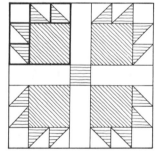

Bear's Paw

beat. Weaving. The beat is the pushing down in place of the **weft** between the **warp** threads. The weaver's hand controls this, whether it is the forward and back movement of the **beater** on a **harness loom,** or a hand held beating instrument in other types of weaving. The beat can make a fabric very dense or like **gauze.** The beat can be executed either immediately after the weft has been inserted in the **shed,** while the shed is being changed, or after the shed has been changed. See **picks per inch, weaving.**

beaten form. Ceramics. Thrown or hand-built pottery that is beaten or **paddle**d to change its form. This may involve flattening the sides, making round forms square, and so on. This is done when the clay is **leather hard,** and can provide interesting decorative textures.

beater. Ceramics. Wooden rulers or flat sticks used for the finer shaping of basically formed pots. See ill.

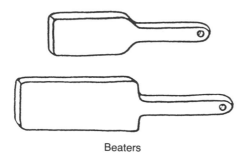

Beaters

beater. Weaving. The movable frame of the **harness loom** located between the **harness**es and the **breast beam.** It is either suspended from the **castle** (called an overhead beater) or propped up on two supports from the bottom of the loom. The beater swings back and forth and beats the **filling pick**s in place after they have been left in the **shed** by the **shuttle.** The beater holds the **reed** in place within its grooved frame. The top part of this frame, called a hand-tree, is removable so that the reeds are interchangeable. Some beaters have a protruding wooden or metal ledge at the bottom of the frame called a shuttle race on which the shuttle travels across the shed. Beater is also known as **batten;** however, the tendency today is to use the latter word in a context with **backstrap** or **frame loom.** Also see **box loom, fly shuttle loom, hand beater, jack type loom, table loom.**

beating. Tincrafting. See **hammering.**

beating. Weaving. The action in weaving of pushing the last **pick** inserted into the **shed** down to meet the other picks in the fabric. On a horizontal loom with an attached **beater,** it is pushed by grasping the beater in the center and pulling forward. If the beater is grabbed at one end instead of the center, there is the possibility of the **web** building up more at one end than at the other. On **vertical loom**s, if there is an attached beater, it slides up and down. On other types of looms, a **batten** or **hand beater** is used, usually with short, swift movements. Also see **beat.**

beat-up point. Weaving. See **fell.**

Beauvais. Embroidery. A type of fine **chain stitch** usually done on a tambour frame with a fine crochet hook or a needle. Originating in Beauvais, France, this work is particularly effective when done on chiffon or other fine, sheer fabric. The tiny chain stitches are done in brilliantly colored silks so that the embroidery has the appearance of painting in enamels. Also see **embroidery frame.**

Bébé buttonhole. Knitting. (Also called eyelet buttonhole.) A simple buttonhole made by using the **faggot stitch,** which creates an opening the size of a small button in the knit fabric.

bede. Beadwork. See **bead.**

Bedford Cord. Weaving. A fabric with a **cord** or **rib** running parallel to the **warp.** The weave for Bedford Cord is a combination of **plain weave** and **filling-faced twill.** There are usually two cords in one repeat of the weave. The **float**s of the filling-faced twill make the rib, and the plain weave holds it together and makes the cord more pronounced. It is a medium to heavy weight fabric used for both apparel and upholstery. See ill. Also see **pique.**

One example of Bedford cord draft

bed rug. Quilts. A rare Early American bedcover of **wool** yarns on a woolen blanket. Nearly the entire surface was covered with yarns, and names and dates were often included. Examples available are mostly from the 1700s. These are sometimes referred to as **wool-on-wool coverlet**s.

bed size. Quilts. See **Quilts: Determining Quilt Size.**

beech. Woodworking. A strong yet flexible wood that is hard, heavy, and **close grained.** Its color ranges from white to pale brown. It is used for hunting bows, furniture, flooring, boxes, handles, mallets, sled runners, and fuel. Because it has very little odor or taste, beechwood is often used for **woodware.**

beech rod. Puppets. Toys. A **dowel** is sometimes referred to as beech rod. Rods are smooth round sticks available from hardware or hobby stores in various diameters and lengths.

beedizi. Spinning. See **Navajo spinning.**

beer. Jewelry. At one time, silversmiths cleaned metal in preparation for soldering, plating, or **coloring** by submerging it in stale beer or ale and then brushing it with a steel or brass brush that also had been doused with beer.

beeswax. Batik and Tie-dye. Beadwork. Bookbinding. Embroidery. Quilts. Stitchery. The **wax** secreted by bees for making honeycomb. Small cakes of beeswax are available in fabric or notions shops to smooth thread. It is sometimes used to coat sewing or **quilting thread,** making it less likely to knot, kink, or tangle. For that reason, beeswax is used to coat the thread used in sewing the **section**s of books together. Beeswax is used in the **batik** process, and is sometimes mixed with **paraffin.** The mixture of beeswax with other materials is called **batiking wax.** Also see **couching.**

beeswax. Candlemaking. A white, fatty substance that darkens with age to a rich, yellowish hue. It is yielded by melting the bee honeycomb at 140° to 150° F. It is estimated that a bee must consume roughly 14 lbs. of honey to produce 1 lb. of beeswax. Beeswax is considered the highest quality wax available for candlemaking but its high cost and relative softness restrict its general use. Its positive qualities include a smooth finish, a slow burning candle, a unique fragrance, and a particular golden coloration. To prevent sticking in molding it must be mixed with small proportions of **paraffin** and **stearic acid.** In earlier times beeswax was held in such high regard that it was considered suitable payment for church tithes and to this day church candles by custom still contain no less than 50% beeswax.

beeswax. Coral Carving. Ivory and Bone Carving. Jet Carving. Wax from honeycombs, naturally yellow-brown but white when bleached. Beeswax melts at 144–151° F and is transparent. Its solvents are petroleum derivatives such as gasoline, benzene, and lighter fluid.

Beeswax is used to lubricate blades and organic fibers and is an ingredient in dopping waxes.

Secure small pieces of stone or bone to a board or workbench with melted beeswax for carving, drilling, abrading, and polishing operations. Before sawing thin concave pieces, fill the recesses with melted wax. The hard wax reduces the danger of breaking the shape. Pry the piece off with a knife. Also see **bead-holding jig, bead-polishing board, bowdrill, carpet underlay, lapsticks, leather-lined vise, wood vise wedge.**

beeswax. Enameling. See **etching, jeweler's saw, resist.**

beeswax. Gem cutting. See **dop.**

beeswax. Jewelry. Wax from bees, sometimes bleached white, but generally used in its natural yellow state. It is available in various sizes in cake form, and is often used as a lubricant when **sawing,** especially on the heavier **gauge** metals. It is used for a lubricant when **drilling** as well. In sawing, the **sawblade** is nicked roughly ¼" through the cake of beeswax on the lower quarter of the blade. The heat produced by friction while sawing melts the beeswax and lubricates the length of the blade. Care must be taken not to add beeswax too often, as it will clog the blade. For example, when sawing 18 gauge sterling silver, about 15–20 strokes can be made before adding more beeswax. **Bronze** will require beeswax more often during sawing to prevent the sawblade from becoming dulled. Gold may require little or none. Experimentation will show how much beeswax is needed for each metal.

When drilling with a **flexible shaft machine** or **drill press,** touch the drill bit to a cake of beeswax occasionally to prevent the drill from burning out. When using a **hand drill,** scrape the drill bit across the beeswax cake from time to time. Also see **high speed drill, resist.**

beeswax. Metalworking. Woodworking. See **wax.**

beeswax. Stained Glass. See **aciding, copperfoiling, waxing up.**

beggar's block. Quilt. Quilt **block**s made up of **fabric** "begged" from friends and neighbors. It was customary to beg the scraps from dresses or neckties to be sewn into these **pieced** designs. Beggar's blocks made use of a great variety of fabrics in small pieces.

begin. Crochet. (Abbr. beg.) The beginning, or **foundation chain,** of any crochet work is made from a series of **chain stitch**es. Into this, the initial **row** of stitches is worked. Also see **Crochet: Basic Procedures, Basic Stitches.**

Beilby effect. Gemcutting. See **polishing.**

Belgian linen. Crewel. Embroidery. A coarse or fineweave linen made in Belgium and suitable as a **background fabric** especially because of its durability.

bell flower. Quilts. See **Quilts: Quilting.**

bell motif. Knitting. See **Knitting: Knitting Stitches and Patterns.**

bellows. Metalworking. A device invented in the Roman empire around the fourth century A.D. that produces a stream of air used to supply increased oxygen to a **forge** or furnace for melting metal, thus increasing the heat of the flames. It has largely been replaced in **forging** by a hand-turned or electrical **blower.** However, bellows are still used to blow away loose sand in making **sandcasting** molds.

bellows toy. Toys. A **folk toy** that goes back at least to 1700, in which a small bellows is used. The bellows, by alternate expansion and contraction, draws in air and expels it through a tube. The air is usually used to produce sound, and sometimes to move parts of a toy. Sometimes the bellows, activated by pressure, was hidden inside a figure or bird. In other toys the bellows was a part of the construction. They were often used in **automatic toy**s and surprise boxes.

bell toy. Toys. Any of a great variety of **sound toys,** including a clanging or ringing **bell.** Some are **rattle**like, others are mechanical toys or **automatic toy**s in which moving parts ring bells at intervals. **Wheeled toy**s, **push toy**s, and **pull toy**s may all be made to include the use of bells.

One of the simplest bell toys had bells attached to the **axle;** others had clappers attached to an axle which, as it turned, struck a gong-type bell.

A popular bell toy is one with a cylindrical cavelike container attached to two wheels, with a long handle. When the toy is pulled the wheels move, turning the cage which is filled with spherical bells or sleigh bells.

Some complex bell toys involved moving figures that struck bells. Some of the animated figures used an eccentric front **axle,** giving a bobbing motion to the figure and ringing a bell with the movement. Bell ringers became especially popular in the last half of the nineteenth century, gaining in complexity of movement and diversity, often representing political figures and events. Also see **musical toy.**

belly. Basketry. The concave surface of a **willow** rod.

belly. Ceramics. See **Ceramics: Form.**

belly. Leather. A term for the underside, bottom part of the **hide,** or **side,** of the leather skin. The belly is the least desirable part of the skin.

Belmont 300 solder. Metalworking. See **solder.**

belt findings. Leather. Metal additions to leather belts which are both decorative and functional, such as loops, D-rings, rings, belt tips, and belt keepers. Ready-made metal keepers are available, or a leather keeper can be made. Cut a narrow strip of belt leather 1″ longer than double the width of the belt. Edge and finish the keeper along with the belt. Skive the ends, overlap them to form a loop, and glue, **rivet,** or stitch the ends together. Slip the keeper over the belt just before you attach the buckle. The keeper may be loose or riveted near the end of the belt from behind. See ill. Also see **finding, skiving.**

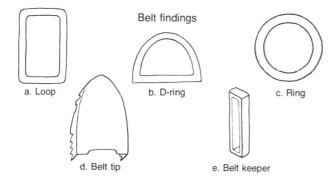

Belt findings

a. Loop   b. D-ring   c. Ring

d. Belt tip   e. Belt keeper

belt loom. Weaving. A narrow width **loom** for the weaving of belts, sashes, ties, ribbons, head bands, bag handles, straps, and tumplines—those long bands used by North and South American Indians to secure loads on their backs by attaching the band around the forehead and the burden. Belt weaving has been found in all cultures around the world and can be done on almost any kind of loom— such as an **inkle loom,** a **backstrap loom** (**rigid heddle** or otherwise), a **bow loom,** a **bandloom,** a long, narrow **frame loom,** and a card loom. It can be quite a unique loom like one used by the Navajos that was made out of a tree-fork. Although the space is minimal, elaborate **pick-up, double cloth, warp-faced, laid-in,** and **tapestry** designs are done on these looms. The narrow strips can be joined together to form wider pieces or articles. Also see **card weaving, joining.**

belt sander. Gemcutting. See **sanding.**

belt sander. Woodworking. See **sanding tool**s.

belt shuttle. Weaving. A version of a **stick shuttle** that is sharply beveled on one edge for use as a **beater.** It is usually 6–8″ long and is used in **inkle** and **card weaving** and other narrow fabric constructions. See ill. Also see **shuttle.**

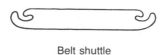

Belt shuttle

bench. Jewelry. (Also called jeweler's bench.) A sturdy table at which a jeweler works; sometimes with drawers and hooks for hanging tools.

bench. Puppets. (Also called operator's bridge.) In the **marionette stage,** a platform on which the **controller** can stand. A bench is sometimes used to provide this platform. For comfort it should be higher than the stage, although the height varies according to the length of the **strings** and the size of the **puppeteer.** Also see **rear bridge.**

bench. Spinning. See **wool wheel.**

bench anvil. Jewelry. (Also called jeweler's anvil.) A small **anvil** used for light **forging** and **forming** operations.

bench anvil. Metalworking. See **anvil.**

bench block. Jewelry. See **steel block.**

bench grinder. Metalworking. Woodworking. See **grinding tool**s.

bench hole. Jewelry. A square hole cut through a sturdy workbench for housing the **tang** of a **stake.**

bench hook. Block Printing. Fabric Printing. Metalworking. Plastics. Woodworking. A stepped board with a wood cleat that is hooked over the edge of a workbench to keep a piece of wood, metal, or plastic stationary while working on it. The bench hook is a device used in block printing and fabric printing on the worktable to hold the **linoleum block** or **wood block** steady while the design is being cut. It consists of a square of wood with a raised wood strip on the opposite sides of two opposite ends. One raised strip is hooked onto the edge of the table and the strip remaining face up is used to brace the block.

To make a bench hook, use a base of ½″ plywood about 12″ square and two strips 2½″ thick and 12″ wide. Glue and screw one strip to one end of the base; turn the base over and glue and screw the other strip to the opposite end. See ill.

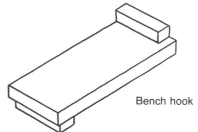

Bench hook

bench-made. Bookbinding. Any work done by hand on the workbench.

bench metal. Metalworking. See **bench work.**

bench pin. Jewelry. A wooden device extending from the **bench** that facilitates maneuverability while working. It often has a V-shaped cut in the end to hold the work. It is used basically for **sawing, filing,** applying **abrasives,** and **hand polishing.** See ill., page 78.

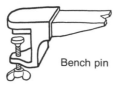

Bench pin

bench plane. Woodworking. See **plane.**

bench rub stone. Jewelry. (Also called carborundum stone, rub stone.) A long, flat carborundum block 12″ × 3″ × 1″, available in coarse through fine **abrasive** grades. It is used to grind away the edges of rings and bracelets to make them flat and true. It is also used to prepare the edges of a piece for soldering where a flat surface is required, as in **box construction.** It is brittle and will break easily if dropped.

The stone should be placed securely on a flat surface before use. The work is rubbed back and forth across the stone or in a circular motion, depending on the shape of the piece, using moderate pressure. More pressure is applied at the point of contact with the thumb; consequently, more metal is removed at this point. This can be avoided by slowly rotating the piece while rubbing, thus slightly changing the position of the thumb pressure against the metal. A more complicated method is to change the pressure of the rest of the fingers to equalize the pressure of the thumb. It feels awkward at first but gives satisfactory results and can be used along with turning if necessary. Metal that is worked for any length of time on the bench rub stone will form a **burr** along the edge; this can be removed with a half-round **needle file.** The stone should be lightly tapped upside-down occasionally to remove metal particles that fill the pores of the stone and slow down the cutting action.

bench saw. Plastics. Woodworking. See **power saw.**

bench shears. Jewelry. Metalworking. A tool used for cutting band or sheet metal. (Do not use on nails, rivets, or bolts, which would nick the blades.) There are two types:

a. With the simpler type of bench shears, the lower arm is clamped in a vise. The cutting line is lined up with the shearing edge of the upper blade, and the upper handle is lowered to cut the metal.
b. Another type of bench shears is also called a shear cutter. It is mounted on the bench, has blades as long as 12″, and is used in blacksmithing and jewelrymaking. It has a long handle for good leverage, and some have a notch toward the back of the blade for cutting round, square, and triangular wire. Sheet metal should be lightly scribed, or have a line drawn with a pencil so there is something to follow, and fed into the shears a length at a time until the full length of the metal is cut. Bench shears cut metal more quickly than **sawing.** However, they tend to curl the metal while cutting whereas sawn metal remains absolutely flat. Straighten out the metal by hammering with a **rawhide mallet** while supporting the metal on a hard wood surface

or on a **steel block.** Take care not to dent the surface. See ill. Also see **foot operated shears, scriber.**

Bench shears

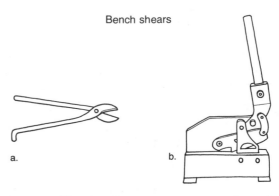

a.   b.

bench stop. Woodworking. A square-topped steel shaft that fits into, and flush with, the surface of a workbench when not in use. When raised it will hold or brace a board to keep it from moving while being worked. It is especially useful for **planing.**

bench vise. Jewelry. A small **vise** that can be attached to a **bench,** available in different sizes and with varying types of jaws. Some have a base that can be swiveled and locked into position while work is being done, and then rotated to other areas of the piece without removing the work.

bench vise. Metalworking. See **vise.**

bench work. Metalworking. (Also called bench metal, cold metal work, hand tool work.) The machining or working of cold metals by hand or with power tools using **hammer**s; drilling tools, **wrench**es, saws, **vise**s, and benders for **cutting, drilling,** forming, **mechanical fastening,** and **finishing.** It includes ornamental metalworking with solt cold metals such as **mild steel, aluminum,** and **copper,** which may involve bending curves, scrolls, or twists in the metals, as in making ornamental window gates or balustrades.

bend. Leather. A term for the part of the **side** or **hide** which is the **back** with the shoulder part cut away.

bending. Jewelry. Metal can be bent in numerous ways. Bending it with the fingers gives maximum control, excellent **support,** and the feeling of whether the metal needs to be annealed or not, and does not scratch or dent the metal. It is surprising how often metal can be bent with the fingers.

If the **gauge** of the metal is too thick or if it is too difficult to bend by hand, these are several other methods. Metal can be bent over a **mandrel,** a **stake,** or a **steel block** by hammering with a **rawhide mallet.**

It can be bent with different kinds of **pliers.** The metal is grasped by the pliers; however, the bending is done by the motion of the metal over one jaw of the pliers rather than by severely twisting the pliers, which would dent the metal. In this sense the single jaw of the pliers acts as a mandrel.

Depending on how heavy the gauge of the metal is, how tough it feels, and how much bending is necessary, heavy wire or **sheet metal** may require **annealing** before or during bending, especially when complex multiple curves are desired. No matter how little or how much bending is being done, support is absolutely necessary. Also see **box construction, brake.**

bending. Metalworking. See **Metalworking: Cold Bending, Blacksmithing.**

bending. Plastics. A forming process for plastics. **Thermoplastic** is heated with a **strip heater** along the line to be bent, or is completely heated in an oven and pressed into the desired form. Sheet **acrylic** can be bent without heating by being held in a curved frame but will not keep the bend when released from the frame, and may **craze** if bent too sharply. Also see **Plastics: Thermoforming and Molding.**

bending. Tincrafting. See **Tincrafting: Preparing the Tin can.**

bending brake. Stained Glass. A tool used to bend **copper sheeting**, particularly for making decorative tops for stained-glass lanterns. The brake allows the metal to be bent into different angles, so that only one seam has to be soldered. Also see **solder.**

Ben Hur's Chariot Wheel. Quilts. See **Princess Feather.**

benitoite. Gemcutting. A mineral found in San Benito County, California. It has **hardness** of 6½, **specific gravity** of 3.655, and refractive indices of 1.757 and 1.804. It is transparent and occurs in white and blue varieties. Benitoite can be **facet**ed. It is polished on a tin **lap** with tin oxide. Also see **faceting, polishing, refraction.**

bent gouge. Woodworking. See **gauge.**

bent-handled scissors. Rugmaking. (Also called shearing scissors.) Scissors with the handles curving higher than the blades. They are used for shearing and trimming **pile** on woven, embroidered, and **hooked rugs** and were developed particularly for the last category. Because of the bend in the scissors, the blades are able to lie flat on the pile surface and level it off evenly while cutting. See ill. Also see **shearing rugs.**

Bent-handled scissors

bentonite. Candlemaking. A claylike, white substance used as a filler in the making of **sand candle**s to strengthen and bind the sand.

bentonite clay. Ceramics. See **Ceramics: Clay.**

bent-tip tongs. Metalworking. See **tongs.**

benzene. Woodworking. See **solvent.**

Berian method. Weaving. A method of **dressing the loom** where the **reed** is used in place of a **raddle**. It is named after the French-Canadian weaver and teacher who perfected it. The **lease sticks** are inserted in the **cross** and tied to the **breast beam** with the short loop of the **warp** facing the **beater**. Groups of warp **end**s are quickly and roughly sleyed from front to back through a widely spaced reed. **Dent**s are skipped where necessary so that the warp is maintained in a straight line from cross to dent. When all ends are through the reed, the back **apron bar** is put through the warp loop and the warp is beamed. The lease sticks are usually transferred to the back of the loom before **beaming**, but they can just as well be transferred after beaming is completed and before **drawing-in** and **sleying**.

Berlin canvas. Needlepoint. See **Berlin wool work.**

Berlin wool. Needlepoint. A soft **yarn** made from the merino sheep of Saxony and used in **Berlin wool work.** **Aniline dye**s are used to produce the brilliant colors typical of this style of work.

Berlin wool work. Needlepoint. A method of working needlepoint by following color **charts**. This method was invented in the early 1800s by a printer in Berlin, Germany. The Berlin canvas was designed with blue lines every 10 meshes for ease in counting the pattern from the charts onto the canvas. This type of needlework was so popular in the Victorian era that all needlepoint was known as Berlin work. The patterns were primarily geometric and worked in **cross stitch**, cushion stitch, **gobelin stitch, satin stitch,** and **tent stitch.**

BernzOmatic. Jewelry. Metalworking. See **propane torch.**

berry knot. Macramé. (Also called hobnail pattern.) The berry knot is a three-dimensional, buttonlike knot that is a combination of **square knot**s and rows of **diagonal double half hitch**es.

Begin with eight **cord**s. Tie two square knots and pin them in place on the knotting surface (**a.**). Use the inside cord in the right square knot as a **holding cord** to tie a row of diagonal **double half hitch**es with the four left cords (**b.**). Make three more rows of diagonal double half hitches, using the other three right-hand cords in succession as holding cords (**c.**). Tie a very tight square knot with the four left-hand cords against the four rows of diagonal double half hitches; these cords are below the half hitches. Tie a very tight square knot with the four right-hand cords against the four rows of diagonal half hitches (to the left of them) (**d.**). They will bunch up to form a "berry" (**e.**). See ill., page 80.

Berry knot

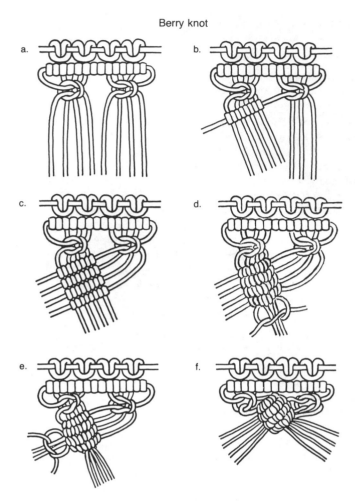

a.   b.   c.   d.   e.   f.

beryl. Gemcutting. A mineral composed of beryllium and aluminum silicates **crystal**lized in the hexagonal system with **hardness** of 7¾, **specific gravity** of 2.7, and refractive indices of 1.57 and 1.58. Beryl is dissolved by hydrofluoric acid, but is immune to others. It has conchoidal fracture and vitreous luster. It is often **facet**ed to display its rich **color** with crown facets at 42° and pavillion mains at 43°. It is polished on a metal **lap** with tin oxide and Linde A.

Emerald (green beryl) is seldom found without imperfections, making it one of the most expensive gem materials. Aquamarine is blue beryl; Morganite is salmon colored; and Goshenite is colorless or white beryl. All varieties possess some dichroism and sometimes exhibit a six-rayed star.

Synthetic chatham with **inclusion**s so closely resembles the natural emerald that gemological analysis is necessary to detect the difference. Also see **abrasive, cabochon, faceting, fracture, luster, polishing, refraction.**

beryllionite. Gemcutting. A mineral with transparent, clear to yellow **crystal**s used for **facet**ed gems. Berryllionite has **hardness** of 6, **specific gravity** of 2.8, and refractive indices of 1.553 and 1.577. It is polished with tin oxide on a tin **lap**. Also see **faceting, polishing, refraction.**

best quilt. Quilts. A quilt set aside for special occasions and not used daily by the household. Some were put out only for guests, or when company could see them. Because of this custom of carefully packing, storing, and preserving quilts, there are many prized specimens in private and museum collections today.

beta brass. Jewelry. See **brass.**

between. Stitchery. See **needle.**

bevel. Gemcutting. See **cabochon, facet.**

bevel. Metalworking. Woodworking. A sloping cut, or angle other than a right angle, that extends through the entire thickness of the end or edge of a piece of metal, wood, or other material. A chamfer is a sloping surface often confused with the bevel but different in that it only extends through part of the edge thickness.

In metalworking a bevel is cut into the edges of metal to be joined by **forge welding** so the edges may be overlapped without a lump of metal at the **weld.** See ill. Also see **blacksmithing technique.**

a. Bevel   b. Chamfer

beveler. Leather. A leather **tooling** instrument available in different sizes and textures, used to depress or bevel down background areas, producing three-dimensional relief work, in which the surrounding areas appear to be raised. Bevelers are usually held perpendicular to the damp leather and struck with a rawhide **mallet.** The depth of design depends on the degree of force of the mallet.

beveling. Jewelry. **Filing** at an angle other than a right angle. This procedure can be used to make a **joint** in preparation for **soldering.** It can be used effectively on the edges of metal to enhance the form and make a piece of sheet metal appear to have more weight.

beveling. Metalworking. See **blacksmithing technique.**

beveling. Rugmaking. See **shearing rug.**

bevel point knife. Leather. A versatile knife for cutting and **skiving** leather. Also see **skiving knife** and **Leatherwork: Tools and Materials.**

bevel square. Woodworking. See **squaring tool**s.

Bewick, Thomas (1753–1828). Block Printing. Découpage. An eighteenth-century English engraver whose intricate wood engravings of rural scenes have been widely used for découpage. Bewick was apprenticed to a metal engraver and at that time became familiar with the graver, an engraving tool. He adopted the graver for use on the end grain of hardwood blocks, producing wood engravings of such technical innovation and charming detail that his work, known as the technique of **wood engraving**, became extremely popular. He drew directly with the graver on the wood block with a skillful use of linear shading that produced subtle tones of gray. He combined these with the dark areas traditionally used in block printing. His renderings of figures, animals, and birds were based on a keen observation of nature. Most of his prints are miniature vignettes, measuring only 2 or 3″. The work produced by Bewick and his students in the shop at Newcastle is known as the Bewick School.

bezel. Jewelry. (Also called closed setting.) A metal wall that follows the outline of the base of a gemstone and holds it in position on a piece of jewelry. The gemstone is usually a cabochon, although any shape stone can be bezeled. **Bezel wire** is usually made of **fine gold** or **fine silver** because of their **malleability.** Do not use **gallery wire** to bezel. The bezel is soldered to the **baseplate** at a right angle. The stone is set within the bezel, which holds the stone in place permanently.

The bezel must be prepared on a hard, level surface such as a **steel block.** If a round stone is used, begin to bend the bezel wire anywhere around the stone. To fit an oval stone begin in the middle of the long side of the stone to facilitate manipulation of the bezel wire. Place the bezel wire against the base of the stone and at a right angle to the steel block. Hold the stone securely against the steel block and bend the bezel wire around the base of the stone, using a **bezel pusher** or the thumb nail. Press the wire firmly against the bottom edge of the stone. The bezel wire must remain at a right angle to the steel block while bending. Do not allow the top edge of the bezel wire to cant inward toward the stone. Cut the bezel wire where the ends overlap (**b.**). Make sure the ends are perfectly square and even. Manipulate the two ends into a **butt joint.** To prevent the bezel from springing while fitting, bend the bezel wire so that ends overlap and then pull the wire ends apart. This will produce a **spring temper** which will hold the ends together. It is not necessary to secure the ends with **iron binding wire** while **soldering.** Solder the joint using tiny **pallion**s of solder. Place the solder on the top edge of the bezel joint and use a small, but not too hot, needle **flame.** The solder will flow along the seam by capillary action. If the joint is not complete, turn the bezel over and add a piece of solder at the other end of the joint. **Pickling** is not necessary as the temperature for soldering is reached quickly, because the metal is thin. Fine gold and silver produce very little, if any, **firescale.** After soldering the joint is completed, pickle, rinse, and dry. Correct the shape of the bezel using a **bezel mandrel** or by pushing the stone through the bezel upside down, allowing the rim of the stone to act as a **mandrel.** In order to adjust the bezel to its correct shape, push the stone through the bezel from both sides. Use a half round **needle file** to remove any excess solder around the bezel joint.

To test the bezel for a perfect fit, place it on the steel block. Adhere a piece of double-faced masking tape to the back of the stone and place the stone in the bezel, keeping the base of the stone parallel with the top rim of the bezel. The stone should fit. Reverse the bezel and do the same to make sure the stone fits from either side. Once the bezel is soldered to a baseplate the stone can only be put in from the top. The stone will not have a good seat against the baseplate if the stone cannot fit through both sides of the bezel.

Roll the bezel with a **burnisher** on a steel block to enlarge a bezel. Keep refitting and checking the stone to make sure the bezel is not stretched too much. To correct a bezel that is too large, saw precisely through the seam, making sure to remove all the solder. File or snip away the excess metal in the bezel and resolder. It is easier to begin again.

Level the bottom of the bezel with **emery paper, carborundum paper,** or a **bench rub stone.** Place the bezel on a finger tip for easy handling (**c.**). If a **bur** is produced while leveling the bottom, remove it before soldering.

Flux the baseplate; use hard solder **flux** on the area where the bezel is going to be soldered. Hard solder flux does not bubble as easily as paste flux, and will not move solder out of position. Paste flux can be used on the other areas of the baseplate. Support the work on **carborundum grains** in a rotating **carborundum pan,** or on a **steel screen** placed on the carborundum pan, depending on the shape of the work. Coat the bezel with hard solder flux using a **flux brush** or by dipping the bezel in the flux with tweezers and place on the fluxed baseplate. The flux on the bezel will dissolve the dried flux on the baseplate. Clean, cut, and flux easy **solder** and place it on the inside of the bezel. The solder pallions should be square or slightly rectangular. Place the pallions flat on the baseplate with one edge touching the inside bottom edge of the bezel. If the pallions are slightly rectangular, place them in the same fashion, but with the longest side against the bezel (**d.**). Heat slowly. Solder into position keeping the flame in indirect contact with the bezel. Aim the torch on the inside of the bezel in order to get the baseplate in that area hot enough. Solder flows toward the hottest point; consequently, the solder will melt inside the bezel and flow out because of the heat and capillary action, making a perfect seam.

Insert the stone into the bezel using the masking tape as described above. Support the work securely on the **bench pin,** or **V-board and clamp.** Use a stone pusher or bezel pusher to shape the bezel to the stone. Rotate the work, supporting and pushing the bezel in the opposite direction

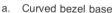

a. Curved bezel base

b. Overlap of bezel wire in
    preparation for cutting

c. Leveling the bezel bottom

d. Solder placement

e. The four opposite pushes to
begin positioning a bezel

f. Continuing pushes around
the stone

Bezel pusher

g. Correct and incorrect position of bezel pusher

until the entire bezel is in position (**e.**, **f.**). Repeat the process to push the bezel in contact with the stone. Press and tighten the bezel around the stone using a curved burnisher with medium pressure. The bezel is smoothed and polished simultaneously. See ill. Also see **reverse bezel.**

bezel mandrel. Jewelry. A small, tapered, steel **mandrel** that can be used for forming and stretching a **bezel.** See ill.

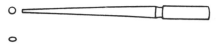

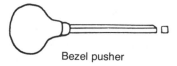

Round, oval, and square bezel mandrel

bezel pusher. Jewelry. (Also called bezel setter, stone pusher.) A square-shanked tool approximately ⅛″ square and 2¼″ long with a rounded wooden handle used for pushing **bezel**s and prongs into position. See ill. Also see **prong setting.**

Bezel pusher

bezel setter. Jewelry. See **bezel pusher.**

bezel shears. Leather. **Scissors,** generally used for metal cutting, used in leatherwork for cutting out small pieces of leather for **appliqué** designs.

Bezold Effect. Rugmaking. Weaving. See **color blending.**

bianco. Coral Carving. See **coral.**

bias binding. Crewel. Embroidery. Needlepoint. A commercial fabric cut on the bias in narrow strips suitable for edging **background fabric.** Also see **Crewel: Preparation and Layout, Needlepoint: Preparation and Layout.**

bias binding. Quilts. Stitchery. A **finishing** strip of **fabric** cut on the bias which is used to **bind** or cover **raw edge**s. A bias binding might be a narrow bias strip cut from matching material, or a standard commercial **bias tape.** Any **panel** or cut fabric piece which has rounded corners is easily bound with a bias binding, though bias pieces are difficult to fit on a right-angle corner.

bias knitting. Knitting. A method of knitting based on **increasing** and **decreasing** to create a bias (or diagonal-pattern fabric). The increasing and decreasing are always separated by several **regular stitches** and must be consistent, with the increases and decreases always vertically above their own kind. (For example, if every odd-numbered row begins with an increase of one stitch and ends with a decrease of one, every even-numbered row would begin with one decrease and end with one increase.)

To bias knit:
Row 1: ml b; Knit across row, k2 tog.
Row 2: K or P across row.
  or
Row 1: K1; S1, psso, across row, ml b.
Row 2: or P across row.

Also see **diagonal knitting** and **Knitting: Knitting Stitches and Patterns.**

bias stocking stitch. Knitting. This is simply **bias knitting** using the **stocking stitch.** In bias knitting, several methods of increasing or decreasing may be used.

right bias: Row 1: K2 tog, knit to last stitch, ml b.
Row 2: P across row.
left bias: Row 1: Ml b, knit to last two stitches, k2 tog, psso.
Row 2: P across row.

Also see **Knitting: Knitting Stitches and Patterns.**

bias tape. Quilts. Stitchery. Long strips of **cotton** or **cotton blend fabric,** cut on the **bias,** which are commercially made and prefolded so that **raw edge**s are on the inside. Bias tape is made in single or double folds and is used as a **binding** in **finishing** raw edges.

In using bias tape the weight of the fabric used for the bias should correspond to the weight of the fabric being bound. Bias tape is available in standard widths of ¼″, ½″, and ⅞″ in a great variety of colors. Because the edges are already turned under, bias tape is sometimes used for **appliqué** where straight lines or **band**s are needed.

bias tent stitch. Needlepoint. See **basketweave stitch.**

bib. Stitchery. A term used to describe any 2- or 3-dimensional creation which may be worn over the chest and attached around the neck. It allows the designer a free play with form while relating it to the human figure. It is used in the same way that a **breastplate** might be used. The bib is cut in a shape that is somewhat reminiscent of a baby's bib.

Bible quilt. Quilts. (Also called Scripture quilt.) A quilt that depicts biblical scenes as the major decorative element of design. Most are made with **appliqué** on **blocks.** Some are **pieced** quilts with biblical verses embroidered or written in India ink on them.

bicarbonate of soda. Stained Glass. Baking soda. Also see **hydrofluoric acid** and **Stained Glass: Safety Precautions.**

bicentennial quilt. Quilts. A quilt designed and made especially to commemorate the 200th anniversary of the United States, 1976. Historical events and significant dates and names are often included. A red, white, and blue color scheme is usually used in the quilt design. Also see **centennial quilt.**

bichromate of potash. Dyeing. See **chrome.**

bichromate of soda. Dyeing. See **chrome.**

bick. Metalworking. See **blacksmithing tool.**

bidri. Jewelry. An **inlay** technique developed in India and named after the town of Bidar. A special nonferrous zinc alloy base is first cast and then inlaid with **fine silver,** in designs ranging from fine, delicate lines to bold shapes. The zinc alloy is then blackened, producing a strong contrast between the silver and the black base metal.

Biedermeier style. Découpage. A nineteenth-century style of decorating furniture with precolored, embossed **cutouts.** The term comes from "Papa Biedermeier," a cartoon character of the time, and was applied sarcastically to middle-class adaptations of French Empire and Directoire furniture designs. Biedermeier was considered heavyhanded, with its symmetrical arrangements of massive flower bouquets, cupids, and doves resembling embossed valentines. The style was Austrian in origin; in later English adaptations it grew more and more dimensional until it was more like **paper sculpture** than découpage.

Bienefeld, Heinz. Stained Glass. A contemporary stained glass artist who created a wall in the church of St. Mary the Queen near Cologne that is considered a significant work of outstanding beauty.

bifurcated rivet. Jewelry. A type of **rivet** with a preformed head attached to a shank divided into two lengthwise. The shank is placed through the holes in the pieces of metal to be joined and opened like a paper fastener.

bight. Weaving. See **bout.**

bilbouquet cut. Toys. A **toy,** very much like **cup-and-ball,** that consists of a wood stick that is pointed on one end and cup-shaped on the other. A perforated ball is attached by **string** to the stick. The ball is swung and caught in the cup, or (if possible) the pointed stick is stuck into one of the small holes in the ball. In Victorian times, bilbouquet cups were elaborately decorated and made in a wide range of sizes from tiny ones of ivory just a few inches high and with a ball the size of a pea, to larger lacquered wooden ones.

bilderbage. Toys. See **découpage.**

billet horse. Toys. See **push horse.**

binary alloy. Jewelry. An **alloy** made of two metals.

binca cotton. Crewel. Embroidery. Needlepoint. An evenly woven fabric suitable as a **background fabric** for **counted-thread embroidery** and **petit point.**

bind. Batik and Tie-dye. To securely tie or wrap a **fabric** with **binding** for **tie-dye** so that the fabric being **dye**d will **resist** color in those areas. Also see **binding material, bind-**ing methods and **Batik and Tie-Dye: Basic Procedures for Tie-dye.**

bind. Stitchery. To cover a **raw edge** with **binding** cut either on the straight of the fabric or as a **bias binding.** One way of **finishing** a fabric edge is to bind it.

binder. Basketry. See **weft.**

binder. Bookbinding. One who binds books; a bookbinder.

binder. Ceramics. Materials added to either a **clay body** or **glaze** to increase the green or dry strength of the ware, to aid glaze adhesion, and to protect the fragile glaze coating during the kiln loading. Add 3% **bentonite clay** to increase glaze adhesion. **Gum arabic** or tragacanth are used as glaze binders. Gums deteriorate, so fire ware within a few days. Methocel is a synthetic methylcellulose compound that prevents setting and does not deteriorate as gums will. Sugar, syrup, or wheat flour can be used as binders in an emergency. However, all of these will ferment and lack the deflocculating action of methocel. A glaze containing more than 10% **kaolin** may not need a binder. Also see **defloculent, viscosity.**

binder. Enameling. A cement used to hold **enamel** in place until **firing.** Binders should burn away cleanly in the **kiln.** In liquid form, binders are brushed and sprayed onto the surface, or are mixed with the enamel and applied.

Klyrfire is a water-base commercial product used as a binder; agar from seaweed is used in some compositions. Gum arabic or gum tragacanth powder is mixed with methyl (wood) alcohol to form a paste, then diluted with water. After stirring, boiling, or shaking vigorously, the gum solution is allowed to stand until the heavier concentration settles to the bottom. Squeegee oil, oil of sassafras, and oil of turpentine are used as binders for finely ground enamels in delicate designs such as portraiture and **grisaille.** Oil of cloves or oil of lavender as binder gives a softer edge. A few drops of distilled water produces varied effects.

Oils must be dried slowly and carefully. Hold the work in front of the opened kiln door and take it away; repeat until the piece is heated and oil vapors are no longer visible. Also see **atomizer, cleaning metal, cloison, color testing, counter enamel, overglaze, sgraffito, spatula** and **Enameling: Basic Operations, Tools and Materials.**

binder's board. Bookbinding. Chipboard or similar heavy board used for the cover **board**s of books. It is sold in red or black in sizes 20″ × 26″, 20″ × 30″, and 20″ × 34″, in rigid or flexible stock.

binder thread. Weaving. The **pick**s in a fabric construction that hold together **filling floats** or **pile** effects. They are most often woven in **plain weave,** but they can also be in a **twill** if the fabric is very fine. Binder picks are found in fabrics like **overshot** where they lie between the rows of pattern floats. The usual arrangement is one pattern, one binder, etc. In pile fabrics or rugs, the binder thread weaves between the rows of pile, spacing the pile and holding it in place.

bindery. Bookbinding. A place where books are constructed or bound.

binder yarn. Spinning. Weaving. See **novelty yarn.**

binding. Batik and Tie-dye. The **binding material** used to tie or **bind fabric** for **tie-dye.** Also, a basic tie-dye process in which parts of a fabric are tightly bound or tied with thread before being immersed in a **dyebath.** Binding prevents the tightly **tied** portion of fabric from dyeing, and therefore preserves the original color. Binding may be used on a fabric that has already been treated by **marbling** or twisting, in which case those colors are preserved in the additional dyeing. Binding can be tied in various patterns, each of which gives a distinct design to the fabric. Among these patterns are **crisscross binding, spiral binding,** and **band tying.** Also see **Batik and Tie-dye: Basic Procedures for Tie-dye.**

binding. Jewelry. Metal is often bound with **iron binding wire** to hold it in position while **soldering.** The iron wire will not solder to the work; although it may adhere, it can usually be pulled off with **pliers,** and sometimes a small amount of filing is necessary to remove the iron wire and any **solder** that may have built up around it. The work should be bound with the iron wire and then **flux**ed. Iron binding **wire** must be removed before **pickling** to avoid contaminating the **pickle.**

binding. Quilts. Rugmaking. Weaving. Sewing a narrow woven tape to the raw edges of a hem around a rug or a woven piece to give a finished edge and to prevent the edges from raveling. The tape, called **rug binding,** is used on non-**selvage** edges on **rug backing**s or woven rugs or tapestries, and is sewn to the finished edges on **knitted, crocheted,** or **braided rugs** where extra strength and stability are required. The binding is sewn first to the edge or hem and then to the back of the backing or piece. It can be left open at two sides to be used as a holder for an inserted rod so that the rug, **tapestry, wall hanging,** or Navajo blanket can be hung. See ill.

In quilts binding refers to the strip of material that is used to bind or finish raw edges, as on the outside edge of the quilt. Also see **blanket, hemming.**

Sewing rug binding to back of rug hem

binding. Stitchery. One method of **finishing** the **raw edge** on a **wall hanging.** A cut-through or **reverse appliqué** is almost always finished by binding, usually using a bias strip. Binding for a larger **panel** may be done using strips of **fabric** cut on the **straight.** Also see **Stitchery: Finishing.**

binding edge. Crewel. Embroidery. Needlepoint. See **Crewel: Preparation and Layout, Needlepoint: Preparation and Layout, Finishing.**

binding material. Batik and Tie-dye. The cord or string used for **binding fabric** in **tie-dye.** Numbers 18, 35, or 45 **linen thread** are excellent as a binding thread. Other suitable binding materials are **bast,** string, cord, yarn, **raffia,** tape, rubber bands, flexible wire, twine, waxed cord, nylon stockings, polyethylene, thong, or carpet thread. The binding must remain tight throughout the dyeing if it is to be effective.

binding methods. Batik and Tie-dye. See **band tying, rolling, spiral binding** and **Batik and Tie-dye: Basic Procedures for Tie-dye.**

binding off. Knitting. See **casting off.**

binding rug edges. Rugmaking. See **finishing.**

binding single sheets with cloth-hinged boards. Bookbinding. Place sheets first between single **endpaper**s of the same size as the sheets, then between **boards** ½″ wider. **Jog** the sheets, endpapers, and boards to square the **head** and **back,** and insert in the **lying press** with the back projecting 1″ above press. Apply **glue** to the back and work it between the sheets. Remove the book from the press, remove the boards, and set to dry. Cut the boards to the same size as the sheets. Cut two strips of cloth to the same length as the sheets and 2″ in width and apply paste to the cloth. Place one of the ⅝″ strips of board onto the pasted side of the cloth so that it is even with the edge. Position the rest of the board on the cloth, leaving a space between it and the ⅝″ strip equal to a little more than twice the thickness of the board. Press firmly. Repeat for the other board and strip. Lay the boards hinge side up and cover the hinges with a **pasting guard,** except for a ½″ margin on the back edge. Apply glue to the margin, invert the boards, and paste them to the **back edge** of the book, checking that the head is level for boards and book. The cloth hinge will be on the inside of the book.

Place the book in **stabbing clamp,** drill holes, and proceed as directed for **sewing a single-section book.** Cover with **cloth.** See ill. Also see **casing in.**

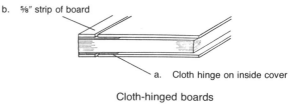

b.   ⅝″ strip of board

a.   Cloth hinge on inside cover

Cloth-hinged boards

binding stitch. Embroidery. A simple, strong, decorative and professional-looking whipping stitch that crosses back and forth in the same manner as a **long-armed cross stitch** over the edge of the **canvas.** It can be used to attach two separate pieces of canvas or to finish off any raw edges on a completed piece. It is especially useful for finishing work such as belts, eyeglass cases, rugs, etc., and eliminates the need for costly professional finishing. The binding stitch also works well as a **border stitch.** Also see **binding edge, joining canvas.**

binding wire. Jewelry. See **iron binding wire.**

birch. Woodworking. A group of over 24 species of hardwoods grown in Asia, Europe, and North America used for cabinet work, veneer **plywood,** interior trim, and **dowels.** It is tough, heavy, elastic, finely grained, and strong but is a difficult wood to work because the **grain** is irregular and very hard. Its color is light creamy brown to near white. It is not recommended for exterior work because it lacks resistance to the elements. Birch is also **stained** and used as a substitute for **walnut** and **mahogany.** Common varieties are the yellow birch, gray birch, silver birch, and swamp birch. Hop hornbeam, a member of the birch family, is so hard it is often called ironwood; it is similar to common birch, but tougher.

birdcage snap. Leather. See **snap.**

Bird of Paradise. Quilts. Any large elaborate bird **appliquéd** in brilliant colors to a single piece of **background** fabric for a quilt. In such Early American quilts there were **wreath**s, flowers, and festoons of leaves and vines surrounding it.

birdseye. Stitchery. A **cotton** or **linen fabric** with a woven-in pattern of **geometric** shapes in which a dot appears at the center, resembling a bird's eye. It is an absorbent **pique**like material, at one time used primarily for towels, runners, and diapers.

bird's-eye maple. Woodworking. See **maple.**

bird's-eye pattern. Weaving. A name used in the past to refer to a **twill weave** pattern, but today it pertains mainly to a specific category of **threading plans.** These threadings are based on the **point draw** and, depending on the **treadling** used, give small, repeated patterns. There are traditionally two treadlings—one that gives the diamond effect, and the other, a horizontal zigzag. However, as early as 1827, weavers experimented with the treadling and came up with different types of all-over designs which were used in table and bed linens, woolen shawls, and cotton cloth. Also see **diamond twill.**

Birds in the Air. Quilts. See **Birds in Flight.**

Birds in Flight. Quilts. (Also called Birds in the Air, Flock of Geese, Flying Geese, Wild Geese Flying.) Any of a variety of arrangements of squares and triangles **pieced** in such a way as to suggest the flight patterns of birds. This is an extremely popular **block** design, usually used without solid or plain blocks to offset the pieced ones, making an **all-over pattern.** In some variations the triangles are **set** in long rows separated by strips of printed fabric. The design is sometimes called **Wild Goose Chase,** but this name is

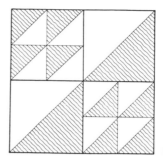
Birds in Flight

also sometimes applied to another design known as **Pineapple.** See ill.

bird toy. Toys. Any toy that has as its basic form the egg-shaped body of a bird. Folk carvers and toymakers from all over the world have used the bird in a great variety of ways, **stuffing** it in **fabric,** carving it from wood or ivory, or forming it from **clay.** The bird is used in the **pecking chickens** toy, found in almost identical form in Czechoslovakian wood carving, Eskimo ivory carving, and Mayan clay forms. The similarity of the chicken shape to the egg shape becomes apparent in different versions of the **chicken-and-egg** toys.

bird whistle. Toys. See **whistle.**

biscuit. Toys. See **bisque.**

biscuit quilt. Quilts. A puffed quilt made up of many small biscuitlike pillows that are formed individually so that each has a back, **filler,** and top. These puffs, or pillows, are prestuffed, and no actual **quilting** is done, so technically this is a **coverlet,** not a quilt.

The process involves sewing large squares, often of **silk,** to smaller ones, usually of **muslin.** The sizes of the puffs can vary, although usually if the smaller (**backing**) square is 2″, the top square in 3″. The larger square is placed over the smaller one, and its sides are tucked or folded to make it fit. Three sides of the square are sewn, and then **batting** is stuffed through the remaining open edge before the fourth side is sewn shut. These finished puffs are then joined by placing right sides together and sewing so as to conceal the first line of stitching. The puffs are sewn in rows, and rows are joined to make the **all-over** top. It is then placed over a backing material and bound. The assembly is similar to that used in the **pillow quilt.**

biscuit ware. Découpage. See **bisque ware.**

bismuth block. Jewelry. Used to support work during **soldering.** It does not conduct heat and can be carved to fit the form of the work; however, it is rather messy to work with and does not last very long. **Steel pins** can be used to hold work to the block. Also see **carborundum pan, charcoal block, powdered asbestos.**

bisque. Ceramics. (Also called biscuit.) Unglazed fired clay, usually porous. Ground-up bisque is called **grog.** Also see **bisque fire.**

bisque. Toys. (Also called biscuit.) Fired but unglazed **earthenware**, china, or porcelain. In **dollmaking** several variations of bisque were once used for making unglazed doll heads or even whole dolls. Those that had only a moderate amount of color added were known as blonde bisque; highly colored examples were known simply as bisque. When a coarser clay was used that produced a bisque with a grayish cast it was termed "stone bisque." White heads, produced with no coloring matter at all, were called **Parian;** they were delicately colored by hand painting.

Bisques varied not only in color, but in degree of fineness. This was determined by the grinding of the **clay** before it was mixed and fired. The doll manufacturer best known for bisque work was the **Jumeau** family firm, which produced some of the finest examples in existence between the middle and the end of the nineteenth century. Also see **all-bisque, ball joint, bisque doll, breast-plate doll head, doll head** and **Toys: Dolls.**

bisque doll. Toys. A doll made of **bisque.** Usually the head, neck, and shoulders were made of bisque and were added to a body of cloth or some other soft material. Arms and legs were either cloth or **composition.** Some bisque dolls, such as **Frozen Charlottes,** are made entirely of bisque and have no movable parts. Any unglazed fired **clay** is actually bisque, so included in this group would be those dolls referred to as **Parian,** as well as **earthenware dolls, clay dolls,** and unglazed china dolls. Also see **joint.**

bisque fire. Ceramics. The firing of clay into ceramic or **bisque.** It is usually the first of two firings; the second is the **glaze fire.** The bisque fire is a slow fire that removes moisture, burns out extraneous matter, and makes the **ware** easy to handle for glazing. Also see **Ceramics: Firing, glazing.**

bisque ware. China and Glass Painting. Ceramics that have been fired after drying without a glaze. Bisque ware can be decorated with **on-glaze color** mixed with glycerine and water. Painting on bisque ware is usually done in light tints. **Matte color** may be used. For best results, the decorated piece should be given five **firings** in a **kiln.**

bisque ware. Découpage. (Also called biscuit ware.) Clay pieces that receive only one firing and no glaze are called bisque ware. Because bisque is not a finished or waterproof surface, it can be given a découpage **finish.** The bisque surface must be given a coat of **sealer** and two coats of semigloss enamel paint as a ground on which to apply découpage **cutouts** and finish. Also see **découpage on ceramics.**

bissonette edge tool. Leather. (Also called safety edge.) An edging tool with the front of the cutting edge safely protected. It is used like a **common edge beveler** to round off the edges of leather. See ill. Also see **dressing, safety beveler.**

Bissonette edge tool

bi-stake. Basketry. See **bye-stake.**

bit. Woodworking. See **drill bit.**

bit brace. Woodworking. See **drilling tool**s.

bit gatherer. Glasswork. See **gaffer.**

bit gauge. Woodworking. See **gauge.**

bit stop. Woodworking. See **gauge.**

bitumen paint. Stained Glass. See **aciding.**

blackboard eraser. Crewel. Embroidery. A compact firm pad usually made of felt, generally with a wood handgrip. It is used in needlework to rub powdered charcoal through a perforated paper pattern. Also see **Crewel: Preparation and Layout.**

black body. Ceramics. A **clay body** that fires black due to **iron oxide** and **manganese oxide** deposits in the clay. Also see **engobe.**

Blackburn, Amelia. Papercrafts. An eighteenth-century Englishwoman whose papercut pictures of flowers, full of exquisite detail, became so famous that soon all papercuts were referred to as "Amelias."

black core. Ceramics. Blackening within the walls of a pot, usually caused by rapid firing and usually in a high iron clay. This effect has been found in primitive pottery and is sometimes a result of sawdust firing. Also see **smoked ware.**

black glaze. Ceramics. A black **earthenware glaze** is achieved by adding 4% each of **iron chromate, cobalt carbonate,** and **manganese oxide.** At higher temperatures, black glazes are hard to control and tend to vary. Also see **pigment oxide.**

black helmet. Shell Carving. (*Cassis madagascarenis.*) One of the most desirable shells for **cameo carving** because it provides a dark **ground color** of chocolate brown. Culled from the coast of North Carolina to the West Indies, it is not always easy to procure. It has a chalky-white exterior layer and a snowy-white **middle color.** The various shades of dark brown in the ground color sometimes give way to lighter shades when removed, increasing the possibilities of innovation. Also see **cowrie, helmet,** and **Shell Carving: Shell.**

black maple. Woodworking. See **maple.**

Black Maul. Basketry. See **willow.**

black oak. Woodworking. See **oak.**

black pigment. Ceramics. Black pigments are used as **underglaze**s or **stains.** A black pigment is hard to mix and tends to spread out unevenly. The most common black pigment oxides are iron, cobalt, and manganese. Also see **black glaze, pigment oxide.**

black powder steel. Metalworkings. See **gun metal.**

black rouge. Jewelry. See **buffing compounds.**

blacksmithing. Metalworking. (Also called ironworking.) The making or repairing of objects in iron or "blackmetal," particularly by shaping it while it is hot and soft. This craft is distinct from redsmithing (working in **copper** or **bronze**) and whitesmithing or tinsmithing. Historians place the origin of blacksmithing at about 6000 years ago in the Caucasus. It spread throughout Europe and replaced bronzeworking for the production of weapons and tools in Britain shortly before the Roman invasion. There were close ties between the work of the early blacksmiths and the occult sciences. Also see **Metalworking.**

blacksmithing hammer. Metalworking. See **hammer.**

blacksmithing techniques. Metalworking. Methods of **forging** used primarily for **blacksmithing** or working with iron, but used with other metals as well. These techniques are for forged work, which is work-hammered when the metal is hot.

Rounding up (also called cogging, or packing) is the hammering of a metal **ingot** or a **blank** to rearrange the structure of the metal grain and to compress the central core of the piece. Roughing is a type of rounding up used to break down the ingot into a rough shape.

Cutting (also called chiseling, cleaving, slicing, or splitting) is the cutting or dividing of a hot metal without losing any of it by hammering the metal over a **hardie** or a **chisel plate,** using a hot or cold **set** (**a.**). When cutting an edge, start from the edge and work inward to avoid cracking the metal; when cutting inside the piece, start from the center and work out.

Drawing out (also called forging down, setting down, or fullering) is the process of making a thick piece of stock thinner in diameter while increasing its length. It is a basic operation in blacksmithing. Setting down is the process of thinning the diameter of only a part of the metal instead of its entire length (**b.**). Drawing out is used especially for scrolls, brackets, screens, and balustrade fences.

Fullering is a form of drawing out using top and bottom fullers and a sledge hammer to hit the fullers (**c.**). It requires two persons to accomplish.

Flattening is the smoothing of metal with a **flatter** or **slick** after it has been fullered. Punching is the making of a hole with a punch and hammer.

Drifting is the enlarging or shaping of a punched-out hole by hammering a **drift** into it (**d.**). Swaging is the hammering of the metal in combination with **swages** or a **swage block.**

Upsetting is the hammering of a piece of metal to thicken its diameter at any place on the piece (**e.**). Bradding is a form of upsetting in which the end of a rod is broadened to prevent it from pulling out of a hole.

Shrinking is the joining of two pieces of metal by inserting a cold rod or bar into a hole in a hot piece of iron. When the iron hole cools, it shrinks and holds the rod securely.

Scarfing (also called beveling or chamfering) is the tapering of the end of a piece of metal in preparation for forge welding (**f.**). This makes possible a smooth **lap weld** without a lump of metal at the seam.

Forge welding is the joining of two pieces of metal at their scarfed ends by hammering the two pieces together without a **welding rod** while they are molten hot. See ill. Also see **blacksmithing tools** and **Metalworking: Blacksmithing.**

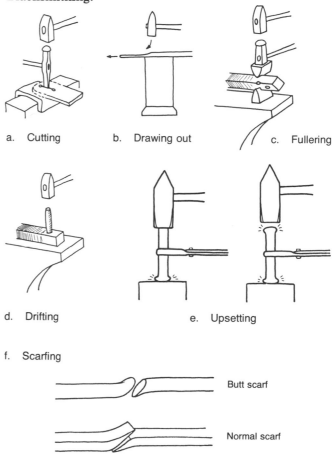

a. Cutting   b. Drawing out   c. Fullering

d. Drifting   e. Upsetting

f. Scarfing

Butt scarf

Normal scarf

Simple scarf

Scarf for thin stock

blacksmithing tools. Metalworking. Tools used for **blacksmithing** or forging **iron,** including forge tools, anvil tools, and set tools. Forge tools are used to tend the **forge.**

POKER Usually made of a ½" diameter rod with a ring handle in one end, its main use is to tend the fire in the forge. It is also used to test the surface of iron heating in the forge or to apply iron filings to heated iron for **brazing.**

RAKE   Similar to the poker, with three or four teeth on the end, it is used to tend a coal fire.

SHOVEL   Used to rearrange or pack coal in the forge.

Anvil tools are attachments that usually fit into the hardie hole on a blacksmith's **anvil.** They are used for forming and forging metal, often in conjunction with corresponding set tools (see below).

HARDIE   Also called cutter or hardy, this inverted chisel is the most important anvil tool, used for cutting or splitting bars. The hot hardie is sharpened for cutting hot iron, and the cold hardie has a duller edge for use on cold metal (**a.**).

FULLER   Tools used with a sledge hammer to thin metal.
  The bottom fuller is similar to the cold hardie with a blunt, rounded edge (**b.**). It can be used in combination with the upper fuller (**c.**), to make grooves, hollows, and concave shapes, or to spread or stretch metal. The top fuller may be used alone to make depressions in metal lying flat on the anvil face. The top fuller usually weighs 3½ lbs. The small fuller has no handle (**d.**).

ANVIL BICK   A small horn on which to hammer small pieces of metal (**e.**).

SWAGE   Swages come in a variety of shapes to form and smooth welds. The metal is placed on the lower swage (**f.**), and the upper swage (**g.**) is placed on top and struck with a hammer to shape the metal.

CHISEL PLATE   This does not fit into the hardie hole; it is an iron plate with bent-down edges that fits over the anvil face to protect the anvil while chiseling.

Set tools are tools hit with a hammer and are often used in pairs with corresponding anvil tools for cutting, splitting, and shaping grooves and depressions in hot metal. They resemble hammers in that they often have rod or wire handles, but the handles are used to hold the shaped end to the metal while the other end is struck with a hammer.

CHISELS   The terms "chisel" and "set" are often interchangeable, as in cold chisel or cold set. Chisels often have handles to keep the hands away from the red-hot iron. The hot set or splitting (or cutting) chisel is sharp and is used on hot iron; the cold set or flogging (or packing) chisel is duller (**h.**). The cape chisel (or gouge, key chisel, or round cape chisel) is used to cut grooves. The chipping chisel has a wide blade and is used to chip away rough metal on a weld to smooth the surface.

WITHY   A wood or wire handle or wire wrapped around a set tool and secured with a wire coupling to facilitate handling.

PUNCH   There are two forms of punches, those without handles and those with handles at least 2' long. Punches come in diameters from ¼" to 1½" and are used to make holes of various shapes in red-hot iron. Punching hot iron is faster and easier than drilling (**j.**).

DRIFT   Although this is not a true set tool and is more related to the swage, it is also used in combination with a hammer to enlarge and punch out holes (**k.**).

FLATTER   Also called slick, this set tool resembles a hammer but has a larger and slightly rounded face, which is approximately 3" square (**m.**). The flatter is placed on hot rough iron and struck on the back with a **sledge hammer.** This process usually requires two people, one to hold the flatter and another to strike it. See ill. Also see **blacksmithing techniques** and **Metalworking: Blacksmithing.**

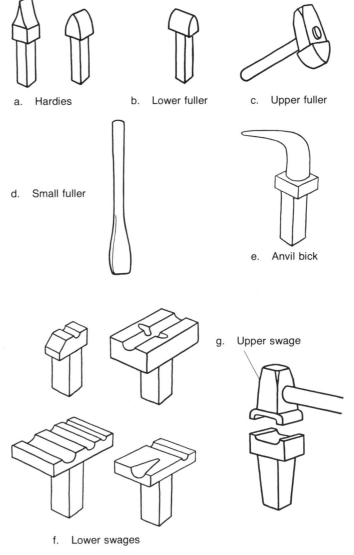

a. Hardies   b. Lower fuller   c. Upper fuller

d. Small fuller   e. Anvil bick

g. Upper swage

f. Lower swages

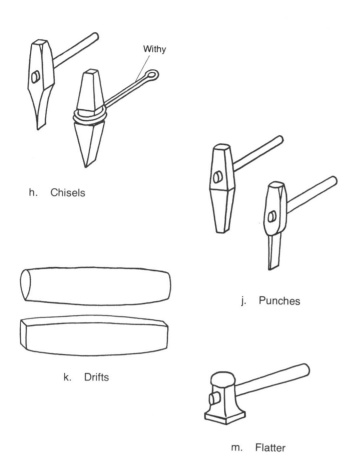

h. Chisels

Withy

j. Punches

k. Drifts

m. Flatter

blacksmith's anvil. Metalworking. See **anvil.**

blacksmith's helper. Metalworking. A portable stand made of wood or metal that is used to support a long piece of metal while one end of the piece is heating in the **forge.** See ill.

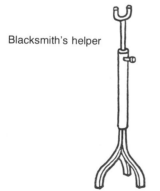

Blacksmith's helper

black walnut. Batik and Tie-dye. The dark brown or black stain from the hull of the nut. Also see **natural dye.**

black walnut. Woodworking. See **walnut.**

blackwork. Embroidery. Embroidery traditionally done in black thread on white **linen** with an **even weave.** It originated in Spain, where natural black wool was abundant, and was probably influenced in design by the geometrical Moorish architecture. It is said to have been brought to England by Catherine of Aragon when she mar-

ried Henry VIII, but this has been disputed. During the reign of Elizabeth I, it became increasingly popular. Hans Holbein painted so many portraits with his subjects wearing clothing decorated with blackwork that certain types of patterns are known as Holbein stitch to this day. Holbein stitch generally refers to close designs carried out in **double running stitch,** as distinct from patterns filled in with basic **back stitch, cross stitch,** or **darning stitch.** The Elizabethans added **gold metallic** thread to the embroidery to enrich it.

The effectiveness of blackwork relies on the juxtaposition of lacy patterns of varying intensity, or solid black patterns contrasted with light, open areas. Contemporary blackwork can be carried out in any monochromatic color scheme with or without metallic threads.

Because blackwork patterns are geometric, they must be counted out on an evenly woven **fabric.** Geometric patterns to fill areas can be created or copied from early **samplers.** See ill.

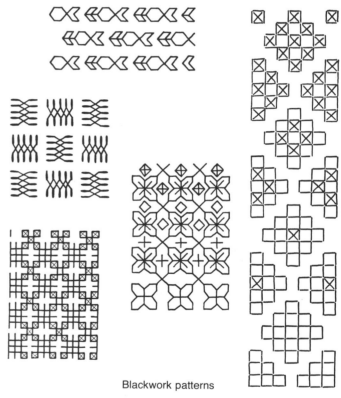

Blackwork patterns

blade. Woodworking. The textured or sharpened edge of a tool that is used to cut, **saw, plane,** or reduce wood. Blades are available in a countless variety of shapes and sizes, depending on the function of the tool it is part of. Blade may also refer to the short leg of a **squaring tool.** Also see **whittling tools.**

blank. Gemcutting. See **cabochon, preform.**

blank. Jewelry. A commercially available punched out metal shape that can be decorated and further processed to produce a finished piece.

blank. Metalworking. A precut, often stamped, metal shape that is used for **raising** and forming metal objects and which must be finished by the traditional metal **finishing** processes.

blank. Stained Glass. Flat glass pieces cut for **sagging** molds. Also see **lampshade mold.**

blanket. Weaving. See **sampler blanket.**

blanket binding. Quilts. A commercially made **binding** cut on the straight of the material that has **selvage** at each edge. It is available in a standard 2″ width and is most commonly used to bind **coverlet**s, **quilt**s, and blankets. Some blanket bindings come prefolded, and most have a **satin** finish.

blanket stitch. Crewel. Embroidery. Needlepoint. See **buttonhole stitch.**

blanket stitch. Quilts. Stitchery. A **stitch** which covers a turned-over edge, as in **appliqué,** or one which may be used to outline or emphasize a shape. If worked in a circle, the stitches radiate out to form a flower. It is often worked in yarn or several strands of floss for a decorative effect.

The blanket stitch is worked from left to right. First the thread is pulled through from the back and held down with the left thumb. The **needle** is inserted slightly above and to the right of the starting point. It is brought out directly below so that the needle has made a short stitch straight down. The needle comes out on top of the first thread to make a right angle corner. The same stitch is repeated to make a row of short vertical stitches. See ill.

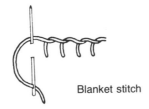

Blanket stitch

blanket stitch. Rugmaking. A finishing **stitch** for rug edges. The stitch is identical to the **buttonhole stitch,** but the name changes when it is made around a larger item and the spacing of the stitch is wider. The stitch can be used as the finished edge itself or it can be made around a rug that is designed to have a **self-fringe.** In either case, it is easier to do the edging stitch before working on the rug itself. If the stitch is used as a finished edge, the color of the yarn used in making the stitch is determined by the design of the rug and by what color will work the best with the design. In the case of a self-fringe, the blanket stitch is made with a strong yarn or **carpet thread** in a matching color to the rug or unraveled **rug backing** thread. The stitch is worked around the entire edge of the rug to secure the edges. Once the stitch is in place, the unused backing around the rug is unraveled and the remaining threads form the self-fringe. At least 4″ of backing should be allowed for the fringe. If this fringe is too sparse, more yarn can be inserted in a **lark's head knot** under the stitch. See ill.

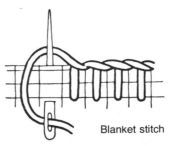

Blanket stitch

Blazing Star. Quilts. An eight-pointed star in **pieced patchwork.** When this pattern is varied to produce a star of many points, it is known as **Blazing Sun** and Sunflower. See ill. Also see **star patterns.**

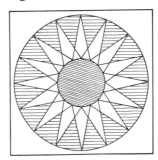

Blazing Star

Blazing Sun. Quilts. A **pieced block** design consisting of many diamond points radiating from a central circle. See ill. Also see **Blazing Star.**

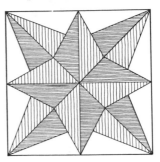

Blazing Sun

bleach. Batik and Tie-dye. Stitchery. A whitening agent or chemical compound used to remove color from fabric. Most household bleaches have a chlorine base, and **bleaching** with them tends to weaken fabrics when a large amount is used. When sparingly used and thoroughly mixed with water, bleach has no apparent adverse effect on fabric. A nonchlorine bleach is safer for fragile or delicate materials; chlorine bleach can be used on denim or other heavy material.

Among the best known bleaches are lemon juice, chlorine, and hydrogen peroxide.

When used in **tie-dye,** bleaching is called **discharge dyeing.**

bleach. Woodworking. See **bleaching.**

bleaching. Batik and Tie-dye. Dyeing. Quilts. Stitchery. Softening, lightening, or removing color by using a bleaching agent. Blue denims or blue jeans, popular in **stitchery** and **patchwork,** are often preferred in a gradation of colors achieved by varying degrees of bleaching.

There are various bleaching agents, among the most

common being **lemon juice,** a safe bleach. Hydrogen peroxide mixed with water is also an excellent gentle **bleach.**

Standard household bleaches will not harm most white or off-white fabrics if they are treated carefully, but a non-chlorine bleach should be selected. Use only a small amount of bleach—about 1 teaspoon to a quart of water to start with. It is better to soak a fabric in a weak solution for a longer period of time than to use a strong solution for a short time.

Spots that occur when **natural fiber**s break down chemically cannot be removed by bleaching. If such a piece is to be incorporated into a **wall hanging** and the spots are disturbing, **stitch**es taken over that area in a matching color will minimize their appearance, or the spots can be touched up with tiny, carefully placed dots of matching **acrylic paint.**

Denim material is very durable and sturdy and may be heavily and deliberately bleached to soften colors. Bleach must be thoroughly mixed in the water before adding the fabric if an overall even color is desired. To bleach a pair of blue jeans, fill a washer with hot water and detergent. Then add about a cup of liquid bleach and agitate well. Drop the denims into the water and stir. If that solution does not adequately fade the material, remove it from the water, add more bleach, agitate well, and reimmerse the material.

To achieve a complete gradation of color, put all the denim pieces into bleach water for a short soak. At the end of a half hour, remove one and add more bleach. Continue this process of removing one piece and adding more bleach until all pieces are finished. Rinse each as it is removed. Remember that colors appear to be much darker when they are wet.

Bleaching leaves denim with a light muted color that does not have the same softness of color and texture as when the denim is faded by the natural color loss due to normal wear. It is therefore not as desirable for patchwork, but certainly more speedy.

In **tie-dye,** the bleaching process is called **discharge dyeing.**

bleaching. Woodworking. **Wood** is most commonly bleached with oxalic acid to remove dark spots, streaks, and natural color. Wood that is already light in color, such as **ash, birch, oak,** and **maple,** is always much easier to lighten than dark wood.

To bleach, dissolve approximately 3 oz. of oxalic acid crystals in 1 quart of hot water. Let it cool, and apply with a brush. After the bleaching solution has dried, neutralize by washing it off with 1 oz. of borax dissolved in a quart of water, and allow 48 hours for final drying. If the wood **grain** becomes raised, sand lightly until smooth. Protect with a **shellac, lacquer,** or **varnish finish.** If a stronger bleaching agent is desired, a commercial two-part solution of caustic soda and hydrogen peroxide should be obtained; follow manufacturer's instructions carefully.

When bleaching, wear eye protection, rubber gloves, and a rubber apron. Mix only as much as needed. Apply with a rope brush or a cellulose sponge—never with rags; apply only in a well-ventilated room. Discard any unused solution immediately. Also see **finish** and **Woodworking: Finishing.**

bleb. Glasswork. The thickened drop of glass left at the center of glass tubing that has been closed off by heating and stretching one end. For most further operations in **flamework** it is necessary to remove the bleb. This is done by heating both the area and a glass rod, and when the bleb becomes soft enough, winding a thread of glass from the bleb around the glass rod. One or two such operations should be enough to "eat up" the bleb.

bleeding. Batik and Tie-dye. Dyeing. The running or fading of a substance from one area to another. Bleeding is usually unintentional but it may be used to advantage in design. The bleeding of **dye** colors is characteristic in **tie-dye.** In **batik,** the **wax** (especially if it is too hot and thin) may bleed beyond the edges of a design. To prevent this bleeding a thin layer of starch can be ironed onto the fabric. If the wax does not thoroughly penetrate and cover the fabric, dye will bleed onto those areas. Also see **dyeing.**

bleeding. Plastics. Woodworking. The spreading or penetrating of **colorants** into areas not intended to be colored, or a color's showing through a covering coat. Keep colorants within a definite area by **masking** adjacent areas with **masking tape** or **cellophane** tape.

In woodworking bleeding refers to the unwanted staining or blotching of a painted wood surface or finish as a result of the soluble salts or resins in knotty or resinous wood coming to the surface. Bleeding will also occur when a colored **wood stain** is covered with a wood finish that contains the stain's **solvent.** Oil-base stains will also slowly bleed through dried matte water-base paints. To prevent bleeding, both natural resinous woods and artificial stains must be covered with a **sealant** like **shellac.** Also see **Woodworking: Finishing.**

bleeding ink. Découpage. Stenciling. Printing ink that is alcohol-soluble and will become blurry after a **sealer** is applied. Inexpensive printed material often has bleeding ink, and is therefore unsuitable for use in découpage. To test prints before using, spray both sides with clear acrylic spray. If the printing from the back side (verso) shows through to the front, don't use it.

In stenciling bleeding refers to the paint that runs under the edges of the stenciled design because the paint has been applied unevenly or because the stencil is held too tightly. Also see **Découpage: Selecting Prints; Stenciling: Printing.**

bleeding the line. Metalworking. In **welding** practice, the draining of the gas hoses to the tank before disconnecting **oxyacetylene welding** equipment or merely shutting it off at the end of the day's work. First close the tank valve, and then open the torch valves one at a time. Open the acetylene valve and empty this hose first. Close it when the hose is empty. Repeat the operation for the oxygen line or hose.

blend. Batik and Tie-dye. Quilts. Stitchery. A term applied to either **yarn** or **fabric** indicating that it is a combination of **fibers**, usually of **natural fibers** and **synthetic fibers**. Such blends offer some of the advantages of each fiber used. Much of the yardage currently available is blended. The information regarding it is available on the fabric bolt; for example, a blend label might read: cotton 65%, orlon 35%.

Blends are sometimes a problem for **hand appliqué** because synthetics tend to be springy. This makes it difficult to turn edges under. For most hand-sewn **stitchery** any fabric that is at least half **cotton** will be easier to **appliqué** than one with a larger percentage of synthetic. For **machine appliqué** blends are satisfactory.

blended solvent. Plastics. See **solvent**.

blending. Metalworking. A **finishing** operation in **pewterworking** in which the scratches made by **cutting** the metal with an **abrasive** during polishing are blended and smoothed by using a **buffing wheel** and tripoli **polishing compound**.

blending. Spinning. Incorporating various colors, textures, or fibers into one yarn. This can be done as early as the **teasing** when colors or fibers can be mixed together as they are picked. They can also be integrated in the **carding** or **combing**. Generalizing, the earlier the blend is made, the more uniform it will be. Textures result during the spinning process.

Blenko Antique. Stained Glass. Handblown glass made by the Blenko Glass Co., Milton, West Virginia. They produce a series of beautiful amber glass by adding table sugar to the molten glass.

blind. Shell Carving. A condition in mother-of-pearl characterized by a lackluster, porcelaneous appearance, as opposed to its normal highly reflective iridescence. It occurs in shells that have been attacked by worms and disease, or from exposure to the sun. This adverse effect of sunlight is evidenced in the dullness of the shells culled from the shore or fished already dead from the water. **Grubby** shells are often blind.

A healthy shell that has been carved is also prone to falling blind, so owners of shell pieces should shield them from the sun as much as possible. Also see **porosity**.

blind appliqué. Stitchery. **Appliqué** in which the attaching **stitch**es are not visible. This requires skillful sewing but may be accomplished with experience. Either the **blind stitch** or **hidden whip stitch** is used. Also see **blind work**.

blinded-in. Bookbinding. A design that has been impressed on a book cover with heated tools without color is said to be blinded in. This is sometimes done to ensure even spacing before applying metallic foils or color. Also see **blind tooling**.

blind mortise-and-tenon joint. Woodworking. See **joint** and **Woodworking: Jointing**.

blind stitch. Quilts. Stitchery. Toys. An **appliqué stitch** in which the thread is concealed and which gives a smooth puffy or raised look to the material edge. In the blind stitch, the length of each stitch occurs within the **folded hem** or **seam allowance** of the **appliqué fabric**. As the **needle** emerges, exactly on the folded edge, it dips down to pick up a thread or two of the **background** material, then immediately goes back into the fold. In appliquéing with a blind stitch a little fullness should always be kept in the piece of fabric being appliquéd. There should be no stitch showing on the surface of the material. Sometimes the stitching arrangement is reversed, with the length of each stitch going behind the background fabric and the needle picking up just a thread of the appliqué piece. This may be faster to sew, but for **hemming** and appliqué the first gives a smoother, fuller, neater stitch. See ill. Also see **hidden whip stitch**.

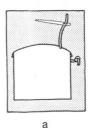 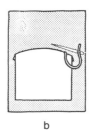 

a   b   c

Blind-stitch appliqué

blind tooling. Bookbinding. (Also called antiquing.) The process of making impressions with hot finishing tools without leaf or color onto the cover of a book. This process is especially effective on light-colored leathers as the heated tool makes the impressions darken. Care must be taken not to burn the cover. To make straight lines across the **spine**, the friction of a thread drawn repeatedly back and forth is sufficient to burn an impression.

blind work. Stitchery. Very delicate detailed hand stitching or embroidery from the East, and most commonly from China, so called because the fineness of the work reputedly caused a loss of eyesight to the embroiderer. Any delicate stitching, so fine that the **stitch**es can scarcely be seen is referred to as blind work. Also see **blind stitch**.

blistered paint. Stained Glass. A paint fault that develops in the **kiln** and is caused by an excess of **gum arabic** in the paint formula. It can sometimes be corrected by rubbing raw powdered glass paint into the blistered area and then refiring the piece. If the blistering is too severe and the glass cannot be recut, the piece can be placed in a mild **hydrofluoric acid** solution, weaker than that used for aciding. After the paint has peeled away, wash, dry, and repaint the glass. Also see **painting on glass**.

blistering. Ceramics. An undesirable effect caused by bubbles of gas escaping from **glaze** in the firing. Blisters do not disappear when the firing is over. Also see **bloating, crater glaze**.

blistering. Enameling. See **Enameling: Repair and Care.**

bloating. Ceramics. Swelling or air pockets that develop on the body of a pot, caused by gas pockets in the **clay body.** This usually occurs in high-fired pottery. Also see **blistering.**

block. Glasswork. The wetted hardwood mold used in forming blown **glasswork.** Also see **blocking.**

block. Quilts. (Also called patch, quilt block.) A single complete unit in the design of a quilt. The block may be **pieced** or **appliqué**d, and may be a **square,** a **diamond,** a **rectangle,** or a **hexagon.** In the case of **pieced quilts,** the block is almost always composed of a number of smaller **patches** or pieces. In **appliqué quilts,** the block is the **background** piece to which the appliqué design is sewn.

As an example, in **Drunkard's Path** the basic unit consists of two patches, a quarter-circle sewn into one corner of a square. This block is then repeated and may be **set** in any of a great variety of ways. Each set of the blocks produces a different quilt design. Fool's Puzzle and Falling Timbers are simply different sets of the Drunkard's Path block.

In designing pieced quilts, it is the arrangement of the parts within the basic patches that produces the **block pattern.** The block is then used in a repeat design to make the **quilt top.**

The motif of a quilt is usually carried in the design that is repeated to produce pattern, and it offers an element that can be developed or expanded upon. A block might also have a basic or central motif along with less dominant or secondary motifs. Also see **module.**

Block Circle. Quilts. See **Rolling Stone.**

block design. Quilts. See **Quilts: Identifying Old Quilts.**

blocked joint. Woodworking. See **joint** and **Woodworking: Jointing.**

block forming. Jewelry. Carving simple forms into a hardwood, then hammering thin sheet metal into the form with **punch**es. This is a form of **dapping die** that has the advantage of allowing you to create your own forms in the wood.

blocking. Bookbinding. The mechanized process of **stamping** a book cover.

blocking. Crewel. Crochet. Embroidery. Needlepoint. The process of shaping a finished (or newly washed) piece of crochet. Use a piece of **Celotex** covered with heavy paper or cloth marked off in 1″ squares. Stretch the finished crochet to the desired size; pin it with as many rustproof pins as is necessary to obtain a smooth edge. Place a dampened cloth on top. Hold a hot iron close to the dampened work to produce steam but do not let the iron rest on the work. Be sure the blocked crochet is dry before unpinning it. If the work has become soiled while being crocheted, wash it carefully before blocking.

In crewel, embroidery, and needlepoint, blocking is a means of stretching and flattening a finished piece of needlework by tacking or stapling the **background fabric** taut on a board or stretcher strips frame. The stretched piece is then dampened and allowed to dry. This straightens the individual stitches and fabric back to its original shape. Also see **Crewel: Finishing; Needlepoint: Finishing.**

blocking. Glasswork. A forming operation in glassblowing whereby the blown form is shaped by turning it in a concave surface of wetted hardwood (beech or fruitwood). The interior surface of the **block** becomes charred with use and the layer of soft carbon has a polishing effect on the glass surface. This shaping operation is an intermediate step in glassblowing and is used especially for shaping the **parison,** preparatory to further blowing. Blocking molds can be spherical for round blown forms or conical for cone shapes; they are usually shaped by hand to meet the individual glassblower's needs. See ill.

Two sizes of blocking mold

blocking. Knitting. Quilts. Blocking is the process of drying and shaping a sewn or knitted object in such a way that it dries smoothly, evenly, and in the proper dimensions.

To begin, roll the washed pieces (sleeves, front and back, in the case of a sweater) in a towel to remove excess moisture. On clean padding, such as a towel or blanket, spread out the wet knit pieces front-side up. Using a ruler, and with the pattern dimensions (which should be specified at the top of the pattern) as a guide, gently push the pieces into the proper size. Check length as well as width and straighten all edges so that they dry evenly.

When all the knit pieces match the pattern measurement exactly, smooth out any bumps with your fingers and then gently press down all over each piece with the palms of your hands to flatten them. Use rustproof pins to pin the work to the padded surface.

Leave the knit pieces to dry thoroughly before removing them from the blocking surface. See ill.

In quilts blocking refers to pressing the quilt. This may be done while the **blocks** are still separate or after they are joined. It is always done before the layers are stacked and the **quilting** begins. If the quilt is blocked before **set**ting, then pressing is required to flatten the seams after it has been set. Also see **Quilts: Pressing.**

Blocking

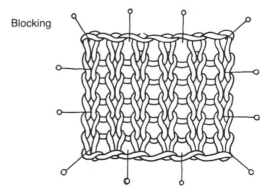

blocking. Metalworking. See **raising techniques** and **Metalworking: Raising.**

blocking. Rugmaking. Weaving. The process of reshaping or stretching a finished **flat rug** or **tapestry** by applying moisture and then fastening it securely to the desired shape and size. The piece should be clean before beginning the process and, if not, this can be done by dipping it into a lukewarm, soapy bath rinsing, and then air-drying it on a flat surface or sponging it with either soapy water or carbon tetrachloride if the yarns are not colorfast. The cleaning process can lead into the blocking process. The actual blocking is done on a flat surface such as a table, floor, or piece of plywood. Wrapping paper or plastic sheets over layers of newspaper can be put on first to protect the working surface or to mark out the shape and size. The item to be blocked is dampened, then tacked on all four sides with nonrusting pins to the flat surface. The amount of moisture is the effective factor in blocking and may have to be extreme if the piece is badly misshapen. If the piece cannot be dipped into water itself, then a bath towel, which has been wrung out in warm water and is still quite wet, is placed on top of the piece. A hot iron is pressed lightly over the towel. It is moved very slowly and with a minimum of pressure, since the object is to force as much steam as possible through the piece and yet not flatten out the piece. If a slight cushion of air space is left under the iron, this will force out more steam than with the iron resting on the towel. This is done over the entire piece with the steaming never going on after the towel has become dry. The damp piece is left to air dry.

The piece may require only repeated **sponging** without steam to get the right shape or at the least a light **steam pressing** with a steam iron, or an ordinary iron and damp cloth.

Blocking is done prior to **hemming** or **binding.** No other **finishing** should be attempted on the rug or woven piece until it is completely dry.

blocking board. Crewel. Embroidery. Needlepoint. Any soft board that tacks can be pushed or hammered into easily for **blocking** a finished piece of needlework. **Chipboard** (or particle board) is recommended.

blocking mold. Glasswork. See **blocking.**

blockout stencil. Silkscreen. The simplest of several methods of producing a **stencil** for silkscreen printing. The screen is blocked, or filled in, in nonimage areas by painting lacquer, glue, or shellac onto the **screen** with an artist's brush. When the material dries, the screen is ready for printing. This method does not lend itself well to intricate work, and the medium used for the blacked areas tends to become brittle and to develop pinholes. However, it is simple to understand and to work, and for some purposes, detail is not important or even desirable.

block pattern. Quilts. The way in which **block**s are **set** together, or joined. Some patterns use blocks on a diagonal; others use them in straight vertical, or horizontal rows. Still other designs are based on interlocking patterns of blocks. The block pattern is an essential aspect of the quilt design. Block design can be set in a number of different block patterns, each giving a new quilt design. Also see **Baby Blocks.**

block patterns. Weaving. **Double cloth** patterns that are possible to make on an 8-**harness loom** that resemble checkerboard effects. This effect is comprised of solid color blocks that appear on both the face and back of the fabric. The blocks can be any width, and the color placement is the weaver's choice, so that it is possible to have blocks alternating between only two colors, or to have them all different colors. The back side could be in totally different block colors from the front if desired, but the size of the blocks would be the same as those on the face side of the fabric. Also see **double cloth.**

block plane. Woodworking. See **plane.**

block print. Block Printing. A print made from a **printing block** on which a design has been cut, inked, and printed on **paper** or fabric. The characteristics of the print largely are determined by the material of the printing block, which can be a **linoleum block, wood block,** or a potato (see **potato block printing**).

BLOCK PRINTING

A printing technique in which designs or patterns are cut in **relief** on a **printing block,** which can be of various materials. Once cut, the block is inked or painted, and printed or stamped on fabric or paper.

Wood block printing is the oldest technique for making relief prints, dating back to Japan around 780 A.D., and has an ancient history in **fabric printing.** Woodcuts were not generally used in Europe until the early fifteenth century, when black line, roughly cut prints were first used for devotional pictures and playing cards. Many of these early prints were colored by hand.

During the early years of block printing there was a division of labor between the artist and the cutter, or engraver. The pen or brush drawings of artists were faithfully reproduced on the block by the engraver. The woodcut was used largely as a means of reproduction, rather than as an art form in itself, as it is today. The prints of Durer and Holbein are astonishing feats of the technical achievement of engravers, reproducing the delicate drawing lines of the artists with skill and accuracy.

In the nineteenth century, artists rediscovered the unique qualities of the woodcut. Artists like Paul Gauguin and Edvard Munch approached the woodcut with a directness of expression that had been lacking; they approached it as an art medium rather than as just a means of reproduction.

Wood engraving, the technique of engraving on the end grain of hardwood, developed toward the late eighteenth century. The work of **Thomas Bewick,** who skillfully used end grain of boxwood to produce detailed engravings, made wood engraving popular and influenced printmaking during the nineteenth century. Contemporary with

Bewick were Edward Calvert and William Blake, both of whom produced original wood engravings. During the nineteenth century, engraving again assumed the primary function of reproduction, with engravers copying artists' work. Later, with the arts and crafts movement in England, came the recognition of the woodcut as a medium of artistic expression.

Perhaps the greatest impact on printmaking in the Western world was the introduction of Japanese woodcuts to Europe in the nineteenth century. Woodcuts, commonly produced in Japan as popular prints, were not highly regarded there, and were sometimes used as packing paper for the porcelains shipped to Europe. These prints were done by a school of painting known as Ukiyoye, which translates as "The Mirror of the Passing Show," and had as its subject matter the humble scenes of daily life. These prints were first drawn by an artist, cut onto the wood block by an engraver, and then printed by a printer.

Oriental art had long been a familiar commodity on the European market (it had been imported since the eighteenth century). However, the style of these colored woodcuts was entirely new. Their solid, flat areas of color and use of common scenes as subject matter were exciting to the eyes of Europeans schooled on the dark tones, modeled volumes, and noble subject matter of academic realism. Artists such as Degas, Cassatt, Toulouse-Lautrec, Van Gogh, Manet, and Whistler were influenced by them.

TOOLS AND MATERIALS For designing, a supply of scratch paper, pencils, tracing paper, tape, India ink or black poster paint, and an eraser will be needed. For cutting blocks, cutting tools and a sharpening stone are necessary. The following materials should be on hand for printing: block printing ink; thinner and solvent; a piece of glass or metal for rolling up ink; a dauber or brayer; a spatula or palette knife for mixing color; the printing paper, with scrap paper for proofs; a burnisher for printing, such as a spoon or a toothbrush handle; and a mallet for cutting woodcuts. Prints should be dried separately to prevent sticking. They can be hung on a clothesline with clothespins or paper clips. For cleaning up, paper towels, newspaper, rags, solvent (benzine, turpentine, or mineral spirits), and water will be needed.

SETTING UP A WORKSHOP Block printing can be done in any well-lighted area where the materials can be permanently stored that is near a source of water for cleaning up. A large work table with solid legs is necessary for cutting and printing. The table should be high enough to work at either standing or sitting on a high stool. All printing materials should be placed within easy reach when the printing begins. The equipment needed for specific techniques will be listed under that particular entry, such as wood block printing.

DESIGNING AND TRANSFERRING In designing for block printing, the characteristics of each medium, such as linoleum block printing, potato block printing, wood block printing, or wood engraving must be considered. Besides the traditional block printing techniques, many variations, such as found object printing, can be experimented with for special effects.

In all block printing techniques the motif is reversed when printed. In some designs this may not be noticeable, but it would be a serious error for lettering to be backward. So a design should be reversed when tracing it to the block: when the final design is completed on paper, it can be transferred to strong tracing paper with India ink or poster paint so that it is visible on the back side as well. A soft pencil is rubbed heavily over the front of the design. When the tracing paper is placed face down on the printing block and the design is traced on the back side, it will be transferred in reverse onto the block. The sheet of tracing paper should be firmly taped to the block, and lines traced with a hard, sharp pencil. When the tracing paper pattern is removed the design on the block can be strengthened with brush or pen and India ink. The block is then ready to be cut.

In designing, remember that the areas cut away will appear as the color of the paper, and the areas left will receive the ink and print. For a positive print the design is cut in relief, protruding from the background, while all areas not to be inked are cut away (a.). For a negative design the pattern is incised, or scooped out of the block (b.). It will be too recessed to receive ink, and therefore will appear white, or the color of the paper, surrounded by an inked background. See ill.

Plans for multicolored prints must be made during the designing stage. A simple version of color printing can easily be achieved by overprinting. Each color is allowed to dry before another one is printed over it. In general, light colors cannot be printed successfully over dark colors; dark colors should be printed over light colors. For prints with several colors, a master design must be executed in poster paints, matching the colors of the block printing ink to be used. Then, using tracing paper, a pattern is made for cutting a separate block for each color. An accurate system of registration is necessary for printing these separate color blocks for a final multicolored fitted print.

CUTTING Before cutting a linoleum block or wood block, experiment with the cutting tools on scraps. Each tool leaves a characteristic mark on the block. Cutting should be done in a comfortable position, with the block supported by a bench hook on the work table. Care must be taken to keep the hand supporting the block behind the knife, away from the direction in which you are cutting. To avoid accidents, never cut with the knife pointing toward your hand. Another common cause of accidents is dull tools, which tend to slide. Always keep cutting tools sharpened with the sharpening stone. Replaceable blades of linoleum tools should be changed as soon as they become dull.

A couple of important points, discussed under Designing and transferring, should be kept in mind. The block will print in reverse, so the pattern must be reversed during tracing. The design may be cut in relief for a positive print, or incised into the surface for a negative print.

When cutting linoleum blocks the edges of the design should be cut at an angle away from the pattern, and care taken not to cut underneath the pattern; if the edges are undercut they may break away. It is sometimes easier to cut the design edges vertically, and perpendicular to the block.

To begin the cutting, first cut lightly, then press more heavily. First cut close to the outlines with a knife. If the pattern is positive, cut outside the drawing line; if it is negative, cut inside the drawing line. All edges are cut with the knife or with a V-shaped tool. Cutting should be about ⅛″ deep, almost down to the web backing of a linoleum block, but not into it. The V-shaped tools are also used to cut small areas, cutting out the fine points of the design by cutting away from the shape. After all the edges are cut, scoop out the background areas with U-shaped tools, always working away from the design and removing the background gradually, in layers. If the background is not cut deeply enough, it will pick up ink and print in an irregular texture. (At times this textured area may be desired as part of the design.) Finally, trim any rough edges on the finished design with the knife blade, then trim the block itself with the knife to clean up the outer edges.

If you should happen to cut into the design by mistake, try to eliminate the mistake by changing the design. See ill.

PRINTING TECHNIQUES Basic printing methods are the same for printing **linoleum block prints** and **wood block** prints as for **wood engravings.** Though a printing press can be used, the block can be printed by burnishing the back of the paper to be printed while it is placed on the inked block. If the **paper** is thin, place a piece of thin cardboard between the **burnisher** and the paper. In burnishing, the tones can be controlled as desired; some parts can be rubbed lightly for a gray tone, while others can be burnished heavily for a dense black. Textures also can be added by uneven burnishing.

To prepare for printing, spread the **block printing ink** on a piece of glass and mix with a spatula, then roll with a **brayer.** Roll the inked brayer backward and forward over the block until the whole surface is evenly covered. Make a test print, called a proof, on scrap paper. The ink is usually used straight from the tube, but it can be thinned with a drop or two of thinner or turpentine. If the print seems weak, the ink may be too dry or there may be insufficient ink on the block. If the color has filled small spaces between the lines of the design, the ink may be too thin. Any corrections in the cutting of the design should also be made at this time.

After thoroughly inking the completed block, the paper is placed over the block and pressed onto it. Pressure must be applied on the back of the paper for a clean print. A clean brayer can be used to press down the paper on the inked design, but usually a burnisher is used. Care must be taken to keep the prints clean. After the block has been inked, the work area should be wiped clean so that no ink is smudged onto the margin of the print.

To dry prints, place them on newspaper to dry or hang them from a line with clothespins or paper clips, keeping the prints separated so that they don't stick together.

A variation of the traditional printing method is printing without ink for a shaped print of white on white forms. The printing paper is soaked in water for five minutes, then excess water is removed between sheets of toweling. The damp, pliant paper is placed on the clean printing block and pressed into the linoleum **relief** shapes with the thumb and the heel of the hand, until the paper has the same shapes as the block. Allow the paper to dry on the block before peeling it off.

Another technique, **offset printing,** is sometimes useful for printing delicate **found object printing** materials, such as feathers.

CARE AND MAINTENANCE OF TOOLS To clean oil-base inks from brushes and tools, rinse them immediately after use in paint thinner or turpentine and rags, then wash in warm, soapy water, rinse well, and dry. The final washing is important; brushes will rot if cleaned only with turpentine. To clean up water-base paints, wash equipment and brushes with soap and water. Then rinse well and let dry.

For the maintenance of **cutting tools,** sharpening is extremely important. The tools should be stored wrapped up in cloth or in a box with a division or section for each tool.

Printing blocks should be cleaned with a stiff brush. Before storing, cover the blocks with cardboard to protect the printing surface from scratches. Store wood blocks away from moisture and heat. The brayer can be dusted with talcum powder when dry.

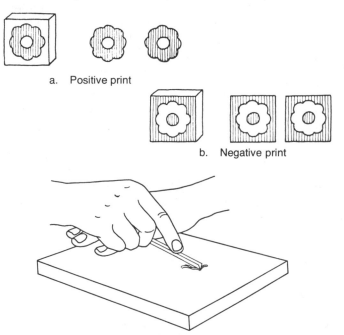

a. Positive print

b. Negative print

Correct position of hands when cutting a block print

block printing. Fabric Printing. The process of **stamping** color by hand on cloth with a **linoleum block, wood block,** or other material into which a design has been cut. Block printing is one of the basic processes in fabric printing; the general block printing procedures are followed using **textile color.**

block printing ink. Block Printing. Oil-base block printing inks with smooth, uniform consistency and varied, bright colors are available in tubes. Water-base block printing inks are also available in tubes. They are opaque and bright, with a smooth, uniform consistency. They are thinned and cleaned with water, and dry very quickly. Textile color is available for printing on fabric.

Ordinary printer's ink, available from printing supply houses, can also be used. Printer's "mixing white" ink can be combined with artist's oil colors or painter's tinting oil colors by mixing about 1 part oil color to 4 parts mixing white.

block quilting design. Quilts. See **Quilts. Quilting.**

blocks. Bookbinding. The dies used to mechanically apply the **title** to a book.

blocks. Toys. (Also called building blocks.) Cubes usually of wood, for building simple structures. These **eternal toys** are a basic type of **constructional toy.** Also see **acrobat, alphabet blocks, architectural playthings, building toy, fabric block** and **Toys: Construction Toys.**

block shading. Crewel. Block shading is extremely effective as a solid filling stitch. The shaded color bands should fit closely together, slightly overlapping the previous row. When used as a **filling stitch** follow the same directional lines as for **long-and-short stitch.**

Outline the shape to be worked with the split stitch to make a firm, even edge. Work the satin stitches over the split stitch foundation. Keep all the stitches close and even (**a.**). Work the second row between the stitches of the previous row (**b.**).

To work around a curve, place the stitches slightly wider apart on the edge and closer in the center to fan them, leaving no visible space between, however. Occasionally slip in a shorter wedge stitch to help fan them (**c.**). See ill. Also see **shading stitch.**

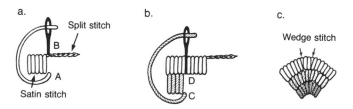

a. Split stitch / Satin stitch   b.   c. Wedge stitch

block weaves. Weaving. **Pattern weaves** whose **drawing-in drafts** are based on a block arrangement. The blocks, in turn, are based on unit combinations of threads. The great variety of the block weave patterns is due to the limitless possibilities in arranging the blocks next to each other and in determining their width. Blocks become **floats** or large areas in a design and stand out as the strongest elements of the pattern. The simplest block weave is **monk's belt** which has a two-block design, 1-2 and 3-4. It belongs to the **overshot** family whose unit combinations of threads are derived from the **twill treadling. Crackle weaves** have some of the more complex block structures, in that it is based on a **point twill drawing-in draft,** which needs extra care in arranging the blocks so a smooth flow in the pattern is achieved. Also see **crackle**

weaves, incidental, monk's belt, overshot, Summer and Winter weave.

bloodstone. Gemcutting. See **quartz.**

blooming. Jewelry. Placing jewelry made of precious or **noble metals** in an **acid** solution to produce a special **matte** surface. The formula for one such solution, **matte dip,** is: 65% concentrated nitric acid, 35% concentrated sulfuric acid, and 1 lb. zinc sulphate ($ZnSO_4$ commercial) per gallon of solution. This formula works especially well on gold and was first used in the Victorian period.

Immerse the complete, polished piece in the solution for several minutes. Agitate it occasionally, and rinse thoroughly. A **resist** such as **asphaltum varnish** can be used to block out areas that are to remain shiny.

When the solution is worn out it should be replaced, or metals in the solution will redeposit on new work and create discoloration. Also see **bright dip, pickling tongs,** and **Jewelry: Safety Precautions.**

blooming. Rugmaking. Weaving. Dyeing. The opening up or swelling of a yarn when it comes into contact with water. With some man-made fibers, it need only be the moisture in the air that will bloom out the cut ends of a yarn.

Also, the brightening of a dyestuff due to exposure to air (**indigo**) or a certain **mordant** (**tin**).

Blooming Leaf of Mexico. Weaving. See **overshot.**

blossom filling. Lacemaking. See **leaf stitch.**

blow. Metalworking. See **blow hole.**

blower. Glasswork. See **gaffer.**

blower. Metalworking. A mechanical or electrical fan device that has largely replaced the **bellows** for directing a stream of air into the **forge** for **blacksmithing.** When **forging** small items, an electric hair dryer may be used, or other equivalents may be devised from home appliances with fans.

blowhole. Jewelry. A small hole left within a **box construction** or **hollow construction** to prevent the construction from imploding or exploding. An implosion will destroy the work; an explosion can destroy your eyesight. Also, an unwanted pit or hole left in a **casting** caused by gas trapped during the pouring of the metal.

blow hole. Metalworking. (Also called blow.) A hole in welded or cast metal caused by gas, steam, dirt, or grease trapped within the metal. In casting it may be caused by insufficient **venting** of the mold, or excessively hard **tamping** of the **molding sand** in a sand mold (which prevents the escape of these materials). It can also occur when welding **cast iron** when too-rapid melting of the metal vaporizes bits of matter in the metal. Watch for these cavities in the weld **puddle** area and get rid of them by making the puddles large and hot enough so that the metal under the hole liquefies, closes the hole, and floats any particles to the top of the molten metal.

blowing iron. Glasswork. (Also called blowing pipe.) The hollow mild steel (or better, stainless steel) pipe used to draw molten glass from a tank furnace and through which the glassblower blows to fill glass vessels. The iron is usually 5′ long and ¾″ in outside diameter and has an enlarged nose at the glass-gathering end. Before drawing a **gather** from the furnace, the nose of the iron is heated to just short of red heat so that the glass will stick to the iron without scale forming, and leaving impurities in the molten glass. Also see **parison.**

blow molding. Plastics. A **thermoforming** process in which a heat-softened sheet of plastic is shaped by blown air pressing it against a **mold.** One may use a vacuum cleaner for the air source in home studio use, but the piece must be very small because the air tends to cool larger pieces before they form thoroughly. For larger pieces, an air compressor and heating element are necessary. Blow molding is also an economical commercial method for the mass production of hollow plastic parts.

blown egg. Toys. See **hollow egg.**

blowpipe. Enameling. See **torch.**

blow pipe. Glasswork. See **blowing iron.**

blowpipe. Jewelry. Typically a hollow tube of tapered metal that is curved at one end. The broader end is placed in the mouth, and the smaller curved end is placed at the source of flame, which can be an **alcohol lamp,** oil lamp, or a bunsen burner. The flame is produced by blowing through the blowpipe into the flame source. It produces a fine, pointed flame that is hot enough to solder small intricate work. There are several types of blowpipes. One collects saliva in a small, removable hollow ball and one can be hooked up to a gas tube.

Blowpipes take some getting used to as far as breath control goes. You must learn to breathe only through your nose and expel the air through the blowpipe. Never inhale through the blowpipe especially while it is in the flame, as you will pull the flame into your mouth and possibly your lungs.

The blowpipe is one of the earliest tools used to control and direct heat in soldering, and it is still widely used throughout the world today.

blowpipe. Toys. A hollow tube, such as a section of bamboo or cornstalk, through which air can be forced or blown. The **peashooter, whirligig,** and **flipperdinger** all use blowpipe construction.

blue jeans. Stitchery. Pants, made of **denim** or **jean,** usually blue in color. Popular from the 1940s into the 1980s, denim art developed as jeans were painted, embroidered,

stitched and **appliqué**d. This art form is related to "pop" or funk and people's art.

blue-jean quilt. Quilts. Any quilt made up primarily from worn blue **jeans** or faded blue **denim** pants. The soft blues are usually used for the **blocks,** with embroidery or **appliqué** on top of them. Occasionally old quilts are found that are **pieced** from all denim **patch**es, but it wasn't until the early 1970s that blue denim was so in vogue that it was used frequently in quilts.

blue paper. Lacemaking. A lightweight blue tissue paper used in **appliqué** lace construction.

blue pencil. Stitchery. A pointed marking pencil, similar to **tailor's chalk** for marking white **fabrics.** It supposedly rubs off, though occasionally blurs remain which stubbornly resist brushing. To mark a line or an area for embroidery or **appliqué** it is sometimes helpful to make a series of dots or broken lines rather than a heavy solid line. That avoids the possibility of a smear on a **panel** which would not ordinarily be laundered.

blue resist quilt. Quilts. Any Early American **coverlet** made by a resist process of dyeing, one of the oldest methods of fabric design. A gum or paste that resisted dye was applied to a fabric, usually **homespun.** The fabric was then put into a dyebath of contrasting color. After dyeing, the resist was removed, leaving the two-color pattern. Such coverlets are associated with the Hudson River Valley, where many beautiful specimens were made.

bluing. Metalworking. The process of dulling and darkening a shiny metal to a bluish-black color to improve its appearance and reduce rusting (Note: it will not entirely prevent rusting). The process is most often used on guns to dull the shiny metal parts that would reflect light and thus frighten game or attract the attention of an enemy. Browning is an old English term synonymous with bluing in the United States.

There are several basic methods of bluing. The first method—painting on a ready-mixed paint or **lacquer**—is temporary. The second, the time-consuming traditional method of bluing, uses chemicals, heat, and water to give a permanent finish. Wood parts must first be removed from the metal because bluing ruins the wood. The old metal finish and rust should be removed with an **abrasive** cloth and the surface brought to a high polish before the metal is cleaned with benzine or gasoline and wiped dry. The metal is then dipped in a hot bath of caustic soda (lye) in a **galvanized** tank to further clean and degrease it. This is followed by a thorough rinsing in boiling water. Now the metal is ready to be dipped in or swabbed with any of several basic bluing solutions, which may be either purchased ready-made from a gun supply house or prepared from purchased chemicals mixed together at home. After soaking for 20 minutes the metal is dried and rubbed with steel wool or a soft wire brush to remove any rust. The dipping or swabbing process may have to be repeated up to 10 times until the desired finish is obtained. When ready, the blued metal is dried and rubbed with linseed or mineral oil while it is still warm.

Parkerizing is another darkening process, similar to bluing, in which the metal is first sandblasted and then boiled in a mixture of powdered **iron** and phosphoric acid.

Heat-treated metals may not accept the bluing. If so, the metal must be swabbed with nitric acid until it turns black, then rinsed in hot water before bluing. **Stainless steel** also requires special preparation. Grease and oil must be removed with alcohol. Then the metal is swabbed with a coppering solution of **sulphuric acid**, distilled water, and dissolved copper sulphate until a **copper** coating appears. Next the metal is treated with **nitric acid** until it turns black, and then rinsed. Then it is ready for the bluing process.

blunger. Ceramics. A machine used to mix clay and water to produce **slip.** It has paddles which turn at slow speeds and agitate the slip, breaking down the chunks of coarse clay and thoroughly mixing them. The drawback to the blunger is that it is time consuming. Also see **dough mixer, propeller mixer.**

blunt needle. Crewel. Embroidery. Needlepoint. See **tapestry needle.**

blunts. Stitchery. See **needle.**

blur. Plastics. See **crazing.**

blusher. Toys. Powdered makeup in rose and pink tones that can be used to add color to stuffed **nylon stocking doll**s. The blusher is brushed on to give a lifelike color to the face.

blushing. Plastics. See **cloudiness.**

board. Bookbinding. The rigid material used to cover books. Various weights are used, depending on the material being bound. Boards, such as **binder's board,** are commercially available but they may also be made by laminating layers of thin cardboard to the desired thickness; a board made by this method will be stiffer than a single sheet of the same thickness. Boards are covered wholly or partially with **paper, cloth, leather,** or a combination of these materials. Also see **backing board, casemaking, cutting board, flexible cover, grooving board, pressing board, split board.**

board. Woodworking. See **wood.**

board foot. Woodworking. See **wood.**

board game. Toys. A **game** played on a specially marked **game board** over which pieces move. Chinese checkers, chess, and backgammon are well-known board games.

boarding. Leather. Folding and rubbing two skins against each other to produce a **grain.** Boarding is done by hand and is mostly used commercially.

board paper. Bookbinding. A single sheet of paper glued to the inside of the **board**s that covers the overlap of the material used on the outside of the boards and cloth **hinge**s or **joint**s. It is trimmed to ⅛" of the **head, tail,** and **foredge** and overlaps the cloth hinge or jointed **endpaper** by approximately ⅛". See ill.

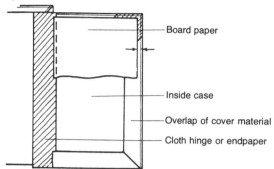

board swing. Toys. The most common kind of **swing,** made from a board and two ropes. The board should be wide enough to accommodate the rider and deep enough to be comfortable. A hole is drilled near each end. A single rope may go down through one hole, under the seat, and up through the other hole, tying the ends of the rope to a tree or beam. Two separate ropes may be used, one at each side, each of which is knotted under the board. In either case it is referred to as a double **rope swing,** as there are two points of connection on the tree.

boart. Gemcutting. See **diamond.**

boat. Toys. A small floating toy craft that may be moved by sails or by pulling an attached **string,** by pushing, or by letting it ride with a current. These floating toys, made of wood or plastic, are often used as **bath toy**s.

A few **wheeled toy**s are made in the form of boats without being intended for water. Some **Noah's ark**s, for example, are not meant to be set afloat. **Folk toy**s include boats propelled by **paddle wheel**s, some of which use tightly wound **rubber band**s to set the paddle wheels in motion. These **rubber band toy**s are easily operated or repaired. Other small boats, set in motion by the action of camphor, are known as **camphor toy**s. **Magnetic toy**s include boats moved over the surface of the water by magnetic attraction. Also see **beach toy, paddle wheel boat.**

boat shuttle. Weaving. (Also called roller shuttle, throw shuttle.) A shuttle in a shape resembling a boat and with a hollowed-out section in the center containing a small spool or **bobbin** containing the **filling** yarn. Boat shuttles are made of wood and used on **loom**s giving a **shed** wide enough so that they can be thrown through the shed from **selvage** to selvage. There is a slot or hole in the center of one side of the shuttle through which the filling yarn comes. This slot faces the weaver during the weaving process. The yarn winds off the center of the bobbin which rotates automatically (a.). Boat shuttles come in a variety of shapes, styles, and sizes. The average size is about 11"−13". There are shapes that leave the bobbin completely open, which allows it to carry a little more yarn, and others that enclose it on one side. A roller shuttle is fitted with rollers on the underside that propel it very quickly through the shed. It is especially useful for weaving wide fabrics (**b.**). A double bobbin shuttle has open sections for two separate bobbins so that two colors can be used simultaneously (**c.**). An industrial model carries a spool that does not rotate and the yarn feeds off through one end of the shuttle (**d.**). See ill. Also see **bobbin winding**.

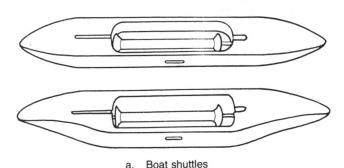
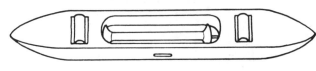
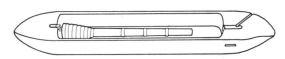

a. Boat shuttles

b. Roller shuttle

c. Double bobbin shuttle

d. Power loom boat shuttle

bob. Lacemaking. See **picot**.

bob. Stenciling. One of the earliest tools used in stenciling, a bob is used to apply paint through stencils to achieve effects of shading and texturing. It consists of a piece of fine wool fabric wrapped around a small pad of cotton and tied to the end of a stick. See ill.

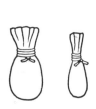

a. Small and large wool bobs

b. Chamois bob with stick handle

bobbin. Kites. See **reel**.

bobbin. Lacemaking. A tool used in **bobbin lace** upon which thread is wound; slightly weighted, it also aids in pulling the fine thread into position. Bobbins are made of wood, bone, metal, glass, or plastic. A bobbin is basically a shaft 4″–5″ long with an area for winding the thread, called the spool, and a head.

Beads or **spangle**s are not only beautiful, decorative additions to bobbins, but also functional ones. Not all bobbins have these; their use depends on the type of lace being made. The beads or spangles are strung on a fine wire, which goes through a hole in the tip of the butt end of the shaft. There are usually seven beads, three on each side of a larger and more decorative bead. The beads serve to give added weight and to keep the bobbin from rolling on the **pillow** (which would untwist the thread) during the lacemaking. Each bobbin design had a functional origin, depending on the use of the bobbin in the particular type of lace.

At the beginning of the lacework, wind the bobbins and place a pin into the start of the pattern, which is in position on the pillow. Hang one **pair of bobbins** on the pin; hang the other pair around the same pin so that the middle threads cross; twist the pairs and cross. This makes a **cloth stitch** around the pin, and is known as hanging two pairs from a pin.

To add a pair of bobbins, place a pin in the lacework where another pair is needed, hang the new pair as a **passive** on the pin, and work the twisted **worker**s through. When adding on a curve, add the new pair on the outside of the curve. To take out pairs on a curve, do it on the inner side of the curve.

When taking out a pair of bobbins, place the pair back out of the way and cut it off later when the work is quite thick and the passives will not unravel. Always add or take out one pair at a time, spaced evenly throughout the row. See ill. Also see **bobbin head, bobbin winding**.

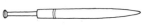

a. Single-head Belgian bobbin

b. Single-head Honiton bobbin

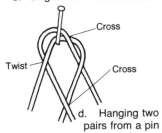

c. Double-head bobbin with spangles

d. Hanging two pairs from a pin

bobbin. Macramé. Small rectangular pieces of cardboard, plastic, or wood—narrower in the middle than at the two ends—around which macramé **cord** or yarn is wound to prevent tangling as the macramé is knotted. As the work progresses, the yarn is gradually unwound from the bobbin. Also see **butterfly, hand bobbin**.

bobbin. Spinning. Weaving. A wooden or plastic **spool** about 4″ long that is used to carry the **filling** yarn in a **boat shuttle**. The flanged edge, or rim, prevents the yarn from slipping off the spool during **bobbin winding** or weaving.

Sometimes the term "bobbin" is used when referring to large spools used for **warping**. It also has become a form of habit to call a **paper quill**, a bobbin.

Also, a general term used in **tapestry** weaving when referring to any one of a number of **tapestry tools** used to carry the assorted and numerous filling yarns. Chief among these would be the **Goeblin bobbin, Swedish bobbin,** and Aubusson bobbin or **flute**. Also see **bobbin winder, butterfly, flyer assembly, shuttle, spindle, spindle shaft, treadle wheel.**

bobbinet. Stitchery. **Cotton net** made up of hexagonal openings which appear to be round. Sometimes made of **nylon** or **silk,** it comes in a variety of colors.

bobbing. Jewelry. Metalworking. The removal of scratches from metal either by **hand polishing** or with a bobbing wheel used on a **buffing machine**. Also see **bobbing compound, buffing, buffing compound, polishing compound.**

bobbing compound. Jewelry. An abrasive compound used with a solid felt or leather **bobbing wheel** with rounded edges. Bobbing compound can be used on all metals, but as it is very abrasive and wears metal away quickly, care must be taken when using it, and the work checked frequently to make sure that too much is not being removed too quickly. Also see **buffing compound, cutting compound, greaseless compound.**

bobbin head. Lacemaking. The part of the **bobbin** that holds the **half hitch,** which in turn holds the thread on the bobbin during lacemaking.

After the thread is wound on the bobbin, make a half hitch and place it directly under the head (if it is a single-headed bobbin). If it is a double-headed bobbin (a bobbin with a groove or indentation in the bobbin head), the half hitch is placed in the groove.

bobbin knitting. Knitting. When more than one color is used in geometric or **Argyle knitting,** the different colors of yarn are wound on individual plastic bobbins rather than worked from separate balls of yarn. This is done to keep the colors separate when they are not being worked. Bobbins are used in these types of knitting because the colors tend to be used in isolated blocks, or sections, rather than continuously. As the knitting progresses, the yarn can be unwound one turn of the bobbin at a time. Also see **geometric knitting** and **Knitting: Tools and Materials.**

bobbin lace. Lacemaking. Lace made on a **pillow** by **twist**ing and **cross**ing threads attached to **bobbin**s. It is sometimes called pillow lace, but because **needle lace** may also be made on a pillow, it is more correctly referred to as bobbin lace. Pin lace and bone lace are other terms sometimes used; bobbin lace may be worked around a support of pins, and bone is used as a material for making bobbins.

Sometimes a bobbin lace of extremely fine quality is called point lace; "point" more correctly is applied to **needle lace.** Also see **Lacemaking.**

bobbin lace. Weaving. See **meshwork.**

bobbin lace filet. Lacemaking. **Filet** lace done with bobbins having the same square mesh look as **knotted lace filet.** It is an uncommon type of lace.

To make this filet **mesh, twist** and **passive**s once or twice, depending on the size of the mesh and thread used. Then pass the **leader** through the passives. Place a pin at about every other crossing of the passives and leader to keep the filet in alignment. Then, with the **darning stitch,** work in the design as done in the knotted lace filets.

bobbin pulley. Spinning. A small, round, grooved piece called a **whorl** on the **spindle shaft** of a **treadle wheel.** The **driving band** goes around it, as well as around the **spindle pulley,** so that when the wheel is activated the **bobbin** will revolve. Also see **flyer assembly.**

bobbin quill. Weaving. See quill.

bobbin rack. Weaving. See **spool rack.**

bobbin winder. Weaving. A machine for winding yarn on **bobbin**s or **quill**s. It can be operated either by hand or electricity. A hand bobbin winder is attached to the rim of a table or shelf, and consists of a tapered metal shaft to place the bobbin or quill on, and a handle with which to turn the shaft by way of interlocking gears (**a.**). An electric bobbin winder also has a metal shaft which can be either tapered or made in two sections that hold the bobbin or quill between them. The shaft and motor are on a stand which sits on a flat surface. A foot pedal activates the electric motor that spins the shaft. An electric bobbin winder is expensive, but it turns much faster than a hand operated one and also leaves both hands free to guide the yarn (**b.**). See ill.

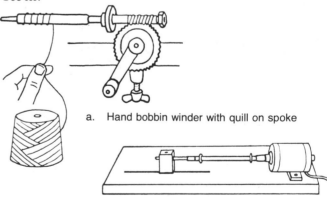

a. Hand bobbin winder with quill on spoke

b. Electric bobbin winder holding an empty plastic bobbin

bobbin winding. Lacemaking. Wind the thread on the shaft section of the bobbin. It is best not to overwind the **bobbin;** the thread may become entangled or slip off it. Wind the thread either by hand or with bobbin winders, obtainable from lace suppliers. Place a firm even pressure on the thread as it is being wound; a soft winding will tend to become very loose, and the thread will become tangled. Also see **bobbin head, half hitch.**

bobbin winding. Weaving. The process of winding the **filling** yarn on a **bobbin** or a **quill** using a **bobbin winder.**

Both yarn carriers fit on a pin set into the grooved-out center of a **boat shuttle.** The yarn must be wound in such a manner that the yarn carrier will fit into the center groove and feed off smoothly through the slot in the shuttle's side. In starting the bobbin winding, the filling yarn is wound around the center of the bobbin or quill, rather than tied to it. The edges are wound and built up first, and the center filled in last. (In weaving, the yarn feeds off the center first and then the sides.) The hand guides the yarn in a back and forth movement so that no uneven, lumpy areas appear. In addition, the hand controls the tension of the filling yarn as it comes off the **spool, cone,** or **skein** so that the bobbin or quill is firmly wound. "Spongy," or too tight bobbin winding, will only result in a poorly wound yarn carrier that will give trouble during weaving. Bobbins should be wound straight across and no wider than the flanged edges of the spool. A quill is fuller in the center and, in addition, must be quite firmly wound so that the yarn does not roll off at the edges and become tangled around the shuttle pin. See ill.

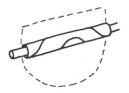

a. Homemade quill

b. Quill with yarn around it

c. Quill during bobbin winding

d. Wound quill inserted in boat shuttle

bobble. Knitting. (Abbr. mb.) A bobble is an embossed (or raised) **motif** somewhat similar to, but more versatile

Bobble

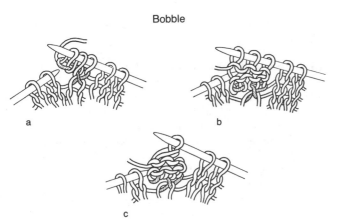

a

b

c

than, a popcorn pattern. The bobble is based on **increasing** (or adding stitches) within one existing stitch, and working the increased stitches backward and forward several times (according to the particular pattern) to create the raised bobble before knitting all the increased stitches together to complete the original stitch. See ill. Also see **knitting: Stitches and Patterns.**

bobble. Macramé. (Also called bead knot, flat knot, shell knot, small ball.) A small, tightly worked "ball" made of square knots.

Begin the bobble by making a **sennit** of 4 or more square knots. (In working this, remember that the bobble will be located at the point of the first square knot. Choose your beginning point accordingly.) Bring the two center cords of the sennit up and put them between the two center cords above the first square knot worked. Pull these 2 cords down tightly behind to make the sennit loop back over itself, forming a small, raised "ball." To finish and secure the bobble, tie one final square knot tightly underneath the bobble. See ill.

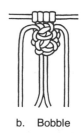

b. Bobble

a. Square knots

bodkin. Basketry. A tool, like an **awl** used to make spaces in the weaving of a basket for adding **stakes** for strength, **handles,** etc. Use a bodkin as you would any ordinary hand awl. Hold both the basket and bodkin firmly. Place the tip of the bodkin into the opening that you want to enlarge and push slowly, exerting pressure with the palm of the hand until the desired depth is reached. Bodkins come in a variety of sizes and shapes. The choice of bodkin depends on the size and strength of the material being woven. The most common type is the straight bodkin. See ill.

Bodkin

bodkin. Rugmaking. Weaving. A term of uncertain but very old origin with a range of meaning from a dagger to a **blunt needle.** In Shakespeare, there is a reference to "a bare bodkin," meaning a dagger. In needlework, a bodkin refers to a sharp, pointed implement made of steel, bone, wood, or ivory and used to pierce holes into cloth—an "eyeleteer."

Also, a needlelike instrument with a large eye and a blunt, knobbed point used for drawing tape or ribbon through a loop or **hem.** When used this way, it is sometimes known as a tape needle.

Bodkins are used in rugmaking for lacing braids together in making **braided rug**s and in weaving for working on **Frame** or **cardboard loom**s. They can be homemade from a toothbrush with the brush part snapped off and the remainder sanded down to a blunt point. Its counterpart is now found in some weaving supply stores, and it is a wooden needle with a large eye for carrying heavy yarn, and is often much longer than the toothbrush bodkin. Also see **needle weaving, rug needle.**

bodkin. Stitchery. Toys. A thick blunt **needle** of steel, ivory, or bone, used as an awl (to force holes through **fabric**) or for sewing. Some Alaskan bone bodkins have an eye at the center with points on each end, and are in addition marked in increments for measuring. Bodkins are ancient devices, serving as **stiletto**s or stitching tools.

body. Batik and Tie-dye. Quilts. Stitchery. The degree of stiffness and bulk in a **fabric**. A fabric with good body tends to hold its own shape and is therefore easier to handle. A heavy body is suitable for **machine appliqué** and a medium body for **hand appliqué.**

body. Ceramics. See **clay body** and **Ceramics: Form.**

body. Puppets. See **skeleton.**

body art. Any art form applied directly to or related specifically to the shape of the human figure. Both **tattoos** and **body paintings** are forms of body art. Many **body coverings** are referred to by this more general term, particularly those which are shaped for the body such as **breastplates** or helmets.

body coverings. A term used to loosely describe and include anything which covers the body. It suggests a flexible approach to clothing, free of set ideas or restrictions, and many encompass the entire range from **tattoos** to blankets. In exhibitions, body coverings or **body art** refer to highly individualized, creative garments which are usually, though not always, wearable. Sometimes called body wear, these costumes are in general a reaction against anonymous mass-produced clothes. Also see **Stitchery: Stitchery Forms.**

bodyless puppet. Puppets. A **puppet** that consists of a head only and for which the **puppeteer**'s hand is the body.

body loom. Weaving. See **backstrap loom.**

body putty. Plastics. An **epoxy** putty with **fillers** designed to repair dents in automobiles. In craftwork it may be used with **reinforcing material** and rods to cast objects in **molds.** It may be easily sanded and painted.

body stain. Ceramics. The use of oxides and prepared **stains** to produce colored bodies. Colored clay bodies produce interesting results when **glazed** because some of the color of the **clay** body shows through, and also may alter the colors on the glazes used.

Bohemian glass. Glasswork. A variety of **soda-lime glass** that includes potash, which gives the glass exceptional clarity. Bohemian glassmakers in the eighteenth century perfected this type of glass, burning acres of trees to produce small quantities of the necessary potash. Bohemian glassware was often ornately decorated with **prunt**s and **knop**s and fluted stems.

Bohus knitting. Knitting. A style of knitting developed by peasant knitters in Bohus country on the outskirts of Götenborg, Germany. Bohus knitting is characterized by embossed effects obtained by knitting some of the stitches in reversed stocking stitch background. This style of knitting cleverly employs the use of the **slipped stitch** to achieve a multicolored effect. Also see **color knitting.**

boilfast color. Batik and Tie-dye. Stitchery. A term used on the labels of yarns, threads, or **fabric**s to indicate that they will not lose color in boiling. This does not necessarily indicate that the color is fast to other conditions, such as sunlight.

boiling. Batik and Tie-dye. A simple means of **removing wax** from the **batik fabric.** While wax removal can be accomplished in a variety of ways, boiling can be used only on those **dyes** that are **colorfast** and will not be removed by boiling. Fabric dyed with **vat dye**s and **fiber-reactive dye**s can be boiled; those with all-purpose **household dye**s cannot. Some wax can first be shaken or flaked off. The fabric is then placed in a large container (any metal) of hot water to which soap powder or mild detergent has been added, using about a teaspoonful per pint of water. Strong detergents should be avoided, as they may weaken the color. As the water boils, wax moves to the surface and can be skimmed off. The material should be constantly agitated as it is boiled. When all wax has been boiled out, remove the fabric and rinse thoroughly.

boiling-off. Spinning. Weaving. See **degumming.**

bolt. Basketry. (Also called bundle.) The quantity in which commercial **willow** is sold. A bolt is 37" in girth, measured 8"–12" from the **butt** end.

bolt. Metalworking. Woodworking. A straight metal shaft, usually with a head at one end, used to fasten two or more pieces of any hard material (such as wood, metal, or plastic) together. All or part of the shaft may be threaded, and a nut with corresponding threads is twisted onto the headless end. (In distinction, a screw is tapered and thus cannot take a nut.) A washer may be used to distribute the pressure of the head and nut over a larger area if the materials being joined are relatively soft, or to help keep the nut from working loose.

  a. Stove bolts are small and fully threaded; the round or flat heads are slotted to accept a screwdriver. Common sizes are from ⅛" to ½" in diameter and ⅜" to 6" long.
  b. Carriage bolts have unslotted round heads with smaller square collars to keep them from turning in the

wood. The shanks are threaded only on the end. Common sizes are from $^3/_{16}''$ to $^3/_4''$ in diameter and $^3/_4''$ to 20" long.

c. Machine bolts have square or hexagonal flat heads, no collar, and are only partially threaded. Common sizes are from $^3/_{16}''$ to $^3/_4''$ in diameter and $^3/_4''$ to 30" long.

d. A stud bolt is a machine bolt without a head. Both ends are threaded to accept nuts, which permits extra tightening. Sizes are similar to machine bolts. See ill.

e. Lag bolts, being tapered, are really **screws** with unslotted heads.

Molly bolts and toggle bolts are really stove bolts with expanding nuts that may be inserted and secured from outside a hollow wall.

To use a bolt, drill a hole the size of the shank through the pieces to be joined. Place a washer, if needed, over the shank and insert the bolt into the hole. Place the second washer over the threaded end and start the nut by hand, turning it clockwise. Use the appropriate screwdriver and wrench, or two wrenches, to tighten.

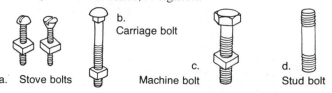

bolting. Metalworking. Woodworking. The process of fastening metal, wood, or other materials together using **bolts**. It is used where a semipermanent joint is desired so that the assembly may be taken apart if desired.

bolt tongs. Metalworking. See **tongs**.

bond. Mosaics. (Also called bonding agent.) Any **adhesive** material such as **glue** or **mortar** used to bind or fix **mosaic** materials to the **backing**. Also see **Mosaics: Tools and Materials, Setting the Material.**

bonded fabric. Stitchery. Toys. A term given to **fabric**s or **fiber**s which have been treated in either of two distinct ways. One is a process in which fibers are pressed into thin sheets and are held together by adhesive or plastic. In this sense, **interfacing**s and webbings are bonded. The second is a process in which a woven fabric has a layer of some other material adhered to it, such as the adhesive added to **cotton** in an **iron-on tape**. The bonded fabrics made by the second process are also referred to as **laminated fabric**s. Also see **backed material.**

bonded mat. Plastics. See **glass fiber**.

bonded polyester filler. Quilts. See **glazed polyester filler.**

bonding. Plastics. (Also called joining.) The joining of pieces of plastic. The four basic types of bonding are: mechanical fastening by means of metalworking or woodworking hardware; **adhesive** bonding; heat or thermal bonding by use of a heating device that softens the plastic surfaces and welds them together; and **cementing,**

using solvents to soften the surfaces and fuse them together. Also see **fastening device, heat bonding,** and **Plastics: Cementing.**

bonding agent. Mosaics. See **bond**.

bonding leather. Leather. See **Leatherwork: Gluing and Bonding Leather.**

bonding material. Gemcutting. See **grinding wheel**.

bonding tape. Stitchery. A tape which has an adhesive backing, usually set by heat. Some bonding tapes are heavy-duty and may be used for **hemming** heavy materials in **banner**s. Other bonding tapes are made of lightweight **fabric**s and are referred to as **iron-on tape**s. Bonding tapes may also be used for mending or for reinforcing areas where **grommet**s are to be attached.

bone. Beadwork. See **found object beads**.

bone. Ivory and Bone Carving. Bone is organic matter in a framework of calcium and phosphorus that forms the skeletons of vertebrates. Bone has a hardness of $2-3$ and a specific gravity of $1.90-2.10$.

Bone has agricultural, industrial, culinary, and craft application. It produces fats for soap, candles, and glue; oils; and gelatin. Ground bone is used as a fertilizer; bone ash is used in the manufacture of porcelain and, treated with acid, can be used as a substitute for cream of tartar in baking. Heated bone furnishes us with bone black, which is used in shoepolish and black varnish; this charcoal is also used as a filter to purify numerous materials. In crafts, bone is used for beads, buttons, tool handles, body ornaments, and for carving and inlay.

Bone is sometimes blatantly misrepresented as being **ivory,** but is considered inferior as well as less romantic and refined. It is harder, more porous, more likely to break, and yellows more slowly than ivory. It acquires black streaks that ivory does not. Bone has been used in many of the ways that ivory has, such as for tool handles, inlaying material, and **scrimshaw;** they are similarly worked. Also see **Ivory and Bone Carving.**

bone ash. Ceramics. Refined calcium phosphate. Bone ash is used as a body ingredient in **bone china.** When used as a **glaze flux,** bone ash lowers the recommended firing temperature and increased translucency.

bone china. Ceramics. A **china** similar to **porcelain** that includes bone ash to lower the maturing temperature at which it is fired. It is extremely hard and very translucent. The **clay body** has a low level of **plasticity** and cannot be used for throwing.

bone folder. Bookbinding. A smooth flat blade of bone or ivory with a square, curved, or pointed tip. It is used to crease folds in paper and for **smoothing,** forming **grooves, rubbing down,** and slitting paper along a fold. Plastic folders are also available but are not recommended because they can streak materials. Also see **polisher.**

bone folder. Leather. See **folder.**

bone lace. Lacemaking. See **bobbin lace.**

Bony, Paul. Stained Glass. The stained glass craftsman who executed the window designs of **Matisse** and **Rouault.**

bookbinders press. Bookbinding. See **book press.**

BOOKBINDING

Bookbinding is done to join separate leaves or **sections** into a unit, to provide a protective cover for the material so that it may be shared and used by many and still endure, and to carry upon the cover and **spine,** its identification. **Forwarding** includes the operations of **folding, collating, trimming,** preparation of **endpapers,** sewing the **sections** together, **backing,** and **back lining**—i.e., all the necessary steps to make a book except for the finishing operations. Finishing procedures involve the final decorative aspects of the craft: **titling,** stamping, and decorating the edges and cover of the book. The craft of bookbinding is quite often applied to the rebinding of books.

Before beginning, consideration must be given to the size, thickness, and number of books to be bound and the type and amount of **paper** and other materials that will be used. Planning is necessary as to the particular requirements related to the usage of the text (in terms of the degree of abuse it must withstand, or whether or not it must lay flat when opened to be most useful, etc.). Materials are expensive, so amounts should be carefully calculated to avoid waste. The time, output of labor, and money for each task must be measured against the value of the material to be bound or rebound. Bookbinding is a slow and unvarying process, and a great deal of experience is necessary to execute the task successfully. Through inexperience it is easy to permanently damage what it is intended to salvage or protect.

Rarely is bookbinding as an art or craft exhibited in museums or galleries, except where illustrations within the binding are the focal point or in cases where special editions have been commissioned by famous artists employing book binders to execute their designs. It is expensive to have bookbinding done for you, and expensive to do yourself. What most draws people to the craft is the wish to repair a treasured volume, or to consolidate notes, manuscripts, drawings, journals, or magazines. It is possible to bind books using little equipment and a lot of imagination; machines can be adapted to perform several functions instead of one by the addition of a few accessories. Bindings can be made without any tools at all, as exemplified by bookbinding's history.

The oldest writing was "cunei-form," meaning "wedge-shaped" and was executed with a wedge-shaped stylus pressed into clay and then baked to produce clay tablets. On such tablets were recorded the laws and history of ancient Assyria. They were kept in the king's library and were accessible to only a chosen few. Bookbinding did not develop until centuries after these first books, but the as-

sociation between writing and binding is inseparable. The birth of the one necessitated the development of the other.

The most primitive binding together of separate pieces began with Brahmin scriptures. These were strips of bark with characters engraved in them with a stylus and bound together with string. In later varieties the characters were executed on linen, brass, copper, and gold. The Indians also marked palm leaves, rubbed black pigment into the marks to accentuate them, and strung the leaves together with cord. Bark and palm leaves were too perishable to provide enough permanence for the records people desired to keep.

Five thousand years ago it was discovered that the sturdy papyrus plant that grew along the banks of the Nile River in Egypt could be rendered into an enduring medium for writing. Thin strips of the papyrus plant were pounded until flat, then pressed into matted layers. They were then polished with ivory until soft, pasted end to end, and rolled on a stick. They were unrolled to be read and then rerolled for storage. Papyrus scrolls were drawn with hieroglyphics (or "priests' writing") and were owned only by kings, priests, and a few scholars. The ancient Greeks and Romans used papyrus.

A more efficient method than rolling was eventually devised—the folding of single sheets of papyrus in half and tying them together. This form of book is called a "codex." Most of the early Christian writings were in codices. Thus the book in the form we are familiar with today emerged.

In the Middle Ages sheep or calfskin parchment replaced papyrus. The famous illuminated manuscripts were lovingly and artistically rendered from the papyrus to parchment by Christian monks. In fact, there was a monastic monopoly on literary activity from the fifth to the fourteenth century. With colored inks they recopied the biblical books, decorating the borders with elaborate designs in colors and gold leaf. Leather covers were made to protect the manuscripts and keep the parchment from curling, and book boxes, the forerunner of **slipcases,** were constructed to keep them in. Some bindings were designed to accept chains that shackled them to the walls of the monasteries so that they couldn't be stolen. Some manuscripts were bound in carved wood covers held together with metal clasps or leather lacing; the wood most often used was beech, which in German is *buche,* the probable derivation of the word "book."

The Benedictines were leaders in copying manuscripts and building libraries. They had unlimited time and the finest materials to provide unrivaled workmanship in their bindings. Because parchment was reserved for pious writings, many a pagan author's work was painstakingly removed from the parchment, which was then reused by the monks. These writings can be detected under the writings of the monks with the aid of fluoroscopes and infrared photography. These documents are called palimpsests.

The Byzantine bindings are remarkable for their lavish use of color, gold, and ivory. In A.D. 332 Emperor Constantine commanded that 50 magnificent and elaborate manuscripts of the scriptures be distributed to the churches of the realm. When Constantinople fell in 1453, Byzantine books were carried to Italy where they enriched Western culture enormously because they had successfully preserved the texts of most of the surviving Greek and African literary works from ancient times. In late medieval times the Egyptians produced impressive bindings of complicated geometric designs. The Persians at this time also developed their own craft of bookbinding, along naturalistic lines, using landscapes to decorate their texts.

Books printed before 1501 are called incunabula, from the Latin word for "cradle." The Chinese are credited with having printed the first book, called the Diamond Sutra, a Buddhist scripture dated 868. They also invented the earliest form of paper as we know it, using rags, fishing nets, and the inner bark of the mulberry tree.

Movable type was invented by Gutenberg in the fifteenth century and revolutionized bookmaking; suddenly, volume book production was possible. In Venice in 1450 Aldus Manutius printed the first pocket-size novel. He was also the first to print the works of Homer. Christopher Plantin (1541–1589) printed works in Latin, French, German, English, Italian, and Dutch. Both Plantin and Manutius began using **title** pages, bringing the name of the book from the end of the text to the beginning. Plantin's print shop continued to print fine books for 300 years and then became the Plantin-Moretus Museum in Antwerp, Belgium.

Bookbinding itself continued to be a manual process. A great emphasis was placed on decoration and a variety of expensive materials, including jewels, were employed. Numerous styles of bindings are the result of commissions by the aristocracy and royal families of Europe to skilled binders to bind books for their private libraries. Usually the main feature of these bindings was the coat of arms, crest, or badge of the family. The bindings were named after the people who commissioned them and not the binders who executed or created them.

In the nineteenth century the production of books was speeded up with faster presses and it was necessary for the time-consuming task of hand binding to give way to machines that could keep pace with book production. Ingenious machines were invented and binding became a factory process but it did not eliminate hand bookbinding altogether. A few small publishing houses, small print shops, and several individuals continued to bind books by hand. In recent years, the task of preserving old books has been made more expedient by the use of microfilm. Nothing, however, will replace the beauty and art of a handbound book.

SETTING UP A BINDERY   One doesn't need a lot of space or equipment for setting up a workshop. An evenly lit workbench, 36″ high, 30″ wide, and 72″ long, is the minimum workspace for one person. An additional surface is desirable for laying out work and for storing work between operations. The surfaces should be clean, smooth, and waterproof. Electricity or a gas source is necessary for heating glues and **finishing** tools, and it is helpful to have a water source nearby. A stool for comfort while performing certain operations is desirable.

Most binding operations require a press; a **lying press** and **plow** will perform virtually all the operations of the several simpler presses. The other tools required are all simple and easily obtainable: a **sewing frame, backing**

hammer, **guillotine cutter, back saw, awl, try square,** straightedge, **bone folder, French paring knife,** mat knife, **burnisher,** decorative **tool**s, and a **stabling clamp** and **hand brace.** It is also helpful to keep on hand scissors, a leather strop, and pliers.

The materials you will need include several kinds of **board**s; **adhesive**s, glue pot, and brushes; **beeswax, thread,** and needles; **paper, cloth,** or **leather; kraft paper; cord**s and **tape**s; **super;** mending tissue; wax paper; metal leaf; and a quantity of clean waste paper.

Some of these tools and materials will not be necessary depending on the type of binding being done and how elaborate it will be.

REBINDING   Books that are in need of rebinding must first have their covers removed. Open the front cover and front flyleaf. Leaning on the body of the book and pressing down on it firmly, pull back the **endpaper** flyleaf until the **slips** and **super** are visible. With a sharp penknife slit the super and slips and unhinge the **case.** Repeat the procedure for the back cover. If the book has a tight back, care must be taken when pulling the cover. If the **board**s are in good condition they can be reused after removing old **cloth, leather,** and **boardpaper**s (dampen and scrape off unwanted coverings). With great care, so as not to damage the backs of the sections, remove the **back lining**s. Turn the leaves until the **thread**s at the center of each section are visible, and cut them. As each section is cut loose, pull firmly but carefully to separate it. Continue until all sections are free. Remove old glue by brushing paste onto the back of the sections and allowing it to soak until the old glue softens; scrape it off with a knife and wipe the backs with a rag. The creases left from the old backing must be removed by gently hammering them out on the **knocking down block,** gripped firmly in the lying press, or on any hard smooth surface. Protect the section from hammer marks with a piece of paper. Take care to strike with the face of the hammer so that you do not tear the paper. Square the sections and press overnight between **pressing board**s.

Magazines are either **sidestitch**ed or saddlestitched. They can be bound as sections or cut and bound as single sheets. When binding several magazines together, the front covers are usually bound into the book and the back covers are discarded.

For magazines that will be bound as sections, remove the staples (and covers if you wish to discard them), **jog** the magazines at their backs and heads, allowing the backs to protrude slightly, and insert into the **lying press.** Tighten the press; remove old glue from the backs as described above. Remove the sections from the press and **strip repair** any torn sheets; when the repaired sheets are dry, return them to their right order in the section. Place the sections in the press, alternating backs and **foredge**s, and leave in the press overnight. Take the sections out of the press and stack them so that the backs line up; jog, insert in the lying press foredge-down, and tighten the wingnuts of the press. Mark the backs for **sewing on tape**s.

For magazines that will be bound as single sheets, remove the staples; place the magazines between two sheets of **kraft paper** or heavy white paper, and jog. Clamp them in the lying press, trim off the backs with the **plow,** coat the freshly cut backs with flexible glue, and proceed to binding.

REPAIR AND RESTORATION There are numerous means to spruce up old bindings and repair the damage caused by careless handling, age, and contaminated air.

To repair a torn page, place a sheet of wax paper with a tissue on top of it under the tear, mix paste as for **strip repair,** and apply it to the edges of the tear. Place another tissue and sheet of wax paper over the tear. Close the book and press for 24 hours. Remove the book from the press and carefully lift the tissue from both sides of the **leaf.** Fibers from the tissue work into the tear to hold the repair. Loose fibers can be removed with a pencil eraser. When there are many tears on one leaf, cover the entire page with a thin coat of paste and apply tissue to the whole page. Repeat for the underside of the page. When dry, trim the tissue flush with the other pages.

To remove grease and oil stains, saturate the stain with benzine, place the page between heavy blotters, and iron with a hot iron. Small spots may be dabbed away with solvent on a Q-tip. Commercial liquid or powder eradicators are quite efficient for removing ink.

Cellophane tape can be removed with a hot iron; clean off the residue with alcohol. Remove dust and fingerprints with a gum eraser; for more stubborn spots use a fine grit eraser. Refurbish a tarnished metal leaf title with a solution of 2 parts vinegar and 1 part water gently sponged across title printing. Clean book edges with an eraser, fine sandpaper, or steel wool.

For loose endpapers repaste and press until dry. For wrinkled or water **cockle**d pages, smooth with an electric iron on a low setting. If this fails, place a sheet of wax paper with a damp blotter on top of it under the page before ironing. Place on the press overnight. If a page is damp, sandwich it between blotters and iron with a medium-hot iron until dry. Repeat until all pages are dry and then place the book in the press to prevent curling.

Torn-out pages can be replaced by **guarding.** Torn backs of sections can be fixed by strip repair.

CARE AND MAINTENANCE Leather Protector, a trademark for a buffer-salt solution containing a small amount of potassium lactate and paranitrophenol, preserves goat and calfskin covers by making them acid-resistant to airborne contaminants. Cleaning leather bindings and dressing them with a combination of neat's-foot oil and anhydrous lanolin in a 60% to 40% ratio will prevent decomposition caused by the leather's gradual loss of oils. Heat the lanolin in a double boiler and add the neat's-foot oil; mix until blended into a clear creamy emulsion. Let cool before applying. After application let the binding dry for a couple of days. Retouch any dry-looking areas, or the whole book if you feel it is necessary. Repeat every two years. Suede, powdery goatskin, and calfskin may be sprayed with Krylon Fixative for protection.

Proper daily care will prolong the life of a binding. There is less strain on the binding if the book is standing in an upright position. When removing a book from a shelf, don't pull at the top of the spine; push the neighboring

books to either side, freeing the book you want. A piece of cotton saturated with oil of lavender and placed at the back of the bookshelf retards mold.

book cloth. Bookbinding. See **cloth.**

book press. Bookbinding. (Also called bookbinder's press.) A simple construction consisting of two boards with adjustable wingnuts at each corner and a brass strip of metal along one edge of each board. The book is sandwiched between the boards and the metal projection on the edge impresses a **groove** along the **back edge** of the book. A **lying press,** used with pressing boards, may be used instead.

Boondoot. Basketry. See **cane.**

borax. Ceramics. The major low fire **flux** other than lead. Borax can be used in small amounts in high fire **glaze**s that tend to be overly viscous. Borax is very soluble in water and should not be used on raw ware. Also see **frit, viscosity, white lead.**

borax. Enameling. See **frit.**

borax. Jewelry. Metalworking. See **flux.**

borax. Stained Glass. See **bubbles, painting on glass.**

border. Basketry. Any of a variety of patterns or weaves used to finish the edge, sides, **foot,** or **lid** of a basket. There are three basic types of borders: braided, trac, and rod. These borders are mainly used for **woven basketry,** but in some cases may be adapted for **plaited basketry. Coiled basketry** borders are usually finished off in the same stroke as the rest of the basket or simply wrapped or tied off. Borders provide a structural edge for the rim of the basket. Most are fairly simple, but some are elaborate and decorative.

The braided border (also called plaited border) is a fairly simple but decorative border. The pattern is derived from the common braid form in which three or more rods are interwoven. It is most common to woven basketry.

The trac border (also called track) is used where heavy wear is not expected and strength is not needed. It is commonly used on woven baskets that will receive a lid and can be used as an additional border on top of a lower one to support the lid.

The following are types of trac borders. The inverted border is generally used on plaited baskets employing flat **diagonal weaving** or **diagonal plaiting** in which **winding reed** or flat **splints** are used. The back trac border (also called trac back) is a simple trac border added to another border but woven in the opposite direction. It is commonly used to thicken the edge of a basket that is to receive a lid. The base border (also called foot border) is worked on the bottom of a wooden base as a means of fixing the stakes in place. It has the same weave as a regular trac border. The scalloped border is used on small and delicate baskets in which the upright stakes are simply looped over and pushed down beside the adjacent stake (**a.**). The madeira border is woven with flat **winding reed.** It is also used as a common border on **plaited palm baskets (b.).** See ill.

The rod border is the most common type of border on woven baskets. It is particularly well suited for **willow** baskets because it requires few tight turns. Variations in thickness of this border result from the number of rods used. Rod borders may be made with from two to six rods; the most common is the 3-rod plain border, constructed with three rods in sequence and used when a border of the same size or thickness of the **siding** is desired. It is well suited for small baskets and trays in cane but is also common for large, simple borders in willow. Also see **Basketry: Woven Basket Construction, Plaited Basket Construction.**

a. Scalloped border

b. Madeira border

border. Crochet. The finishing of a piece of crochet by adding a decorative crocheted edge, not always of the same **pattern** as that used in the body of the crochet work. Also see **edging.**

border. Knitting. The knit areas added to the edges of a knitted fabric. Depending on the use of the fabric being knit, the border may be purely decorative or may have a functional purpose as well (as in the case of a sweater border reinforced with a **ribbed** pattern to help the garment hold its shape).

The actual method of knitting any border depends on the size, purpose, and **pattern** of the particular piece of knitting. A curved border involves the **picking up** of stitches to finish the neck or sleeve of a garment. Stitches are picked up every other **row** according to pattern. For a straight border, stitches are picked up along a straight finished edge, either in the same color as the body of the knit fabric or in a contrasting color.

A frilled border is made by **increasing** stitches at selected intervals from the **knitting up** row to the desired size of frill, and **casting off.** A picot, or scalloped, border is made by systematically increasing and **decreasing** after picking up stitches along the edge.

border. Quilts. The final decorative **band** on a quilt before the **binding.** Not all quilts have borders; **all over patterns** often go right to the edge and touch the binding. In the Amish **border quilts,** the border is the only decorative **piecing.**

The border, or borders (sometimes two, three, or more are used) are part of the **quilt top.** The strips of fabric that make up the border are joined to the edges of the top so that they are quilted along with the body of the quilt. The

borders are often elaborately quilted, adding rich pattern and texture to solid areas of color.

Other borders are **pieced** or **appliquéd.** These patterns are usually variations of the patterns used on quilt tops. The **sawtooth,** for example, is a popular border pattern derived from the **block** design and may be added by piecing or appliqué.

A few of the most common pieced pattern borders are: Birds in Flight, Cat Track, chained square, diamond, **Irish Chain,** rickrack, and Sawtooth.

Some of the most common appliqué border patterns are feathered plumes, festoons and bowknots, grapevine and grapes, looped ribbons, lovers' knot, **serpentine, swag,** swag and bow, various appliqué motifs, and vine. Also see **Quilts: Binding.**

border lead. Stained Glass. See **cartoon, fitting** and **Stained glass: Glazing.**

border quilt. Quilts. Quilts originating with the Amish, in which the **piecing** is of the simplest possible design. A solid-color center, outlined by a wide **border** of another color, is one basic style. There is almost always a change of color in each corner where the **pieced** lines intersect. Other designs consist of an inside border or a double inside border, giving the effect of a square outlined by **band**s of two to four colors. The quilts are usually made of **wool,** always in rich solid colors, and exquisitely patterned with **quilting stitch**es. Also see **Amish quilt.**

border stamp. Leather. A variety of **stamp.**

border stitches. Crewel. Embroidery. Needlepoint. A variety of stitches used to frame the central design of a piece, to edge the total piece, or as a broad line in the design.

Crewel and embroidery stitches effective as border stitches are: **braid stitch, buttonhole stitch, chain stitch** (all variations), **coral knot stitch, couching, Cretan stitch, cross stitch, fishbone stitch, guilloche stitch, herringbone** (all variations), **Pekinese stitch, Portuguese stitch, Roumanian stitch, stem stitch** (all variations), and **Vandyke stitch.**

Needlepoint stitches are: **bargello, binding stitch, cross stitch, flat stitch, gobelin stitch, long-armed cross stitch, old Florentine stitch variation, rice stitch.** Also see **drawn thread border.**

boric acid. Ceramic. Boric acid is often used in place of **white lead** as a **flux.** Boron, a chemical component in boric acid, lowers the expansion coefficient and increases elasticity in a glaze. Also see **silica.**

boring. Woodworking. Small holes are drilled, whereas larger holes—over ¼"—are bored. Any type of **drill bit** may be used for boring: auger, spade, twist, or expansion. Bored holes are commonly made for inserting large dowels or bolts, or for a starting place when a keyhole or saber **saw** will be used to cut a larger hole. Also see **Woodworking: Boring and Drilling.**

boron carbide. Gemcutting. See **abrasive.**

borosilicate glass. Glassworks. Any glass characterized by resistance to **thermal shock, hardness,** and chemical inertness. Michael Faraday is given credit for the introduction of boric oxide to glass, but the varieties of very useful glasses marketed under the brand name Pyrex were developed at the Corning glassworks in Corning, N.Y., around 1912.

Borosilicate glasses rely for their exceptional resistance to thermal shock on the addition of approximately 13% boric oxide (B_2O_3) to a melt that also includes potassium oxide (K_2O), sodium oxide (Na_2O), aluminum oxide (Al_2O_3), and the "glassformer" silica (SiO_2). These glasses are useful to the studio glassworker for their hardiness in **flamework** especially, even though higher temperature **glass fires** are necessary to work them. Most laboratory glassware is borosilicate glass.

borrow and return. Quilts. See **hearts and gizzards.**

bort. Gemcutting. See **abrasive, diamond, drilling jig.**

bossing. Jewelry. See **embossing.**

bossing tool. Jewelry. A series of steel tools with a smoothly polished end used for forming metal and a sharp end for sticking with a hammer, such as a **ball-peen hammer.** Bossing tools are very similar to **repoussé** tools and, in fact, the two can be used interchangeably. Also see **embossing.**

bottle candle. Candlemaking. See **glass bottle candle.**

bottle cutting. Glasswork. Useful and attractive products can be made from refuse bottles by cutting parts of the bottom away. The tools now used for cutting bottles are much more effective than traditional cutting methods. At least three different types of bottle-cutting kits are commercially available, and all are capable of cutting bottles with a high rate of predictability. They use a variation of a steel wheel glass-cutting tool, which is held in position so that a bottle can be rotated against the tool, inscribing a line on the outside of the bottle that meets itself after a full rotation.

The next step is to produce the necessary tensile stress at the inscribed line. One kit offers a device that taps the bottle from the inside at the inscribed line; another kit supplies a transformer and a piece of wire that is wrapped around the bottle at the score line and then heated. **Thermal shock** from the heated wire provides the stress necessary to break the bottle at the score.

After removing necks from bottles to make tumblers, the inventive bottle cutter can go on to more ambitious projects, experimenting with cementing bottles or parts of bottles together with epoxy glue.

bottled gas. Ceramics. See **kiln fuel.**

bottle glass. Glasswork. See **soda-lime glass.**

bottle stone. Gemcutting. See **moldavite.**

bottom dyeing. Dyeing. See **top dyeing.**

bottom fuller. Metalworking. See **blacksmithing tools.**

bottoming. Dyeing. See **top-dyeing.**

bottoming. Metalworking. See **raising techniques** and **Metalworking: Raising.**

bottoming stake. Metalworking. See **anvil.**

bottoming tap. Metalworking. See **tap.**

bouclé yarn. Knitting. (From the French, *boucler*, to buckle.) A multiple yarn with one thread, or **ply,** looser than the other. Knitting with bouclé yarn produces a rough, loopy knit fabric.

bouclé yarn. Spinning. Weaving. See **novelty yarn.**

bouging. Jewelry. Metalworking. A hand hammering technique of smoothing surface imperfections, usually by tapping the surface with a rawhide mallet.

boulle. Découpage. A technique of inlaid decoration for furniture invented by **André Boulle,** using natural tortoiseshell as a background for inlaid fine-gauge brass scrolls. Contemporary adaptations of this technique use **gold paper trim** and braid arranged on **decorative paper** backgrounds coated with découpage **finish.**

Boulle, André Charles. (1642–1732) Découpage. A French craftsman who made fine furniture during the reigns of Louis XIV, Louis XV, and Louis XVI. His style of decorative **inlay** work, characterized by ornamental brass inlays in rich wood and tortoiseshell pieces, became known as **boulle.**

Boulle work. Ivory and Bone Carving. Shell Carving. (Also called buhl work.) A term applied to furniture ornamented with tortoiseshell inlay. Generally of the cabinetwork associated with André Charles Boulle (1642–1732), famous French cabinetmaker.

boulle work. Woodworking. See **marquetry.**

bouncing horse. Toys. A **rocking horse** suspended from springs on which a child sits and bounces to set the horse in action.

bound book. Bookbinding. A book which has the **boards** attached during the process of **forwarding,** or the making of the book. The covering material is applied after the boards have been attached to the text. Bound books require an **endpaper** with an outside spare sheet that is attached to the board. The endpapers are sewn to the first and last section of the book. Tipped endpapers are not strong enough.

bound edge. Rugmaking. Weaving. See **argatch.**

bound seam. Stitchery. A **plain seam, press**ed open, which has a **seam binding** or **bias tape** sewn over each of the **raw edge**s. If the raw edges are joined, a **double bound seam** is made. See ill.

Bound seam

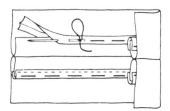

boundweave. Rugmaking. Weaving. A thick, highly patterned or colored fabric in which the pattern or color effects are obtained by the **filling** completely covering the **warp**. This is not a **tapestry** weave where threads are picked up individually, but a **loom-controlled** technique where the filling runs **selvage** to selvage and the **threading** and **treadling** are important to the final design. Boundweave offers unlimited design possibilities in creating rugs, wall hangings, bags, and pillows. The rigidity and weight of the fabric make it impractical for any use requiring a pliable cloth. The warp is usually cotton or linen and is widely spaced, so that the filling can be packed down to cover it. Wool is recommended as the best filling since it beats down so well. Threadings, or **drawing-in drafts,** often used for boundweave, are **point draw**, herringbone (broken) **draw, summer and winter weave** and **overshot.** A variety of treadling patterns can be tried with each threading. They are all based on the **twill weave** and, if the normal twill sequence is followed with the right color placement, a flamepoint effect is achieved. A popular Swedish method is to weave on **opposites.** This with the point draw gives smaller, more formal geometric patterns. With any of the mentioned threadings and a little experimentation, it is possible to obtain stylized buildings, trees, flowers, figures, and animals. Also see **herringbone, opposites, overshot, point draw, summer and winter.**

bouquet. Quilts. See **Quilts: Quilting.**

bouquet weave. Weaving. See **Brooks Bouquet.**

bout. Weaving. (Also called bight.) The group of **warp ends** tied together in a **tie-on knot** around the front **apron bar.** Also see **tying-on.**

boutoné. Rugmaking. Weaving. (Alternate spelling boutonné.) The name of a type of French-Canadian rug woven in **flat weave** with looped patterns. Geometric forms are raised in loops against a **plain weave** background. Also see **looping.**

boutonné. Rugmaking. Weaving. See **boutoné.**

bow. Basketry. (Also called bow rod, handle bow.) A stout **rod** that forms the foundation of a basket handle. Also see **Basketry: Woven Basket Construction.**

bow. Ceramics. See **harp.**

bow. Woodworking. See **wood.**

bowdrill. Coral Carving. Jet Carving. A simple tool for drilling, forming, and polishing; different shafts inserted into the spool turn it from a drill into a tool for forming and polishing beads. A shaped **lapstick,** designed to accept rough or semiformed beads, is inserted into a drilled hole in the bottom of the spool; it is revolved by moving the bamboo bow back and forth. Below the lapstick is the material to be shaped (dopped or wedged in place), fitted into a depression in a stone slab or wood block. It is revolved in various grits of abrasives. With graded depressions in the slab you may form graded beads or, by using one size, produce beads of uniform size. See ill. Also see **bead-holding jig** and **Coral Carving: Working the Material.**

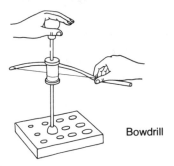

Bowdrill

bowenite. Gemcutting. See **serpentine.**

bowing. Kites. The bending of the two sides of a kite surface back along a center **spine** or keel to create a **dihedral angle.** Bowing places the side tips of the kite farther back than the center, softening the impact of the air's resistance by dividing its flow in the same way that a ship's bow divides resisting water. Bowing also improves flight stability—the kite pivots along the center spine in a strong gust of wind and then returns to normal position. Also see **Kites: Construction.**

bowing. Rugmaking. Weaving. See **bubbling.**

bowing string. Puppets. See **back string.**

bow loom. Beadwork. The most primitive **loom** design used in **American Indian beadwork,** the bow loom is made by bending a single branch into an arc and tying the warp strings between the two ends. The warp is pulled taut by the tension of the bow. A few sticks, called weft sticks, are inserted at one end of the warp to keep the strings evenly spaced until several rows of beading are woven to take over this function, at which time the sticks are removed. The loom is held between the knees, and **bead weaving** is started near the body and worked to the far end.

bow loom. Weaving. Perhaps the most primitive of **looms** made out of two boughs or pieces of wood, or of one piece of wood split in two and tied at the ends to prevent further splitting. In this last version, two small pieces of wood are inserted into the split to prop it open. There are no **heddles, harnesses, beater,** or **reed.** The wood or boughs merely provide a place to stretch the **warp** yarns. In the split wood type, the loom resembles a conventional bow and arrow, and carries a **continuous warp** that is wound around the widest section in the center of the loom. A crude wooden **needle,** darning in and out, inserts the **filling.** Bow looms are still in use in some Pacific Islands in the making of bast **fiber** mats, in the northwest Amazon basin for beadwork aprons, and among one or two North American Indian tribes for belt weaving. See ill.

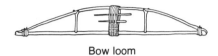

Bow loom

bow mark. Basketry. The space held open by a short **rod** or **stake** (the **handle liner**) for the bow while weaving the basket. It is used to facilitate deep insertion of the bow for a secure handle. Also see **Basketry: Woven Basket Construction.**

bow rod. Basketry. See **bow.**

Bows and Arrows. Quilts. See **Steeplechase.**

bowtie quilt. Quilts. A design for a **pieced quilt** consisting of small **blocks,** each made up of two triangles. When the blocks are placed so that certain dark or light triangles touch, they suggest bowties. There are many possible ways of arranging the blocks. Also see **block pattern, set.**

bow tongs. Metalworking. See **tongs.**

box construction. Jewelry. A construction with top, bottom, and sides which entirely enclose a space, such as a cube. Whatever the form, when the last side is soldered on, a **blowhole** somewhere within the construction may implode, or explode, causing injuries. The hole need be no larger than the head of a pin to allow for the escape of the gases and steam which form during the heating process. The hole could take the form of a decorative element or a series of small pierced designs. To make an actual box form for the first time start with a size no larger than 2″ × 2″ × 2″. The easiest method is as follows: Cut two pieces of sheet metal approximately 4¼″ × 2″. Using the steel rule as a straightedge, **scribe** a line across the length, dividing the pieces in half. Scribe several times lightly at first and then harder, to begin a groove. Deepen this groove by **filing** with a square **needle file** at a 45° angle or by using a triangular file. Begin filing at a slight angle; maintain this angle to prevent slipping while following the scribed line. File the metal deeply, almost, but not all of the way through. Using the filed groove as a guide, bend the metal over a **steel block (a.).** Use a **rawhide mallet** to hammer and perfect the right angle of the corner if necessary. Bend both pieces to make the four sides of the box. The grooved corners will be thinner and weaker; it is wise to **flux** the work and reinforce them with medium **solder.** After soldering,

pickle in the usual fashion. Position the pieces (**b.**) and file all edges to form good **joints.** A **bench rub stone** is good for this purpose or **carborundum paper** can be placed rough side up on an absolutely flat surface and used in the same manner as the bench rub stone. The **baseplate** should be cut slightly larger all the way around than the sides when they are in position. Use **iron binding wire** to secure the baseplate. Flux. Position solder along the outer edge of the baseplate; the extra allowance on the baseplate will permit space to do this. Place the solder in the same fashion as for soldering a **bezel** to its baseplate, placing a little extra at the corners that are not soldered together and a small piece of solder at the top of each of these corners. Have a **soldering point** handy while soldering to facilitate pulling the solder along the seam. Remember that solder flows toward the hottest point. Consequently, after the entire work is heated and the solder is ready to flow, angle the **torch flame** at the solder in the joint to help pull it along. Capillary action will take care of the corners that have not been soldered, and the baseplate. Remove binding wire, and pickle. If the entire seam is not soldered and if there are small spaces, turn the box upside down and tap lightly along the edge with a rawhide mallet to close the gap. Reflux. Solder. Add a little extra solder at these spaces if it seems necessary. File off almost all of the extra metal in diag. b—parts one and two and the flange of the baseplate. Remember, this is the last side, and the box will be closed. There must be a small hole somewhere, or the box will explode during the soldering of this last part. During soldering, do not get your eyes in direct line with the hole. The gases can build up and rush out of the hole, especially if it is very small, at a tremendous velocity. Pickle. The box will fill partially with pickle due to the hole in the construction. Fill the box with water to dilute the pickle; shake, and pour out. Repeat several times until the box is clean and empty. If there are any spots which have not soldered, redo them, being especially careful this time, as there will surely be liquid inside, producing even more gas and steam than when soldering the first time. File off rough edges. Emery. Finish with **buffing.** See ill. Also see **capillarity.**

a. Filed groove relative to   b. Box construction
steel block for bending metal

box drum. Toys. See **drum box.**

"boxed in." Puppets. Enclosed within the box or framework of the hand-puppet puppet stage. The **puppeteer** may be behind the **proscenium,** under the **playboard,** and concealed from view at the sides. The puppeteer's voice may not carry from this boxlike enclosure to the audience, so provision must be made to allow sound to carry through openings or vents.

box kite. Kites. A rectangular boxlike kite with a covered **cell** at either end and an open space between. Lawrence

Hargrave, an Australian, invented the box kite during the last decade of the nineteenth century. He combined several principles of **aerodynamics** to create a kite that would serve as a practical lifting machine. The extent to which these principles function depends in part on the way the kite's **bridling** system is arranged. Strung to fly flat, the kite has two flying surfaces or planes, stacked one above the other as in a biplane, that produce far more **lift** than the single surface of the **diamond kite.** Hargrave flew his kites flat; bridled to fly on edge, however, the box kite offers a right-angled **dihedral angle** to the wind that greatly increases the stability of flight. The box kite illustrates another aerodynamic principle known as **venting.** In this case, the venting is the open middle section between the two covered end cells. Also see **Kites: Construction.** See ill.

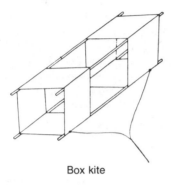

Box kite

box loom. Beadwork. See **loom.**

box loom. Weaving. A **loom** modeled after the **frame loom** but using an open box rather than the frame. Usually the two longer sides are much lower than the short sides that the circular or **continuous warp** is wound around. In rough versions all sides are the same height. The depth of the box makes the loom suitable for **rigid heedle** weaving. An alternate **shedding device** would be to use a **heddlebar** and **shed stick**s.

Also a loom with boxes for the **shuttle** on each side of the shuttle race on the **beater.** The loom may be a power loom, or a semimechanical loom like a **dobby loom** or a **fly shuttle loom.** In the latter case, the shuttle is transferred from box to box across the **warp** by the weaver pulling on a cord or levers connected to the boxes. The number of boxes may vary. In some looms, there is only one box on each side of the beater. In other looms, there is one box on one side and as many as seven on the other side. In this case, a maximum of seven different colors can be used, but each one that goes across the warp must return before the next color is shot through, so that the solitary box on one side is always empty and waiting to receive the next color. The average number of boxes on each side is four. Also see **bandloom.**

box nail. Woodworking. See **nail.**

box quilt. Quilts. (Also called Heavenly Steps, Pandora's Box, **Patience Corner,** Stairsteps.) A **pieced quilt** design made up of squares and parallelograms. It resembles Baby

Blocks and has similar optical possibilities. The distinction between these two similar patterns is that the Box Quilt is made up of two shapes, while the Baby Blocks uses only diamonds. Also, the Box Quilt suggests steps, whereas the diamonds of Baby Blocks combine to form six-pointed stars.

A variation of the Box Quilt is **Attic Windows,** which gives a different optical illusion.

box swing. Toys. Any **swing** that uses a wood box, a galvanized tub, a boiler, or any similar box or container as the seat. It is usually attached by **rope**s at the four corners through holes drilled into the box. The four ropes can then be tied together and suspended from another rope to make it a single rope swing. Care must be taken to assure that the container or box is strong enough to support weight and that the tying is securely done. A **nylon rope** or strong **manila rope** can be used.

box tongs. Metalworking. See **tongs.**

boxwood. Woodworking. A fine-textured, heavy, extremely hard, dense, and close-grained wood common to Asia, Africa, and South America. It ranges in color from white to deep yellow. Because it is available only in small pieces, it is highly prized for **wood engraving.** It is also used for small **wood turnings** and **woodcarving**s. The sawdust of the South American variety is said to be toxic.

box wrench. Woodworking. See **wrench.**

brace. Woodworking. See **drilling tools.**

bracelet mandrel. Jewelry. A round or oval tool made of hardened steel used as a **stake** over which a bracelet can be bent, by striking it with a **rawhide mallet.** See ill. Also see **mandrel, ring mandrel.**

Oval bracelet mandrel

brad. Woodworking. See **nail.**

brad awl. Basketry. A tool like an awl used for pinning a basket to a work board or a **lap board.**

brad awl. Woodworking. See **drilling tools.**

bradding. Metalworking. See **blacksmithing techniques.**

bradel binding. Bookbinding. (Also called cartonnage á la Bradel.) A temporary type of binding, believed to have originated in Germany and first employed in France by a **binder** named Bradel.

braid. Crewel. Embroidery. Needlepoint. An interlacing of three groups, or bundles, of threads. The three bundles are knotted together and the knot is firmly anchored. The outside bundles are then repeatedly brought across the center bundle, alternating left and right.

Braids may be sewn down as a decorative trim, added to a design where a textured three-dimensional detail is needed, or used to hold precut strands of embroidery yarn neatly together. Used in this way, braids prevent the yarn from tangling and allow the strands to be pulled out individually as they are needed.

braid. Lacemaking. (Also called plait.) A braid in **bobbin lace** is made with two pairs of **bobbins**. The bobbins **cross, twist,** and repeat the cross-twist motions with the same pairs of bobbins to make the desired length of braid. Also see **bar.**

braid-aid. Rugmaking. (Also called rugbraider.) An optional tool used to facilitate the making of cloth strip braids in a **braided rug.** They are funnel-like holders made of metal or plastic which, when threaded onto the end of a roll of fabric strips, automatically turn the raw edges of the strips in and fold the fabric while they are being braided. Braid-aids come in different sizes to properly accommodate the width of the braiding fabric.

braided bar. Lacemaking. See **bar.**

braided border. Basketry. See **border** and **Basketry: Woven Basket Construction.**

braided candle. Candlemaking. A candle formed by braiding together three or more thin **tapers** formed by **dipping.** The braiding process should begin while the wax of the tapers is still warm and malleable.

braided fringe. Rugmaking. Weaving. Yarn ends or equal groups of yarn ends criss-crossed together to form a braid as a **finishing edge.** Braids can be three or more strands or groups of strands. Depending on the yarn and **sett** used, these groups can be of 2 or more strands each. However, if the strands are too far apart, there may be a gap between the start of the braid and the edge of the weaving or rug. While **braiding,** pull tight to minimize the gap and to attain a firm braid. Ends of the braid are knotted with an **overhand knot** or whipped to prevent the braid from undoing. A **fringe** can be braided for its entire length or just partway. The braiding can be turned into a network or lacy effect by having the strands of one braid criss-cross with another. Also see **whipping.**

braided rug. Rugmaking. Rugs made out of narrow cloth strips that have been braided into long strands which are then sewn or laced together to form a solid surface. The sewing is done edge to edge starting in what would be the center of the rug and proceeding outward around and around into an oval, round, or rectangular shape. These are the traditional shapes, although **free-form** contemporary **rug**s can also be constructed from the braids.

The history of braided rugs also involves the history of **braiding**—one of the oldest crafts known to man. As early as 6000 B.C. braiding was being done with reeds and rushes. Mats made out of grasses are still used in Mexico and South America while braided cornhusks were a farm answer to doormats. They are still made as a selling commodity in some areas of Kentucky and the Appalachians. At the tail end of the eighteenth century, a Providence, Rhode Island, milliner discovered the craft of braiding rye and oat straw for making women's bonnets. It became a cottage industry with all the members of a family braiding in their spare moments to earn extra money or to use the braids as barter in the local general store. Eventually, braiding factories with the braiders all under one roof and working fulltime replaced the cottage industry method. The step from straw to the use of other material for braiding was a very natural one, and it is speculated that this gave rise to the braiding of rags for use as rugs. The usual source for cloth for braiding rugs was discarded and outgrown clothing. However, since the first American woolen mills were established in New England, it is possible that there were remnants or wool scraps available to these early braiders. The same sources of cloth formed the basis of woven **rag rug**s. Of these two techniques utilizing cloth strips, braided rugs were considered far superior. As America spread westward, so did braided rugs. Today they are found all over the United States and are strongly associated with early American decor.

Braiding is a rugmaking technique where just as much time can be spent on preparing the materials as on the actual craft, which in itself is not time consuming. How well the finished rug looks and how easily the braiding goes depends on the preparations beforehand—the cutting, **piecing** together, and folding of the fabric strips. A fabric **strip cutter** can be used to cut the cloth into lengths or they can be torn by hand. The widths are from 1¼ – 3" in order to obtain braids from ⅝ to 1½" wide. Lightweight fabrics would be cut wider, and medium and heavyweight fabrics, narrower. Very often the cloth is dyed before cutting, since a wide assortment of remnants and **mill end**s can be used and the **top dyeing** unifies the various colors. The strips are pieced and wound into a flat roll with the seams kept to the underside. The roll is prevented from unrolling by securing with a large blanket pin or a string that runs through the center. It is unwound as braiding proceeds and lengths are added to the strips as needed. The raw edges of the strips are turned in either by hand or with **braid-aids,** which are slipped on at this point. The ends of three lengths for a three-strand braid are pinned, sewn or tied together, or a T-start is made as illustrated (**a., b.**). Braids can also be made of 4–7 or more strips if the fabric is very fine.

Fingers are the main tool used in braiding and other equipment is incidental. However, to make the process go smoothly and quickly, a hook, chair knob, or a weight or clamp on a table is used to anchor the braid so that there is something stable against which to pull while braiding. During Civil War times, a "sewing bird" was used. This was basically a clamp that could be attached to a table or shelf. It was made of metal in the size and shape of a little bird with usually a velvet pin cushion on its back. Its beak had a spring in it and this held the sewing or braid. Some variations on this appeared in the 1930s and 1940s and it is still possible to find them in thrift or antique shops.

After a braid of a desired length has been made, it is

secured with a clothespin so that it will not unbraid, and the core or center of the rug is constructed. The length of this core and the manner in which it is braided or laced depend on the length of the rug and whether it will be round, oval, or rectangular. For a round rug, the center is braided by starting left strand over center strand, left over center again and right strand over center, tightly. This is repeated so that the braid automatically turns into a circle. When the circle is about 3″ in diameter, the normal sequence of braiding is resumed for a short length and then laced to the circle. For an oval rug, a length is braided that is equal to the difference between the width and the length of the rug. (For example, a 4′ × 6′ rug would need a 2′ center starter length.) At the end of this length, a turning is made as for a round rug and then a normal braid is continued until equal in length to the center one. This new length is laced to the center and regular braiding is resumed. For a square or rectangular rug, a braid is made for an arbitrary desired length and a square corner is manipulated by braiding left strand over center, left over center again, then once again, and right over center tightly. Two such square corners are needed, and then normal braiding is continued to the length of the center strand. These are laced together and a third square corner is made. A few loops are braided and a fourth square corner is made. This procedure is followed to the completion of the rug with square turnings being made whenever a corner is reached. Although some braiders sew their braided strips together, **lacing,** by using lacing cord and a **lacer** or a blunt needle gives a much better looking and a firmer rug. The connections between braids are hidden and there are no lumps or ridges due to overlapping fabric or a poorly manipulated turn (**c.**).

When a strip runs out during braiding, the tip should be cut on the bias and the new strip hand or machine sewn to the previous one as in other piecing of strips. These piecings should all be staggered. To join braids, the individual strips of one braid are matched and sewn to the strips of the other—again using a bias piecing technique. **Butting** can be done to make distinct color changes and to avoid "cupping" or small bumps in the rug which occur frequently at the braid joinings. The rug is finished by cutting the last 6″ or more of each strip to a long, tapered point. Braiding is continued until the strips are too thin to be held by the braid-aids. The raw edges are folded in and sewn together and pulled through the loops and secured with invisible stitches (**d.**).

In addition to the above shapes, a simple rug can be made of equal long lengths of braids which are laced together to form vertical stripes in a rectangular rug. The strips can form a fringe at both ends if desired. **Interbraiding** also gives a square or rectangular rug, but no stitching or lacing is required. Braided rugs are made as hit-or-miss rugs by choosing strips at random, or are carefully planned bands of color that are put together one hue to another. Small designs, such as arrowheads, can be formed by combining in one braid 2 strong colors with a light one. Although woolen cloth is usually associated with braided rugs, they can also be made of heavy rug yarn, heavy cord or string, grasses and jute or hemp for outdoor use. See ill. Also see **plaiting.**

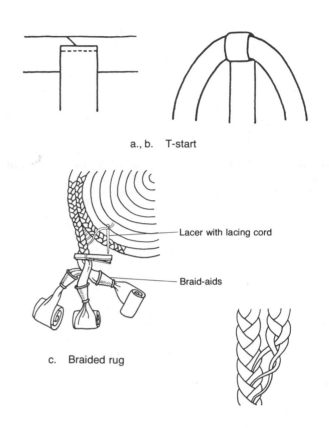

a., b.   T-start

Lacer with lacing cord

Braid-aids

c.   Braided rug

d.   Finishing off with tapered points

braided wick. Candlemaking. A **wick** the tip of which bends outside the flame area and dissipates of its own accord. Before its invention by Cambaceres in 1825 it had been necessary to cut away the carbonaceous matter of the burning wick with scissors to eliminate smoking. The braided wick represents a significant breakthrough to the candlemaking industry. Today all wicks sold are of the braided or plaited variety.

braiding. Rugmaking. Weaving. A method of criss-crossing yarns or rag strips to form a long coil. This coil can be used alone as a trim, a handle, a belt or a **finishing edge** on a **fringe.** Many coils can be sewn together to become a mat, rug, bag, pillow, or wall hanging. Braids are composed of 3 or more strands or strips or groups of strands. They can be thick or thin, round or flat. For a 3-strand braid, go left, strand over center and under, then right over center and under. This procedure is repeated for the length of the braid. With a 4 or more strand braid, the interlacing pro-

3-strand braid

4-strand braid

ceeds from the left over, under, over, etc. The same order is repeated by the other strands. See ill. Also see **braided fringe, braided rug, plaiting.**

braid stitch. Rugmaking. An edging stitch used to finish off the edges of an embroidered rug. It has the appearance of a braid and is much more prominent than other edging stitches. Therefore, the color of the yarn used in making the braid stitch should harmonize with the colors of the rug design. In working the braid stitch, the needle moves from back to front shifting to the left with each stitch, and then back to the right. For example, on **canvas mesh,** the needle would be inserted back to front for the initial stitch, then moved one hole to the left, inserted back to front, sewn and the tail of the yarn caught. The next stitch is a return to the first hole, insert stitch, move three holes to the left, insert stitch, move back two holes to the right, insert stitch. Continue in this manner around the entire rug, compensating in the number of holes moved forward and back at the corners so that a smooth transition is made around the corners. See ill.

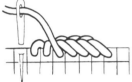

a.   Side view of braid stitch in canvas mesh

b.   Top view

brake. Jewelry. A rather large, heavy, floor-standing piece of equipment used for **bending** angles in **sheet metal.** It's a marvelous piece of equipment but expensive, and only very well-equipped studios will have one. Sheet metal shops usually have a brake, and will often allow a craftsperson to use it.

brake. Spinning. See **flax.**

brake. Weaving. See **friction brake.**

branch loom. Weaving. A **loom** made out of a tree branch. Although this is a simple loom in which the fingers are used to open up the **shed**s and manipulate various techniques, it is not a **primitive loom.** Rather, the concept is an artistic one in which the loom becomes part of the finished woven object. The shape of the branch is an important part of the aesthetic qualities of the object and is instrumental in determining the shape of the object. However, it is not necessary that what is woven follow exactly the configurations of the tree limbs. That is the choice of the weaver and he can weave in only small portions between the limbs, hide the limbs completely, make two or more layers of fabric (depending on the number of limbs), wrap the limbs, knot on various constructions, or do anything else that his imagination dictates.

In addition to shape being an important factor, the branch loom must be sturdy and have limbs in a position around which some type of **warp** can be maneuvered. Usually this warp is a continuous one going between two of the limbs, but a warp-weighted arrangement of yarns can be also used. In some cases where the branches are thin and pliable, they can be bent to a desired shape and even into a **circular loom.** Size is a relative factor depending on what the end result is to be, and what the weaver is able to handle successfully. Since there is nothing to hold a warp in place the yarns chosen for warp are usually somewhat fuzzy so that the fibers will cling to the wood and not shift around too much. The weaving is most often done with needle and yarn or a **butterfly.** See ill. Also see **continuous warp, finger-manipulated, needle weaving, warp-weighted loom.**

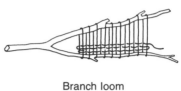

Branch loom

Braque, Georges. Stained Glass. A leading artist of the cubist movement who also designed a series of small windows at Varangeville, France.

brass. Enameling. See **metal.**

brass. Jewelry. A copper-zinc **alloy** that, for specific purposes, has small proportions of other metals added to it to obtain increased strength, hardness, or resistance to corrosion. **Tensile strength** increases with the addition of zinc, but in excess of 43.5% zinc the alloy's strength begins to fail and it becomes brittle. The alloys with a 2–5% zinc content are known as "zinc deoxidized copper" and can withstand severe cold working.

Alpha brass contains up to 36% zinc and is yellow in color. It is used in cold forming and is suited to wire drawing, beads, chains, rivets, and stamping. Its melting point is 1660° F, and its annealing temperature is 800–1100° F.

Beta brass contains above 37% zinc content and is suitable for hot working. The most commonly used beta brass is called Muntz metal; it is 40% zinc, with a melting point of 1650° F and an annealing temperature of 800–1100° F.

Red brass contains 15% zinc, although this figure may vary slightly, and occasionally small amounts of tin are added—always less than the zinc content. It is the contemporary version of **pinchbeck** metal, and is used for costume jewelry. Pinchbeck metal is a copper-rich alloy containing 12% zinc. It is similar to gold in color and was commonly used as a substitute in Victorian costume jewelry.

Gilding metal contains 5% zinc, and is golden in color, resistant to corrosion, and very malleable. It is commonly used in jewelry that is to be gold-plated.

Nickel silver, also known as German silver, is not silver at all but a series of copper-zinc alloys that have nickel added. The nickel silver alloy most often used in jewelry is 62% copper, 33% nickel, and 5% zinc. It possesses an attractive white color, takes a good polish, and has good working qualities for forming and joining. It is used either alone or silver-plated for eating utensils and jewelry. Also see **buffing compound.**

brass. Metalworking. The name given a group of **alloys** of **copper** and **zinc,** sometimes with small amounts of other metals such as **tin** and **lead.** It is less **malleable** and **ductile** than copper; in general, greater amounts of zinc proportionately decrease those qualities. Hammering work-hardens brass rapidly and it must be **annealed** often. It may be joined by hard **soldering** or **brazing.**

Red brass (approximately 85% copper and 15% zinc) is very soft, malleable, and ductile, has little tendency to crack, and has high corrosion resistance. It is recommended for artwork formed by **raising techniques.** Yellow brasses (27–35% zinc) are less ductile than red brass; one yellow brass is cartridge brass (used for small arms cartridges; about 20% zinc), good for **metal spinning.** Other alloys include standard commercial brass (about 10% zinc), 1 leaded brass (65% copper, 34% zinc, 1% lead), forging brass (60% copper, 38% zinc, 2% lead) for **forging,** and fine casting brass (90% copper, 7% zinc, 2% tin, 1% lead).

Brass may be purchased in sheet form for craft use in **tempers** of soft, quarter-hard, half-hard, and hard, and in many **gauges** or thicknesses. The stock sheet size is 24″ x 76″; it is also sold by the **linear foot** from rolls or by weight.

Historically, brass objects have been found that date from about 1000 B.C., but the early alloying may have been accidental because ores for copper and zinc are often found near each other and the ancient languages did not distinguish between copper, brass, and **bronze** (which alloys copper with tin). Brass remained relatively rare until the time of the Roman Empire, when brass money was produced with a zinc content of 21–28%, and decorative brass with less zinc (11–20%) was used, often hammered into a thin foil. In later times, brass foil of similar composition was known as **gilding metal** and Dutch leaf because it resembled gold leaf. Brass was often used in church reliquaries and sculptures by the eleventh century, and was crafted by braziers into utilitarian objects such as andirons, candlesticks, bells, works for guns, ship items, and furniture hardware.

Early alloys of brass were produced with calamine or cadmia—a zinc carbonate—but in 1781 a process of refining zinc was discovered that simplified the alloying procedure and opened the way for the large-scale production of brass.

brass. Stained Glass. Used in sheets, it can be cut into **filigree** for decorating lamps and windows. Stained-glass supply houses sell brass filigree and embossed **brass banding** in a variety of forms that can be used to decorate the edges of lampshades. They can be **tinned** if a lead color is desired.

Brass has more rigidity than copper and is second only to **galvanized steel** in providing sound structural support. Also see **lampshade construction, tinning.**

brass banding. Stained Glass. Embossed strips of brass filigree used for decorating the edges and seams of lamp shades. Also see **brass.**

brayer. Block Printing. Découpage. Fabric Printing. (Also called inking roller, squeegee.) A heavy rubber roller with a sturdy metal handle used for inking all types of printing blocks. The brayer is used to evenly apply ink over the surface of the block. The ink is first rolled out on a piece of glass or metal, then when the ink has been rolled to an even consistency, it is rolled onto the printing surface of the block. A hard roller distributes ink only on the top level of the printing surface; a softer roller can be pushed down to reach lower levels of the printing surface. Brayers are generally from 3″ to 6″ long, but larger ones are available. A brayer is also used to transfer the design from the printing block to paper in **offset printing.** See ill.

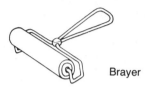

Brayer

braze. Metalworking. See **welding.**

braze welding. Metalworking. See **welding** and **Metalworking: Welding.**

braze welding flux. Metalworking. See **flux.**

Brazilian sol lace. Lacemaking. See **sol lace.**

brazilwood. Batik and Tie-dye. An East Indian redwood tree from which a **colorant** is extracted for use in **dyes.** The extract from this **dyewood** produces red and red-purple **natural dyes.**

brazing. Jewelry. A type of **hard solder**ing using a **spelter solder.** Also see **soldering.**

brazing. Metalworking. See **welding.**

brazing alloy. Metalworking. See **solder.**

brazing rod. Metalworking. See **welding rod.**

brazing solder. Jewelry. See **spelter solder.**

brazing solder. Metalworking. See **solder.**

bread clay. Toys. A malleable **inedible dough** used for modeling small objects such as **bead**s, flowers, and ornaments. It is a dough art, although it is not baked as are most products of the **baker's art.** Bread clay is simple to mix; once modeled it must be thoroughly dried before it is painted with **oil-base paint**s, **acrylic paint**s, or stains. Marking pens can be used to add details to the dried dough.

Break one loaf of sliced white bread with all crusts removed into tiny pieces. Add 1 scant tablespoon **white glue** per slice of bread. Mix to a puttylike consistency. Glycerine may be added to give a smooth surface to the dough. Keep unused bread clay in a plastic bag; it will keep in the refrigerator for several days. Add **tempera** paint or **food coloring** a drop at a time for color. Also see **baker's clay; bread-crumb doll, salt clay, salt dough,** and **Toys: Ephemeral Toys.**

bread-crumb doll. Toys. A doll that has a head modeled from a mixture of dry bread crumbs and **white glue.** The bread crumbs are crushed with a rolling pin to a very fine powder. White glue is added to make a malleable dough that is thick enough to assure that the head will hold its shape. It is similar to **bread clay.**

After the head is formed, a wire can be inserted and left there to dry. The wire provides a means of attaching the rest of the figure. Sometimes a wire **armature** is made and the bread-crumb mixture is formed over the portion of the wire that will be the head.

Hands may be made either of the crumbs or from fabric. The dolls are usually dressed in fabric clothes. The dried face can be painted with **acrylic paint** or **tempera,** and a **finish** of **lacquer** or **fixative** can be added.

bread dough. Toys. Bread baking is not only a necessity of life, but also a medium for inventive design and a symbol in ancient folk art and superstitious traditions. Dough is malleable and pleasant to work with. It can be rolled, formed, braided, cut into shapes, pressed into molds, incised, or perforated with designs. The preparation of breads and cakes for holidays has traditionally been a time for experimenting with innovative shapes and forms symbolic of the occasion, and embellishment with seeds, candies, frosting, and so on. Many cook books give basic bread recipes that can be used for dough sculpture.

As an extension of this ancient craft, there are recipes available for making inedible dough mixtures such as **baker's clay** to produce hard, permanent dough sculptures. Whether preserved in their natural golden brown tone or painted in bright colors, these dough sculptures maintain the sense of immediacy, easy malleability, and naiveté associated with bread baking. To ensure permanence, the completed pieces should be coated with a **protective finish;** the dough absorbs moisture from the atmosphere and becomes soft if it is not so sealed.

bread dough clay. Découpage. A claylike mixture made of bread and glue used to stuff raised areas in **repoussé** pictures. It is also used to make miniature sculptures, such as flowers, for adhering to the découpage surface before the **finish** is applied. The dried sculpture may also be painted before the application of the découpage finish.

bread dough sculpture. Toys. An ancient form of dough art in which shapes are formed or sculptured from yeasted **bread dough,** then baked. Designs traditionally related to festivities or holidays.

A wedding bread from Crete, for example, might include wheat (a symbol of life and fertility) along with other symbolic decorations. The bread is used in the wedding ceremony. There are Finnish bread twists, similar to the German pretzel, bread rabbits and figures from Switzerland, alligators from Italy, and animal or human bread forms from Sicily. A bread with less leavening, or sometimes no leavening, is used for the Ecuadorian and Peruvian bread figures. In Mexico, All Soul's Day is celebrated with elaborately decorated bread figures and animals. Almost every religious holiday has specially shaped and decorated breads made in celebration. Also see **baker's art** and **Toys: Ephemeral Toys.**

breadfruit. Quilts. See **Hawaiian quilts.**

break. Weaving. A recess in the cloth caused by a weave structure that puts **warp end**s (**raiser**s) against a long or short **filling float** (**sinker**). Complex weave patterns can be based on "breaks," but the one most encountered by handweavers is the **broken twill** or **herringbone.**

break-away mold. Plastics. See **mold.**

breaking. Spinning. See **flax.**

breaking. Stained Glass. See **Stained Glass: Cutting Glass.**

breaking in a buffing wheel. Jewelry. Although ready-to-use **buff**s are available, most must be prepared for use by removing loose dust and fibers and applying **buffing compound**s.

It is advisable to wear protective glasses, a face mask to protect your eyes and prevent inhalation of the fiber dust, and an apron to protect your clothing while changing the wheel. While the **buff** is in rotation, apply a small amount of the desired compound, most of which will fly out along with fiber dust and threads. Turn the motor off, and when the buff stops, rotate it by hand, burning the strings and loose fibers off with a match. Do a small section at a time but continue around the entire circumference of the wheel. Pat the flame out with your fingers using a quick slapping motion. If the flames or little fire spots are not completely out when you turn the motor on, they will instantly burn through to the center of the wheel.

Turn on the buffing machine and charge the buff with buffing compound. Slightly more will adhere each time. Repeat the singeing and charging procedure until the strings stop sticking out. Use a piece of **sheet metal,** such as copper, to test the buff. The wheel is ready when it remains compact, and the test metal is buffed smoothly. Any strings left sticking out of a buff will create grooves or **feathering** in the metal. Depending on the size of the wheel the breaking-in time can run from 15 minutes to hours. Fortunately, once they are broken in they can last for years. Breaking in compressed felt buffs takes little time. Simply apply the compound, and buff a piece of sheet metal or a flat, smooth piece of wood. Apply the compound and continue buffing until the compound is evenly distributed across the buff. Also see **buffing, charge.**

breast beam. Weaving. The breast beam is the upper one of two **beam**s located in the front part of the **loom** where the weaver sits. The cloth, after being woven, passes over the breast beam and is guided down to the **cloth beam** where it is wound and stored. The breast beam is the front counterpart to the **back beam** located in the rear of the loom. It is parallel to the back beam and perpendicular to the **warp,** thereby making the right angle interlacing of warp and **filling** easier. Sometimes in old looms the breast beam is omitted and the cloth passes directly to the cloth beam which is then set higher. Also see **harness loom, jack type loom, table loom.**

breast piece. Weaving. See **breast beam.**

breastplate. Stitchery. A large decorative collarlike form similar to a **bib,** which is worn over the chest. Often heavily **stitch**ed and padded, the breastplate is not jewelry, nor is it really a **garment.** This name does not limit the kinds of work that can be included, since it allows for any two or three dimensional construction which can be worn over the chest.

breastplate doll head. Toys. A **doll head** or bust head, manufactured with the neck and shoulders attached. There were often perforations in the breastplate to attach a **kid** or **cloth body.** Most breastplate doll heads were made of **bisque** or **composition.**

brick filling. Lacemaking. See **leaf stitch.**

brick pattern couching. Crewel. Embroidery. A method of couching **metallic thread**s. The positioning of the stitch gives the appearance of a brick wall. When used as a background stitch on material other than **evenly woven** fabric, mark horizontal lines lightly with a pencil before beginning stitching to ensure even rows. Fill the area with horizontal rows, placing the lines of metallic thread close, but not so tightly packed that they overlap one another. As you turn at the end of each line, hold the corners square by placing two stitches on the outer thread and one on the inner, then continue along the line, alternating the stitches to form a brick pattern. See ill. Also see **couching.**

Brick pattern couching

brick stitch. Crewel. Embroidery. An upright stitch of uniform length used as a **filling stitch.** If worked on a background fabric that is not evenly woven, parallel lines should be lightly penciled onto the fabric to aid in maintaining an even stitch. The finished effect is like a row of bricks. See ill. Also see **shading stitch.**

Brick stitch

a.   b.   c.

brick stitch. Needlepoint. (Also called Irish stitch.) An upright stitch of uniform length, usually worked over two or four threads on **canvas** and giving the appearance of a brick wall. It is an easy, well-wearing stitch and is especially useful for filling in background areas. Brick stitch is the basis for **bargello.** Come up at A, go down at B, 4 threads above. Come up at C, level with A but 2 threads to the left, then down at D, 4 threads directly above C (**a.**).

Repeat across the canvas. Work the next row beneath the first, coming up at E, 2 threads below and between A and C, then going down 4 threads above at F. See ill. Also see **filling stitch.**

Brick stitch

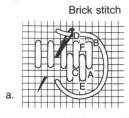   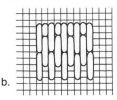

a.   b.

brick stitch. Rugmaking. See **Hungarian stitch.**

brick wall. Quilts. See **brickwork.**

Brickwork. Quilts. (Also called Brick Wall.) A **one-patch** design using rectangles set together in the fashion of bricks.

brickwork inlay. Weaving. See **laid-in.**

Bridal Wreath. Quilts. An **appliqué block** depicting a **wreath** made up of numerous delicate leaves that surround a central flowerlike form of hearts. Bridal quilts almost always included hearts. See ill. Also see **bride's quilt.**

Bridal Wreath

bride. Lacemaking. See **bar, buttonhole bars, ground.**

bride's quilt. Quilts. A quilt, usually the last and best of a series, traditionally made by the bride-to-be for a girl's dowry. The bride's quilt was meant to be used in the master bedroom of the new home. The quilt was started when a girl's engagement was announced, and it was not unusual in the 1880s, when these were popular, for the girl to have ten or twelve quilts completed by that time.

The bride's quilt could also be a collection of **block**s, similar to the **Friendship Medley,** each different and each sewn by a friend of the bride-to-be. The quilt then served as a series of samples from which new quilts could be patterned. When made as a collection, it was similar to the **album quilt.**

It was considered to be an especially lucky sign if the groom designed a block or did a drawing that was incorporated into the quilt. Hearts were commonly included in the design.

bridge. Basketry. A **rod** or series of rods wrapped or woven to make a partition inside a basket or a support for a hinged **cover** across the top of the basket. The rods are usually cut to size and then are attached with the same procedures used for making a regular **handle.**

bridge. Découpage. (Also called stay.) Fine strips connecting delicate elements of intricate designs to hold them in position for cutting.

Draw the bridges onto the **print**s. Cut the interior spaces first (**a.**). Then cut outer edges of print, leaving bridges attached as shown in illustration by dotted lines (**b.**). Leave strips uncut until ready to apply **glue** (**c.**). See Ill. Also see **ladder** and **Découpage: Cutting.**

bridge. Puppets. A post-and-lintel arrangement of two upright supports joined by a horizontal board or bar at the top. In the **marionette stage,** the bridge is securely attached to a base and provides the structure behind which the **controller** stands. The bridge has a **backdrop** hung from the top to conceal the **puppeteer**s. A marionette stage often has more than one bridge. A bridge at the front, from which the **proscenium curtain** is hung, is called the **front bridge.** The **bridge bar** is the top bar of the middle bridge, usually just called "the bridge," over which the **marionette**s are hung. The **rear bridge** is behind the **bench.** Also see **Puppets: Marionette Stage, Puppet Stage.**

bridge bar. Puppets. (Also called leaning bar.) The top cross-piece or horizontal bar that joins the vertical posts or supports of a **bridge.** The **controller** of the **marionette** reaches over the bridge bar to manipulate the figure. Also see **Puppets: Marionette Stage.**

bridle. Kites. The bridle is the line or lines that make up the **bridling** system that connects the kite to the flying **line.** The strings are often referred to as **legs**—a simple bridle with two strings attached to the kite is a two-legged bridle. The bridling system is crucial because it determines the angle at which the kite will meet the wind, and thus whether or not the kite adheres to the principles of **aerodynamics.**

bridling. Kites. The construction of a **bridle** or system of strings determine the angle at which the kite will meet the wind. If the kite is set to fly on a perfect horizontal plane, the wind will pass above and below it with equal force, and the principle of **aerodynamics** will not come into play.

On the other hand, too upright a position will result in more resistance or **drag** than the kite can handle. Ideally the bridling system should hold the kite at an angle to take maximum advantage of the wind and to create optimum **lift** with minimum drag. Experience shows that the proper angle is somewhere between 20° and 40°. Bridling systems vary with kite design and wind conditions. See ill. Also see **Kites: Construction.**

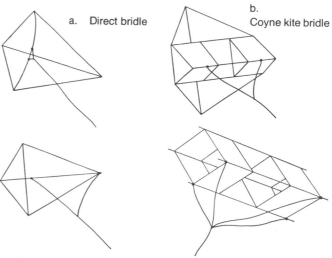

bright annealing. Jewelry. **Annealing** done in the controlled atmosphere of a **kiln** so that a minimum of **fire-scale,** or surface oxidization, is produced on the metal. This method is especially appropriate for annealing wire because the heat in a kiln is quite even, and hot spots, which easily occur when using a torch, and may melt the wire, can be avoided. Make a smooth, loose coil of wire so that it won't kink, and wrap the two ends loosely around the coil to hold it together. **Flux** as usual. Paste flux is more appropriate for this purpose than hard solder flux. Heat the kiln first, then place the wire on a heating frame and put it into the kiln, using tongs. Heat the wire until it just begins to turn red, then remove it and **quench.** Take care not to overheat and melt the wire.

brightboy wheel. Jewelry. A wheel composed of an **abrasive** substance and rubber used to grind away metal slowly. It is available in many shapes and sizes. Small brightboy wheels can be used on the **flexible shaft machine,** large ones on the **buffing machine.** It's a good idea to wear a face mask and protective glasses because the brightboy throws off an extremely fine grit of the abrasive and rubber.

bright dip. Enameling. A solution of 1 part concentrated nitric acid, 1 part concentrated sulfuric acid, and a pinch of table salt used as a quick bath for metals to produce a shinier surface under transparent enamels. This mixture generates heat and should be allowed to stand 24 hours before use. Immerse, remove, and rinse the metal, held by copper tongs. To avoid contaminating the metal with grease and oil, scrub it with a glass brush and a few drops of soapless detergent to alkalinize it under running water. Do not touch the surface or use steel wool. Also see **cleaning metal.**

bright dip. Jewelry. An acid solution that produces a bright, clean surface on metal. The formula is 25% concentrated nitric acid, 60% concentrated sulfuric acid, 2% concentrated hydrochloric acid, and 13% water. This solution should be used at room temperature.

Pickle the metal clean, then dip the work; remove almost immediately, and rinse at once under running water. Too long a time in the solution will result in spotty surfaces due to the hydrochloric acid. This is a very strong **acid** solution, and after the piece is rinsed clean under running water, it is advisable to boil it in a solution of **baking soda** and water for at least 15 minutes to neutralize all the acid residue that will otherwise attack the **solder** and eventually cause the piece to fall apart at the solder **seam**s. Also see **blooming** and **Jewelry: Precautions.**

brightness. See **value.**

brilliance. A quality of color usually considered synonymous with **saturation.** Sometimes brilliance is used loosely as a characteristic of color that is both highly saturated and of high **value.**

brilliant. Gemcutting. See **facet, faceting, preforming.**

brine. Metalworking. A solution used for **quenching** hot metals made by adding 5–10% common salt to water. Quenching in brine creates a more uniform hardness, wets the surface more quickly, and gives the metal a more delicate **temper** than water alone. Rinse the brine off with clear water when the metal is cool because brine accelerates corrosion.

brine curing. Leather. See **curing.**

brioche knitting. Knitting. A style of knitting attributed to the Breton peasants in France that produces a thicker fabric and a deeper ribbing than usual. The brioche stitch is based on a ⅛ yarn over, a slip stitch purlwise, and a knit stitch ⅛, repeat ⅛ to ⅛ the width of the first row. The second row (which is repeated for all even rows) is based on a yarn over, slip stitch purlwise, knit 2 together (these 2 stitches being the slip stitch and the yarn over of the first row). See ill. Also see **Knitting: Construction.**

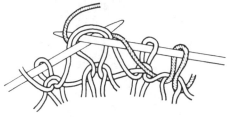
Second-row brioche stitch

brioche stitch. Knitting. See **brioche knitting.**

briolette. Gemcutting. See **facet.**

bristle brush. Jewelry. Brushes made of nylon, horse or hog's hair and fiber used for **polishing** and texturing metal on buffing or flexible shaft machines. The brushes are available in a large assortment of shapes and sizes. Their chief virtue is that they are very flexible and can reach into difficult areas. Short bristles produce a stiffer brush; longer bristles provide more flexibility. Charge the brush lightly with red rouge to polish metal. Brushing can also remove scratches and burrs (scratch brushing). They are particularly appropriate where a fine surface treatment has been applied, such as **engraving,** polishing, **stamping, reticulation** or any other technique in which metal is not removed. Used with emery paste, brushes can produce a **matte** finish. Protective eye shields should be worn when using a bristle brush as the bristles occasionally fly out. Also see **buffing compound, wire brush.**

bristol glaze. Ceramics. A medium firing temperature glaze containing **zinc oxide.** It was developed to avoid the use of **white lead** which is toxic. A difficult **glaze** to control, it is subject to **crawling** and **pinhole**s.

Britannia metal. Jewelry. See **copper.**

Britannia metal. Metalworking. See **pewter.**

britch wool. Spinning. See **sorting.**

brittleness. Metalworking. (Also called shortness.) The tendency of a metal to break easily. For example, certain kinds of **cast iron** will break when dropped. Hard metals are more brittle than soft ones. When a metal becomes **work-hardened** from hammering it becomes brittle and **annealing** is necessary to resoften it and prevent it from cracking.

brittleness. Plastics. Plastics often become brittle because of the inherent formulation of the plastic material, low outdoor temperatures, oxidizing effects of ultraviolet rays in sunlight, and stress and pressures put upon the plastic. In general, high-density resins are more brittle than low-density ones. Brittleness can be reduced by mixing **additive**s, such as **antioxidant**s, **plasticizer**s, and **filler**s, into the **resin,** or by **annealing thermoplastic**s.

broach. Jewelry. See **reamer.**

broaching. Jewelry. The use of a tapered, sharp tool, a broach or **reamer** to create or enlarge holes in metal.

broad chain stitch. Crewel. Embroidery. See **chain stitch.**

broadcloth. Quilts. Stitchery. (Also called cotton broadcloth.) A closely woven **cotton fabric** of smooth, even texture. It is a **fabric** that handles very easily for **appliqué** and is therefore commonly used in quilts and in stitchery. Broadcloth is the name also applied to similar weaves of **wool** and **synthetic fiber**s.

broad rope stitch. Crewel. Embroidery. See **rope stitch.**

brocade. Crewel. Embroidery. A woven **fabric** with low or matte design areas juxtaposed with raised or shiny design areas. It can be quite dramatic when used as a **background fabric** with the brocade design itself used as part of the overall design.

brocade. Stitchery. Heavy, rich-looking **fabric**s in which floral or figured patterns are raised, emphasizing changes in surface and colors. The design appears on the **right side** of the fabric in more contrast and detail than of the **back.**

brocade. Weaving. (Also called brocading.) Originally brocade was a term used to designate a particular type of figured or patterned fabric in which an elaborate and sumptuous embroidered effect was achieved with a **supplementary** filling thread—often of silk, gold, or silver. The word "brocade," a noun, was changed through colloquial handweavers' usage to a verb, "brocading," indicating a method of fabric structure. It has come to mean various types of structures to various schools of weaving. About the only common point these assorted meanings have is that the fabric is patterned with a third element being introduced into a basic two element (**warp** and **filling**) **ground** structure. The brocading yarn is understood to be heavier and softer than the ground cloth threads—a departure from the original method of constructing brocade. Among handweavers, there are three types of brocade weaves that appear—warp brocade, filling brocade, and **laid-in** or **discontinuous** brocade. A warp brocade has a pattern or decorative warp threaded on certain **harness**es so the design element appears as a warp stripe or squares or rectangles formed by interrupting the warp stripe with the filling ground thread. After each pattern warp **end,** there is a warp end that will weave with the filling to form the ground. In filling brocade, the pattern thread weaves **selvage** to selvage with a **pick** of ground filling after every pick of brocade. **Overshot** falls into this type of brocade category. Laid-in has the brocading element weaving back and forth only in the design sections planned by the weaver. The pattern yarn is not continuous from one selvage to the other, hence the name, discontinuous brocade. These classifications are all open to controversy. Some weavers acknowledge the warp and filling brocades as true brocades, and laid-in is cited as not being a true brocade because of the discontinuous pattern yarn. Other weavers feel that laid-in, with an effect similar to embroidery, is closer to brocade than other structures. Most of the weaves falling under the brocade umbrella have their own weave structure categories, so there is no need for them to have a second classification as a brocade weave.

brocade knitting. Knitting. **Color knitting** that uses a change of **stitch**es and a change of color. This is done to introduce more texture and to emphasize the design. Silk and metallic threads are commonly used in this type of knitting. One of the most famous examples of this knitting was worn by Charles I of England on the day of his execution in 1649. Also see **Knitting.**

brocading. Weaving. See **brocade.**

brocading yarn. Weaving. See **brocade.**

brochure. Bookbinding. A sewn book with a paper cover.

Broderie Anglaise. Embroidery. See **whitework.**

broderie Perse. Quilts. Persian embroidery, or the name given to the **appliqué** of **fabrics** imported from the East Indies. The **palampores,** hand-blocked and richly painted exotic fabrics, were exported even though the British Parliament strictly prohibited it. The unusual forms and exciting colors of the fabrics were adapted by the women of late Colonial days, who cut designs from these fabrics and appliquéd them to handwoven **linen.** Embroidery was added, and the finished **coverlet**s were called "broderie Perse." The term is sometimes used to refer to any appliqué in which floral arrangements or trees are cut out and appliquéd to another **backing.**

Broder Medici wool. Crewel. Embroidery. Needlepoint. (Also called French wool, Medici wool.) A two-ply tightly twisted French tapestry yarn with a silky sheen, considered one of the finest quality wools available. It is extremely fine in texture and is available in a range of antique colors very similar to those used in sixteenth-century tapestries.

broken color. A color that has been mixed with some of its **complementary color** to partly gray or "break" the full value of the **hue.** Broken colors tend to look complex or sophisticated and when used with elements of a **shadow series** can produce elegant color harmonies.

broken dishes. Quilts. See Windmill.

broken ends. Weaving. **Warp end**s that break while weaving either due to too much or uneven tension or weak fibers in the yarn. To repair, do not tie a knot, but put in a new warp thread the length of the remaining warp. Tie it in a bowknot to the broken thread at the back of the **loom.** With this new end, replace the broken one in the **reed** and **heddle**s and bring it to the front of the loom, so that about 4″ overlaps the **fell.** Secure to the fabric, by winding in a figure-8 around a pin stuck into the cloth about 1″–2″ down from the fell. Untie the bowknot and adjust the tension of the new warp end to match the other warp ends. As the weaving progresses and the warp moves forward, the bowknot will come closer to the back **harness.** Untie it and retie at the **back beam.** When the fabric is off the loom,

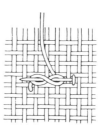

New warp thread secured to fabric

pull the loose ends to the back of the fabric by **darning in** with a needle and then trim. See ill.

Broken Star. Quilts. See **Dutch Rose, Eight-pointed Star, Star-within-Star.**

broken threads. Lacemaking. See **weaver's knot.**

broken twill. Weaving. See **twill.**

Bronson weave. Weaving. A name given by the American weaver Mary Meigs Atwater, to a group of weaves found in an early nineteenth century weaving treatise written by J. and R. Bronson. The treatise was American, but the weaves are actually English in origin, although credit is given to the Germans for introducing them to colonial America. They fall in the spot and **lace weave** groupings and are made up of **plain weave** with **float**s in specific areas to give the spot designs or the lacy openings. Spot Bronson (also called Barley-Corn) has either an all-over textured look, or the spot floats are grouped in patterns to give a specific surface design (**a.**). Lace Bronson is often mistaken for **Swedish lace,** to which it has a close similarity. The lacy effect may be either in spots or in grouped pattern areas. Lace Bronson differs from spot Bronson in that it is **sley**ed more loosely, and the float spot is doubled in order for the open effect to appear (**b.**). The Bronson weaves were frequently used in colonial America for household linens. Today Bronson weaves are woven in cotton and wool and used in upholstery, blankets, afghans, pillows, wall hangings, scarves, stoles, and women's apparel fabrics. See ill. Also see **spot weave.**

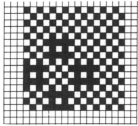   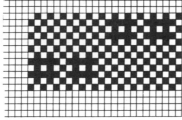

a. One repeat of a pattern in spot Bronson

b. Lace Bronson draft

bronze. Enameling. See **metal.**

bronze. Jewelry. A **copper-tin alloy** that is the oldest alloy known to man. It was used in England 2,000 years before the Roman invasion. Although sometimes called bronze, they are better described as high tensile brasses. Modern phosphor bronzes contain 1.25–10% tin; 5% tin with 0.35% phosphorus is the most commonly used. They have superb resiliency, hardness, fatigue endurance, and resistance to corrosion. Phosphor bronze melts at 1550–1900° F. It can be joined by soft soldering, silver soldering, **brazing,** and oxyacetylene welding. When overheated, bronze becomes **hot-short,** or brittle.

bronze. Metalworking. An **alloy** used most often in the casting of sculpture composed of about 90% **copper** and 10% **tin,** with traces of other metals. Its melting point varies from 1300° F to 1900° F, depending on the proportions of the various metals. Sometimes sculptors add small amounts of lead to the molten bronze to lower the melting point and soften the metal. Its color ranges from golden or lighter (if zinc is added) to gray-blue (if lead is added) when it is first cast. It then turns with age to golden, reddish, or dark brown, or to light green when sulfates form on the surface.

Bronze casting alloys expand as they solidify, forcing the molten metal into the crevices of the **mold,** and then slightly contract when cool, facilitating the removal of the metal from the mold. **Tin** or **aluminum** added to the alloy increases strength and corrosion resistance; the addition of **nickel** lightens the color. The bronze surface takes on a **patina** from oxidation in outdoor weather, but this film of corrosion does not usually penetrate far beneath the surface.

Bronze is sold in sheets for **raising** and **metal spinning.** Bronze may be welded, soldered, forged, and cut with saws or shears. Casting alloys may be braze-welded with bronze **welding rods** but they become brittle when heated past red hot.

The name "bronze" is derived from the Italian word for brown (*bruno*). It is impossible to pinpoint the first producers of bronze, but bronze objects from Mesopotamia have been dated at about 2900 B.C., from Egypt at about 2400 B.C., and from China (Shang ritual vases) at 1523 to 1028 B.C. The ancient Greeks often cast sculpture in bronze, but most of these statues were later melted down for the metal by Romans, Turks, and other invaders. Large Greek statues were sometimes made in sections, which were soldered or riveted together. Sheets of bronze plate were also nailed and riveted over wood carvings, and large wooden patterns were sometimes **sandcast** in bronze.

bronze powder. China and Glass Painting. A metallic powder for decorating handles and vases (but not durable enough for use on tableware); it provides a dull, matte luster after **firing.** It is available in various shades from gold-bronze through green-gold bronze; combine and apply it in the same way as matte **gold.**

bronze powder. Découpage. Stenciling. Tincrafting. Metallic powders and paints are available from art-supply and paint stores in a variety of shades. The dry powders are dissolved in turpentine with a bit of **varnish** or in a specially prepared bronzing **solvent,** also available from paint stores. These metallic colors have a tendency to tarnish. Also see **Stenciling.**

bronze red. Metalworking. See **welding rod.**

bronze solder. Jewelry. See **spelter solder.**

bronze welding. Metalworking. See **welding.**

bronzing. Tincraft. The application of metallic powders or paints to metal surfaces. The powder is mixed with a solvent to the consistency of milk and applied with a brush. The metallic bronzing colors as well as the solvent are available from art supply and paint stores in a variety of shades, from light gold to deep bronze and in lustrous blues and greens. The liquid colors come ready to use. Also see **bronze powder** and **Tincraft: Finishing.**

bronzite. Gemcutting. See **hypersthene.**

Brooks Bouquet. Weaving. An **openwork technique** that creates the open spaces by taking the **filling** yarn around groups of **warp** threads and knotting them tightly together. It is an ancient technique going back to the time of pre-Inca Peru, where it was used to create a fine, mesh fabric that was used as a base for embroidery and was thought to be **netting.** In this version, it is sometimes referred to as Peruvian knotting. The more commonplace version is not so fine, nor so open that it resembles a mesh. Each group that is knotted together is comprised of many more warp **end**s than the Peruvian type (which consisted usually of two or three warp ends held together), and as this group is pulled together, it looks like a bouquet. Hence, it is also called a bouquet weave, or a wrapped weave, due to the wrapping of the filling around the warp ends to form the knot. However, the name Brooks Bouquet (after Marguerite G. Brooks, an expert in bobbin lace who created many variations on the bouquet technique), is in more general and widespread use.

Brooks Bouquet uses a **plain weave** with the **shuttle** brought out of the **shed** at the point where the bouquet is to be formed. The shuttle is taken back over the warp threads to be included in the bouquet and then under them, going through the loop made by the filling yarn. The yarn is pulled tightly to draw the warp ends together. The shuttle is reinserted into the shed and the next bouquet is formed. This wrapping and pulling tight procedure is continued for as many bouquets as desired. The bouquets are spaced apart by bands of plain weave. The closer the spacing, the more open the effect. See ill.

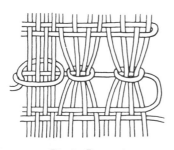

Brooks Bouquet

broom-handle horse. Toys. See **hobbyhorse.**

brown. Basketry. See **willow.**

Brown. Quilts. See **Gray Goose.**

Brown and Sharpe gauge. Jewelry. Metalworking. See **gauge, sheet metal gauge.**

brown-bag puppet. Puppets. See **paper bag puppet.**

Brown Goose. Quilts. See **Gray Goose.**

browning. Metalworking. See **bluing.**

brown pigment. Ceramics. An oxide that provides the color brown in **glazes** and **slips. Iron oxide** is the most common brown pigment. Also see **burnt sienna, iron chromate, ochre, pigment oxide, sienna.**

brown sculpture wax. Stained Glass. See **aciding.**

Brunswick Star. Quilts. (Also called Chained Star, Rolling Star.) A **block** design for a **pieced quilt** that features a central six- or eight-pointed star made up of triangles or diamonds. It has long been a favorite pattern. See ill.

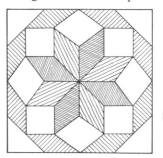

Brunswick Star

Brunswick wheel. Spinning. See **treadle wheel.**

brush. Batik and Tie-dye. Découpage. One of the few tools used in the **wax-resist** technique. **Natural fiber** brushes are preferable, as **synthetic fiber**s are easily affected by overheating. A small wire rack in the bottom of the hot wax container will keep bristles from resting against the source of heat, avoiding the overheating and bending of bristles.

Regular paintbrushes, 1″–3″ wide, can be used for **waxing** large areas. Bristle brushes are also excellent for this. A brush with angled bristles (you can cut your own from a straight-end brush) is helpful in waxing close to design lines. Assorted artist's brushes, both flat and pointed, can be used for **direct-dye painting** and waxing. Japanese ink brushes or Oriental ink brushes are excellent where fine lines or pointed areas are to be painted.

Q-Tips, toothpicks, spatulas, paste brushes, and stencil brushes can all be used to give different effects in the application of **dye** or wax.

Wax-stiffened brushes become flexible again when they are dipped back into the hot wax. Wax may be removed from brushes with mineral **solvent**s, but generally brushes once used for batik are best kept for only that use because it is difficult to remove all the wax.

In découpage fine pointed watercolor brushes are used. They should be natural bristles and of an appropriate size for the design. Flat brushes of good quality from the hardware store can often be used for finishing. Use each brush for only one purpose.

brush. Ceramics. A variety of brushes are used in applying **glaze** and **wax resist.** Cheap brushes generally work better for applying glaze. Japanese brushes are also recommended for decorating. It is worth noting that once a brush has been dipped in hot wax it can only be used for wax painting and it will be destroyed if it is dipped in hot wax when wet.

brush. China and Glass Painting. Many brushes, usually sable or camel's hair mounted in brass, wire-bound quills, or lightweight wooden handles, are available for painting china or glass. There are different shapes designed for various painting techniques. Each shape is available in several sizes.

Pointed brushes, called pointed shaders, are used for shading or modeling (**a.**). The small, fine-pointed brushes, called scrollers and liners, are used for lining and for intricate work such as gold lines over **raised paste** (**b.**).

Brushes with straight ends are background color brushes (**c.**). Lettering quills may also be used. Slant-cut brushes are used to blend and soften and for lining and **banding** (**d.**). Wide, blunt brushes are used for stippling (**e.**). See ill.

Camel's-hair brushes for china decorating

a. Pointed brush   d. Slant-cut brush

b. Scroller   e. Stippling brush

c. Straight-cut brush

brush. Jewelry. There are many types of brushes used in jewelry, each having their own specialized use: **flux brush** for **fluxing**, an old toothbrush for washing off **buffing compound**s, other types of brushes that fit on a **buffing machine** or on a **flexible shaft machine.** Also see **bristle brush, wire brush.**

brush. Stained Glass. Many varieties of brushes are used to achieve different effects in **painting on glass.** The following is a basic list:

Broad hog-hair brushes and stiff-haired scrubs are from 1"–6" wide. The bristles are 1½"–2" long and hold a lot of paint. They are like those used for house painting (**a.**).

Oil painting brushes.

Broad-headed, flat, soft-haired brushes. These brushes provide a delicate touch, but the bristles often separate into two or three bunches that produce parallel lines of paint. They do not hold much paint and are useful with enamels ground in an oil base (**b.**).

Riggers, liners, pencils are long, thin, flexible-haired brushes. They are good for drawing, hatching, shading, and drawing crisp lines. The long-haired brushes help to free up the brush stroke (**c.**).

Calligraphy brushes are the nearest modern counterpart to the brushes used for glass-painting in the Middle Ages. Larger brushes are better and are very versatile. They produce sharp, easily controlled brush work (**d.**).

Badger brush (also called stippling brush). These are among the most important tools used in painting on glass. They are used to smooth and manipulate the paint when it is already on the glass. They create a dull matte out of the paint, which can then be treated to let light through. They range from 14" to 4" wide at the base of the handle, but the badger hairs, which are quite bushy, spread out much farther. They are very flexible brushes and their elasticity is not affected by water. If properly cared for, they can last 40 or 50 years (**e.**).

Other materials. These are for the individual to experiment with. Such things as toothbrushes, cut-down housepainter's brushes, and cut-down oil brushes are sometimes useful. Goose and turkey feathers or quills; small paint-rollers; small, stiff brushes; pot-scrubbers, and other ingenuities can also be used. See ill. Also see **matting, stippling.**

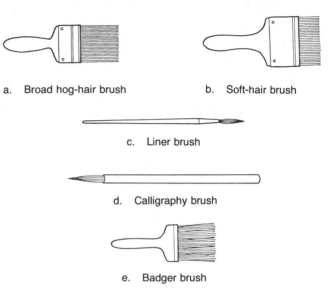

a.   Broad hog-hair brush   b.   Soft-hair brush

c.   Liner brush

d.   Calligraphy brush

e.   Badger brush

brush. Stenciling. See **stencil brush.**

brush finish. Jewelry. See **Swedish finish.**

brushing. Weaving. See **napping.**

brushing flame. Jewelry. See **flame.**

brushing glaze. Ceramics. See **Ceramics: Glazing.**

brush-on dye. Batik and Tie-dye. See **direct-dye painting.**

brushwork. Ceramics. A type of ceramic decoration. The most common methods are brushing one **glaze** over another, decorating with **oxide**s, and **wax resist.**

bruting. Gemcutting. The process of grinding **facet**s into a **diamond** by abrading it with another diamond. **Diamond powder** is used to polish the facets. Also see **Abrasive.**

bubble. Stained Glass. (Also called glass bubble, pinhole.) Bubbles appear in antique glass when the blowpipe is removed from the pot before the **silica** sand, borax, and colorants have boiled away the sulphurous gases. The longer the pot of molten glass is heated, the cleaner is the glass produced.

bubble blower. Toys. Any device used for **soap bubble blowing.** It must offer clear passage for air blown in at one end to form bubbles from soap film placed over the other end. Any soap or detergent water will do, although a little glycerin added to the water extends the life of the bubbles. Commercial bubble mixes are available.

Most children readily discover that by curling the fingers around to the palm to form a circle, a simple soap bubble blower is formed. A plastic or wooden spool, such as a thread spool, works well. Straws, particularly plastic ones, can also be used. In short, any waterproof or semiwaterproof tubular-shaped form through which a person can blow makes a good bubble blower. Handmade blowers are of wood or clay. Coat hangers, bent in the shapes of circles with handles attached, can be used as bubble blowers. The circle is dipped in the soapy water, then swung through the air to leave behind a stream of bubbles. Also see **bath toy, ephemeral toy.**

bubbling. Candlemaking. A surface defect in the finished candle formed by **molding** that shows up as a complete ring of tiny **pitmark**s (air bubbles) around the candle. It is caused by adding water to the **water bath** after the molded candle and mold have been immersed. Also see **Candlemaking: Molding, Possible Flaws in Candles.**

bubbling. Rugmaking. Weaving. (Also called arching, arcing, bowing, curving, waving.) Placing the **filling** in the **shed** as a series of small arcs. This keeps the filling very slack so that it can cover the **warp** completely and also prevent the fabric from drawing in and narrowing at the edges. The arcs are formed in the open shed by pushing the filling every 2″–3″ toward the **fell** or the last **pick** of weaving. This can be done with a finger or the point of a pencil or scissors. Care should be taken that the arcs do not touch the weaving, or little beads of filling yarn will form at the point of touching after the filling is beaten down. The technique of bubbling is used primarily in rugs, whether **flatweave** or **pile.** It also is used in wall hangings, or other fabric, where there is difficulty in covering the warp. It is usually associated with working **selvage** to selvage, instead of in just small areas. See ill.

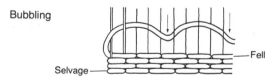
Bubbling / Fell / Selvage

bucket. Basketry. A container used to hold water for soaking the **reed** in order to soften it in preparation for basketmaking. Also see **Basketry: Preparing the Materials.**

buckram. Bookbinding. See **cloth.**

buckram. Crewel. Embroidery. A coarse linen or cotton cloth stiffened with glue, used for backing or interfacing lightweight or soft embroidered fabrics. Also see **Crewel: Finishing.**

buckram. Stitchery. A heavy and somewhat stiff **plain weave** cotton or **linen** mesh material that is heavily **sized** and is used for **stiffening** and shaping. It is used as interfacing in banners and wall hangings and as stiffening in **soft sculpture**s, **three-dimensional stitchery,** and **stuff**ed animals.

buckskin. Leather. A term for skins of deer and elk from which the outer or **top grain** has been removed.

buff. Basketry. See **willow.**

buff. Enameling. See **polishing.**

buff. Jewelry. Metalworking. Plastics. To refine a surface by removing scratches or by **polishing.**

Also, a disk of felt, cotton flannel, rubber, wool, muslin, various leathers, or canvas that is attached to the spindle of a **buffing machine** (also called buffing wheel) or to a **flexible shaft machine** for the **buffing** and polishing of metal or plastic. Closely sewn buffs are harder than unsewn buffs and are used with coarse polishing and **cutting compound**s such as **Lea's compound** and **tripoli**; softer, unsewn buffs such as muslin and loosely sewn wool are used for final buffing operations. Stitched muslin and loosely sewn wool are used for final buffing operations. Stitched muslin buffs are applicable to many situations, whereas other kinds of buffs have specific uses. To determine the correct buff to use for a piece of work and with which compound, consult your jewelry supply house.

A buff once charged with a compound cannot be used with another compound. Charging the wheel refers to the application of a compound to it. An overcharged buff may be cleaned with a wheel rake. Except for **felt buff**s, fabric buffs that are dirty or have become contaminated with the wrong compound may be laundered with detergent in a washing machine and dried in a dryer to restore them. When a sewn buff wears down, a layer of stitches may be removed to refurbish it. Although it is possible to purchase ready-to-use buffs, most of them must be broken in before use. See ill. Also see **breaking in a buffing wheel, buffing compound, charge.**

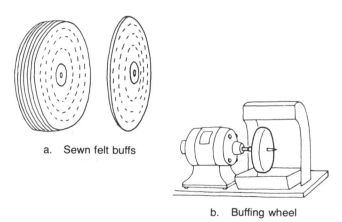
a. Sewn felt buffs
b. Buffing wheel

buffalo skin. Leather. See **water buffalo skin.**

buffing. Candlemaking. A finishing process in candlemaking in which the completed candle is buffed with a wet paper towel to accentuate the waxy shine. Great care should be taken during buffing not to mar the surface of the candle. Also see **Candlemaking: Finishing.**

buffing. Enameling. See **polishing.**

buffing. Jewelry. Metalworking. Plastics. The process of shining metal to its final surface luster, following **polishing** operations. **Polishing cloth**s are used for delicate work that needs hand polishing. Buffing wheels constructed of various soft or loose materials are used with power tools for less delicate work.

The surface finish desired, the speed and size of the wheel, the **buffing compound** used, the material the **buff** is made of, and the surface condition and the type of metal to be buffed are all considerations that dictate the techniques used.

To prepare for machine buffing, **charge** the wheel with the proper compound. Support is extremely important during buffing. Hold on to the work tightly, but in such a fashion that if it gets caught in the wheel it can be pulled from your hands without catching your hands and fingers. Buffing and polishing are done on the lower third of the wheel. The buff is gentle to the skin, so if you are holding a piece of work securely and the wheel runs over part of the skin, it may get hot but will not burn.

A piece of **sheet metal** can be buffed by holding it with the thumbs on top of the metal and the fingers fully supporting the area from underneath. The buffing wheel will polish the areas between the thumbs. Direction of the metal must be constantly changed during buffing, or **feathering** will occur. A fairly firm pressure must be exerted against the wheel in order for the buff and its compound to work effectively. If the metal should become too hot to hold, it can be dipped into a bowl of water to cool it. Dry the work before continuing buffing, as the compounds cut too fast when they are wet for good control to be maintained.

When buffing, allow the wheel to run over (a.), but not into (b.), edges; the latter may not only ruin the form of the work, but it can also jerk it out of your hands.

It is normal for some compound to collect on the surface of the metal. However, as you turn the metal the rotation of the wheel will pull most of it back onto the wheel. If the compound builds up it can cause feathering as it moves around and digs into the metal. Excess buildup of compounds should be removed from the work with **ammonia** and an old toothbrush. Then rinse and dry off the work, and continue buffing. When buffing is completed, all buffing compounds can be washed off in the same way.

Be careful not to overbuff. You want the metal to remain crisp. This applies both to organic and geometric forms. Overbuffing rounds off edges and forms in an uncontrolled manner, producing slurred, mushy-looking forms and edges.

To change a buff, turn off the motor, allow it to stop completely, and unwind the buff by hand. To put on a different buff, turn the motor on and place the buff lightly against the tapered spindle, making sure the larger part of the hole in the buff goes on toward the motor. It will grab hold of the tapered spindle and wind itself on. Be prepared to let go of the buff the moment it takes hold.

It takes a short while to get used to buffing. There are a few practical rules that will enable you to avoid injuries. The wheel should always rotate toward the operator. Never wear anything loose. Remove all jewelry and accessories. If your hair is long, tie it back and tuck it up under a close-fitting cap. Button or roll up long sleeves above the elbow, or wear a short-sleeved shirt. Do not wear gloves of any kind. Do not turn your back on a running motor; turn it off first. Wear shatterproof eyeshields or goggles. See ill. Also see **bobbing**, **chain polishing**.

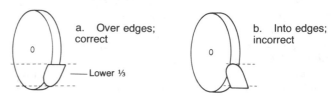

a. Over edges; correct
b. Into edges; incorrect
—— Lower ⅓

buffing. Leather. Leather is buffed with a soft cloth or shoebrush after applying finish coats to bring up luster and remove any excess finish. Also see **Leatherwork: Finishing Leather.**

buffing compound. Jewelry. Compounds used for the final **polishing** and **buffing** of metal. There are two primary divisions of buffing compounds. The first group consists of compounds which are considered **cutting compound**s, in that they slowly cut metal away to remove the scratches left by previous forming methods. The second group consists of preparations which are considered **polishing compound**s in that they do not cut, and cannot remove scratches. They are used to produce a higher polish on metal surfaces. Polishing compounds are used after the cutting compounds have produced a smooth, perfect surface on the metal. Included in this group are **coloring composition**s, which are final polishing agents which affect color changes in the metal. Each compound should be confined to a **buff** which is used specifically for that compound. After a piece of work is buffed with a cutting compound, it should be thoroughly washed with a diluted solution of soapy household ammonia, dried, and then polished. This washing and drying should take place after each compound used to prevent contaminating the next buff, and after the final polishing to remove any residue left from the final compound.

Cutting compounds are generally applied to hard, close sewn, cloth buffs made from coarser materials such as muslin, felt, wool, canvas, or leather.

Polishing compounds are generally applied to softer, loosely sewn, more flexible fabric buffs, or to string or sheepskin buffs.

Listed below are some of the compounds available, their uses, and some of the metals and buffs with which they are used. If you run into a situation where you are not sure which compound to use for a specific metal or wheel, refer to your jewelry supply house.

CUTTING COMPOUNDS
  Super Tripoli, a cutting and polishing compound that can be used on all metals.
  tripoli, used on all metals, generally with a muslin buff.
  Lea's compound, used for cutting or finishing **copper** or **silver.**
  bobbing compound, used on all metals and applied to small leather or small, hard, felt buffs.
  crocus composition, used for fast cutting of silver, **brass**, and copper.

white diamond, used for cutting, polishing, and coloring brass, aluminum, and copper and applied to a muslin buff.

powdered pumice, removes excess oxidation when **liver of sulfur** has been used, and with a muslin buff produces a **satin finish.**

emery paste, fast cutting mixture of **emery** and grease, used with a muslin buff.

stainless compound, used for fast cutting of steel, copper, silver or plastic, as well as being excellent for polishing **stake**s and **hammer**s.

POLISHING COMPOUNDS

red rouge, produces a high polish on gold, silver, brass, copper, and bronze. One of the most commonly used polishing compounds.

yellow rouge, has good polishing qualities for gold, silver, and stainless steel, and with extra pressure exerted will achieve a cutting action.

porcelain rouge, produces a fast mirror finish on all metals which require red rouge, except high **karat** gold.

white rouge, used with white gold and platinum.

green rouge, used with gold and silver.

black rouge, polishes silver and darkens it.

gray compound, cuts and colors most metals.

pink compound, cuts and colors most metals.

Also see **coloring composition, greaseless compound.**

buffing machine. Jewelry. A motor-driven device of ⅜ or ½ horsepower used to polish metals by means of rotating spindles with attached buffs of various materials charged with cutting or **buffing compound**s. They are available with fixed and adjustable speeds ranging from 1750 rpms to 3500 rpms. Higher speeds are used for normal polishing, and lower speeds are used for **chain polishing,** wire, long strips of metal, as well as for **grinding** operations. The more sophisticated polishing machines contain excellent motors that have lights in the polishing hoods, and are equipped with suction blowers and filters to eliminate the dust and dirt that result from polishing. They can have one shaft, but usually have a shaft extending from both sides of the motor so that two buffs can be used.

If you purchase a buffing machine, read the directions thoroughly. They sometimes come without information, so you should know the following. Tapered spindles are marked for use on the right side marked R, or left side, L. Do not interchange them or the wheel used will not stay tight and can fly off. It is important that the wheel always rotate toward the operator.

If the speeds are variable and the machine goes slowly enough for grinding and chain polishing, at least one tapered spindle has to come off for grinding and be replaced with an arbor, which is also not interchangeable from right to left. Check when purchasing a buffing motor to see if the shaft can house both tapered spindles and arbors. When a motor has only one speed, say a low speed, 1750 rpm or less, the choice of the buff size is important. The larger the diameter of the wheel, the faster its outside edge goes in terms of feet per minute. For example, a motor

with a speed of 1750 rpm, with a wheel 1″ in diameter, will have a perimeter speed of 450 feet per minute; a wheel 4″ in diameter will have a perimeter speed of 1800 feet per minute; a wheel 6″ in diameter will have a perimeter speed of 2750 feet per minute. See ill. Also see **bristle brush, buffing, chain polishing, files, flexible shaft machine, hand polishing.**

Buffing machine

Shank

Tapered spindle in position on shank

buffing spindle. Jewelry. See **tapered spindle.**

buffing wheel. Gemcutting. See **polishing.**

buffing wheel. Jewelry. Metalworking. Plastics. See **buff.**

buff top. Gemcutting. See **facet.**

bugle beads. Beadwork. A type of **glass bead** that is used for **bead embroidery.** They are thin and cylindrical, approximately ½″–¼″ long, and are available in a wide variety of colors, lined or unlined. **Lined beads,** because they are painted with a tinsel lining inside, tend to fade after constant exposure to sunlight. Unlined bugle beads, also called satin bugle beads, are permanent in color.

Bugle beads were introduced around 1600 for use as **trade bead**s; they were less valuable than other beads, and sold by weight. Also see **Beadmaking.**

buglework. Beadwork. **Bead embroidery** tapestries using cylindrical bugle beads, in which the motif as well as the background are solidly filled with rows of beads.

buhl work. Shell Carving. See **boulle work.**

building blocks. Toys. See **blocks.**

building brick. Toys. Building **blocks** shaped like **brick**s. They are a popular construction toy, easily made at home from blocks of wood. Some commercially available ones are made of rigid cardboard or fiberboard, sometimes paper-covered or painted in a brick pattern. Also see **constructional toy.**

building toy. Toys. See **constructional toy.**

Bulgarian knitting. Knitting. **Color knitting** in the style and traditional patterns of Bulgaria. Bulgarian patterns are often used for knitting socks.

bulk. Stitchery. A thick or unwieldy mass. In sewing, **fabric**s are often trimmed close to **seem**s to get rid of excess bulk. This is especially helpful and important when bulky materials have been used.

bulked yarns. Spinning. Weaving. Synthetic **filament** yarns which have gone through a texturizing process that displaces the filaments from their natural closely packed position. The processes either mechanically loop or crimp the yarn so that it has a greater volume and a softer **hand** or touch. The bulking processes were developed to give synthetic filament yarns some of the advantages of **spun yarn.**

bulldog clip. Batik and Tie-dye. A hinged metal clip that is held shut by a spring. Two flat, short lengths of metal form the clamping jaws. It is commonly used on clipboards or to hold many sheets of paper together. In **tie-dye** the bulldog clips are used to hold **pleat**s, folds, or **gather**s in the **fabric.**

bullion. Stained Glass. See **crown glass.**

bullion knot. Crewel. Embroidery. Needlepoint. (Also called caterpillar stitch, coil stitch, knot stitch, post stitch, Puerto Rico rose, roll stitch, rose stitch, worm stitch.) A decorative knot deriving its name from a resemblance to **bullion thread.** The bullion knot is attached to the fabric only at points A and B; therefore, if the coil is longer than the original distance between A and B, the knot will be raised from the surface. This simple stitch is useful for leaves, petals, or rosebud effects when coiled around one another, and is effective worked on the top of a needlepoint background. It is best worked on an **embroidery frame.** Double thread is usually best for this stitch. The knots may be used individually, or worked side by side. They should not be too long, or they will curl instead of lying flat on the material.

Bring the needle up at A, go down at B, but do not pull the thread through (**a.**). Stab needle up at A again but bring it only halfway through the material (**b.**). Holding the needle from below, twist the thread round the needle at A, until the number of twists equals the distance between A and B (**c.**). Holding the top of the needle and threads firmly with the finger and thumb of the free hand, draw the needle through loosening the coil of threads with the free hand as you do so, to allow the needle to pass through freely (**d.**). Then place the needle against the end of the twist, at the same time pulling on the thread, until the knot lies flat on the material. If any "bumps" appear in the knot, flatten these by stroking the underneath of the twist with the needle, at the same time pulling on the thread (**e.**). Put the needle in close a' .he end of the twist and pull through firmly (**f.**).

To make roses, work three bullion knots to form a triangle. Then work one bullion knot to wrap around one corner of the triangle, putting a few extra twists on the needle so that the knot curls around instead of lying straight. Next, add another bullion, overlapping halfway over the previous one. Work round the triangle in this way, until the rose is formed (**g.**). The **stem stitch** and **detached chain stitch** make the leaves and stem respectively. See ill. Also see **crewel point.**

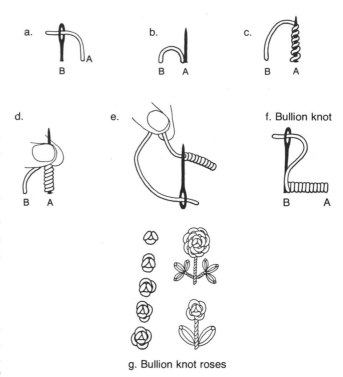

f. Bullion knot

g. Bullion knot roses

bullion stitch bar. Crochet. (Also called roll stitch.) The bullion stitch bar is composed of a series of **yarn-over**s and creates a hard, solid barlike row of crochet.

Wind the yarn evenly around the hook for as many yarn-overs as it takes to reach the desired height of the bar (**a.**). This may be as many as 10 or 12 times. Insert the **crochet hook** into the **loop** below in the **foundation chain,** make a yarn-over and draw it through all the yarn-overs except for the last two on the hook. Make another yarn-over and draw it through the last two to finish the bar (**b.**). See ill.

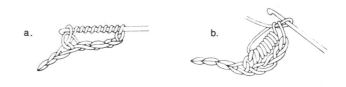

Bullion stitch bar

bullion thread. Embroidery. (Also called purl.) A **metallic thread** that is a fine wire wrapped very tightly to form a smooth coil or fine spring. This hollow tube may be cut into short lengths and sewn down to fabric like a bead, using a fine needle and waxed thread. Care must be taken not to catch the thread in sewing it down, as it will pull out and will not return to its original shape.

Purl or bullion thread is generally available in three distinct types: rough, a coil with a matte satin finish; smooth, a coil with a high sheen; and check, an angular, checker coil that reflects the light in different facets, giving a sparkling effect.

Sizes vary with the diameter of the coil; bullion thread is available in silver and gold purl. See ill. Also see **metallic thread embroidery, pearl purl.**

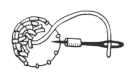

Sewing down bullion thread

bull-mouth helmet. Shell Carving. (*Cassis rufa Linn.*) One of the less reliable shells used for cameos, as regards strength and consistency of color. It has a brown outer layer and a soft creamy-white middle layer over a tawny reddish-brown **ground color**. A shell will often yield only one cameo. The concentration of ground color is near the lip, so it may be checked before purchasing or cutting by inserting a light into the mouth of the shell. It does not separate or easily fade. Also see **cowrie, helmet** and **Shell Carving Shell, Cameo Carving.**

bullnose rabbet plane. Woodworking. See **plane.**

bull-roarer. Toys. (Also called buzz, buzzer, hummer, moaning stick, thunder-spell.) A **sound toy** made from a slot of wood attached to a **thong** or cord. It is held at the end of the thong and whirled. The whirling motion causes the slot to produce an intermittent roaring sound. The toy must be used outdoors in a clear area. The wood piece can be cut in a variety of shapes, no two of which will produce the same sound. In primitive societies the bull-roarer was used for various magical purposes or religious rites. The thunderbolt is similar to a bull-roarer, but it has a rounded form. The Czechoslovakian **folk toy** variation of the bull-roarer is called a wolf, and in New Caledonia it is referred to as a monster. In the Appalachian area of the United States it is known as a hummer, swish, or thunderstick.

bull's eye. Beadwork. See **rosette.**

bull's eye. Quilts. See **David and Goliath.**

bull's eye. Toys. A **target used in various shooting toys or target toys**. It usually consists of a series of rings in a radiating pattern printed in alternating black and white lines. Most **dart** games use a bull's eye target.

bundle. Basketry. See **bolt.**

bundle. Batik and Tie-dye. The **fabric** after it is folded and **tied** for the **tie-dye** process. Also, the individually tied area in **bundle tie-dye.**

bundle tie-dye. Batik and Tie-dye. A **tie-dye** method in which objects are tied up inside **fabrics**, offering a firm surface against which threads and strings can be pulled taut. Small stones and other rigid objects can be used. In **gadget tie-dye** coins, buttons, spools, or found objects may be tied into a single piece of cloth. Sometimes all the fabric

is wrapped and bound in repeated stages until a single bundle is produced for dyeing. Also see **clump-tying.**

bunting. Stitchery. A loose, porous, thin material of **cotton** or **wool** often used in **banner**s or curtains. It is similar in weight and weave to **cheesecloth.**

bur. Jewelry. A grinding tool that fits into the handpiece of a **flexible shaft machine**. There are many varieties, some with specific uses. Entire sets are available with differing sizes that coincide with the sizes of the pointed bottoms of faceted stones. The types of burs available are round (**a.**), bud, flame, cone, inverted cone, wheel, cone square cross cut, cup, hart bearing (**b.**), 45° bearing cutter, etc. A good part of using burs is deciding which bur is best for the desired purpose. Make tests on metal before attempting to apply a bur to any work that you are doing. Since burs are driven by motor, they remove metal very quickly and can grab the metal and zip across its surface, scratching it very badly. They can as easily run across the skin of your hand, so use caution. Some of the burs used in jewelry making are identical to the ones your dentist uses. As he can only use them for a short time, and as a jeweler can get a great deal of use out of them after they are no longer useful to him, ask your dentist to save them for you. See ill. Also see **router.**

a. Round metal bur   b. Hart bearing cutter

burden stitch. Crewel. Embroidery. A technique combining **laidwork** and **brick stitch** and having a finished effect like weaving. This stitch can be worked either closely, so the laidwork is hardly seen, or openly, to give a lacy effect. By changing the color yarn used, different patterns and shadings will take shape. It is helpful to outline the finished shape all around with a **split stitch** or **stem stitch**. Work the brick stitch over laidwork. The ends of the brick stitch touch but do not pierce the laidwork ground (**a.**). Work a second row, keeping the brick stitches at right angles to the laidwork (**b.**). Complete the top row last, working the brick stitch over laidwork (**c.**). See ill. Also see **shading stitch.**

a. Laidwork-brick stitch   b. Second-row brick stitch   c. Burden stitch

Burgoyne's Surrender. Quilts. See **Double Nine-patch.**

Burgoyne Surrounded. Quilts. A **block** design for a **pieced quilt** that is based on the actual plan of a battle. The small blocks represent military regiments, and the pattern shows central squares surrounded by smaller squares. This name was used during Revolutionary times.

It was later called **Wheel of Fortune** and still later Road to California and Homespun.

burin. Jewelry. See **graver.**

burin. Metalworking. Plastics. Woodworking. A pointed tool with a hard steel blade used to obtain and maintain the **burr** on **scraper**s. See ill. Also see **Plastics: Carving.**

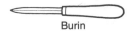
Burin

burl. Woodworking. An abnormal wart or domelike growth on a tree from an infection or wound. It results in a hard, swirling, and highly **figured** wood that is often used for pipe bodies or, because of its beauty, cut into thin slices for **veneer**ing.

burlap. Crewel. Embroidery. Needlepoint. Rugmaking. A coarsely woven fabric made of jute, flax, or hemp. As a **background fabric** it can be used effectively with heavy wools to achieve a coarse, rough effect. Although it is not an evenly woven fabric, it can be used effectively for needlepoint rugs. Also see **embroidered rug, jute, plain weave.**

burlap. Plastics. See **reinforcing material.**

burlap. Stitchery. (Also called gunny sack, sacking.) A **plain weave,** coarse, heavy **fabric** of single **jute** yarns that is commonly used as sacking material. Usually available in natural or brown, better grades are **bleach**ed and dyed bright colors. Many stitchers use it as a background for yarn embroidery, though it is too coarse and open for appliqué. It is frequently given to children beginning work in stitchery since a **needle** will easily pass between the threads rather than through them.

burning. Metalworking. The process of oxidizing a metal by overheating it to the point where sparks are emitted from it and the **grain** structure is damaged. It is the basis of **flame cutting** with a gas cutting torch. Avoid burning the metal while welding it by continuously moving the welding torch over the area to be heated and joined so that the heat will not accumulate in one small area and burn it.

Burning the metal can occur in metal casting if the metal is overheated in the **foundry** furnace to the point where it seems to boil. Avoid this by checking the temperature of the metal frequently with a **pyrometer** as you melt it.

Burning may also occur while grinding or polishing metals with power tools, especially with metals such as pewter that have low melting points. Avoid overheating the area by constantly moving either the tool or the object as you work and by using recommended tool speeds for the particular wheel and operation.

burning test. Spinning. Weaving. A simple test to determine **fiber** content. It is somewhat primitive and inconclusive in some areas, especially when a yarn is of mixed fibers. Only a well-equipped laboratory can do a complete and absolutely correct fiber analysis.

Vegetable or cellulose fibers burn with certain similarities. **Cotton** has a yellow-orange flame that tends to mauve in the center. The smoke is bluish and does not appear until the flame is out. The odor is of burning paper. Cotton ignites easily and burns very fast and then smolders indefinitely. It is not self-extinguishing and leaves the fiber ends spread apart slightly in a fine gray or black ash.

Linen smells like burning grass and has a sparkling yellow and orange flame with the orange appearing more toward the edges. The smoke is bluish, and appears after the flame. Linen ignites easily, burns with a crackle and has a short smoldering, after which it extinguishes itself. The fiber ends remain short and clean in a delicate gray ash.

Rayon, a cellulose fiber, also smells like burning paper and is fast burning, but tends to orange sparks with yellow-orange edges. A bluish smoke appears after the flame is out. Rayon ignites and burns fast and is not self-extinguishing. A black or gray ash is left.

The animal fibers, **silk,** and the various types of animal hair smell like burning hair or feathers. **Wool** has a yellow flame with an orange center tending to blue or purple edges at the bottom. A bluish-gray cloud or wisp appears when it is removed from the flame. It ignites easily, but is self-extinguishing. The burned edges of a cloth tend to stick together and have a thick coating of carbon.

Silk has a sparkling orange-yellow flame with an orange center and gives off a grayish-blue smoke after its removal from the flame. It is similar to wool in that it ignites easily, but it is self-extinguishing. It burns with a faint sizzle.

Nylon has a distinct odor of fresh celery as it is hissing and burning with a blue flame surrounded by orange. It gives off grayish-blue puffs while burning. Nylon does not so much catch fire, as it melts. It tends to shrink from the flame and is self-extinguishing. No ash is left, but the melting leaves a bead. Orlon also leaves a bead, but it does ignite rapidly and is not self-extinguishing. It burns with an aromatic odor and a yellow flame tipped with orange and emits black smoke. The same odor, flame and smoke characteristics are true of dacron, but it tends more toward nylon in that it is difficult to ignite and is self-extinguishing. It melts forming a bead.

Acetate can be tested by burning, but it is more common to drop a bit of acetone (nail polish remover) on it. The acetone will dissolve the acetate. If burning acetate the flame will be pale yellow and mauve or blue at the bottom. Small, wispy bits of blue smoke rise after the flame is out. The odor is acetic and it ignites easily and is not self-extinguishing. It tends to melt rather than burn and leaves a charred bead.

burning tool. Silkscreen. A hobbyists' wood-burning tool resembling a miniature soldering iron that is used to stipple or burn away areas of film used for **cut-film stencil** work. The heated tip of the tool melts the film on contact and creates an area that will print when the film is transferred to the screen. An Ungar or similar iron that has a variety of sizes and shapes of replaceable tips is the most useful.

burnisher. Block Printing. Bookbinding. Any tool with a hard, blunt end (e.g., a spoon, a toothbrush handle, an agate burnisher, a bookbinder's bone folder) used to apply pressure to the **paper** when placed over the inked block in block printing.

In bookbinding it refers to the tool that is used to affix and polish gold or silver titles and designs that have been applied to the cover of a book.

burnisher. Jewelry. Metalworking. A hand tool used for smoothing, **polishing,** and sometimes, shaping metal, as in fitting a **bezel** around a stone. Some are oval in cross-section and made of polished hardened steel with a wooden handle, and are available with straight (**a.**), tapered, or curved blades (**b.**). Burnishers with an agate, bloodstone, or hematite top are used for polish **burnishing,** the final finish on metal. This process compresses the surface of metal, producing, in the case of silver, a brilliant surface that remains lustrous. See ill.

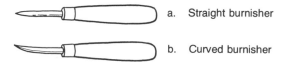

a. Straight burnisher

b. Curved burnisher

burnisher. Leather. A flat piece of plastic, ivory, or bone used for burnishing beveled edges of cut leather and smoothing down rough fibers. Sometimes a round plastic tool with a grooved rim, called a **circle edge slicker,** is used as a burnisher. Also see **dressing, hardwood wheel** and **Leatherwork: Cutting and Edging Leather.**

burnishing. Ceramics. Burnishing forces the hard particles such as **grog** into the body of the pot to give a smooth surface. It is also used for **polishing** the surface of **leather-hard** clay or **gliding.** Burnishing tools can be plastic, metal, wood, or stone.

burnishing. China and Glass Painting. A technique of polishing fired **gold** areas on china to attain a high luster. Burnishing is easily done on china that is still warm from **firing.** After firing, allow nothing to touch the gold until the burnishing is completed, as fingerprints made before burnishing will show. There are three methods of burnishing: polishing with sand, with an **agate burnisher,** or with a **glass brush.**

For general polishing, the sand method is used, using siliceous sand available for burnishing gold. Do this in a separate work area, keeping all sand away from other equipment. Place some white burnishing sand in a saucer and moisten well with water. Dip a soft cloth into the sand, then rub it lightly over the gold areas, keeping the cloth thoroughly moistened. Burnish with light, circular strokes. Rinse piece thoroughly in water to remove sand. Burnishing with sand is good for hard-to-reach areas, such as interiors of pieces and under handles.

Use the agate burnisher to polish small areas and linear patterns, and gold-covered **raised paste** decorations. A light rubbing motion will turn the gold shiny.

The glass-brush method produces a lovely finish but is difficult and hazardous. Rub a glass brush over gold areas with a circular motion. After burnishing, rinse the china to remove every particle of glass. Take care not to breathe in or expose the skin to the tiny particles of glass that result. Wear gloves, and, ideally, try to hold your breath while working. Burnish over a newspaper, well away from the work area.

burnishing. Jewelry. Metalworking. A hand polishing method used especially on **silver, gold,** and pierced work. Begin with hardened polished steel **burnisher**s and then with rounded or curved agate, bloodstone, or hematite burnishers. This helps shape the metal and produces a high, lasting luster by compressing the surface.

Metal should be lubricated while it is being burnished, and although the best lubricant varies according to the metal, generally a neutral soap and water will work. Saliva works well for gold. Work a small area at a time until you obtain the desired luster. Burnish the surface of a three-dimensional piece after pickling to highlight certain areas of the dull pickled surface. Burnishing can be followed by **mirror finish buffing.** Use only a buff in excellent condition or it may remove the burnished finish. Also see **piercing.**

burnishing. Leather. See **burnisher, circle edge slicker, hardwood wheel.**

burnishing tool. Découpage. A steel or agate burnishing tool (a stainless steel spoon or a melon scoop may be substituted) used in découpage for pressing down the edges of glued-on **cutouts** to bevel and imbed the edges into the wood or **gesso** background. This process smooths the surface so that not as many layers of **varnish** will be needed to finish the piece. An **agate burnisher** is also used for polishing water-gilded **gold leaf** surfaces to a high sheen. See also **gilding.**

burnite. Gem cutting. See **azurite.**

burn out. Enameling. See **overfiring.**

burn out. Jewelry. Metalworking. The process of heating a plaster **mold** in a **kiln** or furnace to remove a **wax model** inside by melting it out of the mold. The mold is turned upside down to allow the wax to flow out of the **pouring basin, vent**s, and any other openings, and heated for about a day. The burn-out also prepares the mold for the molten casting metal by removing the moisture from the plaster.

burn-out kiln. Metalworking. A **kiln,** oven, or furnace used to burn wax out of molds. It generally has some sort of exhaust system leading outdoors to siphon off the fumes from the melted wax. Do not attempt to **burn out** wax in your kitchen oven; it has no provision for draining off the wax or fumes and may cause a fire.

burns. Jewelry. See **Jewelry: Safety Precautions.**

burnt clay. Toys. A **clay** that has been fired. When antique toys are referred to as made of burnt clay, it suggests a fired clay, but not necessarily of a high-temperature firing. **Earthenware doll**s may be said to be of burnt clay.

burn test. Batik and Tie-dye. A test used to aid in the identification of fibers in which a fiber or piece of **fabric** is subjected to flame. Various kinds of fibers exhibit different properties and characteristics as they burn. The specific results from the burn test, sometimes called the flame test, are discussed in **Batik and Tie-dye: Identifying Fibers.**

burnt sienna. Ceramics. A reddish-brown **calcine**d **ochre** pigment that can be used as a **glaze** or **slip** colorant.

burr. Jewelry. A thin, sharp edge on metal that can occur after **sawing, cutting, filing,** or using a **bench rub stone.** Make sure all burrs are removed or else the piece will be rough and possibly cause injury. Do this before **soldering,** as the burr can solder in position and become difficult to remove. Support the metal firmly and run a flat **needle file** at a slight angle along the edge. The burr will seem to peel away. Sometimes burrs can simply be peeled off with the fingers and the last of the roughness rubbed lightly with a fine **emery paper.** If the piece is nearly finished and all that is required is **buffing,** that operation also will remove the last of the sharpness. Do not count on removing a burr entirely with the buffing wheel, as this can make the metal of the piece mushy-looking.

burr. Metalworking. Woodworking. The curled edge that forms on the back of a metal **chisel** or **gouge** during **sharpening** and **grinding.** It is removed for fine carving. This same curled edge or burr is desirable on some **woodturning tool**s and on cabinet **scraper**s. A **burnisher** is used to obtain and maintain the burr. See ill. Also see **Woodworking: Grinding and Sharpening.**

Burr

bury a print. Découpage. See **sink a print.**

bust head. Toys. See **breastplate doll head.**

butt. Basketry. See **willow.**

butt. Stitchery. To join end-to-end without overlapping. In **appliquéing fabrics,** pieces are sometimes butted. This eliminates the added **bulk** of overlapping materials, especially when appliquéing fabrics such as **velveteen, sailcloth,** etc. In **machine appliqué,** cut pieces of fabric are usually joined end-to-end, to make a flat, flush seam.

butt chisel. Woodworking. See **chisel.**

butted round. Rugmaking. See **butting.**

butterfly. Macramé. Rugmaking. Weaving. (Also called finger bobbin, finger hank.) A hand or finger-wound arrangement of yarn used as a yarn carrier in place of a

bobbin or **shuttle.** In macramé, the butterfly is a **hand bobbin** used to prevent tangling the ends of the macramé cord while working. It is very handy to use when experimenting with yarns or colors, when only small amounts of a yarn are needed, or in such techniques as continuous **knotted pile** and **soumak** where a pliable yarn carrier is necessary. Butterflies are used extensively where the **filling** does not travel **selvage** to selvage—such as in **tapestry** or **laid-in weave**s. They can be used on any kind of loom. A butterfly is made by winding the yarn in a figure-8 arrangement between the thumb and little finger. Stretching the hand wide open gives a large butterfly, while holding the fingers close together gives a smaller butterfly. The starting end of the yarn, as it comes from the **cone** or **skein,** is clasped between two fingers. The yarn is then brought in back of and around the thumb and around the little finger from back to front. On its return trip to the thumb, the yarn should cross in the center. This will keep it in order and free from tangles (**a.**). When the desired amount is wound, cut the yarn from its source and wind the loose end around the center of the butterfly, half-hitching it twice so that it will not become undone (**b.**). In use, it is pulled from the inside of the butterfly by the loose end that was being held between two fingers. See ill.

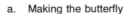

a.   Making the butterfly   b.   Finished butterfly

buttering. Mosaics. The application of a **bond** such as **glue** or **mortar** to the back of an individual **tessera** with a **palette knife** or small **trowel** before setting it into the **mosaic** design. The buttering is often used when the amount of detail in the mosaic slows down the work to such a degree that it becomes impractical to cover a large area of the **backing** with the glue or mortar. Buttering is used both in the **direct method** for fixing the **tile** to the backing and in the **indirect method** for gluing the tile to the **mounting paper.** Also see **Mosaics: Setting the Material.**

butting. Candlemaking. In **molding** a candle, any mars or seam marks on the mold will be transferred to the finished candle. Butting is the process in which any obvious seam lines or imperfections are scraped away with a sharp knife. Also see **Candlemaking: Finishing the Candle.**

butting. Rugmaking. A technique used in **braided rug**s where separate braids are joined in order to introduce colors in the middle of the rug or to end the finished rug in a different color. A braid is first made into a "butted round," meaning that the ends are rounded off by tucking the separate, tapered strands of the braid back into the braid.

Tweezers or pliers may be needed to pull back these strands if the loops of the braid are pulled tight. If the ends of the strands protrude from under the loops of the braid, they are trimmed off and stitched down, and then the butted ends are sewn through the loops from one to another until secure. After the braids are joined, **lacing** is resumed on the rug. Butting must be done carefully to ensure that there are no bumps in the finished rug.

butt joint. Fabric Printing. See **Fabric Printing: Designing.**

butt joint. Jewelry. A joint made between two pieces of metal lying edge to edge in the same plane. This tends to be a difficult joint, especially with thin-**gauge** metals, because the pieces must be on exactly the same plane. If they are not, metal must be removed from both sides after **soldering** to even them out, which will make the metal too thin. A butt joint in which the edges meet over only a small area, for example, 18-gauge round wire or flat sheet that will be bent later, tends to be weak. Also see **capillarity.**

butt joint. Stained Glass. See **joint.**

butt joint. Woodworking. See **joint** and **Woodworking: Jointing.**

button. Jewelry. See **sprue button.**

buttonhole. Knitting. A **horizontal** buttonhole is the most frequently used buttonhole and is simply a horizontal hole next to the edge (usually center front) of a knitted garment. It is the best buttonhole for knit clothing.

> Row 1: Knit to the position for the buttonhole (3 or 4 stitches from the edge), cast off 3 or more stitches and continue to the end of the row.
> Row 2: Work in pattern to the cast-off stitches, cast on as many stitches as were cast off (see **casting on**) and continue to knit following the pattern.

A vertical buttonhole is recommended for use in the closing of pockets. Begin by knitting to the position of the buttonhole. At this point, the work is divided into two sections, so that each section can be worked separately. Work the right side (the left side may be put on a stitch holder) back and forth in garter stitch for at least three rows. The number must be uneven so the work will continue across the row after the left side of the buttonhole is worked. Attach a new piece of yarn and work the left side for an even number of rows (one number less than the right side because the work is continued from right to left when the two sides are joined). When the desired number of rows on each side is completed, cut the yarn on the left side to a length of about 8″. Continue working across the row with the original ball of yarn. After the piece of knitting is completed, work the beginning end from the left side into one stitch of the right side before working the end in an overcast fashion up the right side of the buttonhole. The end yarn at the top can be worked into one stitch on the right side and then the end of yarn can be worked in an overcast fashion on the left side.

buttonhole. Leather. Buttonholes may be made in leather garments using various methods. A simple method is to reinforce the back of the leather with a small rectangle of light leather where the buttonhole will be. Stitch around the buttonhole position in a rectangle; cut in the center of the stitched rectangle by slitting through the two thicknesses of leather with a razor or knife, taking care not to cut the stitching.

buttonhole bar. Lacemaking. (Also called bride.) A **joining** in the **ground** of **needle lace.** To make a buttonhole bar, place a foundation thread or threads across the space attaching two areas of the pattern, depending on the thickness of the **bar** desired. Work **buttonhole stitches** over this foundation. A bar may or may not have a **picot** ornament. See ill.

Buttonhole bar

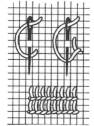

Foundation threads

Buttonhole stitches

buttonhole stitch. Crewel. Embroidery. Needlepoint. (Also called attached buttonhole stitch, blanket stitch, button stitch.) This **filling stitch** can be used to create many other effects. It can form a circle or scallop shape when worked radiating from a central hole; and it can be used as an outlining or **border stitch.**

The buttonhole stitch is used as the basis for many other stitches, such as the **coral knot** stitch. It can be worked effectively on any **background fabric,** including **canvas.** The needle comes up at A, goes in at B, and up at C, directly below B and level with A. The thread is under the needle as the needle is drawn through. See ill. Also see **crewelpoint.**

a.   b. Curved   c.
Worked on canvas

buttonhole stitch. Lacemaking. The stitch used most in **needle lace. Point de Venise** and **reticella** are good examples of its use. It is used in the **ground** as well as in the **filling** of the **design.** The buttonhole stitch is worked very closely and tightly; when it is done loosely, it is called the tulle stitch.

Attach the first row of buttonhole stitches to a foundation thread, or a section of the lace. Then attach the second row to the first row, and so on.

To begin the stitches, bring the threaded needle from the back to the front of the lace.

Make a **loop** with the thread by placing the tip of the needle toward you, and under the foundation structures to which the first row of stitches is attached.

Bring the needle over the loop and draw the thread out tightly.

Continue the second stitch, same as the first.

On the next row, make a stitch that catches each stitch of the previous row.

Work with small stitches, closely placed. See ill.

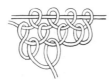

Buttonhole stitches in construction

buttonhole stitch. Leather. See **single buttonhole stitch.**

buttonhole stitch. Quilts. Stitchery. A closely worked loop stitch used to reinforce an edge, as around a buttonhole. See ill.

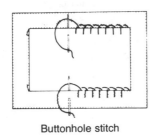

Buttonhole stitch

buttonhole twist. Embroidery. Needlepoint. A tightly twisted rayon or mercerized cotton thread with a high sheen used in embroidery or needlepoint. This thread is an excellent substitute for silk.

buttonhole twist. Stitchery. A strong **silk** thread made especially for hand-sewn buttonholes. It has a special twist and is heavier than regular **sewing thread.** It is sometimes used in shisha embroidery and other decorative work.

button-on-a-string. Toys. See **buzz button.**

button rug. Rugmaking. See **shirred rug.**

button stitch. Crewel. Embroidery. Needlepoint. See **buttonhole stitch.**

button test. Ceramics. A behavior test for ceramic materials. Damp **glaze** sample are formed into small balls and fired on a **slab** of **clay** to obtain an idea of their qualities, such as hardness, porosity, color after firing, and **shrinkage.** See ill. Also see **firing.**

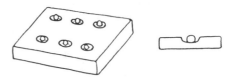

Button test

butt weld. Metalworking. See **weld.**

buzz. Toys. See **bull-roarer.**

buzz button. Toys. (Also called button-on-a-string, buzz saw, hummer button, illusion circle, moon winder.) A simple traditional toy made from either a button or a pierced wood disk and some **string.** A string is run through one hole in the disk, out to a handle, and back through the second hole; the two ends are secured to the second handle. A flip will start the button or disk rolling, then a seesaw motion will keep it going. By pulling out on the handles the string is made taut and the button unwinds. Relaxed, the button goes in the opposite direction and re-winds. When spirals, wedges, or other geometric designs are used on disks the images tend to blend or merge, creating visual patterns similar to those of the **thaumatrope.** Also see **sound toy, visual toy** and **Toys: Folk Toys.** See ill.

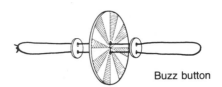

Buzz button

buzzer. Toys. See **bull-roarer.**

buzz saw. Toys. See **buzz button.**

bye-stake. Basketry. (Also called bi-stake.) An extra **rod** inserted by the side of a **stake** to strengthen, decorate, or enlarge the basket. See ill.

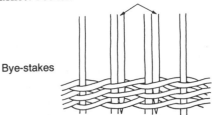

Bye-stakes

by-the-spool. Quilts. A method by which quilters sometimes charge for their **quilting** services. When the lines of quilting are close together and complex, more thread is used. Therefore, paying "by-the-spool" keeps an appropriate relationship between the amount of time and energy expended, the amount of thread used, and the charge made for quilting.

Byzantine art. Mosaics. See **Mosaics.**

Byzantine enamel. Enameling. Mosaics. See **glass, smalti,** and **enameling.**

Byzantine glass. Mosaics. See **glass, smalti.**

Byzantine stitch. Needlepoint. A stitch that gives an effect of a zigzag stripe, worked similarly to the **slanting gobelin stitch.** The stitches can vary in size as long as they are worked over an equal number of threads horizontally and vertically. The number of stitches can also vary as long as it is worked with the same number in both directions. See ill. Also see **Jacquard stitch.**

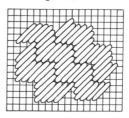

Byzantine stitch

C

cabinet chisel. Woodworking. See **chisel.**

cabinet clamp. Woodworking. See **clamping tools.**

cabinetmaker. Woodworking. A person who performs both hand and machine operations in the making of cabinets and finished furniture for home and office. The cabinetmaker's skills include the ability to read working drawings and specifications, and operate such machines as the circular **saw,** band saw, **jointer,** and **router** in cutting and shaping parts, and glue up, assemble, and finish a piece. Today as few as 100,000 persons are employed strictly as cabinetmakers.

cabinet rasp. Woodworking. See **rasp.**

cabinet scraper. Woodworking. See **scraper.**

cabinet varnish. Woodworking. See **varnish.**

cable. Spinning. Weaving. The term "cable" can refer either to the heaviest **rope** manufactured, or to a firm, round **yarn** formed by twisting together two or more **ply** yarns.

cable casting on. Knitting. See **Knitting: Casting On.**

cable chain stitch. Crewel. Embroidery. See **interlaced cable chain stitch.**

cable cord. Rugmaking. Weaving. See **Seine twine.**

cable knitting. Knitting. Cable knitting is a variation of the **stocking stitch** that creates the look of a vertically twisted rope. It is perhaps best known as one of the patterns used in a **fisherman's knit** sweater. Two or a greater even number of stitches (usually six) are selected from the worked stocking stitch. The first half of these stitches are transferred to a **cable needle** or hook, and become held stitches, or **stitches in waiting,** either at the front or the back of the work. The second half of the stitches are knit first, then the remaining stitches are knit—off the cable needle and back onto the regular needles. There are many variations of this **one over one** (two over two, three over three) **principle.** Common variations are: **plaited basket stitch,** twisted cable rib, basic cable rib, simple cable, snaky cable rib, corded cable rib, reverse cable rib, plaited cable rib, and mock cable rib. See ill.

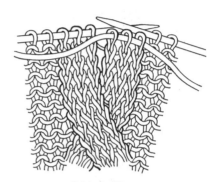

Cable knitting

cable needle. Knitting. A short curved **knitting needle** used to hold **stitches in waiting** when making a **cable knitting** stitch. Also see **Knitting: Tools and Materials.**

cable twine. Rugmaking. Weaving. See **Seine twine.**

cabochon. Gemcutting. A non**face**ted gem with a domed surface atop a geometric flat shape, such as an oval, circle, triangle, rectangle, heart, or cross. The cabochon cut is used primarily on opaque stones for display of color, design, and **luster.** Its form developed from the Egyptian scarab (**a.**).

Translucent and transparent stones are cabochon cut to feature chatoyant and star phenomena (**b.**). Cabochon shapes vary in the height of the convex top, referred to as **spread,** to display the material to its best advantage. For example, moonstone is cut very high (**c.**), while moss agate is cut thin (**d.**).

Double cabochons, rounded on opposite faces, are used for pendants and are sometimes cut from transparent gems, such as amethyst, **tourmaline, beryl** (emerald and aquamarine), and **corundum** (ruby and sapphire) (**e.**).

If slabbed material is used, place the template over the portion of the stone chosen and draw the outline with a sharp **aluminum pencil,** keeping the point as close to the edge of the template as possible. Trim the blank from the slab with the trim saw around the line drawn on what will be the bottom of the finished gem. (If a rounded beach pebble or an irregular-shaped rough is used, grind a **flat** on the edge of the **grinding wheel,** finishing it on the side of the wheel with light pressure and a lot of water. Then mark the outline as above.) Shape and smooth the bottom (girdle) on a 100 grit wheel to within a millimeter of the line. A thin bevel at a 45° angle is ground back toward the bottom to prevent chipping and to allow for solder in the jewelry mounting. Unless the stone is large, it is best to **dop** it to a stick for safety and visibility.

Grinding should be done wet to reduce the heat buildup which could crack the gem. Hold the stone at an angle of 30° from the horizontal at a point just below the middle of the wheel (**f.**). Keep the work moving and rotating. Round the top, working from the bottom up, until the shape curves evenly in all directions. The angle of the sides at the girdle should be 15° if the mounting will be made of silver, or 27° if gold will be used (**g.**). Finish grinding on a 220 (or 320) grit wheel.

The stone is smoothed on a **sanding** disc or drum with silicon carbide cloths of 320 to 600 grit **abrasive.** Check the stone for size with the template and examine the surface for scratches with a **loupe.** If any appear, it is necessary to return to coarser through finer sanding. Clean the stone, the **dop stick,** and your hands between each grit and before **polishing.**

Polishing is done on a leather or felt disc or buff using compounds of tripoli or 1,000 grit silicon carbide for pre-polishing and tin or cerium oxide for final polishing. Separate buffs are used for each compound, with water as vehicle and coolant. The bottom of a cabochon cut from transparent or translucent material is also polished.

Chatoyant stones are cabochon cut for best effect. The phenomenon of a single shining ray of light across the surface of a gem is due to small inclusions of fibers or tubes arranged along the **C axis.** The base of the cabochon is oriented parallel to the plane of the C axis with the long dimension of an ellipse shape at right angles to the fibers. When the chatoyant band is strongly contrasted to the dark color of the stone the gem is called cat's eye. Gems, such as **chrysoberyl, scapolite, tourmaline, beryl,** nephrite, **jade, serpentine quartz, spodumene, sapatite, calcite,** crocidolite, **fibrolite, iolite,** enstatite, and **corundum,** exhibit chatoyance.

Some chatoyant gems have very open and porous surfaces which require protection to prevent the oils of sawing and the compounds of polishing from discoloring them. Soak the rough in warm sodium silicate solution (such as water glass) for several hours and repeat until the pores are filled and dry. The stone should be sawed in water. Retreat the stone with water glass before polishing; when finished leave it soaking in clean warm water for several days. Fibrous gems are sanded and polished across the grain to avoid material sloughing off.

Material with a chatoyant star is cut with the base at a right angle to the C axis. The orientation of material exhibiting asterism is done by grinding a rough **sphere,** sanding, and polishing enough so that no opaque areas remain when the stone is wet with oil or water. Look through the stone at a direct bright light and rotate it in all directions until a six-rayed star is apparent; turn it slightly until the length of the rays appears equal and the center is as small and well defined as possible. Mark the spot where the center is. Turn the stone 180° and mark the other side. The two points are ends of the C axis. Join them in a circle around the stone; draw in the equator at right angles and saw in half on this line for two cabochon blanks with perfectly centered stars.

Rough shape corundum cabochons with a coarse grit silicon carbide grinding wheel shape and grind the hard gemstone on a diamond lap. Polish star sapphire and star ruby gemstones on grooved wooden wheels with 1200 to 8000 grit diamond powder compound. Grooves of ½" and 1" diameter in the edge of a ⅛" wooden disc are used for vertical operation (**m.**) and grooves of ¼", ½", and 1" for horizontal operation (**n.**). See ill.

Doublets are made by fusing or cementing two materials together; **triplet**s are made by cementing three units into a stone. The crown is generally the gem material, and the back is glass or inferior material. **Opal** doublets are made to simulate black opal by cementing a thin section of precious opal to a gray or black opaque back with black cement. After the cement dries, the doublet is cabochon cut in the usual manner.

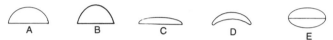

a. Side view of cabochon
b. High cabochon shape for some chatoyant stones
c. Thin or shallow spread, for display of design or luster
d. Hollow-shaped for translucency or color
e. Double cabochon

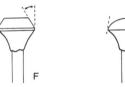

f. Grinding the curve on a cabochon at about 30°
g. The angle at the girdle is finished at 27° if the gem will be set in a gold bezel; 15° if a silver mounting is used
h. The back-bevel at the base ground at 45°

j. Top views

k. Side views

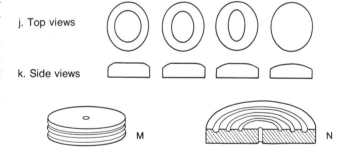

m. Grooves of ½" and 1" diameter in the edge of a ⅛" wooden disc used for vertical operation
n. Cross section of a wooden wheel with grooves ¼", ½", and 1" used for horizontal operation

cabosil. Plastics. A brand name for a fine grade of silica used as a **filler** and thickening agent for **polyester, epoxy, silicone,** and **urethane** resins. It causes irritation to the skin and lungs. See **thixotropic.**

cabretta. Leather. A term for light, supple Brazilian sheepskin, generally used for making gloves and shoes. Also see **glove leather, lining leather.**

cachalong. Gemcutting. See **opal.**

cacoon yo-yo. Toys. See **twirling yo-yo.**

Cactus Flower. Quilts. A **geometric** flower form designed for a square **block**. It is first **pieced**, then **appliquéd**. It depicts a four-petaled flower on the diagonal of the block.

The Maple Leaf block is formed when four Cactus Flower blocks are **set** with stems meeting in the center.

Cactus Rose. Quilts. See **Peony.**

caddy. Toys. (Also called pewee, tippy.) A traditional **American folk toy** of very early origin. Examples have been excavated in the American Southwest and dated at A.D. 1100. It became popular in this century when Laurel and Hardy used it in the 1930s movie of **Babes in Toyland.**

The **game** consists of a short square stick of wood about 4″ or 5″ long. It is sharpened at each end, and is called the caddy. The caddy is placed on a hard surface, such as pavement or hard ground (away from windows and small children) and is struck with another stick. A length of broomstick-size **dowel** will do. If the caddy is struck on the pointed end it will fly into the air, where it can be struck again. There are many variations of this game.

cadmium salts. Stained glass. See **antique glass colorants.**

Caesar's Crown. Quilts. A **pieced** wheel pattern that forms a new four-leaf pattern when **blocks** are **set** together.

caftan. Batik and Tie-dye. Stitchery. The flowing **garment,** a native **costume** from eastern Mediterranean countries, consisting of a long gown or robe with very wide sleeves. Sometimes, with very wide **fabric,** no sleeve is added; instead the side **seam** is left open at the top for the armhole. The caftan may be tied with a belt or sash or left long and loose. Because of the extremely simple lines, the caftan lends itself to garments of batik, tie-dye, **appliqué,** direct-dye painting, or silkscreen printing.

cairngorm. Gemcutting. See **quartz.**

calabrian laid-in. Weaving. See **laid-in.**

calcine. Ceramics. A process used to preshrink a **glaze** or ceramic ingredient before its use by putting it through an initial firing between 750° and 1050° C. This eliminates **crazing.** Also see **burnt sienna, ochre, umber.**

calcite. Gemcutting. A mineral composed of calcium carbonate, with a silky fibrous appearance, often occurring as veins in shale. It has **hardness** of 3 and **specific gravity** of 2.95. It is white, brown, or red, and is often banded in several **colors.** The fibrous structure may exhibit a chatoyant effect when cut in **cabochon** form.

Aragonite is a variety of calcite found in caves as stalactites and stalagmites deposited by mineral springs. It is also the main constituent of coral, shell, and pearl.

Mexican onyx (also called travertine) is a calcite which is easily carved and dyed.

Polishing is done on a carpet **lap** with tin oxide and 10% solution of oxalic acid.

Also see **lapis lazuli, luster** and **Gemcutting: Hand Grinding and Polishing, Rough Shaping.**

Calcomine. Batik and Tie-dye. See **direct dye.**

calculating yarn. Rugmaking. Weaving. See **yarn calculation.**

Caledon dye. Batik and Tie-dye. See **leuco, vat dye.**

calendering. Batik and Tie-dye. The final process in treating **fabrics** to add sheen or luster and remove wrinkles. It is a fabric **finish** that does not affect the receptivity of **fibers** to **dye** because it is essentially the same as **ironing.** It is usually removed by washing before the fabric is used for **tie-dye** or **batik.**

calendering. Plastics. A commercial rolling process involving controlled heat. It is used to give a variety of surface textures on **thermoplastic** sheets or to **laminate** plastic films onto other materials, such as paper or cloth.

calf. Bookbinding. See **leather.**

calfskin. Leather. A term for leather from the skins of young cattle. It is very durable and supple, vegetable tanned, and has a fine **grain.** It is suitable for **embossing** or **tooling.** Calfskin is generally used for making small leather articles, such as wallets. Also see **glove leather, lining leather, vegetable tanning.**

Calgon. Batik and Tie-dye. A commercially packaged common household water softener used to prepare **soft water** for the **dyebath.** About ¼ teaspoon Calgon is added to each pint of water before it is mixed with the dye powder or **pasted** dye. It is also used in making a **chemical water** solution. Also see **mordant formula.**

calico. Quilts. Stitchery. A **plain-weave,** light, inexpensive **cotton** fabric brightly printed on one side. The name comes from the Indian city of "Calicut," from which it was first imported. Early calicoes were **all-over** prints of elaborate detail, but later the name was used to mean any cotton fabric or to indicate cotton **percales** that are printed in the **all-over patterns** so popular in quiltmaking.

Calico is usually sized, so that it feels crisp, but the sizing washes out. The crispness of the sizing makes it easier to handle in turning under edges of a hem for **appliqué.** It is a favorite fabric for quiltmaking.

Calico Cat. Toys. See **Gingham Dog.**

California rose. Quilts. See **combination rose.**

California star. Quilts. A **pieced block** design identical to the **Feather star** except for the center block. Only when the **nine-patch** is used in the center is it known as the California star.

calimanco. Quilts. A colonial **fabric** of glazed **linen** that had a pattern showing on one side only.

calipers. Ceramics. A curved-arm compass of metal, wood, or plastic, used for measuring inner and outer circumferences of pots on the **potter's wheel** when throwing. It is used most often when throwing a lid to assure that it will fit the diameter of the pot opening. Also see **Ceramics: Throwing.**

calipers. Metalworking. Woodworking. See **measuring tools.**

calligraphy. Ceramics. A term used to describe **brushwork** or decorating that uses the movement and shape of the brush itself to determine the character of the design. It is most often associated with the quick, fluid strokes formed by the soft-pointed brushes in Oriental brushwork.

calligraphy brush. China and Glass Painting. See **brush.**

calme. Stained Glass. See **lead came.**

calyx-eyed needle. Stitchery. See **needle.**

cambium. Woodworking. See **wood.**

cambric. Quilts. A fine **cotton** or **linen** that has a **plain weave** and a glossy, smooth luster on the face side. It was once a popular **fabric** with quiltmakers.

Cambridge style. Bookbinding. An English style of book-cover decoration typified by double panels with a flower tooled on each of the outer four corners.

came. Stained Glass. See **lead came.**

camel's hair. Knitting. Spinning. Weaving. The hair shed every summer by the two-humped Bactrian camel of Asia. The outer hair, which is coarse, tough, and wiry, is made by the natives into tents and **cordage.** The underhair is similar to wool and can vary in color from light tan to reddish-brown. It is lustrous and extremely soft and is used by itself or combined with wool in apparel fabrics, blankets, and Oriental rugs. The fabrics are lightweight, warm, and long-napped. Also see **Knitting: Tools and Materials.**

camel's hair brush. Enameling. A tool used for applying **flux, firescale** treatment, and **resist** to metal surfaces, when **etching, electroplating,** and **electro etching.** Also see **Enameling: Tools and Materials.**

cameo. Gemcutting. A technique of engraving a figure or design in relief on gem material. This style was popular in the Roman era for portraits and for crests and coats of arms in the Middle Ages. Generally, stones chosen for cameos, such as onyx, sardonyx, and carnelian onyx, have alternate bands of two or more **colors.** The figure is carved in one layer and material removed around it to provide a contrasting background. The carving is done with a **point carver,** or **flexible-shaft machine,** and **carving points.**

The chevet is a modern cameo in which the cameo is carved below the stone's surface for protection. Chevets may be carved in a stone with three different layers.

Also see **doublet, intaglio, quartz.**

cameo. Shell Carving. A technique of low-relief carving of shells with different-colored layers so that the raised design is of one color and the background another. Also, a gem so cut. Also see **cowrie, helmet,** and **Shell Carving: Shell, Cameo Carving.**

cameo carving. Shell Carving. See **Shell Carving: Cameo Carving.**

camouflage tool. Leather. A **stamp** available in various patterns for texturing leather, generally arc shaped, with a face marked by vertical lines. Also see **stamping, tooling.**

camphor toy. Toys. A **toy** in which the power is provided by camphor. A small chunk or pellet is placed in the toy in such a way that it comes in contact with water when the toy is set in a bathtub or a bowl of water. The chemical action of the camphor on water forces the water to move through an open channel at one end, propelling the floating toy in the opposite direction. The use of camphor was at one time popular in both homemade and manufactured toys. Also see **boat.**

Canada balsam. Amber Carving. This is the best cement for joining pieces of amber. The balsam is heated to evaporate excess volatiles in the resin; it is ready when a pin touched to the surface draws out a thin, brittle thread. Parts to be joined should be warmed and joined with a sliding action to eliminate air bubbles. Canada balsam dries perfectly transparent. Its solvents are turpentine, benzine, and acetone.

cancel. Bookbinding. A page printed to replace a page in a book that contains errors or requires alterations.

canceling. Bookbinding. Cutting out a leaf of a book in order to substitute another leaf in cases of misprints or to make alterations.

candle. Candlemaking. A solid mass of tallow or wax that is burned to give light. It contains a **wick,** a combustible, porous core usually made of cotton or linen threads and the part that takes the flame. The heat of the flame melts the wax, which is absorbed by the wick by capillary action and acts as fuel to the flame. The size of the wick must be correctly proportionate to the quantity of the wax ("the fuel pool"). Too thick a wick or too low a **melting point** for the wax produces **guttering** or smothering of the flame. Too small a wick produces a flame that is too small to burn up the wax as it melts. In the perfect candle the wax keeps pace with the wick's capillary and vaporizing action.

candle-drip batik. Batik and Tie-dye. A simple **batik** process in which the **wax resist** is applied from a burning and dripping candle. Its advantages are that it avoids the necessity of heating and melting the wax in a container and eliminates the need for **brush**es or a **tjanting.** The disadvantage is the limitation on the kinds of lines and patterns that can be made. The burning candle is held over the **fabric,** and by tilting the candle the flow of drops can be controlled to some extent. The hot wax penetrates the fabric to form a resist to the **dye.** This drip batik method can be combined with other batik processes.

CANDLEMAKING

The origins of candlemaking are lost in the dark void of prehistoric times. How man came to control fire and how he made the transition from the crude torch to the **wick-**burning predecessor of the modern candle is purely a subject for speculation. We can at least safely assume that once man learned to put fire to practical use he realized that fatty substances from cooking animals gave off considerable light as they dripped into the fire.

Archeologists digging in Egypt have uncovered clay candle holders dating as far back as the fourth century B.C. Recorded Egyptian history also shows that soft-centered reeds were dipped in fat to increase their burning capacity. In early Roman times plant material, such as papyrus, was twisted into wicklike rope to burn liquid **tallow** or **beeswax.**

The role played by candles in modern Christian religious ceremonies goes back to its symbolic use in earlier, pagan forms of worship, when candles were lit to protect departed souls against evil spirits. To demonstrate the magnitude of the part played by candles during the medieval Christian era, it should be mentioned that beeswax served as an acceptable tithe during that time and that the church of Wittenberg used in excess of twelve tons of candles annually.

By the thirteenth century candlemaking had reached such proportions that in Paris candlemaking guilds were established to regulate and protect the traveling candlemakers.

In the fifteenth century Sieur de Brex, a French candlemaker, developed the wooden **mold,** introducing the **molding** technique to candlemaking. Prior to that time all candles had been made by **dipping** or **rolling.**

The nineteenth century saw a series of discoveries that were of paramount importance to candlemaking: the discovery of **stearic acid** by Michel Chevreul; the discovery of **paraffin** in 1830 and its application to candlemaking by James Young; and the development of the **braided wick** by Cambaceres in 1825. But that century also saw a series of discoveries that led to the demise of the candle as the primary source of light. Kerosene, a by-product of petroleum, and eventually electricity replaced the candle in most homes.

Nothing, however, can replace the warmth and softness of the light produced by a well-made candle, and candlemaking continues to thrive both as an industry and a craft to this day.

SETTING UP A WORKSHOP   A relatively small area can be used as a workshop. Good lighting, access to a sink and stove, a table or counter, and sufficient storage space are necessary.

There are four methods for forming a candle: **dipping, pouring, rolling,** and **molding.** Basically the same materials and instruments are used for all of them.

The basic constituent of candles is wax; nowadays paraffin, rather than beeswax and tallow, is the wax most commonly used. Stearic acid or **Krystalline** are necessary **additive**s. Coloring agents and fragrances, although not essential, enhance the product and should be kept on hand. It is useful to have a supply of wicks in several lengths and thicknesses. Basic wax-melting equipment, such as a double boiler or an electric frying pan with a **melting pot,** is mandatory; wax should never be melted over an open flame. Because **temperature**s for melting wax can be crucial, it's handy to have a heat-resistant **thermometer,** such as a candy thermometer. For molding, at least one **mold,** either a commercial or a **found object mold,** is necessary. The number of molds available allows for greater variety in the finished product. A **mold release,** either **silicone spray** or vegetable oil, greatly facilitates removal of the candle from the mold. Immediately after pouring, or **casting,** the candle in the mold should be placed in a warm **water bath.** Any leak-proof container, such as a plastic bucket deep enough to hold the immersed mold, will serve. An **ice pick,** skewer, or knitting needle to pierce the wax during the refilling of the mold, plus **clay** or **caulking compound** to seal the mold at the base opening for the wick, are also necessary. The entire work area should be completely covered with old newspaper to avoid damaging the work surfaces with hot liquid wax.

SELECTING THE WAX   Most candles are a mixture of paraffin and 5–10% stearic acid. For specialty candles beeswax or bayberry wax, either alone or combined with paraffin, can be used.

A wide variety of waxes is available at hobby shops. Paraffin is usually sold in 10-pound slabs that can be broken into pieces for easy melting.

MELTING THE WAX   A double boiler or an electric frying pan partially filled with water into which a melting pot is set is standard equipment for melting the wax. See ill.

Powdered baking soda and a tight-fitting lid for your heating vessel should be kept handy in the event that a fire should start.

Different waxes have different **melting points;** even paraffin, the basic wax component for most candles, melts at different temperatures, depending on how well it was refined.

Most candles are poured at 180–190° F. To reach these levels the heat should be raised gradually and a constant check should be kept on the temperature with a heat-resistant candy thermometer. As a general rule, the hotter the wax, the finer the candle. This rule, however, must be tempered with common sense, an awareness of the heat-resistant properties of your mold (when molding), and certain safety limitations. The temperature of the hot wax should rarely be allowed to rise above 212° F, the temperature of boiling water.

One pound of wax melts roughly to the equivalent of two cups of water. In molding you can estimate your mold's capacity by filling it with water and then emptying it into a measuring cup; be sure, however, to dry the mold before pouring in the hot wax.

Professional metal molds are usually marked with the amount of wax they require.

ADDITIVES   Most candlemakers today add stearic acid to their basic wax to improve the quality of the candle. Stearic acid hardens the candle, increases its **opacity,** and makes it burn better. The greater the percentage of stearic acid, the more opaque the candle. For most candles a 5–10% level of stearic acid is satisfactory. Personal preferences in terms of the whiteness or translucency desired for the candle can be worked out with experimentation.

A variety of **coloring** additives is available. Wax **crayons** can be used, but solid color buds formulated for candlemaking are preferable because some crayons contain additives that adversely affect the candle's performance. Color buds are available from most hobby shops in a large range of colors. They are added to the melted wax by shaving off small amounts until the desired color is achieved. Because wax usually hardens to a lighter shade, it is practical to run color tests on small wax samples before pouring your candle.

To add scent to your candle, any oil-based perfume or special candle scent may be used. The fragrance can be added to the melted wax or the wick may be dipped in the liquid essence. If the scent is to be added to the hot wax, this should be done just prior to pouring the wax, as continued heating will dissipate the potency of the perfume. An excess of oil-based essence will cause **mottling** in the finished candle.

SELECTING THE WICK   Braided wicks that have been treated with a **mordant** are available in a wide variety of sizes and lengths. The size of the wick depends on the diameter of the candle. Too small a **wick** will result in excessive **dripping,** and too large a wick can cause **smoking.** Wick sizes are stated in number of ply. As a general rule, candles of 1–3″ in diameter take a 15-ply wick and candles of 3–4″ take a 24-ply wick. Anything larger requires either a 30-ply wick or a multiple wicking system. Your hobby shop can advise you on your needs.

Melting the wax

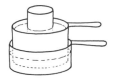

a.   Double boiler   b.   Electric frying pan with melting pot in water

DIPPING   Dipping is the oldest method of candlemaking. A weighted wick is repeatedly dipped into a hot **wax bath.** The temperature of the hot wax is crucial. Low temperatures allow the greatest wax buildup but make the candle lumpy and uneven; high temperatures tend to melt previous wax accumulation. Approximately 150° F works well; experimentation will, however, determine the best heat range.

After the candle is formed it is rolled on a smooth flat surface to even out any lumps. **Rolling** should be done while the candle is still warm and malleable.

POURING   Pouring is similar to dipping, except that the hot wax is poured over a weighted wick. The temperature of the wax should be 150–165° F. If the wax is too cool, it won't flow, and if it is too hot, it will melt the previously poured layers. Each successive layer should be allowed to cool completely before the next one is poured. Unless a natural look is preferred, the **taper** can be rolled after each pouring has partially cooled to smooth the surface.

ROLLING   Honeycomb sheets of beeswax are cut to the desired length, warmed slightly to increase their malleability, and rolled around a wick tightly crimped in position along one edge. If sheets of different colors are used, each sheet should be pressed slightly to eliminate any air pockets. Squeeze the completed candle gently and roll it on a flat heated surface to seal the ends.

MOLDING   Sieur de Brex, a French candlemaker in Paris, produced the first candle **mold**s out of wood in the fifteenth century. Prior to that time all candles had been formed by dipping. By the beginning of the nineteenth century candlemakers began to develop equipment that allowed for the mass-produced molding used by the candle industry today.

Although many people specialize in making candles by dipping or pouring, molding is by far the most popular method of candlemaking. In molding, the candle is formed by casting hot melted wax into any container or receptacle that will not melt or break when subjected to heat. The candle may be cast in the mold with or without wicking. If the wick is positioned before casting, care must be taken to assure it is centered and held taut throughout the molding procedure. With certain molds the wick, by necessity, is inserted after the candle has been cast and cooled.

SELECTING THE MOLD   An almost limitless number of molds is available to the creative candlemaker. Basically they fit into two categories: the professional mold (or purchased mold) and the **found object mold.** Professional molds come in many different materials, including heat-resistant plastic, ceramic, plaster, and rubber, but the most common (herein referred to as the professional mold) is made of metal.

Metal molds come in numerous shapes and sizes and can be purchased at hobby shops and candle-supply stores. Found object molds can be of almost any material that will hold up under the relatively high **temperature** of the melted wax. The only restriction on mold shape is that no point on the mold can be narrower than any point between it and the opening unless the mold is made of a material that can be cut, torn, or broken away. The handling of a found object mold depends on the material it is made of. **Paper molds** or **cardboard container candle** molds may be pierced with a small hole and wicked in the same manner as the professional mold. They also usually serve as one-time-only molds in that they are most often torn away after the candle has hardened. **Glass mold**s, such as bottles or drinking glasses, metal found object molds, and **gelatin mold**s that cannot be pierced for wicking produce candles that must be wicked after the candle has been poured and allowed to harden. In selecting a found object mold it should be kept in mind that in addition to yielding different shapes, different mold materials result in subtle variations in the surface of the finished candle. Metal molds tend to produce glossier surfaces than wax containers, whereas plastic or glass containers tend to result in a dull, soft sheen. Also see **ceramic mold, plaster mold, plastic mold, rubber mold, sand candle.**

CLEANING THE MOLD   After each use the mold should be carefully cleaned with a wax **solvent** or dry-cleaning fluid unless the mold is of the one-time-only type or is made of a material that might be adversely affected by chemical compounds. If the wax resists, it should be rubbed very carefully with a cloth dipped in the solvent. Extreme care must be taken at all times to avoid denting or scratching the mold surface. The slightest mar on the mold will show up on the candle and probably seriously impede removal of the candle from the mold. Just before pouring the wax, the mold should be carefully wiped to remove any foreign material, such as lint or dust.

PREPARING THE MOLD   Once the mold has been wiped free of any foreign material it should be lightly coated with either **silicone spray** or a vegetable oil, such as olive or peanut oil. This should facilitate the release of the candle from the mold. Any excess oil, however, should be wiped from the mold with paper towels to eliminate mottling on the finished surface of the candle.

WICKING THE MOLD   Most professional molds are equipped with a small hole at the bottom center point through which the wick can be threaded and drawn up to the top of the mold. If found object molds are to be wicked before casting, a method must be found to pierce the bottom center point. With cardboard container candle molds this is a relatively simple operation, requiring only a sharp, pointed object, such as an **ice pick,** for piercing. If no hole can be made, the wick can be inserted after the candle has hardened. In any case, the wick must be positioned to run exactly through the center of the candle and held taut throughout the entire pouring and cooling process.

To wick a mold with a hole punched in the bottom, tie a small knot at one end of the selected wick and thread the wick up through the small hole at the bottom of the mold. The knot should be large enough to keep the wick from slipping through the hole (**a.**). Some metal molds come with a small retainer screw that fits into the wick hole, eliminating the need for the securing knot. In either case the hole must be sealed with **clay** or a **caulking compound,** such as Mordite, to prevent the liquid wax from leaking out. Then draw the secured wick up through the mold and knot it to a rod that rests across the top rim of the mold (**b.**). By adjusting this rod the wick can be pulled taut and positioned in the exact center of the mold. Either a slip knot or tape to secure the rod will assist in this effort. The mold is then ready to receive the hot melted wax. See ill.

To wick an already hardened candle, bore a small hole with a heated ice pick through the center of the candle; dip the wick in hot wax to stiffen it and insert it in the bored hole. A small amount of hot wax poured into the hole sets the wick for burning.

WARMING THE MOLD   Metal molds should be warmed before the wax is poured into them to avoid **pitmarks** on the surface of the finished candles. An oven heated to 150° F or a hair dryer can be used.

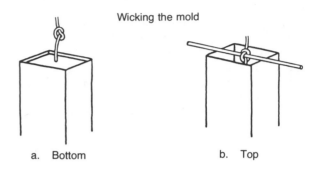

Wicking the mold

a. Bottom   b. Top

POURING THE WAX   Once the selected dye and scent are added to the hot wax and the desired temperature reached, the wax is poured into the mold. Using a hot pad or oven mit, tip the mold at a slight angle so the wax runs down the side of the mold. Gradually bring the mold to an upright position and continue pouring until the candle reaches the proper height. Tilting the mold during pouring reduces splashing and also reduces the amount of **bubbling.** Retain from two-thirds to a full cup of wax for **refilling the mold.**

COOLING THE MOLD   Several minutes after the candle has been poured the mold should be placed in a **water bath** of lukewarm water. Any large leak-proof container will serve. The water in the bath must be slightly above the level of the wax in the mold but it must not be allowed to overflow into the mold itself. It's a good idea to premeasure the water level by placing the mold in the bath before you get to the pouring step. Water added to the bath after the mold has been immersed will create a fine bubble ring around the candle. The cooling mold should remain in the bath for thirty to forty minutes or until a slight film forms across the top of the candle. The water bath permits a gradual cooling of the wax that allows any trapped air bubbles to rise and escape from the candle. Place a weight on top of the mold to prevent it from floating while in the water bath.

REFILLING THE MOLD   Because wax shrinks as it cools, a **depression** at the top of the candle surrounding the wick and **cavities** inside the candle will form. Remove the candle from the water bath when a thin film forms across the top of the candle and prepare for refilling. Using an ice pick, skewer, or knitting needle, deep holes should be punched all around the wick. These holes should be close to but not through the bottom of the candle. Melted wax heated to approximately 185° F is then poured into the punched holes. Care should be taken to prevent the refilling wax from overflowing the level of the original candle, as the new wax may hinder mold release or may damage the surface of the molded candle. The refilling process should be repeated as often as is necessary to fill the cavities and depression.

FINAL COOLING PROCESS The refilled candle should be allowed to cool overnight at room temperature.

REMOVING THE CANDLE FROM THE MOLD If the mold is completely cold to the touch, it is an indication that the candle is hardened and is ready to be removed from the mold. The retaining screw or securing knot and clay or caulking compound must be removed from the bottom of the mold. The wick knot around the rod at the top of the mold must also be untied. Ideally, at this point, the candle should easily slip free of the mold. If it resists, the inverted mold should be tapped gently over a thick bed of cushioning napkins. Never bang or hit the mold to release the candle. Any dents or mars in the mold itself will make it useless for future use. If necessary, refrigerate the mold for 30–45 minutes and attempt to release the candle once more. If this fails, place the mold in hot water. This method may damage the surface of the candle but will not ruin the mold. Possible reasons for resistance are dents in the mold that are holding the candle, the use of an inferior grade of wax, or too complex a mold structure.

With paper or cardboard container molds, the mold itself can be torn away. Glass molds should be carefully wrapped in toweling or paper bags and then cautiously broken. Extreme care should be taken to avoid damaging the candle surface.

FINISHING Your molded candle is now complete. Remove any obvious mold seam lines with a sharp knife, trim the bottom of the wick flush with the base, and trim the upper wick to within ½" of the top of the candle. If the candle fails to sit straight after trimming, the base can be leveled by holding the candle in a vertical position on any suitable hot surface, such as a pie plate inverted in a dish of boiling water. See ill.

Polish the candle with a nylon stocking, or buff the surface with a wet paper towel if the stocking fails to yield an ample shine.

Leveling the base of a candle by rotating it on a pie pan inverted in a pan filled with boiling water

POSSIBLE FLAWS IN CANDLES Hopefully your candle will be perfect, but flaws do appear. Bubble lines ringing the candle may have been caused by adding water to the water bath after the candle was immersed. Cave-ins may occur during burning if the candle was not properly refilled after the initial pouring. An unplanned mottled or speckled effect on the surface can be the result of too slow cooling, the use of wax that had been reheated too often, or an over-eager use of an oil-based scent. (If mottling is desired, it can be obtained by the use of a **mottling oil** additive.) **Frost**

marks on the surface can be the result of too low a temperature for the melted wax or the use of an unheated mold. Prewaxed cardboard container molds often produce frost-marked candles, most likely because the container wax itself is partially melted by the heat of the hot wax. **Pitmarks** on the surface are usually caused by air bubbles trapped within the mold, either because the wax was poured too rapidly or because the mold was too cold. Lint or dust in the mold can also cause pitted surfaces. Internal breaks in the candle are the result of too rapid cooling, inadequate refilling, or refilling after the wax has hardened.

The candle should be allowed to cure for several days before it is burned. Sometimes a candle will not burn well. Excessive **dripping** reflects too soft or poor quality wax, or a wick too small to absorb the melted wax. **Smoking** is the result if the wax is of poor quality, or the wick is too large and the flame consumes the wax faster than the wick can draw it up. If the candle burns too rapidly, it may be because of excessive air in the candle caused by too rapid cooling or too low a melting point for the wax used.

SAFETY PRECAUTIONS Wax is highly flammable. It should never be melted over an open flame. Baking soda and a lid for the pan should be at hand to extinguish any fire that might accidentally occur. Never use water to extinguish a wax fire because it will spread the flame.

If hot wax splashes on your skin, apply cold water to harden the wax, and treat as a burn. Consult your doctor if the burn is severe.

Candlemas. Candlemaking. The second day of February. A church feast day honoring the Virgin Mary with the burning of candles as a sacred symbol of her purity. Candlemas dates back to the eleventh century.

candlepower. Candlemaking. The intensity of illumination produced by a source of light, expressed in candles. One candlepower is based on the light given off by one pure **spermaceti candle** weighing one-sixth of a pound and burning at the rate of 120 grams per hour.

candlesnuffer. Candlemaking. Before the invention of the **braided wick** by Cambaceres in 1825, which allowed the **wick** to drop outside the flame area, it had been necessary to snip away the smoking top of the candle with scissors. The trimming of the candles in public lamps was the responsibility of men called candlesnuffers. Today the term applies to a tool resembling a small inverted cup on the end of a long pole used to extinguish a candle. The cup is placed over the candle, suffocating the flame.

candlewick. Embroidery. A type of needlework formed by sewing heavy cotton thread, the kind used for candle wicks, through a tightly woven **background fabric,** leaving loose loops on the fabric face. These loops may be cut to form a pile that stays in place because of the combination of the thick thread and the close weave of the fabric.

candlewick. Weaving. A yarn used as a pattern **filling** in a candlewick fabric. It can be either a thick, soft, lightly spun cotton yarn or a multi-**ply** cotton that is used for the wicks in candles.

Also, a fabric woven with a design in tufts on a fine, unbleached cotton **plain weave ground.** The tufts are achieved through **tufting** or **looping,** while being woven. Then the fabric is washed for shrinkage to secure the cut loops into the ground; the washing also fluffs out the cut yarn ends. This candlewicking was originally to make bedspreads. Today the tufts are usually needleworked into a muslin-ground fabric.

candlewick fabric. Quilts. An unbleached **muslin** sheeting used as the base for **tufting** or **candlewicking.** A **homespun cotton** twill was traditionally used. The fabric is not preshrunk. After the completion of the tufting, the candlewick fabric is washed; the shrinking helps to hold the **tufts** in place.

candlewicking. Quilts. A term used to describe both the process of **tufting** and the cord used in that process. The candlewicking is a special heavy, soft **cotton** cord used in sewing the tufted designs. Originally it was the cotton wick used in candles. Now a similar cord is known as **roving** and comes in various diameters.

candlewick needle. Embroidery. A large, pointed needle with a long eye for holding the heavy, rounded candlewick thread used in **candlewick** embroidery.

candlewick spread. Quilts. A **coverlet** or bedcover in which the design is made by embroidering with **candlewicking.** The cut ends of the candlewicking form soft balls, or **tufts,** making a series of dots for the design. Also see **roving, tufting.**

candy thermometer. Candlemaking. See **thermometer.**

cane. Basketry. (Also called rattan, reed.) A very popular and useful **basketry material** that comes from the tropical rattan palm, a climbing plant growing to a length of 300−500′. Almost all the cane varieties mentioned here are commercially available, sold in coils or **hanks** in lengths from 50−500′. Round reed and winding reed are the most popular and are generally available.

Whole cane has not been processed and retains its outer skin. Kooboo, whole cane grown commercially in Malaysia, is yellow and glossy, and may be purchased in sizes from 5−13 mm in diameter. Malacca is a variety of whole cane that is not quite round, has a rib on one side, and has larger leaf joints than the other rattan-palm canes; it is used primarily for walking sticks. Nilghiri, grown in India and very hard and difficult to bend, also is used for walking sticks. Tohiti ranges from 12−30 mm in diameter and is used primarily for furniture and hamper frames because of its thickness. Palembang is a whole cane that has not been stripped or processed, comes in two basic thicknesses, 3−5 mm and 5−8 mm, and has a red-brown color, **unkind** texture, and a slightly ribbed surface.

Boondoot is similar to Palembang but is harder and lighter in color.

Round cane, also known as pith cane, center cane, pulp cane, reed, round reed, and split reed, is cut from the tough, fibrous core or **pith** with circular knives into various uniform sizes. It is easy to work and accepts color readily. It is numbered in sizes from 000 to 16 (0 is about ¹/₆₄″ in diameter; 5 is about ⅛″) (**a.**).

Oval cane is essentially the same as round cane.

The hard, glossy surface of the rattan palm is used to make wrapping cane, split reed, flat cane, or winding reed (used, for instance, for wrapping handles). Chair-seating cane is fine-quality wrapping cane, also sometimes known as glossy cane or glossy wrapping cane. When it is enameled in various colors, it is called enameled cane. Flat reed comes in diameters of ¼″, ⅜″ and ½″. Winding reed comes in ⅛″ and ¼″ sizes (**b.**). Sarawak is a commercially grown cane ranging from 8−18 mm in diameter. It has a fine, yellow, glossy surface, and the outer part of this cane makes excellent chair-seating or wrapping cane. Segah, another commercial cane, ranges from 4−10 mm and is used for pulp cane and glossy chair-seating cane. See ill.

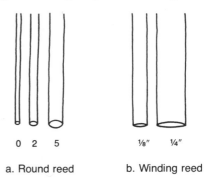

| 0 | 2 | 5 | ⅛″ | ¼″ |

a. Round reed   b. Winding reed

cane. Glasswork. Solid glass rod, frequently colored, used in **flamework** for melting and **drawing,** or gathered in bundles for fusing in glassforming or for **latticinio** work.

cane handle. Ceramics. See **Ceramics: Form.**

cane pair. Basketry. See **chain pairing.**

canopy. Puppets. A framework that sometimes extends out in front of the **proscenium.** The canopy may have tracks or rings from which a **curtain** is suspended and drawn, or it may provide a structure to which lighting is attached. Also see **Puppets: The Puppet stage.**

canopy. Stained Glass. The decorative plate that attaches to the ceiling and through which the electric wiring passes for a hanging lamp. It covers the hole in the ceiling where the electric box is located, and it provides the hook from which the chain can be hung.

canvas. Needlepoint. A sized, evenly woven fabric made originally of linen or hemp, and now of either cotton or manmade fiber, for use as a **background fabric** in needlepoint or canvas work. Canvas can be purchased in two varieties: a double-thread canvas called penelope, double-mesh, or duo canvas; and a single-thread canvas called mono. The sizes of penelope and single canvas most readily available are: 5, 7, and 8 (**gros point**): 10, 12, 14, and 16 (**demi point**): and 18, 20, 22, and 24 (**petit point**). Penelope canvas can be worked over one or two threads.

Interlocked canvas is a two-threaded cloth similar to penelope, but the two threads are so close together that they appear as one, and are worked that way. The interlocking mesh makes this canvas extremely rigid and not susceptible to warping.

A new plastic canvas offers many advantages over cotton canvas. With the plastic canvas, there is no need for blocking, no need for a frame, and no need to bind the edges, and it can be cut and attached to another piece of plastic very easily. Three-dimensional needlework can be built with this new material, as it needs no special backing for stiffness.

Plastic canvas comes in sheets of 10½″ × 13½″ with mesh 7 to the inch, and in smaller shapes such as circles, diamonds, and squares, but it is not readily available by the yard. Other sizes and qualities may be available in the future.

Canvas comes in white (most popular), cream, ecru, and brown. Also see **joining canvas**, **silk canvas** and **Needlepoint: Basic Operations and Materials.**

canvas. Rugmaking. Weaving. A term loosely given to cotton or linen fabric in a **basket** or other porous weave. It is then sometimes called ''art canvas'' and can be used as a **rug backing (ground cloth)** in hooked or **embroidered rug**s. A better fabric is a heavier canvas, called **rug warp cloth,** that is made especially for use in rugmaking.

In weaving, canvas is a heavy cotton **plain weave** fabric used as the front and back **apron**s.

canvas. Stitchery. A strong, firm, closely woven **fabric,** usually of **cotton.** It is produced in many grades, and may be heavy and stiff or soft. Canvas and **duck** are sometimes used interchangeably, though canvas is heavier.

canvas bag. Ceramics. A sack that is used to thicken **slip.** It is filled with slip and hung from a ceiling until the slip thickens.

canvas mesh. Rugmaking. (Also called mesh canvas, open canvas, scrim canvas.) A stiff, open mesh made up of evenly spaced doubled, vertical and horizontal threads. It came into prominence as a **rug backing** for **latch-hooked rugs,** but its stiffness and open hole structure made it also popular for the counting of stitches while making an **embroidered rug.** It now comes in a variety of sizes (some very fine for fine needlework) and in widths up to 79″. The size is determined by the number of holes per inch. The best for rugmaking would be 3½ or 4 holes per inch. Canvas mesh is known by many different names, some of them trade names and others coined through popular usage. Scrim or open canvas are two commonly used names. Often there are blue lines indicated on the backing that make counting easier.

canvas needle. Rugmaking. See **rug needle.**

canvas pliers. Crewel. Embroidery. Needlepoint. A tool with broad, flat ends suitable for gripping fabric firmly, used in **blocking** a finished piece. These pliers are used also for stretching artist's canvases and are available from art supply stores. Also see **Crewel: Finishing, Needlepoint: Finishing.**

canvas weave. Weaving. A group of weaves with openwork areas and very often having the appearance of gauze or netting. They have a **plain weave** ground with **float** areas and are closely related to **mock leno** and other **lace weave**s. Although some canvas weaves have a firm structure, more often the weave is so loose that it is expected that the **filling** will slide around in the **warp** after the cloth is removed from the **loom.** This is due in part also to the **sleying,** which is usually done in such a way that **dent**s are left empty between ones where the **end**s are crammed in. The filling likewise alternates between open areas and crammed ones. The most common use for canvas weaves is as curtain or casement cloth. Also see **grouped threads.**

canvaswork. Needlepoint. Stitchery worked on a canvas. The term includes **bargello, crewelpoint,** and needlepoint.

cap cut. Gemcutting. See **facet.**

cape chisel. Metalworking. See **blacksmithing tools, chisel.**

capeskin. Leather. A term for leather from South African sheep. Also refers to sheepskin with a natural **grain.** Shelter cape is white sheepskin tanned on the grain side, available in 7–10′ skins with a protective finish to keep it clean.

capillarity. Jewelry. The physical law by which liquids in contact with solids rise, fall, or go sideways as the molecules of the liquid are attracted by those of the solid. An example of capillary action is the movement of solder in a liquid state into a well-fitting **seam** or **joint** of solid metal. Also see **freeze.**

capillary action. Jewelry. See **capillarity.**

capillary cementing. Plastics. See **cementing** and **Plastics: Cementing.**

cap rivet. Leather. See **rivet.**

cap screw. Metalworking. See **screw.**

Captain May in the Mexican War. Quilts. A one-of-a-kind quilt of **appliqué block**s made in 1846. On one of the blocks is depicted the mounted figure of Captain May as he charges the enemy forces. The captain is surrounded by blocks showing cows, hens, horses, birds, and stags. Other symbolic designs are mixed with some traditional block designs. This quilt is in the Shelburne Museum, Shelburne, Vermont.

carat. Gemcutting. A measure of weight used for buying and selling gems. One carat is equal to one-fifth of a gram; there are 141.75 carats in an ounce.

Carat should not be confused with karat, which is a measure of the purity of gold, or with the troy ounce used for weighing precious metals.

carbide. Metalworking. Plastics. Woodworking. A binary compound of carbon. Metal carbides are created by a heat treatment, making the metal on the surface extremely tough and hard. Tungsten carbide steel tips are used on cutting blades, **chisels**, and **drill bits**, which are subject to hard wear or high speeds in power tools.

Carbide blades and drills are recommended over ordinary **iron** and **steel** tools for working plastics, metals, and hardwoods. Carbide-tipped tools last longer, need sharpening less frequently, and, because they keep their sharpness longer, cut more precisely.

carbide glass-cutter. Stained Glass. A **glass-cutter** with a cutting **wheel** made from silicon carbide. It can be re-sharpened by the manufacturer and lasts about five times longer than a steel cutter.

carbide scriber. Stained Glass. A sharp, pointed tool used to sign completed glass pieces. It can also be used to trace around a thick pattern when the **glass-cutter** cannot get close enough.

carbonado. Gemcutting. See **abrasive, diamond, drilling jig.**

carbonetto. Coral Carving. See **coral.**

carbon method. Crewel. Embroidery. See **Crewel: Transferring a Design.**

carbon paper. Batik and Tie-dye. A thin paper that has been coated on one side with a carbon preparation, sometimes containing lampblack, or with some similar dark-colored pigment mixture. It is available at stationers or office supply shops. When the carbon is placed face-down between two sheets of paper the pressure of a tool on the top sheet will transfer the color to the bottom sheet. In **batik,** designs worked on paper are sometimes transferred to **fabric** with carbon paper and a **tracing wheel.** When designs are transferred to **wood,** a pencil, ball-point pen, or dental tool will work.

carbon paper. Crewel. Embroidery. See **dressmaker's carbon paper.**

carbon paper. Jewelry. A thin paper, coated on one side with a carbon preparation, used to transfer designs to metal. Also see **transferring designs to metal.**

carbon ring stick. Jewelry. A tapered stick made of compressed carbon used for holding **ring shank**s in position for **soldering,** and for other small, round, formed work. It is clamped in position between two pieces of metal which are fastened to a **transite board.** Also see **asbestos ring stick, carborundum pan.**

carbon steel. Metalworking. See **steel.**

carbon tetrachloride. Metalworking. A nonflammable, colorless liquid hydrocarbon solvent used to clean wax and grease off **pewter** and other metals, and some plastics. It is also used in fire extinguishers.

carborundum. Gemcutting. See **abrasive.**

carborundum. Jewelry. Metalworking. Woodworking. A hard **abrasive** made of carbon and silicon (**silicon carbide**) that fractures readily, exposing new cutting points while in use. It comes in many forms and is available with paper backing (**carborundum paper**), on cloth (**carborundum cloth**), in wheel form to be used with a motor for grinding, or in a solid block form called a **bench rub stone.** It is also available in grains of numerous sizes and in lump form that can be used to support work in a **soldering pan** during **soldering** and **annealing** processes. Carborundum can be heated to very high temperatures without melting, and it does not burn. Also see **abrasive.**

carborundum blade. Stained Glass. See **glass saw blade.**

carborundum block. Jewelry. See **bench rub stone.**

carborundum cloth. Jewelry. A cutting **abrasive** cloth available in grades from very fine to coarse used to refine metal surfaces. **Carborundum** cloth is more flexible than **carborundum paper.** Also see **crocus cloth.**

carborundum pan. Jewelry. (Also called annealing pan, soldering pan.) A rotating pan on a raised base containing small lumps of refractory material, usually **carborundum** or **pumice**, that retain heat while **annealing** or **soldering.** The work can be supported by propping it against a mound of carborundum grains or by partially burying it. See ill. Also see **asbestos pad, asbestos ring stick, bismuth block, carbon ring stick.**

Carborundum pan

carborundum paper. Jewelry. An abrasive paper used to refine metal surfaces. Also see **carborundum cloth.**

carborundum stone. Enameling. See **stoning.**

carborundum stone. Jewelry. See **bench rub stone.**

carbuncle. Gemcutting. See **garnet.**

carburizing flame. Metalworking. See **flame.**

card. Lacemaking. See **pricking.**

card. Spinning. See **carder.**

card. Weaving. Thin but sturdy cardboard, wood, metal or plastic tablet used in groups in **card weaving.** They can be bought or homemade, but in either case they must have smooth edges and rounded corners to facilitate turning them during the card weaving process. They can be of any geometric shape and have from 2 to 10 holes perforated in them, usually in the corners. Since the **warp** threads are threaded through them, the cards must be of a size large enough so that the distance between the holes makes a wide enough **shed.** In use, the cards must all be of the same size and shape and have the same number of holes. The holes are labeled A, B, C, D, etc., running in a clockwise order from the upper left-hand corner on the front of the card. The most commonly used card is 3½″ square with 4 holes, one in each corner. Cards with other shapes and numbers of holes give different sheds, utilize different weights of yarn, and are used to produce specific effects. See ill. Also see **card weaving.**

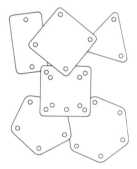

Various shaped cards showing placement of and number of holes

Cardan's rings. Toys. See **prisoner's lock.**

cardboard. Toys. A stiff paper of about the weight used for postcards or heavier. There are several types, all of which remain rigid and can be scored or cut with scissors.

Illustration board, often used in making **models** of buildings, boxes, and for matting pictures, is surfaced on both sides with an even-textured paper. It comes in sheets as large as 4′ × 6′ in a wide range of colors.

Railroad board is a lightweight cardboard with a smooth surface, available in many colors. The surface will spot if care is not taken in gluing.

cardboard container candle. Candlemaking. Cardboard containers, especially waxed milk cartons, serve as excellent **found object mold**s for candlemaking. The center bottom of the container can be readily pierced with an **ice pick** or skewer to allow it to be wicked in the same manner as the professional **metal mold.** Because it is made of paper, a pouring **temperature** of around 135° F is recommended. It is also suggested that the sides of the container be reinforced with tape or braced with wooden slats to prevent sagging or bulging under the stress of the heat and the weight of the hot wax. Cardboard containers, if waxed, leave a dullness on the finish; if unwaxed, they impart a relatively rough texture. Once the candle has hardened the cardboard container is cut or torn away. Also see **Candlemaking: Molding.**

cardboard loom. Weaving. A simple **loom** made out of a rigid, heavy piece of cardboard or illustration board. This board serves as a holding device for the **warp** threads. They are then interlaced with a **filling,** carried by a **needle** because there is no **shed** for a **shuttle** to go through. Finished woven pieces can be made on cardboard looms. If these pieces are large, they are made in sections and joined together.

The main function of a cardboard loom is experimental, as it permits speed, freedom, and spontaneity in weaving. It serves as a good introduction to weaving, a means of trying out new ideas before putting them on a large loom, or as a means of solving design and color problems.

Because large pieces of cardboard tend to buckle easily, most cardboard looms are small, with a 10″ or 12″ square being average. However, even small cardboard looms will buckle if the **warp** and filling yarns are pulled too tightly on the loom. Large cardboard looms must be of extremely rigid cardboard or reinforced with an extra piece of cardboard so that it becomes a double layer of cardboard; or a wooden crosspiece can be attached to the rear of the loom. Usually, when these extras have to be attached to the loom, the weaver opts for a more permanent structure, such as a **frame loom.**

The cardboard used as the loom should be slightly larger than the finished weaving. Slits are cut into the two lengthwise sides of the board. The warp is anchored and spaced in these slits. The warp can go completely around the cardboard, back and forth from slit to slit on the front of the loom, or each **end** can go from slit to slit and then be taped down on the back of the loom. The last is a good method to follow if small scraps of yarn are used. The slits are usually about ¼″ apart and ¼″ deep, but these measurements can vary according to the type of yarn used and the desired result. The filling usually weaves from **selvage** to selvage, but it can also be anchored around slits cut across the width. This method would be preferred if single scrap strands were used; they too could be taped to the back of the loom. The cardboard usually remains attached to the weaving as its frame or support, but it is equally easy to remove the weaving and finish the edges so that the piece will not unravel.

Cardboard looms need not be only square or rectangular; they can be circular or shaped to the form of the desired object. In these cases, slits are made around the entire cardboard piece. A cardboard loom need not necessarily be made of cardboard. Alternative materials are masonite, fiberboard, or Styrofoam. If masonite is used, nails can be pounded in to hold the warp as in a frame loom, or the slits can be made with a saw. Also see **finishing edge, joining, needleweaving, shaped weaving.**

card clothing. Spinning. See **carder, carding machine.**

carded wool. Spinning. Wool with relatively short **staple** fibers that has gone through the process of **carding** and is ready for spinning into **wool yarn**.

carder. Spinning. (Also called card.) A pair of hand implements used to separate and straighten **fibers** before spinning. They are rectangular, with a handle, and somewhat resemble paddles. There is usually a slight curve to the paddle, and on the upward side of the curve is mounted the card clothing, which is the part doing the actual work in **carding**. Card clothing is made up of bent wires or small spikes embedded in a foundation of leather or heavy material. This foundation is nailed or otherwise firmly attached to the paddle so that the wire hooks point toward the handle. The two carders are held and moved in such a manner that the surface of one card clothing against the other catches the fibers on the hooks and transfers them from one card to the other. Card clothing comes in different degrees of coarseness. Ideally, a spinner has three sets of carders in the order of proceeding: a first carding on widely spaced, thick hooks, to a final cording on densely spaced, fine hooks. Prior to card clothing, heads of **teasel** plants were used for this purpose. The French for teasel is *la cardère*, and it is assumed that the terms "carders" and "carding" are derived from it. See ill. Also see **carding, carding machine, rolag, sliver, teasel.**

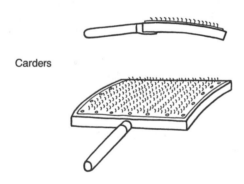

Carders

carding. Spinning. The process in which fibers are prepared for spinning by being brushed up to be more or less parallel. The fibers have large portions of foreign matter still remaining after **teasing**, which are removed and are put into a manageable form known as **sliver**. Carding can be executed with a pair of hand **carders** or a **carding machine**. In using hand carders, one carder has to be first charged or stroked with the fibers so that they are caught against the wire hooks. When the carder is almost full, the second carder is pulled across the first one. The fiber is transferred to the second carder. This is repeated until all the fiber is on the hooks of the second carder. This sequence of transferring from one carder to the other continues until the fibers are thoroughly clean and lying straight across the hooks of the carder. In machine carding, the same sequence happens as the wool passes through two sets of carders that have a cylindrical form. The fibers may be passed through more than once until they are in the desired condition. Wool fibers of 2–5″ are

carded and ready for spinning. Longer wool fibers also have to be combed. See ill. Also see **combing, rolag.**

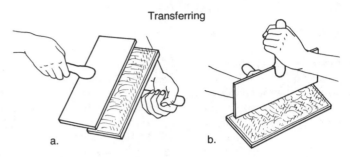

Transferring

a.   b.

carding machine. Spinning. A hand-cranked mechanism that separates and straightens **fiber**s in preparation for spinning. It is somewhat faster than using hand **carders**. The machine consists of two revolving rollers or cylinders, one large and one small. Both are turned by the hand crank. To use it, the fibers are spread evenly in a feed pan next to the small, or licker-in, roller. As the handle is turned, this roller catches the fibers and transfers them to the larger roller, or swift roller. Both of these rollers have card clothing around them. The card clothing, with its embedded wire hooks, is the instrument by which the fibers are caught and transferred, and, in so doing, are separated and aligned. This is accomplished at the moment the fibers move from the licker-in roller to the swift. There are interchangeable rollers with card clothing of varying degrees of coarseness, so it is possible to proceed from a very coarse **carding** to a very fine one. A narrow rod or knitting needle can lift the fiber from the machine when carding is completed. See ill.

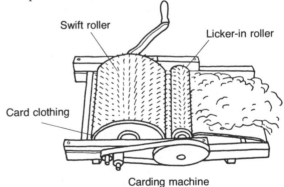

Swift roller   Licker-in roller

Card clothing

Carding machine

card marionette. Puppets. A simple jointed figure cut from cardboard. The head can be a **papier mâché** or Styrofoam ball, or it can be a circle cut from cardboard. The body is cut in one rectangular piece. Legs and arms each have two parts, jointed at the knees and elbows. Hands and feet are added separately. Parts are connected with a single loop of cord or heavy thread. The loops or joints are loose enough so that the figure will bend at the connections. **Strings** are first tied to knees, elbows, head, and hands and then are joined to a **control** above the figure.

In place of the single loops, parts of a card marionette may be joined with cellophane tape. Cardboard parts are together, and then tape is applied over the joint on one side. This allows one-way **hinge joint**s, which work well for a very simple puppet. In either of these versions a weight may be needed to keep the figure's feet on the ground. Drapery weights or a fishing weight can be sewn to each foot. Also see **articulated puppet.**

card weaving. Weaving. A form of warp twining using perforated cards and a **filling.** It is a type of **belt weaving** in that a long, narrow, and firm construction is made. These belts can be joined together to form purses, rugs, apparel, and wall hangings. The construction is a compact **warp-face,** the filling having been beaten out of sight and visible only at the **selvage**s. Card weaving is also weaving without a **loom** because the only equipment necessary is two supports several feet apart and the series of cards, which are square or another geometric shape (**a.**). The supports maintain the tension of the **warp** throughout the weaving. This method can also be used in **backstrap** weaving, where the weaver provides one of the supports.

Following a planned color pattern, the warp is made to the desired length on a **warping board** or similar apparatus. It is then threaded through the cards, which serve as both **heddle**s and **harness**es. The cards are stacked face up with all the holes that are indicated by the same letter aligned on top of each other. The warp is put in position between the two supports and weaving begins, using a small stick **shuttle** for the filling that can also act as the **beater.** The fingers or a comb also can be used to beat down the filling. The **shed** is opened by turning the cards a one-quarter turn. It is formed between the yarns from the top holes of the card and those from the bottom. The cards can be twisted in any combination, so many shed openings are possible (**b.**). After each passage of filling, the warp threads twist around each other and the filling, making an extremely strong fabric. See ill.

The pattern in card weaving is determined by the color plan of the warp, the order in which the holes are threaded, and the direction in which the cards are turned. This can be diagrammed out on **graph paper** before weaving begins. A draft is made in which every vertical row of squares represents a single card and every horizontal row a particular hole. The draft should also contain directions on how to thread the cards, because they can be threaded from front to back, or from back to front. In one card, all the holes must be threaded in the same direction. The number of cards used and the thickness of the yarn determine the width of the fabric. Thinner yarns require more tablets. A smooth, firm yarn must be used because a soft, loose yarn would pull apart easily under the stress of the twist.

Many kinds of designs and structures are possible in card weaving. Double cloth can also be woven with cards by turning the cards on end so that the corners are aligned vertically. This opens up two sheds, allowing the filling to pass first through one shed and then the second.

Card weaving is also known as tablet weaving and Egyptian card weaving. The latter name comes from the belief that card weaving dates back to Egypt as early as 750 B.C. In Scandinavia, cards and warp were found that date back to A.D. 830. Also see **carders, Peruvian ingrain weave.**

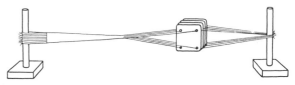

a. Supports used in card weaving

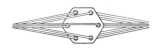

b. Two sheds formed (using 6-sided cards) for double cloth.

care of quilts. Quilts. See **Quilts: Care of Quilts.**

caricature. Puppets. The exaggerated portrayal of a character. **Puppet head**s lend themselves to such satire or parody because the features are individually formed for each figure. The caricature may offer a way of quickly identifying or describing a character if the distortion is only slight. If distortion is extreme, the character may be made absurd or ridiculous. Also see **Puppets: Making the Puppet Head.**

carnauba. Leather. See **Leatherwork: Finishing Leather, Tools and Materials.**

carnauba wax. Woodworking. See **wax.**

carnelian. Gemcutting. See **quartz.**

carousel. Toys. A moving toy made to imitate or suggest a real carousel. It is similar to the **merry-go-round,** with a revolving circular platform on which animals are placed. Some are made as **windup toy**s, with a music box attached. The homemade carousels are often hand-turned, containing no mechanical devices. When the platform is turned, the animals, usually horses, move forward in a never-ending circle.

carpenter. Toys. A **swinging-weight toy** that basically works like the **pecking chickens.** In this case there are two **string**s; one animates the carpenter with an ax, the other man with a saw. It is one of a series of similar traditional **folk toy**s of Eastern Europe. It is similar in action to a **hammer toy.**

carpenter's horse. Woodworking. See **sawhorse.**

carpenter's pencil. Woodworking. See **marking tools.**

carpenter's square. Woodworking. See **squaring tools.**

Carpenter's Wheel. Quilts. See **Star-within-Star.**

carpentry. Woodworking. The craft or trade of cutting and joining **lumber** and **timber** into a structure. The carpenter, as opposed to the **joiner** or **cabinetmaker,** is principally responsible for the stability of the skeleton of a building. The carpenter works mostly with unplaned lumber that is usually hidden by subsequent finishes. The work may be permanent, as in floor or wall framing, or temporary, as in building scaffolds or forms for concrete work.

carpet needle. Stitchery. A strong, heavy **needle** with a large eye. Cord, heavy waxed thread, or string can be used for extra-heavy-duty sewing. It is similar to an upholstery needle, though it has a straight shaft.

carpet thread. Batik and Tie-dye. Stitchery. Toys. An extra-heavy thread for heavy-duty hand sewing. It is excellent for sewing any **seam**s that must support weight, as in **soft sculpture**s, large **banner**s, or **stuffed toy**s. Because it is available only in large spools and in a limited range of colors, usually neutrals, the stitching is rarely used decoratively. Carpet thread is good for **binding** in **tie-dye** since it is strong enough to withstand the pulling required to compact the **fabric.**

carpet thread. Puppets. A strong cord or thread suitable for **stringing** a **marionette**. It is made to join sections of rug or carpeting and has a lightly waxed surface. Also see **Puppets: Stringing the Marionette.**

carpet thread. Rugmaking. Heavy-duty cotton thread used in making **braided rug**s, and for hemming and general sewing on other types of rugs. Sometimes called double-duty thread, it is found on sewing counters in a limited range of colors.

carpet underlay. Amber Carving. Ivory and Bone Carving. Jet Carving. Shell Carving. When working a material by hand that is too fragile to be clamped in the vise it can be of some help to press the piece into a piece of carpet tacked to the bench. It cushions and grips the material. In certain situations it is convenient to fold the carpet over the material and to clamp it with a wooden clamp. Also see **beeswax, wood vise wedge.**

carpet warp. Rugmaking. Weaving. The name given to an 8/4s cotton **rug warp** yarn used traditionally in the weaving of **rag rug**s. It comes in numerous colors and is soft and highly serviceable, but has little body compared to other warp yarns. Also see **yarn count.**

carpet weaving. Rugmaking. Weaving. See **rug weaving.**

carriage bolt. Metalworking, Woodworking. See **bolt.**

carriage clamp. Woodworking. See **clamping tools.**

Carrick bend. Macramé. See **Josephine knot.**

Carrickmacross. Lacemaking. (Also called Carrickmacross appliqué.) A very distinctive **needle lace** made in Ireland, dating from about 1850. It is characterized by a very fine fabric stitched to a **net** foundation, and is classed as an **appliqué** lace.

Trace the **design** onto the sheer fabric, which is mounted into a **hoop** and backed with a layer of net.

Follow the outlines of the design with a line of very small **running stitches** which join the two layers of material.

Make the outlines around the design **motif**s with a round cord sewn on the right side, all around the edge, with a moderately tight **overcast stitch** in fine thread. This cord also forms **picots** around the edge of the lace in a succession of single **loops.**

Work the overcast stitches and the **buttonhole bar**s that join the different parts of the design at the same time.

When outlines and connecting bars are finished cut away the fabric from the ground areas, leaving a **ground** of net against the design.

On the right side, outline the design motifs with a round cord. Sew all around the edge with a moderately tight overcast stitch in fine thread.

carton-cuir work. Leather. Molded decorations made from a malleable mixture of boiled waste leather scraps and waste paper. This technique was popular in fourteenth-century Europe when boiled leather was either stamped in molds or modeled into decorative embellishments, and often combined with **cuir-boulli work.** The designs were generally stained black. The mixture of leather scraps, often bookbinders' cuttings, and waste-paper scraps was often boiled with gum or flour paste for added strength. Also see **embossing** and **Leatherwork.**

cartonnage à la Bradel. Bookbinding. See **Bradel binding.**

carton pierre. Papercrafts. A French term used in the mid-nineteenth century for molded **papier mâché** imitations of plaster decorations on ceilings or walls.

cartoon. Crewel. Embroidery. Needlepoint. A sketch, drawing, draft, or projection on paper of a final design. Also see **Crewel: Transferring a Design; Needlepoint: Transferring a Design.**

cartoon. Mosaics. Stained Glass. (Also called working drawing.) A full-sized drawing that will be transferred to heavy paper to be cut up and used for patterns for cutting desired shapes out of stained glass. A lightweight drawing paper, such as 30 lb paper, can be used.

Be sure to include the outside border lead in the drawing. For example, when using 3″ lead for the border, the dull size of the pattern will be ³/₁₆″ wider than the actual dimensions of the glass. Half the width of the border falls outside the picture. This is important in order to produce the size **panel** desired. A felt-tip pen can be used to draw in the lead lines between the glass in the cartoon. After the **template**s are made, the cartoon is taped to the workboard.

In mosaics, cartoon refers to a preparatory sketch used in planning the **mosaic.** Because mosaic materials such as **tesserae** have uniquely defined qualities, the cartoon should not attempt to be anything more than an indication of the nature of the final colorings and patternings. Too precise a rendering will force the mosaicist to copy the cartoon, thereby stifling creativity in the construction. Thick felt-tip pens or pastel sticks are recommended for cartoon sketching. Above all, the sketching should stay loose and spontaneous. Creativity should be saved for the setting step. Also see **photographic cartoon, squaring up, Mosaics: Creating the Design, Stained Glass: Glazing.**

cartoon. Weaving. Traditionally, a full-scale copy drawn or painted on paper or traced in black paint or ink on tracing paper or tracing linen cloth from the original full-color drawing used in **tapestry** weaving. Today the cartoon usually refers to the working drawing as opposed to the full-color painting or sketch; however, the reference can be to either. Designs can also be drawn in small scale and then enlarged to the desired size by the grid method of **transferring design**s. Another method is to weave a very accurate **maquette** or small model of the intended piece, and then enlarge it photographically to the desired size.

The cartoon is placed behind a **high-warp** loom and below a **low-warp** loom, and is usually followed exactly. Designs should be drawn with the possibilities and limitations of tapestry techniques in mind. Cartoons can be painted in the colors of the finished piece, or numbered to correspond to specific yarn colors. This is done to ensure that the weaver uses the correct colors, especially because the tapestry designer is often not the weaver, as in the case of the well-known tapestries produced at Aubusson in France. Tapestry techniques, such as **hatching** and the use of **slit**s, are often indicated on the cartoon to ensure their proper placement in the finished piece.

In weaving a tapestry, the front side traditionally faces away from the weaver. Therefore, when working in this manner, the cartoon must be drawn in reverse of what the finished tapestry is to look like. The weaver decides the best way to weave the tapestry. This will often be sideways in order to accommodate a large width or to handle shapes and color shadings in the best possible manner. The cartoon is then placed behind or below the loom to be used as a direct guide, or behind or to the side of the weaver for use as a color reference. When placed behind the warp, the design is either pinned to the woven part of the tapestry, suspended by a system of strings from the loom, or taped to the loom. Sometimes the design is copied from the cartoon directly onto the **warp end**s using a series of dots encircling each warp end. A felt-tip pen or india ink is used to do this. This transference is useful in case the cartoon shifts position, which sometimes happens when it is merely pinned to the tapestry. On a low-warp loom, the cartoon is usually pinned underneath to the **selvages** of the tapestry and is rolled along with the tapestry around the **cloth beam** as the weaving progresses. The rolling process often ensures that the cartoon will not shift. Mirrors are used to check the work from below or behind.

Modern tapestry weavers work with the right side facing them and use the cartoon in its front version, not reversed. They also draw the cartoon much more freely, indicating large forms and motifs only, and interpret color shadings and texture as they weave. Cartoons are also used in **rugweaving** and **wall hangings,** but are referred to simply as drawings. Also see **Aubusson tapestry, Gobelin tapestry.**

cartoon booklet. Toys. See **animated booklet.**

cartouche. Découpage. A French term for an Italian word, *cartoccio,* meaning a roll or twist of paper. The term usually refers to an ornamental scroll border enclosing an oval or oblong area. This device of stylized, framed areas, often filled with figures and scenes, is characteristic of eighteenth-century **print**s, which are popular subjects for découpage. Often the scrollwork borders are cut from the original print and rearranged on the surface as a design vehicle for organizing and accenting areas. In coloring the prints, the cartouche can be treated as a separate design element (a vignette) with a different color background outside its borders.

cartridge brass. Metalworking. See **brass.**

cartridge pleating. Knitting. See **corrugated fabric.**

carved wood. Puppets. Toys. Wood that has been shaped, cut, sculpted, or sanded to a desired form. **Puppet** or **marionette head**s are often made of carved wood because it allows for many facial details. Many handcrafted **toys** are made that include portions or areas of hand-carved wood. Some molded **plastic toy**s attempt to duplicate the texture of carved wood in the plastic. Also see **balsa wood.**

carved wood head. Puppets. See **Puppets: Making the Puppet Head.**

carving. Candlemaking. Wax takes beautifully to a well-manipulated carver's knife. For special effects the candle may be dipped before or after carving in a 200° **wax bath.** If the candle is dipped in a wax of another color before carving, the basic **coloring** will be revealed beneath the cutaway dipped layer. If dipped after carving, the coloring of the dipping wax will tend to accumulate in the carved areas, thus softening the cut edges.

carving. Jewelry. A technique of cutting heavy-**gauge** metal with sharp cold chisels. The chisel cuts away the metal, leaving the surface of the work bright and shiny. The work can be faceted like a gemstone to give off bright, mirrorlike reflections. This technique is often used in India.

carving. Leather. Incising **tooling** patterns into dampened leather with a **swivel knife** without actually removing any leather; or utilizing a V-gouge to cut out a channel along design lines. For an added decorative effect the carved lines may be darkened with felt-tip pens.

carving. Plastics. Cutting away and removing material to create a form. Carve plastic sheets and solid forms with **flexible shaft machine** tipped with a **burr** or **tapered drill bit.** Carve **foam**s with hand tools, such as hacksaw blades, knives, **surform** files and sandpaper, or flexible-shaft and power saws for high-density foam. Also see **intaglio process** and **Plastics: Carving.**

carving. Woodworking. See **whittling, woodcarving** and **Woodworking: Woodcarving and Whittling.**

carving point. Gemcutting. A small metal tool held in a **point carver** or **flexible-shaft machine.** It is charged with **abrasive** and used to carve, engrave, and sculpt gem materials. Charge iron nails or needles with diamond powder or silicon carbide by rolling the needle between two flat pieces of agate covered with diamond powder in oil. Material is rapidly removed by small **grinding wheel**s with thin-bladed "saws." Polish the gem material with tools of the same size and shape as used for carving; the polishing points can be made of wood, ivory, horn, tin, copper or bronze. Charge the points with fine diamond powder; tin oxide, or tripoli on small felt, muslin, or leather wheels can also be used. See ill. Also see **charging.**

Carving points

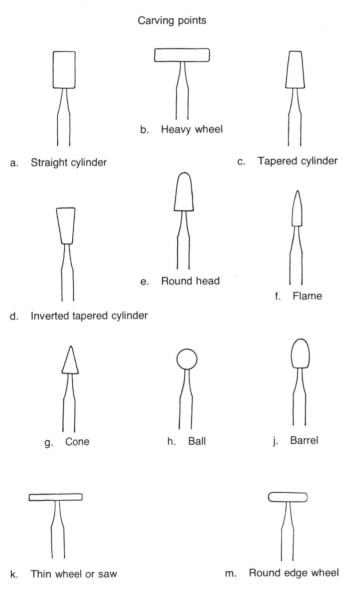

a. Straight cylinder

b. Heavy wheel

c. Tapered cylinder

d. Inverted tapered cylinder

e. Round head

f. Flame

g. Cone

h. Ball

j. Barrel

k. Thin wheel or saw

m. Round edge wheel

case. Bookbinding. A book cover constructed separately from the body of the book and attached to it later.

casebinding. Bookbinding. See **casemaking.**

casebound. Bookbinding. See **casemaking.**

casein. Toys. A paint similar to **tempera** but of better quality and more expensive. It is worked in the same way, with water as the thinner. It is available in tubes from art supply stores.

casein glue. Woodworking. See **adhesives.**

casemaking. Bookbinding. (Also called case binding.) The process of making a cover of **cloth**-covered **board**s, separately from the body of the book, to be attached as the final operation, thus producing a casebound book. Nearly all books now published are casebound.

Cut boards ¼″ longer than the height of the book and ⅛″ wider than the width of the book from the **backing** groove to the **foredge.** Cut cloth ⅝″ wider than the measurement from the front foredge around to the back foredge, and ⅝″ longer than the length of the boards. Cut a lining strip of manila or other heavy paper of ⅛″ less than the measurement from the **back edge** of the front board to the back edge of the back board (across the back) and equal to the length of the boards (not the book). Holding the boards flush with the backing groove, mark the position of the boards and strip on the inside of cloth. Spread hard glue in a dabbing motion from the center of the cloth to the edges. Weight the corners to keep them from curling. Cut off the corners of the cloth at a 45° angle, allowing about ⅛″ between the corner of the board and the cut. Position the boards and lining strip according to the marks you have made on the glued cloth and rub down well. Turn in the overlap first at the **head,** then at the **tail;** tuck in the corner projections and then the foredge overlap. Rub down. Turn the work over and rub down through a clean waste sheet with the **bone folder** and crease the hinges with the folder. **Nip** in the press. Turn the work over and place the book on the **case.** Close the front board over the book and adjust the book square to the boards, with a uniform ⅛″ **square,** or overhang, around the edges. Run the folder along the hinges to set the shape and tie a string around them to hold it. Place the book between **pressing boards** and clamp in the press. Let it dry for 24 hours. Remove the book from press, remove the string, and lay the case face-down on a table. If desired, trim the turn-in to ⅜″, but do not trim across the back between the boards. The book is then ready to be **cased in.**

Boards laid out in position on cloth

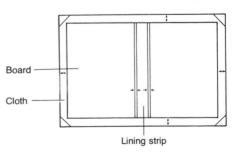

Board

Cloth

Lining strip

cashmere. Crewel. Knitting. The protective covering of the cashmere goat that is spun into knitting yarn. Cashmere fleece, obtained during the moulting season, is soft, strong and very silky. The natural color is a muted brown. Also see **Knitting: Tools and Materials.**

cashmere. Spinning. Weaving. The hair of a mountain goat found in the Himalayan Mountains in Tibet, the Kashmir province in northern India, Iran, Iraq, and China. The hair is very soft, lightweight, warm and silken to the touch. The finest hair comes from the goats living at the highest altitudes. The desirable inner hair, 1¼–3½" in length, is obtained by combing. The coarser, outer hair is longer—3½–4½". During the combing, many long hairs come out; these must be removed by hand. Because some of the long hair remains no matter how much care is taken, its presence has become a characteristic of cashmere yarn. The natural color of cashmere ranges from pure white to gray or brownish-gray, which predominates. The word "cashmere" also applies to the fabric made of this yarn, and to the intricately designed shawls once handwoven by the peasants of Kashmir, India.

cashmere stitch. Needlepoint. A technique of working four diagonal stitches in a sequence of one short stitch, two long stitches, and one short stitch. Come up at A, go down at B, up at C and down at D. Continue working in this fashion, working one short stitch, two long, and one short. See ill.

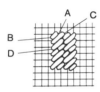

Cashmere stitch

cashmere stitch diagonally. Needlepoint. A variation of the **cashmere stitch**; it is worked so that the last short stitch of one group is the first short stitch of the next group. This stitch is good for backgrounds and filling. See ill.

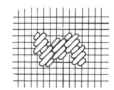

Cashmere stitch diagonally

casing. Glasswork. A process in glassblowing used to color a blown vessel. Because blown work using colored glass has a tendency to become too dark in the thick areas, casing is used so that the applied color appears even throughout the vessel. After a blown piece is formed in clear glass, it is partially cooled and then turned in a tank of molten colored glass, which adheres in a thin film.

casing. Leather. The process of preparing heavy leather for **stamping** or **tooling.** Soak the leather in cold water until completely saturated; wrap it in a cloth or place it in a plastic bag; and leave it 4 hours or longer, preferably in a refrigerator. Unwrap; place the cased leather **grain** side up

until it shows the first signs of drying. The leather is then ready to be decorated. Also see **embossing wheel** and **Leatherwork: Forming Leather.**

casing in. Bookbinding. Joining the **case** to the book. Place the book squarely in the case, with a ⅛" projection on **head, tail,** and **foredge.** Place a sheet of waste paper under the **board paper** and carefully paste the endpaper from the center out on the side facing the board, holding the waste sheet in place so paste does not get under the endpaper; avoid getting paste in the hinge. Lift the endpaper and remove the waste sheet, replacing it with a sheet of waxed paper to prevent moisture from damaging the book. Lay the endpaper flat once more and carefully close the cover on it. Lift the board slightly to ascertain that the endpaper is correctly positioned; if adjustment is necessary, slide the body. Press the board firmly onto the book. Turn the book over and repeat the operation for the other endpaper. Press for at least 24 hours in the **standing press.**

casing nail. Woodworking. See **nail.**

casserole. Ceramics. See **Ceramics: Form.**

cassiterite. Gemcutting. A mineral composed of tin dioxide with **hardness** of 6½ and **specific gravity** of 6.8–7.1. The gems are transparent, **color**ed white, yellow, and brown and have high refractive indices of 1.997 and 2.093. They are **facet**ed with main crown facets at 35° and main pavillion facets at 41°, and are polished with Linde A on a tin **lap.** Also see **faceting, polishing, refraction.**

castile. Batik and Tie-dye. A fine, hard soap prepared from olive oil and sodium hydroxide. When added to the **dyebath** in dyeing **silk,** castile imparts a fine luster to the **fabric.**

casting. Candlemaking. The process of pouring hot liquid wax into a **mold.** See also **Candlemaking: Molding.**

casting. Ceramics. See **casting slip, molding, slipcasting.**

casting. Enameling. A **metal** form made by filling a hollow mold with molten metal. A sterling silver, casting has a thin layer of fine silver on its surface.

casting. Glasswork. Glass can be cast by pouring the molten material into a **mold** made of plaster and sand, or by placing pieces of glass in the mold and placing the mold in a furnace so that glass fuses together and fills the form. It is customary to determine the volume of glass that will just fill the mold so that it will not be necessary to add additional glass while the mold and glass are at full oven heat. This is simple to do. Fill the mold with water and find the volume of water. Add **cullet** to that volume of water in a measuring cup until the difference in the two water levels is the same volume as will fill the mold.

To make a mold:

a. Model the form in clay or wax and fix a funnel-shaped attachment of the same material to the bottom of the model. See ill., next page.

b. Place the model on a flat surface so that it rests on the funnel-shaped foot. Form linoleum or other stiff material into a dam around the model and seal the bottom edge to the surface.

c. Pour refractory plaster into the dam so that it completely covers the model.

d. The level of the liquid plaster should be an inch or so above the model inside. Allow the plaster to set.

e. Strip the clay model and dig it out of the plaster mold. If the model is wax, it can be melted out by placing the mold upside-down in a furnace at low heat.

f. Scrape and clean the funnel with a knife.

To mold a piece:

g. Place the exact volume of glass in the cavity and place the whole thing in a furnace hot enough so the glass melts and flows into the model mold.

h. Break the plaster mold away from the form after it has cooled through the **annealing** cycle.

j. The piece is finished.

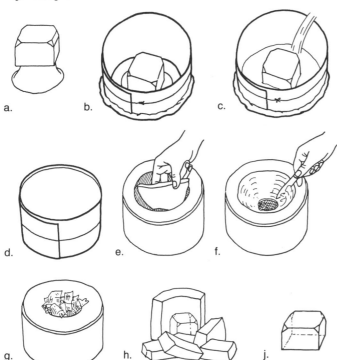

casting. Jewelry. Metalworking. A process in which molten metal is poured into a previously prepared hollow form and allowed to cool, solidifying into the shape of the mold. The mold material that is selected is determined by the types of metal used, the complexity of the pattern, the degree of definition desired, the temperature of the molten metal, and the number of castings to be made from a mold. Some of the various casting methods are: **centrifugal casting, lost wax casting, cuttlebone casting,** core casting, **sand casting,** plaster mold, tufa casting, **steam casting,** and **vacuum casting.** Also see **alcohol lamp, blowhole, burnout, ganging** and **Metalworking: Casting.**

casting. Plastics. The process of making a form by pouring into a **mold** a liquid that solidifies without external heat or pressure. Plastic casts are made by pouring **catalyzed** liquid **casting resin** into a prepared mold. Also see **Plastics: Casting.**

casting brass. Metalworking. See **brass.**

casting concrete. Stained Glass. See **dalle-de-verre.**

casting epoxy resin. Stained Glass. The process of embedding or surrounding glass pieces in a clear plastic resin. The fumes from this resin are toxic. Also see **dalle-de-verre, epoxy resin, lamination, mosaic** and **Stained Glass: Safety Precautions.**

casting flux. Metalworking. See **flux.**

casting grains. Jewelry. Commercially prepared metal pieces that are used in **casting.** The grains are clean and free from impurities, and because of their size and the fact that spaces remain around them when they pile up in the crucible, they tend to melt quickly. If you do not have scrap metal to cast with, it is advisable to buy casting grains as opposed to sheet metal, which is more expensive and which you would then have to cut up. It is even cheaper to use scraps if you have them because when you sell scraps to a refiner you are paid only for the precious metal content and lose the money you paid for the original processing. Also see **shot, shotting.**

casting lead came. Stained Glass. Studios in France and Germany extrude their own **lead came.** It is quite elaborate to make. Piglead **ingots** are purchased from a lead dealer and melted down in a cast-iron crucible or bucket. When the lead is molten and the **dross** has been removed, the lead is poured into molds from lead ladles. When the lead sets up, the mold is opened and the top of the cast is grabbed with pliers and pulled sharply from the mold. When they are cool enough to be handled, the castings are milled through a lead mill and turned into came of various sizes with different-shaped **channels.**

casting metal. Metalworking. See **metal.**

casting off. Knitting. (Also called binding off.) The process of removing stitches from the needles to finish a piece of knitting. Also see **Knitting: Casting Off.**

casting off in pattern. Knitting. See **Knitting: Casting Off.**

casting on. Knitting. See **Knitting: Casting On.**

casting plaster. Metalworking. Plastics. Plaster used to make molds for metal and plastic castings, and to make patterns for **sandcasting.** Casting plaster must be mixed with **refractory materials** to make a mold for molten-metal casting. Ferrous **alloys** may not be cast in plaster or plaster-bonded molds because the high temperature of the molten metal would destroy the mold; alloys based on **copper** or **aluminum** are suitable. Ready-made mixtures for metal casting may be purchased under various brand names, e.g., Match Plate plaster, Hydroperm (a metal-casting plaster made from Hydrocal), and Kastical (designed for casting alloys containing zinc).

To prepare casting plaster:

a. Weigh the powdered plaster carefully and measure out the proper quantity of water at 70–80° F. For maximum strength, use the precise amounts given in the product instructions.

b. Let the water become still in the mixing vessel before adding the plaster; agitation will start the chemical reaction between the water and plaster, and lumps will form before you can add all the plaster.

c. Sprinkle the plaster gently on the surface of the water. As you sprinkle it, the plaster on the surface will soak and sink into the liquid. Do not mix until all the dry plaster has disappeared from the surface.

d. Mix the plaster with your hands in order to feel and squeeze out any lumps. Continue until the mixture is the consistency of heavy cream. Avoid agitating the surface excessively to prevent air bubbles in the mixture. Because plaster tends to dry out the skin, you may wear plastic or rubber gloves, but be sure they are thin and close-fitting so you can feel any lumps.

e. Use the mixed plaster immediately. Mix only as much as you can use quickly. The curing time of the plaster depends on the temperature of the water and the speed of mixing—higher temperatures and faster agitation speed up the reaction and shorten the working period.

casting plaster. Plastics. A variety of gypsum-based materials, such as Plaster of Paris, Hydrocal, and Ultra-Cal, used for **mold**s. Hydrocal is harder and more durable than Plaster of Paris. Ultra-Cal is the hardest of the three and has the lowest shrinkage and **distortion** rate. Coat the plaster surfaces with a **sealant** and **mold release agent** before pouring the **resin** into the mold.

casting plastic. Plastics. See **casting resin.**

casting polyester resin. Stained Glass. See **polyester resin technique.**

casting resin. Plastics. (Also called casting plastic.) A resin designed for casting that contains **plasticizer**s to minimize **cracking** and that has a low exotherm when **curing.** A low exotherm is particularly desirable when making thick casts.

Some casting agents also contain **wax**es that rise to the liquid surface for an **air shield,** and some contain **mold release agents.**

casting sand. Metalworking. See **molding sand.**

casting slip. Ceramics. A **slip** containing a **deflocculent** that is cast in plaster molds. Sodium silicate and **soda ash** reduce the amount of water required to make a slip fluid. A properly deflocculated slip pours easily but has a thick consistency that prevents heavier slip particles from settling and ruining the casting. Coarse-grained **kaolin**s make a faster casting body, while ball clays give a slow cast with a tough surface. Clay bodies with a high degree of **plasticity** are unsuitable for casting. Also see **slip casting.**

casting top. Toys. See **peg top.**

cast iron. Jewelry. A metal that is easily fused and fluid when pouring or **casting.** It is hard and brittle and cannot be bent, hammered, or formed after casting or it will break. Consequently, it should not be used when strength is an important factor.

The interior of cast iron has a texture much like coarse granulated sugar. Getting a block of cast iron to break with a level surface is extremely difficult and mostly a matter of chance. Once a flat piece is obtained, however, **sheet metal** can be placed on its surface and hammered, picking up the surface texture of the iron. The sheet metal can then be formed into jewelry. Some **pitch bowl**s are made from cast iron, and their outside surface, when the bowl is turned upside down, can be used to obtain a similar effect. The sheet metal would of course curve as the pitch bowl does, as the bowl is acting as a **stake.** It will not produce as textured a surface as the broken iron, however.

Hammering sheet metal on a rough concrete surface such as a floor or the sidewalk with a **rawhide mallet** or a **planishing hammer,** each giving a different effect, will produce a similar texture, although not as fine and uniform as that produced by cast iron.

cast iron. Metalworking. See **iron.**

cast-iron crucible. Stained Glass. See **casting lead came.**

cast-iron toy. Toys. An iron toy, especially one produced in America between 1840 and 1940, with the 1880s being the high point of their production. The toys, cast in molds, were heavy and usually in the form of trains or other vehicles with the surface painted. Some are now being reproduced from the original molds.

castle. Weaving. The central framework of a **floor** or **table loom,** in which the **harness**es are housed and the mechanism to operate them is attached. Without the castle structure, a **harness loom** would revert to being a **frame loom.** Also see **jack-type loom.**

Castle Wall. Quilts. A **pieced quilt** based on a central **octagon,** surrounded by numerous cut pieces. They form a star and two more octagonal rings. Also see **star pattern.**

castle wheel. Spinning. See **treadle wheel.**

castor oil. Leather. Castor oil is used by many craftsmen to soften and condition leather. Rub well into the leather with a soft cloth. Also see **Leatherwork: Tools and Materials.**

catalyst. Plastics. (Also called curing agent, hardener.) A chemical added to the **resin** to initiate the **curing** process. The most common catalyst for **polyester resin** is MEK-Px **(methyl ethyl ketone peroxide).** Extreme care should be exercised in the handling, use, and storage of catalysts.

Many are highly flammable and toxic and may cause severe skin irritation or burns. Use only the recommended catalyst for each resin. Also see **Plastics: Casting.**

catalyzed. Plastics. A **resin** that contains a **catalyst** and is in the process of **curing.**

catalyzing. Plastics. See **curing.**

catch. Jewelry. See **finding.**

Catch-Me-if-You-Can. Quilts. See **Swastika.**

catch stitch. Bookbinding. See **kettle stitch.**

catch stitch. Quilts. Stitchery. A single short stitch used to hold something in place. It simply **tack**s it there with a tiny stitch in as inconspicuous a way as possible.

caterpillar stitch. Crewel. Embroidery. See **bullion knot.**

cathedral glass. Stained Glass. Stained glass is produced in two general categories—**antique glass,** which is handblown, and cathedral glass, which is rolled by machine rollers that may or may not be textured. Cathedral glass is generally ⅛" thick, whereas antique glass varies in thickness, and is made in the United States, which makes it less expensive than antique glass. Also see **diamond glass cutter, drapery glass, hammered glass, machine-made glass.**

Cathedral Window. Quilts. (Also called Pin Cushion.) A traditional design for a **coverlet** that combines **muslin** and bright **cotton**s in a diamond-in-circle design. No **filler** is required, and no **quilting** is actually stitched. The muslin is folded in such a way that numerous layers of fabric give the coverlet weight.

The separate units are made by hemming, folding, and refolding squares of muslin, **slip-stitch**ing edges, and turning them inside out. Units are then folded in the center, **tack**ed, and joined. Pieces of bright-colored fabric are set into the areas between units, and the muslin is folded over the raw edges. The finished units show edges rolled back to reveal bright diamonds of color. The units are joined, and no **backing** is required.

cathode. Enameling. The negative pole of a battery or other source of direct current. In **electroetching, electroforming,** and **electroplating** the cathode receives the accumulation of metal. Also see **anode.**

cationic dye. Batik and Tie-dye. See **basic dye.**

cat-on-a-stick. Toys. See **stick rider.**

Cats and Mice. Quilts. A **pieced block** design that contains a diagonal cross formed of squares and triangles.

cat's eye. Gemcutting. See **C-axis, cabochon, chrysoberyl, luster, quartz.**

cattle hide. Leather. Leathers from bull, steer, cow, and **kip hide**s.

cat track. Quilts. See **border.**

caulking compound. Candlemaking. A caulking compound such as Mordite clay should be used to plug the hole at the bottom of a candle **mold** through which the **wick** is threaded. This prevents the hot melted wax from **leaking** during the **pouring** procedure. Also see **Candlemaking: Wicking the Mold.**

caustic soda. Batik and Tie-dye. Sodium hydroxide, or concentrated **lye,** used in mixing the **colorfast** azoic or **naphthol** dye.

caustic soda. Dyeing. Sodium hydroxide or "lye" in white, crystalline form used in dyeing in conjunction with **indigo** and other **vat dye**s. It is readily soluble in water and it is a very potent and dangerous substance. It destroys animal fibers. Keep it away from the skin and eyes.

Cavandoli work. Macramé. A two-color pattern of closely worked vertical and horizontal **double half hitch**es. Cavandoli designs often include small birds, trees, flowers, and primitive figures.

A Cavandoli stitch pattern is usually charted knot by knot on graph paper to determine how the colors will be worked. On graph paper, the background stitch (**horizontal double half hitch**) would be indicated by darkened grid squares and the design stitch (**vertical double half hitch**) by light or blank squares. See ill.

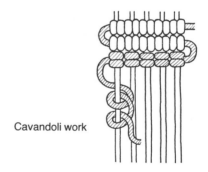
Cavandoli work

cave-in. Candlemaking. Wax has a natural tendency to shrink as it cools. This can produce **cavities** within the candle that unless refilled during the candlemaking process will result in cave-ins when the candle begins to burn. Also see **Candlemaking: Molding.**

cavity. Candlemaking. As it cools, wax has a natural tendency to shrink in volume. This usually results in cavities or air holes along the wick line. These must be completely refilled during the candlemaking process to avoid **cave-ins** when the candle begins to burn. Also see **Candlemaking: Molding.**

C-axis. Gemcutting. The direction of crystal growth; often it is parallel to the length of the crystal. **Cleavage** planes are aligned parallel or perpendicular to or through the

C-axis. Inclusions of dust, tubes, or threads of microscopic size are often arranged along the C-axis. Chatoyance and cat's eye phenomena are caused by **reflection**s from the fine lines formed by inclusions. Two or more chatoyant lines intersecting form stars. The A-axis is perpendicular to the C-axis, transverse inclusions along this A-axis exhibit a centered star. Dichroic **color** effects are most striking viewed from the direction along or across the C-axis. Also see **cabochon, luster.**

C-clamp. Jewelry. A C-shaped clamp used for holding objects firmly in place. A **V-board and clamp** uses a C-clamp to hold the V-board in place. A C-clamp can be used to hold metal in position during **drilling, sawing,** and **filling** operations. Cardboard should be placed between the jaws and the piece to prevent scratching or denting of the metal. C-clamps are necessary when drilling holes with a hand drill, as it takes two hands to operate a hand drill. They are also helpful when using a **flexible shaft machine** or a **drill press,** as the drill can bind in the metal, grab it, and rotate it at high speeds which could be dangerous if you were holding the piece with your bare hand.

C-clamp. Macramé. An adjustable, C-shaped clamp sold in hardware stores. A pair of C-clamps can be used in measuring lengths of **cord** and to clamp work-in-progress to a table.

To measure cords evenly, measure and cut one length of cord by hand. This is usually cut 8−10 times the intended length of the finished piece and then doubled when attached to the **mounting cord** so that it becomes 4−5 times the length when it is in position to be knotted. Screw the C-clamps upside-down on a table to this 4−5 lengths' distance (so that the cut cord will fit completely around the clamps once). Knot one end of the ball or spool of cord you are using to one of the C-clamps. Wind the cord back and forth for knotting. Cut all the cords at the C-clamp where the cord was initially tied. Cords will then be doubled and ready to be attached to the mounting cord or bar.

C-clamp. Woodworking. See **clamping tools.**

cedar. Woodworking. A light **softwood** of many varieties; the most common for craft work is the Eastern red cedar. This wood emits a beautiful odor that repels moths and is therefore used for lining chests, closets, and cabinets. Its color ranges from a light red (the **sapwood**) to a deep brown (the **heartwood**). It is sometimes difficult to **plane** because of numerous knots but is generally straight-**grain**ed and easy to work. Western red cedar and Eastern white cedar lack the aromatic odor but are very durable and suitable for shingles, outdoor garden furniture, and subflooring. Grades C and better may be used for high-gloss interior finishes.

ceinture flechée. Weaving. A plaited sash made by French-Canadians during the nineteenth century to be worn by men of fashion. It was known as the finest weaving produced in French Canada and was very popular among the merchants of Montreal. The most famous weavers lived around l'Assomption, Quebec. The actual origins of the sash are a mystery, but during the early days of the country the northwest voyagers who left Montreal had a ceinture flechée in their possession. To cut costs, the Hudson Bay Trading Company had the sashes machine-woven in England. They could not compare with the plaited ones, but sold well because of their low price and so tended to discourage the home production. Also see **Assumption sash, plaiting.**

celadon. Ceramics. The general name for subtle green to blue-gray **stoneware** and **porcelain glaze**s; the color is due to the reaction of **iron oxide** in **reduction.**

celebrity doll. Toys. A doll made to represent any of various celebrities of stage or screen. In the 1920s they were painted and costumed carefully, and each carried a signature of the character being portrayed. Currently it is any doll made so that the celebrity being portrayed is recognizable. Also see **character doll, nursery character.**

cell. Kites. One of the multiplaned or multifaceted units in a **box kite** (the covered area) or the **Coyne kite** (the covered triangle area). Most kites of the cell construction have at least two cells; some have many more.

cellophane. Plastics. A **cellulosic** transparent sheeting, impermeable to grease, bacteria, and moisture, used as an **air shield** and **mold release agent** for **casting resin**s. Cellophane tape may also be used for **masking** joints before **cementing.**

Celluclay. Toys. A brand of **instant papier mâché** available in powdered form, to which water is added. It dries hard and can be painted or **finish**ed in a variety of ways.

cellular plastic. Plastics. See **foam.**

celluloid. Toys. An early plastic, made from camphor pyroxylin, used in toys in the first quarter of the twentieth century. It was easily adapted to plastic molding techniques, but was disapproved of primarily because of its flammability. Also see **ball, ball joint.**

celluloid toy. Toys. Any **toy** made of **celluloid** or similar plastic material. Normally colorless or ivory-colored, it was brilliantly tinted for toys. Celluloid was used as early as 1880; some of the most delightful toys made with it came from Germany in the early 1900s.

cellulose. Batik and Tie-dye. Stitchery. A substance that makes up the cell walls in most fibrous plants. Cellulose is subjected to **acetic acid** and sometimes other acids in the production of **acetate** or **rayon.** The **cellulosic fiber**s of cotton and wood are most often used for this.

cellulose. Plastics. A carbohydrate that is the principal constituent of all plant tissues and fibers. It is used in making **cellulosics,** paper, and explosives.

cellulose acetate. Plastics. (Also called acetate.) A **cellulose** resin used in lacquers, photographic film, and transparent sheeting. Also see **air shield, cellulosic.**

cellulose fiber. Batik and Tie-dye. Quilts. Stitchery. Any **fiber** that occurs naturally in plants. Cellulose fibers are sometimes called **vegetable fiber**s and include abaca, **cotton, flax, jute,** and others. Also see **alkali test, burn test, oil test** and **Batik and Tie-dye: Identifying Fibers.**

cellulosic. Plastics. A plastic produced by a chemical reaction involving acetic acid and **cellulose.** Cellulose nitrate or celluloid was the first commercially successful plastic. Although highly flammable, it was used for shirt collars, handles, combs, and photographic film. **Cellulose** acetate, developed later, is now widely used in crafts, and commercially for such things as tape, **adhesives,** and fabrics such as acetate rayon and viscose rayon.

cellulosic fiber. Batik and Tie-dye. Stitchery. Either **vegetable fiber**s or **man-made fiber**s that contain a large amount of **cellulose. Cotton** and **linen** are the most commonly known. **Jute, hemp,** and sisal are among other cellulose fibers; they are less commonly used in textiles. **Acetate** and **rayon** are man-made fibers that have a base of natural plant cellulose.

Celotex. Lacemaking. A wallboard sold in building supply stores useful as a substitute for a **pillow** for sample work or large contemporary lacework. Celotex comes in large panels ½″ thick; it is easily cut to size. A board 12″ × 18″ or 18″ × 24″ is a good size to handle. Pad the board slightly with one or two thicknesses of cloth, and cover it all over with another cloth. Either sew or pin the edges of the cloth to the underside. Use a glass-headed **pin** with a large head and strong shaft on this board "pillow."

Celotex. Macramé. An insulating board used as a flat pinning surface for macramé. Used in this way, it is called the knotting surface.

Cover your sheet of celotex with plain, sturdy paper and mark 1″ grid across the entire surface to make it easy to maintain the symmetry of the knotting.

Also see **Macramé: Tools and Materials.**

Celotex. Stitchery. Toys. A fibrous board made of sugarcane waste. Because it is loose-structured, it can be pinned into, and therefore makes a good backing for **mount**ing some **stitchery panel**s or for a **pin-up wall.**

cement. Enameling. See **binder.**

cement. Jewelry. An **adhesive** available in many varieties. One of the most commonly used adhesives today is epoxy. Epoxies are packaged in kits of the resin and a catalyst. It can also be used as a base for **inlay.** There are opaque and transparent epoxies; one of the best is a transparent epoxy called "no-peg pearl cement," made by Ferris. (Pearls are traditionally cemented into position on a peg.)

Cements can be used for inventive new techniques; however, cementing to hold work together seems valid only when there is no other solution for holding the pieces in position. Also see **rubber cement.**

cement. Mosaics. Stained Glass. A powdery substance composed of clay and burned **lime** that, when mixed with sand, water, and, most frequently, **hydrated lime,** produces **mortar,** the traditional **bond** for **mosaic**s. For many craftspeople cement mortar is still considered the most flexible, the most tenacious, and the most durable of all the mosaic bonds. Since cement ranges in color from white to dark gray it should be carefully chosen, unless colored grout is to be used to fill in crevices. If the final work is to be exposed to the elements, a waterproof cement must be used. Also see **dalle-de-verre, frowel, Louis Comforts, Tiffany** and **Mosaics: Setting the Material.**

cementing. Plastics. (Also called solvent bonding.) A **bonding** process using a **solvent** to soften and fuse plastic. In soak cementing the edges to be joined are soaked in a container of solvent until they are soft and then pressed together. In capillary cementing the solvent penetrates the edges to be joined by capillary action. It is applied into a seam with an eyedropper or small brush. Also see **Plastics: Cementing.**

cementing. Stained Glass. (Also called cementing leads.) An alternative to puttying, cementing is a caulking or water-proofing process that follows the soldering of **lead came** in **glazing.**

To make a glass cement compound, mix 6 oz. **lampblack,** 3 oz. red lead, ½ pint boiled linseed oil, 1 cup Japan drier, ¼ cup turpentine, 3 cups **whitening,** and ½ cup **plaster of Paris** in a 2-gallon pail to pancake-batter consistency. Plaster of Paris can be added to thicken, linseed oil to thin.

Spoon out a cup or two of the mixture onto the center of the leaded glass panel. Rub it between the leaves of the lead and the glass to fill in the spaces, as in puttying. Remove excess cement, let the window dry for a few hours, and turn over the panel and repeat the process. Remove any residue of cement with a sharp stick or razor. Also see **graissage.**

cementing lead. Stained Glass. See **cementing.**

centennial quilt. Quilts. Any quilt made to commemorate and celebrate the 100th anniversary of the United States, 1876. It was usually patriotic in nature, including designs of emblems, eagles, stars, and presidents. Some used fabrics printed especially for the occasion. While the **patriotic quilt**s and **commemorative quilt**s were similar in nature, the centennial quilt was the only one specifically made for the anniversary celebration. Also see **bicentennial quilt.**

center cane. Basketry. See **cane.**

centering. Ceramics. See **Ceramics: Centering.**

centering pin. Woodworking. A small metal pin that is placed in the first holes of a **doweled joint** to accurately line up the hole centers on the adjacent piece. Also see **Woodworking: Jointing.**

center point. Crewel. Embroidery. Needlepoint. In **bargello** and **counted thread embroidery** many of the patterns or designs are worked from the center point of the **background fabric** outward to be sure that the pattern is equidistant from the edge of the fabric or area being filled. Also see **Crewel: Transferring a Design.**

center punch. Jewelry. A short steel rod with a squared end for striking and a tapered point used to make small indentations in metal prior to **drilling** to prevent the drill bit from slipping across the surface of the metal and scratching it.

For an extremely accurate center punch mark, use a scriber. Lightly scratch a small x. A felt-tip pen may also be used. Support the metal that is to be center-punched on a smooth block of wood or on the **bench.** Place the point of the center punch on the junction where the lines formed by the x cross. Hold the punch straight up and down and at a right angle to the metal with a firm downward pressure. Tap extremely lightly with a **hammer;** this is to position the hammer for the next strike. It should not make more than the slightest surface scratch. Do not lift the center punch. Give one medium-light tap with the hammer to produce a small dent in the metal into which the top of a drill can fit. If the center punch is struck too hard it will dent the metal over a larger area than will be drilled out. Also see **automatic center punch, transferring designs to metal.**

center punch. Metalworking. See **punch.**

center punch. Woodworking. See **marking tools, punch.**

center rod. Puppets. See **rod.**

centipede knot. Macramé. See **square knot with picots.**

central increase. Knitting. See **Knitting: Increase.**

central rod. Puppets. See **rod.**

centrifugal casting. Jewelry. A method of **lost-wax casting** using centrifugal force by means of a **centrifugal casting machine.**

Place a preheated **crucible** in the centrifugal casting machine, using a pair of **flask tongs;** the crucible fits tightly into a tracklike slot. Wind the centrifugal casting machine. Remove the **flask** from the **kiln** and place it into the centrifugal casting machine using flask tongs. Wear a protective glove to fit the crucible tightly against the flask. The **sprue cone** of the flask and the projection hole in the end of the crucible must align, although absolute centering is not necessary. Hold the machine securely with one hand while you are doing this; it is already wound, and you must keep the tension against the trigger pin. Should the machine slip, get out of the way because there is tre-

mendous force behind it. Put the predetermined amount of metal into the crucible and add a pinch of borax to enhance melting.

Using a Prest-o-lite **torch,** approach the crucible slowly or the torch will blow the borax away. When the borax has melted, continue heating until the metal becomes totally molten. Toss in another pinch of borax to make the metal flow better. Move the torch in an oval motion keeping the flame directed into the crucible to melt the metal quickly so it enters into the cavity in the burned-out **investment.**

Metal pulls in on itself when it is totally molten; there must not be lumps of unmelted metal within the gleaming outer surface. Unmelted metal clogs the opening causing the metal to splash out of the crucible, ruining the casting. To ensure that the metal is completely molten, take a secure hold of the balance arm, pull it slightly away from the trigger pin, and let the trigger pin drop. Hold on to the arm—remember, it is wound—and jiggle it slightly. Look at the molten metal; it should roll back and forth slightly and very easily, indicating that the metal is molten all the way through. While making this test, constantly play the flame of the torch on the metal to keep it molten. If you take the flame off, even for the slightest moment, a thin skin of solid metal or oxide will form. Should this happen, it can be easily remedied by reheating with the torch. Do not overheat the metal, causing it to boil or to create sparks over its surface, as this will cause pits and **porosity** in the casting. There may be some liquid **flux** in colors of red, orange, green, or blue, floating in circles or ovals on the surface; this is all right. When the metal is cast, the flux will all be on the surface of the **sprue button.** Skim off any impurities that float on the surface with a tool made from a wire coat hanger hammered flat. Remove all paint from the coat hanger with emery paper or flame. Let go of the counterbalance arm, allowing for the powerful rotation of the centrifugal casting machine and the **sheet metal shield.** Keep clear of the machine while it is rotating, and turn off the torch.

Using flask tongs, pull the crucible slightly back on its track to get it out of the way. Remove the piece from the centrifugal casting machine with the flask tongs. Check the sprue button; it will be an orange-red or bright cherry-red. This check is best done in a shaded area as a normally lit room will not reveal the true color. As the metal cools, the metal will get a deeper and deeper shade of red until the color disappears and the metal looks cold. In actuality, however, it is still extremely hot and should be handled with flask tongs. Drop the flask into a bucket of water; the investment will break out due to internal stress formed by steam. The flask is dropped horizontally into the water in order to allow the investment to break out from both ends. Do not drop the flask into water before the red color has disappeared from the metal; the metal, at this point, is still too hot and excessive stress would cause the casting to crack.

Although the water may have stopped churning, there can still be extremely hot investment inside the flask; it is possible to get a severe burn underwater. The water will be fairly warm and murky; the flask may not be easily visible. Reach for it cautiously; touch, but do not grasp. Scrub the piece with an old toothbrush to remove the remaining investment, taking care not to scratch the casting. Also see **ganging.**

centrifugal casting machine. Jewelry. A spring-driven machine used to revolve the **flask** and **investment** at high speeds for **lost-wax casting.** The machine is bolted to a heavy, stable worktable, and is equipped with a **sheet metal shield** to catch escaping molten metal. The arm of the casting machine is rotated, usually clockwise, to tighten the spring located within the base of the machine. The arm is turned 3½–6 full turns, depending on the newness of the machine (a new one will tighten with much fewer turns) and the size of the work being cast (3½ is enough for a ring or pin; a bracelet may require 4 or more full turns).

Only wind the machine prior to casting to avoid unnecessary wear on the spring. Also, the machine is potentially dangerous; should it slip, serious injury could occur. If you have never used the machine, a test winding should be made to determine the strength of the spring. Before winding, however, the following steps must be taken. There are two basic sections to the upper portion, or arm, of the machine. One side contains the section in which the flask is placed during casting. The other side contains weights that can be moved forward and backward on a threaded bolt and that act as a counterbalance for the flask. On top of the arm, in the center there is a threaded nut that, when loosened, acts as the fulcrum. Loosen this nut and line up both sections of the arm. Screw the counterweight forward or backward until the arm is balanced; tighten the threaded nut in the center of the arm to maintain the balance. Be absolutely certain it is tightened before releasing the spring or the arm will spin at a great speed—this is dangerous to you and to the machine.

The steel trigger pin in the base of the machine holds the arm in tension after it has been wound. Pull the pin out, gauging how much pin is pulled up to hold the arm in position and how much is left within the base to hold the arm in tension. After the arm has been balanced, test-wind it with one or two turns, remembering that the more turns made, the faster (and more powerful) will be the reaction. Wind with a hand-over-hand motion, always keeping one hand on the arm. After the arm has been wound, raise the trigger pin in position to hold the arm. Pivot the left side of the arm (the section that holds the flask and crucible) at an angle, away from you as far as it will go. It is this angle and the initial thrust, when the spring arm is released, that casts the metal. The rest of the spinning is the machine unwinding. Let the machine spin itself out naturally. In actual casting, the spinning also helps to cool the flask. Also see **burnout, centrifugal casting, investing, sprue, sprue cone, vent, wax.**

centrifugal casting shield. Jewelry. See **sheet metal shield.**

ceramic beads. Beadwork. Clay is a basic material in **beadmaking.** Various types of clay can be modeled or pressed into molds and fired in a kiln. Color is applied with glazes for unlimited variety. Also see **donkey beads, faience.**

ceramic découpage. Découpage. See **découpage on ceramics.**

ceramic mold. Candlemaking. Ceramic **mold**s designed for plaster casting can be used for candlemaking provided they are first coated with several layers of **spar varnish** to keep them from absorbing the liquid wax. Also see **Candlemaking: Molding.**

CERAMICS

The art of making permanent objects of usefulness or beauty by the heat treatment of **clay,** ceramics is derived from the Greek word "keramos," meaning an earthen vessel. It is also referred to as **pottery.** Ceramics include not only pottery, but structural clay, **tile,** brick, sanitary **ware**s, cements, and anything made from clay.

There is much speculation over the first discovery of ceramics or a fired form. Although it would be safe to assume that the earliest and most primitive forms of ceramics do date back to prehistoric times, the belief being that the cave dwellers discovered that the earth beneath their fires became hard, and once extracted from the ground and shaped in some way, the earth could serve some other purpose.

One of the most popular of all handcrafts in the United States, ceramics has experienced phenomenal growth since the end of World War II. The desire to be involved in a creative and functional way has caused this increase in the craft's popularity. Clay is rewarding and easy to work with; the only essential tools are the hands. One need not set up an elaborate environment in which to work to fully appreciate this craft.

All aspects of ceramics covered here are meant as reference and not as a guide to making ceramics.

EQUIPMENT The following is a list of tools needed to become involved in ceramics. For **throwing,** first is the choice of the **potter's wheel**—either a **kick wheel** or a power wheel (it is a good idea to try them both). The basic tools in throwing are a pin mounted on a wooden handle, a potter's knife, called a **fettling knife,** a **rib,** a wooden **modeling tool,** a wire, a ruler, a brush, a bucket for water, a wire trimming tool or turning tool, a paddle, and any interesting tool you may come across. In hand building, a **rolling pin** is also useful. A flat surface for **wedging** clay is needed. See ill.

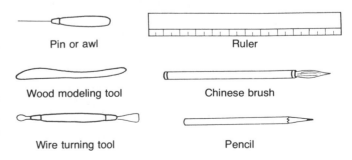

Pin or awl   Ruler

Wood modeling tool   Chinese brush

Wire turning tool   Pencil

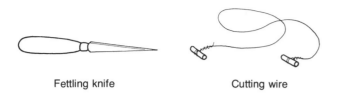

Fettling knife   Cutting wire

SETTING UP A WORKSHOP The size of the workshop and the manner in which it is set up depend on the available space, but keep in mind the relationship of the set-up to your own work procedure; the drying area and the raw materials should be near the forming area and the **kiln** should be located in the far corner of the studio.

Separate tables for working in clay and plaster are recommended since plaster particles in clay will cause it to break in **firing.** A working surface for pottery should be slightly porous so that the clay comes away cleanly.

Shelves are necessary to store tools, materials, and for drying pots; you will find that you can never have enough shelves.

The many models of **potter's wheel**s and kilns that are major items of purchase should be compared for size, quality, and usefulness.

As far as rules for safety and first aid are concerned, clay itself is a harmless material, but the ingredients in **glaze** and stains may be extremely toxic. The best advice is not to eat or smoke when working with glazes and wash your hands after use. Consider all chemicals as poisonous and treat them with the respect that dangerous materials deserve. See ill.

Workshop

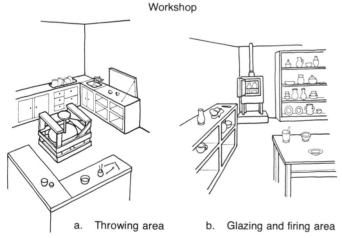

a. Throwing area   b. Glazing and firing area

CLAY An insoluble mineral substance that derives from the decomposition of minerals such as granite, **feldspar,** and **pegmatite.** Through disintegration these rocks release **alumina** and **silica** particles. The combination of alumina, silica, and water produces pure clay (Kaolin).

Clay is classified into two general groups: primary clay (or residual clay) is formed by the decomposition of rocks that have not been moved by water, wind, or glacial action. These clays are the purest because they have had little chance to mix with other minerals. Most primary clay derives from feldspar, which is easily broken down by the action of water. Primary clays are used for their white color and their relative purity; secondary clay (or

sedimentary clay) is clay that is carried by water, glacial, or rock-folding action and has more impurities, smaller particles, and greater **plasticity.**

Clay is made up of tiny crystals that are so tiny that it takes about 50,000 crystals to measure an inch. Each crystal measures 0.7 microns in diameter and 0.05 microns in thickness; a micron measures 1/25,000 of an inch.

A clay particle is roughly hexagonal and platelike in shape. The platelike surfaces become coated with water and adhere to each other, giving clay remarkable and unique plasticity. Air floating is the classification of clay according to particle size using a method of air separation.

The aging of clay refers to a process whereby clay is stored in airtight containers to obtain higher plasticity and greater workability in **clay.** This storage allows the particles of clay to become completely coated with water and it also starts the growth of bacteria, which affects the clay. Frequently, new clay is mixed with old clay to quicken the process.

Lean clay refers to the low plasticity of a clay or clay body.

Short clay refers to clay that has a low level of plasticity and does not handle well.

Fat clay refers to clay that has a high degree of plasticity.

Throwing clay refers to a **clay body** or blend of clays that has a high degree of plasticity and is able to absorb undesirable water without slumping. Also see **potter's wheel** and **shrinkage.**

The **preparation of clay** is a process of **mixing** clay and water done either by hand, for small amounts, or by machine for large quantities. Clay is added to water to ensure that each particle of clay is coated with water. More water is used than is required to obtain the heavy cream consistency of **slip** because evaporation takes place during storage and **wedging** or **kneading** the clay. Wedging, kneading, or **deairing** the clay are done to ensure that the clay has consistency and is completely free of air bubbles. This final step is necessary for the successful forming and firing of the **ware.**

Cutting clay depends on the dryness of the clay. A wire is used on clay having **plasticity,** a **needle awl** on molded dishes, and a knife or **turning tool** on clay that is **leather-hard.**

Adobe clay has little plasticity and a large quantity of sand found near the ground surface, which is used for making sun-dried bricks and adobes.

Ball clay is a fine-grained, highly plastic clay, with high dry strength that is dark gray in color when wet and white when fired. It is not as white as **kaolin.** There is a great amount of shrinkage in ball clay after drying and firing and for this reason, it is mixed with another clay. Because of its plasticity, ball clay is generally mixed with another clay to improve **throwing** and handling. Ball clay was originally sold in fifteen-pound balls, which is its name derivation. The largest deposits of ball clay are found in Kentucky and Tennessee where the clay particles were deposited in swampy areas creating its dark color and fine-grained quality.

Bauxite clay is a highly refractory clay containing a high percentage of **alumina.**

Bentonite clay is a clay having extremely small particles which is mixed in small amounts with other clays and is valued for its plasticity. The clay is not grainy in texture and contains a lot of colloidal matter. Because of its high shrinkage and stickiness when wet, bentonite clay is always used as an admixture. Its origins are volcanic and pits are found in the Dakotas and the Rocky Mountain states.

Diaspore clay, like bauxite clay, is another highly refractory clay that also contains a high percentage of alumina.

Earthenware clay is a common and easily available clay that is found near the ground surface and that can be **fire**d at a low temperature. Because of its abundance all over the world, it has been used in the making of everyday utensils. There is generally a high percentage of **iron oxide** in these clays which serves two purposes: one, as a flux lowering the temperature at which the clay is fired; and, two, as the red, tan, brown, and buff color with which **earthenware** is associated. The clays are found in great quantity in the lower Great Lakes region.

Fire clay contains more flux than kaolin and is fired at a higher temperature. It fires gray or tan and is used in manufacturing **refractory** materials, such as firebricks and **muffle**s for **kiln**s. Fire clay is often very plastic and can be used as an ingredient in **stoneware** bodies.

Flint clay is a highly dense and refractory clay.

Gumbo clay is a clay that is found near the ground surface which has a high level of plasticity.

Red brick clay is a porous clay used for making building bricks. They are usually mixed with a low-**firing** clay and are red or orange in color. In eighteenth-century America, redware pottery was made from these clays.

Sagger clay is a highly refractory clay which resists temperature changes and repeated firings. It fires a light gray or buff color and ranges from medium to high plasticity, which is why it is mixed with **terra cotta** and earthenware clays.

Slip clay is a clay that contains **flux**es and that is used as a **glaze.** It ranges in color from tan to brick red, brown-black, and, occasionally, blue and white.

Stoneware clay is **clay** that generally has good **plasticity** that fires at a high temperature to a buff to gray color. It matures into a dense, hard **vitreous** body. It is usually the main ingredient in a **clay body** and is mixed with ball clay, flint, **feldspar** or earthenware clays to produce certain firing and throwing qualities. It can, however, be used alone, as in the nineteenth century when daily utensils were made from clay dug from a neighborhood pit. Pits are found in New York, New Jersey, through the Midwest and the Pacific coast.

FORM   Since clay is an amorphous and plastic material, it is easily modeled into many practical forms. Ideally the ceramic form should express the plastic nature of clay and the forming method used, whether throwing, **extrusion, molding, pressing, casting,** or any of the several methods of hand-building, and the form should be carefully considered when planning the decoration and **glaze.**

Ceramic forms can be roughly grouped in three classes: utilitarian objects often associated with building;

nonutilitarian ceramic sculpture; and pottery, usually designed to hold liquids or food. Utilitarian ceramic objects include bricks (not adobe, which is unfired); **tile**s for surfacing walls, floors, and even roofs; sanitary tiles used to form drainage pipes; appliances such as toilets; and insulators and other objects made of **electrical porcelain.**

Ceramic sculpture is a broad category of primary decorative objects. Some, such as **della Robbia ware, terra cotta,** and ceramic murals, may be associated with architectural applications; others are more similar to a broad range of free-standing sculptures in other media; still others, such as much **funk pottery,** are more or less related to basic pottery forms. Ceramic **bead**s can take on almost sculptural forms.

POTTERY   The word "pottery" may mean any fired clay object or the place where such objects are made, but it is usually restricted to mean pots and related containers, including tableware. Most pot forms are symmetrical and are derived from the forms made in throwing clay on a **potter's wheel,** although similar forms can be made by other methods.

A pot is any generally rounded vessel for holding liquids or solids—if a hollow fired-clay form has a hole at the top, it is considered a pot. Most of the parts of a pot are named after the parts of a human body. The foot is the base on which the pot sits, often no more than a **foot ring** formed by **turning** after the thrown pot is **leather-hard.** The belly is the widest part of the form. The shoulder is the upper part of a pot, where it turns inward toward the rim or neck. The body includes the belly and shoulder—the main part of the pot. The neck is the narrow point at the top of a pot, such as at the opening of a bottle. The rim or lip is the top edge of a bowl or pot. The lip may also be the pouring lip of a jug, bowl, or pitcher; it may be formed with the fingers immediately after throwing, or it may be made separately in the form of half an inverted cone and be added to the pitcher when leather-hard.

A bottle is a potlike form with a narrow neck. Historically, bottle forms were used as storage vessels for grain or liquids; they were easy to pour from, yet rodents could not get into the small openings to contaminate the contents (**a.**).

A jug is similar to a bottle, but without the flared rim; it should combine a generous and well-defined form with utility (**b.**). If it has a handle, the handle should be visually and physically strong; and if the jug is to be used for hot or cold liquids, it should be able to withstand moderate **thermal shock.**

A vase is any pot designed for holding flower arrangements; it is usually in a bottle form. Weed vases are often much freer in form, designed to hold dry flowers and grasses; they do not have to be waterproof, and are often in the shape of hanging, slab-built pouches.

A pitcher is similar to a jug; it always has a handle on one side and a pouring lip on the other; the mouth is usually wide. The mouth is the opening of practically any pot; its relation to the flaring lip and to the body of the pot is an important element of the overall design.

A jar is a wide-mouthed pot, usually with a short neck or no neck at all, and often with a lid.

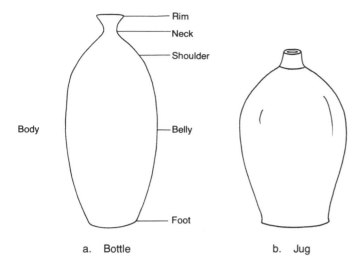

a. Bottle   b. Jug

An amphora is a large, narrow-based or pointed-based pot with two handles. The ancient Greeks used amphoras to transport wine. Such large forms often were, and still are, thrown in two or more sections and joined in the leather-hard stage. (Also see **mending.**)

A handle is purely functional, and should not be added to a ceramic form if there is no need for it (**c.**). Nonetheless, when it is needed—as for a cup, mug, or pitcher—it is an integral part of the design, and many factors should be considered: placement, the number of fingers needed to lift the form, the curve of the handle and of the main form, and balance. In industry, handles are made in molds. Potters make a handle by pulling a coil of clay into a tapered carrotlike shape with wet hands, then holding it by the thick end and allowing it to takee a natural curve; this is called **pulling a handle.** A lug or ear is a small, usually horizontal, handle or a pierced piece of clay for suspending a pot on a rope or for applying a cane handle (**d.**). A cane handle is used on teapots and storage jars. It is made of cane or bamboo, and a ring of the same material or of wire slips over each of the doubled ends to secure them to the lugs on the pot (**e.**).

A teapot is a relatively difficult object to make satisfactorily, since several elements must be considered in the design (**f.**). The tip of the spout must be level with the top of the pot so the liquid won't spill out, and it must pour well; the handle—either of cane, or of clay placed opposite the spout—must be comfortable, keep the pot well balanced while pouring, and keep the fingers cool; and the lid should not fall out while pouring. The several parts of the teapot should be thrown at the same time and from the same batch of clay (so they will shrink at the same speed while drying) and be joined when leather-hard. A spout is a tapering tube, usually thrown as a simple cone shape, then trimmed and attached to the pot when leather-hard (**g.**). Before **scoring** and **joining,** the spot where the spout will join should be marked on the pot, and the body should be punctured there—either one large hole, or a number of small ones to act as a tea strainer. A lid or cover should be designed to match the pot it is for; it may be flat or domed, and with or without a handle, knob, or flange. After it is leather-hard, it may be trimmed to assure accurate fit; it should be dried and **bisque**-fired in place on the pot to

prevent **warping.** A teapot usually has a deep interior flange to keep it in place while tea is being poured. The knob on a lid can be the focal point of a pot; it should accommodate the finger and thumb, and should relate to the overall form of the pot. It may be a simple lump of clay or may be formed more carefully into a disc-on-a-cylinder shape. The flange is a narrow projection near the rim of a pot on which the lid rests; it may project inward beneath the rim, or may be formed as a step beneath a collar. A collar is an abruptly vertical area beneath the rim of a pot; it is usually wider than the area beneath, but a squat, cylindrical neck on a curved jar might be called a collar (**h.**).

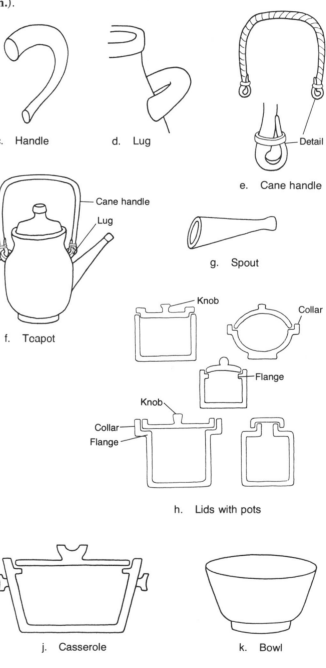

c. Handle   d. Lug

e. Cane handle

f. Teapot

g. Spout

h. Lids with pots

j. Casserole   k. Bowl

m. Plate

A casserole is a broad, covered pot for cooking in the oven; it usually has two lug handles, and a tight-fitting lid with a knob; it must be resistant to thermal shock (**j.**).

TABLEWARE   Tableware is any pottery made for table use, usually restricted to dishes for individual service. Flatware is the industrial term for tableware. The bowl form is one of the easiest forms to throw, yet one of the hardest to throw well (**k.**). A bowl is basically a low, wide cylinder; it may be large or small. If the rim flares out too much, there is danger of the bowl warping in drying or **firing;** if it is bisque-fired upside-down, the danger is reduced.

The Japanese have two basic bowl shapes—the summer and winter tea bowls. The winter bowl is closed in at the top, so as to focus the heat of the tea in the drinker's face; the summer bowl flares out at the top to dissipate the heat, and it is held with the tips of the fingers on the foot ring. A beaker is a drinking vessel without a handle or saucer, but sometimes with a pronounced foot. A mug is a drinking vessel with a handle, usually more or less cylindrical, and without a saucer. A cup should be a comfortable, easily gripped drinking vessel with a handle that permits the cup to be held without the fingers touching the hot sides of the cup. Usually a cup is formed more delicately than a mug, and rests on a saucer. A saucer is a small plate with a depression in the center where the cup is to rest. The design of the cup and saucer should be considered as a unit.

A dish is any thrown, molded, or slab-built shallow container, midway between a bowl and plate. A plate is formed as a very low, wide cylinder when thrown on a wheel, but it is often made with a **jigger** and jolly. Plates (and saucers) tend to flatten during firing; a distinctly curved-up lip helps to retain the shape. It is important to avoid a ridge just before the rim, however. Usually a foot ring is trimmed when the plate is leather-hard. The **foot ring** (or foot rim) is a low pedestal or flat ridge on which a pottery form rests; it is usually trimmed in the **turning** process after throwing. It gives stability and strength to the finished object and imparts a feeling of lightness to the form (**m.**) See ill. on page 163.

FORMING   Before a pot of any kind can be built or thrown, the clay must first be prepared by aging and wedging. After this is done, one can either make hand-built pots or thrown pots.

Hand-building can be done in many ways. Coil building led to the discovery of the wheel. Early storage vessels were made by building up the wall of a pot with large coils while walking around the pot. Later, a turn table was introduced allowing the potter to remain in one spot and to turn the pot as he worked. Further discovery showed that the addition of water on the potter's hands caused the coils to thin, blend, and grow upward; thus, throwing was introduced.

Another hand-built technique is constructing with a **slab.** An even thickness of clay is rolled or pounded out and the rough edges are trimmed off. These slabs can be wrapped and joined to form ceramic vessels.

The **pinch pot** is a hand building method which involves pinching a ball of clay with the thumbs while rotating it in the fingers to build up walls and achieve form. While simple in technique, it takes a great deal of practice to learn control of the clay while pinching.

THROWING   Throwing is the hand forming of soft clay on a revolving wheel to make hollow shapes. An infinite number of shapes can be achieved; a thrown form can be identified by its symmetry and by spiraling grooves or finger marks coming up the pot walls.

Throwing is done in various stages. The first step is wedging the clay, forming it into a ball and literally throwing it onto the wheel. The term "throwing" comes from this method of attaching the clay firmly to the wheel.

During the process of throwing a pot, the hands must be kept wet to keep the clay malleable and to keep the hands from causing friction against the clay and preventing the natural motion of the clay on the turning wheel.

The next step is centering or lining up the mound of clay symmetrically and perfectly in the center of the wheel. This alignment is essential to a properly thrown pot. The mound is opened up with the thumbs or fingers by pressing steadily in the center as the wet clay turns on the wheel. The clay is now raised with two points of contact, one hand inside and one hand outside, to form a cylinder. The cylinder's walls are thinned by applying pressure with the fingers, a small amount at a time, with each additional pull up the wall. Any form that is made on the wheel, whether it is a bottle or a bowl, is first thrown as a cylinder. Once a cylinder with even walls is achieved, any number of shapes can be made from it. Throwing is an art which requires much practice to achieve complete control over the clay. A few tools are needed for throwing: bronze wire (No. 28 gauge) to remove thrown pieces from the wheel, natural sponges of various sizes to moisten the surface while throwing and to absorb excess water from the bottom of pieces, assorted **ribs**, wooden turning tools for shaping and trimming, and calipers for precision throwing.

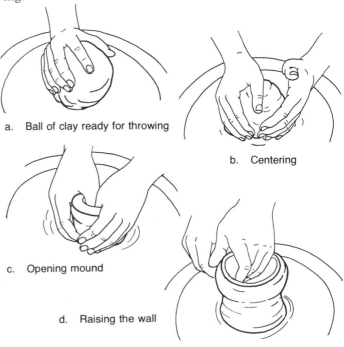

a.   Ball of clay ready for throwing

b.   Centering

c.   Opening mound

d.   Raising the wall

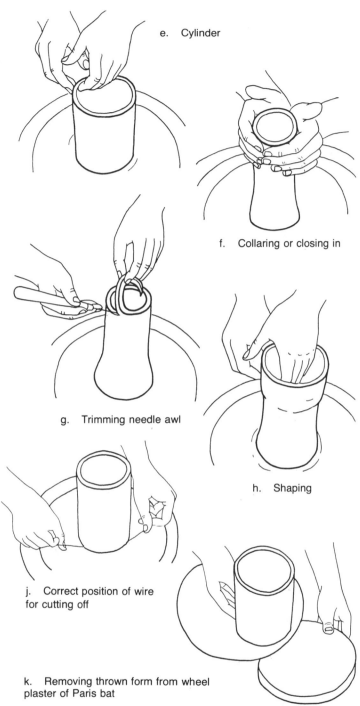

e. Cylinder

f. Collaring or closing in

g. Trimming needle awl

h. Shaping

j. Correct position of wire
for cutting off

k. Removing thrown form from wheel
plaster of Paris bat

Cutting off refers to removing a thrown form from the wheel using a wire. Hold the wire taut and pull it under pot, applying pressure on the wheel to ensure a clean break. Keep thumbs down for better leverage. A strong, fine, and flexible wire, such as nylon fishing line, works well. See ill.

HAND BUILDING Any method of making ceramics without a wheel or cast, using various techniques singly or in combination.

Pinching is probably the simplest hand-building technique; small **pinch pot**s (or thumb pots) are made by hold-ing a ball of clay in one hand and pressing the thumb of the other into the clay. By rotating the clay in the holding hand and gently squeezing the thumb against the developing clay wall, cups and bowls are formed; with practice, large, thin-walled shapes can be achieved. Pinch pots are traditional for **raku** and sawdust firing.

Slab building is a hand-building technique which permits free and imaginative use of clay; slabs of clay are joined together with slip for pots or sculptural forms.

Form slabs by rolling with a **rolling pin.** A dry cloth (canvas or burlap, for instance) is the best surface, is a great aid in moving large slabs, and provides an interesting texture. Pound the clay down fairly flat with your hands, then roll the rolling pin with a firm and steady pressure. For uniform thickness, place strips of wood on each side of the clay to support the ends of the rolling pin (**a.**).

Another method is to pat the clay firmly into a solid block, and then cut slabs off with a wire between the hands (**b.**).

Once the slabs are formed and nearly leather-hard, they may be joined in the desired form. The following steps are used for a chunky covered pot: **scoring** the edges to be joined provides surface for a good join; both edges of the join should be scored (**c.**). **Slip** is added to join the pieces by **luting.** The edges are placed together and the join is secured by pressing with a wooden forming tool. A coil of soft clay is added to the inside of the join and worked in (**d.**). The other sides are joined, using the same steps. Place the four joined sides on a base slab and join as before. Trim the base with a knife. Pinching, a form of **applied decoration,** can be used to secure the joined edges (**e.**). Join a narrow, thinner slab around the inside edge to form a collar. Handles are added to the pot and joined firmly (**f.**). The cover is a flat slab about the size of the base to which handles are joined (**g.**). Place the cover on the pot and loosely shape to fit the collar. Make all pieces from the same batch of clay to ensure proper fit, uniform drying, and successful firing. Trim away any excess on the cover (**h.**).

Slabs are also used in a variety of other techniques, such as **beaten forms, hollow-dish mold**s, hump mold, template, and tiles.

Coil building, or coil method is a method of making pots that is probably the oldest method known to man. It is also a very good method for beginners. Ropelike coils of clay are made by rolling the clay on a table until the desired length is achieved (enough to lay about three circles around the base) (**j.**). The coils are then joined together inside and out with a wiping motion (**k.**). It is important that the inside be kept smooth as the coiling continues. If the coil is laid on the inside edge of the previous coil while building, the pot will close in; if placed on the outside, it will flare out. When coil building a large pot, it is necessary to go in stages, letting the first few layers dry to the **leather-hard** stage before **luting** the next coil on and building further. If this is not done, the weight of too many layers will make the form collapse. After the form is completed, it may be beaten to change its shape. See ill. on next page. Also see **modeling.**

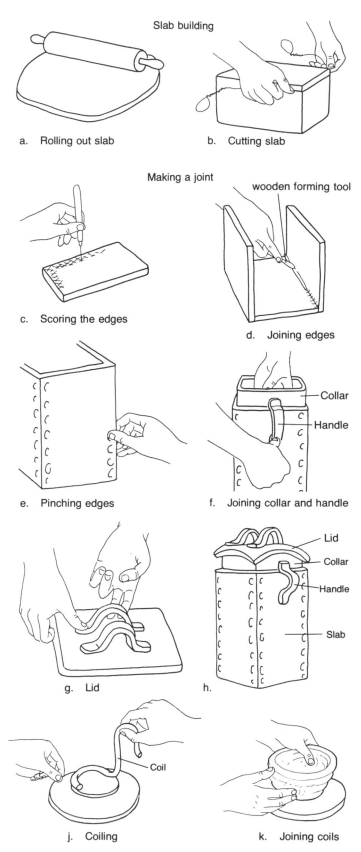

Slab building

a.   Rolling out slab

b.   Cutting slab

Making a joint

c.   Scoring the edges

wooden forming tool

d.   Joining edges

e.   Pinching edges

Collar

Handle

f.   Joining collar and handle

Lid

Collar

Handle

Slab

g.   Lid

h.

Coil

j.   Coiling

k.   Joining coils

FIRING   Firing refers to the heat treatment of ceramic materials to the **sintering** stage in a **kiln.** Chemical and physical changes take place in firing, sintering, and then a series of melts. Speed as well as temperature in firing will affect

the final result. The standard firing procedure consists of a slow **bisque fire** to burn out any organic matter and chemically combined water. The resultant bisque is strong enough to be handled, but still porous enough to absorb **glaze.**

It is important to remember, when packing the kiln, to place the pots as closely as possible, not just to be economical, but because closely packed kilns fire better.

After **glazing,** the ware is fired again in a process called the **glaze fire.** This firing is done at a higher temperature and is a faster cycle. Its purpose is to bring the body to maximum strength and to melt the glaze. The temperature and speed of this firing is more crucial and varies according to the body and glaze used. Remember that glazed surfaces must not touch.

The maximum temperature for earthenware is between 400–600° C. Firing too far below the minimum temperature will result in incomplete vitrification. Above the maximum temperature, the body tends to bloat and eventually melt. Stoneware or fire clay can be fired at any temperature, but maximum strength is reached between 900–1000° C.

Compatibility of the body and its glaze is essential for proper firing; the **maturing** point of the body must conform to the **melting point** of the glaze. The compatibility can be adjusted in the glaze recipe. **Flux** can be added to lower the melting point of the glaze, or a **refractory** material can be added to raise it.

Firing atmosphere, the degree of **oxidation** or **reduction,** also affects the behavior of the glaze and body. To refire incorrectly glazed ware, warm the ware until the glaze is sticky. Refiring may change the character of the ware. Also see **blistering, bloating, cones, cracking, crawling, crazing, dunting, limeblowing, overfiring, pinholes, shivering, smoked ware, underfiring, vitreous.**

FINISHING   Once the clay form has been finished and is allowed to dry, it can be fired and glazed. The first fire is the bisque firing. The ware must be thoroughly air-dry before firing. A good check is to hold the piece against your cheek, if it still feels cold it is not dry enough to fire.

After firing, the final process is glazing, which gives beauty and durability. It is almost as important a technique as making the pot itself.

Once ceramics are fired, they are stone, and the only fact to keep in mind in maintaining a ceramic form is not to drop it.

GLAZING   Glazing refers to the application of glaze to bisque or leather-hard clay. There are several methods of applying glazes. Some of them are the following. Brushing glaze is a method of applying glaze using a wide, flat, brush (**a.**). Dipping glaze is a process of applying glaze to an object that has been moistened and which is immersed into a large container of glaze (**b.**). Pouring glaze is another method of glazing that uses a funnel. The glaze is poured onto or into an object, such as inside a vase (**c.**). See ill. Glaze is also applied using a spray gun. It is important to remember that the ware should be sprayed in a vented box to avoid breathing the glaze vapors. Wear a face mask while spraying if an enclosed box is not available.

Ways to apply glaze

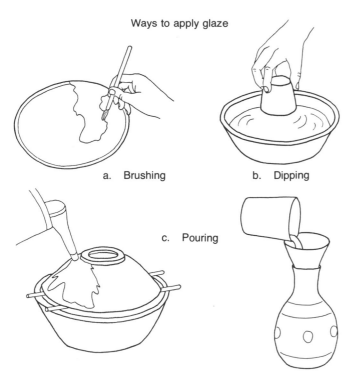

a. Brushing

b. Dipping

c. Pouring

ceramic sculpture. Ceramics. See **Ceramics: Form.**

ceramic tile. Mosaics. (Also called clay tile.) A relatively inexpensive **mosaic** material, designed primarily as a commercial **tile** for bathroom flooring. Ceramic tile is sold in most building supply outlets; it comes in a limited number of colors but a variety of sizes from ¾–6″ squares. Ceramic tile is usually only surface-colored, with matte or glazed finishes. Before use, ceramic tile must be soaked in water for several minutes to prevent the porous, unglazed back from drawing off the water in the **bond.** Ceramic tile can be used very effectively in combination with **smalti** and other mosaic material on large-scale projects. Because ceramic tile is rather difficult to cut precisely, many mosaicists break the tile with a hammer and use the random fragments in their works. Also see **Mosaics: Tools and Materials, Cutting the Material.**

ceremonial doll. Toys. A small figure made for ritual or ceremonial use and not intended as a toy, such as the **Kachina doll** of the American Indian. Many ancient figures and doll forms are believed to be of ceremonial significance and never intended as toys. Crèche figures or **crib set**s are made as religious figures, not as toys.

cerium oxide. Gemcutting. See **abrasive.**

Chagall, Marc. Stained Glass. A modern painter who has designed numerous stained-glass windows in England, Israel, Germany, and the U.S.A. His windows are of glass rather than a treatment of stained glass as a design element in itself.

chain. Crochet. A series of chain stitches into which the initial row of crochet is worked. This chain is the **founda-**tion for most crochet **pattern**s. Also see **Crochet: Basic Procedures, Basic Stitches.**

chain. Macramé. **Half hitch**es worked alternately. The chain can be worked with single or double **cord**s. The chain is used as an integral part of larger macramé pieces or whenever a thin, sturdy, braided cord is necessary. Also see **chain knot, sennit.**

chain. Tatting. (Also called arch.) The chain (abbr. ch.) is a basic design element or **motif** in tatting composed of a number of **double stitch**es. It can be worked with one or two **shuttle**s. When one shuttle is used, there will be a **single thread** joining the two ends of the chain to form an archlike motif. **Working with two shuttles** will eliminate this single thread because the **knot bearer** will be covered by the **loop thread.** When a chain is pulled up tightly so that the two ends of the chain come together, a **ring** is formed. See ill. Also see **scallop.**

a. Detached scallop chain made with one shuttle

b. Chain made with two shuttles

chain decrease. Knitting. See **Knitting: Decreasing.**

chain draft. Weaving. A representation on **graph paper** of the combination and order of **harnesses** to be lifted in each **pick** of **weaving.** The term "chain draft" is interchangeable with peg plan or lifting plan. All stem from the chain in a **dobby loom** that had pegs fitted into it in order to lift the correct harnesses. Because the **warp end**s lifted by the harnesses are **raiser**s or risers on a weave draft, the term "riser sequence" is also used. A chain draft is used for **table looms** that have no **tie-up** and can also apply to **treadling sequence** of **floor loom**s that have a direct tie-up. Although the correct representation of a chain draft is on graph paper, it can also be shown in numbers that correspond to the harnesses to be lifted. Also see **dobby loom, drafts.**

chained. Rugmaking. Weaving. See **soumak.**

Chained Five-patch. Quilts. See **Irish Chain.**

chain edge. Knitting. A chain-like **edge** created in the following manner:

row 1: Slip the first and last stitch as if to knit.
row 2: Purl across row. Also see **selvage.**

chained square. Quilts. See **border.**

Chained Star. Quilts. See **Brunswick Star.**

chainette. Crewel. Embroidery. See **chain stitch.**

chaining. Weaving. The procedure by which the **warp** length is shortened after **warping** so that the warp can be easily transferred to a **harness loom.** The shortened length makes for ease in **beaming** and prevents tangles. The chaining technique is similar to chaining in crochet, with the hand playing the part of a huge crochet hook.

After warping is completed on a **warping board** or **reel,** the weaver starts removing the warp from the board or reel at the end opposite the **cross.** A loop is formed by flipping the end of the warp over itself, or the natural loop formed by the yarn going around the first warp peg can be used (**a.**). The hand goes through the loop and pulls enough warp through to form a second loop (**b.**). More warp is pulled through the second loop to form a third loop (**c.**). This procedure continues until the cross is reached. The last piece of warp is not pulled through the last loop because this would lock the chain and it would be impossible to undo the **warp chain** during beaming (**d.**). As it is now, the chain is easily undone during beaming by pulling on the loops as they approach the **lease stick**s. If the warp is to be saved for some future use, the last loop and the cross are tied together to prevent accidental unchaining.

An alternate method to chaining is to form **slip knot**s in the warp at regular intervals about a yard apart. However, this does not give as compact or short a warp bundle as chaining. See ill. Also see **chain warping, weft chaining.**

a.   Natural loop, or loop formed by flipping warp

b.   Pull warp through

c.   Pull warp through to form a loop

d.   Pull warp through third loop

chain knot. Macramé. (Also called seesaw knot, single tatted chain.) The chain knot is made from **alternating half hitch**es and is worked in a series to form a **sennit.** The **cord**s are worked over each other alternately to form vertical half hitches. The chain knot can be made with any number of cords.

chain pairing. Basketry. (Also called cane pair.) A decorative **wicker weave** that is made by following one **round** of **pairing** with one round of **reverse pairing.** See ill.

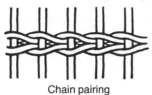

Chain pairing

chain pliers. Stained Glass. Pliers used to open links of metal chain. The nose of the pliers is fitted inside the link of chain, the handles are squeezed, and the nose separates and opens the link.

chain polishing. Jewelry. Wrap the chain securely around a board and nail the loose ends of the chain with small nails to the back of the wood. This holds the chain securely and exposes only a small portion of the chain to the buffing wheel at one time. **Buffing** chain can be hazardous if the chain is not supported and held securely. If it gets caught in the rotating wheel it can catch and break, and possibly cause injury. Also see **buff, hand polishing.**

chain saw. Woodworking. See **power saw.**

chain soldering. Jewelry. To **solder** the links of a simple chain, solder each **seam** separately on each link (**a.**). Solder one new link to each previously soldered link. Position the links so that the direction of the seam alternates with each link (**b.**). See ill. Also see **chain polishing, pick soldering, soldering.**

Chain soldering

a.   Previously soldered seam

b.   Links soldered in groups of two

chain spacer. Weaving. **Weft chaining** done around the **warp end**s at the start of weaving on a **tapestry** or **frame loom** in order to space the warp evenly, keep the warp ends in order, and give a firm starting edge for the first row of **filling.** The chain spacer is removed after weaving is completed and taken off the loom. In place of the chain spacer, weft **twining** can be used instead. Also see **weft chaining.**

chain stitch. Bookbinding. See **kettle stitch.**

chain stitch. Crewel. Embroidery. Needlepoint. (Also called chainette, tambour stitch.) The chain stitch has been used in almost all countries, and for many centuries. In China, it was worked on such a minute scale that the embroiderers often lost their eyesight after working it for any extended period, and it thus became known as the "forbidden stitch." Many of the **palampores,** or "tree of life" designs brought from India to Europe in the seventeenth century utilized a fine chain stitch. In Britain, until the late nineteenth century, the chain stitch was worked on a hoop or tambour frame with a fine crochet hook, and called tambour work.

The stitch is created by drawing loops of thread through one another to form a chain. When filling in an area, one should always start each row at the same end. It can be worked narrow or broad, depending on the desired effect.

Chain stitch is the basis for many other stitches, such as **backstitched chain stitch, detached chain stitch, detached twisted chain stitch, double chain stitch, interlaced cable chain stitch, magic chain stitch, whipped chain stitch,** and **zigzag chain stitch.**

Bring needle up at A. Form a loop and put the needle in at A again, holding loop down with a finger. Then come up at B, directly below A (**a.**). Draw gently through, forming the first chain stitch.

Repeat, always inserting the needle exactly where the thread came out, inside the last loop (**b.**).

The chain stitch may also be worked open (**c., d.**). See ill. Also see **line stitch, shading stitch.**

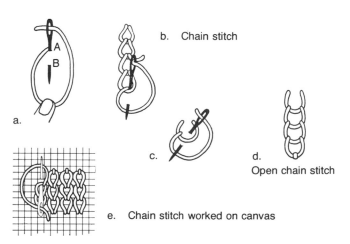

a.

b. Chain stitch

c.

d.
Open chain stitch

e. Chain stitch worked on canvas

chain stitch. Crochet. See **Crochet: Basic Stitches.**

chain stitch. Lacemaking. The stitch used for making the **pattern** in tambour lace. Stretch the **net** on the frame and draw the thread through from the back to the front by the **tambour needle** in a succession of **loops**, with the second loop formed catching or securing the first, and continuing in that manner.

chain stitch. Macramé. The chain stitch in knotting is a horizontal (looping) technique. It can be used within a piece or as a **finishing** technique. Each loop is used as a base for the next **cord.** A crochet hook is used to facilitate making the loops. See ill. Also see **fringe.**

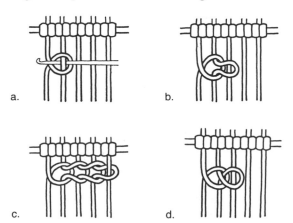

a.

b.

c.

d.

Chain stitch in knotting

chain stitch. Tatting. (abbr. ch st) See **edging.**

chain stitch with crossed loops. Macramé. See **Macramé: Finishing.**

chain wale. Basketry. Similar to **chain pairing** except that it uses one **round** of **waling** followed by one round of **reverse waling.**

chain warping. Weaving. The process of measuring out the entire **warp** at one time on an independent piece of equipment and then transferring it to the **loom.** Usually this is done on either a **warping board** or **reel,** and then the warp is chained in order to compress its length for ease in transferring and **beaming,** and to prevent the threads from tangling. Instead of **chaining, slip knots** can be placed every few inches in the warp. An alternative to chain warping is **sectional warping,** which requires a special **warp beam.** Also see **warping.**

chair. Glasswork. The five-man commercial glassworking team, also called a **shop.** Also see **gaffer.**

chair rocking horse. Toys. (Also called rocking shoo-fly, shoo-fly rocking horse.) A simply made **rocking horse** that consists of two wood profiles of a running horse. Each profile shape is attached so that the horse's feet rest on a rocker. A seat and various braces connect the two horses. The rider sits in the seat and rocks the toy. Occasionally other animals, such as ostriches and camels, are used.

chair-seating cane. Basketry. See **cane.**

chair wheel. Spinning. A **treadle wheel** with four legs, resembling a chair. The **treadle** is divided in half, with each side attached to the lower wheel propelling the **driving wheel.** Both feet are used, making for increased speed and a more constant rotation. This wheel is said to have originated in Connecticut and it is for wool spinning only.

chalcedony. Gemcutting. See **quartz.**

chalk. Ivory and Bone Carving. Scrapings from this snow-white porous rock (essentially calcium carbonate, but commonly contaminated with quartz) are used to polish **ivory, bone,** and other soft substances. Precipitated chalk has been chemically prepared and cleansed of silica. Siliceous chalk is a natural chalky earth, or marl, from Germany. Unlike chalk, it consists of silica (opal) skeletons, and not calcium carbonate. Also see **tripoli, whiting.**

chalk. Quilts. Stitchery. A powdery substance available in sticks or pencils of rainbow colors. It is sometimes used to mark **quilting pattern**s because the **chalk line** can be brushed away without staining or marking the fabric. **Tailor's chalk,** a harder material, is made in flat pieces to facilitate the drawing of sharp lines. Also see **Quilts: Marking and Cutting, Quilting Patterns.**

chalk. Woodworking. See **marking tools.**

chalk bead. Beadwork. See **glass bead, seed bead.**

chalk line. Quilts. Stitchery. A line applied to fabric to serve as a guide in cutting, sewing, or **quilting.** It is especially helpful where long straight lines are needed. A string is rubbed with **chalk** and held taut, keeping the ends at the points between which a straight line is to be drawn. The string is lifted in the middle, and held above the area to be marked. Snap a string means to let go with a snap so that a perfectly straight line is marked on the fabric.

chalk line. Woodworking. See **marking tools.**

chalk stripe. Rugmaking. Weaving. See **stripe.**

chambered kiln. Ceramics. A term generally applied to the **climbing kiln**s of the Orient. Two-chambered kilns are quite common among potters; the second chamber, usually smaller, is used for the **bisque** fire. The heat that escapes from the first chamber is utilized in the second chamber. See ill. Also see **bank kiln, cross-draft kiln.**

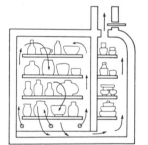

Chambered kiln

chambray. Quilts. Stitchery. A smooth, lustrous **plain weave fabric** with a frosted appearance. It is woven with white threads for **weft** and colored threads for the **warp,** giving it a variable color effect.

chamfer. Woodworking. See **bevel.**

chamfering. Metalworking. See **bevel, blacksmithing techniques.**

chamois. Ceramics. A soft, pliable leather used for smoothing and finishing the edges of **pots** on the **potter's wheel.** Because chamois resembles clay when wet, it is practical to keep it separate from the clay.

chamois. Jewelry. A soft leather used for cleaning and **polishing,** to which an **abrasive** or **buffing compound** may be applied. Also see **hand polishing.**

chamois. Leather. A soft, extremely supple leather made from the underside (flesh side) of sheepskin, called **flesher.** Chamois is often used for making garments, and is commonly used as a polishing cloth. Also see **cuir-boulli work** and **Leatherwork: Tanning and Manufacture.**

chamois polishing stick. Jewelry. **Chamois** glued to one side of a flat wood stick, used with rouge when **hand polishing** for a bright **mirror finish.** See ill.

Chamois polishing stick

chamotte. Ceramics. A term describing heavily **grogg**ed **stoneware** that is often un**glaze**d.

champlevé. Enameling. A technique of enameling in which enamels are fired in cavities etched or carved into the **metal** with the raised portions of the metal exposed. The depressions may be made by engraving, chiseling, **etching** or soldering metal shapes onto a surface, and the exposed metal may be finished by **polishing,** burnishing, **electroplating,** or **mercury gilding.** Also see **resist** and **Enameling.**

chandler. Candlemaking. A dealer in specified goods or equipment. The word stems from the French *chandelier* meaning "one who sells candles *(chandelles),*" which was the original application of the word in English.

channel. Stained Glass. The long groove or furrow in a piece of **lead came.** The lead is channeled, or grooved, in the process of **casting lead came.** The channel's leaves or flanges hold the pieces of stained glass in place and prevent them from falling out. Also see **lathkin, leaf.**

channel setting. Jewelry. A form of **en pave** in which gemstones are set in a single row, which can be straight, curved, tapered, flat, or arched.

character doll. Toys. Lifelike dolls made to represent real people or popular personalities. Some were modeled after babies and children, some were made to resemble well-known figures such as Charlie Chaplin or Shirley Temple and some depicted well-known fictitious characters. Also see **celebrity doll, nursery character.**

charcoal. Horn Carving. Ivory and Bone Carving. Jet Carving. A mild **abrasive** and polishing agent used for soft materials. The finely divided silica (opal) contained in various natural woods is the abrasive agent.

charcoal block. Jewelry. A block of compressed charcoal, used during **soldering** when prolonged heating is undesirable because charcoal retains heat. The work being soldered reaches the temperature at which **solder** flows sooner. Also see **asbestos pad, bismuth block, magnesium block.**

charge. Jewelry. The application of **buffing compound**s to the **buff.** This is done very simply by pressing the compound against the buffing wheel while it is rotating on the **buffing machine.** This operation is referred to as charging the wheel. Also see **breaking in a buff, buffing.**

charging. Gemcutting. A process of embedding diamond powder in a soft metal tool for use in grinding. Though **diamond** is brittle, it has very high tensile strength and if pressed gradually, it will embed in metal. Copper, bronze, or mild steel is charged with diamond for the manufacture of **laps**, **tube drills**, and **carving points**.

charging the wheel. Jewelry. See **charge**.

charlotte. Beadwork. See **embroidery bead**.

chart. Crewel. Embroidery. Needlepoint. A drawing, often on **graph paper,** showing placement of colors and stitches in detail, enabling anyone to complete the needlework design by following the chart. Charts are used instead of transferring a design or painting a design directly onto the **background fabric**.

charting. Knitting. A method of planning patterns stitch by stitch, row by row, on graph paper. The **knit** stitch is always marked with a white square, **purl** with a black square. Different colors are charted with preindicated symbols or numbers. Different stitches can be indicated by abbreviations. Also see **Knitting: Terms and Abbreviations**.

chasing. Basketry. The term used in woven basketry for randing (**checked weave**) with two weavers alternately. Chasing is woven in a **round** around an even number of stakes and when completed will look like randing although woven differently. See ill. Also see **Basketry: Woven Basket Construction**.

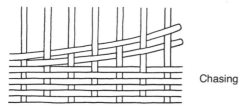
Chasing

chasing. Jewelry. Clarifying form and decoration in metal by placing it in **pitch** and working it from the front with **punch**es of different shapes and sizes. It is an addition or a refining process after **repoussé** has been completed. Chasing can also be done on flat surfaces alone, and in cleaning up and defining forms in a piece of work done through **centrifugal casting**. Also see **matting tools, modeling tool, repoussé hammer, repoussé tools**.

chasing. Metalworking. A mechanical finishing process whereby a cast metal surface is refined or fine details are added to it. It is also a decorative process for hand-shaped or hammered metals. Chasing is accomplished with chisel and punchlike tools used in combination with a lightweight hammer. Also see **Metalworking: Finishing**.

chasing cement. A brownish cement with a lower melting point than stick shellac used by jewelers and silversmiths. It is obtained from jewelry supply houses.

chasing hammer. Jewelry. See **repoussé hammer**.

chasing tool. Jewelry. See **repoussé tool**.

Chatham emerald. Gemcutting. See **beryl**.

chatoyance. Gemcutting. See **C-axis, cabochon, luster**.

chatter. Ceramics. Vibration of the **turning tool** in trimming due to the corrugation of the clay surface. To remedy this, brace your hands, hold the tool firmly, and use only the tip of the tool to smooth off the tops of the ridges.

check. Weaving. A pattern in which the **warp** is arranged as a **stripe** of two alternating colors, and the **filling** is put in the same colors, using the same amounts and the same sequence. This is known as a true check; however, many variations are possible and the pattern is called a check as long as it resembles a check. Some variations include: different colors in the filling, but using the same proportions as the warp; the same colors as the warp, but using different proportions; and in some cases, more than two colors in either the warp or the filling. The amounts of each color can be equal or different. The smallest amount would be two threads of one color. Also see **hound's tooth check**.

check. Woodworking. See **wood**.

checked plaiting. Basketry. One of the three types of **plaiting**. Two groups of parallel elements are used perpendicular to each other and cross over and under each other one element at a time, producing a checked effect. Also see **plaited basketry** and **Basketry: Plaited Basket Construction**.

checked stitch. Knitting. See **Knitting: Stitches and Patterns**.

checked weave. Basketry. (Also called randing.) The most common type of weaving, where the **active element** (or **weft**) is worked around one **passive element** (or **warp**) at a time. The warps are parallel, and both elements are the same size. Also see **Basketry: Woven Basket Construction**.

checkerboard. Quilts. The most simple method of joining **blocks** into a **quilt top**. It utilizes blocks all of one size, and they can be **set** by sewing them first into rows, then joining the rows. The checkerboard pattern can be very quiet or extremely active, depending on color and values used.

The checkerboard is sometimes used as a **border,** with just two rows of blocks. It is usually **pieced,** because these squares are easily joined. Occasionally, examples are found in which the squares are **appliquéd**.

The checkerboard offers a good way to join predesigned blocks that may have been embellished with batik, embroidery, tie-dye, or fabric painting.

In **felt** quilts a background of one color of felt may be used, over which blocks are appliquéd onto alternating squares, giving a checkerboard effect.

checker stitch. Needlepoint. A pattern created by alternating squares of **tent stitch** and **flat stitch**. It can be worked in one or two colors to give a highly textured effect. See ill. on next page.

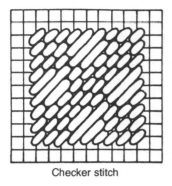

Checker stitch

cheese. Weaving. Yarn wound around a paper or wooden tube in large, indefinite amounts. The form resembles a bulk cheese.

cheesecloth. Stitchery. A plain, thin open-weave **cotton fabric** which is soft, lightweight and strong. It has many household uses, though it is not generally used in stitchery except for unusual effects. In a single layer, it serves as a **transparent fabric.** Used on top of other fabrics its softness allows it to be sculpted or molded by **stitch**ing or tucking.

When dyed, cheesecloth may be called **bunting,** which is used decoratively for swags and draping. Speakers platforms are often bedecked in bunting. While it is variously referred to as gauze, scrim, or tobacco cloth, there are slight differences. Gauze usually comes, bandagelike, in strips with non**fray**ing edges. Scrim, used in stage settings or for curtains, is woven in extra-wide panels. Tobacco cloth is a closer weave and is made in a brown or natural, also woven in wide widths.

cheese hard. Ceramics. See **leather hard.**

chemical dye. Dyeing. See **synthetic dye.**

chemical fiber. Batik and Tie-dye. Stitchery. See **man-made fiber.**

chemical mask. Plastics. A mask for covering the nose and mouth to filter out chemicals and organic compounds. Wear it when working with **casting resins** or spray paints. Fumes from these plastics can be toxic and the effects of repeated exposure may be cumulative. Also see **Plastics: Casting.**

chemical stain. Woodworking. See **wood stain.**

chemical water. Batik and Tie-dye. A solution used for thinning **fiber-reactive dye**s so that they can be sprayed. It consists of 1 teaspoon **Calgon,** 10 tablespoons **urea,** 2 cups hot water, and 2 cups cold water. Mix it in a quart jar by stirring the Calgon and urea into the hot water. When dissolved, add cold water and shake well. When a thick **dye** is needed for **direct-dye painting,** sodium alginate is added.

chemistry of pottery. Ceramics. Ceramic materials are described by the elements that make them up. They are generally noted as abbreviations or symbols. Element symbols are international. An element which contains oxygen is an oxide.

Oxides are classified in three groups. The first group of oxides have **flux**ing action that lowers the melting points of the material to which they are added. These oxides are basic or alkaline in nature. The second group of oxides are **refractory** and acidic in nature, and raise the melting point. The third group of oxides are **amphoteric**s and have an intermediate balancing and uniting role in a **glaze** formula.

A simple glaze might consist of **silica** (glass), lead (a flux to make it melt), and a china clay to make it stick to the pot and not run off when fired. Also see **pigment oxide.**

chenier. Jewelry. Metal tubing used in the making of **hinge**s.

chenille. Stitchery. See **tufted fabric.**

chenille fabric. Rugmaking. Weaving. A fabric that has **pile** on one or both sides. This pile is formed by the use of chenille yarn as **filling.** In weaving, the fringe of the yarn that acts as the pile must be combed out of the **shed** before beating to avoid its being enclosed in the shed. The pile may be much thicker than some knotted pile and it can be of any length; this depends on how the chenille yarn being used was woven. Since chenille yarn is a woven yarn, chenille fabric is often called "twice-woven fabric." Although the fabric can be used any place where a thick, heavy cloth is desired, the most popular use is for rugs. Also see **novelty yarn, shirred rug.**

chenille needle. Crewel. Embroidery. A short sharp-pointed needle with a long eye used in crewel embroidery. It is available in size 13, the largest, to size 26, the smallest.

chenille yarn. Weaving. See **novelty yarn.**

cherry. Woodworking. A hard, straight, close-grained fruitwood. Its color ranges from light to dark reddish brown. The wild black cherry is widely used for cabinets, furniture, and interior finishing. Although it tends to split, its other working qualities are good. It is ideal for **wood-carving** and takes a high polish.

Cherry Basket. Quilts. See **basket pattern.**

Cherry Wreath. Quilts. See **wreath pattern.**

chert. Gemcutting. See **quartz.**

chessylite. Gemcutting. See **azurite.**

chestnut. Woodworking. A light brown, lightweight **softwood** that splits easily and has large pores. It is used for cheap furniture, **core** stock in **plywood,** and (because of its resistance to rot) fence posts and railroad ties. Because of a blight at the turn of the century, chestnuts in the U.S.

were virtually wiped out; most chestnut now available has been imported from Europe.

Chestnut Burr. Quilts. See **Feather Star.**

chevet. Gemcutting. See **cameo.**

chevron. Batik and Tie-dye. A **zigzag** pattern produced in tie-dye by a folding process, usually for backgrounds. It is ideally used on narrow strips of fabric. To make the chevron, folded lengths of fabric are wrapped over a stick on the diagonal (**a.**). When the spiral folding is completed, the fabric is bound so that it will resist dye to produce a series of chevrons (**b.**). See ill.

a.

b.

chevron. Weaving. See **twill weave.**

chevron filling. Crewel. Embroidery. A stitch taken from **bargello,** but worked on any fabric. A series of long threads is laid down and small panels of **satin stitch**es are done over this **laidwork** in geometric fashion to form the chevron pattern. This can be worked and shaded in as many colors as desired. The edges should be kept neat, as the whole stitch looks best when not outlined. See ill.

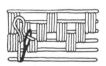

a.   Chevron stitch pattern ¼"   b.   Finished effect

chevron knitting. Knitting. Chevron knitting utilizes paired **increasing** and **decreasing** to form a V-shaped pattern in the knit surface. For example, knit to middle of row, make a **double decrease,** continue across row to next-to-last stitch, M1, K1. Also see **Knitting: Increasing, Decreasing.**

chevron pattern. Knitting. See **Knitting: Stitches and Patterns.**

chevron pattern. Macramé. Double **half hitch**es worked on the diagonal to form a chevron, or V-shape, of solid bars in the macramé work.
   Proper working of the chevron pattern depends upon the **holding cord** being held constant at the proper angle.
   Using either the right or left outer cord as a holding cord, anchor it securely at the beginning of the row. Loop the nearest cord around the holding cord twice and pull tight (**a.**). Repeat, making a row of diagonal double half

hitches (**b.**). Using either the right or the left outer cord as a holding cord, work the second row (**c.**). See ill. Also see **anchoring, diagonal double half hitch with center closing.**

Chevron pattern

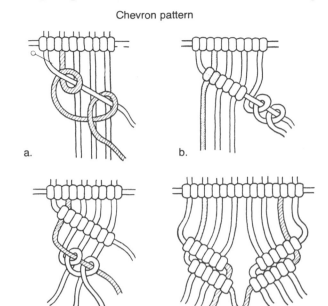

a.

b.

c.

d.   Right and left directions

chevron plaiting. Weaving. A **plaiting** that starts in the center, with the two middle strands plaiting over the outer strands in opposite directions from each other. Each successive **warp end** is taken in rotation from the center and plaited out to the edge. It is known by many other names; one of these is Osage braid, after the Osage Indians. Another name, double band plaiting, refers to the fact that the warp is divided in half and the two halves are joined during the plaiting. Chevron takes its name from the type of design most commonly seen in this method of plaiting. See ill. Also see **multiple band plaiting.**

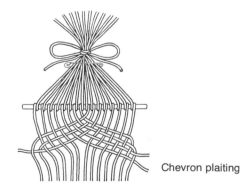

Chevron plaiting

chevron stitch. Needlepoint. This stitch works into an interesting textured pattern that is especially effective when worked in one or two colors. Work vertical stitches in a chevron pattern, one row over four mesh of the **canvas** (**a.**) alternating with a row of vertical stitches in the same chevron pattern over two mesh of the canvas (**b.**).
   The stitch works up quickly and is excellent for backgrounds or filling in large areas. See ill. on next page.

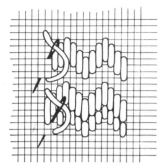

a.   Vertical stitches over 4 mesh

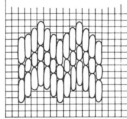

b.   Vertical stitches over 2 mesh

chiaroscuro. Art of design using only black and white. Also refers to the distribution of light and shadow in paintings.

chiastolite. Gemcutting. See **andalusite.**

Chicago Star. Quilts. See **star pattern.**

chicken-and-egg. Toys. (Also called chickens.) Any of several **toys** based on the old riddle of "which came first, the chicken or the egg." Usually **egg**-shaped, the toy opens to reveal a chicken. Sometimes it is made as a nested toy (chicken within an egg, within a chicken, and so on). Also see **archetypal toy, bird toy.**

chickens. Toys. See **chicken-and-egg, pecking chickens.**

chicken wire. Papercrafts. Chicken wire, available from lumberyard or hardware stores in various mesh widths, is often used as a support for especially large **papier mâché** sculptures. The wire is fashioned into a shape by bending the loose wire ends back and twisting them around overlapped meshwork. The chicken wire has a large mesh, which often shows through the papier mâché coating. To achieve a smooth surface, first coat the chicken-wire support with **aluminum foil,** then cover with several layers of papier mâché, using the **paper-strip method.** Heavy wire cutters are needed to cut chicken wire; it is helpful to wear work gloves when working with it.

chief's blanket. Weaving. See **Navajo weaving.**

chiffon. Stitchery. A **silk, wool, nylon,** or **rayon fabric** which is gossamer, **sheer,** and lightweight. It is durable, drapes softly, and is excellent for tie-dye since the soft and light fabric can easily be tied securely.

Chilkat blanket. Weaving. Highly patterned blankets that were finger-woven by the Tlingit Indians of southern Alaska. They were not truly woven but weft-twined across a **warp** hung from a horizontal bar and weighted at the bottom. The warp was shredded cedar bark twisted with mountain goat's wool for stiffness and body. The **filling** was all goats' wool for pliability in twining. The patterns on these blankets, which were worn only by the chiefs, are symbolic stylized animals, birds, and sea monsters in a distinctive blue-green and lighter **natural dye** colors, sharply outlined in black. The men painted the designs on pattern boards and the women copied them in the twining. To achieve this **tapestry**like cloth they made a very tightly packed **weft twining** over alternate warp pairs, going back and forth within each motif. The joinings between motifs are interlooped, which is akin to tapestry **interlocking.** Joinings between sections are hidden under an outline row of three-strand weft twining. There is a long fringe around the bottom border of the blankets. Dress-length dance shirts, leggings and aprons are done in the same technique. Also see **finger weaving, warp-weighted loom.**

Chimneysweep. Quilts. (Also called Maltese Cross, White Cross.) A **block** design for a **pieced quilt** that has an X or a plus sign in the center. This is reminiscent of the four-flue chimney of early American times, from which it takes its name. The plus sign is made of from 5 to 9 **patch**es in a basic **nine-patch,** which is in turn set at a 45° angle within another **square** and is surrounded by a **sawtooth** pattern.

china. Ceramics. A general term applied to **vitreous porcelain** bodies **fire**d at low temperatures.

CHINA AND GLASS PAINTING

The decoration of pottery, ceramics, and china is one of the oldest forms of art. The production of porcelain, dating back to the ninth century A.D. in China, and perhaps earlier, was a well-guarded secret until 1709 when Johann Friedrich Bottger discovered the process in Saxony. Soon, decorated porcelain, with its translucent, lustrous surface, became well known and highly treasured. Chemistry has improved ceramic glazes, and more and more colors have become available. The techniques and materials of china painting are derived from basic ceramic procedures. China painting generally refers to the addition of hand-painted designs on a ceramic piece to which glaze has been added and then **firing** done. Therefore, paint for china painting is called **onglaze color.** The onglaze color is painted onto the glazed, fired surface and fired again to fuse the colors of the added design into the surface. Various traditional techniques are available to the craftsperson, including **acid etching, banding, dusting, ground laying, raised paste,** and **silver resist,** and freehand painting.

SETTING UP A WORKSHOP   The best china for painting is made in France, Germany, and Japan. Old pieces of china are sometimes used, but are not entirely dependable. Equipment for decorating china and glass is available from ceramic supply stores. Powdered or liquid **onglaze color** is available in a variety of colors. An assortment of various sizes and shapes of camel's hair or sable **brushes** and a glass or ceramic palette will be needed.

Grind powdered color on a ground-glass slab. Use a

palette knife to mix it with a **medium,** such as oil of cloves or **lavender oil.** Use pure gum turpentine for thinning some colors and for cleaning up. Have on hand cotton rags and absorbent cotton. Pieces of old silk will be needed to make a **silk pad** used for **ground laying.**

Tracing paper or graphite tracing paper and lead pencil, **china pencil** are used in designing. Use Plasticene or Scotch tape to fasten tracing paper onto china.

Clean china with denatured alcohol before painting. Use a sifter, preferably with brass or bronze screening, for **dusting** powdered colors and **flux.** Use a **crowquill** pen for fine **outlining.**

A **kiln** is necessary for firing. If you don't have a kiln, the painting can be done at home or in the studio, and the piece then taken to a ceramic studio for **firing.** Be sure the firing is done at the required temperature.

Keep the work area and all equipment completely free of lint. Avoid wearing wool sweaters while working. As an added precaution, cut the rags for clean up with scissors; tearing makes lint. Establish a separate work area for messy work such as **burnishing.**

PREPARING CHINA AND PAINT Thoroughly clean the piece to be decorated with soap and water, rinse, and then wipe with a few drops of denatured alcohol on a lintless cloth. Leave it in a dust-free place until ready to paint.

In general, it is difficult to decorate old china, as it may have impurities that will cause blotching during firing. However, it can be done if you carefully remove the original design with a **china eraser.** The colors for decorating china, **onglaze colors,** are available in powder or liquid form. The powdered colors must be mixed with an **oil,** or **medium,** and sometimes need to be thinned to the proper painting consistency with pure gum turpentine. Follow the manufacturer's instructions on the label. Use liquid colors directly from the bottle.

The ceramic surface to be decorated will determine the consistency of the paint. In general, china with a thick, glossy **glaze** requires a thicker color to adhere than does a thinner, more matte glaze, such as earthenware. Tests should be made on scraps of broken china to see the results of **firing** before painting is begun.

Some powdered colors will not have the necessary amount of **flux** to provide a bond with the surface glaze when fired. An **unfluxed** color may be mixed with flux; mix the powders together first before adding the oil or medium.

To mix colors, place the powdered materials, 3 parts color to 1 part flux if necessary, on a glass slab. Add a few drops of turpentine and grind with a palette knife, glass muller, or pestle until all feeling of grit disappears. Then add about 6 drops of **fat oil of turpentine,** lavender oil, or a few drops of any other suggested medium. Stir with a palette knife to the consistency of cream for **tinting,** thicker for painting. The mixture can usually be thinned with turpentine. This formula varies for specific techniques, such as **ground laying. Gold** and **silver** paints require special preparation.

When mixing yellows, use a glass, ivory, bone, or plastic spatula to avoid the discoloring effects of metal on the color.

Designs may be drawn directly on the surface to be decorated by using a **china pencil.** Wipe the china with turpentine and allow it to dry to a thin film. Draw the design on the film layer with a lead pencil.

Designs worked out on graphite tracing paper are transferred to the china by tracing. Adhere the paper to the china with tape or Plasticene. If regular tracing paper is used, slip a piece of carbon paper under the tracing paper and, with a hard pencil, trace the design onto the china. Use India ink to mark the carbon lines clearly on the china (the ink will fire out).

Paint the design with **onglaze color** and a fine brush. Brushstrokes of various sizes and shapes are the basic method of decorating china. Practice brushwork on scrap paper first, trying curves, zigzags, lines, and waves, then combining strokes to form parallel stripes or cross hatching to form shaded areas for tonal effects. Control the width of the lines by the pressure on the brush; wide lines are made with heavy brushstrokes. The painting should always be done delicately, building up color intensity through repeated application. After the paint has dried, wipe the surface lightly with a damp cloth to remove ink lines. Retouch any omitted areas of the design. When dry the piece is ready for firing. Fire the piece after each application of glaze. After each firing, sand the color lightly with extra-fine sandpaper to remove any grit. Also see **banding, ground laying, outlining.**

PAINTING GLASS For decorating glass, use the same general materials and procedures as for china painting. The glass to be decorated must be able to stand a hard **firing.** For painting materials, a ceramic **glaze, enamel** colors, and **ice** are used. Mix the colors to the consistency of cream and thin with turpentine. For more body, add tar oil or damar varnish. Kaolin (china clay) may be added to enamel to help it fuse to glass. The best procedure is to add china clay to white enamel, fire the piece, then apply color over it for a second firing. The result will be an opaque surface similar to painted china. An alternate method is to cover the glass surface with **flux** by **dusting.** Used as a clear glaze, the flux fuses the color to the glass surface and retains the transparent quality of glass.

For transferring the design to glass, the pattern may be placed inside the glass, and guiding marks made on the outside of the glass.

CARE AND MAINTENANCE All equipment for china and glass painting, such as the palette and brushes, should be kept clean with alcohol, turpentine, or paint thinner. Clean the brushes used for paint and oil in turpentine, India ink brushes in water, and luster brushes in turpentine and then in alcohol, brushing back and forth against the hand until the bristles are dry and fluffy. After cleaning, wash all brushes in warm water and soap, then rinse and dry. Keep all the cloths, rags, silk, etc., clean by soaking them in turpentine to remove paint, then washing them in soap and water, and rinsing.

When grinding and mixing colors, clean the glass slab with turpentine and cloth before beginning, and then wipe it again after mixing each color.

After firing, the china or glass should have a permanent

finish that requires no maintenance other than washing in mild soap and water. However, old pieces with worn gold rims and edges may be retouched and refired if the surface is first thoroughly cleaned with water and baking soda.

china clay. Ceramics. See **kaolin.**

china color. China and Glass Painting. See **onglaze color.**

china doll. Toys. A **doll** made from glazed and fired china. Usually just the head was made from china, although sometimes the arms and lower legs were also of glazed **clay.** The body of the doll was cloth, **kid,** or wood. China dolls were first made in 1750 but did not become greatly popular until 100 years later. They were either pressed or poured into molds. These dolls are sometimes referred to as porcelain dolls. Also see **bisque dolls.**

china eraser. China and Glass Painting. A specially prepared liquid available for removing color from china. Apply it to the desired portion of the china with the end of a brush wrapped in a cloth and dipped into the eraser. Its etching action will remove the unwanted designs. Rinse under running water to stop the etching action. Wear gloves, and take care not to get any eraser on the skin. This technique is sometimes used to remove designs from an old piece of china in preparation for painting a new design. However, the new design must go in exactly the same areas as the erased ones, as a faintly etched design will remain. To remove paint that is dry but unfired, apply a mixture of several drops of fresh oil of tar (from the drugstore), thickened with hard-soap shavings, to the area to be erased. Allow the mixture to stand for a few minutes, then wipe off both mixture and paint with a cloth. Also see **China and Glass Painting: Preparing China and Paint.**

china grass. Weaving. See **ramie.**

china pencil. China and Glass Painting. (Also called lithographic pencil.) A waxy pencil used for marking on china or glass surfaces. Also see **China and Glass Painting: Setting Up a Workshop.**

Chinese embroidery. Embroidery. Because silk thread is as common in China as cotton or wool is in other countries, **silk embroidery** is usually associated with Chinese needlework. Chinese embroidery designs have influenced the needlework of other countries throughout history. The designs are masterpieces of stylization. To quote Coomsawary, "To delineate a real bird, feather for feather, that would be barbarous, but to communicate all that makes up the essence of a bird—that is art." Because of the use of silk thread, the stitching is generally extremely fine, and is often combined with **metallic threads.**

Typical stitches used are **long and short, French knots, Pekinese stitch,** and often **satin stitch** worked in blocks or bands with a **voided line** between each one.

Besides **silk embroidery** and **metal thread embroidery,** a great deal of beautiful, fine white work has been done in China. See ill.

Symbols used in Chinese embroidery

Chinese rings. Toys. See **prisoner's lock.**

Chinese thimble. Stitchery. An open-ended thimble which slides over the middle finger and rests between the first and second joint. This **thimble** is used in a sideways movement against the blunt end of the **needle.** It was designed in this way to allow for long fingernails, since among the Chinese short nails were considered undesirable as a sign of manual labor.

Chinese white. Jewelry. A solid cake of white water-base paint used for transferring a design from paper to metal. Wet the fingers and rub them across the solid cake. Dab the metal surface evenly. Allow to dry thoroughly. Transfer the design. Also see **transferring designs to metal, yellow ochre.**

chinoiserie. Découpage. A French term for work done in the style of Chinese art popular in eighteenth-century Europe. The designs were inspired by **lacquer ware**s imported from the Orient. While they lacked the cohesion and meaning of the Chinese originals, they had their own delightful style. Designs were generally arranged in a fantastic rococo format with figures, pagodas, and arched bridges hovering inside **cartouche** borders. **Jean Pillement** popularized this style. Chinoiserie **print**s have always been a favorite subject for use in découpage.

A fantastic variation of this style is singerie (from the French word *singe* meaning monkey), a style depicting monkeys fancifully dressed, in similar arrangements to chinoiserie.

chintz. Quilts. Stitchery. A **plain-weave cotton fabric** that has a glazed surface. It is usually printed in brightly colored patterns, and the glaze remains after washing.

chintz quilt. Quilts. Any quilt or **coverlet** made from printed **chintz** or blazed **calico** of the late 1700s or early 1800s. The designs depicted historical events or pastoral country scenes. These designs were emphasized through **quilting,** which gave further dimension to the printed patterns. A similar kind of quilting is not uncommon now, using prints depicting children's toys, circus animals, and the like, in which the quilting merely outlines the printed pattern.

Another kind of chintz quilt and one similarly adapted to contemporary quilting involves the use of portions of a printed fabric. Specific shapes, such as leaves, figures, flowers, or trees, are cut out from the material and **appliqué**d to a **background.**

The designation **chintz quilt** also used to refer to any quilt in which white **blocks** were separated by areas of printed fabric, whether or not that fabric was chintz.

chipboard. Crewel. Embroidery. Needlepoint. (Also called particle board.) A material made up of small particles or chips of assorted woods compressed together to form a soft board that is excellent for **blocking.** This type of board does not warp.

chipboard. Woodworking. See **particle board.**

chip carving. Woodworking. See **woodcarving** and **Woodworking: Whittling and Woodcarving.**

chip knife. Stenciling. See **stencil knife.**

Chippewa. Weaving. See **Ojibwa weaving.**

chipping. Plastics. Chipping is caused by drilling plastic with a drill bit that is dull or too coarse, by cutting with a saw that has uneven teeth, by **feeding** plastic into a blade too quickly, or by not clamping forms securely enough when cutting.

chipping hammer. Stained Glass. See **dalle-de-verre.**

Chips and Whetstones. Quilts. Any of several **pieced block** patterns that incorporate a **sawtooth** pattern in a circle. It is representative of the pioneer tasks of splitting rails or firewood. See ill. Also see **Circular Saw.**

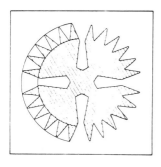

Chips and Whetstones

chisel. Leather. A chisel is used for general leatherwork, such as setting **nailheads.** Also see **thonging chisel.**

chisel. Metalworking. A wedge-shaped tool with one end hardened and sharpened for cutting, shearing, and chipping metal. There are four basic shapes of chisels used for common **bench work:** flat cold chisel (**a.**), diamond-point chisel (**b.**), cape chisel (**c.**), and roundnose chisel (**d.**). See ill. These are especially useful for **chasing** rough metal castings.

Chisels used for **forging** may have handles or wires attached to them, and are called set tools.

To use a chisel, secure or clamp the object to be chiseled on a protected work surface (covered with a metal plate or wood). Put on **eye protectors** or a **face shield.** Mark a layout line on the area to be chiseled with a pencil or scriber. Hold the chisel with your thumb and fingers around the body. Strike the tool lightly with a hammer, keeping your eye on the cutting edge, not on the tool handle. Go back over the line with firmer blows to cut through the metal, or turn the piece over and cut from the other side. When

chisel-cutting an internal hole, drill small holes around the inside circumference, then cut the line with a chisel.

To sharpen a flat cold chisel:

Grind one cutting edge on a bench grinder at an angle of 60°–70° by moving one side of the cutting edge lightly back and forth against the revolving grinding wheel. Do not allow the surface to overheat or it will lose its hardness. If it gets hot, pause to let it cool. Do not use heavy pressure.

Grind the other side to a sharp edge. Also grind off any deformation or mushrooming of the soft head of the chisel to prevent this metal from cutting your hand while working or from flying off while chiseling (**e.**). See ill. Also see **blacksmithing tools.**

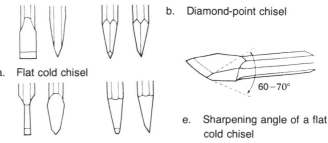

a. Flat cold chisel

b. Diamond-point chisel

e. Sharpening angle of a flat cold chisel

60–70°

c. Cape chisel   d. Roundnose chisel

chisel. Tincrafting. A solid metal shaft with a flattened and sharpened cutting edge at one end used to make cuts in the tin sheet that cannot be readily made with the **snips,** or to punch out rectangular openings in an overall tincraft design. Also see **Tincrafting: Cutting the Tin.**

chisel. Woodworking. A wood-cutting tool with a straight cutting edge on the end of a flat blade. Chisels vary according to their use in **carpentry, wood carving,** and **woodturning.** Handles on chisels are of two types: tang, in which the end of the blade opposite the cutting edge tapers and is wedged into the handle (**a.**), and socket, in which the handle fits into the cupped end of the chisel blade (**b.**). It is used for heavier work, often with a **mallet.**

Carpentry chisels vary according to size and use. Most have parallel sides that are **chamfered.**

The cabinet (or pocket) chisel is the standard carpentry chisel, with blades that range from ⅛–1½" wide and from 4–6" long (**c.**).

The butt chisel is similar to a cabinet chisel but with a shorter blade.

A slick chisel is a chisel with a 3 or 4" blade, used for heavy **roughing out.**

A mortise chisel has a narrow blade ⅛–½" wide; it is used for cutting **mortises** in **mortise-and-tenon** joints (**d.**).

To use a carpentry chisel, clamp the wood securely. Mark out or visualize the area of wood you want to remove. If possible, **stop cut** beside or behind the desired area with a **backsaw** or the chisel itself. Place the beveled edge of the chisel up, or in the direction you want to remove the wood. With your hand or a **mallet,** strike the end of the chisel so that it is cutting in the direction of the **grain** or diagonally to it.

Woodcarving chisels are generally straight-sided, without chamfers.

Straight (or firmer) chisel is the standard wood chisel for carving. The sides are straight and parallel, and the blade is 6−8″ long and ⅛″ wide (**e.**). See ill. The fishtail chisel is similar to the straight chisel, but the sides taper down suddenly behind the cutting edge.

A skew chisel is also similar to the straight chisel, but its carving edge is not at right angles to its sides. The bevel is also ground on both front and back (**f.**). See ill.

Wood-turning chisels are not all true chisels. Most are scraping tools, with the exception of the gouge and skew chisel.

A skew chisel is similar to a woodcarving skew, but, as with all wood-turning chisels, it has a heavier blade and longer handle. Also see **wood-turning tools.**

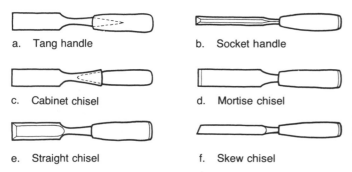

a. Tang handle   b. Socket handle

c. Cabinet chisel   d. Mortise chisel

e. Straight chisel   f. Skew chisel

chisel cut. Woodworking. See **whittling.**

chisel cutting. Jewelry. A direct method for cutting very intricate designs into very thin **gauge** metals using small, sharp, "cold chisels." These chisels are available with different cutting edges and are struck with a **ball-peen hammer.** Support the metal while chisel cutting on a soft steel or heavy-gauge brass or bronze plate. Originally, chisels were used to cut or split metal before the advent of the **saw frame** and **saw blade.**

chiseling. Metalworking. See **blacksmithing techniques.**

chisel plate. Metalworking. See **blacksmithing tools.**

choke. Weaving. A tight tie around the total **warp ends** made after **warping** is finished but before the warp is removed from the **warping board** or **reel.** There are usually a series of chokes in a warp placed at approximately one-yard intervals. They are of a contrasting color yarn and are usually tied in a bowknot for easy removal. They are tied as tightly as possible around the warp because the purpose of chokes is to hold the warp together as it is taken off the board or reel. Chokes also separate the warp groups so that, in **chaining,** threads from one group are not accidentally picked up with another group.

chopped strand mat. Plastics. See **glass fiber.**

christening quilt. Quilts. A special quilt made for the christening ceremony at which a baby is baptized and named. It is usually delicate in color and exquisitely sewn. The name and birthdate of the baby are occasionally incorporated into the design.

chromatrope. Toys. An **optical toy** developed in the early 1800s in which a series of colored discs is flicked quickly past the eye on a rotating drum, creating an illusion of movement. Geometric patterns are sometimes used, and in series or rapid succession the visual image is one of melting shapes in which the geometric forms dissolved. It is not unlike a self-operating **kaleidoscope.** Also see **animated booklet.**

chrome. Ceramics. See **chromium.**

chrome. Dyeing. The orange-colored crystals used by dyers as a **mordant.** These metallic salts are either potassium or sodium dichromate and are the same as those used in photography. They are also called bichromate of potash or bichromate of soda. Chrome gives a warm underglow to many colors and brings out reds and oranges. In greens, however, it mutes them to a grayish tone. Too much chrome will soften and darken wool. This chemical is light sensitive and must be kept in opaque or dark glass jars.

chrome calf. Leather. A smooth, lightweight chrome tanned **top grain** leather used for linings, belts, and shoe tops. Also see **chrome tanning.**

chrome tanning. Leather. A leather **tanning** process in which skins are soaked several hours in tanks with soluble chromium salts (or compounds of metal chromium) before washing to make leather stronger and more water resistant and to increase its **tensile strength.** Chrome tanning is a much faster process than **vegetable tanning** and therefore less costly. Chrome-tanned leather is widely used for footwear. It cannot, however, be used for **tooling** or **stamping.** Also see **chrome calf, combination tanning** and **Leatherwork: Tanning and Manufacture.**

chrome-tin pink. Ceramics. A **pigment oxide** used in **earthenware underglaze** painting as a stain. It is produced by a reaction between tin and chrome in the glaze mixture. Used in the eighteenth-century, it was originally called English pink.

chromium. Ceramics. A **pigment oxide** of chrome that is used to produce green colors in **glaze**s. A very versatile pigment oxide, especially when fired at low temperatures, the color is always opaque and tends to be rather heavy and flat. Do not place tin-glazed and chrome-glazed pieces next to each other in the kiln.

chromium. Jewelry. A steel-gray metal obtained from the mineral chromite. It is **alloy**ed with **copper,** steel, and nickel because of its high resistance to atmospheric corrosion at elevated temperatures, its resistance to **acid**s and alkalines at normal temperatures, and its high **tensile strength.** It is used only for plating because it is extremely brittle.

chromium. Metalworking. See **steel.**

chromium. Stained Glass. See **antique glass colorants.**

chrysoberyl. Gemcutting. A mineral composed of beryllium and aluminum oxides with **hardness** of 8½ and **specific gravity** of 3.6 to 3.7. Chrysoberyl occurs in transparent **crystal**s of the orthorhombic system and has conchoidal **fracture** and vitreous to greasy **luster.** Its refractive indices are 1.75 and 1.76 and it is colored light and dark green with some dichroism.

Alexandrite is a variety of chrysoberyl which appears dark green in daylight and red or violet in candlelight. Synthetic alexandrite is actually synthetic **corundum** which exhibits a similar color change.

Cymophane is translucent chrysoberyl with microscopic inclusions arranged in planes parallel to the **C axis.** An oval **cabochon** cut from this material oriented properly to the chatoyant reflection accentuates this phenomenon into a thin, brightly shining band of light contrasted on a gray-green background called cat's eye.

Main crown **facet**s are cut at 37° and main pavillion facets at 40−42° with 1200 grit **diamond** powder. Traditionally, **polishing** is done with tripoli on a tin **lap;** however, 1400 diamond powder can be substituted. Also see **faceting, refraction.**

chrysocolla. Gemcutting. A hydrous copper silicate with **hardness** of 2−4, amorphous structure, and blue-green **color.** Also **quartz** with chrysocolla inclusions.

chrysolite. Gemcutting. See **olivine.**

chrysoprase. Gemcutting. See **quartz.**

chrysotile. Gemcutting. See **serpentine.**

chuck. Ceramics. A ring or block of clay supporting a pot or a bowl on the **potter's wheel** when **turning.** The technique is referred to as "throwing a chuck." Also see **cup head.**

chuck. Jewelry. The part of a tool that is tightened by hand turning. It is threaded and as it's turned it closes down on a **collet** which in turn holds tools such as drill bits, **bur**s, wire, and **reamer**s. Also see **flexible shaft machine, hand drill, pin vise.**

chuck. Metalworking. Plastics. Woodworking. A revolving holding attachment on the end of the spindle of a **lathe** or drilling tool. It is usually tightened by hand on hand tools, and with a key on power tools. In **metal spinning,** chuck is the term for the (usually **hardwood**) pattern over which the metal is forced.

chuck key. Metalworking. Woodworking. A tool used with a drill press or portable electric drill to secure or tighten a **drill bit** into the drill's **chuck.** Also see **drilling tools.**

chun glaze. Ceramics. An **opalescent** Chinese **glaze,** with a milky bluish tint, that is derived from wood ashes. Chun glaze does not contain oxides.

chunk candle. Candlemaking. A variation of the molded candle in which colored chunks or molded forms of solid wax are packed in a **mold** and then covered with hot molten wax. The **temperature** of the heated pouring wax determines the final effect—the hotter the wax, the more dispersed the color chunks. The chunk candle can be wicked as in any **molding** method or a thin **taper** can be inserted in the center of the mold. Also see **Candlemaking: Molding.**

Churn Dash. Quilts. A **pieced four-patch** pattern consisting of squares and triangles. One of the many **quilt** names taken from familiar household utensils. See ill. Also see **Pinwheel.**

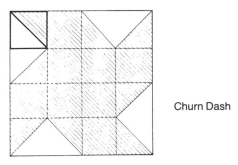

Churn Dash

churning scene. Toys. A **swinging-weight toy** based on the system used in **pecking chickens.** In this, the weight alternates the movement of the animated figures of a woman churning and a cat lapping milk. It is a traditional **folk toy** of Eastern Europe.

cigar-band quilt. Quilts. Those **quilt**s that utilize **silk** cigar bands in their structure and design. At a time when fabrics, especially brightly colored ones, were expensive and hard to find, these bands were deemed too valuable to be thrown away. The lettering on them also contributed to the design; they were usually **pieced** in strips to take full advantage of the silk. Because the amount of material available was somewhat limited (unless the quilter knew a chain smoker of cigars), these were often made as **throws,** smaller than quilts. Also see **making do, tobacco-bag quilt.**

cinnabar. Gemcutting. Mercury sulfide with **hardness** of 2¼, **specific gravity** of 8.1, scarlet **streak,** and red **color.** Cinnabar crystals are in the orthorhombic system and have perfect **cleavage** in one direction parallel to the **C axis.**

circle. Batik and Tie-dye. A round shape or rounded pattern on a **tie-dye fabric** created by a particular method of tying. To produce the circle, a point of fabric is picked up on the desired spot. It is pulled straight up, and the remaining material is drawn down over it so that it looks like a folded umbrella. The pointed column of fabric is then **tied** with **binding** in any of the **binding methods** (a.). The distance from the top of the point to the end of the tying determines the size of the finished circle. If a pattern of circles is desired, a dot should mark the center of each before tying begins, as the material is distorted in shape by the tying and it will be difficult to control the spacing. Concentric circles can be made by continuous bands of tying (**b.**).

Another method of making circles is **tritik,** which involves first drawing a circle on the fabric. A line of running stitches is then sewn around the line and pulled tight. The inside area of the circle is pulled into a peak, and it can then be tied with any of the binding methods.

Small circles can be made by pricking and then lifting a tiny bit of fabric with a threaded needle. The tip end is then stitched through and tied off. A number of such small circles can be worked in series to produce patterns. See ill.

circle. Papercrafts. By folding and cutting a square of paper, a perfect circle can be made. Fold the square in quarters, then fold again to form a triangle (**a.**). Using the short side as a radius, measure, then cut, an arc (**b.**). Unfold for a circle. See ill. Also see **concentric circle.**

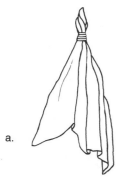

a. Fold lines

b. Cut arc

Cutting a circle

circle cutter. Jewelry. (Also called disk punch set.) A tool composed of several **punch**es of hardened steel that fit into a steel block with corresponding holes. The block has a slot into which the metal that the circles are to be made from is inserted. The proper punch is inserted into the corresponding hole and struck several times with a hammer, cutting the circle. The punch is then removed by pushing it through the hole. Check the **gauge** of the metal to be certain it falls within the maximum gauge the circle cutter can handle. It is imperative that the cutting end of the punch be placed into the hole; reversing it can destroy the cutting edge when it is struck with the hammer. See ill.

Punches and pierced steel block units that comprise the circle cutter

circle cutter. Metalworking. Plastics. (Also called fly cutter.) A cutting attachment used in a drill press or portable electric drill for cutting large circles in plastics, laminated material such as **Formica,** and **plywood, hardboard** (Masonite), and sheet metal. Use it on metal, plastic, or wood as you would a **drill bit,** at a machine speed of near 7000 rpm. See ill. Also see **drilling tools.**

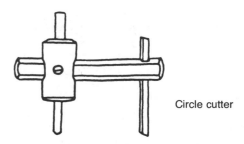

Circle cutter

circle cutter. Stained Glass. A compasslike tool that **scores** the glass in circles ½–5″ in diameter. The glass is then also scored at right angles to the circle, and the sections outside the circle are removed with glass pliers. Circles may also be cut free hand with a regular **glass-cutter.** See ill.

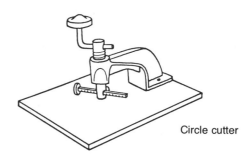

Circle cutter

circle edge slicker. Leather. (Also called edge slicker.) A small plastic tool that serves as a **burnisher** for the edges of leather which have been beveled; for example, the edges of a belt. It is a small plastic disk with a hole in the center and a grooved rim. The tool is held with the thumb and forefinger through the hole and the grooved rim is run along the edges of the belt with some pressure to smooth down rough fibers left from cutting and edge beveling operations. See ill. Also see **hardwood wheel** and **Leatherwork: Cutting and Edging Leather, Tools and Materials.**

Circle edge slicker

circle swing. Toys. (Also called circular swing.) A single **rope swing** made from a disk of heavy plywood that has a hole drilled through the center. The rope is run through the hole and tied underneath, then the other end of the rope is hung from a tree or beam. To be hung outdoors, an exterior plywood should be used and all cut or drilled edges should be sealed before being undercoated and painted.

Circling Swallows. Quilts. See **Falling Star.**

circular flathead stake. Metalworking. See **anvil.**

circular knitting. Knitting. (Also called round knitting.) A piece of work knit on **circular needles** or on three or more

double pointed needles. Circular knitting produces a knitted fabric without seams.

circular loom. Weaving. See **cardboard loom, hoop loom, needleweaving.**

circular needle. Knitting. Circular needles can be used for all knitting, including **circular knitting.** Many knitters prefer circular needles because the weight of the work is held in the lap instead of on the end of the needles. Circular needles are used for knitting clothing and wide pieces such as afghans and wall hangings.

circular netting. Lacemaking. A **knotted lace filet** done in a circular shape. The **mesh**es of this lace are worked in a similar fashion.

Start with the **foundation loop** as in regular knotted lace filet. When there are a sufficient number of meshes on the loop to make a circle of the desired diameter, tie the ends of the foundation loop together with a **reef knot** to secure tightly. Proceed as in meshed filet, but going around and around instead of back and forth, increasing the number of meshes as needed to keep the circle growing, occasionally making two meshes for each one in the previous row. Tie colored thread into the mesh at the beginning of the row, and at the places where increases would be needed. Remove the thread as the work progresses or when it is finished.

Variations in the pattern may be made by changing the size of the **mesh stick,** to increase or decrease the size of the meshes. A **buttonhole stitch** is not needed for a finish, as the natural looping of the meshes makes a good edge.

Circular netting is suitable for flat doilies or for bags, and does not have a **filling stitch.** See ill.

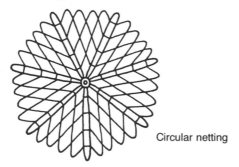

Circular netting

circular pouring shank. Metalworking. See **tongs.**

circular rug. Rugmaking. See **braided rug, hooked rug, hoop loom, rug weaving.**

circular saw. Plastics. Woodworking. See **power saw.**

Circular Saw. Quilts. (Also called Four Little Fans, Oriole Window.) Any of several old-time **quilt block** patterns that suggest the disk of a circular saw blade. Each requires the skillful **piecing** of tiny triangles, as well as the sewing of curved lines. These **blocks** are sometimes sewn in a combination of piecing and **appliqué.** Also see **Chips and Whetstones.**

circular swing. Toys. See **circle swing.**

circular warp. Weaving. See **continuous warp.**

circular weave. Weaving. See **tubular weave.**

circus toy. Toys. Any **toy** based on circus animals, acrobats, or performers. Some circus **wagon**s were cut from wood and carried cutout animals; others were solid wood with printed paper sheets glued to the sides. Circus toys of the 1800s consisted of paper sheets to which paper cutouts were added. Later circus toys were of wood, metal, paper, **celluloid,** rubber, or plastic.

cire perdue. Jewelry. See **lost-wax casting.**

citrine. Gemcutting. See **quartz.**

clamp. Jewelry. Holding tools that free the hands for working or that hold parts of tools or equipment together. There are many types of clamps among jewelry tools, e.g., the **thumbscrew** and nut on a **sawframe** that hold the **sawblade** in place, and a **bench pin** or **V-board and clamp,** which are different versions of the same tool and are clamped to the **bench** (although there are types that can be secured permanently). The **ring clamp, c-clamp, peg clamp, engraver's block, engraver's sharpener, cross-locking tweezers,** and the **third hand** are all clamps.

clamping tools. Metalworking. Woodworking. A variety of tools used to hold material stationary while working on it or to hold two or more pieces of material together while being fastened. All-metal clamps are used in metalworking because of the hard materials being worked on and the high heats sometimes generated; in woodworking, many clamps are made of wood or protected by wood or leather to prevent damaging the wood. The first two clamps below are used most commonly in metalworking; all are used in woodworking.

a. C clamp or carriage clamp. The metal C comes in maximum opening sizes of from 3–16″; the clamping pressure is provided by the screw. Because the force is concentrated on a small gripping face, it tends to dent wood if not padded with scrap wood.

b. Spring clamp. A clothespin-type metal clamp used for light clamping.

c. Hand-screw clamp. The basic wood clamp, useful for irregular, flat-sided objects. Both the angle and the distance between the wooden jaws are adjustable up to 12–14″.

d. Bar (or pipe or **cabinet**) clamp. Used for clamping across a large expanse. The fixed jaw has a screw adjustment; the other jaw slides along a bar or pipe. They are available in lengths of 1–12′, or you can buy the jaws alone and fit them on any length standard pipe.

e. Band clamp. A canvas or nylon strap with an adjustable metal buckle for holding large or odd-shaped pieces of up to 10′ in girth.

f. Woodworker's vise. A flat-faced clamping vise anchored permanently to the edge of a workbench with the top edge of the jaws flush with the workbench surface. Some are made entirely of wood; most are of metal with wood-covered jaws 6–12″ wide that open to about 12″. See ill. Also see **vise** and **Woodworking; Gluing and Clamping.**

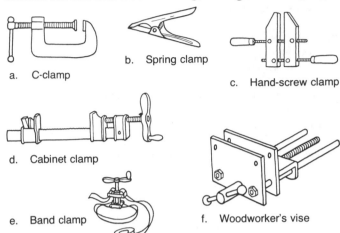

a.   C-clamp

b.   Spring clamp

c.   Hand-screw clamp

d.   Cabinet clamp

e.   Band clamp

f.   Woodworker's vise

clamp kiln. Ceramics. (Also called pit firing.) A firing technique similar to a bonfire. A pit is dug, lined with firewood, and a fire is lit. Fully air-dry **pot**s are placed on the coals and more fuel is added. The process takes about twenty-four hours. See ill.

Clamp kiln

clamp-on vise. Jewelry. A **vise**, either swivel or stationary, that can be clamped onto a solidly constructed worktable.

Clamshell. Quilts. A **pieced quilt** pattern of concave and convex curves that is exceedingly difficult to make, even for the skillful quilter. The clamshell pattern, rows of **scallop**s that touch, is more commonly used in **quilting.** Also see **Quilts: Quilting.**

clapper. Toys. See **rattletrap.**

clarify. Amber Carving. To make opaque amber clear by slowly bringing it to a boil in rapeseed oil and then cooling it slowly to prevent fractures. Opaque **amber** is often clarified to increase its value. Color may be added to the oil to dye the amber. The oil fills the cavities, allowing light to pass through the material unhindered (opacity is caused by small bubbles of air in fissures that obstruct the passage of light). Incorrectly executed, the clarifying process can produce fissures that resemble fish scales. Iridescent at first, they become increasingly more conspicuous until the cracks shine a bright gold, at which point they are called sun spangles. These can help differentiate between naturally clear and clarified amber. Large pieces of opaque amber may require repeated heatings to clarify it.

clasped weft. Weaving. (Also called locked weft.) A method of weaving that gives two distinct **filling** colors in a **shed** but does not interrupt the **selvage**-to-selvage passage of the filling. One color is carried by a **shuttle**; it enters the shed on the right and, after going through the shed, picks up a yarn that is on a **cone** or in ball form at the left side of the **loom.** The shuttle returns in the same shed, carrying with it the picked-up yarn, which is brought into the shed for the desired amount, then the shed is changed and the two yarns are clasped or looped together. Their meeting point can be moved from side to side in the shed with each **pick.** The same procedure is repeated in the next shed with the same colors or with different ones on one or both sides of the loom. Any **weave** can be used. The technique allows free patterning and its potentials are almost limitless. It can never approximate the detail found in **inlay** or **tapestry,** but within its scope it offers as much speed as ordinary weaving. See ill.

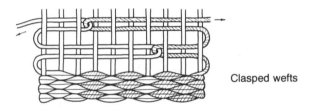

Clasped wefts

clasp knife. Woodworking. See **whittling tools.**

classification of lumber. Woodworking. See **wood.**

clatter blocks. Toys. See **Jacob's ladder.**

claw hammer. Woodworking. See **hammer.**

clay. Candlemaking. Clay or a **caulking compound** such as Mordite can be used to seal the hole at the bottom of a candle **mold** through which the **wick** is threaded. This step is taken to prevent leakage of hot molten wax during **casting.** Also see **Candlemaking: Molding.**

clay. Papercrafts. Modeling clay or plasticene, shaped into desired form, provides an excellent base on which to apply **papier mâché** by the **paper-strip method.** Details of the clay model should be large and exaggerated so that they will not be obliterated after the application of several layers of newspaper. The completed clay model is lightly coated with petroleum jelly before the paper is applied, so the dried papier-mâché form can be easily removed. The clay may be remodeled for another design. This technique is especially suitable for **relief** projects, such as making a **mask.** Also see **molding.**

clay. Puppet. Toys. **Puppet** and **marionette head**s may be modeled from clay and fired, then decorated either by glazing or painting. The primary concern in making these heads is that of weight; if the **puppet head** is too heavy, it will droop.

Many small **toys** for children are made from clay. These are often low-fired clay or **earthenware**. Large-scale toys, or sculptured clay animals on which children can climb and play, are usually high-fired and very durable. Large forms, because of their weight, are very stable and cannot be tipped or moved by children. Also see **all-bisque, burnt clay** and **Toys: Dolls.**

clay beads. Beadwork. See **ceramic beads** and **Beadmaking.**

clay body. Ceramics. A mixture of clays and other materials designed to meet the properties of **plasticity,** firing, **color** and **texture** in the making of an object.

If a clay is low in plasticity, ball clay and bentonite clay are added. If a clay is overly plastic with a tendency to be sticky and to not stand up, flint clay, **grog,** or fire clay may be added to open up the clay. This also promotes even drying, avoids cracking, and reduces shrinkage.

Fluxes, such as **iron oxide, frit,** and **talc,** are added to clay to lower the temperature at which a piece **matures** when fired. If a clay body contains too many fluxes, it must be mixed again; or fire clays which mature at a high temperature may be added.

clay doll. Toys. A **doll** made of fired **clay.** Clay dolls have been made since ancient times. Early Roman clay dolls had **joint**ed arms and legs. In the middle 1800s, clay dolls were unearthed in Nuremberg that were dressed in costumes of the fourteenth century, suggesting they were in common use as early as the 1300s.

While the **bisque,** porcelain, or **Parian** dolls of the nineteenth century are all actually made of clay, they are referred to by those specified designations—not as clay dolls. The clay dolls are usually unglazed (although they may be painted) and are usually low-fired or **earthenware doll**s. Some contemporary toy and dollmakers are again making clay dolls.

Clay's Choice. Quilts. See **Star of the West.**

clay tile. Mosaics. See **ceramic tile.**

cleaning. Amber Carving. See **Amber Carving: Finishing.**

cleaning. Metalworking. See **Metalworking: Finishing, Care and Maintenance.**

cleaning. Plastics. See **Plastics: Care, Cleaning and Maintenance.**

cleaning and care of lace. Lacemaking. See **Lacemaking: Cleaning and Care of Lace.**

cleaning crewel. Crewel. See **Crewel: Care and Maintenance.**

cleaning embroidery. Crewel. Embroidery. Needlepoint. See **Crewel: Care and Maintenance, Needlepoint: Care and Maintenance.**

cleaning fluid. Batik and Tie-dye. Any liquid **solvent** used to **dissolve wax** in the **batik** process. Wax may be removed from brushes or the finished fabric by dipping into a **vat** of white gasoline, carbon tetrachloride, kerosene, or other solvent or commercial cleaning fluid. Cleaning fluids do not damage the fabrics. This treatment removes the wax more thoroughly than does **ironing,** but special precautions must be taken when dealing with these flammable and sometimes toxic solutions. To avoid handling the hazardous cleaning fluids, the batik fabric can be run through a **dry cleaning** machine or taken to a dry cleaning establishment. Either method immerses the fabric for a thorough cleaning.

cleaning metal. Enameling. **Metal** surfaces must be cleaned before applying **enamel, binder, flux,** or **resist.**

As a preliminary step to burn off grease, wax, and oils, heat the metal with a **torch** or in the **kiln** to about 1400° F, or until it begins to glow red. While the metal is still hot, but after the color has faded, quench it in cold water. More thorough cleaning is achieved by bathing the metal in an acid pickle; use a solution of 1 part nitric acid to 3–8 parts water, always adding acid to water, never vice versa. Sulfuric acid in 10 parts water is also used. Because iron contaminates the pickle, causing copper to cover gold and silver, pickling is done in Pyrex bowls and copper or wooden tongs are used to manipulate the pieces. Copper turns pink, and silver turns white when they are pickled. Acid will dissolve silver solder and may cause enamels to lose their gloss or to discolor.

Action can be increased by heating the solution and stirring and brushing away the bubbles of hydrogen that form with a feather. The fumes produced are hazardous. The pickle turns blue when it is exhausted. Discard it carefully, flushing well with water to avoid damaging the drains. A commercial granular compound called Sparex #2 is used similarly to the acid pickle.

After pickling, alkalinize the metal with soapless detergent or saliva and rinse with water. A clean metal surface will allow a stream of water to flow across it without beading. Wipe the surface dry and avoid touching it with your fingers. Some enamelists keep cleaned pieces under water until needed to avoid further oxidation.

Metals are also cleaned with abrasives such as fine steel wool, emery, pumice, or salt and vinegar. A **glass brush** is often used for cleaning silver. Also see **bright dip, polishing.**

cleaning needlepoint. Needlepoint. See **Needlepoint: Care and Maintenance.**

cleanliness. Jewelry. One of the most important considerations in the successful making of jewelry is cleanliness.

Always use an absolutely clean **flux brush** and uncontaminated (clean) **flux,** and clean, greaseless metal. Remove as much **firescale** as possible after **pickling.** Clip solder on clean white paper. The ink on lined paper may dissolve and contaminate the solder, preventing it from flowing. Clean off solder prior to every use with **emery paper.** If time has passed since you have used the solder, it will have oxidized and it does not flow when dirty.

Work must be absolutely grease-free before oxidizing, coloring, or creating a **patina.** After using **steel wool** or **abrasive**s before **buffing,** rinse the work well with water to free it of particles that could contaminate the **buff.** Clean the work well after using **buffing compound**s; use sudsy household **ammonia.** Keep in mind that all tools should be kept clean and dry.

clear acetate. Stitchery. Puppets. Toys. See **acetate sheet.**

clear banding. China and Glass Painting. See **banding.**

clear pine. Woodworking. See **pine.**

clear plastic grid overlay. Crewel. Embroidery. Needlepoint. (Also called overlay.) A clear grid used to enlarge and reduce a design by the squaring method, or to work out a needlepoint design by counting the squares. Grids are available in small sheets printed in various mesh sizes, measured in squares per inch. To copy a design or photograph, lay the grid on it and, working on the same size **canvas** mesh as the grid, count out the stitches from the painted design onto the canvas. Also see **enlarging and reducing a design.**

clear select. Toys. A grade applied to lumber to indicate wood of the best grade; this is free from knots, defects, knotholes, or dark lines and streaks in the wood. Pine can usually be purchased in this grade for toymaking.

clearstory (clerestory) window. Stained glass. A window placed high up on the wall of a structure that acts as a lighting source. Traditionally, it was a window above the lower portions of the church roof that cast light into the nave, or the central part of the building. The first church of St. Peter, built by Constantine in 326, used clearstory windows, which in time became transformed into the stained-glass church windows known today.

cleavage. Gemcutting. A property of some **crystalline** gem materials to separate along plane surfaces in one or more directions parallel to their crystal faces. This property is used to cut these stones to approximate size and shape.

Cleavage planes are avoided as surfaces (**facets**) in the finished gem because they are difficult to polish and material often sloughs off.

To cut a stone along its cleavage plane, scratch a notch in the correct place, place a steel knife or chisel in the notch, and strike the knife with a hammer.

Gems which do not possess cleavage are said to **fracture** when broken. Also see **C axis** and **Gemcutting: Orientation.**

cleave. Basketry. (Also called shave.) A tool used in **willow** work for cutting or splitting the dry willow **rod**s into **skein**s. See ill. Also see **Basketry: Tools and Materials.**

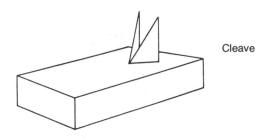

Cleave

cleaving. Metalworking. See **blacksmithing techniques.**

cleek. Toys. A device used to roll the **hoop** in a variation of **hoop roll.** It is sometimes called a gird because it links or girds the stick or **skimmer** to the hoop with a ring bent into the end of the stick.

Cleveland Lilies. Quilts. A **quilt block** design that depicts three lilies on a stem, set diagonally on a **square.** It is usually sewn in a combination of **piecing** and **appliqué.** The design was named for President Cleveland. See ill. Also see **presidents' quilt.**

Cleveland Lilies

Cleveland Tulip. Quilts. See **Tulip.**

click reel. Spinning. See **reel.**

climbing bear. Toys. An **American folk toy** that consists of a flat wood cutout of a bear that climbs up two cords. The bear is sawed out from ½" wood and a hole is drilled from the outside edge of each hand to the inside edge, pointing up at a 45° angle. Cords are run from a bar at the top, down through the hand holes, and down to **wood**

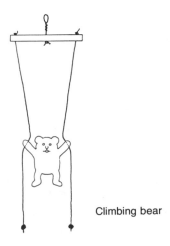

Climbing bear

beads attached at the ends of the cords. When the bar is hung and the cords are pulled alternately, the bear climbs up the cords. When both cords are relaxed, the bear slides back down. See ill.

climbing kiln. Ceramics. Wood burning **kilns** built on a slope with more than one connected chamber. Heat is drawn from one chamber to the next, which is further fed with fuel. The second chamber can be used for **bisque** firing since it will have a lower temperature, or, fuel can be added to provide an additional **glaze** chamber. Also see **bank kiln, chambered kiln.**

Climbing Rose. Quilts. See **Kansas Troubles.**

clinching. Woodworking. See **nailing** and **Woodworking: Nailing.**

clip blade. Woodworking. See **whittling tools.**

clippers. Metalworking. A hand cutting tool used to cut wire or rod. Cut wire or rod is sometimes used in **blacksmithing** to make large **bolts** and **nails.** Insert the metal between the two pincerlike jaws and press the handles together to cut. See ill.

Clipper

clippers. Mosaics. (Also called cutting tool, nippers.) Tool specifically designed for cutting or, more accurately, fracturing mosaic **tile** or **tesserae** into smaller chips. The best clippers are the spring type, with toggle joint and carbide-tipped cutting edges. Most craft shops or tile shops carry a wide range of tile-cutting clippers. Also see **Mosaics: Tools and Materials, Cutting the Material.**

clipping. Jewelry. The cutting of wire or round, flat, square, or thin sheet metal into lengths with clipping **pliers.**

clock reel. Spinning. See **reel.**

clockwork. Toys. Having the machinery of a clock, containing geared wheels of small size and springs. **Clockwork toys** or dolls are usually operated by a key or other winding device that puts tension on a spring, which is then gradually released to activate the toy. Also see **automatic toys, autoperipatetikos.**

clockwise toy. Toys. (Also called key windup toy.) Any **toy** operated by **clockwork.** In most, the clockwork device propels the toy in some way by turning wheels, paddles, or propellers. In some, the mechanism animates some part of the toy. Clockwork dolls, which became popular in the 1860s, are usually wound with a key. Also see **automatic toys, autoperipatetikos.**

cloison. Enameling. A fine metal wire shaped for use in cloisonné technique. Cloisons may be soldered in place with hard solder or adhered to a fired coat of **flux** enamel. A **metal foil** background is often used to add brilliance. Rectanglar wires in sizes from 20–30 gauge (.30–.010″) by 18 gauge (about 1 mm) are available, or cloisons may be sawed out of sheets of metal. The wires are stood on their narrow edges touching one another, each slightly bent to allow it to stand. Round cloisons made of wires as fine as 34 (.006″) are also used. These will stand by themselves, but stoning should be kept to the same level to maintain a uniform-width cloison. Round wire may be drawn through a die into a rectangular shape.

A flux or other background enamel is fired first. Then the wire cloisons are set in place with **binder** and fired until they sink firmly into the base. Because **firing** on fine gold or silver requires no flux, cloisons on such pieces may be wet-inlaid with the first coat of enamel and fired simultaneously.

Copper mesh or screening used for cloisonné requires cleaning between firing to remove firescale. Silver cloisons may melt or blacken if they are overfired. Also see **overfiring, wet inlay** and **Enameling: Tools and Materials.**

cloisonné. Bookbinding. A type of enamel inlay work, sometimes used for decoration.

cloisonné. Enameling. A technique in which small metal wires called **cloisons** are fused into the enameled surface to accent the design and separate the colors. The cells formed between the wires are filled with enamel, using the **wet inlay** technique, and fired, often several times. The enamel may be built up until it is slightly above the height of the wires, then stoned to a smooth surface, or the cloisons may be ground down to the enamel. The exposed wires may be polished, electroplated, mercury gilded, or darkened with **liver of sulfur.** Also see **electroplating, mercury gilding, plique-à-jour, polishing, stoning,** and **enameling.**

close. Tatting. (abbr. cl) See **ring.**

closed kiln. Stained Glass. See **kiln.**

closed satin stitch. Stitchery. See **machine satin stitch.**

closed setting. Jewelry. See **bezel.**

closed silhouette. Papercrafts. See **silhouette.**

closed zigzag stitch. Stitchery. See **machine satin stitch.**

close grain. Woodworking. See **wood.**

close herringbone stitch. Crewel. Embroidery. Needlepoint. (Also called plaited stitch.) A variation of the **herringbone stitch,** worked very close together. This stitch is smoothest if kept slanting. Space the stitches a little apart when the needle goes down, and keep them close together (almost touching) when the needle comes up on the edge. This will help maintain the slant, and make a sharp V in the center. It can be worked to form a band or a leaf shape, and can be effectively worked on **canvas.** See ill., next page.

a. Working the stitch   b. Finished effect   c. Leaf shape

close rand. Basketry. Tight **randing**, which is obtained by tightly compressing the rows of randing with a **rapping iron.**

cloth. Bookbinding. Cloths made specifically for bookbinding are available in both woven and compressed fiber materials in a range of texture, color, and quality. Whether cloth is used for decorating the **board**s or for reinforcing the **joint**s and **back,** it is essential that it be of good quality or it will stretch out of shape when dampened with **paste** or be stained by penetrating water. It is best to consult your binder's supply house to find what is best suited for your project.

Buckram is available in both cotton and linen varieties, the latter being by far superior in quality. It is sturdy and recommended for large, heavy books or books that receive constant handling, such as school and library books. Lacqroid is a cotton and plastic blend that simulates leather. It is durable, waterproof, and resistant to dirt and grime. It can be tooled, printed, or silk-screened. **Linmaster** is versatile, high-quality, comparatively inexpensive, hard-wearing nonwoven material. It comes in solid, wear-proof colors. Muslin is a gauzelike fabric used for reinforcing book joints and backs. Also see **cutting cloth, super.**

cloth. Stitchery. See **fabric.**

cloth. Weaving. A word originating from Greek mythology; Clotho was one of the Three Fates weaving one **web** of human destiny. Cloth is synonymous with **fabric;** the word was once used mainly in connection with products of weaving. Now includes knitting, crocheting, knotting, **plaiting, braiding, felting,** or any means of interlocking yarns and fibers to produce a finished textile.

cloth analysis. Weaving. See **fabric analysis.**

cloth beam. Weaving. The rotating **beam** in the front of the loom on which the woven cloth is wound and stored. In old looms it often took the place of the **breast beam** and was located almost parallel to the **reed.** In some primitive looms the cloth beam is a cloth roller that is a separate piece from the loom structure. In most contemporary handlooms the cloth beam is underneath the breast beam and is either round, hexagonal, or octagonal. At the right end there is a handle for turning the beam and a **rachet** and **pawl** to hold it in place. An **apron** is attached to the cloth beam and the unwoven warp is tied to the **front apron bar,** which acts as the pulling mechanism when the woven cloth is ready to be wound. Also see **harness loom, jack-type loom, table loom.**

cloth beam rod. Weaving. An alternate term for the front **apron bar.** Also see **apron.**

cloth body. Toys. A soft **doll body** of fabric stiffened with **batting, sawdust, wood wool,** or rags. Cloth bodies have always been popular because they are easily made, can be cuddled and comfortably held, and are durable.

Cloth bodies were traditionally used with heads of various materials, and sometimes with half-limbs of **composition** or wood. They were both hand-sewn and commercially manufactured. **Stockinet** and woven fabrics were used to make the cloth bodies.

cloth cutting machine. Rugmaking. See **strip cutter.**

cloth doll. Toys. See **fabric doll.**

clothespin. Basketry. A useful tool to secure or hold loose ends while weaving **border**s, wrapping **handles,** etc. Also see **Basketry: Tools and Materials.**

clothespin doll. Toys. Any **doll** that uses the old-fashioned round-top clothespin as its base. The shape of the clothespin suggests a head, neck, body, and two legs.

The dolls can be painted directly with acrylic, enamel, or watercolor; **marking pen**s work well, and even a fountain pen or a pencil can adequately suggest the features.

If the bottom or split end of the clothespin is sawed off even, it will stand up, or, that end can be **glue**d to a block of wood or a checker to provide a base. Arms can be added by drilling a hole through the clothespin, then inserting a cut section of **dowel.**

Clothing the dolls is simple; fabrics can be tied or glued to the wood, or stitched in place. When fabric is used, arms may be added with cloth or cord. Hair can be of yarn, floss, or **batting** can be glued to the wood, or it can simply be painted.

The clothespin figure will readily sit astride a horse cut from thin wood. Or, if the legs are exposed, as with the painted figure, they can sit astride a wire or line. Clothespins can be sawed off at various lengths to suggest babies or children to accompany the long-legged adults.

clothespin wrestlers. Toys. A simple **toy** made from two clothespins and a rubber band. Two old-fashioned round-top clothespins are used, although any pieces of wood about the size of a piece of chalk will do. Faces may be drawn on for added realism in suggesting figures, although that is not essential to the function of the toy. A rubber band is slipped around one clothespin, tied by means of a slip knot (**a.**), and the second pin is then slipped into the remaining loop (**b.**). If there is too much slack to just hold the pins loosely together, a smaller rubber band is needed. The two figures are then twisted in opposite directions until the rubber band is tight and kinked. When set loose on a smooth hard surface, the wrestlers will flail and thrash in a wrestling match until they lie unwound and exhausted. It is a toy that children find greatly amusing since they can make, operate, or repair it with relative ease and no expense.

The **dancers,** sometimes called clothespin wrestlers, is another toy made from the wood clothespin. See ill. Also see **animated toy.**

a.   Clothespin wrestlers   b.

cloth glass fiber. Plastic. See **glass fiber.**

clothing construction. Stitchery. The methods by which **garment**s are usually made. There are standard construction procedures for cutting, sewing, **press**ing, and joining particular parts. Construction directions accompany most clothes patterns. In the making of body coverings, many of the usual construction methods are bypassed for simple designs, such as **caftan**s, **poncho**s, and other ethnic clothes.

cloth-jointed endpaper. Bookbinding. An **endpaper** that is attached to a strip of cloth and sewn into the book instead of being tipped in. This form of endpaper is used with **bound book**s and with **split board**s. It provides a waste leaf, a paste-down leaf, a colored, lined fly leaf, and a white fly leaf. To execute cloth-jointed endpapers apply **glue** to a strip of good-quality book cloth the length of the book and one inch wide. Attach a folded piece of medium-grade white book paper the size of the text to the strip of book cloth, covering two-thirds of the width of the strip. Attach a second folded sheet of the same paper to the remaining section of the glued strip, leaving a gap $^1/_{16}''$ between the back folds of the two attached papers. Next, cut two sheets of colored or decorative paper so that they overlap the cloth by ⅛", glue over the entire surface of their backs, and position them over the white paper and the remaining exposed strip of book cloth. **Nip** in the press; remove and allow them to dry thoroughly under weights. This will produce the endpaper for only one side of the book; the process is repeated for the second endpaper. When attaching the endpaper to the text, position the two-thirds width of the book cloth away from the body of the book. Also see **fly leaves, tipping.**

cloth marionette. Puppets. A simple **string puppet** like a doll made of **stuffed fabric.** Dolls may be strung to become **marionette**s themselves. These may not be **manipulate**d with the same refinement as a specially designed marionette, but they are an excellent way of learning the **control**s. Also see **stuffed marionette** and **Puppets: Making the Marionette Skeleton.**

cloth stick. Weaving. Another name for the front **apron bar.**

cloth stitch. Lacemaking. (Also called linen stitch.) A stitch in **bobbin lace** made with two pairs of **bobbin**s. To make this stitch, **cross, twist,** and then cross the bobbins (abbr. C.T.C.). Some lacers call the cloth stitch the **whole stitch;** however, the latter is worked differently.

When working an area in cloth stitch, a pair of bobbins advances horizontally; this pair is called the worker pair or the **worker**s.

cloud filling stitch. Crewel. Embroidery. A two-art stitch done in two colors with a blunt needle. First lay down rows of evenly spaced straight **tacking stitch**es with a double thread in **brick stitch** fashion. With a single thread of a contrasting color and a blunt needle, interlace the thread through a tack stitch on the top row, then drop down through the stitch below, and return through the next stitch above. Continue in this manner from right to left. This is a very attractive **open filling stitch;** it should always be worked on an **embroidery frame.** See ill.

Cloud filling stitch

                 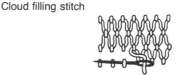

a.   Tacking stitches   b.   Interlaced tacking stitches

cloudiness. Enameling. See **Enameling: Repair and Care.**

cloudiness. Plastics. (Also called blushing.) In the case of incompletely **cured resin,** cloudiness is the result of moisture in the **mold.** Fully cured plastic will cloud if exposed to excessively chlorinated water. To prevent clouding, keep molds and tools dry and dust-free; wet sand only after the plastic is fully cured, using distilled water from a plastic water jug.

clove hitch. Macramé. See **double half stitch.**

clump tying. Batik and Tie-dye. A method of tying in which fabrics are bunched together. Sometimes objects are placed on the fabric (pebbles, marbles, seeds, pieces of wood, grains, etc.), and the material is bunched and **tied** around them, as in **bundle tie-dye.** Then several of these tied pieces are bound together by further tying, clumping them together with additional **binding.** If an entire piece of fabric is to be treated in this way, the inside areas should be tied first. This method is an excellent one when only one **dyebath** is used as it gives a complex pattern. Using **dyed binding thread** adds to the color and design without requiring an additional dyebath.

clung. Basketry. Partially dried **hedgerow** woods and other **stuff** that is ready for use.

cluster. Crochet. A group of two or more stitches worked either into one common stitch or into several consecutive stitches to create a raised, bumpy pattern. The cluster is usually worked between rows of **double crochet.** The cluster is one of the most popular crochet motifs and is often found in patterns for crocheted sweaters, caps, and mufflers.

Cluster patterns vary, but a cluster made of 3 double crochets would be worked like this: dc, holding the last 2 loops of the **stitch** on the hook; **yarn over,** dc, pulling the thread through the first 2 loops and retaining the last 2 on the hook; yo, dc, bringing the yarn through the first 2 loops; yo and bring it through all the loops to form a cluster. Also see **bullion stitch bar, Crochet: Basic Stitches.**

cluster. Macramé. See **overhand knot.**

clustering. Knitting. The highly decorative cluster pattern is formed when three or more stitches are knit onto a separate needle, and either the working yarn or a separate color is wrapped around these held stitches several times before transferring them onto the right-hand needle and then continuing the pattern. See ill. Also see **embossed knitting.**

Clustering

cluster stitch. Crochet. See **Crochet: Basic Stitches.**

coal. Ceramics. See **kiln fuel.**

coal crystals. Toys. See **crystal garden.**

coal-tar dye. Batik and Tie-dye. Any of a variety of synthetic or **aniline dye**s derived from a distillation of coal containing coal tar.

coarse grain. Woodworking. See **wood.**

coarse weave linen. Crewel. Embroidery. A **linen fabric** woven of relatively heavy threads and suitable as a **background fabric** when using medium-weight yarns such as **Persian yarn, tapestry yarn,** and **worsted yarns.** Also see **linen fabric.**

cobalt blue. Stained Glass. See **antique glass colorant.**

cobalt oxide. Ceramics. A **pigment oxide** used to produce blue. **Frit** with lead or **alumina** and lime to produce low fire **underglaze** colors. The frit permits a lighter and more even color dispersion.

cobalt oxide. Stained Glass. See **antique glass colorant.**

cobra skin. Leather. Full cobra skins (around 6′ – 10′ long and in a wide range of colors) are available already laminated to a cloth backing for easy handling and durability. Also see **snakeskin.**

cochineal. Batik and Tie-dye. A red-violet **dye** obtained from the ground dried bodies of the female cochineal insect. It is a **natural dye** that has been used for hundreds of years.

cochineal. Dyeing. An ancient scarlet-red dye used in the Americas and unusual in that it is made from a cochineal, a female insect that lives on a cactus, indigenous to Mexico and Central America. In the Near East, a similar red dye is made from an insect that lives on a Mediterranean oak tree and is the same species of shield louse as the cochineal. The insects, called kermes, are dried and powdered for use as a dyestuff. Cochineal works best with **mordants,** whereas kermes needs no mordant at all. Alum, with cochineal, gives rosy to pink colors; chrome gives a warm pink to purplish-red; iron, a purple; copper, a claret; and tin, a very strong scarlet. The early Mexicans used this red for textiles not to be exposed to constant, bright sunlight, because the color is not extremely fast. On the other hand, the kermes dye is a very fast color, as can be seen from the fresh reds in the Coptic textiles of the fourth and fifth centuries A.D. Both cochineal and kermes are excellent for use with silk and wool. In medieval days, kermes was also used for cotton, leather, and as a nonpoisonous food color. Kermes was much sought after in Europe until America was discovered, and then cochineal replaced kermes as the principal source of red.

cock horse. Toys. A **push horse** that stands erect on four legs. Cock horses were sometimes made with the heads of other animals.

cockle. Bookbinding. The puckering that occurs when leaves, **boards, tapes,** or other bookbinding materials are moistened with **adhesives.** Paper folded along the grain will shrink back to its original size when dry, whereas paper folded **against the grain** will stretch considerably more and will not flatten when dry. Also see **leaf.**

cocklebur butterfly. Toys. An **American folk toy** or object that uses a cocklebur to suggest the body and tissue paper decorated with paints or inks for the wings.

cocoa butter. Metalworking. See **wax.**

cocobolo. Woodworking. A heavy, hard, oily Central American wood. It is difficult to glue and is commonly used for small **wood turnings** and **woodcarvings.** It ranges in color from reddish-orange to black.

cocottes. Toys. See **paper folding.**

coefficient of expansion. Ceramics. The ratio of change between the length of a material mass and the temperature. Also see **thermal shock.**

coefficient of linear expansion. Metalworking. Plastics. (Also called coefficient of thermal expansion.) The amount material expands when heated. When planning outdoor constructions of solid sheets of metal or plastic, allow for flexible fastening with screws and bolts by a slight space between the edges to provide for expansion and contraction. The manufacturer's specifications include this expansion rate.

coefficient of thermal expansion. Metalworking. Plastics. See **coefficient of linear expansion.**

coffee. Quilts. Stitchery. A common household item which may be used to color, stain, or dye old laces or **fabric.** Any piece which needs to be antiqued or aged to match other old fabrics can be dipped in a pan of water to which a cup of brewed coffee has been added. Repeated dippings will continue to darken the fabric. Coffee adds a warm yellowish cast to the material and will always appear darker while it is still wet. **Tea** can also be used as a stain.

cogging. Metalworking. See **blacksmithing techniques.**

coil. Basketry. The process of turning an **active element** or material back upon itself in a spiral motion; it may also be used to refer to one **round** or row of a series of coiled rows.

coil basketry. Basketry. One of the three types of basket-weaving structures. It consists of a **foundation** material or structural element **coil**ed in successive rows and a **binding** element that keeps the rows together. There are a number of different types of coiled baskets, all of which depend on variations in the type and number of foundation material employed, and the type of stitching used to bind the coils together. Also see **Basketry: Coil Basket Construction.**

coil building. Ceramics. See **Ceramics: Hand-building.**

coiled asbestos. Jewelry. **Asbestos** that has been made into a long continuous strip and wound into a coil. It is placed in a tin pan and used to hold work in position during **soldering. Pins** can be easily inserted into the coiled surface. Pieces of the strip can also be torn off as needed to deflect **flame** and heat when soldering work that has a delicate area that needs to be protected. The strip is very thin and can be folded over numerous times to provide the desired thickness. However, as the asbestos is torn off, the coil begins to unwind and can no longer be used to support work.

coiled pot. Ceramics. An object made by **coil building.**

coiled wire end. Beadwork. A finishing technique for wire ends of flower stamens in **bead flowermaking** in which the **wire** is wrapped around needlenose pliers or a darning needle, pushing the coils close together. The coiled wire is removed from the pliers and cut away at the tip end. See ill.

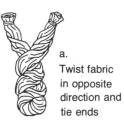

Coiled wire end

coiling. Ceramics. An age-old method of making **pot**s by laying clay ropes one upon another and working them together. Also see **Ceramics: Hand-building.**

coiling and twisting. Batik and Tie-dye. A method of preparing **fabric** for **tie-dye** by twisting lengths of material into a tight coil. A length of material is folded with **selvage**s together and then **gather**ed and **tied** at each end. The length must then be twisted—either by two people, or by securing one end to a stable object so that one person can twist the opposite end (**a.**). The length is then twisted so tightly that it begins to coil back on itself (**b.**). The raw ends are placed together and the double coils are bound (**c.**). The entire bound piece is dyed, rinsed, dried, and untied. This process may be repeated for additional colors. See ill.

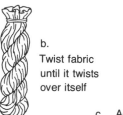

a.
Twist fabric
in opposite
direction and
tie ends

b.
Twist fabric
until it twists
over itself

c. Add binding

coil stitch. Crewel. Embroidery. See **bullion knot.**

coin silver. Jewelry. In the United States, a silver **alloy** that is 900 parts **silver** and 100 parts **copper.** In the Far East, coin silver may be as low as or lower than 800 parts silver.

coke. Ceramics. See **kiln fuel.**

cold chisel. Metalworking. See **blacksmithing tools, chisel.**

cold-cure silicone rubber. Plastics. See **silicone plastic.**

cold dyeing. Batik and Tie-dye. A process of coloring or dyeing fabrics in temperatures not over about 100° F. Also see **cold-water dye, direct dye, oil resist.**

cold flow. Glasswork. The slight tendency of glass to deform and run at room temperatures. For theoretical purposes, glass is best considered to be liquid at all temperatures. As its temperature is increased, the viscosity of glass becomes lower. Even though glass is harder than many metals at room temperature, it does flow under the influence of gravity. However, a measurable flow could take billions of years.

cold flow. Plastics. See **distortion.**

cold forging. Jewelry. A method of **forming nonferrous metals** without heating them (except for **annealing** purposes) by hammering them with **forging hammers.** Also see **forging.**

cold forming. Plastics. A method of temporarily bending or curving plastic at room temperature by springing the sheet into a **jig.** The sheet will regain its original shape after release. Sharp bending may cause **crazing.** Cold forming cannot be used with all plastics. Also see **thermoforming.**

cold-metal casting. Plastics. See **resin-metal casting.**

cold-metal spinning. Metalworking. See **metal spinning.**

cold-metal work. Metalworking. See **bench work.**

cold resin resist. Batik and Tie-dye. A relatively new **resist agent** for batiking. It is used with **dyes** requiring **hot dyeing.** The clear resins are applied in a liquid form by brush or from squeeze bottles. The fabric should be left on absorbent paper until the resin resist is dry. It can then be immersed in a hot **dyebath** (at least 125° F). The heat solidifies the resin and turns it white. It can be simmered or heated further. The resin remains flexible so that it does not have the **crackle** pattern characteristic of most batik.

When the dyeing process is finished and residual dye has been rinsed out the resin can be removed with cold water. Also see **Batik and Tie-dye: Batik.**

cold rolled. Metalworking. See **metal.**

cold set. Metalworking. See **blacksmithing tools.**

cold-water detergent. Crewel. Embroidery. Needlepoint. A soap especially designed to dissolve in cold water and used to wash wool without shrinking or matting. Cold-water detergents often contain bleach, so it is a good idea to test a corner of the fabric in the solution first.

cold-water dye. Batik and Tie-dye. Any **dye** used for **batik** that does not require heat during the dye process. High-temperature dyes cannot be used because the resist areas of **wax** would melt. The only dyes made specifically for **cold dyeing** are the **fiber-reactive dye**s, and it is recommended that they be used in a 100° F **dyebath.** Their **lightfast**ness and **washfast**ness are excellent and the colors are brilliant. Other dyes may be used with less permanent results.

Cold-water "reactive" dye is the most satisfactory **dye** for the beginner in batik or **tie-dye.** It is **colorfast** and safe. Some can be applied in cold water, but others require dry heat or steam to **set** them. They do not all work simply with cold water as the name suggests. Also see **oil resist** and **Batik and Tie-dye: Dyes.**

cold-water dye. Dyeing. Dye that needs no heating to impart color to fiber. Also see **procion dye.**

collage. A usually abstract two-dimensional composition in which the artist assembles bits of various types of fabric and paper by gluing them to a surface. The "real" materials are often combined with lines or forms of the artist's devising in paint, crayon, pencil, etc.

collage. Crewel. Embroidery. Needlepoint. A mixed media design made by combining different types of needlework, or by combining needlework with other crafts.

collage. Papercrafts. A technique of adhering paper, fabric, and other materials to a background **support,** generally paper or cardboard. The art of collage began around 1912 when Braque and Picasso produced pictures containing incongruous materials such as newspaper, string, and sand with paint and charcoal in what seemed a revolutionary technique; indeed, this inclusion of unconventional materials in paintings began as a revolt against the academic painting traditions of the time. Later, around 1916, collage was also used by the Dada movement for revolutionary, antirational paintings in mockery of established culture. Collage was further developed by Kurt Schwitters, who combined bits of paper, newspaper, tickets, and other scraps in compositions.

Collage has since become widely used by artists as a means by which reality can be incorporated in a picture by the inclusion of mementos of daily life. Fabric, paper, or almost any material is glued to the picture, integrated into the composition, and often combined with paint or other media. **Tissue paper** is sometimes used for its transparent effect in collages.

collar. Ceramics. See **Ceramics: Form.**

collaring. Ceramics. (Also called necking.) A method to close in the neck of a **pot** on the **potter's wheel** while throwing. This tends to reduce the diameter, thicken the walls, and increase the height of the form. See ill. Also see **Ceramics: Throwing.**

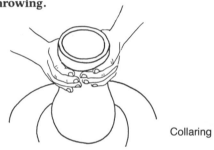

Collaring

collate. Bookbinding. (Also called gather.) To put into the correct order all the various elements that constitute the book, such as **sections**, plates, and leaves, and to verify that composition. **Back marks** and **signatures** are specific aids to collating.

collecting knot. Macramé. See **gathering knot.**

collet. Jewelry. The part of a **hand drill** or an electric drill such as a **flexible shaft machine** that opens or closes to fit the shanks of different-size bits, **burrs**, and other drill accessories. See ill. Also see **chuck.**

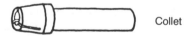

Collet

collet hammer. Metalworking. See **hammer.**

colonial lead came. Stained Glass. See **lead came.**

colonial overshot. Weaving. A name given to a type of Early American pattern weaving. These patterns were woven, or developed, from the beginning of the seventeenth century to the beginning of the nineteenth century, when power-loom weaving was introduced. They were usually woven for coverlets on **four-harness sinking shed loom**s. Most of the patterns are highly ornate and consist of **twill**

float combinations held together by a **plain weave ground.** Some of these patterns were woven as brought from England, some were modified in America, and some invented in America. They have interesting names based on their design construction—for example, "Star and Wheel," "Blooming Leaf," and "Bow-Knot." Although colonial overshot patterns have become classical and well established in American weaving right up to the present time, the overshot principle of patterning is not exclusive to colonial America. It appears all over the Western world under local or national names. Also see **overshot.**

Colonial Tulip. Quilts. See **Tulip.**

colophon. Bookbinding. An inscription at the end of a book or manuscript that gives the title and details of the book's production, such as place and time of printing, author's, illustrator's, and designer's names', names of typefaces, and kinds of paper and binding employed. Most of this kind of information, if it appears at all now, is included on the title page at the beginning of the book. Colophon has also come to mean the identifying symbol or trademark of a publisher, or less often, artist.

color. Ceramics. The range of color is very wide and generally adheres to the natural color of rocks and earth; pure white, buff, tans, orange-reds, reds to browns and blacks. Iron **oxide** is the most common colorant and generally gives a warm tone. Color is highly dependent upon the temperature of firing and the method of firing. A single clay will fire any number of colors depending upon how it is fired. **Reduction** firing, for example, tends to fire cool tones.

Red iron oxide burns red or brown color. Black iron oxide burns gray color. Iron oxide and manganese dioxide burn gray-brown color with specks. Iron, manganese, copper, and cobalt burn black color. Cobalt blue oxide burns blue color. Copper and chrome burn green color. Antimony, uranium, **vanadium,** iron, and chrome burn yellow. Also see **pigment oxide.**

color. Enameling. See **metal oxide.**

color. Gemcutting. A primary feature of all gems is their color. Idiochromatic stones have a color essential to their composition; color is a fixed and invariable characteristic of the material. **Azurite, malachite,** and **hematite** are examples.

Allochromatic stones are colored due to **inclusion**s of pigment or trace elements. Hue, degree, and dispersion of color vary within the same mineral species.

Ordinarily, compounds of aluminum, barium, potassium, sodium, and lithium are colorless; minerals composed of these chemicals in pure form are clear and transparent. Elements that are colored in mineral form appear in clear materials either as pigments (in bands, patches, or zones) or as trace constituents of the material. Large inclusions of pigments often create attractive markings, as in banded, moss, and dendritic agates. Sometimes inclusions of **rutile** in **quartz** take needle and hairlike forms. Chromium imparts the blue-green color in **beryl** (emerald)

and the red in **corundum** (ruby). Copper colors green in **malachite** and blue in **turquoise.** Iron produces yellows, greens, browns, reds, and black in citrine quartz, **epidote, axinite, almandine,** and hematite respectively; iron also combines with titanium to color **spinel** purple. Manganese is responsible for the pink color in **rhodochrosite** and **rhodonite.** Nickel imparts a yellow-green that is warmer than the green rendered by chromium. Sulfur imparts a blue color to sodalite and **lazurite.** Titanium produces blue in corundum (sapphire). Cobalt imparts red and blue colors.

Some gems exhibit different colors in different light. For example, alexandrite, a variety of spinel, appears green in daylight and red in candlelight. Actual changes in color of some stones is caused by heating and dyeing.

Dichroism and pleochroism are properties of gems showing two and more different colors when viewed in different directions. For example, cordierite appears dark-blue, light blue, and yellow-gray when viewed from three positions perpendicular to each other. All dichroic materials are anisotropic; determinations made with a **dichroscope** are an aid in gem identification.

Transparent gems are cut with the deepest color at the bottom for best effect; if possible the colorless and pale portions are removed.

The color of set stones can be altered by using colored metal foil as backing; use purple foil to remove the pale yellow in a transparent stone. Also see **luster.**

colorant. Batik and Tie-dye. The coloring matter added to **dye** or paint to impart hue. Colorants may be derived from natural sources or they may be synthetic. The colorant in pigment is nonsoluble and is mixed with a vehicle such as oil, water, or synthetic material to make paint. It coats the area to which it is applied. Dyes are soluble colorants that allow the coloring agent to combine permanently with **fibers.** Colorants are derived from a variety of sources. Following are some of those sources along with a single example of a colorant extracted from it: **aniline (coal tar dye**s), **dyewood**s (fustic), plants (**madder**), insects (**cochineal**), ores (ocher), and minerals (zinc white).

colorant. Plastics. Colorants come in dry colors, pellets, pastes, and liquids which are usually added to the **resin** before **catalyzing** it. Colorants are dyes, pigments, or metal fillers. In both dyes and pigments, different colors have varying endurance to weathering.

Dyes are generally transparent and have high color saturation, but may also be unstable and deteriorate under sunlight and heat. Neozapon is a brand name of metalized organic dyes which are relatively stable when used in **polyester, epoxy,** and **urethane** resins.

Pigments are usually opaque and come in organic and inorganic bases. Inorganic pigments are more permanent for outdoor use. Opaque inorganic pigments also act as antioxidants by helping to screen out ultraviolet sun rays.

Special-effects colorants contain metal flakes, usually aluminum or copper; pearlescent ones contain lead and bismuth. Metal-flake pigments can shorten the **shelf-life** of polyester resin. Zinc, tin, and lead compounds interfere with curing of **silicone plastics.** Metallic colorant containing free copper, zinc, manganese, and magnesium should not be used with **polyvinylchloride** plastic.

Fluorescent colorants lose their fluorescence with time.

Plastics may also be painted with a wide variety of products. Also see **Plastics: Casting, Coloring.**

color blending. Rugmaking. Weaving. The mixture of many colors of yarn to form a one-color effect so that the color is made richer, more alive, and more interesting. For example, if a blue is the desired color, then a number of blues of almost the same **hue** or adjacent hues are used, and a new blue color is the result. The color **value** of the yarn used must be the same; i.e., all light hues, medium hues, or dark hues. Mixing lights and darks gives a tweedy or flecked effect. Color blending can also be done using various closely related **shade**s, **tone**s, or **tint**s of one color. Often a color that does not work well by itself can be enhanced through blending. Pointillism, the art of painting with small, differently colored dots that merge into one color, is an example of color blending done with paint on canvas. Seurat and Signac were its great masters. In the study of color theory this is known as the Bezold Effect after Wilhelm von Bezold (1837–1907), who, in his rug designs, recognized this illusion of a new color forming through the mixture of many colors.

Color blending can be used in all **flat** and **pile rugs,** in **tapestry** weaving, and in fabric weaving. In **flatweave rug**s, **shuttle**s can be wound holding a mixture of different colors. In **embroidered rugs,** the needle would carry the mixture. Pile rugs, whether they are hooked, woven, needleworked, or latch hooked, all lend themselves to blending. The yarn can be in long strands for continuous **knot**s or **precut** for individual knots. In making individual knots, color can be blended differently for each knot. This is how the lush coloring of the Scandinavian **rya** rugs is achieved. In tapestry, blending can be achieved through **hatching, alternating pick**s, or combining two or more color strands in a **shed.** In fabric weaving, a **warp** can be a mixture of all different colors to obtain a one-color look. It can also be planned as a mixed **stripe** of different colors, with mixtures going on in each stripe so that, for example, in a red and green striped warp each color would be a blend of many reds or many greens. With the use of textured yarns, the colors assume even more diversity, and surface interest is added to the cloth. Also see **mixed warp, rug design.**

color bud. Candlemaking. See **coloring.**

color chart. Crewel. Embroidery. Needlepoint. See **chart.**

color clash. A combination of colors that appear to repel each other. For example, a purple and a green, both secondary colors that share a common **primary color** (blue), are seen as distinct from each other. Including the shared primary color with green and purple in a composition, weave, or whatever, can be harmonious. However, in the absence of the primary blue, and if the green is nearer to a chartreuse shade (closer to yellow than to blue) and the purple is blue-violet (closer to blue), then the blue-violet and the chartreuse can be said to clash, often even in the presence of the shared primary color.

The operating principle is that while the common primary color, blue, exists in both colors, in chartreuse the blue is secondary to yellow, whereas in the blue-violet the primary blue is dominant. Similarly a reddish-yellow and a yellowish-blue would clash.

Clash is not necessarily bad. In certain kinds of compositions the strong mutual repulsion of colors that clash can be used for dramatic effects. Usually the inclusion of the shared primary color in the same design tends to quiet the violence of color clashes since the eye perceives the structural relationship of the shared primary to the other colors. Also color clashes are rendered less repellant if both colors have been weakened by adding gray to them. Also see **color, color harmony, complementary colors, discord, spectrum.**

colored-wax batik. Batik and Tie-dye. A **batik** process in which color is added by means of colored wax, made from crayons or colored **paraffin.** Each color of melted wax is "painted" directly onto fabric.

After the designs are painted in the various colored waxes the fabric is **dye**d, usually a single color. The fabric is then placed between layers of newspaper so that the wax can be ironed out. As the fabric is ironed the wax is melted out but the wax color remains in the batik fabric. This method is often used for school children because only one **dyebath** is necessary. It also takes advantage of broken or leftover crayons.

Colorants used in crayons and colored wax are usually not permanent, so fabric batiks made by this method should be **dry clean**ed, not washed.

colorfast. Batik and Tie-dye. Dyeing. Quilts. Stitchery. (Also called fast color.) A term applied to **fabric,** thread, or yarn to indicate that colors are permanent. Colorfast dyes resist the deteriorating effects of washing, cleaning, light, perspiration, or abrasion. However, **dye**s are sometimes fast to one condition and not to another. It is more helpful when a label reads "fast to sunlight," "boilfast," or some other terms giving the specific situation under which the color will not fade or bleed.

Natural dyes are fast only under certain conditions when used on a certain fiber. The method of dyeing is also a determining factor. Rarely does a dye, natural or otherwise, prove fast in all the above circumstances. Some natural dyes become permanent with the use of specific **mordant**s. In some cases, a mellowing or fading of a color is desirable in order to get a soft effect. Of all the fibers, wool combines with the greatest number of dyes for the longest-lasting color. Cotton is the direct opposite, and only complicated processes produce fast colors. A **dyestuff** should be tested for colorfastness by dyeing small swatches prior to dyeing large quantities.

A standard reference for the permanence, or colorfastness, of a dye to light and washing is the **Color Index.**

colorfast. Batik and Tie-dye. See **fiber-reactive dye** and **Batik and Tie-dye: Dyes.**

colorfast salts. Batik and Tie-dye. See **fast-color salts, naphthol dye.**

color guide to kiln temperature. Enameling. See **firing.**

color harmony. An arrangement of colors or a choice of colors that the eye recognizes as ordered. Any two colors used together are likely to be pleasing, especially if they are near to being **complementary colors** and one of the two colors predominates both in size and **saturation.**

The addition of a third color to any two chosen should be related to the others in terms of interval in the **monochromatic color triangle,** or by virtue of equal spacing around the **hue circle. Proportion** is as important to color as it is to shape.

Color Index. Batik and Tie-dye. A standard reference on the **colorfast**ness, or permanence, of **dye**s to various conditions. It is a resource published by the American Association of Textile Chemists and Colorists. These volumes are available in most large city libraries or in the chemistry libraries of colleges or universities. Variations occur from one color to another even within a single dye class or type, and this information is of special interest to anyone working in **batik** or **tie-dye.**

coloring. Basketry. See **Basketry: Dyeing and Coloring.**

coloring. Candlemaking. Candle dyes come in solid, powder, and liquid form. Solid dyes (also called color buds) are added to the melted wax by shaving off small amounts until the desired color intensity is achieved. It is advisable to run tests with small amounts of hot colored wax before **pouring** the final candle because the color becomes lighter as the wax hardens. Liquid dyes are added to the hot wax drop by drop. Powdered dyes are added to a small amount of hot wax; after the wax hardens it is added to the hot wax the way solid dyes are. **Crayon**s of the true wax variety can be shaved or broken into small pieces and added to the melted wax until the desired color is obtained. It should be noted, however, that most crayons contain additives that will adversely affect a candle's performance. Food coloring will not dye candles.

coloring. Jewelry. Metals can be colored to enrich or change their quality, provide contrast for surrounding areas, and, quite simply, to provide more color if desired. Listed below are a few of the hundreds of formulas for coloring different metals and the techniques for doing so. It is an important consideration when coloring metal to remember that the metal will retain the quality it had before coloring; that is, metal that has been highly polished will carry this quality through to the surface of the coloring, and a metal that has a rough or unpolished surface will maintain that quality. Most coloring processes are not permanent, in that they continue to change by exposure to air. Coloring, which is sometimes referred to as **patina,** rubs off metal quite easily. Consequently, it is more appropriately used in areas that are protected from being rubbed. Work to be colored must be immaculately clean.

KARAT GOLD, SILVER, COPPER Brown to black: Dip into a heated solution of **liver of sulfur.** Liver of sulfur used con-centrated will produce a patina that will eventually peel off. Dilute with water to produce a slower, more permanent, denser, colored film. Heat gold and dip before applying liver of sulfur solution to produce black. It is the copper in the gold which reacts to the chemical.

Deep black: Dilute 2 oz. of liver of sulfur and ¼ oz. of aqua ammonia in 1 gallon of water. Use solution at room temperature. The work can be dipped or areas can be treated with a brush.

COPPER AND BRASS Sage green: Combine 48 grains of ammonium chloride and 48 grains of calcium chloride, and 48 grains of copper nitrate in 3 oz. of water. Apply the heated solution with a brush and allow to dry. Several applications may be required. Rinse and dry when desired color is reached.

Reddish-brown: Make a solution using 120 grains of copper sulphate and ½ pt. of water. Dissolve copper sulphate in boiling water, neutralize mixture with sodium nitrate, and add 150 grains of red iron oxide. Submerge work in solution and watch until color change begins. Remove work and heat on a hot plate to deepen color. Repeat procedure for deeper color. **Casting**s will be higher.

BRASS Blue: Lacquer work to seal color. Mix 2−4 oz. lead acetate, 4 oz. acetic acid, and 8 oz. of sodium thiosulphate in 1 gallon of 180° F water.

Yellow to bright red: Combine 2 parts copper carbonate, 1 part caustic with 10 parts water. Dip until desired color is achieved, then rinse thoroughly in water.

BRONZE Black: Mix together one part ammonium sulfate with 2 parts water and dip or paint piece.

All of the above solutions produce their colors through painting, dipping, and heating. Another method for creating a patina on metal is to place a solution of household ammonia in a glass bowl and set a block of wood in the center with the piece of work on top of it. Cover the top of the bowl tightly with plastic food wrap. Set it in sunlight, which politely heats the solution. Brass will turn quite black in a few hours, and the color is difficult to remove. Bronze can produce colors ranging from brown to green, depending on the alloy. However, this may take several days or even weeks to obtain the desired color. But it is a far more lasting patina, although it too can be removed by excessive rubbing. Keep the bowl covered and look through the food wrap to check the progress of the coloring without removing the piece. Uncovering the bowl will slow the procedure. This bowl method may possibly work quite well with other solutions than ammonia. Also see **Antiquing, buffing compounds, coloring composition, cupric oxide, heat oxidizing.**

coloring. Plastics. See **Plastics: Coloring.**

coloring. Woodworking. See **paint, wood stain** and **Woodworking: Finishing.**

coloring composition. Jewelry. A **polishing compound** used to achieve a final luster on metal, at the same time imparting color to or affecting the color of the metal. Also see **buffing compound, coloring.**

coloring compound. Jewelry. Metalworking. See **polishing compound.**

coloring metal. Jewelry. See **coloring, liver of sulfur.**

color knitting. Knitting. The use of two or more colors in one knitted fabric. Color knitting was one of the earliest means of adding variety to knitting. In color knitting, the various colors are stranded, or carried, across the **back of knitting** side of the work when they are not being used in

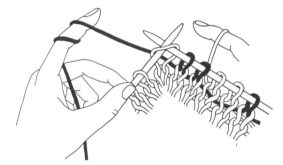

a.   Knit stitch, second color stranded on backside of work

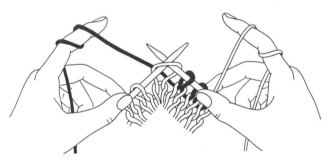

b.   Knit stitch, correct position of yarn

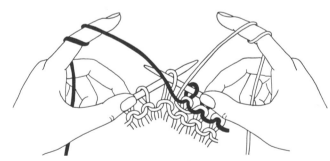

c.   Purl stitch, correct position of yarn

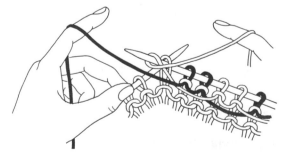

d.   Purl stitch, stranding colors on backside of work

the pattern. The **stocking stitch** is the stitch most commonly used, with the design created through the use of color rather than through the use of various stitch patterns.

When working with two colors, the most advantageous way is to hold one color in the right hand and one color in the left hand (continental method). The main color is usually held in the right hand. **Tension** is of the utmost importance if an uneven surface is to be avoided. Follow the diagrams carefully as to the position of the yarn in the right and left hands when not in use or the front of the knitting will be incorrect.

The **Bohus** style of color knitting combines the stocking stitch with **purl** stitches. See ill. Also see **Albanian knitting, Argyle knitting, Bulgarian knitting, Fair Island knitting, Faroe Island knitting, Florentine knitting, jacquard knitting, Scandinavian knitting, Shetland knitting.**

color pattern. Crochet. Any crochet **pattern** that is worked in more than one color. Often takes the form of **tapestry crochet** and may involve **stranding,** done to carry the various colors along the back side of the work in place. **Granny square**s can be worked as a color pattern.

color pencils. Découpage. (Also called oil pencils.) Oil-based colored pencils, available from art-supply stores, are used to tint black-and-white **print**s to be used in découpage. The **hand coloring** is done before cutting and gluing the **cutout**s to the surface. Some brands are Colorama pencils, Derwent English pencils, and Prismacolor pencils. Water-based pencils must be avoided because the découpage **finish** may make them smudge or run.

color remover. Batik and Tie-dye. A commercial product sold under various trade names including Putnam, Rit, or Tintex that can be used as the bleaching agent in **discharge dyeing.**

color test. Batik and Tie-dye. A sample made by dyeing a small piece of **fabric.** This experimental work is important where controlled color is essential as there are many variables affecting the final color. Type of **fiber,** strength of **dyebath,** duration of dyeing time, temperature, and other variables are all factors affecting the **dye penetration** and intensity of color.

color testing. Enameling. Because enamel colors after **firing** are different from their powdered forms, samples are made for reference when matching colors and values. Although firing is difficult to control, notes made of firing temperature and length of firing time may be helpful. Cut out, clean, and **counterenamel** small pieces of 18-gauge copper sheet, about 1″ × 2″. Then clean the front, spray it with **binder,** and dust with the opaque enamel to be tested, leaving a space at the top for marking the identification number of the test. Fire this coating at temperatures above that required for maturity (**a.**). This is called **overfiring.** Then redust half the enameled surface with the same color and fire it just to maturity to achieve the true color (**b.**).

Color identification may also be made by firing a black, gold, or platinum **overglaze** figure. True opaque colors can also be produced by firing over an opaque white if the enamel being tested is softer than the white. Firing a harder color over a softer requires higher temperatures on the second firing and causes the first coating of white enamel to bubble through.

For color-testing transparent enamels, cut rectangles of 18-gauge copper about 1″ × 3″ to allow space for the various tests of each color. Clean the copper and counter-enamel it, protecting the top convex surface with **fire-scale** treatment, or clean the copper after firing. Each enamel should be tested over grounds of bare copper, opaque white, gold **metal foil**, silver metal foil, and **flux** enamel (**c., d., e.**). A **scriber, underglaze,** or overglaze is used to identify each plaque.

Other tests of experimental and special effects should be made as needed. See ill. Also see **Enameling: Basic Operations.**

Testing opaque enamel

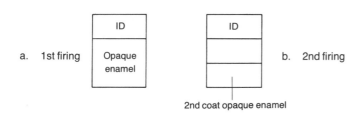

a.   1st firing

b.   2nd firing

2nd coat opaque enamel

Testing transparent enamel

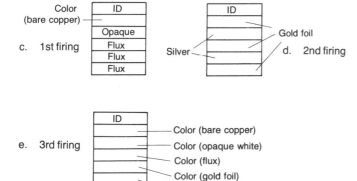

Color (bare copper)

c.   1st firing

Silver

Gold foil

d.   2nd firing

e.   3rd firing

Color (bare copper)
Color (opaque white)
Color (flux)
Color (gold foil)
Color (silver foil)

color wheel. See **hue circle.**

comb. Rugmaking. Weaving. See **hand beater, tapestry tools.**

comb. Spinning. A traditional long-toothed implement through which wool **fibers** are pulled during the **combing** process. Combs were used in pairs and were known as hand, wool, or **worsted** combs. They are difficult to obtain today, so a dog comb or any comb or rake with strong steel teeth can be used. The wool comb consists of a flat wooden piece with several rows of very long metal tines and a handle. When in use, the combs are attached in succession

to a post support or to some other stationary object. Whatever is being used as a substitute for the comb must also be clamped or tied to something stationary. See ill.

Comb

comb-dovetailing. Weaving. See **dovetailing.**

combed wool. Spinning. Wool that passes through a process called **combing,** which comes after **carding** but before spinning. Only wool with a **staple** fiber 5–12″ long is used. Spun combed wool is a firm, smooth, lustrous yarn called worsted.

comber board. Weaving. See **draw loom.**

combination blade. Woodworking. See **power saw.**

combination candle. Candlemaking. A candle formed by combining together several molded candle elements to produce a more complex design. For example, a candle resembling a mushroom can be constructed by combining two pieces formed by **molding**—one, molded in a half-round mold, serving as the mushroom cap; the other, molded in a cone or cylinder, acting as a stem. The hardened forms are joined together by heating the top of the conical candle on a hot surface and fusing it to the half-round candle. The joined pieces are then wicked as one. See ill. Also see **Candlemaking: Molding.**

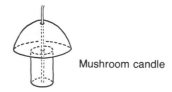

Mushroom candle

combination punch. Leather. A leatherwork tool with attachments for punching various sized holes and slits. See ill. Also see **punch, single tube spring punch.**

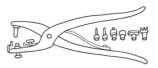

Combination punch

combination rasp. Woodworking. See **rasp.**

Combination Rose. Quilts. (Also called California Rose.) A **block** design for an **appliqué quilt** depicting four rose buds branching out to the edges. When this block is worked in yellow, it is called the Texas Yellow Rose. See ill. Also see **flower designs.**

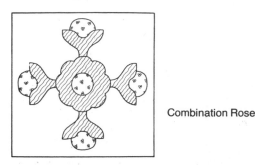

Combination Rose

combination sander. Woodworking. See **sanding tool.**

combination square. Woodworking. See **squaring tools.**

Combination Star. Quilts. (Also called Ornate Star.) A **split nine-patch block** utilizing squares and triangles to form a **pieced** eight-pointed star. Also see **star patterns.**

combination stone. Woodworking. See **sharpening stone.**

combination tanning. Leather. Any **tanning** process in which more than one tanning agent is used, such as **chrome tanning** followed by **vegetable tanning.**

combination weave. Weaving. A weave composed of two or more simple weaves and used as one in a fabric structure. They are often originated by the weaver and open up almost limitless possibilities. Given enough **harness**es and the right combinations, effects such as horizontal stripes, vertical stripes, plaids, checks, or textures can be obtained through weave alone. Combination weaves can also be woven in **double cloth,** the weave structure of which is a combination of **filling-faced** and **warp-faced** weaves. There are some standard combination weaves such as **satin brocade** or satin-striped **rep weave;** their names tell what the combination of weaves is.

combing. Ceramics. A decoration achieved by scoring with a toothed or pronged instrument, similar to a hair comb. The term also applies to **sgraffito**-like decoration through a **slip** or **glaze.** See ill.

Combing

combing. Spinning. A process similar to **carding,** used only with high-quality, long-**staple wool** or **cotton fibers** after carding. It separates the longer fibers from the shorter ones by combing the longer ones away from the shorter ones. At the same time, it straightens the longer fibers and sets them in uniform, parallel order for spinning. If two wool **comb**s are used, one comb is attached to a rigid support and is spread with fibers by stroking the carded wool across the tines so that it is caught in the comb. The second comb is then drawn repeatedly across the fiber group, picking up more and more fibers as it combs closer to the stationary comb. To doff, or remove, the combed fibers, the second full comb is attached to the support and the fibers are gradually drawn out in a thick strand called a **top.** What remains in the teeth is the **noil,** or short fibers, which can be removed and kept for carding with other wool. Fibers should be combed and recombed until the fiber arrangement in the tops is parallel.

If a substitute comb is used, it is made stationary and the fibers are pulled through it by hand. This is done repeatedly, and then the fiber group is turned over and drawn through a few more times. See ill. Also see **comb** and **Spinning: Wool Preparation.**

Doffing the fibers in combing

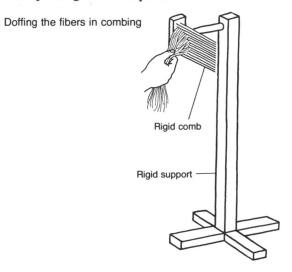

Rigid comb

Rigid support

Comb of Princess Kaiulani (Ke Kahi O Kaiulani). Quilts. See **Hawaiian quilts.**

comforter. Quilts. A soft, fluffy bedcover made of a top, **filler,** and **backing.** The layers are usually tied, which means a much heavier filler can be used than when it is quilted. The term is sometimes used more broadly to include any quilted bedcover. Also see **tied quilt.**

comic-strip toy. Toys. A **toy** or figure derived from a popular comic strip or "funny paper." These toys are similar to **nursery character**s in the way they became popular, first in written or pictorial form, then as **stuffed toy**s, balloons, wood toys, printed fabrics, etc. The Toonerville Trolley, a somewhat rickety and comic train, grew out of a comic strip a generation or two back. Little Orphan Annie and her faithful Sandy were popularized in comics, but originated in a poem by James Whitcomb Riley. There are toys patterned on comic favorites such as "Peanuts" characters Charlie Brown and his Snoopy. Toy two-way wrist radios and ray-guns certainly were developed from the funnies.

commedia dell'arte. Puppets. An extemporaneous form of drama that developed in Italy around the end of the fifteenth century. It grew out of performances by troupes of buffoons and acrobats, called "**zanni**," and eventually included **stock characters** around whom the dramatic action always centered. **Pulcinella** was a creation of this theatre. Also see **Punch, Punch and Judy show.**

commemorative quilt. Quilts. Any quilt that is designed to celebrate or commemorate a historical occasion or patriotic event. Some depict portraits, state flags, symbols, dates, emblems, buildings, monuments, and other memorabilia. These are highly personalized, one-of-a-kind quilts. **Centennial quilts** are commemorative, as are most **state quilts.**

Some specific well-known commemorative quilts are the **Hudson River quilt,** the **Oregon quilt,** the **Peace and Freedom quilt,** and the **Oberlin quilt.**

commercial brass. Metalworking. See **brass.**

commercial dye. Dyeing. See **direct dye.**

common. Woodworking. See **wood.**

common edge beveler. Leather. (Also called edge beveler, edger.) An edge tool, similar to a **bissonete edge tool** or **edge cutter,** available in several sizes for finishing, rounding off edges of lightweight leather straps, or taking a sliver of leather off the top edge of heavy leather to give a beveled edge. See ill. Also see **Leatherwork: Cutting and Edging.**

a. Edge beveler   b. Using a common edge beveler

common nail. Woodworking. See **nail.**

common solder. Metalworking. See **solder.**

compact half hitch. Macramé. The compact half hitch produces a finished edge. It can also be used within a piece. Each cord is looped onto the next cord in succession across the row of knotting cords. See ill. Also see **finishing, fringe.**

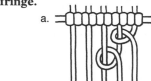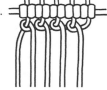

Compact half hitch

compass saw. Woodworking. See **handsaw.**

compatibility. Ceramics. The agreement of a **clay body** and a **glaze** with regard to firing temperature. All bodies, whether **earthenware** or **stoneware,** can be fired between 1500–1800° F., but the glaze ingredients melt at different temperatures. The body must be capable of firing at a temperature high enough to melt the glaze without shattering the body.

complementary colors. Colors that, when mixed as **pigments,** produce a neutral gray. Blue and yellow, and green and magenta are two sets of complementary colors. Theoretically every color has its complement. The complement for any color can be suggested by staring at a patch of the color for which a complement is desired for a period of about 30 seconds and then immediately focusing on a piece of white paper. The afterimage that appears on the white paper is an optical effect produced by fatigue of the eye's sensory mechanism, and indicates the kind of color the complement must be. This exercise works best with colors that are near maximum **saturation.**

Color schemes are most pleasing when the complementary of the dominant color is included in the design. Children tend to color their drawings using pairs of complementary colors because it "looks right." Care must be taken, however, to keep from using too nearly equal amounts of complementary colors, especially if they are touching and at the same saturation and **value,** or else the colors will "vibrate" in their demands for your attention. Also see **color harmony.**

complementary yarns. Weaving. See **compound weave.**

composition. Toys. A mixture that hardens on setting that is sometimes used to form the heads or bodies of **dolls** or for molding other **toys. Papier mâché** is a composition, although it suggests the use of paper strips. Composition usually refers to mixtures of **glue** and wood pulp. Sometimes resins, starches, plaster of Paris, bran, or **sawdust** are added. Composition was reportedly first used in the 1700s, but became better-developed and more popular in the middle 1800s. By 1900, some French doll bodies were made from a composition material that included cardboard, rags, and gum tragacanth. By 1920, composition had become a common replacement for the papier mâché.

Dollmakers all had their own composition formulas. The most common were composed of wood flour, resin, and starch; they were moistened and then molded in a gas-fired press similar to a waffle iron. Composition was a sturdy material and was used until hard plastics were developed and became popular in the 1930s. **Sawdust mâché** is a similar kind of molding composition used for the sawdust-head doll. Also see **ball joint, breast-plate doll head, joint.**

compound weave. Weaving. Weaves that have more than one set of both **warp** and **filling** threads. These extra sets can be used as in **double cloth,** which is a perfect example of where two entire sets of warp and filling are needed. The sets are equal to each other in the fabric structure and in amount, and they interlace with each other. **Triple cloth** and **multiple-layered cloth** are in this same group. Double-faced fabrics have either two sets of warp, or two sets of filling, interlacing with either one filling or one warp. These extra sets, called complementary yarns, are not used as an addition to a **ground** weave, but rather all three elements combine to weave one fabric with a different color, texture, or pattern on each side. The last group of compound weaves is that which has extra warp or filling only in sections. These warps or fillings, added to a basic ground or foundation weave, are called **supplementary yarns.** They are added for color, pattern development, decoration, weight, or reinforcement. If added to the filling, they may be woven back and forth in a given area in order to fulfill a pattern shape. These are called discontinuous picks, as opposed to the continuous ones weaving **selvage** to selvage. Float patterns such as **overshot** have supplementary continuous filling. **Pile weaves** such as **terry cloth** or **corduroy** are other examples of an additional element woven in with the ground weave. In these cases it is made to protrude to give surface decoration. Also see **brocade, double cloth, laid-in weave, overshot.**

compressed metal forming. Metalworking. See **raising technique** and **Metalworking: Raising.**

compression. Jewelry. The ability of a metal to be reduced in volume and its resistance to buckling or cracking while being compressed. Also see **annealing.**

concentric circle. Papercrafts. A three-dimensional **circle** formed by slitting a circle to the center and **scoring,** then folding, concentric circles. When the edges are overlapped to form a **cone,** the scored lines form alternating convex and concave planes. On a paper circle draw 3 inner circles, 2 on one side of the paper and one on the other. Score these lines. Cut a slit to the center and cut out a small segment of the circle to form a cone (**a.**). Bend the scored lines in alternating directions and overlap the edges to form a shallow cone shape. Glue the overlapping edges (**b.**). The design can be varied by making more circles within it. See ill.

Concentric circle

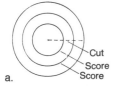

Cut
Score
Score
a.   b.

conchoidal fracture. Gem cutting. See **fracture.**

conchoidal fracture. Glasswork. Certain noncrystalline materials such as glass break along imprecise planes that leave smooth concavities and convexities similar to the insides of some sea shells. Glass-cutting techniques minimize these effects. The natural fracturing of certain kinds of rocks into conchoidal patterns enabled primitive man to make very sharp tools from flint and similar materials by striking the edges of the work with other rounded rocks.

conchyolin. Shell Carving. The horny brown organic material that makes up the outer layer of shell. It is harder than the **nacre,** with a hardness of 5 on the Mohs scale. It is generally removed before working mother of pearl. Also see **Shell Carving: Tools and Preparation.**

concrete. Mosaics. A mixture of cement, sand, water, and stones or crushed rock. Concrete, when poured out as a slab, makes an excellent backing for mosaics. Although exact proportions are a matter of preference, a good guideline is 1 part cement, 2 parts sand, and 3 parts ¼–½″ pieces of stone or crushed rock. Stir the mixture before adding water until the mixture becomes doughlike in consistency. Add water slowly and conservatively, as too much will definitely weaken the final concrete base.

concrete. Stained Glass. See **dalle-de-verre.**

concrete backing. Mosaics. A backing for mosaic materials poured from a mixture of **cement,** sand, stone, or crushed rock, and water. Many professional mosaicists prefer a **concrete** backing over plywood or masonite because it tends to be stronger, more rigid, more durable, and more resistant to the elements. The only drawback to a concrete base is that it is heavy, and if it is to be hung, its weight must be taken into account.

To form a concrete backing, concrete is mixed to a doughlike consistency and poured approximately 1″ deep onto a previously constructed plywood frame. Wire reinforcing mesh is then embedded in the concrete, and the remaining mixture poured on top to the desired thickness. Once the concrete has set for several hours, the surface should be crosshatched with a trowel to provide a better gripping surface for the **mortar** bond. To ensure the gradual curing of the concrete, the slab should be sprinkled occasionally with water and covered overnight with a damp cloth. The curing step, which should take a minimum of three days to be most effective slows down the drying to prevent cracking. When completely cured, the frame can be removed and the backing prepared to receive the **mortar bond.** It is necessary to wet down the slab before applying the mortar to prevent the concrete from drawing off the water in the mortar mixture. Also see **Mosaics: Tools and Materials, Setting the Material.**

conditioner. Leather. See **lexol, neat's foot oil.**

cone. Ceramics. A cone, or pyrometric cone, is used to measure the heat in a **kiln.** A cone is actually a slender pyramid of ceramic materials that is compounded to bend and melt at a specific temperature, enabling the potter to determine when the firing is complete. A ceramic material will mature in a slow-heating kiln at a lower temperature than it will at a rapid rate of heating, and a cone is better for indicating this heat work than is a **pyrometer.**

cone. Papercrafts. This three-dimensional geometric form can be shaped by rolling a segment of a paper **circle.** The radius of the circle determines the height of the cone and the portion of the circle used determines the size of the base of the cone; the greater the segment of the circle used, the fuller the cone. A paper circle is slit to the center, and the overlapped edges are glued, or a pie-shaped segment is cut out of a circle, rolled, and the overlapped edges are glued. See ill.

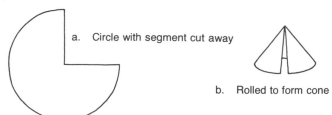

a.   Circle with segment cut away

b.   Rolled to form cone

cone. Weaving. A package of yarn wound around a tapered cardboard cylinder. It is one of the most common ways in which weaving yarns are sold. It has an advantage over **skeins** or **spools** in that the yarn winds off very smoothly and without revolving the cone, so that **warping** or bobbin winding is made easier. Also see **doubling stand.**

Cone pat. Ceramics. See **cone socket.**

Cone plaque. Ceramics. See **cone socket.**

cone socket. Ceramics. (Also called cone pat, cone plaque.) A device that is available commercially to hold **cone**s. Commonly, potters use a small amount of **grog**ged clay to make a small block to hold cones while firing.

coning. Ceramics. A process in centering when throwing **clay.** The clay is raised into a cone-shaped column on the rotating wheel by using the pressure between the palms of the hands.

construction. Jewelry. See **box construction.**

constructional toy. Toys. (Also called construction toy.) A **toy** made up of many parts that can be fitted together to make structures or building forms. Building **block**s of all sizes, with arches, windows, and triangles, are a popular kind of constructional toy. There are many ingenious connecting, or joining, devices for these toys, from the notched pieces of **Lincoln Logs** to the snap-together design of **Lego building bricks. Erector set**s, geodesic structures, and **Tinkertoy**s are other popular construction toys with fitted connecting devices. Some **building bricks** have connecting notches, but most are simple rectangular shapes of wood, cardboard, or fiberboard. Also see **Toys: Construction Toys.**

construction paper. Toys. An inexpensive, heavy paper available in a wide range of colors. It is not permanent in color or durable so it is best used in working out designs or for items of relatively short use, such as decorations. It can easily be cut with scissors and is the standard children's craft paper.

construction toy. Toys. See **constructional toy** and **Toys: Construction Toys.**

contact cement. Plastics. See **adhesives.**

contact cement. Stitchery. Toys. An **adhesive** for joining wood to wood. It is semiliquid and of rubbery consistency,

and must be used with adequate ventilation. In applying it, both surfaces must be coated and left to dry. When the two surfaces are pressed together they form a permanent contact, so care must be taken to assure that placement is accurate. Contact cement can also be used to join some fabrics to wood; only coarse-textured fabrics work well, and only the wood is coated with the contact cement. If the adhesive soaks through a fabric, it will spot or mark it.

contact cement. Woodworking. See **adhesives.**

contact paper. Batik and Tie-dye. Stitchery. Toys. **Adhesive**-backed colored or patterned paper with a smooth surface. It is manufactured as shelf paper, but has many other decorative uses. On simple **building brick**s, **blocks,** or **toys,** decorative details may be added from cut pieces of the contact paper.

Transparent contact papers may be applied to fragile papers, photographs, or tissue to make them more durable, especially if they are to be incorporated into **stitchery** or toys. The contact paper can itself be adhered or sewn to another material so that the original paper remains undamaged. Contact paper, however, is not completely permanent.

Contact paper can also be used to make a self-adhesive **stencil** in the application of **wax** in **batik.**

container candle. Candlemaking. Candles that remain in the **mold,** or container, after they have hardened. Goblets, glasses, pottery bowls, and tin vessels make attractive container candles. As a general rule, container candles are poured with a relatively low **melting point** wax (130° F) that contains no **stearic acid,** so that all the wax is consumed as the candle burns. A **wire wick** is used because it offers the rigidity desired. As an alternative, a weighted wick or metal **wick holder** can be used. With the latter technique, just enough wax should be poured into the container to solidify and secure the wick before it is drawn taut with a securing rod positioned across the top of the mold. Also see **sand candle** and **Candlemaking: Molding.**

contemporary quilt. Quilts. See **Quilts: Definition.**

contemporary stitchery. Stitchery. The use of various embroidery and **appliqué** techniques as a means of personal, expressive work. It contrasts to traditional work in terms of purpose. Contemporary stitchery offers an outlet for creative energy in an unconstrained approach and an inventive use of the established methods. It is also open or receptive to the use of new materials, new concepts, and new methods. "Contemporary" often suggests a breaking away from what is standard and accepted. Thus some works, actually antiques in terms of their ages, may be regarded as "contemporary," while some work produced today may be traditional.

conterie. Beadwork. See **trade beads** and **Beadmaking.**

continental casting on. Knitting. See **Knitting: Casting On.**

continental stitch. Needlepoint. A form of **tent stitch,** worked horizontally from right to left and then turned upside-down for the return row and worked right to left. The stitch can also be worked from top to bottom as a vertical continental stitch. It is recommended that continental stitch be worked on an **embroidery frame** because the stitch pulls the canvas out of shape in the direction of the stitch. When working on the frame, the stitch is worked upside-down on the return row rather than turning the frame. If the continental stitch is worked in the hand, the piece can be returned to its original shape by **blocking.** It can be worked on either penelope or mono canvas. See ill. Also see **Needlepoint: Finishing.**

a.   Horizontal continental stitch   b.   Vertical continental stitch

continuous crossover loop. Beadwork. See **crossover loop.**

continuous filament. Spinning. Weaving. See **filament.**

continuous-firing kiln. Ceramics. (Also called tunnel kiln.) A long tunnel-like **kiln** in which unfired ceramic **ware,** loaded on "cars" is carried through, in continuous movement, on tracks. The kiln is at peak temperature in the center. Most commercial **pottery** is fired in this way.

continuous loopback. Beadwork. A technique used in **bead flowermaking** in which the loops are formed on either side of a **basic loop.** Make the first loopback on the left side of the basic loop. Bring the wire back over the front of the beginning wire at the base of the first loop. Add the second loopback on the right side of the center loop, wrapping the wire across the front of the stem. The third loopback is formed to the left side again, and so on, alternating sides until the desired number of loops is completed. Wrap the beading wire around the beginning wire. Twist the two wires together and cut for stems. See ill.

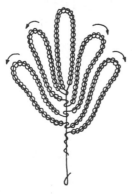

Continuous loopback

continuous single loop. Beadwork. A technique used in **bead flowermaking** for flower centers or repeated loops in flowers such as marigolds and carnations. Place the desired number of inches of beads on **spool wire,** crimping the open end of the wire. Move the beads to within 4″ of the crimped end and make a loop by twisting the wire close to the base of the loop, below the lowest bead. Form the second loop close to the base of the first loop in the same way. Repeat for the desired number of loops, making the wires twist in a consistent direction. Leave 4″ of bare wire for the stem and cut it from the spool. Twist the two wires under the loops for the stem. See ill.

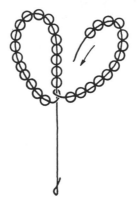 

a.   Forming loops   b.   Completed flower

continuous warp. Weaving. A **warp** that is made directly on the **loom** of one continuous length of yarn, rather than consecutively measured out on a separate piece of equipment, such as a **warping board** or **reel,** and then transferred to a loom. In actuality, just about all warps are continuous no matter where the **warping** is done, because noncontinuous would imply that each warp **end** is cut and separately put on. However, the term "continuous warp" is associated with the particular method of putting a warp on a frame, tapestry, ground, box, hoop, bow, inkle, or **Navajo loom.**

There are various types of continuous warps. Some are made so that there is provision for tension adjustment. The **shed**s are usually opened with a **shed stick** and a **heddle bar.** A **chain spacer** or **twining** spreads the warp. In weaving the full length possible on each type of continuous warp, a tapestry or wooden **needle** is used to insert the last **filling pick**s as the sheds can no longer be opened.

One type of continuous warp looks like a figure eight when viewed from the side and is called a figure eight warp. It cannot be moved around the loom and, therefore, the length of the weaving is determined by the distance inside the frame of the loom. The easiest method of warping is to turn the loom on its side and, with the warp yarn wound in a tight ball, carry the yarn over the top of the loom, forward and down in back of the bottom frame. Then the yarn goes under the bottom frame, up in front of it, and through the center of the frame, there to cross with the first end. This **cross** in the center holds the threads in order. The yarn continues up in back of the top frame and the sequence begins all over again. If one starts at the left of the loom, the yarn is initially tied to the top frame at the left, and when the desired number is wound the yarn is cut and tied to the frame at the right. The warp should be lightly but evenly tensioned so that there is enough slack for **take-up** and for the sheds. The warp is actually separated at the top and bottom into ends that go in front or in back of the frame. These ends are all brought together through twining so that the weaving can begin.

Another type of continuous warp is a circular warp, or ring warp. This looks like a circle when viewed from the side. There are many variations on the circular continuous warp, and in most of them there is some provision for tension adjustment. Either the warp is made around a frame loom with a built-in **tensioner; tension stick**s are added under the warp as it is being wound; or some sort of homemade tension devices are added to the bar or bars that are used in some versions of the circular warp (**a.**). In its simplest version, the warp yarn is wound around and around the frame continuously and, when completed, the beginning warp end and the last warp end are tied together to make the circle complete. The circular warp is revolved around the loom as weaving progresses and the weaving length is almost twice the length of the loom. If there is a tensioner on the loom it should be extended a little beyond its midpoint. This will then allow for giving slack to the warp as it tightens up during weaving and for tightening the tension if it needs adjusting at the outset. If there is no tensioner, tension sticks are added to the frame as the warp goes around. They will later be removed when there is too much take-up. There is no cross to hold threads in order, so the weaver may wish to file shallow grooves on the top and bottom frame (or tensioner) to help space the warp and keep order. These grooves are either ½" or 1" apart.

In a variation on the circular continuous warp, a **warp-end bar** is used around which the beginning and end of the warp yarn goes, which makes for ease in pushing the warp around the loom as weaving progresses. Tension sticks, or a tensioner, are used; grooves are filed to space the warp; and weaving length is the same as for the above-mentioned circular warp. At the outset the bar is taped temporarily to the loom to keep it stable until the warp ends are around it. The beginning and end of the warp are tied to the bar. The warp yarn is wound into a ball or huge **bobbin** and held in the hand as it goes down from the warp end bar in the rear of the loom around and up the front of the loom to the top frame. It goes over the top frame and down to the warp-end bar, around it, and back to the top frame (**b.**). From here the warp yarn travels over the top, down the front, and under and up the back to the warp-end bar. It goes around the warp-end bar and then repeats the entire previous journey. This is continued until the entire desired number of ends is attained. A variation on the warp-end bar calls for two warp-end bars spaced apart with cord and homemade tension dowels that unwind the cord and loosen the bars as more slack is needed during weaving.

Perhaps the very simplest type of continuous warp is one that goes around nails in the top and bottom frames of the loom. The nails are used to hold and space the warp. The warp yarn is tied around the nail where the warp is to begin and then the yarn is brought back and forth across the front of the loom between the nails. When the desired width has been reached the warp yarn is tied off at the ending nail. There is no attempt at tension control but, as the weaving length is limited to the length of the warp running between the nails, in this short length great problems of tension adjustment do not usually arise. See ill. Also see **bow loom, box loom, frame loom, ground loom, hoop loom, inkle loom, shedding device, tapestry loom.**

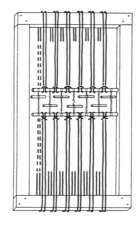

a. Variation on circular or ring warp using a home-made tension device between 2 warp-end bars

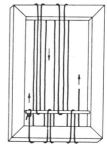

b. Variation on circular continuous warp

continuous wraparound loop. Beadwork. A technique used in **bead flowermaking** for flower centers, petals, and leaves using the **continuous single loop** method with an additional loop of beads around the outside of each loop, giving the flower a double row of beads.

Place the beads on the **spool wire** and crimp the open end. Move the beads to within 4" of the crimped end and make a loop by twisting the beaded wire close to the base of the loop below the lowest bead. Then wrap the beaded wire around the outside of this loop of beads. To join, twist the bare spool wire around the beginning wire at the base. Make another loop next to the first petal and continue in the same way until as many double-row loops as desired are finished. See ill.

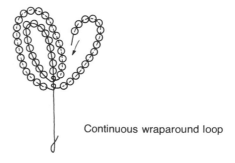

Continuous wraparound loop

contremarche loom. Weaving. See **countermarch loom.**

control. Puppets. The arrangement of **rod**s and bars by which a **marionette** is **manipulated**. The control may be either a **vertical control** or a **horizontal control**. Also see **arm bar, crossbar, head bar, playing the puppet, rocking** and **Puppets: Stringing the Marionette.**

control bar. Puppets. (Also called main control, string control.) The primary rod or central bar of either the **horizontal control** or the **vertical control** to which **crossbars** are attached. The **puppeteer** grasps this central bar of the **control** in order to **manipulate** the **marionette.** Also see **back string, gallows, galvanized wire, horizontal rod, shadow play, shoulder bar, simplified horizontal control, stringing, vertical rod** and **Puppets: Stringing the Marionette.**

controller. Puppets. The **puppeteer** or manipulator of the **string puppet** or **marionette.** The controller grasps the **control bar** in one hand and maneuvers the puppet by using both hands to operate the strings. Also see **bench, bridge, bridge bar.**

controlling pyrometer. Ceramics. A mechanism similar to a thermostat that can control the firing process automatically. The simplest form is merely a switch which turns off the power supply at a given temperature.

control point. Puppets. The spot or point on a **marionette** to which a **string** is attached and by which the figure is **manipulated.** The control points for the head, for example, are at the sides of the head just in front of the ears. The **head strings** are then attached to these control points, usually by means of **screw eyes.** Also see **Puppets: Stringing the Marionette.**

Conventional Tulip. Quilts. See **Tulip.**

cookie art. Toys. A form of dough art used to produce **edible toys** and decorative cookies, usually for some festive or holiday occasion. Cookie art includes the use of both light and **dark dough.** Gingerbread boys are one of the most familiar forms of cookie art. Sugar cookies are often cut with cookie cutters into a great range of shapes and sizes. Dough can be used in flat pieces or bricklike shapes to build cookie castles or gingerbread houses. **Marzipan** is more of a candy than a cookie but is considered a cookie art.

Some familiar cookie art forms of other countries are **lebkuchen, springerle,** and **tirggeli.** Pressed cookies are made from **cookie molds** or **cookie boards; translucent cookies** are made from hard candies; and three-dimensional figures are made by assembling preplanned parts to make freestanding cookie sculptures. Also see **ephemeral toys.**

cookie board. Toys. A decorative board onto which cookie dough is pressed to imprint a design. Traditional cookie boards were elaborately and intricately carved; museum examples date back to the 1700s. Subject matter for the designs included animals, birds, buildings, historical events, portraits, saints, mounted riders, and proverbs. They were particularly popular in Germany, but were also abundant in Belgium, Switzerland, Holland, and Austria.

Some cookie boards have a single large design. Others may have a series, over which the dough was probably rolled. The **springerle** cookie is made by rolling a carved rolling pin over the dough—the reverse process.

Cookie boards are sometimes called **cookie mold**s, although molds may be made of a variety of materials. Gingerbread boards usually depicted a single figure, as did some Swiss tirggeli cookie molds.

The **edible toy**s produced as cookie art have been popular for centuries. Some were used as gifts rich in symbolism, others were ornaments. Cookie toys are an example of ephemeral art.

cookie-cutter quilt. Quilts. Any quilt in which some of the basic motifs are traced from cookie cutters. It is a method most often reserved for children's or babies' quilts. The cutters may provide a pattern for the **appliqué,** the **quilting,** or both.

cookie mold. Toys. Any of a variety of forms used to help shape a cookie into some decorative figure. One kind of mold is the **cookie board.** Another type of mold is the cookie cutter, of which a seemingly endless variety of designs has been made. Some molds are rolled over the dough, such as the **springerle;** others are pressed. Some simple cookie molds, handcrafted of ceramic, are pressed onto a rounded lump of dough, leaving an impression much like that of a seal on wax.

Many commercially made cookies are poured into molds. Among them are the old favorite Animal Crackers. Few are eaten without having first had a brief life as a **toy.** Also see **edible toy.**

cookie pellet. Plastics. See **fusible thermoplastic.**

cool color. Blue, blue-green, and blue-violet colors. Cool colors are opposed to warm colors, which include red and orange.

cooling. Stained Glass. See **firing.**

cooling cracks. Stained Glass. See **firecrack.**

cop. Spinning. Weaving. In spinning, the cone of yarn formed by winding the **spun yarn** on a **wool wheel** or hand **spindle** during the spinning process.

In weaving, another word for the paper **bobbin** of a **boat shuttle.** It also sometimes refers to a cone-shaped paper **spool** or to the cone of yarn wound on the spool. Also see **bobbin, quill.**

copal. Amber Carving. A brittle, aromatic resin from various tropical trees used for varnish and lacquer. Copal is often used to imitate **amber.** It can be tested by rubbing; when amber is rubbed it becomes electrified and when copal is rubbed it becomes sticky.

cope. A vestment which resembles a cape and which is worn for certain ceremonies, usually in an ecclesiastical setting. The cope has traditionally used some needlework or embroidery, often employing **metallic thread**s of gold or silver, as in much ecclesiastical needlework. Recently the design of copes for some religious observances have been brilliant in color and very contemporary in design.

cope. Metalworking. See **sandcasting molding equipment.**

coping saw. Woodworking. See **hand saw.**

copper. Enameling. See **electrolyte, etching, metal.**

copper. Jewelry. (Cu) Specific gravity 8.96; melting point 1083° C, 1984° F; boiling point 2595° C, 4703° F; and **annealing** temperature 700–1200° F. Copper was the first metal known and used by man, starting around 8000 B.C. It is found in workable quantities in masses and veins. Pure copper possesses high thermal and electrical conductivity, is malleable, has good working strength, and has a fair resistance to corrosion. Cold-working operations harden copper, simultaneously reducing ductility and increasing its tensile strength. Work-hardening also reduces its conductivity. Annealing restores its softness and permits further cold working.

Combined with varying amounts of zinc, copper produces the wide range of **brass alloy**s. In combination with tin, often with additional elements of nickel, zinc, phosphorus, and lead, it forms **bronze.**

Silicon enhances its strength, ability to take a weld, and resistance to acid and atmospheric corrosion.

Britannia metal is the name applied to contemporary pewter; it is a **ternary alloy** of copper, tin, and antimony. Also see **buffing compound.**

copper. Metalworking. A very soft, **malleable,** reddish metal with high **ductility** and good **tensile strength,** used much for art work. When exposed to the weather, a green protective film forms on the surface that inhibits further corrosion. **Raising techniques** cause it to **work-harden** and become brittle, but softness can be restored by **anneal**ing. Copper stretches easily but is difficult to machine; for instance, it is easier to cut threads on **mild steel** rod than on copper rod.

Sheet copper may be purchased in 24″ × 96″ stock sheets in different **tempers** and **gauges,** with its cost based on the weight in pounds per square foot. Its hardness gradings are soft temper—¼, ½, or ¾—and hard temper.

Copper may be joined by braze-welding, welding, and soldering. It becomes molten and a lemon-yellow color at approximately 1960° F; when cooled, its color changes, often unpredictably, making it difficult to duplicate. Welding is accomplished without the aid of a **welding rod** while the pieces are molten. When braze-welding copper, a bronze rod may be used if it is not important to match the color of the joint to the **base metal;** to match the color, a rod of deoxidized copper or of phos-copper is used.

Several varieties of copper are produced with small amounts of other metals or elements in them. Tough pitch copper contains oxygen to increase its tensile strength and reduce its ductility, and is used for general purpose work. Deoxidized copper has a high phosphorus content, is tougher, and is recommended for hot working processes including annealing, brazing, and welding. Oxygen-free

copper is very ductile in the hard-temper form. Copper combines easily with other metals; several hundred copper **alloy**s are produced, among them **bronze, brass, nickel silver,** and **aluminum bronze.**

Copper is one of the few metals commonly occurring as a pure metal and not as a mineral compound out of which the metal must be extracted. Historically, the Phoenicians are credited with the discovery of copper, and it was used in predynastic Egypt; because it is a component of bronze, it would have been in use before the Bronze Age. The name of the metal derives from the Latin *cuprum,* from *aes cyprum,* meaning "metal of Cyprus," where there were abundant copper deposits. In alchemical writings, the symbol for copper is the one used for Venus; Cyprus was the legendary birthplace of the goddess.

The Japanese had replaced their wooden shrines with copper ones by the eighth century A.D., and Italian Romanesque and Gothic artists mercurially gilded copper for art works. Redsmithing, as copperworking is called, was a thriving trade until the nineteenth century. Copper utensils were tinned for use with food, especially in colonial America. Paul Revere was the first American to devise a commercial method for rolling copper sheets for sheathing ship hulls.

copperas. Dyeing. (Also called green vitriol.) It is iron or ferrous sulfate; it tends to darken colors and harden the wool during **mordanting.**

copper carbonate. Ceramics. A **pigment oxide** used in **glaze**s to produce green. Copper carbonate is preferred to **copper oxide** in the production of blue-greens or copper red under reduction conditions with an alkaline **flux.** Red glaze must be fluid; small amounts of tin or **zinc oxide** are recommended in a low **alumina** glaze base.

copper foil. Stained Glass. Thin sheets of copper manufactured in rolls of precut strips of ³/₁₆″, ¼″, and ⅜″ wide with adhesive backing and in sheets of foil 6″ wide in thicknesses from .001–.005″. The foil sheets come with or without adhesive backing and can be cut precisely to need. Copper foil is used as a lead substitute. Also see **copper foiling, template** and **Stained Glass: Tools and Materials, Planning a Piece of Glass.**

copper foiling. Stained Glass. (Also called foiling.) The process of cutting copper foil into strips and wrapping them in the form of a U around the edges of pieces of stained glass. The strips are then **solder**ed together over a pattern or mold to form stained-glass panels, lampshades, boxes, free-form hangings, and so on.

The technique evolved during the **Tiffany** era and is sometimes called the Tiffany foil method.

Copper foil is best for achieving very delicate effects and depends on solder for its structural rigidity. Soldering copper foil differs from soldering lead **came** in that foiled pieces are completely coated with solder, whereas lead came is soldered only at the **joint**s.

When using sheets of foil by the pound, unroll a piece about 18″ long and fold it over into three or four layers 3–6″ long (**a.**). Hold the cut piece of glass to be foiled on edge along the foil packet, leaving room for about ⅛−¹/₁₆″ overlap on either side of the glass. Make a mark with a pushpin at the top and bottom of the folded foil, and then with a straightedge **score** a straight line on the foil (**b.**). Using either a razor blade or scissors, cut along the score line. Wrap 9 strip of copper foil around the edge of a piece of glass (**c.**).

If the foil does not have an adhesive backing, open the strips, lay them on newspaper, and spray them with a permanent adhesive. When the adhesive becomes tacky wrap the foil around the edges of the stained-glass pieces. For sheet foil without adhesive rub petroleum or beeswax on the glass edge, to hold the foil strip on the glass. See ill. Also see **double glazing, floated solder seam** and **Stained Glass: Planning a Piece of Glass.**

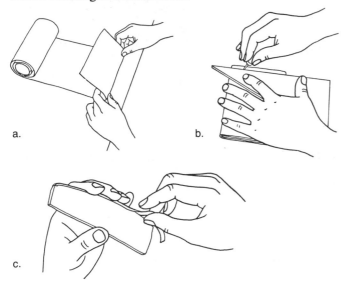

a.

b.

c.

copper oxide. Ceramics. A slightly **fluxing pigment oxide** producing a variety of green glazes under oxidizing conditions. Copper used with a lead flux produces a blackish green. Also see **copper carbonate.**

copper oxide. Jewelry. See **cupric oxide.**

copper sheeting. Stained Glass. Heavy sheeting, used to cut **filigree,** leaves, and so on, that can be embossed. The designs are then tinned and soldered to lamps and **panels** or other work for decorative effects. Also see **solder, tinning.**

copper sulfate. Enameling. See **electrolyte.**

copper sulfate crystals. Stained Glass. See **antiquing solution.**

copper ties. Stained Glass. Ties are 4″ long pieces of 16−18 gauge copper wire used for **banding.** They secure the stained-glass window to **saddle bars** outside or inside the window. The ties are soldered onto the lead along the line of the saddle bar at **intervals** of no more than three inches. They are twisted around the saddle bar and their ends cut off. The ties should be placed where there is a joint in the lead, or **joints** should be provided for them during **glazing.**

To make copper ties, take a long piece of copper wire, stretch it out, and clean it with emery cloth. Then cut it into 4″ pieces, lay them side by side (but not touching), and **flux** the center of each wire. Place a small bit of solder on the center of each wire; with the **soldering iron** roll each wire until the center is completely tinned. The places on the lead where the wires are to be attached should be cleaned and fluxed first. See ill. Also see **division ties, tinning** and **Stained Glass: Glazing.**

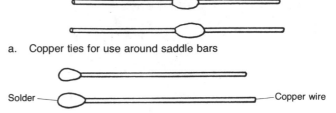

a.   Copper ties for use around saddle bars

b.   Copper division ties for use around division bars

copper tongs. Jewelry. See **pickling tongs.**

copper-wheel engraving. Glasswork. See **engraving.**

copyright notice. Bookbinding. A statement that indicates ownership of the book by the author or publisher, that two copies have been placed in the Library of Congress, and that a Library of Congress card catalogue number has been assigned.

coral. Beadwork. A skeletal secretion of certain marine polyps that is deposited in reefs in tropical seas. Although coral comes in various shades, the orange-red is most commonly available. Coral has been used since ancient times in beadmaking.

Rich red coral has not only inspired jewelry of great beauty, but also aroused myths and superstitions throughout the centuries. The Greeks and Romans thought that a few beads of red coral would save a sailor from storm or shipwreck, or a traveler from accident. In Asia, coral was believed to repel lightning, tempests, and whirlwinds, and to protect against spells of witchcraft. In England, a string of coral beads was tied around the throat to stop a hemorrhage; it is said that the coral would turn pale if the wearer were in danger of death.

coral. Coral Carving. Coral is the formation of the calcareous skeleton of colonies of the coral polyp. These colonies attach themselves to any solid surface, but prefer steep rock faces with a southern exposure (never northern) and grow perpendicular to that surface, be it up, down, or sideways. Healthy coral is a compact, homogeneous solid, free from internal cavities (although it may have **inclusion**s of other marine organisms), built of thin concentric layers into a branching structure. The organism lives five years; but it takes ten years of layers of dead polyps to produce a decent-sized piece of coral (a 3 lb mass is considered a good size). It is fished for only six months of the year, from spring to fall (before the seas become too dangerous) from coral fields or banks, usually located from four to nine miles out to sea and from depths of 90–900'. The deeper the bank, the paler and more brittle the coral is. The majority of coral fished is from the Mediterranean, the African coast, and Japan, although it grows in many waters. Pacific Ocean coral is more compact and harder than Mediterranean coral and weighs four to five times more. Before the coral color is exposed it is covered with a flaky outer covering called the **sarcosoma;** after this is removed it reveals a ridged surface with small circular depressions and the small pinholes of boring animals; this surface can be made smooth by polishing.

Although there are countless varieties of coral, the coralium rubrim is the material generally used for carving. It has a hardness of 3¾ and a specific gravity of 2.6–2.7. It is also known as jeweler's coral, noble coral, and precious coral.

The value of a piece of coral is dictated by its color, size, and shape. The quality of the polish it will take is not as important as its color. The fishing and working of the rough material is almost entirely an Italian industry, so the color classifications are given Italian names. The names of the various shades of Mediterranean coral are:

pure white: bianco
pale flesh-pink: pelle d'angelo
pale rose: rosa pallido
bright rose: rosa vivo
second color: secondo coloro
red: rosso
dark red: rosso scuro
darkest red: carbonetto or ariscuro

The color is generally uniform throughout a piece, although sometimes pieces that have died and begun to turn black are combined with red. Coral that has died can also turn white or yellow.

Black coral is called akabar or king's coral because it was used for scepters by certain African tribes. It is pitch black and shiny, and is composed of a horny (instead of calcareous) substance that is capable of being molded.

Most coral consists of fine branches, with pieces thicker than a finger being relatively rare. The largest piece of the coral stock is the disc-shaped foot by which the coral is attached to the sea bottom; this provides enough material for a bowl or dish.

Coral is imitated by red gypsum, which can be scratched with a fingernail, while coral cannot. Coral will effervesce when sulfuric acid is applied; imitations will not. Other coral impostors are bone, burned and dyed red, and powdered marble mixed with isinglass and colored with cinnabar, red lead, or red sealing wax. Also see **Coral Carving.**

coral. Toys. Baby toys made of coral, usually pink or red in color. Because they were smooth and hard, corals were used as teething rings. The coral was also frequently used on **rattles**. The rattle made of silver and coral was considered to be a **princely toy.** Also see **cradle toy.**

coral beadmaking. Coral Carving. See **Coral Carving: Working the Material.**

CORAL CARVING

The myths and history of **coral** have been associated with toil, suffering, and violence; it has often had magical properties attributed to it, and it has been treasured throughout history.

A thousand years before Christ, the wild Gauls of Western Europe decorated their helmets and weapons with branches of coral, and coral was bound with strips of sealskin to the mastheads of ships to ward off storms.

The ancient Greeks called coral "the blood of the Gorgon," referring to the Gorgon Medusa, the sight of whom would turn any living creature to stone. Legend relates that Perseus decapitated Medusa and used her head to aid in rescuing the fair Andromeda; he then laid the bloody head on the seashore to wash his hands. Blood seeping from the head colored the seaweed red and turned it into stone, producing coral.

Coral was the basis of trade between Greece and India after Alexander the Great; the Indians believed it protected the wearer from danger and healed scorpion and mad dog bites. The Romans believed that drinking pulverized coral cured many diseases and that its ashes healed diseased eyes; it was also thought to be strong protection against lightning. Amulets of coral were given to newborn babies in ancient Rome, and even in this century, teething rings of coral are still popular.

Various cultures have used coral as protection against falling sickness, whirlwinds, fire, shipwreck, sorcery, fits, evil eye, and to keep evil spirits from inhabiting the bodies of the dead.

Chinese mandarins wore a button of coral on the hat as a sign of rank; because large pieces of coral were rare, these buttons were often made of tiny beads strung and knotted into solid balls in the process called "passementerie." The beads were also used in Chinese embroidery.

Despite the popularity of coral, its nature and origin puzzled the users; the ancient Greeks thought it was a stone tree. This explanation was accepted until 1775, when two English scientists, Ellis and Solander, identified it as the skeleton of a marine polyp.

The search for coral formed the basis of the French commercial empire in North Africa; France, Italy, and Spain vied for the coral-fishing rights off West Africa, until Italy gained the upper hand in the eighteenth century. To this day Italy controls the coral industry, while India, China, Iran, and Japan are the largest consumers of coral.

The size of coral limits its use, but coral products through the years have included mosaics; murals; weapon ornaments; decorative harnesses; handles for canes, umbrellas, and tableware; pipes; and beads for rosaries and jewelry.

TOOLS AND MATERIALS   Although coral is soft enough to be scratched with copper, it is brittle and is splintery and uneven when fractured. It must be worked carefully and slowly with steel hand tools and various abrasives and polishes.

The tools used for coral are the same as those used for **Amber Carving,** with a few additions to accommodate the greater hardness and different nature of coral and the slightly different operations.

A pen is used with India ink to outline designs. Coral may be carefully gripped in a leather-lined vise, or attached to a dopstick. An electric drill may be used with an abrasive head and rotary files. **Emery** is the first abrasive used.

Other miscellaneous tools needed for working coral are: thin sheets of waste wood, and some small boards; a **bead-polishing board;** nylon string; tacks; a block of sandstone; a **needle drill;** abrasive-covered boards; hydrogen peroxide; and a wood-carving knife.

WORKING THE MATERIAL   If rough coral is used the first operation is to remove the pink, flaky **sarcosoma** using a scraper, knife, or wire brush. Beneath the sarcosoma, the surface of the coral is finely ridged. The surface can be flattened with a round file, needle file, and knife, then sanded with coarse sandpaper.

Clamp the saw—a hacksaw for large pieces, a jeweler's saw for smaller ones—in a vise. Move the coral across the blade, rotating it between your fingers to prevent chipping the edges. When sawing thin, flat pieces of coral, first glue them to a thin sheet of wood to prevent breaking them.

Coral is polished with emery, **pumice powder,** tripoli powder, jeweler's **rouge, tin oxide,** and **crocus** powder. Coral may be abraded and polished with almost any abrasive compound.

One of the most common uses for corals is coral bead-making; rough-formed, **negligé,** and shaped beads are made. A traditional method for rough-forming beads is to string the drilled blanks on a steel wire stretched tight across a work surface. A block of abrasive sandstone is moved back and forth across them until they are sufficiently formed to be further worked with files.

A **lapstick** is used with a **bowdrill** for further shaping and polishing. The coral is dopped to the end of the lapstick and rotated in the hemispherical depressions of a **bead-polishing board.** Successively finer abrasives are brushed into the hollows.

Coral beads may be gingerly held in a **leather-lined vise** or in a **bead-holding jig** while drilling. A hand twist drill is excellent for boring holes in coral, but for slender pieces a **needle drill** may be necessary.

Pieces of coral used for coral mosaics, coral inlay, and similar techniques must be flat on one or both sides. This is easily accomplished by gluing the pieces to a board and sanding them with an electric drill with an abrasive head. Thus a number of workable elements of uniform thickness can be produced simultaneously.

The pieces may be glued onto a waste piece of wood and sawed to shape, then placed on a dopstick for filing and polishing.

After mounting the coral to a suitable surface with cement, the excess glue may be removed with a scalpel.

To restore color and to clean coral, bathe it for twenty-four hours in a solution of one part hydrogen peroxide and two parts water.

coral inlay. Coral Carving. See **Coral Carving: Working the Material.**

coral knot. Crewel. Embroidery. (Also called bead stitch, coral stitch, double coral stitch, German knot stitch, scroll stitch, snail trail.) A knotted stitch that can be used as a line stitch or filler. In the latter case, the knots of one row fit between the knots of the previous row in a brickwork fashion and is called a double coral stitch. The knots may be spaced close or far apart, but should always be at right angles to the line. When several rows are worked close together the effect is solid and resembles rows of fat **French knot**s. Insert the needle in at A and up at B at right angles to the thread. Holding the needle over the thread, draw through and pull gently to form a knot (**a.**). To make the coral knot effectively, it is best to use a double thread. See ill.

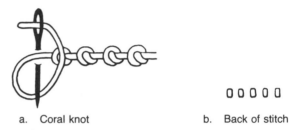

a.   Coral knot   b.   Back of stitch

coral mosaic. Coral Carving. See **Coral Carving: Working the Material.**

coral stitch. Crewel. Embroidery. See **coral knot.**

cord. Bookbinding. The sections of books may be sewn onto cords positioned across the **back** in the same manner as tapes to strengthen the back. The cord used is usually a four-ply unbleached linen, unpolished hemp, or nylon cord. Also see **band, sewing on cords.**

cord. Macramé. The yarn or twine used in the knotting of macramé. In general, macramé cord should be strong, fairly smooth (so that the actual knotting predominates rather than the texture of the cord), and have as little elasticity as possible. This rules out most knitting yarns, as they are generally fairly elastic.

Cords are made from both natural and man-made fibers and include cotton seine twine, **jute, linen,** navy cord, polished raffia, rug wool, silk, **sisal** (all natural fibers), nylon braid, nylon seine twine, **marline twine,** polypropylene cord, rattail (or **satin cord**), and ribbons (all man-made). Also see **bobbin, hand bobbin** and **Macramé: Tools and Materials.**

cord. Spinning. Weaving. A term given to yarns of two or more **ply** that have been twisted together. The term can also be given to the raised **rib** that appears in certain woven fabrics.

cordage. Spinning. Weaving. A general term covering **string, twine, cord, rope,** and **cable** implying that it is made of a **bast fiber.** Cordage of a thick diameter is often used in wall hangings and **fiber sculpture.**

corded fabrics. Weaving. See **Bedford Cord, piqué, rib.**

corded fringe. Rugmaking. Weaving. See **plied fringe.**

corded seam. Stitchery. A **plain seam** which has a **band** of **cording** inserted to exaggerate the importance of the **seam.** It is often used decoratively on knife-edge **pillows** or boxed pillows. See ill.

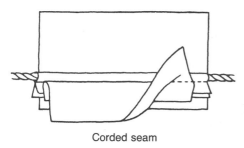

Corded seam

cord for tie-dye. Batik and Tie-dye. Any string or **rope** long enough to be wrapped around a **bundle** and strong enough to be tightly **tied** can be used for **tie-dye.** This includes household or butcher's string, yarn, **raffia,** heavy-duty thread, tailor's thread, crochet cotton, buttonhole thread, linen thread (especially nos. 18 and 35), and carpet thread. Sometimes nylon stockings or tape can be used.

cordierite. Gemcutting. See **iolite.**

cording. Embroidery. A technique in **metallic thread embroidery** using a thread of braided, twisted, or woven strands. Cording is usually sewn, tacked, or couched down with a waxed thread. Also see **couching.**

cording. Macramé. The process of working a row of **double half hitch**es on a **holding cord.** The cording direction may be horizontal, vertical, or diagonal. Work rows of cording close together to form solid fabrics or alternate with other knots and beads. Also see **diagonal double half hitch, horizontal double half hitch, vertical double half hitch.**

cording. Quilts. See **roving.**

cording. Stitchery. A **bias**-cut strip of **fabric** which has been **fold**ed **lengthwise** through the center and has a **cotton** cord placed in the fold. The fabric is folded with the right side out and a row of basting or stitching holds the cord in place. This cording can then be inserted in a **plain seam** to add a decorative effect to **pillows, costumes,** or to any finished edge. Cording can be made with any lightweight fabric, or it can be purchased ready-made in a limited range of colors. See ill. Also see **corded seam.**

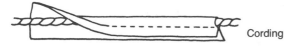

Cording

cord joint. Toys. A **joint** commonly used in connecting the parts of a **doll body** to allow movement in the head and limbs. It was developed in China and perfected by German dollmakers. A cord, especially **elastic** cord, was drawn through the hollowed portions of the doll to make connections at the joints. It is similar to a **string joint,** but the flexibility of the elastic greatly increased the possible doll movements.

cordonnet. Lacemaking. In **needle lace** particularly in **point de Venise,** a raised stitching to outline a **motif.** A padding of coarser threads is stitched and built up to the thickness desired. Over this padding a series of fine **buttonhole stitch**es are worked to cover the padding completely.

cordovan. Leather. A term originally denoting the heavily worked and decorated leather of the Arab craftsmen in Cordoba, Spain, now more commonly used in reference to leather from a section of **horsehide** called the shell.

cord quilting. Quilts. A variation of **Italian trapunto.** Cord quilting uses one layer of fabric, not two, and gives a raised linear effect on the surface of the fabric. It is sometimes used in monogramming. The stitching is done from the top over a double-line pattern. The cord is held in place, under the fabric and between the double lines, with a series of **backstitch**es that cross under the cord on the back side. In a free-form approach, no lines are used and the "drawing" is done freehand over the surface of the material.

corduroy. Rugmaking. Weaving. Originally, a fabric with **filling float**s forming a **warp**-wise ridge normally cut to have a soft, velvety **pile.** In recent years the term has come to mean a loom-controlled method of making a **shag** pile rug with an appearance akin to that of a **knotted pile rug.** In both fabric and rug, the construction follows that of **overshot—twill** float combinations that give the pattern and which are held together by a **plain weave ground.** The twill floats form the ridges which are woven in a heavier, softer yarn than the ground. The difference from overshot is that, due to the **sett** being more open and the placement of the plain weave coming less frequently, the ground is completely covered by the floats. The difference between the fabric and the rug is in the size yarn used, which governs the sett, and the filling floats, which in the case of the rug are put in in large groups and pulled down in loops so that when cut a higher pile results. The floats are cut in the center of the loops either on or off the **loom.** In order for the pile not to be pulled out, the filling float must interlace an amount of warp equal to that over which it skips. In addition, a heavy **beat** must be maintained. Filling float patterns can vary so that, with correct color placement, pile patterns can be attained. Corduroy as a rug technique was popularized by the British weaver Peter Collingwood in the 1960s. However, the idea of using corduroy as a rug has been around much longer under the name of fluff rugs—rugs with fluffed-up **cut-float** pile, used mainly as bedside rugs or bath mats. Mr. Collingwood developed many ingenious refinements, such as double cutting (mixing a short and long pile for design effect) and **inlaying** the float yarn groups so that a wider variety of designs could be achieved. He coined the terms "single corduroy," which refers to the simplest version directly related to the ridged corduroy fabric, and "double corduroy," which staggers the ridges for a thicker pile. See ill. (p. 208). Also see **laid-in.**

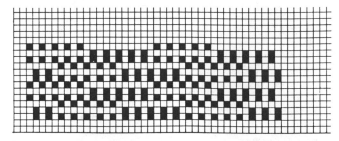

"Double corduroy" weave draft; empty horizontals are the staggered floats

corduroy. Stitchery. Toys. A **cotton** or cotton **synthetic fabric** which is sturdy, warm, and heavy. There are ridges in the **warp** threads giving it a characteristic texture. These ridges vary from very narrow lines in the fine-wale corduroy to the flat area of wide-wale corduroy. Cut corduroy has a deep, smooth **nap** over the entire surface of the fabric.

Corduroy was not used in traditional **patchwork,** but contemporary designs have been adapted to include this heavily textured material. Frequently used in **banners, panels,** and **soft sculpture,** it is also a favorite material for **stuff**ed animals.

core. Metalworking. A quantity of sand, **investment material,** or clay used to fill the interior cavity of a mold when making a hollow casting. There are several basic methods of making a core. The **wax** or **foam** model (to be burnt out later) may be built directly over this core, or the core may be positioned inside the hollow model and supported on metal pins or nails during the process of making the mold. Sometimes the core is left inside the finished casting when its removal is impossible. The function of a core is to reduce the amount of metal needed for a casting, to keep the metal walls of the casting as close to between $1/16''$ and $1/8''$ thick as possible (preventing undue shrinkage and **distortion**), and to lessen the total weight of the finished casting.

The following is a method of making a core for **sandcasting:**

Shape the moist **molding sand** over an armature of iron rods and wire mesh. Test it for size by fitting it carefully into the hollow pattern or into the sand mold. Adjust its shape and size. Add small bits of sand (called flies) to the surface about 1″ apart on the core. Place the core in the sand mold and close the mold. Reopen the mold. If any of these flies is crushed, it indicates that the core must be made smaller at that point. Remove the flies. Coat the core with graphite. Place several layers of soft tissue paper (up to ⅛″ total thickness) on the sand mold. The smaller the object to be cast, the thinner the wall may be. Fasten the core onto the tissue-covered mold with pins or nails. Close the mold.

Bake the mold to remove the moisture. The tissue paper will also burn out, leaving the core suspended at the proper distance from the mold surface.

core. Woodworking. The material or structure that makes up the majority of the inner body of a fabricated door or **hardwood veneer** panel. This core is usually an inexpensive grade of filler wood in **plywood** panels, or a honeycombed cardboard structure in hollow doors.

core end. Macramé. Any cord end that a **knot** is tied over. Also see **alternating square knot, square knot.**

core yarn. Spinning. Weaving. See **novelty yarn.**

cork gun. Toys. See **popgun.**

cork printing. Block Printing. A printing technique in which a whole cork is cut, inked, or painted on **fabric** or paper. Because of its crumbly nature, a cork print is only suitable for simple patterns. Corks of various sizes can be collected from the household, or corks of sizes up to 3″ diameter are available at drug stores. The surface of the cork must be smooth for cutting a design. Paint the pattern on the cork with black paint or ink, then cut away the cork around it. Always cut with the knife slanting away from the edge of the design because, if the edge is undercut, the design may break away. The design should be cut about ½″ deep. The cork may be printed uncut for irregular, textured circles. Also see **Block Printing: Printing Techniques.**

corkscrew yarn. Spinning. Weaving. See **novelty yarn.**

Corn and Beans. Quilts. See **Shoo-fly.**

Corn and Peas. Quilts. See **Windmill.**

corn dollies. Toys. Small figures used in harvest festivities that have their origin in ancient fertility customs in certain rural areas of England. The dolls were made of flax, hemp, or straw; at least one museum example remains of such a talisman, brought to America by early settlers. These dolls were made as fetishes, not as **toys**; they did not, however, have the ominous import attributed to them in Thomas Tryon's chilling novel "Harvest Home," which offers a view of the survival of the figures in contemporary times. The dolls were sometimes called kern maidens.

cornelian. Gemcutting. See **quartz.**

corner. Bookbinding. **Leather, cloth,** or heavy **paper** corners are often added to the cover of a book for decorative purposes and to strengthen these areas of the case, which tend to receive more wear and tear than others. Also see **library corner, mitered corner, pasting leather.**

corner. Knitting. Corners in a piece of knitting are made by controlled **increasing** and **decreasing.** A mitered corner has a 45° angle, with the shaping done on the angled edge so that the opposite edge is left to be knitted into the pattern.

To knit a corner based on 11 stitches, the center stitch is the axis of the angle. Row 1: k 4, m 1 b, k 3, m 1 b, k 4. Row 2: purl all stitches. Row 3: k 5, m 1 b, k 3, m 1 b, k 5. Continue until the desired width.

To decrease, k 2 tog. at beginning of every knit row to desired width.

corner-round bit. Woodworking. See **router bit.**

corner weld. Metalworking. See **weld.**

cornhusk dolls. A traditional American craft using dried cornhusks as a material for creating simple fold doll figures. Remove the husks from the ear of corn, dry them in the sun, and soften them by soaking them in warm water for 10 minutes, or until pliable. While the husks are wet, form them into desired shapes by folding, braiding, or twisting them, and secure by tying with thread. For a lady doll, fold a husk in half. Place a small rounded form, such as a nut, inside the fold and pull the husk down over it, tying thread tightly under it for the neck. Insert a twisted husk under the neck for the arms and tie at the wrists. Tie thread tightly around the doll's waist; add a skirt by tying on additional, overlapping husks around waist. Trim arms and skirt top and hem with scissors. Additional details may be added, such as a shawl around the shoulders, or corn silk may be stitched to the head for hair. Let the doll dry overnight; pins may be used to hold the husks in place while drying.

cornhusk and corncob doll. Toys. An **American folk toy** made since the 1700s, consisting of a corncob body with husk head, limbs, and clothes and corn silk hair. These **doll**s were first exhibited at the New Orleans International Exhibition in 1884, and are still made today.

cornice. Woodworking. See **molding.**

Cornish bridal sweater. Knitting. A sweater knitted by a Cornish fisherman's sweetheart to be worn at his wedding and on all holidays and celebrations.

cornstarch dough. Toys. A malleable **inedible dough** used for modeling small figures and ornaments. The ingredients for the **cornstarch dough recipe** are available in any kitchen, and the mixture is safe for children to handle. It is used in **baker's art** or dough sculpture and is often cut with cookie cutters.

In saucepan blend 2 cups baking soda, 1 cup cornstarch, and 1⅜ cups water to a smooth paste. Cook, stirring constantly, over medium heat for about four minutes. Cover with plastic and let cool for ½ hour.

Roll out the dough ¼–⅜″ thick. If it is too thick it will crack when it dries. The dough can be cut into shapes by using cookie cutters, or original shapes can be cut with the point of a knife. The cut shapes can be left to dry overnight. If shapes begin to curl or warp they can be turned with a spatula.

The process can be hastened by baking the shapes in a warm oven (about 150° F) for 20 minutes until dry to the touch. Decorate with **acrylic paint**s or **marking pen**s. Also see **Toys: Ephemeral Toys.**

cornucopia. Quilts. The name given to several different modern quilt designs, each showing a cornucopia form with flowers of **geometric** or naturalistic shapes emerging from it. The name is given to **blocks** of **pieced** or **appliqué**d techniques, or a combination of the two.

coronation. Quilts. A **pieced quilt** pattern of diamond shapes that form square **blocks** that are **set** on end or on the diagonal. The pieced blocks are alternated with plain ones. This pattern was called **King's Crown** in the days of Sir Walter Raleigh. Later, in New England, it became Coronation. Still later it became President's Quilt, Washington's Quilt, or, in 1830, Potomac Pride.

corozo nut. Ivory and Bone Carving. See **vegetable ivory.**

correction. Tatting. To open a **ring** to make a correction, go back a few **knots,** usually to a **picot,** and with the tip of the **shuttle** or with a **crochet hook,** pick up the **knot bearer** and lift up. Go back a few stitches at a time, lifting the knot bearer until enough thread has been taken up to make the ring slide open easily so the hand can be placed inside the **loop** made by the **loop thread.** Then take out the **knots** one at a time. Do not try to open the ring at the closing.

From time to time while tatting, check to see that the knots are sliding freely on the knot bearer; if they are not, take out the tatting in the manner described above. If the knots do not slide easily, it is usually because two **left half hitch**es or two **right half hitch**es were inadvertently made together, instead of a **double stitch.**

corrodibility. Metalworking. The degree to which a specific metal will corrode when exposed to weather. This characteristic must be considered when planning a piece for outside use and when calculating maintenance cost. Some metals such as **stainless steel, aluminum,** Cor-Ten **steel, bronze,** and **copper** have a high resistance to corrosion. They form a thin surface layer of oxide that protects the metal underneath. **Galvanizing** also reduces the corrodibility of **ferrous** metals, but this protection is destroyed where the joints are welded or soldered after galvanizing. In general, **alloys** resist corrosion better than pure metals. The following list is a sample of metals arranged from the most corrodible to the least corrodible when exposed to an urban industrial atmosphere: **iron, zinc, tin, aluminum, lead, copper.** Silver, gold, and platinum are almost immune to atmospheric corrosion.

corrosion. Jewelry. The oxidation of metals that occurs when the surface of the metal is exposed to moisture, atmosphere, gas, or other conditions. It can be caused by both chemical and electrochemical action. The **precious metals** are some of the least sensitive to corrosion. Also see **liver of sulfur, patina.**

corrugated fabric. Knitting. (Also called cartridge pleating.) The basic fabric is knit in two colors, with three stitches of one color followed by three stitches of the second color. While knitting in this equal-strip fashion, the yarn is kept under very tight **tension.** This tension along the **back of knitting** side causes each stripe to pucker out slightly, creating a corrugated or pleated effect.

corrugated fastener. Woodworking. A small, corrugated steel strip about 1″ long that is sharp along one corrugated edge. It is used to fasten **butt joint**ed or **miter**ed pieces of wood together. To use, place it upright (with teeth down) across the joint, and drive it into the wood with a **hammer** until flush. See ill.

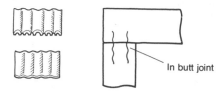

Corrugated fasteners

Cor-Ten. Metalworking. See **steel.**

corundum. Gemcutting. A mineral composed of aluminum oxide with **hardness** of 9, **specific gravity** of 4.02−4.08, and refractive indices of 1.76 and 1.77. Corundum occurs in transparent and cloudy **crystals** of the hexagonal system with some **cleavage** between twinning surfaces and conchoidal fracture. It has vitreous luster and occurs colorless, green, yellow, violet, red (called ruby), and blue (called sapphire). When deeply **color**ed, corundum exhibits dichroism. Synthetic corundum is produced to resemble ruby, sapphire, and alexandrite. Some stones display asterism and are **cabochon** cut in proper orientation to best exploit this effect. Main crown **facet**s are cut at 37°, and main pavillion facets are 42°. Corundum gems are polished on a lead **lap** with tripoli, or a tin lap with 6,400 grit diamond powder. Also see **abrasive, faceting, fracture, luster, polishing, refraction** and **Gemcutting: Applications of Gems.**

corundum. Jewelry. See **aluminum oxide, emery.**

corundum. Metalworking. See **abrasives.**

costume. Stitchery. Whatever is worn in the way of a garment or apparel. Costume usually indicates a garment of more elaborate meaning and detail than does the simple designation of clothes. A costume may have some special significance, as would a uniform or ethnic clothes. Body coverings are costumes in the sense that special consideration is given to the planning, fabricating, and arranging of the materials.

Cottage Tulip. Quilts. See **Tulip.**

cottage wheel. Spinning. See **German wheel.**

cotter. Jewelry. U-shaped **steel pins** of varying lengths used to hold metal parts together during **soldering.** Also see **jig.**

cotter pin. Tincraft. A split pin that is inserted through two or more pieces of tin and then has its ends spread apart to hold the pieces together. See ill.

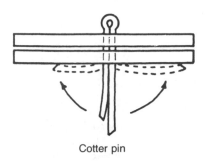

Cotter pin

cotton. Plastics. See **filler.**

cotton. Quilts. Stitchery. A **natural fiber** found around the seed of the cotton plant. The term applies to any of the **fabric**s woven from cotton **fiber**s. The cotton fiber is durable and long lasting, withstanding repeated washing and ironing. Also see **cotton fabric, pima cotton, sea island cotton.**

cotton. Spinning. Weaving. A vegetable **fiber** that was used in India as early as 5000 B.C. A cotton industry developed in Egypt from about 1500 B.C. and, even today, some of the best long **staple** cotton is grown in the Nile delta. The Pima Indians were growing it when the Spaniards came to America and Columbus brought back a hank of cotton yarn to Queen Isabella.

The cotton plant belongs to the mallow family, which relates it to the hollyhock and hibiscus. It is found only in warm climates and grows to 3−4′. The fiber comes from the fluff surrounding the seeds of the plant. After the blossoms appear, wither, and fall off, a small pod called the cotton boll is left. Inside the boll are seeds from which the fiber grows. Cotton can, therefore, be classified as a seed hair fiber. When grown and ripe, the boll splits open and the fluffy white cotton stands out like a powder puff. It is then ready to be picked by hand or machine. After picking, the fibers are separated from the seeds in a process done by the cotton gin called ginning. The fibers are eventually cleaned and carded and formed into a rope called a **sliver,** which sometimes can be bought for handspinning. Cotton can also be combed to produce the best cotton yarn.

Raw cotton is creamy white in color. Its quality depends on many factors, almost all affected by the natural conditions under which it is grown. The staple length of cotton ranges from less than one inch to about 1⅝″. The short lengths produce a coarser fabric and the extra-long staples make a cloth that is smooth and almost silky. American cotton is usually medium to long in staple length. Despite its relatively short length, when compared to other fibers cotton is one of the most spinnable of all fibers, due to a natural **crimp** that enables the fibers to adhere to one another.

Cotton yarn is easy to work with, low in cost, versatile, comfortable, and washable. It is strong, elastic, and resistant to friction, and can be spun very thin. It takes a wide range of dyes and finishes and blends well with man-made fibers. On the negative side are its poor absorbing and insulating qualities, and a dull look that can only be remedied by mercerization. Also see **carded wool, combed wool, mercerized, yarn count.**

cotton batting. Dolls. Quilts. Stitchery. Toys. A soft, fluffy **cotton filler** that comes in bags for **stuff**ing or in sheet form for **quilting**. Because it tends to hold water and to shift or get lumpy unless there are many lines of quilting securing it in place, many quilters prefer the nonabsorbent **Dacron polyester batting.** Also see **batting, glazed polyester filler.**

cotton blend. Quilts. Stitchery. A combination of **cotton** with some other **fiber,** usually a **man-made fiber.** The two are usually combined before spinning. The label will give the name of the dominant fiber first, and will state percentages of fibers. For example, cotton 65%, **polyester** 35%.

cotton boll. Spinning. Weaving. See **cotton.**

cotton broadcloth. Quilts. See **broadcloth.**

cotton canvas. Needlepoint. A sized, evenly spaced mesh of woven cotton threads. Also see **canvas.**

cotton cording. Quilts. See **roving.**

cotton count. Spinning. Weaving. See **yarn count.**

cotton embroidery floss. Crewel. A highly polished mercerized cotton thread with the appearance of silk, available in skeins of six 2-ply strands. These strands are easily separated, enabling the embroiderer to work with as many strands as needed in a design. Also see **cotton tapestry yarn, D.M.C.** and **Crewel: Yarns.**

cotton fabric. Batik and Tie-dye. Quilts. Stitchery. **Cotton** is an excellent all-purpose **fabric** used in **appliqué,** batik, dollmaking, quilting, and tie-dye. It is inexpensive and is available in a wide range of colors and weaves. Many cottons now come in **blend**s of cotton with **synthetic fibers.** Some of the most commonly used cotton fabrics are **cotton broadcloth, calico, cambric, chintz, corduroy, denim, duck, gingham, hopsacking, muslin, organdy, percale, sailcloth,** and **velveteen.**

For batik and tie-dye, all cotton fabric is excellent, especially if **colorfast**ness is required. Only fabrics of natural **vegetable fiber,** like cotton, will take the colorfast dyes. Also see **fabric.**

cotton flannel. Quilts. Stitchery. A **flannel** or lightly **nap**ped fabric, usually 100% **cotton.** Some materials identified as cotton flannel are **blends** of **cotton** and **synthetics.** Cotton flannel is an excellent **filler** for baby quilts and **coverlet**s and is used to pad small areas of **appliqué.** Also see **baby flannel.**

cotton roving. Quilts. See **roving.**

cotton tapestry yarn. Needlepoint. A soft rounded cotton thread imported from France. A single thick strand has an effect similar to wool. Compared to **cotton embroidery floss,** this yarn is heavier and has a matte finish. Cotton tapestry yarn is especially useful for needleworkers who are allergic to wool.

cotton yarn. Knitting. Cotton yarn is processed from the fibers surrounding the seeds of the cotton plant. It is one of the oldest natural fibers known to man and is valued primarily for its strength and durability. Some of the most common cotton yarns and cords are Seine twine, Pearl cotton, and cotton cord. Also see **ply.**

couched stitch. Beadwork. See **overlay stitch.**

couché rentré. Embroidery. Surface **metallic thread**s couched in straight lines over linen or **canvas.** When using an openweave linen as a **background fabric,** cut the threads and plunge them at the end of each line. This makes an easier and neater edge than turning them at the end of each line. Stretch the fabric firmly in an **embroidery frame;** use a strong waxed double silk or cotton thread to couch the pairs of metallic threads. See ill. Also see **couching, Opus Anglicanum.**

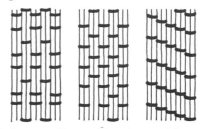

Various couching positions for couché rentré

couching. Crewel. Embroidery. This stitch derives its name from the French word *coucher,* which means "to lay down or set in place." Couching is a method of tacking threads at intervals to a **background fabric** by a small **straight stitch** worked at right angles to the laid threads. A single or double thread may be used in the needle, any number of threads may be couched down, and contrasting colors may be used. Couching can be worked in patterns and may be used as a **border stitch** or a **filling stitch.**

Lay a bundle of threads on the fabric. Come up at A, go over the threads, and go down at B as close to A as possible pulling thread tight (**a.**). Come up again about ¼" from

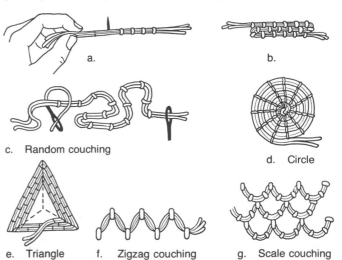

a.

b.

c.   Random couching

d.   Circle

e.   Triangle

f.   Zigzag couching

g.   Scale couching

that stitch, and continue working. See ill. Also see **brick pattern couching, couché rentré, Italian shading, laidwork.**

couching. Quilts. Stitchery. A means of applying a linear pattern of **yarn**, string, floss, or thread to a **fabric background.** Usually a heavy thread or yarn is placed on a fabric, then a lightweight thread is used to **stitch** or **tack** it in place. The stitches of the attaching thread can be angled to match the twist of the yarn, which makes the attaching thread virtually disappear, or the thread may be stitched at right angles to the heavier yarn, making a pattern. To achieve a very heavy line, several yarns or cords may be attached at one time. Also see **star stitch.**

couching cord. Crewel. Embroidery. A technique of attaching any type of cord or braid to the surface of a **background fabric** using a small slanting **couching** stitch. See ill.

Couching cord

count. Spinning. Weaving. See **yarn count.**

counted-thread embroidery. Embroidery. A variety of embroidery done by counting the threads of an evenly woven **background fabric** to form geometric patterns. The design is formed from the structure of the cloth, and the stitches, such as **cross stitch, running stitch,** and **satin stitch,** become an integral part of it.

Counted-thread embroidery is the traditional embroidery of Denmark and Sweden, and today beautiful table linens, baby dresses, and accessories are still made in these countries in both color and **white work.** The basic thread used is a polished linen thread that washes and wears well and comes in a magnificent range of colors. The designs are counted out from a graph and must always be done with a **tapestry needle** to avoid splitting the threads of the linen background. Also see **blackwork, drawn-thread border, evenly woven fabric.**

counter. Weaving. The **warp** counting cord that is situated at the **cross** and used to count off groups of warp yarns during **warping.** The cord is a long piece of fairly sturdy yarn in a color contrasting to the warp. It is looped around the outside of the yarns at the cross and then crossed over them every time a predetermined number of warp ends is made. For example, if the predetermined number is 20, then after every 20 **ends** the 2 ends of the cord would cross each other, thereby encircling and separating every group of 20 ends. The warp will be divided into small groups that make the counting of total warp ends easier and aid in spreading the warp when it is put on the **loom.** The counter can be placed either at the **portee** or **porrey cross,** depending on which the weaver finds easier and whether both crosses are being used.

A counter is also a device placed on the **tension box** during **sectional warping** to count off the number of yards per turn. This is to assure that all sections are the same length. The counter has a resetting system for each beginning of a new section. It is not a permanent part of the tension box but can be removed at will.

Finally, counter is the number used to count off interlacing points in a **satin weave.**

counterbalanced loom. Weaving. A **floor loom** in which the **harness**es are lowered when a **treadle** is pressed. Because of the method of attaching the harnesses, those harnesses not tied to a treadle will be raised by the counterbalance cords at the top of the loom. Pairs of harnesses are suspended together by a common cord wound over **rollers** or **pulleys** or attached to **horses.** The end result is that **warp ends** are both lowered and raised. However, it is the action of the lowered threads that determines the reading of **pattern drafts** for this type of loom. Based on this, it is known as a **sinking shed loom.** Counterbalanced looms are made usually with only 2 or 4 harnesses in widths of 27″ or more. The looms work best when **balanced weaves** are woven, i.e., in a four-harness loom, two harnesses are raised

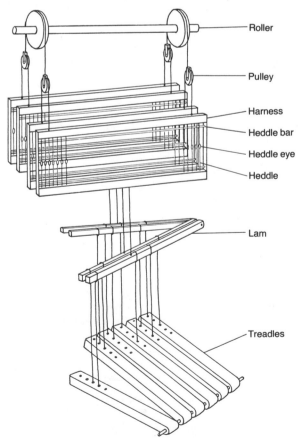

Roller

Pulley

Harness

Heddle bar

Heddle eye

Heddle

Lam

Treadles

Counterbalanced loom

and two are lowered. Raising three harnesses against one is difficult, but a **shed regulator** will help to keep a clear shed. Balanced weave sheds open easily and are wide. The motion of the warp ends going in two directions when a treadle is pressed is good for yarns that tend to stick together. The looms are quiet and sturdy, with a simple construction that makes them cheaper than other floor looms. Counterbalanced looms have been in America since colonial times, when they were brought over from Europe. They are the type of **harness loom** most found in rural or backwoods areas of the world today. See ill. Also see **foot-power loom.**

counterbalance toy. Toys. See **balance toy.**

counterenamel. Enameling. (Also called backing.) To apply a coat of **enamel** to the reverse surface of an enameled piece to lessen warping and cracking after firing, or the coat of enamel itself. Differences in the rates of expansion and contraction between metal and enamel cause the enameled surface to become convex; counterenameling equalizes this stress. On concave surfaces, counterenameling isn't necessary; on flat or convex surfaces, it is advisable to counterenamel first.

Apply **binder** and then dust on the counterenamel. On steep-sided surfaces, spray the binder and dust twice. A thin counterenamel coat is recommended for transparent enamels, a thicker one when working with opaques. Be sure all **metal** is covered evenly and allowed to dry completely. Counterenamel may be underfired, relying on subsequent firings to mature it. When cooling, hammer with a rawhide hammer or clamp or weight the piece to prevent warping. Also see **color testing.**

countermarch loom. Weaving. (Also called countermarche loom, double tie-up loom.) A loom that combines the features of the **counterbalanced loom** and the **jack-type loom.** It has a double **tie-up** that produces both a **sinking** and a **rising shed,** as in a counterbalanced loom. In similarity with the jack loom, it has an unbalanced raising of **harness**es (three against one in a four-harness loom). To be able to have a double tie-up, there are two sets of **lams** placed horizontally under the harnesses, one set below the other. One set of lams pulls down the harnesses and the other set pulls up on the remaining harnesses. A sinking and a rising shed is achieved at one time. Each harness has two lams. Because no harness remains stationary, but will move either up or down, it must be tied to either one lam or the other. Every **treadle** operates both sets of lams, so that when a treadle is stepped on some warp ends will go up and others will go down. One treadle is used at a time. Such a tie-up produces a clear, wide **shed** for even the largest **shuttle**s to go through. The tie-up, which is complex and tedious, is a major disadvantage of this sturdy loom, on which heavy and large pieces can be woven. The looms go up to 75″ in width and have 4–16 harnesses. There are some American-made countermarch looms, but most come from Sweden or Finland. The word "march," or "marche," is the English, Scotch, and Scandinavian term for "lam." See ill. Also see **foot-power loom, harness loom.**

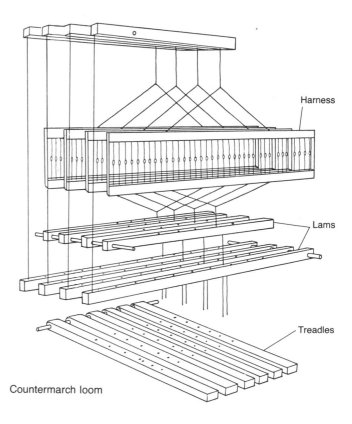

Harness

Lams

Treadles

Countermarch loom

counterpane. Quilts. A term describing a bedcover that is neither **pieced** nor **appliquéd** but achieves its design entirely through the **quilting.** Sometimes it is used to denote any quilt or bedcover. Also see **all-white quilt.**

countershed. Weaving. The second or opposite **shed** in **plain weave** from the one that has been first opened. For example, the first shed would be 1–3, the countershed 2–4. In **primitive loom**s, the first shed would be picked up over, under, and the countershed under, over.

countersink. Metalworking. Plastics. Woodworking. The funnel-shaped enlargement at the outer end of a hole made to receive the head of a **screw, bolt, rivet,** etc., or the drill bit used to make that hole. Also see **drill bit** and **Woodworking: Screwing.**

countersinking. Metalworking. Plastics. Woodworking. The process of **drilling** a conical hole with a **countersink** bit to accommodate the head of a flat-head **screw, bolt,** or **rivet** flush with or below the surface of the material (wood, metal, or plastic); also the process of sinking the head. In plastics and metals, the head is most often left flush with the surface of the material. In woodworking, the head is often countersunk below the surface and the remaining hole filled in with **wood filler** or a **plug.** In the latter case, an **auger bit** of the appropriate size is used rather than a countersink bit. Also see **drill bit** and **Woodworking: Screwing.**

counter twining. Rugmaking. Weaving. A term in **weft twining** referring to twining rows of weft in alternative directions. If one row of **half-turn**s is twined going right to left, the next row is twined left to right. This results in the half-twists lying in opposite directions so that a knitted or **soumak** look is produced. This effect can also be obtained in warp twining. See ill.

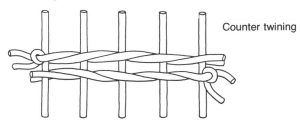

Counter twining

counting cord. Weaving. See **counter**.

Country Husband. Quilts. See **Drunkard's Path**.

County Fair. Quilts. See **Mrs. Cleveland's Choice**.

course. Metalworking. A complete cycle of hammering, **bouging**, and **annealing** in **raising**. The course is worked as the object is hammered and revolved on a **stake, anvil, mold,** or sandbag, and annealed when the metal becomes **work-harden**ed. An object may require many courses during the process of fabrication.

course. Weaving. See **tapestry**.

Courthouse Square. Quilts. A quilt pattern in which five **blocks** are **pieced** to form a cross, which is then surrounded by squares. Triangles are added to finish the block.

Courthouse Steps. Quilts. An arrangement of the **pieced Log Cabin block,** in which strips are added in pairs at the opposite sides of the center block.

couvette. Beadwork. See **sequins**.

cove. Woodworking. A groove with a curved cross section that may be cut along the length of a board or around the middle of a **wood turning**. Coves are commonly used for a decorative molding effect or as a functional hand pull or knob on the face or edge of a drawer.

cover. Basketry. The name for the lid of a basket. It is almost always woven in the same manner as the basket itself. For example, a round coiled basket woven with a **Lazy Squaw** stitch would receive a round lid also woven with a Lazy Squaw stitch. Occasionally the lid is woven so that its sides fit snugly down over the top edge of the basket, at which times it receives a **border**. As with picnic baskets, the cover is sometimes **hinge**d and utilizes a **hasp, noose,** and **peg** to hold it closed.

cover. Bookbinding. The protective or identifying outer casing of a text. Also see **board, case, tight-backed**.

cover. Ceramics. See **Ceramics: Form**.

cover cloths. Lacemaking. Two cloths of washable material for the **pillow** in **bobbin lace**. One is pinned over the **pattern** and finished lace, and the other is placed over the part of the pattern on which the **bobbins** lay. They keep the lace clean and prevent the thread from catching on the **pins**. Also see **dressed pillow**.

covering. Kites. The material used to cover the framework of a kite. A wide variety of covering materials can be used, from the traditional **silk** of the Far East to the most modern synthetics. Also see **Kites: Tools and Materials, Construction**.

coverlet. Quilts. A **bedspread** or bedcover that does not involve **quilting**. It may use **piecing** or **appliqué**, but the term is most often associated with the woven bedcover. In a few instances, coverlet is used to designate a bedcover of small size, covering only the top of the bed and a few inches on each side.

Making coverlets is a traditional American folk art that began with the founding of the colonies in the seventeenth century. Women not only wove these coverlets but also grew the fibers from which they were made. Using **cotton** meant field work—planting, hoeing, and gathering—before the final steps of carding and spinning. Using **wool** involved raising sheep, which had to be sheared before the wool could be washed, carded, and spun. Flowers were gathered and dried for dyes, as were roots and barks.

Coverlet patterns developed in much the same way as quilt patterns. Names changed from one locale to another. Also see **tied quilt**.

Cowboy Star. Quilts. See **Arkansas Traveler**.

cowhair yarn. Rugmaking. Spinning. Weaving. A Scandinavian yarn made of a mixture of wool and cowhair. A **singles** yarn, it has a firm body and a nice sheen, and is hard wearing. These qualities make it popular for rugweaving.

cowhide. Leather. Leather from the hides of cows, available with a smooth surface or with a **grain**. The grained cowhide is very durable.

cowrie. Beadwork. See **shell**.

cowrie. Shell Carving. A species of shell used for cameo carving. It was used during the Renaissance but fell from popularity until reinstated by the School of Coral around the turn of the century. Cowrie was a cheaper material than the **helmet**, which was traditionally used for the students to learn upon.

Cowries have a thinner outer layer of shell that is more easily removed than the helmet **conchyolin**. Cowries are smaller than helmets but not as flat. They are easier to carve and have a broader color range, including violet colors unobtainable in the helmet. Also see **abalone, bullmouth helmet, cameo, gold ringer, cowrie, money cowrie, panther cowrie, poached egg, snake's head cowrie, tiger cowrie** and **Shell Carving: Shell**.

Coxcomb. Quilts. An **appliqué block** of a three-flowered plant in a pot. Also see **flower designs.**

Coyne kite. Kites. A triangular **box kite,** in which each **cell** has three rather than four sides. The Coyne kite was invented by an American, Silas Coyne, in the first decade of the twentieth century. In simplest terms it is an edge-flown triangular kite. A **spar** stretched across the upper base supports a pair of outstretched wings. The inverted triangle tip provides the **dihedral angle** for stability, while the outstretched wings give added **lift.** The French army used this kite so extensively that it is sometimes called the French military kite. See ill.

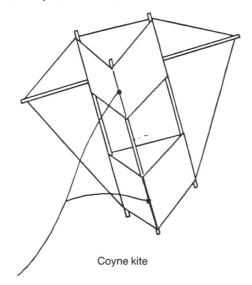

Coyne kite

crack. Stained Glass. See **firecrack.**

cracking. Ceramics. See **dunting, shivering.**

cracking. Enameling. See **counterenamel** and **Enameling: Repair and Care.**

cracking. Plastics. Shrinkage during **curing** causes cracking in **casting resins.** Prevent cracking by reducing the amount of **catalyst** in thick pours; add a **plasticizer** to rigid casting resin; or, if the plastic is to be opaque, add an inert **filler** such as wood flour (fine sawdust), glass, or cotton.

cracking off. Glasswork. The operation whereby molten glasswork is separated from the **punty** or **blowing iron.** The groove formed by the **jack** during the process of **necking down** constitutes a natural weak point in the glass. This area is encouraged to be even weaker by dripping water into the groove, which sets up tension in the glass due to the natural shrinking through cooling. A smart rap on the blowing iron with a file or the handle of a jack is sufficient to fracture the glass at that point.

Alternatively, in the operation of attaching the punty, the necked-down area is scored with a wet file. The cooling effect of the water on the file in combination with the score is somewhat more reliable in cracking the piece off at the proper point. The score is made by sawing with the file in a kind of rocking motion while the work is turned by rolling the blowing iron on the arms of the **glassworker's chair.**

cracking the tank. Metalworking. The process of opening and closing the valve very quickly on the oxygen or acetylene tank in order to blow out any dust in the tank connections. Also see **oxyacetylene welding equipment.**

crackle. Batik and Tie-dye. (Also called veining.) The characteristic veining created in **batik** when **dye** penetrates cracks or **fractures** in the waxed areas. The more brittle the **wax,** the more pronounced the crackle will be. Heavy overall crackle can be achieved by placing the waxed fabric in the freezer to make the wax extremely brittle before cracking it. Stirring the batik frequently and thoroughly while it is in the final **dyebath** will also help make the crackle dominant. To avoid crackle a more flexible wax is used. **Paraffin** hardens and cracks, whereas **beeswax** stays pliable, so a mixture can be adjusted in proportions to help exaggerate or diminish crackle.

crackle. Ceramics. (Also called craquelé.) A term for **crazing** of **stoneware** or **porcelain glaze**s. Considered decorative on some forms, the technique is not recommended on tableware. Crackle can be achieved by using a glaze that shrinks more than the body. Also see **coefficient of expansion, compatibility.**

crackle. Enameling. See **enamel.**

crackle glass. Stained Glass. An **antique glass** that is dipped into water immediately after being blown. The dipping causes fracture lines throughout the sheet. The glass is removed from the water before the lines go all the way through and break it. It is cheap glass that is not particularly unusual or attractive when the crackling is done in large quantity.

crackle weave. Weaving. Weaves derived from a pointed **twill drawing-in draft,** but with a smaller repeat structure so that the direction of the diagonal is constantly changing. The resulting weave has **float**s of three **ends,** as opposed to two in an ordinary twill. Patterns are made up of four blocks of threading units with each one a set of small twills. Each unit can be repeated any number of times; therefore, the blocks of pattern are variable in size. However, when joining two blocks an extra thread, or **incidental,** must be inserted to preserve the continuity of the diagonal. The incidental is a repeat of the first thread of the block. There is a definite progression from block A to block B to block C and to block D. If, in designing the threading, a skip is made from block A to block C, then the incidental from block B must be inserted as well as that from block A.

There are many ways to **treadle** crackle. A common way is to **square off** the weave as for **overshot** and use the overshot format of one pattern, one **plain weave.** However, crackle weave bears no resemblance to overshot when woven. It can also be treadled like **Summer and Winter Weave,** which it does resemble, or **boundweave,** on **opposite**s.

Sweden is the origin of these weaves but the name "crackle" was coined by an American weaver, Mary Meigs Atwater, whose writings helped to make it popular in the

States. She named it so for the fissures, or cracks, in the texture of the pattern. See ill.

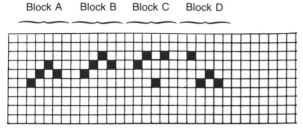

Block threading units in crackle weave

cradle gym. Toys. A colorful toy hung above a cradle or crib so that it will attract a baby's eye and increase hand/eye coordination by encouraging the baby to reach for or move the toy. It is based on a Shawnee Indian toy that consisted of a wooden hoop hung with attractive toys attached to a cradle board above the baby's head. "Cradle gym" was a trademark, but it became the common name for any similar toy. Some have **bell**s, moving parts, and **elastic** string to add to the baby's interest.

cradle quilt. Quilts. See **Quilts: Determining Quilt Size.**

cradle toy. Toys. (Also called baby toy.) Any toy given to a very small baby, usually one not yet walking. Among the most common are the **cradle gym, rattle**s, or **coral**s, and teething rings.

craft clay. Puppets. Toys. Mixture of synthetic resins and fillers that may be fired in a kitchen oven, often referred to as self-hardening clay. They are strong and hard, and superficially resemble fired clay, but not durable or impervious to water. They are intended for amateur use, especially by children.

Craftool. Batik and Tie-dye. See **acid dye, direct dye.**

craft renaissance. The recent tremendously popular revival of interest in handcrafts and folk arts which developed during the 1960s and has continued to grow, revitalizing many of the old crafts which had virtually disappeared. Craft fairs, renaissance fairs, and crafts classes are evidence of an ever-growing interest which seems to reflect a disenchantment with the mass-produced products of a technological society as the final or best or only solution. Some craftsmen follow a purist's approach, in the sense that they limit themselves to using only native materials and traditional methods. They eschew the use of power tools and plastic paints in favor of the more primitive methods, thus leading to a revival of hand spinning, raku firing, and dyeing with lichens. Other craftsmen, using modern tools and in some cases modern materials, are recapturing a spirit of personal commitment to their work which has characterized folk art throughout the world. Both are valid approaches. There is an excitement in the varied personal and expressive work of all these fresh, original artists working within the traditional crafts.

craft stick. Toys. (Also called popsicle sticks.) A flat wooden stick with rounded ends, similar to the tongue depressor but smaller. It is used as a tool or construction material in toymaking and various other crafts. They are also used as paint-mixing sticks.

cram. Basketry. (Also called cram off.) The method used to finish off a **rod border** when the stake is sharpened or **slype**d and then turned down at right angles and inserted beside the next stake. So as not to crack the stake, it is advisable to first prick it. Also see **pricking.**

cramming. Weaving. See **sett.**

cram off. Basketry. See **cram.**

crank. Ceramics. See **kiln furniture.**

crank mixture. Ceramics. See **kiln furniture.**

crapaud. Weaving. (Also called ressort.) An **outlining** technique in **tapestry** often found in Coptic weaving. It is a free technique in which a line of filling thread makes short skips from place to place in a manner resembling superimposed embroidery. In addition to outlining, the technique can be used to do line patterns in tapestry.

craquelé. Ceramics. See **crackle.**

crash. Bookbinding. See **super.**

crater glaze. Ceramics. A thick decorative **glaze** finish derived from burst bubbles in a glaze. These bubbles are sharp and can be dangerous. Also see **blistering.**

crawl. Plastics. See **distortion.**

crawling. Ceramics. The effect which occurs when a **glaze** bunches up or gathers in places leaving other parts of the surface bare. Crawling is caused by dusty or greasy **bisque**, an incorrectly fired bisque, or a thickly applied glaze.

crayon batik. Batik and Tie-dye. See **colored wax batik.**

crayon quilt. Quilts. Any quilt in which the colored decorative work is applied by means of **fabric crayon**s.

crayons. Candlemaking. Common school crayons may be added to hot wax for an expedient way to color candles. One crayon will color approximately one quart of liquid wax. Commercial solid dyes (color buds) are preferred to crayons in that the latter often contain additives that may cause a chemical reaction that will affect the wick and possibly extinguish the flame. Pure wax crayons do not cause this problem. Shave or break pieces of crayons into the hot wax until an approximation of the desired color is attained. If a fairly precise color is required, you should be aware that wax tends to lighten in color as it hardens. Color tests with small quantities of the wax may be needed to produce the desired hue.

crazing. Ceramics. Small cracks or fractures in a **glaze** caused by tension between the **clay body** and the glaze while cooling. Often called **crackle,** when used as a decoration, crazing is most apparent in clear glazes.

Crazing is prevented by increasing the amount of flint (**silica**) used in making the body. If the body composition cannot be altered, increase the amount of flint, or **boric acid,** while decreasing soda or potash to ease contraction in a glaze.

Test the craze potential of a glaze by repeatedly heating and plunging the glazed ware into cold water; increase the kiln temperature each time this is done. Also see **Harkort test.**

crazing. Enameling. See **enamel.**

crazing. Glasswork. Hairline fractures in glass or pottery, which constitute a weakness along those lines but along which lines the material has not actually separated. Also see **crizzling, Venetian glass.**

crazing. Plastics. Tiny internal fracturing of plastic caused by chemicals or pressure. Stress crazing is caused by bending a material too sharply during **cold forming,** or by insufficient heating and softening before shaping when thermoforming. This crazing may not appear for months after forming. Alleviate stress crazing by **annealing.** Chemical crazing, called blur, is caused by solvents attacking the surface. Also see **Plastics: Cementing.**

Crazy Ann. Quilts. A **pieced block** design of triangles and squares that gives windmill effect. See ill.

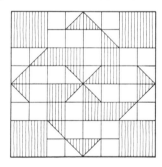

Crazy Ann

crazy quilt. Quilts. The utilization of every scrap of material was a necessity when fabrics were scarce and the production of fibers and the carding, spinning, and weaving were all done at home. When scraps of every size, color, and fiber were collected into one quilt, the crazy quilt was the result. Some crazy quilts consist of squares or rectangles of **muslin** to which smaller **patch**es are **appliqué**d. Others are **all-over pieced** patterns of assorted fabrics, although many of these are also assembled from smaller **block**s. Yarns and flosses are used to add exquisitely detailed decorative stitches at the joining lines of the blocks. Sometimes commemorative ribbons, hand painting, embroidered flowers, names, and various memorabilia are added on the fabric.

The term "quilt" is erroneous in this case because most are not quilted at all, but tied.

Also see **making do, tied quilt, Victorian crazy quilt.**

crease. Batik and Tie-dye. To make a fold semipermanent by **heat-set**ting or applying pressure. **Fabric**s are usually creased by **ironing.** Paper can be creased by running over the folded edge with a fingernail or finger pressure.

creasing. Leather. A leathercraft technique in which belts and straps are incised with a line even with the edge for a finished look. An **edge creaser** is used for this **tooling** variation. Also see **Leatherwork: Creasing, Scoring, and Folding Leather.**

creative bead knitting. Knitting. See **bead knitting.**

crèche. Toys. See **crib set.**

creel. Basketry. A pouch-shaped fishing **basket** with a hinged lid that has a hole to put the fish through.

creel. Weaving. See **spool rack.**

creep. Metalworking. (Also called creeping.) A term describing the increasing of the pressure gauge or regulator readings on a gas tank or cylinder when the pressure continues to build up quickly when the torch valves are closed. This indicates a faulty valve or fitting in the regulator. It is dangerous to continue **welding** when the pressure gauge is creeping. Have it repaired before using it for further welding. Also see **oxyacetylene welding equipment.**

creep. Plastics. See **distortion.**

Creil. Découpage. A technique developed by John Sadler, an English engraver, for transferring ornamental designs in black ink directly to white porcelain from an engraved copper plate. Later the black motif was applied to yellow or ocher pieces. Soon the style became popular in France, and in 1796 the Creil factory was established. The wares were so popular that the style became known as Creil, though there were many other such factories in France. The Creil factory continued production until 1895.

Creil-ware motifs are varied, with scenes based on events of the time, such as processions, street vendors, and views of cities. Madame Blanchard's balloon ascension was a popular subject. The central motif was usually enclosed by a classic border of leaves or garlands. Tinware, called **toleware,** is often decorated in Creil style.

crepe. Weaving. See **plain weave.**

crepe paper. Papercrafts. A thin, crinkled paper available from the dime store in sheets and rolls of strips in bright colors. Crepe paper is very elastic and can be formed into shapes such as flower petals. The colors bleed when moist, so care must be taken when gluing.

crepe-spun yarn. Spinning. Weaving. See **twist.**

crepe weave. Weaving. **Derivative weave**s that give a mixed or uniformly mottled or textured appearance. In their simplest form, they derive from the **plain weave** with certain **raiser**s left out so that a **float** effect is interspersed with the plain weave. The **drawing-in draft** is usually rearranged to help place the floats where desired.

crepe yarn. Knitting. A tough twist yarn made of cotton, silk, wool, or other fibers and having a "crimped" appearance. This yarn is used primarily in ladies' garments.

crescent wrench. Woodworking. See **wrench.**

Cretan stitch. Crewel. Embroidery. (Also called feather stitch, long-armed feather stitch, Persian stitch.) A technique for creating a leaf shape or band with a braid down the center. The stitch is named for the isle of Crete, where it was used to decorate embroidered skirts. Cretan stitch can be worked close or widely spaced (feather stitch), and can be used as a border or filling. It can also be worked to resemble the **fishbone stitch.**

Come up at A; go down at B a fraction below and to the right of A. Form a loop and come up at C inside the loop (**a.**). Go down at D, a fraction to the left and below A. Form a loop and come up at E, inside the loop (**b.**). E is a little to the left and below C. Repeat **a.** going down at F and up at G, inside the loop (**c.**). F and G are a fraction to the right and below the previous stitches. Repeat **b.** The needle goes down and comes up at a fraction to the left and below the other stitches, coming up inside the loop each time (**d.**). Continue in this way so that a plait is formed down the center of the shape. Keep the stitches very close together on the edge to maintain the slant and the center stitches on an even line below one another (**e.**) See ill.

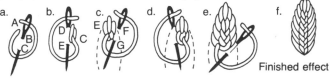

Finished effect

CREWEL

Crewel embroidery rose to the height of its popularity in the seventeenth century in England, and in the eighteenth century in America. In England, typical designs fell into roughly three groups. First, the allover "sprigged" designs, in which small motifs "powdered" the whole area. Second, scrolling or wavy stem designs, with flowers growing from or being enclosed by the stems. And third, Indian Tree of Life designs with stylized flowers, animals, birds, and fruits often growing from a single stem. These designs were fanciful and imaginative interpretations of exotic plants and trees, the exuberance and variety of which were perfect partners for the patterns and textures formed by crewel stitches such as **bullion knot**s, **buttonhole stitch, chain stitch, squared filling**s, **fishbone stitch, french knot**s, **long and short stitch**es, **satin stitch, stem stitch,** and **straight stitch,** to name some of the most basic ones.

American settlers translated the traditional European crewel embroideries into their own more simple and open style. Worked in glowing home-dried colors on homespun linen, these designs have a charming naiveté. There were several reasons for the great popularity of crewel in seventeenth-century England and eighteenth-century America. After the invention of the steel needle in the sixteenth century, England became the center for its manufacture. This meant that all kinds of new skills could now be more easily achieved in needlework, and for the first time the embroiderer, working with crewel designs, discovered the satisfaction and freedom of surface "decoration" as distinct from surface "covering," for example, bargello and needlepoint, in which the background canvas must be entirely covered with close stitching, is surface covering. The East India Company, formed by London merchants in 1600, soon found that embroideries were an important part of its trade, and the large and beautiful handpainted or chain-stitched Tree of Life designs, called **Palampores,** became increasingly popular designs for crewel embroidery. The fashion for four-poster beds furnished with curtains, valances, and coverlets was at its height. According to Hampton Court records, Cardinal Wolsey had 230 beds, most of them hung with brocaded silks and needlework. At first, needlepoint was used as a variant to woven tapestry, but the bold scale of the Tree of Life designs worked in textured crewels seemed perfect for bed hangings, and they became increasingly fashionable.

Early settlers brought crewel to America, where the four-poster bed was still the most popular place for its use. Many of the English embroideries were done in workshops, so that the designs, always exquisitely stitched, had a certain professionalism and compactness. The American settler who had to spin and dye her own yarn and often weave her own linen, lent a personal touch to her crewelwork, interpreting the traditional designs with refreshing primitive directness and beautiful color combinations still greatly admired today. Even though many of the petticoat borders, chair seats, bedspreads, and hangings have worn out because they were in everyday use, those that remain in museums such as Shelburne in Vermont, The Museum of Fine Arts in Boston, and the old Gaol Museum in York, Maine, retain their brilliant colors.

Recipes for vegetable dyes made from plants, berries, or barks, such as butternut, goldenrod, onion skin, sumac, black walnut bark, etc., were passed from hand to hand although some were closely guarded secrets. Colonial crewel embroidery, done all in shades of blue and white, may have been inspired by Canton, China—or perhaps it was simply this restrained palette that appealed to the Puritan mind, together with the ease of producing beautiful shades of blue from the wild indigo plant, which grew in profusion. At any rate, because of the monochromatic color scheme, full emphasis could be given to the varied stitches, and the blue and white crewel was so popular that it was revived in the nineteenth century, when a successful workshop was started by two ladies, Margaret C. Whiting and Ellen Miller, at Deerfield, Mass.

Today, crewel embroidery is enjoying another revival. People have discovered the joy of personal expression in an age of mass production, and many outstanding pieces of needlework are being produced, both in America and Europe. Today's concepts have broadened the meaning of crewel to include bold stitchery with rug wool on heavy tweedy fabrics, close stitching that gives the effect of oil painting, and fine stitching using both wool and cotton threads. Crewel is used for soft furnishing such as curtains, valances, bedspreads, and quilts. It is used on wing chairs; pillows; pictures; articles of wearing apparel such as evening skirts, vests, shirts, handbags, and slippers; bell pulls; rugs, table linens (using washable **acrylic yarn** and **cotton embroidery floss**); wall hangings; eyeglass cases and pincushions, to illustrate the great variety of articles that may be embellished by this form of needlework.

MATERIALS The traditional fabric, a twill weave cotton and linen combination, is still an excellent background fabric for any crewel embroidery that is to receive hard wear. It is generally available in white or natural (although it may be dyed to any color) in widths of 36″, 54″, and 72″.

Deciding on where the article is to be used is the first step before choosing a fabric for crewel embroidery. Because crewel can be used for such a wide variety of objects, the range of fabrics is extensive. The following fabrics are good for soft furnishings such as curtains, chair seats, bedspreads, and pillows: worsteds, linens, nylon and acrylic mixtures (smooth or brushed), upholstery satin, antique satin, tweeds, and linen twill. For clothing, pictures, mirror frames, coasters, etc., cotton velvet, flannel, corduroy, denim, and linen are recommended. Fine fabrics such as damasks and brocaded silks may also be used for crewel, but first should be backed with muslin or fine linen by **basting** the two fabrics together.

Crewel needles are generally sold in packages of assorted sizes, either called "crewel" or "embroidery." They have sharp points and long eyes, making them easy to thread. Practicing a few stitches will determine which is the best size needle for the yarn and fabric being used. The needle should be large enough to open a clear hole in the fabric, allowing the wool to pass through easily, yet not so large that it has to be forced through. Needles are numbered to size, and as the number increases, the size of the needle decreases. For instance, a 3 or 4 crewel needle is an average-to-large-needle, and a number 10 is very fine (**a.**).

For working on an **embroidery frame**, particularly with heavier yarn, a **chenille needle** is ideal. These are short needles with longer, larger eyes than crewel needles, and are very easy to pass quickly back and forth through the fabric when it is stretched tightly in a frame. Chenille needles range in size from 26 (the smallest) to 13 (the largest) (**b.**).

Tapestry needles are also used for crewel embroidery, and are exactly like chenilles except that they have blunt points (making them useful for weaving and darning stitches worked on the surface of the fabric) and only pass through the fabric at the beginning and end of the line of stitching. Rug needles are useful whenever heavy yarn is being used on large-scale designs. Even though their points are blunt, the background fabric, to be suitable, must necessarily be of a fairly open weave so that the yarn and the needle can pass through easily (**c.**). See ill.

The traditional crewel yarn was a lightly twisted two-ply wool. Today, various versions of this basic fiber are on the market. The most universal is known as **Persian yarn.** Three threads of two-ply wool are lightly twisted together to form a strand of wool approximately the thickness of

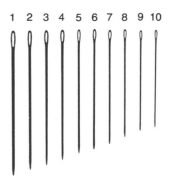

a. Crewel needles

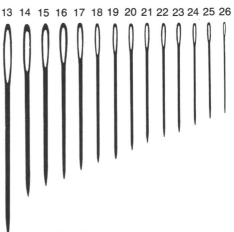

b. Chenille needles (sharp points)

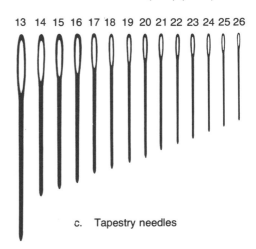

c. Tapestry needles

one strand of **knitting yarn.** This strand can easily be separated to work with one, two, or three threads in the needle according to the effect desired. Because of its loose twist, Persian yarn has an attractive slightly irregular handspun look. It comes in a wide range of good colors.

English **Appleton crewel wool** is finer and more tightly twisted, and comes in close shadings of colors. Like the Persian, it is sold in small skeins of approximately 40 yards.

French (**Broder Medici wool**) crewel wool is finer still. As the article made with this yarn is used, the wool takes on a lustrous silky sheen. The colors available are the muted yet glowing shades of French tapestries.

Rug wool comes in various weights in both real wool

and acrylics, and is useful for bold-scale stitching and in combination with other textures.

Knitting yarn, sport yarn, and fingering yarn are all available in wool and acrylics. The latter takes vivid dyes very well, and may sometimes be combined with wool to highlight a design. For instance, the clearest, brightest white is available only in acrylic yarn.

Cotton embroidery floss is extremely versatile; it may be easily separated to use as many strands in the needle as necessary. It is attractive used in combination with wool or where a design should be washable. The most universally available is six-strand cotton, made by such manufacturers as **D.M.C.,** Coates and Clark, or the American Thread Company. The cotton made by these companies is boilfast. There are many different methods of applying a design to fabric. The method you choose depends on the type of material you are using (smooth or bulky, light or dark, etc.).

TRANSFERRING A DESIGN If you are transferring a design only once and your design is not exceptionally large, the **light box** method is the most accurate. This is an age-old method of transferring by holding the fabric and pattern against a window so that the light shines through, making it easy to trace the design onto the cloth. An easier method is to do this with an electric light and a glass-topped table. With masking tape, secure the background fabric to the table. Center the design on top and place a light underneath the table.

Trace the design with a permanent felt-tip marker. Alternatively, mount the fabric onto **stretcher strips** or into an embroidery hoop. With masking tape, hold the design in place on the reverse side, and position a table lamp (the flexible kind is best) behind it so that it will clearly silhouette the design, then trace with a permanent felt-tip marker. This method is often more convenient than the table top—it eliminates the need for a sheet of glass, and it is easy to shift the position of the design as you go along so that the light clearly silhouettes the part on which you are working.

For light-colored smooth fabrics, the carbon method of transferring is quick and simple. First mark the center of your **background fabric** by creasing it in half both horizontally and vertically. With a thread of a contrasting color, baste over the folds. Fold the design in the same manner and place it on top of the first fabric with the centers matching. Secure the fabrics to a flat hard surface by taping the edges with masking tape. Lay the pattern face-up on top, lining up the creases in the pattern with the basting threads on the fabric to center the design. Hold it in place with books or weights and slide **dressmakers' carbon,** wax-side down, between the pattern and the cloth (**a.**). Trace the design with a dull pointed object, such as a soft pencil or stylus. It is important to press firmly, drawing with short smooth strokes so as not to tear the paper (**b.**). Constantly check by lifting a corner of the paper to make sure that the pattern is transferred clearly. Any weak lines can be made heavier by using a permanent felt-tip marker afterward. See ill.

Certain heavy, nubby materials are difficult to transfer with dressmaker's carbon, so the net method is often used.

Transferring a design

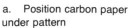
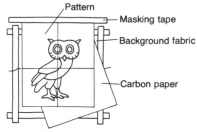

a. Position carbon paper under pattern

b. Trace design onto background fabric

Trace the pattern with a permanent felt-tip marker onto net or tulle. Lay this over the background fabric, centering the design. Trace the design again with the marker. The ink will penetrate between the holes of the net, leaving a clear impression on the fabric.

An excellent method for sweaters is to transfer the design with basting stitches. Fine silks or stretchy fabrics such as knits are best backed with muslin or crinoline to prevent stretching while the embroidery is in progress. The stitching is then worked through both layers. It is relatively simple to transfer the design at the same time. First, trace the pattern onto the organdy or muslin or whatever transparent material you are using for backing; pin this to the reverse side of the fabric and baste through both layers along all the outlines, using small stitches and contrasting thread. Work the design, covering the basting stitches, then cut away the excess transparent material from around the edges of the pattern on the reverse side.

A quick and easy method of transferring is to use a transfer pencil. The drawbacks are that the resulting line is rather heavy and apt to smear as the needlework is being done. It should only be used on washable fabrics, as the pink transfer line can be completely removed with soap and water. Using a lead pencil, trace the design onto layout or tracing paper. With the transfer pencil, retrace it onto the reverse side of the paper. Center the pattern on the background fabric with the pink transfer side down. Make a few test lines on the corner of the paper and, with a fairly hot iron, transfer these to a corner or an odd scrap of fabric. When the iron is hot enough, the wax of the transfer pencil will melt and penetrate the fabric. Iron on the design, "stamping" rather than rubbing with the iron to make sure the pattern will not slip out of place and smudge the lines as you are transferring. At first the paper tends to stick to the cloth, but later, when the wax has melted, it will lift off easily.

A perforated pattern is the most difficult and time-consuming method of transferring a design, but is very useful when several repeats of the same design are desired. The design must first be traced onto perforating paper, layout paper, or sturdy tracing paper. Break a pointed needle in half and set the broken end in an eraser of an ordinary pencil. Lay the design onto a thick pad of felt or any thick layer of material. With a spiked pencil or a tailor's wheel, prick small, evenly spaced holes all around the outlines of the design.

Find the center point of your fabric and perforated pattern by folding them in half horizontally and vertically.

Tape the fabric to a flat surface with masking tape and center the perforated pattern on top. Keep it in place with weights. With a blackboard eraser or a rolled pad of felt, rub powdered charcoal (known as "pounce") through the pattern. Rub lightly with a circular motion, using only a small amount of charcoal. Lift a corner of the paper, and if the line is not clear, rub again, using more charcoal. If too much has been used already, lift off the pattern and lightly blow off the excess.

Using a fine watercolor brush (#3 or #4) and a blue watercolor or gouache paint, lightly paint around the lines. It is recommended that this is first practiced on another piece of fabric, because it takes time to get the proper mixture of water and paint. If a permanent line is needed, oil paint and turpentine may be substituted for the watercolor.

WORKING ON A FRAME   Because of the soft nature of the background fabrics on which crewel embroidery is worked, it is particularly important to use an **embroidery frame.** By this means, the fabric is stretched out tightly and the needle is taken back and forth vertically through it. Both hands are used, one above and one below the frame, so the work is done speedily and with even tension.

All crewel embroidery stitches are easily worked on a frame, and for some of them a frame is essential; for example, **burden stitch, laid work, long-and-short stitch,** padded satin stitch, **split stitch,** and **squared fillings.** Others, namely the American crewel stitches, were traditionally done in the hand and have a completely different effect when worked on a frame. The stitches are the same as the ones primarily used for toughness and wearability on peasant costumes—short, interlocked, and looped stitches that can be held down by the thumb and fingers of the free hand while the other hand controls the action of the needle. They are primarily **rope stitch, buttonhole stitch,** coral stitch, **Roumanian stitch,** and all narrow banding stitches that will not draw the fabric together and pucker it.

PREPARATION AND LAYOUT   If your design is not the correct size, it may be enlarged or reduced by the squaring method. The quickest and most accurate way to arrive at the right size is to photostat it. Photostating services are available in most large towns and are relatively inexpensive. It is only necessary to request one final measurement—either vertical or horizontal—and the rest will follow in proportion. The design can then be traced onto firm tracing paper, using a black felt-tip marker. The lines should be clear-cut and flowing so that there will be no haziness about the areas for stitching. If the design is complex and the photostat dark, clear acetate is a good substitute for tracing paper. If acetate is used, a permanent fine-tipped felt marker or drawing pen should be used to trace the design.

After the design has been drawn or traced it is necessary to find suitable fabric. To determine the amount to buy, add at least four inches to each side dimension of the design (less may be allowed if the pattern comes close to the selvage).

In the case of a wing chair, each pattern piece should be measured and cut out in paper or muslin, preferably by the same person who will upholster the chair. These patterns should be large enough to include turnbacks, and should be marked with a pencil outline all around, showing the design area. The pieces should then all be laid out on one length of fabric, fitting them in to avoid waste, yet paying attention to the straight grain of the fabric, which should run vertically through the center of each piece regardless of its shape. The designs should then be transferred and embroidered without cutting out the separate pieces. Finally, the whole piece should be blocked, then cut and mounted.

The same procedure may be followed for sets of chair seats or clothing. If the length of fabric is too unwieldy, it may be cut into easier-to-handle pieces. The only basic rule to follow is to cut the fabric as far as possible with straight edges around each pattern. If you cut them exactly to shape, they may stretch and flute where the fabric is cut on the diagonal while they are being worked. Remember that the cost of an extra length of material is comparatively inexpensive compared with the value of finished embroidery. It is easy to cut away extra fabric, but extremely difficult to add! Also see **enlarging and reducing a design.**

COLOR AND DESIGN   Traditionally, color in embroidery was influenced by dyes available to the needleworker. Early crewel embroidery had clear yet soft coloring. Aniline dyes of the Victorian era had a revolutionary effect on color in embroidery. Climate has a distinct influence on color in embroidery. For instance, the primary colors are used in Mexico because of their sunny, strong contrasts; soft, shaded colors are used in needlework in England, and the warm earth tones are used by the desert-dwelling Indians around the Grand Canyon.

With the wide range of colors available to the embroiderer, color decisions are often confusing. In general, it is a good idea for the beginner to restrict the palette so that full emphasis can be given to the texture of the stitches. It is difficult at first to select from a wide range of colors and stitches without the result losing impact.

Design ideas for embroidery are almost unlimited, but the best tools of the embroiderer are color and the materials. As William Morris said, "Now indeed it is a delightful idea to cover a piece of linen cloth with roses and jonquils and tulips all done quite natural with the needle, and we can't go too far in that direction if only we remember the nature of our craft in general, and since we're using especially beautiful materials, that we shall make the most of them and not forget we are gardening with silk and gold thread."

FINISHING   Blocking is by far the best method for finishing crewel embroidery, but the work should be color tested first for fastness. If the colors are not fast, the embroidery should be pressed on a soft pad on the reverse side of the fabric using a damp cloth under the iron. If the colors are fast, block on an old piece of board, preferably particle board or **chipboard.** The **blocking board** should be covered with heavy-duty brown paper to keep the needlework clean and to avoid splinters in the fabric. With a right angle and ruler or a compass, depending on the shape of the piece, draw the finished shape on the brown paper. Using **canvas pliers** and rustproof carpet tacks, nail the embroidery to fit the outline. Nail the corners, then the centers, and finally complete the outline by placing nails at evenly spaced intervals of approximately ½–1″. Instead of a board, **stretcher strips** can be used and instead of tacks, a heavy-duty staple gun is often easier to handle. After the fabric is stretched square and taut it should be soaked thoroughly with clean cold water and allowed to dry.

Crewel can be used for chair seats, soft coverlets, curtains, pillows, clothing, etc., so the methods of finishing cover every form of soft furnishing in the home. It would be impossible to go into every detail about every type, but a few basic rules should be remembered. Crewel to be hung on a wall should never be glued to the cardboard or plywood backing, but should be mounted like a canvas oil painting on stretcher strips. If a board is covered it should be stretched, either by lacing the back with a **herringbone stitch** or by stretching it tightly with masking tape. The board should first be covered with a sheet to give it a slight padding and a softer look. Pillows can be mounted as a knife-edge pillow with a single welting, or as a box pillow with a gusset to give added thickness. The pillow backing should be color coordinated, and the fabric should be substantial, such as velvet or corduroy. If the piece is not blocked well before mounting, it will probably not be as square as the pillow.

CARE AND MAINTENANCE   Crewel embroidery can be washed with cool water and a mild, pure soap. Some detergents contain small amounts of bleach that could make the colors fade, so check the label. Before washing, also check the piece for colorfastness.

Crewel should be treated with as great care as any fabric of fine quality. A chair seat or footstool should not be vacuumed too frequently, as certain long stitches can be pulled apart by the suction. Curtains or drapes should be interlined with a sunscreening material to prevent fading. Crewel pictures are best framed without glass so that full dimension is given to the texture of the stitch; they should not be placed in strong sunlight where they might fade, and should be taken down periodically to be beaten on the reverse side to loosen any particles of dust.

crewel needle. Crewel. Embroidery. (Also called embroidery needle.) A needle of medium length with a long eye, available sizes 1–10 (the higher the number, the finer the needle). The needle should always be somewhat thicker than the thread used so that yarn passing through the **background fabric** will not wear. Also see **Crewel: Materials.**

crewel needle. Stitchery. See **needle.**

crewel on canvas. Crewel. Needlepoint. See **Crewelpoint.**

Crewelpoint. Crewel. Embroidery. Needlepoint. A combination of needlepoint and crewel stitches on **canvas.** Nee-

dlepoint in smooth **tent stitch (petit point)** has been traditionally enriched with a few touches of raised crewel stitches. The eighteenth-century carpet owned by Lord Salisbury at Hartford House in England has magnificently stylized flowers on a dark blue ground as its central design. French knots are worked on top of the needlepoint flower centers for an effective restrained textural emphasis.

Today all kinds of crewel stitches are being added to needlepoint, or the crewel stitches are worked alone to give a tapestried effect. The most useful stitches are **Turkey work, satin stitch, fishbone stitch, chain stitch, buttonhole stitch, stem stitch, bullion knot,** and **French knot.**

crewel stitch. Crewel. Embroidery. See **stem stitch.**

crib set. Toys. (Also called Christmas crib, crèche, manger scene, Nativity set.) A collection of figures, animals, trees, and buildings used to set up a Nativity scene to celebrate the Christmas holidays. The sets are religious in nature, but children are often allowed to arrange or play with the crib figures. They are made from many different materials; the finest are handcarved wood. **Clay,** plaster, paper, and other materials are also used. Usually there are figures of the Christ Child, Mary, Joseph, the Wise Men, angels, shepherds, sheep, cattle, trees, and buildings that vary with the locality in which they are made.

cricket. Toys. A small **sound toy** made of thin metal, usually in the shape of a cricket or other insect. When stepped on or pinched, a dome-shaped piece of metal is forced out of shape and the buckling of the metal makes a noise. Released, the metal springs back into shape, repeating the noise.

crimp. Spinning. Weaving. The natural wave or curl found in wool fibers. The waviness varies in different breeds of sheep, with a shorter-haired sheep such as the **Merino** having more crimp than a longer-haired breed. **Mohair** has very little crimp. The more crimp, the finer the wool. A uniform crimp indicates a superior wool. Wool with much crimp will spin into a soft, fluffy yarn, whereas wool with little crimp will spin into a smoother, harder yarn. Also see **bulked yarn, loft, wool.**

crimping. Metalworking. See **raising techniques** and **Metalworking: Raising.**

crimping stake. Metalworking. See **anvil.**

crinoline. Stitchery. Originally a **stiffening fabric** of **linen** and horsehair. It is now made of a coarse medium-weight fabric that is **sized** to give it stiffness. It is used in **stuff**ed **stitchery** forms or **doll**making to add **body** and give shape to certain areas.

crisscross binding. Batik and Tie-dye. A **binding method** that gives a partial resist in **tie-dyeing.** The crisscrossing pattern of the threads makes a meshwork design on the fabric. It is sometimes called lattice binding. See ill.

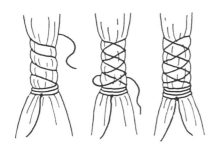

Crisscross binding

cristallai. Beadwork. See **Beadmaking.**

cristobalite. Jewelry. See **investment.**

critical angle. Gemcutting. See **refraction.**

crizzling. Glasswork. The process in glassblowing by which the surface of the glass is crazed by sudden cooling and then reheating. Molding blown-glass vessels in ice molds will produce this effect. Also see **crazing.**

CROCHET

The term **crochet** comes from the French word *croc*, which means a "hook." Crochet is a method for making lace. One of the most famous crocheted laces is **Irish crochet.** Irish crochet lace derives from the Irish imitation of expensive Venetian lace of the nineteenth century.

Crochet was initially used for embellishment. It has been referred to as "nun's work" because it was made by nuns from the thirteenth through the sixteenth centuries—primarily for altar cloths and vestments, for which it is still used today. Nuns who became missionaries carried their craft to foreign soils where it was used to produce lace and articles for the home.

Men have played an important part in the production of crocheted lace—not only in the design, but also in the fabrication. Traditionally, both boys and girls were taught lacemaking in school.

Crochet is a single interlooping element that is worked with a hooked implement. Basically, crochet is a kind of chaining. Each successive horizontal row is built up by a series of loops that are simultaneously worked vertically and horizontally. In most cases, when crochet is worked back and forth the two sides of the fabric are identical. When crochet is worked around, the two sides of the fabric are different. These two facts apply to all crochet in its pure form.

In this century crochet has been used to produce collars, cuffs, antimacassars, doilies, bedspreads, tablecloths, lace, pillow covers, afghans, and clothing. During the 1960s a new awareness of crochet as a means of producing art grew. The use of large hooks, heavy yarns, and cords that commonly had other uses resulted not only in crocheted wall hangings but also in an exciting new approach to clothing.

MATERIALS The variety of yarns that can be used for crochet is endless. Children's clothing needs a soft, durable yarn, which can be wool or one of the many synthetic fibers available today. For table mats, doilies, tablecloths, bags, and bedspreads, cotton or linen thread of various weights is recommended. Afghans, pillow covers, and adult clothing can be crocheted of wool, mohair, alpaca, camel's hair, synthetics, or a combination of these.

Specific pattern directions usually recommend the type of yarn, the size of crochet hook, and the stitch gauge. Recommended fibers may include alpaca, angora, camel hair, cotton yarn, jute, linen, llama yarn, mohair, ramie, and rabbit hair. The new uses of crochet—wall hangings, avant-garde clothing, hats, blankets, pillow covers, and bags—involve the use of materials traditionally used for weaving. The range of materials is vast and the choice determined by the craftsperson.

Crochet hooks are made of steel, wood, plastic, and aluminum, and are available in a variety of sizes and lengths. Size primarily refers to the size of the hook and the shank toward the hook end. The material used is a matter of personal preference and size availability. With the exception of a wooden or an **afghan hook,** all crochet hooks have a flattened finger indentation midway along the shank of the hook. The hook size and brand are usually printed on this flattened area. Afghan hooks have the same numbering as aluminum hooks for sizes F through K. The following is a comparison chart of American and international hook sizes.

CROCHET HOOKS: COMPARATIVE SIZES (Afghan hooks have same numbering as aluminum hooks in sizes F to K.)

American (in inches)	International (metric—mm)
K or 10½"	7 mm
J or 10	6½
I or 9	6
H or 8	5½, 5
G or 6	4½
F or 5	4
E or 4	3½
D or 3	3
C or 2	2¾
B or 1	2½

Aluminum hooks are 6″ long and are available in sizes B through K. Plastic hooks are 6″ long and are available in sizes D through K. Steel hooks are 5″ long; sizes range from 00, the largest (and not listed above), to 5, the smallest. Wooden hooks are 10″ long and come in sizes 10−16. There is a giant plastic or casein hook available, measuring ⅝″ in diameter (size Q) to ¾″ in diameter (size S) and 8″ long.

Afghan hooks are either 9″ or 14″ long, have no finger indentation along the shank, and have a knob opposite the hook end to keep stitches from slipping off. There are also some flexible crochet hooks that hold more work than regular crochet hooks. See ill.

Some miscellaneous items are necessary or useful for crochet. You will need a pair of scissors for cutting yarn, a ruler or tape measure for determining **gauge,** and **tapestry needles** for working loose ends of yarn into the fabric.

Small, colored plastic rings can be used as a row or pattern marker. A notebook is helpful for keeping a record of stitches, patterns, and supply sources. If you are going to do **hairpin lace** you will need a U-shaped steel hairpin lace fork.

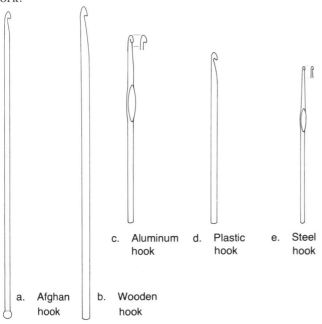

c. Aluminum hook   d. Plastic hook   e. Steel hook

a. Afghan hook   b. Wooden hook

ABBREVIATIONS

beginning	beg
chain, chain stitch	ch, ch st
cluster	cl
decrease	dec
double crochet	dc, dcr
double triple crochet (double treble)	dtr
half double crochet	hdc
increase(s)	inc(s)
inclusive	incl
long double crochet	l dc
loop(s)	lp(s)
open mesh	om
picot	p
pattern	pat
previous row or round	pr r
repeat	rep
repeat ⅛ to ⅛	rep ⅛ to ⅛
row round	r rnd
single crochet	sc, s cr
skip	sk
space(s)	sp(s)
stitch(es)	st(s)
together	tog
triple chain	tr ch
triple crochet (treble crochet)	tr, tr c
triple triple crochet (triple treble)	tr tr
wool round hook (yarn over)	wrh
yarn over hook	yo

BASIC PROCEDURES   Hold the hook however it is comfortable for you. Most people hold the hook as if it is a pencil, with the hook end forward, but many grasp the entire shank in the fist and use the thumb for leverage.

The yarn is held in the free hand while working. It is usually placed between the last two fingers, taken over the little finger, brought over the next two fingers and over the forefinger, and held taut by the thumb and forefinger. Bend the little finger over the yarn to help control the tension.

To begin, make a **loop** (**a.**), pull the yarn coming from the ball through the loop (**b.**), and pull tightly to close. This is called a **slip knot** (**c.**). Insert the hook through the loop, pick up the yarn, and pull it through the loop; continue in this manner until the desired number of stitches are on the needle. This is called a **chain** (**d.**).

To close a **chain,** insert the hook through the beginning loop and pull the yarn through (**e.**). This closure is used as a base for some medallion work.

To increase, or to add additional stitches to the existing ones, you simply make 2 sts into any one existing stitch. Whenever you do this, you will add one extra stitch to the number in the **row** of crochet.

To eliminate one or more stitches at a time from the crochet work is to decrease. This is done by working two stitches together as you normally would work one. See ill.

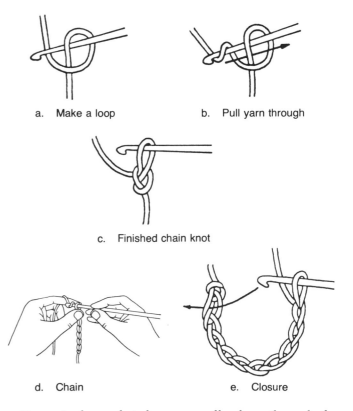

a. Make a loop   b. Pull yarn through

c. Finished chain knot

d. Chain   e. Closure

For a single crochet decrease, pull a loop through the next two stitches, yarn over, and pull the hook through the three loops (**f.**). Skip one stitch and make a single crochet on the next stitch (**g.**).

For a double crochet decrease, work a double crochet into the next two stitches, keeping the last loop of each stitch on the hook. Bring the yarn over and pull the yarn through three loops (**h.**).

For a triple crochet decrease, work a triple crochet into the next two stitches, keeping the loops on the needle.

Yarn over and pull the yarn through the three loops (**j.**). See ill.

f. Single crochet decrease, start

g. Single crochet decrease, finish

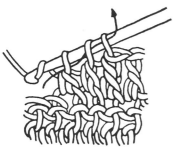

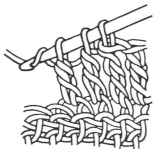

h. Double crochet decrease   j. Triple crochet decrease

To determine whether your stitch gauge matches that specified for a piece of crochet, work a sample piece measuring 16−20 stitches across and a minimum of four rows down. Follow the **blocking** procedure before measuring (counting the number of stitches vertically and horizontally).

To block, use a piece of **Celotex** that has been marked off in a grid of 1″ squares. Stretch the finished crochet work to the desired size and pin with T-pins often enough to obtain a smooth edge. Place a damp cloth on top. Hold a hot iron close to the cloth to produce steam, but do not let the iron rest on the work. When the work is completely dry, unpin it, and wash it with mild soap and water if the work has become soiled. Remove any excess moisture with terry-cloth towels, pin the work to a blocking surface while still damp, and let it dry.

After the first row of stitches, unless otherwise stated, insert the hook through the top two loops in the direction of front to back. One loop is always left on the hook at the end of the row. When counting completed loops, do not include the loop on the hook.

To **turn** work at the completion of a row of crochet, reverse it to begin the next row. It is important at this point that a chain of one or more stitches is made before beginning the next row of crochet. This chain raises the yarn to the level of the row to be worked and prevents puckering. The number of chain stitches to be forked for the various crochet stitches are as follows:

single crochet: chain 1 and turn
half double crochet: chain 2 and turn
double crochet: chain 3 and turn
triple crochet: chain 4 and turn
double triple crochet: chain 5 and turn
triple triple crochet: chain 6 and turn

To join together finished pieces of crochet, place them either face to face or back to back. Insert the crochet hook through the front loop of the piece facing you, and then insert the hook through the back loop of the second piece and make a single crochet stitch*; repeat * to * across the work. The slip stitch may be used for the same method.

BASIC STITCHES The following basic stitches are arranged approximately in order of difficulty.

The slip knot is the single **loop** knot that starts all crochet. It is used to cast the yarn onto the hook. Form a small, U-shaped loop with one end of the **yarn.** Bring the short end of the yarn around the longer end once and then bring it through the circular opening it has formed to make a loose knot. The loop at the side of this knot can be loosened or tightened to fit onto the **crochet hook,** where the knot is then pulled tight. It is from this knot that the **foundation chain** is worked.

The slip stitch (abbr. sl st) is a crochet **stitch** that adds no height to the work and that is used to shape or strengthen **edges,** to join a **chain** when making a **ring** in a **motif** or **medallion,** or to join two pieces of finished crochet together. Insert the **crochet hook** into a stitch, catch the yarn strand on the hook, and draw it back through the loop.

Single crochet (abbr. sc or s cr) and the **chain stitch** form the basis for all crochet work. Single crochet makes small even stitches and can be used to join sections of a crocheted item together. Place the **crochet hook** through the two top threads of the stitch in the **previous row. Yarn over** and draw this through both the loops on the hook in one movement. The new **loop** remaining on the hook is used to work the following single crochet, and so on (**a.**).

Half double crochet (abbr. hdc) is a crochet stitch that is halfway in length between the single and double crochet stitches. Skip 2 ch, * yo, insert hook into next ch (**b.**), draw through loop (**c.**), yo, draw through the three loops on the hook (**d.**)*, repeat * to *, ch 2, turn.

The double crochet (abbr. dc or d cr) is one of the most basic and widely used crochet stitches. Make a foundation chain, sk 3 ch, * yo, insert hook in next chain, draw through loop, yo, draw through 2 loops, yo, draw through last 2 loops * (**h.**), repeat * to *, ch 2, turn.

Triple crochet (abbr. tr or tr c) is worked as for **double crochet** except with **2 yarn-overs** (rather than the 1 yo of double crochet). To make triple crochet, working on a foundation chain, yo twice, insert hook in 5th ch from hook (**k.**), pull up loop, * yo, pull through 2 loops * (**m.**), repeat * to * twice (**n.**). Chain 4 before turning. Be careful that yarn-overs don't slip off the hook.

Double triple crochet (abbr. dtr) is worked as for **triple crochet,** composed of **over**s, and loops with the height of 6 chain stitches. Five chain stitches are done before turning for the next row.

To make a double triple crochet, work a foundation chain, yo 3 times, insert hook in 6th chain from hook, yo, draw through loop * (**p.**), yo, draw through 2 loops * (**q.**), repeat * to * 3 times (**r.**).

Triple triple crochet (abbr. tr tr) creates rows of long vertical bars in the crochet **pattern** or design.

To make the triple triple, yo 4 times, insert hook in 7th chain from hook, pull loop through, * yo, pull through 2 loops * (**s.**), repeat * to * 5 times (**t., u.**); chain 6 to turn.

Double foundation chain is a **foundation chain** created by a series of two loops and a yarn-over. After the completion of the first **stitch** a base is provided for working additional stitches. Two stitches are always involved; the left stitch is the base for the new stitch. Pick up the left stitch (**v.**), yo and pull through one loop (**w.**), yo and pull through two loops (**x.**).

For a triple foundation chain, ch 3 yo (**y.**), insert hook into first chain stitch and complete as for double crochet (**z.**). Insert hook in the edge loop of the dc and continue to the desired length.

Many patterns and motifs can be made by combining the basic stitches. They can be worked on a **foundation chain** or incorporated into an existing piece of crochet fabric. The use of more than one color greatly enhances the effect of a pattern; **stranding** is employed to hold a color of yarn when not in use.

Popular patterns include the alternating shell stitch (**a.**), the around the post stitch (**b.**), a stitch that is worked around the stitch of the previous row, the cluster stitch (**c.**), the **lover's knot stitch,** the **popcorn stitch** (**d.**), **picot** edging (**e.**), the rose stitch, the afghan stitch, and the shell stitch. Two of the most popular motifs are the granny square and the pinwheel. See ill.

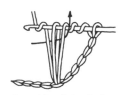
p.   Insert hook in chain

q.   Draw through a loop

r.   Finished double triple crochet

s.   Pull through first two loops

t.   Repeat five times

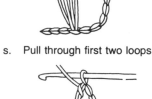
u.   Finished triple triple crochet

v.   Pick up stitch

w.   Pull through first loop

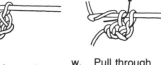
x.   Finished double foundation chain

y.   Yarn-over

z.   Finished triple foundation chain

a.   Single crochet

b.   Insert hook into chain

c.   Draw through loop

d.   Pull through three loops

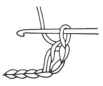
e.   Finished half double crochet

f.   Insert hook in chain

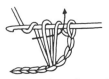
g.   Draw through two loops

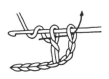
h.   Draw through last two loops

j.   Finished double crochet

k.   Insert hook in chain

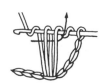
m.   Pull through two loops

n.   Finished triple crochet

crochet. Lacemaking. A single-**filament** technique done with yarn and a **crochet hook.** Crocheted lace is made with usual crochet stitches but in such a manner as to give an

a.   Alternating shell stitch

b.   Around the post stitch

c.   Cluster stitch

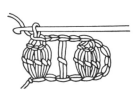
d.   Popcorn stitch

e.   Picot edging

open or "lacy" look. Use this method for large wall hangings and clothing. The yarn used may be cotton, linen, silk, synthetic, metallic, wool, or any other suitable fiber. See ill. Also see **crochet filet, Irish crochet.**

crochet cotton. Needlepoint. A glossy, tightly twisted two-ply cotton floss. Crochet cotton provides an attractive contrast with wool yarn on needlepoint.

crocheted rug. Rugmaking. Rugs made with a crochet hook and yarn. Some are given a surface trim such as **knotted pile** or embroidery, or used as a base for other materials to be threaded through it. Small sections can be crocheted and then sewn together. The yarn used is a heavy wool, cotton, jute, rayon, or other synthetic. Rag strips can be used also. A large hook is used, such as a K(10½) or J(9). Aluminum or wooden hooks are the best to use to support the weight of large rugs. The rug need not be hemmed, bound, or lined unless desired. The stitches in crochet are basically a few foundation ones from which other stitches have been developed. One very simple rug that has become popular, because of its thrift in the use of materials, is made of a crocheted filet mesh base into which are threaded old stockings and panty hose or felt, leather, vinyl, cloth, or fur strips—all items that can come from previously used garments or objects. Another thrifty rug is made by combining objects. A chain stitch with strips of material forms a **shirred rug.**

crochet filet. Lacemaking. A **filet** worked to have the same square-meshed look as **knotted lace filet,** and to imitate its designs. The background and design areas are all worked in **crochet** stitches.

crochet hook. Crochet. See **Crochet: Materials.**

crochet hook. Lacemaking. Tatting. A long shaft for a handle with a hook on one end. Crochet hooks are made of bone, plastic, metal, or wood in varying sizes. They are used in lacemaking for picking up **sewing**s in **bobbin lace.** An extremely fine-hooked **tambour needle** is used for **tambour lace.**

Use a crochet hook to **attach** tatted **motifs.** Insert the crochet hook through a **picot** from a previously made **ring** or **chain** and pick up the **loop thread** from the ring or chain and draw it through the picot. Bring the **shuttle** from the **knot bearer** through this **loop** and continue tatting.

crocheting with beads. Beadwork. A technique incorporating beadwork with crocheting in which the yarn is threaded with beads and is worked as usual, slipping the beads into position with the desired stitch.

crocking. Batik and Tie-dye. Dyeing. The loss of color from a yarn or fabric due to rubbing or abrasion. Sometimes this is excess coloring matter chipping off. Other times it can be the result of imperfect penetration or fixation by the **dyestuff** due to the method of **dyeing** used or the un-

suitability of the dyestuff to the fiber. Also see **color fastness,** and **Batik and Tie-dye: Dyes.**

crocking. Leather. The "balling up" of small fibers on new suede or **split** leather when it is first being worked or worn, much as a wool sweater does. Crocking is normal; it can be lessened by brushing the excess fibers out with a wire brush.

crocus. Amber Carving. Coral Carving. Jet Carving. An iron oxide **abrasive** produced with the same technique that simultaneously produces **rouge.** Crocus differs in that it is black, harder, and of coarser grain. It is used particularly for polishing metals and is bonded to paper and to papers covering sticks for fine filing operations.

crocus cloth. Jewelry. A fine **abrasive** cloth used to remove scratches from metal. Also see **carborundum cloth, emery cloth.**

crocus cloth. Leather. A fine abrasive cloth used for finer honing of tools after they have been sharpened on a whetstone. A crocus cloth can also be used to clean and polish **stamps.**

crocus cloth. Metalworking. See **abrasives.**

crocus composition. Jewelry. Metalworking. A **cutting compound** used on a **buff** or on a **felt polishing stick** when **hand polishing** for fast cutting of aluminum, **brass,** and **copper.** Also see **abrasive, buffing compound, polishing compound.**

crocus martis. Ceramics. Purple red oxide of iron used as a red-brown glaze colorant. Also see **pigment oxide.**

crocus paper. Jewelry. A fine **abrasive** paper used to remove scratches from metal. Also see **carborundum paper, emery paper.**

crofting. Stitchery. See **grass bleaching.**

cropped. Bookbinding. A book is said to be cropped when its margins have been injured in cutting.

cross. Basketry. A start, or type of beginning formation, of **spokes,** used in **cane** and **wicker bases.** Also see **Basketry: Woven Basket Construction.**

cross. Lacemaking. (abbr. c.) A basic movement in **bobbin lace,** done by placing the right **bobbin** of the left pair over the left bobbin of the right pair and dropping it on the **pillow.** A cross is always from left to right, between pairs. Bobbins #2 and #3 of two pairs are interchanged and after the movement is completed assume their regular **numerical order of bobbins.** See ill. next page.

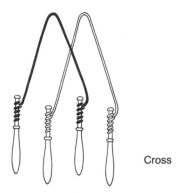

Cross

Cross. Quilts. (Also called Cross-within-a-Cross.) A **pieced block** design that has a square set on end within another square. A plus sign is pieced within the smaller square, and where the bars of the plus sign overlap, a small square appears.

cross. Weaving. (Also called lease, leash.) The alternate criss-crossing of **warp ends** between two pegs of the **warping board** or **reel** as the warp is being wound. The cross is used to maintain order among the warp threads so that they wind on without bother and lay in a straight line from the **apron bar,** that they are attached to on the **warp beam** to the apron bar that attaches them to the **cloth beam.** If the warp has a color or yarn pattern, the cross assures that this pattern will not be lost when the warp is transferred to the **loom.** The cross is made of single warp ends, in pairs or in repeat groups. After the warp is made the cross is tied with a lease cord so that it will not be lost as the warp is being **chained** and taken to the loom. **Lease sticks** are later inserted and the cord removed. The lease sticks can stay in the cross during the entire time of weaving, or they can be removed before tying the warp to the front apron bar. Also see **warping, warping board.**

Cross and Crown. Quilts. See **Bear's Paw, Crown and Cross.**

cross bar. Puppets. (Also called bar.) A short piece of wood attached at right angles to the **control bar** in either the **horizontal control** or the **vertical control.** The **shoulder bar** is one of the cross bars on each of these controls. Also see **arm bar, head bar, heel bar, leg bar** and **Puppets: Stringing the Marionette.**

crossbar. Quilts. See **Quilts: Quilting.**

crossbarred carpet. Rugmaking. Weaving. See **rag rug.**

cross cut. Gemcutting. See **facet.**

crosscut. Woodworking. The process of cutting across a board perpendicular to the wood grain. Also see **hand saw** and **Woodworking: Cutting and Sawing.**

crosscut saw. Woodworking. See **hand saw.**

cross-draft kiln. Ceramics. A variation on the **down-draft kiln.** Also see **bag wall, chambered kiln.**

cross dyeing. Dyeing. See **piece dyeing.**

crossed corner stitch. Needlepoint. See **rice stitch.**

crossed purl stitch. Knitting. (abbr. p 1 b.) A stitch made by **purling** into the back of a stitch, which therefore is crossed when completed. Also see **Knitting: Knit Movements.**

crossed slab glass. Stained Glass. This glass is similar to **Norman slab glass** but is made differently. Molten glass is rolled out on an iron table that has an indented pattern, as does the roller or rolling pin. The result is an irregular-surfaced glass. It is very hard to obtain and is not sufficiently stable to be fired. Also see **firing, slab glass.**

crossed stitch. Knitting. (Also called cross-stitch cable.) This knitting pattern employs the **one-over-one principle,** and is used mainly in **Aran Isle** sweaters. It is a small, simple **cable pattern** and can be made without a **cable needle.** The same principle is used in **cable knitting,** which involves more stitches and usually the use of a cable needle as well. Also see **plaited basket stitch** and **Knitting: Construction.**

crossed stitch cable. Knitting. See **crossed stitch.**

crossed stocking stitch. Knitting. (abbr. K 1 b.) A crossed stocking stitch is made by knitting into the back of the **stitches** on both the **knit** and **purl** rows. Also see **Knitting: Knit Movements.**

crossed warp. Weaving. A term most often used in conjunction with **gauze weave, leno,** or **Mexican lace.** However, it can also refer to **transposed warps** or to warps that are woven as individual strips and then criss-crossed to interweave with each other, and can be joined to form a wider strip or to give a spatial illusion. This kind of crossed warp is seen in **wall hangings** done on **frame looms.** The early work of Olga de Amaral of Colombia shows a mastery of this technique with warps crossing, joining, splitting, and recrossing.

Crosses and Losses. Quilts. (Also called Fox and Geese.) A **block** design for a **pieced quilt** made up of squares and triangles. The effect is one of complexity, although it is not difficult to sew. Each block consists of 16 squares joined together. The squares alternate between two designs. One square is made up of two triangles, the next of four smaller squares. They are **set** together to suggest a diagonal pattern. This block is similar to variations of the **Letter X** block. See ill.

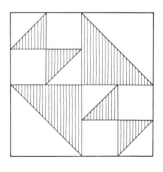

Crosses and Losses

cross-filing. Metalworking. Ordinary filing of a surface to remove material or to smooth the surface by pushing the file forward across a piece of stock. Also see **Metalworking: Filing.**

cross handle. Basketry. A rigid handle that arches from **border** to opposite border of a **woven basket** and is usually wrapped or roped. Also see **rope handle, wrapping,** and **Basketry: Woven Basket Construction.**

cross-lap joint. Woodworking. See **joint** and **Woodworking: Jointing.**

cross-locking tweezers. Jewelry. **Tweezers** with tightly closed ends, considered to be self-locking. They are used to hold work during **soldering** because it does not require a constant pressure to keep them closed. They are available blunt or pointed, curved or straight. See ill. Also see **clamp, jig, third hand.**

Cross-locking tweezers

cross loop stitch. Leather. See **cross stitch.**

crossover loop. Beadwork. (Also called continuous crossover, crossover petals.) A technique used in bead flowermaking for shapes such as lilacs or wheat. It is basically the same as the continuous single loop method except that each loop is filled with additional rows of beading. The initial loops should be uniform in size.

Begin with a narrow loop and twist the wires at the base of the loop twice. Bring the beaded wire up the front of the loop and fill in the center of the loop with beads, pushing the extra beads away. Bring the bare wire in between the beads at the top of the loop, then down the back of the loop and wrap it around the base of the loop for a three-row crossover petal. Flatten the petal with the fingers so all three rows are showing. Repeat for the desired number of petals (**a.**). Allow 4″ of bare wire at the bottom for the stem, then cut the wire from the spool and twist the stem wires together.

For a four-row crossover, add beading up the front and down the back, instead of just bringing the bare wire down the back (**b.**). Then flatten the petal so that all four rows are visible. See ill.

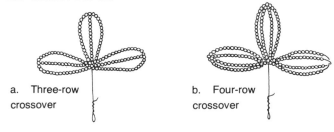
a. Three-row crossover   b. Four-row crossover

crossover petals. Beadwork. See **crossover loop.**

cross-peen hammer. Metalworking. See **hammer.**

cross reel. Spinning. See **reel.**

cross rod. Weaving. See **lease peg.**

cross stick. Weaving. See **lease stick.**

cross stitch. Crewel. Embroidery. Needlepoint. A **counted-thread embroidery** stitch that can be worked on any **evenly woven fabric**—cotton, **linen,** or **canvas**—using a **tapestry needle** to avoid splitting threads. The stitch was a favorite of early American embroiderers, and is the foundation of other stitches such as the **herringbone stitch** and the **rice stitch.** It can be used either as a **filling stitch** or **border stitch;** however, one should be careful that all the crosses are crossed in the same direction. Only the imagination of the needle worker limits the variations possible with this stitch. See ill. Also see **blackwork, long-arm cross stitch, Montenegrin cross stitch, oblong cross stitch.**

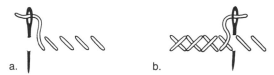
a.   b.
Cross stitch worked on background fabric

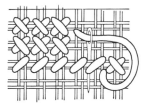
c.   Cross stitch worked on penelope canvas

cross-stitch. Knitting. An embellishment embroidered onto a finished piece of knitting. Cross-stitch is an X design made over a single complete stitch of knitting with a tapestry needle and embroidery floss or thin yarn. Usually a series of cross-stitches are applied to the knitted piece to form a decorative pattern—either over-all or on the garment borders, cuffs, or yoke. Also see **Swiss darning.**

cross stitch. Leather. (Also called baseball stitch, cross loop stitch, cross whipstitch, shoelacing stitch, X-stitch.) An X-shaped stitch used for decorative stitching on leather. Punch holes or slits for stitching. **Whipstitch** all along the seam, in one direction, forming diagonal stitches; return, whipstitching the other half of the crosses, forming an X. If a **lacing pony** is used, this can be done as a **double needle stitch,** to save time. See ill. Also see **edge stitch, lacing** and **Leatherwork: Sewing Leather.**

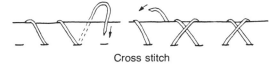
Cross stitch

cross stitch. Rugmaking. A square stitch composed of two diagonal stitches crossing exactly in the center. The lower stitch acts as a padding for the upper. The easiest way to work cross stitch is to do all the stitches in one direction in one journey across the canvas and then cross them in the return journey. Throughout the work, all under stitches should go in the same direction and all upper stitches cross in the same direction. To work cross stitch in **canvas mesh,** bring the needle back to front and insert diagonally at upper right of the desired square that the stitch will occupy. Emerge at lower right and then continue on in this manner for the rest of the row. At the end of the row, emerge at lower right and cross over the understitch and insert the needle front to back at the upper left. Emerge at the lower right and continue on until all the understitches have been crossed. There are variations on the cross stitch; one of the most popular for rugs is the Smyrna stitch or double cross stitch, which provides a texture and a "cushy" underfoot to the rug. The cross stitch is made and then a straight vertical and horizontal cross is added in the spaces left empty by the regular cross stitch. It is a large stitch usually occupying 3 or 5 holes, depending on the size of the backing. See ill.

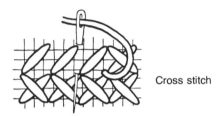

Cross stitch

cross stone. Gemcutting. See **andalusite.**

Cross-Upon-Cross. Quilts. See **Three Crosses.**

cross weave. Weaving. Any **weave** in which the **warp end**s are crossed and half-twisted around each other by the fingers or with the aid of a **pick-up stick, doup**s, or beads. The simplest and most total cross weave is a **gauze weave. Leno** is another type of cross weave, but has areas of **plain weave** among the **crossed warp** areas. Depending on the placement of the plain weave or solid areas in relationship to the cross weave or open areas, there are specific names for the pattern. For example, if in the warpwise direction there are stripes of cross weave alternating with stripes of plain weave, the pattern is called Pickets. Blocks of cross weave totally surrounded by plain weave give a design called Riddles. Today, however, these names are seldom used. Also see **bead leno.**

cross whipstitch. Leather. See **cross stitch.**

crosswise. Quilts. Stitchery. Cross-grain or across the **fabric,** from **selvage** to selvage. The **weft** threads are those which run crosswise in a woven fabric.

Cross-within-a-Cross. Quilts. See **Cross.**

crow bead. Beadwork. A type of large **glass bead,** over ¼" in diameter and of various colors, associated with the Crow Indians (although they are not unique to them). Crow beads were not usually used for weaving or stitching but as an accent in stringing necklaces, when a few were interspersed with other beads.

crow call. Toys. A **whistle** or horn used originally by hunters to attract crows. It is a traditional **American folk toy** made of a tubular wood piece, notched at one end, containing a reedlike section that vibrates when the whistle is blown. This **sound toy** or **noisemaker** is similar to the **turkey call** in origin and use.

crown. Gemcutting. See **facet.**

Crown and Cross. Quilts. A **pieced block** pattern of a large cross overlapping a square. It is sometimes called Crowned Cross or Cross and Crown, although those two names usually refer to a completely different block. Also see **Bear's Paw.**

Crowned Cross. Quilts. See **Bear's Paw, Crown and Cross.**

crown glass. Glasswork. **Soda-lime glass** formed into sheets in a historically important way. A thickening at the center and a **punty** mark are characteristics of crown glass. Some examples made in American colonial days can be seen above doorways in old sections of Boston.

First a bulb is formed on the **blowing iron,** and then it is transferred to the punty. The work is turned on the punty slowly while the mouth of the vessel is opened with a jack (**a.**). After reheating the glass on the punty, the work is whirled into a bowl (**b.**). Continuing to spin the work at high speed will result in a nearly flat circular sheet of glass, as large and thin as required (**c.**). See ill.

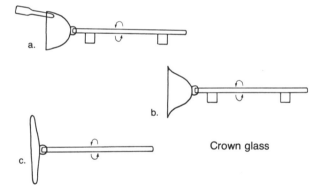

Crown glass

crown glass. Stained Glass. A type of **antique glass** made by gathering a blob of molten glass on the end of the blowpipe and blowing a bubble that is then transferred to a pontil pipe and spun out through rotation of the pipe into a disk measuring up to 5' in diameter. The disk is then broken off the pontil pipe. The result is a thin disk with a thick, knotted knob in the middle. It is thought that this is the way ancient glass was made. Crown glass was used often in the seventeenth and eighteenth centuries for window panes. The knobby part in the middle was sliced off and sold cheaply for use in public and farm buildings. This part of the crown was known as bullion.

Crown of Thorns. Quilts. (Also called Georgetown Circle, Memory Wreath, Single Wedding Ring.) A **geometric pieced block** with the 12 points of a star surrounding an angular circle form. See ill. Also see **star pattern.**

Crown of Thorns

crown setting. Jewelry. A metal form with prongs or claws into which slots are filed to receive a stone, usually faceted. Crown settings are available ready-made in a large range of shapes and sizes and as such are considered **findings.** See ill.

Crown setting

crowquill pen. China and Glass Painting. A small, fine-pointed drawing pen used for **outlining** and monogramming on china.

Rather than dipping the point of the pen into the paint, scoop up the paint with the edge of the pen. Practice the strokes until the pen feels comfortable. See ill.

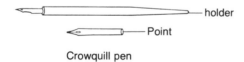

holder

Point

Crowquill pen

crucible. Jewelry. A container made of a refractory material used for melting and holding metal during **casting.** It is advisable to warm the crucible either on top of the **kiln** during **burnout** or inside the kiln for the last 15 or so minutes of the burnout. This will help the metal to melt more quickly, as an unheated crucible pulls a great deal of heat from the torch and melting metal for the first casting takes quite a while. Metal is melted directly in the crucible with a pinch of borax added to the metal to help it flow. The melted metal is poured through the bottom of the crucible into the pouring gate of the mold. See ill. Also see **casting grains, centrifugal casting, plumbage.**

Crucible

crucible. Metalworking. A container for melting ores or metals that is able to withstand great heat. It may be made out of clay, graphite and clay, cast **iron,** cast or wrought **steel,** or other **refractory material.**

crucible tongs. Metalworking. See **tongs.**

crude coil. Basketry. A **coiled basketry** weave that is built spirally but where the **foundation** and **binding** element is a single unit. The material is usually branches gathered together. The stout ends, hooked together, unite the foundation element. The leafy ends of the same branch, used as the binding or **active element,** are wrapped inside, holding the entire foundation to the previous **coil.**

crumb stitch. Crewel. Embroidery. See **seed stitch.**

crushed glass. Stained Glass. See **gemmaux, lamination.**

Cryla. Plastics. See **acrylic paint.**

crystal. Gemcutting. A mineral bounded by plane faces of regular form, distinct from amorphous materials (called massive) whose structure is without definite external form. Crystalline bodies have internal structure whether the plane faces are visible outwardly or not. Examples of amorphous gem materials are **opal,** amber, and **obsidian** which sometimes occur in rounded or nodular forms.

Crystals are regularly bounded by plane faces. Crystalline stones also occur as portions of crystals and as aggregates of many crystals. Extremely compact aggregates, often opaque, which require microscopic examination of thin sections to see their crystalline structure are called crypto-crystalline; examples are chalcedony, agate, and **turquoise.**

Crystal forms are classified by the number of directions they may be split into equal halves; these are called planes of symmetry.

Crystals of the isometric system have nine planes of symmetry and develop into cubes, octahedrons, and dodecahedrons.

Crystals of the tetragonal system have five planes of symmetry and take the form of rectangular or octagonal prisms, tablets, and pyramids.

Crystals of the hexagonal system have seven planes of symmetry and occur with hexagonal cross sections in plate, tablet, pyramidal, and rhombohedral forms.

Crystals of the orthorhombic system have three planes of symmetry and develop into boxlike, thin wedge shapes or pyramids with lozenge-shaped cross sections.

Crystals of the monoclinic system have one plane of symmetry and form prisms with rectangular cross sections and pointed terminations; sometimes thin shapes develop sprays and tufts.

Crystals of the triclinic system have no planes or symmetry and occur in various boxlike, tabular, and elongated prismatic shapes.

Tabular form means that the opposite faces are parallel to each other. Prisms are forms in which opposite faces aren't parallel, that is, wedge-shaped. Pyramids have triangular faces that terminate in a point. A rhombus is a parallelogram. A lozenge is diamond shaped.

The interfacial angles of crystals are measured with a contact goniometer by mineralogists for identification. Also see **C-axis cleavage.**

crystal. Glasswork. See **lead-crystal glass, quartz glass.**

crystal bead. Beadwork. (Also called **cut beads, faceted beads.**) In the final **beadmaking** processing of **glass bead**s, instead of rounding and polishing, beads are cut or faceted to give them mirrorlike flat surfaces that sparkle in the light. Crystal beads are available in many colors and in round or long shapes.

crystal garden. Toys. (Also called coal crystals, salt garden.) An **educational** toy that allows a child to watch salt crystals form. To start the garden place 2 lumps of coal in a shallow glass dish. Mix 1 tablespoon salt with 1 tablespoon water, to which 1 tablespoon bluing has been added. Pour the mixture over the coal. Within one or two days, blue crystals will spread over the coal. Mercurochrome can be used to give a red color. When the solution starts to dry it can be renewed by pouring more saltwater solution into the bottom of the dish.

Cubework. Quilts. See **Baby Blocks.**

cuir-boulli work. Leather. A technique of molding designs on rawhide leather which has been softened by soaking and boiling in water and alum or salt. When dry, the leather is extremely hard. A relief pattern in leather may be molded on an incised design cut into a wood board by pressing wet, thin leather or leather pulp (made from scraps) into the mold. Other materials may be used for molding with leather, such as plaster of Paris, that has been oiled to prevent sticking. Wet leather may be molded over bowls, plates, or other objects, particularly an undecorated, smooth glazed surface, or used to cover objects made from other materials. Raised relief designs are filled from the back with waste leather pulp (any combination of leather scraps boiled with paper, wool, or cotton scraps as in **carton-cuir work**). The addition of glue, gum, or flour paste to these mixtures will make them firm and durable when dry.

Another method of producing relief designs in leather is to press wet leather over a cutout design of heavy cardboard or thin board, pressing the leather with a dry sponge and the fingers into the negative areas. To facilitate placing leather over a relief pattern, the back side of the leather is sometimes glued to the pattern with gum. When the leather is pressed in place, the outline of the design is worked with a tracer or wheel and the ground is stamped. If the leather is removed from the board pattern it will need to be reinforced to make it hold its shape. A waste leather pulp may be used. The back side is then covered with cloth or leather.

The leather relief work was usually finished by staining black with dye or writing ink applied in several thin coatings. When dry, the surface is rubbed with a **chamois** skin, then lightly oiled. Also see **Leatherwork.**

cuir-cisele binding. Bookbinding. A leather binding with designs cut into its surface rather than stamped or tooled.

culet. Gemcutting. See **facet.**

cullet. Ceramics. A cheap but variable **flux** in the form of small broken pieces of colored glass, used in decoration. Also see **milled glass decoration.**

cullet. Glasswork. Broken or refuse glass intended to be remelted. Studio glassmakers rarely make glass from **silica** and the necessary **flux**es because broken glass is available cheaply and in variety from glass factories. Also see **cullet bin.**

cullet bin. Glasswork. A metal box, preferably lidded, into which scraps of hot glass are thrown and allowed to cool and to crack or shatter without injuring anyone.

cultured pearls. Beadwork. The process of producing cultured **pearls** was known in ancient times by the Greeks and the Chinese, then apparently lost until fairly recent times. A piece of **mother of pearl** is inserted as a foreign irritative body inside the oyster shell by pearl growers. The size of the resulting pearl is determined by the size of this core, around which the pearl grows, rather than by the length of time it is allowed to grow. The oysters are then returned to the sea in cages and allowed to grow. After three to five years the pearls are harvested. The cultured-pearl industry produces great quantities of these pearls, which are widely used for beads and jewelry.

cumdach. Bookbinding. A book box that resembles a casket, sometimes called a **book shrine,** used in Ireland in medieval times.

cup. Metalworking. See **pouring basin.**

cup-and-ball. Toys. (Also called ball-and-cup, flip ball.) A **folk toy** known throughout the world in many variations. The toy consists of a wooden cup on a handle and a small wooden **ball** attached to the handle by a cord. The object is to swing the ball up and into the cup. **Bilbouquet cup** is a variation of cup-and-ball. See ill. Also see **Toys: Games and Other Toys.**

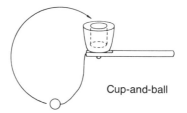

Cup-and-ball

cup head. Ceramics. A **wheel head** with a hole in the center used for supporting **mold**s and for turning small necked pots. Also see **chuck.**

cup lawn. Ceramics. A small cup-shaped sieve, usually made of metal, that is used for sifting **glazes.**

cupping. Rugmaking. See **braided rug.**

cupping. Woodworking. See **wood.**

cuprammonium rayon. Stitchery. See **rayon.**

cupric oxide. Jewelry. (Also called copper oxide.) Liver of sulfur reacts to the film of cupric oxide left on the surface of low karat yellow gold after **casting** and **pickling** and creates a black **patina.**

A thick film of oxide can be formed on higher-karat golds, but not 24K, by heating to a high heat with an oxidizing **flame,** which will produce a dark brown color. Liver of sulfur can be added for a still darker brown, but black is not quite obtainable. The technique works best on cast pieces, as the oxides are formed automatically during the casting process. Also see **coloring.**

cuprite. Gemcutting. Copper oxide crystallized in the isometric system with hardness of 4, specific gravity of 6.1, green color, and uneven fracture. Also see **fracture** and **Gemcutting: Rough Shaping.**

cure. Plastics. See **curing.**

curing. Candlemaking. Candles should be allowed to cure (age) in a cool place for a minimum of one week before burning. The reorientation of the molecules during that time improves the quality of the candle.

curing. Leather. (Also called brine curing.) An early process in leather **tanning** in which the skin is washed, then soaked in vats of salt crystals for twelve hours to stop bacteria action and prevent the skin from decomposing. Also see **bating** and **Leatherwork: Tanning and Manufacture.**

curing. Plastics. (Also called catalyzing, cure, set, setting up.) The chemical reaction whereby a liquid **resin** becomes solid by the addition of a **catalyst.** When the resin first starts setting it resembles partially set gelatin; it is referred to as soft gel and can be **gel-mold**ed. Later it resembles completely set gelatin and is referred to as "hard gel." If it is cut with a knife at this stage, the edges will fracture. Finally, when tapping the surface with a stick produces a clicking sound, the resin is referred to as "hard," or "clicking hard." At this stage the plastic must still be kept weighted to prevent **warping.** In the case of some plastics, curing continues for up to seven days after the resin reaches the hard stage, during which time it may still be easily marked or scratched. One may sand plastic twenty-four hours after hardening, but it is recommended that polishing and machining be done only after a full cure of several days. The curing plastic heats as a result of the chemical reaction. This is called **exotherm.** When pouring thick pieces use a type of **casting resin** that causes less internal heat buildup. Also see **Plastics: Casting.**

curing. Woodworking. See **wood.**

curing agent. Plastics. See **catalyst.**

curious glass. Stained Glass. The name given to sheets of **antique glass** considered "seconds" by the manufacturer.

They are sold more cheaply, but sometimes their irregularities are hard to incorporate into a stained-glass window.

curling. Papercrafts. A paper construction technique in which strips of paper are drawn tightly over the edge of a ruler or scissors blade to produce curls, scrolls, and spirals. Since most papers have a **grain,** rolling the sheet by hand should be done first to determine which way it will curl most easily. Tight spiral curls can be made by rolling paper around a pencil. The paper curls should keep their shape. The process may be repeated to tighten the curling. See ill.

Curling

curling. Tincrafting. See **Tincrafting: Cutting the Tin.**

curtain. Puppets. The cover for the front of a stage is called the curtain. The most common type is the **draw curtain,** and sometimes more than one such curtain is used. There may be a curtain covering the **proscenium** with only an opening for the stage; another curtain may open to reveal the stage **set.**

The curtain is usually decorative, partly to entertain the waiting audience. It may be painted, stitched, or appliquéd, depending on the type of performance or stage and the material used. Some curtains are designed to announce the names of plays, performers, and characters, or to depict a scene from the play to be performed. A curtain can, of course, be a plain piece of fabric, although even a minimal tassel or fringe will heighten the effect. Also see **bridge, canopy, sheeting, topdrop.**

curved border. Knitting. See **border.**

curved-claw hammer. Woodworking. See **hammer.**

curved life-eye needle. Leather. See **lacing needle.**

curved sewing awl. Leather. See **awl and haft.**

curved scissors. Crewel. Embroidery. Needlepoint. Scissors with curved tips used to snip off loose thread ends when working on an **embroidery frame.** The upward curve of the scissors ensures that the **background fabric** is not accidentally cut. Also see **embroidery scissors.**

curved snips. Metalworking. See **snips.**

curving. Rugmaking. Weaving. See **bubbling.**

Cushing's Perfection. Batik and Tie-dye. See **household dye.**

cushion filling. Lacemaking. See **leaf stitch.**

cushion stitch. Crewel. Embroidery. See **satin stitch.**

cusping. Stained Glass. These are the small stone points that stick out around the areas of Gothic **tracery.**

cut. Jewelry. Metalworking. The grade—coarseness or fineness—of a **file.**

cut acid. Metalworking. (Also called killed acid, killed spirits.) Cut acid is made by adding **zinc** to **hydrochloric (muriatic) acid** in a glass or earthenware container. It is placed outdoors until the zinc is dissolved in the acid (about 24 hours) because the compound gives off noxious fumes. The final compound is zinc chloride and it is used as a **flux** when soldering **tin plate, copper, brass, lead, stainless steel,** and **nickel.** Since it is corrosive, the metal must be thoroughly washed after using it.

cut and color compound. Jewelry. Metalworking. See **polishing compound.**

cut beads. Beadwork. See **crystal bead.**

cut corner. Bookbinding. See **mitered corner.**

cut-edge book. Bookbinding. A book with evenly cut edges. Also see **trimming.**

cut-film stencil. Silkscreen. A kind of **stencil** for silkscreen printing using proprietary two-layered film products.

The original material, called Pro-film, consists of a shellac composition glued to a backing of glassine paper. Portions of the shellac layer are cut away with the use of **stencil-cutting tools** and lifted off the glassine backing sheet. A hot clothes iron can be used to adhere the finished design to the mesh in a **screen frame** (a.). The screen is lowered onto the cut stencil, which lies on layers of newsprint on the **printing base** (b.). The hot iron is used to press and partially melt the shellac material into the screen fibers. As the shellac material melts and becomes wedded to the screen, it becomes darker, indicating that the adhesion is complete. When the pressing operation is complete, the screen frame is raised and the backing sheet is peeled away from the screen to open the mesh (c.). The stencil can also be fixed to the screen with an adherer (d.). See ill.

Pro-film, Nu-film, Ulano film, Blu-film, and green film are all similar but have different stencil-forming lacquer portions for special use. Blu-film resists the chemical action of cellulose inks. Green film adheres well to synthetic fibers and stainless steel meshes; these stencil films come with plastic backings. Aquafilm and Nu-film water soluble products use water as an adherer, avoiding the danger and expense of the usual lacquer solvents. These screens also can be reclaimed by soaking and spraying with water,

whereas other types of film stencils require a special **removing thinner** to loosen the material from the mesh.

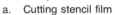

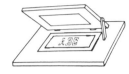
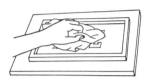

a. Cutting stencil film   b. Positioning the film stencil

c. Removing the film backing

d. Adhering the film stencil to the screen

cut flax. Spinning. See **Spinning: Process.**

cut-float. Weaving. **Filling floats** cut to form a **pile,** as in **corduroy** fabrics. Another kind of cut-float is found in **brocade,** where a motif is woven **selvage** to selvage even though it appears only in certain areas. Between these areas are long floats of filling that can be cut and trimmed off after weaving, provided the filling yarn in the motif is safely anchored in the **ground weave.** Also see **float.**

cut length. Weaving. The length of the **warp** as it is being measured in a taut position on a **warping board** or **warping reel.** It also refers to specific lengths of finished cloth as woven on a power loom. Also see **yarn calculation.**

cut-line. Stained Glass. Cut-lines designate the outlines of the separate pieces of glass in a **cartoon.** The cut-line is followed in **glazing** the stained glass **panel.** The English, who do not cut out **templates** for cutting their glass, place the glass over the cut-line and follow it with the cutter. They become skilled enough to cut just inside the line, leaving room for the **heart** of the **lead came.** A light table is often used beneath the panel so that the cut-line shows through the glass. Templates are used for very dark pieces. Also see **cutting bench.**

cut-lining. Stained Glass. (Also called lead-lining.) A traditional method for transferring the cartoon onto tracing paper or tracing cloth with a brush and India ink or a felt-tip pen.

A piece of plate glass is placed on top of the finished cut-line and ⅜″ lead lines are traced onto it with a paint made of **lampblack,** water, and **gum arabic.** The thin black line represents the **heart** of the **lead came** and is drawn wherever a new piece of glass is used.

The plate glass is turned over and set up at an easel or window. Little balls of **plasticine** are attached to the plate glass at intersections. Cut pieces of stained glass are pressed onto the glass as they are completed. The glass should be covered when not in use to prevent the plasticine from getting dirty.

An alternate method for attaching the cut pieces of

stained glass to the lead-lined plate glass is to use very hot, melted beeswax and to spoon it with a waxing tool between the joints. This method was used during the nineteenth century for many of the Gothic Revival windows in England. See ill.

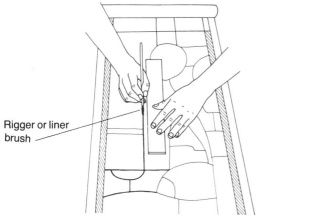

a. Lead-lines being painted on clear glass placed over the cartoon
rigger or liner brush

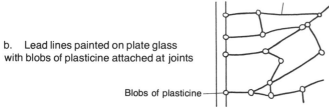

Painted cut-lines

b. Lead lines painted on plate glass with blobs of plasticine attached at joints

Blobs of plasticine

cut nail. Woodworking. See **nail.**

cut-off pen blade. Woodworking. See **whittling tools.**

cut-off saw. Gemcutting. See **slabbing saw.**

cutout. Papercrafts. (Also called papercut.) A term used for a design cut out of paper, using any of various techniques. Cutouts can vary from a simple **symmetrical cutting,** made by folding the paper once, to intricate **repeat pattern**s and freehand designs.

cut-out figure. Puppets. The flat figure of a **puppet** cut from paper, card, leather, or any similar material. The **silhouette puppet** and **shadow puppet** are examples of traditional cut-out figures. The **flat puppet,** or **penny plain and tuppence colored,** was a popular English version of this kind of figure.

cutout printed doll. Toys. A doll printed on **fabric** to be cut out, sewn, and **stuff**ed to make a **rag doll.** The **art fabric doll**s were of this type. Some are now silk-screen printed on **felt** or fabric and sold either as kits or already assembled.

cutouts. Découpage. **Prints** on lightweight paper are cut out with intricate detail and adhered to the surface to be decorated with découpage. Lightweight paper, folded and cut in symmetrical or repeated patterns, can also be used for découpage designs. In the découpage process, the term "cutouts" refers to the print, colored with hand-coloring if desired, coated with a sealer, and cut, with the exception of the bridges, preparatory to gluing. Also see **Découpage: Cutting, Selecting Prints.**

cutouts. Toys. Figures of people, animals, or buildings from magazines or books that are cut out and glued to a cardweight paper backing. A tab may then be added at the back to support the figure and make it stand; or, another piece of **cardboard** or heavy paper is slotted and set into a matching slot on the base of the figure to make it stand. **Paper doll**s are sometimes made in this way. Children can make villages or farms by using paper cutouts. Printed, ready-made cutouts can be also purchased.

Cutout sheet paper toys have been made since the early eighteenth century. These include paper buildings, **architectural playthings,** three-dimensional scenes and settings, and figures. The **penny plain and tuppence colored** "cut-and-color toy" sheets were of this variety. Paper dolls were also made as cutouts and became quite elaborate. Figures had costumes of great variety and accessories of every kind. Also see **Toys: Construction Toys.**

cutout village. Toys. A series of buildings or houses printed on paper to be cut and **glue**d to **cardboard.** Also see **cutouts** and **Toys: Construction Toys.**

cut-paper stencil. Silkscreen. A kind of hand-cut **stencil** for silkscreen printing, similar to **cut-film stencil,** that is suitable for amateur and short-run commercial work.

A piece of thin bond paper or its equivalent is taped to the **printing base** over the design to be reproduced so the lines of the design are visible through the paper. **Stencil cutting tools** are used to cut out shapes as required, but the cut-out areas are left in place. When the whole design has been cut, the tape is carefully removed and the **screen frame** lowered into printing position (**a., b.**). One or two passes of ink with the **squeegee** are usually sufficient to allow the ink to adhere the whole piece of paper to the bottom of the screen (**c.**). The ink acts as a sort of glue. Then the screen is lifted and the cut areas carefully peeled away, opening the stencil (**d.**). Stock to be printed is then set into guides on the **printing base,** and printing can begin (**e., f.**). Many studio printers experiment with various kinds of paper for the stencil.

The technique is disarmingly simple and can make stencils capable of runs of several hundred copies with good sharpness. Some porous papers will leak ink onto the print with reproducible and sometimes interesting effects. Reclaiming the screen after the run is a simple matter of washing out the ink; the paper comes free and is discarded. A disadvantage of the method is that reruns of the same design are not possible unless a new stencil is made. See ill. next page.

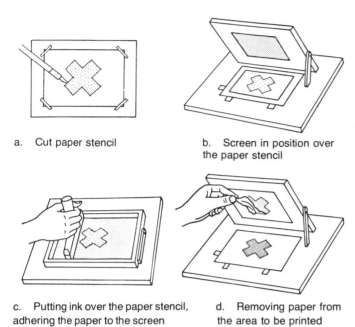

a. Cut paper stencil

b. Screen in position over the paper stencil

c. Putting ink over the paper stencil, adhering the paper to the screen

d. Removing paper from the area to be printed

e. Open stencil, ready for printing, with stock to be printed in place

f. Making the first print

g. Finished print ready for removal

cut pile. Rugmaking. Weaving. See **flossa, pile, rya.**

cut system. Spinning. Weaving. See **yarn count.**

cutter. Metalworking. See **blacksmithing tools.**

cut-through appliqué. Quilts. Stitchery. A method of decorative **appliqué** design in which pieces of **fabric** identical in size are stacked and are then cut and sewn. It is different from the usual appliqué procedure in that there is a reversal of forms. The areas which are cut away, that is the **negative shapes**, become the dominant design areas. The **positive shapes** become the background. Designs are cut first into the top layer, then into layers beneath. Anywhere from two to seven or eight layers may be used, though three or four are most commonly used.

The cut-through appliqué stitchery or **reverse appliqué**

approach was developed by the Cuna Indian women on the San Blas Islands. They use the colorful decorative work on their **mola**s. In this original **San Blas appliqué** a **cotton fabric** is used and very intricate complex patterns are formed. An **overcast stitch** or **whip stitch** is used. In adaptations of these molas, other stitchers use a variety of **cottons**, **cotton blend**s, or **felts**. **Blind stitch** or whip stitch are used on the woven fabrics, and **running stitch** or whip stitch is used on felt.

Cut-through appliqué is executed by first stacking several layers of fabric all cut the same in size. A cotton fabric, or cotton blend, works better than a **synthetic fabric** for the intricate cuts, since either is easier to turn under and sew. The stacked layers are pinned, then **baste**d together. Designs are then cut through the top layer to reveal colors of the second layer. **Trimming scissors,** because they are small, may be the easiest to handle and control in this careful cutting. Further cutting can be done through the second layer to reveal colors beneath it. Seldom are more than four or five colors used in the stack. A greater variety of colors can be added by inserting small sections of fabric into cut-out areas or by appliquéing them on top.

When some portions of the designs have been cut they must be sewn before the cutting is continued. If all the cutting is done at one time there are too many loose pieces and the panel is difficult to handle. All cut **raw edge**s are eventually turned under and appliquéd.

When felt is selected for the cut-through appliqué, a running stitch or whip stitch can be used. Finishing of the outside edges of this work in either felt or fabric is usually done with a narrow **binding.** A **backing** fabric can also be added to face or finish the reverse side.

Cut-through appliqué is a more complex way to work than the usual appliqué. The stitching is more difficult, especially when woven materials are used, but the method is intriguing and inviting. Part of its appeal lies in the fact that a cut-through **panel** cannot be completely planned at the beginning. It must develop and grow as the work continues. This approach is used for work on **wall hanging**s, **quilt block**s, or clothing and is occasionally referred to as slit appliqué. Also see **lace appliqué.**

cutting. Bookbinding. See **trimming.**

cutting. Jewelry. See **shears, snips.**

cutting. Metalworking. A **blacksmithing technique** for splitting metal. Also a process for finishing pewter in which an abrasive is used to wear down metal around a crack or blemish until the surface is level. Also see **pewterworking** and **Metalworking: Cutting.**

cutting. Mosaics. See **Mosaics: Cutting the Material.**

cutting. Plastics. See **Plastics: Cutting.**

cutting. Tincrafting. See **Tincrafting: Cutting the Tin.**

cutting anvil. Stained Glass. (Also called wedge.) A rigid metal shape with a sharp point over which slabs of glass are broken. See ill. Also see **dalle-de-verre.**

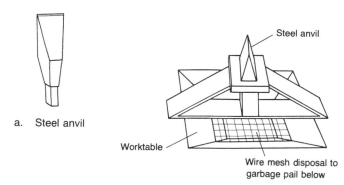

a. Steel anvil

Steel anvil

Worktable

Wire mesh disposal to garbage pail below

b. Manufactured cutting anvil and worktable

cutting bench. Stained Glass. The table at which **stained-glass** pieces are cut. It should be a comfortable height for working while standing—usually just below the ribs so that it is possible to lean over it—and it should be made of a smooth, level, hard surface that supports the glass when it is being scored.

An alternate cutting bench is in the form of a light box or light table. The top of the box is made of a long piece of ¼″ glass or **plexiglass**. The back and two sides are made of wood and the front is open. It catches daylight reflected upward by a large mirror placed inside the box at a 45° angle. Another way of lighting the table is to use fluorescent lights and to paint the underside of the glass white or to use translucent plexiglass. Also see **portable light box**, and **Stained Glass: Setting Up a Workshop.**

cutting board. Bookbinding. Wedge-shaped **board**s, usually of beech with a squared top, used to hold the book in position while **trimming** it with the **plow**. Cutting boards are available in various lengths—8″, 12″, and 15″ being the most commonly used.

cutting board. Leather. See **Leatherwork: Setting up a Workshop.**

cutting board. Stitchery. A flat surface of cardboard or composition board on which **fabric**s may be cut. Commercially made cutting boards have inches marked off on the edge or an all-over **grid pattern** of one-inch spaces. An improvised cutting board may be **Masonite**, plywood, or any smooth surface on which the material may be spread. For cutting small pieces, a bread board or other similar flat area may be used. The cutting board, if small, often doubles as a **lapboard**.

cutting chisel. Metalworking. See **blacksmithing tools, chisel.**

cutting clay. Ceramics. See **Ceramics: Clay.**

cutting cloth. Bookbinding. Lay out the cloth with the lengthwise **grain** running from the book's **head** to its **tail**. Maintain a steady pressure on the straight edge while cutting; do not move it until the material has been cut clean

through the entire desired length. Use a smooth-surfaced firm board underneath the cloth when cutting. The knife blade you cut with must be very sharp; do not try to force the blade through the cloth; instead, use several light strokes.

cutting compound. Jewelry. Metalworking. An abrasive compound used with the **buffing machine** or in **hand polishing** operations to slowly cut away the surface of the metal, thus removing scratches. It can be used either as a final finish or as a preparation for a **polishing compound**. Also see **bobbing compound, buffing compound, greaseless compound.**

cutting curve. Stained Glass. See **Stained Glass: Cutting Glass.**

cutting fluid. Metalworking. See **lubricant.**

cutting glass. Stained Glass. See **Stained Glass: Cutting Glass.**

cutting lead. Stained Glass. Lay the glazing knife on top of the **lead came** and, with gentle pressure and by rocking it from side to side, cut through the came. The lead should be measured before it is cut by laying it where it is to go and marking it with a slight notch. Also see **joint** and **Stained Glass: Glazing.**

cutting leather. Leather. See **Leatherwork: Cutting and Edging Leather.**

cutting nippers. Jewelry. A kind of **pliers** used primarily to cut wire; they can also be used to cut small pieces of thin-**gauge** metal and solder. They are made with side-cutting, end-cutting, and diagonal-cutting blades.

cutting off. Ceramics. See **Ceramics: Clay.**

cutting out. Basketry. See **Basketry: Preparing the Materials.**

cutting scissors. Stitchery. (Also called cutting shears.) Large **scissors**, 6″ to 8″ long, for all major cutting. The handles may be bent, but usually scissors are straight-handled, **shears** are bent-handled. Cutting scissors are larger than **trimming scissors**, smaller than shears.

cutting the warp. Weaving. See **warping.**

cutting tool. Mosaics. See **clippers.**

cutting tool. Stenciling. See **stencil knife.**

cutting tools. Block Printing. Sets of gouges and knives are available from art supply stores for cutting **printing block**s. The best ones have the blade fixed permanently into a handle. The cheaper variety comes with a wooden handle with interchangeable blades or nibs. For cutting a **linoleum block** either type is adequate, but for cutting a **wood block** the blades should be permanently mounted in the handles. Sets usually have two V-shaped and two U-shaped gouges, and a straight knife. A utility knife or a pocket knife may also be used. Each tool produces its own shaped groove in the linoleum.

To cut a line with a knife requires two strokes, clearing away the background on either side of the line, leaving the line raised to receive the ink. With a V-tool (also called a scribe or scriber), a linear channel can be cut with only one stroke. The V-tools, available in various sizes, are used for cutting lines and for clearing corners. They are valuable for drawing directly on the block.

The U-gouge, available from a small U shape to a nearly flat scoop, comes beveled and sharpened on the inside of the curve (for drawing on the block) or beveled and sharpened on the outside of the curve (for clearing spaces).

A **chisel** is used for clearing spaces on a wood block.

All cutting tools must be frequently sharpened on a **sharpening stone.** See ill.

a.   Wood and linoleum block cutting set

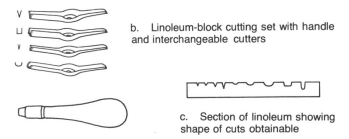

b.   Linoleum-block cutting set with handle and interchangeable cutters

c.   Section of linoleum showing shape of cuts obtainable

cutting tools. Papercrafts. Various tools are used to cut **paper,** scissors being the most common. Any average-sized scissors may be used for general work, and small manicure scissors for detailed cutting. Heavier paper is cut with a **knife** or a single-edge razor blade. For making holes, a punch is often used.

cutting torch. Metalworking. See **oxyacetylene welding equipment.**

cuttlebone casting. Jewelry. A type of **casting** in which forms are cut directly into cuttlebone (the medium hard inner shell of the cuttlefish) and molten metal is poured directly into the cavity. Carving and casting are done on the flat side. Forms can be cut out with a sharp steel tool or with **burr**s.

It is also possible to file and sandpaper two flat surfaces on two different pieces of cuttlebone so that they fit flush against one another. Forms can then be carved into both halves, producing a more fully three-dimensional object. The form of the jewelry to be cast is carved into the cuttlebone. The form, let us say a ring, will be in the negative and should also include a negative area to act as a **sprue** and **sprue cone.** There should also be some small grooves carved into the cuttlebone coming out of the area of the ring to allow for the escape of gases. These grooves should not extend to the edge of the cuttlebone. It is important that the two halves fit precisely together. To ensure this, short metal pins can be inserted into one-half of the cuttlebone in the flat side; the other piece of cuttlebone is then pressed firmly against the pins, of which there should be at least three placed in a triangular arrangement. The halves are then pulled apart, leaving holes corresponding to the pins in the second half. These pins are referred to as "key pins," and will ensure exact realigning of the cuttlebone after carving. The key pins should be put into position before any carving is done in the cuttlebone. The two pieces of cuttlebone are bound tightly together with **iron binding wire** in at least two places. A **crucible** in which the metal will be melted can be carved out of a piece of charcoal. A channel must also be carved out of the charcoal and adjoining cuttlebone to allow the metal to flow from the charcoal to the sprue cone. The charcoal should also be carved so that it fits snugly against the cuttlebone. It is bound to the cuttlebone with iron binding wire. It is imperative that all joints be tight, or molten metal will leak out.

Either complete works or sections of pieces that can undergo further **fabrication** can be cast from cuttlebone. Further fabrication can utilize **sheet metal, tubing,** wire, or other materials. Cuttlebone casting imparts a unique texture to the cast work and can also reproduce accurate detail. It is generally believed unwise to have deep undercuts in this type of casting, although these can cast beautifully. Also see **centrifugal casting.**

cutwork. Lacemaking. Cutwork is a form of needle embroidery; the term was given to some of the earliest known laces. Cutwork was made by drawing or pulling out threads from fine cloth; then the **buttonhole stitch** was worked into this structure of the remaining threads. As areas were worked some sections were cut away, leaving open spaces; hence the name cutwork. From this beginning, the **needle lace reticella** developed.

In **bobbin lace** a **filling,** worked in the **leaf stitch,** is called cutwork. It closely resembles the spot stitch, and is worked the same way.

cutwork with a hole. Lacemaking. See **leaf stitch.**

cylinder. Ceramics. The basic form that is built up in throwing a pot on a **potter's wheel.** See ill. Also see **Ceramics: Throwing.**

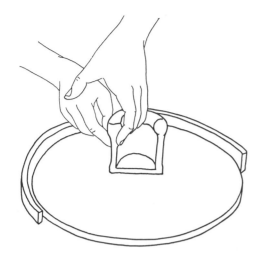

Cross section of the cylinder with position of hands when throwing

cylinder. Metalworking. See **oxyacetylene welding equipment.**

cylinder. Papercrafts. The three-dimensional form shaped by rolling a sheet of paper into a tube (**a.**) and **fastening** the overlapped edges (**b.**). See ill.

Making a cylinder

cylinder glass. Glasswork. A kind of sheet glass made by a historically important process. A bubble of glass is formed on a **blowing iron** to the required size and then **marver**ed cylindrical. The ends are then cracked off and a fracture is made the length of the cylinder. On reheating in an oven, the glass sags and rolls out flat from the fracture. Sheet glass made in this way has waves in the surfaces that distort objects seen through it. The Lubbers process, a semimechanical method of forming the cylinders used about 1900, made cylinders as long as 40′. Another old method for making sheet glass results in **crown glass.**

cymophane. Gemcutting. See **chrysoberyl.**

cypress. Woodworking. A lightweight **softwood** that grows well in the swamps of the southern United States. The **heartwood** is dark brown and the **sapwood** creamy white. It has a peculiar odor and oily appearance. Cypress **plane**s easily and weathers well. It is used for shingles, railroad ties, water tanks, outdoor planters, and boats.

d

Dacron. Plastic. See **filler, reinforcing material.**

Dacron polyester batting. Puppets. Quilts. Stitchery. Toys. A fiber fill that is soft, white, resilient, nonallergenic, and odorless. It can be unrolled and used as **filler** for a quilt. It is also available in nonlayered form that is more convenient for **stuff**ing fabric dolls and animals.

Dacron wadding. Embroidery. A fluffy synthetic fiber used as pillow stuffing and stitch padding, as in **appliqué** and various **stumpwork** stitches.

dado. Woodworking. A square or rectangular groove that is cut across the **grain** slightly in from the end of a board. It is usually made to accept or secure the end of another board to make a dado **joint.** Also see **Woodworking: Jointing.**

dado head. Woodworking. An assembly of blades used on a table or radial-arm **power saw** to cut **dado**es. One type consists of two fine-toothed side blades, which cut the edges of the dado, with a variable number of thicker chipping blades sandwiched between; the width of the groove depends on the number of blades assembled together.

dado joint. Woodworking. See **joint** and **Woodworking: Jointing.**

daedelum. Toys. An **optical toy** patented in England in 1833. In it, a picture train is carried inside a revolving drum and the pictures are viewed or glimpsed through slits in the drum wall. The **zoetrope,** or **wheel of life,** was made in a similar way. The **toy** probably took its name from Daedalus who, in Greek mythology, was concerned with creating clever or cunning devices, moving figures, and flying devices. Daedalus and his son Icarus escaped the Cretan labyrinth (designed by Daedalus) by flying out on wings made of feathers.

dagger. Rugmaking. Weaving. See **bodkin.**

Dahlia Wreath. Quilts. See **wreath patterns.**

daisy. Quilts. See **Quilts: Quilting.**

dalle-de-verre. Stained Glass. (Also called dalle.) Glass that is 8″ × 12″ and 1″ thick and was first used by the French in the 1930s. The dalles may be used as they are or broken into chunks. They are usually set into **epoxy resin** or **cement.** Though often used for casting **slab glass,** cast-

ing concrete is not particularly suited to outdoor architectural work because it can crack due to stress caused by extreme temperature changes. The glass is made in France, Germany, England, and America. Dalle-de-verre in French means "paving stone of glass."

TOOLS AND MATERIALS   The cutting tools are a steel anvil, which can be homemade, and special dalle hammers (**a., b., c.**). A mason's hammer can be substituted for a dalle hammer. The homemade anvil is made from a steel T-angle screwed down to a wood log or beam 18″ and 8–10″ in diameter. The T of the angle should be at least 3″ long and should be ground to a point that feels like a dull ax. The anvil should then be placed on a box to make it 30″ high or a comfortable height to work at (**d.**). See ill.

Safety goggles are important for protecting your face from flying chips. Other equipment includes heavy-duty rubber gloves, a **glass-cutter** for scoring the dalle, a rubber **spatula** or **trowel,** gallon-size plastic buckets, and plastic bags or hot-liquid paper cups for squeezing out or pouring out the epoxy.

Dalle is more expensive than **antique glass.** Broken pieces of dalle with no choice of color can be purchased for about 50¢/lb. Purchase at least 10–20 lbs. at first to give yourself a selection of colors to work from.

Fine sand, washed, and free of impurities is needed for use with epoxy.

Epoxy resin is sold in gallon cans; a smaller can of hardener is included. One gallon is sufficient for the beginner; use extenders or **ballast**s to extend epoxy.

Also needed are ¾″ plywood about 20″ × 30″ for a start and enough 1″ × 2″ stripping for building a mold around the four sides of the plywood.

Coarse sand or fine **marble chips** are often used to add an attractive finish to the concrete or epoxy.

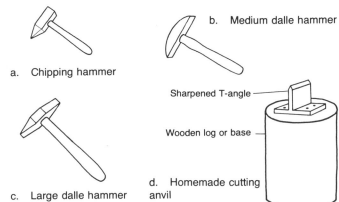

a. Chipping hammer

b. Medium dalle hammer

Sharpened T-angle

Wooden log or base

c. Large dalle hammer

d. Homemade cutting anvil

CUTTING THE DALLE There is a smooth side and a textured side to the dalle; the smooth side should be on the outside of the window.

In designing the first piece of dalle or slab glass keep the shapes bold and simple and large enough not to get lost in the epoxy or concrete. Straight shapes and slight curves should be attempted at first. Cut out **templates** as in cutting glass and place one on the dalle. **Score** around it with the glass cutter. When cutting straight lines, place the dalle over the **cutting anvil** with the **cut line** over the point and with hands on either side (**e.**). Raise the piece and bring it down sharply over the point, snapping it in two (**f.**). For cutting curves use the dalle hammer. Place the glass on the anvil at the score and gently tap away at the edge, chipping away pieces to the desired shape. Sometimes, for small, irregular cuts, it is useful to lay the glass on the block of wood on which the anvil is mounted and chip with the hammer (**g.**). When cutting curved or irregular shapes, the only way to get even cuts all the way through the glass is to use a **masonry saw. Faceting** is created by using the hammer to make side chips around the edge of a piece of dalle (**h.**). It gives a sparkling appearance to the glass. See ill.

TECHNIQUE When all the dalle pieces are cut, build a box the dimensions of the finished panel, using the ¾″ plywood for the bottom and nailing the wood strips to form the sides. Grease the sides of the box with a mold release agent (see **releasing agent**) such as a latex sealant, which also seals the box so that the epoxy does not run out. Place the **cartoon** on the bottom of the box.

Cutting dalle-de-verre

Score made with glass cutter

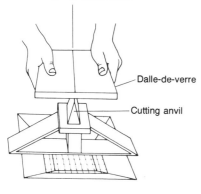

e. Place scored piece of dalle on cutting anvil point

f. Snap dalle in two over cutting anvil

g. Chipping a piece of dalle with a chipping hammer

h. Faceted dalle

Clean off all the cut pieces of dalle with **alcohol.** Coat the bottoms with rubber cement and stick them in place on the cartoon. If there are faceted pieces as part of the design, put **plasticene** in the gouges before setting them in place or they will be filled with epoxy. Sticking the pieces down helps prevent epoxy from running underneath them. An alternative and better solution is to pour fine sand around the dalles about halfway up their sides and to the borders of the piece. Smooth out the sand with a piece of cardboard or brush.

The epoxy, a monomer and a polymer, usually in separate containers, should be mixed thoroughly in the plastic bucket, using a rubber spatula or strong stick. Fumes from epoxy resin are toxic; prepare epoxy in a well-ventilated room. Once the mixture is prepared, you have about 10 minutes to work with it until it sets up. Wearing rubber gloves, use a homemade heavy kraft-paper funnel held together with masking tape or a plastic bag with a hole cut in one corner, or a half-gallon waxed milk carton; fill it with the epoxy mixture, and let the mixture flow evenly around the dalles to about ⅛″ below the tops of the pieces. It should extend to the edges of the frame. Be sure the epoxy fills every irregularity around the dalle. A small piece of cardboard will help to push it around. Sprinkle coarse sand or small marble chips on top for texture.

Wait 24 hours for the epoxy to dry. Then remove the strips from around the piece. If the first method of cementing the dalles to the cartoon is used, the piece is finished when the epoxy dries. The side which was attached to the cartoon will have a rough, uneven surface. If fine sand is poured around the glass, the piece must be turned over and the sand brushed away. A thin layer of sand will remain bonded to the epoxy; it will act as a gripping surface to hold the next batch of epoxy.

The second side has epoxy applied in the same way as the first, with a texture of sand or marble chips sprinkled on top. In this procedure, both sides of the panel are textured.

Premixed casting concrete is less expensive than epoxy and, used in the proper setting, is worth working with. A 25 lb. bag costs about $1 at most hardware stores and building suppliers. Also buy coarse sand or small marble chips to texture the outer surfaces of the concrete and give the piece an attractive finish. The sand should be washed and screened for impurities.

The casting worktable can include a **vibrator** for settling the concrete around the glass.

The other important equipment for concrete is **armatures**.

Use a wooden mold as in **casting epoxy resin.** The sides should be made independently so that they can be knocked away from the concrete when the casting is dry. This can be done with wing nuts on bolts that stick up through the base of the mold. The seams of the mold can be sealed with a mold release to prevent leakage.

If a vibrator is being used, the base of the mold will have to be attached to the worktable so that it doesn't shake off.

Set the armature in place on prefabricated concrete blocks, which can be made by pouring concrete into small matchboxes. These supports will prevent the armature from being exposed through the concrete. The bottom of the mold can be lined with foam rubber or styrofoam to prevent the concrete from running under the dalles (**j.**). See ill.

Color can be added to the mixed concrete; natural colors look best. The concrete can also be black or white.

When using concrete, wear rubber gloves. Shovel the mixed concrete with medium-sized trowels, pushing it around the glass.

If you use the vibrator, add some concrete, vibrate, add some more concrete, vibrate again, and so on, until the mold is filled and there are no bubbles rising to the top of the liquid concrete. Add the final textures of sand or marble.

To remove concrete that may have gotten on the glass, wait until it has set up but not hardened and then wash or wire-brush the glass. All extra water and **laitance** lying on top of the concrete and glass should be removed. Cover and insulate the mold and let it stand for 3−4 days until it is thoroughly dried. Then remove the sides of the mold and the bottom, keeping the concrete and glass supported when it is not upright. Also see **acetone** and **Stained Glass: Cutting.**

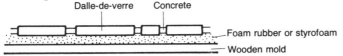

j. Casting dalle-de-verre on foam rubber or styrofoam to prevent concrete from running under the dalles

dalle-de-verre mold. Stained Glass. **Mold**s made for enclosing **dalle-de-verre** slabs vary, depending on the casting material and the size of the finished piece. The material used for sides or bases can be wood or steel. The sides are made to the exact size of the panel, plus its overlap. Each side should be constructed so that it can be removed without disturbing the casting while it is drying.

Molds used with casting concrete are usually made of wood. If a **vibrator** is used the base of the mold must be attached to the worktable with **armature**s to keep the mold on the table. Also see **dalle-de-verre, shuttering, vibrator.**

dam. Glasswork. A temporary support for plaster while the plaster hardens. In the **casting** of glass pieces, the model made of wax or clay is surrounded by **refractory** plaster. An adequate dam can be made by curling a piece of linoleum into a cylinder, securing it with a length of twine, standing it on end, and pouring the plaster into it.

damascene. Jewelry. A process of decorating metal that involves the application of one metal to another by **appliqué** or **inlay.** Also see **kuftgari.**

Damascus edge. Rugmaking. Weaving. A **finishing edge** used in rugs and weavings and formed by a row of continuous knots running from **selvage** to selvage. It protects the first and last **pick** of **filling** and is called a weft protector. The Damascus edge is knotted in two stages with the first stage starting at the right-hand side of the work and proceeding to the left. This first series of knots can be used as a finishing edge without going on to the second stage. It is then called a half Damascus edge. Different effects can

be obtained just with the numbers of rows of this first series. One row will secure the filling and the ends can be darned into the fabric. Three rows will roll the band to the back of the fabric with the warp ends pointing upward. Successive rows will create a band that can be hemmed back.

The first step in the Damascus edge is begun at the right side by wrapping end #1 around and under #2, emerging between #1 and #2 (**a.**). This is repeated across the width always picking up a new end on the left and dropping the end that now points upward on the right. The second stage is done by turning the work so that the fringe points downward and working the knots from the left-hand side in the same wrapping manner as with the first stage (**b.**). This results in ridges on both sides and the finished fringe hanging downward away from the cloth in the normal fringe position. If using this edge for a rug, it should be determined through trial whether there are enough **warp ends** for the edge to be wrapped securely without pulling the rug edges in. See ill.

a. Half Damascus— first stage worked right to left

b. Full Damascus—second stage worked left to right; the half Damascus is not visible in the second drawing

damask. Weaving. True damask is a figured fabric made up of a combination of **warp-face** and **filling-face satin**s. It originally came from China via Damascus, Syria. Marco Polo encountered it in the thirteenth century. Since the satins are true satins, they require at least 10 harnesses to weave both of them simultaneously. If the **ground** is warp-faced, the patterning is filling-faced with no floats crossing over from pattern to ground. Since warp and filling are usually in the same color, the patterning stands out because of the contrast between the two weaves. To be able to do the intricate floral, bird, animal, and figure designs damask is known for, it is usually woven commercially on a **Jacquard loom.** Handweavers who attempt true damask use a **draw loom,** also known as a damask loom. There is an 8-**harness** cloth known as false damask. It has the contrast between 4-harness warp and filling faced **twill** weaves, but the design is a very simple block pattern and the long floats that add luster to a true damask are missing. Handwoven damask is traditionally used for table linens, but it is also used for ecclesiastical fabrics, upholstery, and drapery. Also see **draw loom, satin.**

damask loom. Weaving. See **damask.**

damp-cupboard. Ceramics. (Also called damp room.) A cool, tight cupboard that maintains a saturated atmosphere and is used for keeping pots damp until they are leather hard. Clay is kept damp more often by covering it with polyethelene sheeting.

danburite. Gemcutting. A transparent, white or yellow mineral with hardness of 7, specific gravity of 3 and refractive indices of 1.630 and 1.636. Facets are polished with tin oxide on a tin lap. Also see faceting, polishing, refraction.

dancers. Toys. (Also called wrestlers.) A two-figure toy that moves on a string. The bodies and legs are cut from wood clothespins and the arms are made from craft sticks. Holes are drilled to allow for a small wire to be inserted to loosely connect the arms and legs. The craft sticks are notched to suggest hands. A black string or sewing thread is tied to one notched hand with the other end of the string going to a chair leg or any similar object. A string is then tied to the other craft stick hand and the end of it is held in the hand. The figures should be supported by the strings so that they are just above floor level. When the hand-held string is jerked, the figures dance or wrestle excitedly. See ill. Also see clothespin wrestlers.

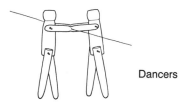

Dancers

dancing man. Toys. (Also called limber jack, stomper doll.) An articulated toy made of wood with a varying number of joints, all of which move when the figure "dances." The legs, arms, and knees are usually jointed and sometimes there are added joints at elbow, wrist, ankle, and waist. All joints must be loose. A dowel is attached at right angles to the figure's back so that it can be held out in front of the person operating it. The operator sits on the back end of a paddle, a quarter-inch-thick piece of wood, thereby holding it steady. The free end of the paddle projects out in front over the edge of a chair. The figure is held over the paddle so that its feet just barely touch the wood. When the paddle is drummed or tapped with the fingers it vibrates, causing the figure to dance. This toy is often operated by an adult to amuse a child, rather than played with by the child. See ill.

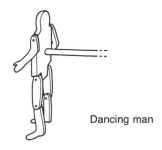

Dancing man

dancing top. Toys. A top made in the form of a girl's figure or a ballerina. The point of the top on which it spins is the dancer's "toes."

Danish hedebo. Embroidery. See whitework.

Danish Hedebo lace. Lacemaking. See sol lace.

Danish Medallion. Weaving. A finger-manipulated openwork technique that produces openings in the fabric by a technique of encircling the filling in groups. The encircling produces an effect of woven roundels or medallions. The basis of the technique is plain weave with the medallion shape formed during the right-to-left movement of the shuttle in the shed. The outside right selvage thread should be lying in the top section of this shed. The shuttle is actually brought up out of the shed and, with the aid of a finger or a crochet hook, a loop of the yarn on the shuttle is brought down to the point where the medallion shape is to begin, and under that filling yarn that will serve as the lower boundary of the shape. The shuttle is then passed through the loop and the loop is pulled closed tightly. The tighter it is pulled, the larger the openings become. It is also possible not to pull tightly at all and then the medallion becomes a surface decoration, rather than a lace effect. One medallion is thus shaped, and the shuttle goes back into the shed passing to the left for a few ends up to the point where it is to emerge from the shed again for the next medallion. This procedure is repeated across the warp for as many medallions as are desired. If the technique is found to be too clumsy with a shuttle, the weaver can use a blunt tapestry needle or a netting shuttle for the encircling yarn.

The medallions can be placed directly above each other or staggered. They can also vary as to width (by having more warp ends included in each medallion) and height (by having more plain weave between the beginning and ending picks of the medallion). Often a heavier yarn or one of a different color is used for the first and last picks of the medallion which serves to accentuate the shape. There are other variations as to possible shape, especially when using this technique as a surface decoration.

This type of openwork lace effect is found in many countries, but is called "Danish Medallion" owing to its popularity in Scandinavia. It is used in wall hangings, curtain fabrics, room dividers, and as trim on placements, napkins, scarves and stoles. See ill.

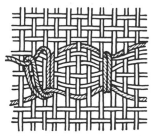

Danish Medallion with heavy yarn to outline the shape

Danziger glass. Stained Glass. See streaky glass.

dapping. Jewelry. A technique of forming metal domes. Also see dapping block, dapping die, dapping punch, doming.

dapping block. Jewelry. A cube-shaped dapping tool usually made of shell, with semicircular depressions of various sizes on all sides. It is used in conjunction with **dapping punch**es to make semicircular domes of sheet metal. See ill. Also see **dapping die, doming.**

a.   Assorted dapping punches   b.   Dapping block

dapping block. Tincrafting. A hard, wood block with various sized concave depressions cut into each of the six surfaces. It is used for **hammering** in conjunction with a **ball-peen hammer** to create raised or depressed round areas on the metal. The hammering should begin at the outer rim of the area to be raised or lowered and then gradually worked inward as the metal gives. Also see **Tincraft: Preparing the Tin can.**

dapping die. Jewelry. The same thing as a **dapping block,** only not necessarily in cube form. In addition, a dapping die may have any negative form cut into its surface, whereas the dapping block has only concave hemispheres. Also see **doming.**

dapping punch. Jewelry. Dapping tools used in combination with a **dapping die.** Also see **dapping block, doming.**

dapping tool. Jewelry. See **dapping block, dapping punch.**

dark dough. Toys. A cookie dough used in dough art or **cookie art** that is dark in color. Gingerbread figures are traditionally dark, the color resulting from the ginger and other spices as well as the use of molasses and brown sugar. Blackstrap molasses and dark brown sugar will add even deeper color to the batter. Traditionally, white frosting is used to make linear patterns on the rich brown cookies.

Dark doughs are sometimes made with chocolate cookie recipes. When the chocolate and white doughs are combined, as with standard icebox cookies, the two colors add greatly to the design possibilities of the cookie art. Also see **Toys: Ephemeral Toys.**

darkening metal. Enameling. See **firescale, liver of sulfur.**

dark quilt. Quilts. Any quilt that could be made from all dark fabrics. These were usually **one-patch** and gave an **all-over** effect. Patterns depending on contrasting colors to be effective required light materials, and these were less common in colonial times. Light colors were almost always required for **appliqué quilt**s, so most dark quilts are **pieced.**

dark wood. Puppets. Toys. A way of referring to the color of wood without reference to whether it is a **softwood** or **hardwood.** When wood is left with a natural finish, not painted or stained, the dark woods offer rich variety.

Those woods with a reddish cast are redwood, red cedar, and mahogany. Rosewood ranges from a light red to a deep purple. Both walnut and teak are brown; the latter may also have darker brown streaks. Ebony is black.

darning. Knitting. A method of outlining knit stitches with a contrasting colored yarn. This type of darning is used for its decorative rather than practical value. Techniques may vary slightly but primarily require that a tapestry needle threaded with very thin yarn be threaded in and out of the actual knit stitches in whatever design or outline you have chosen. Also see **Swiss darning.**

darning head. Ceramics. A wooden, mushroom-shaped tool used for pressing clay into **mold**s.

darning in. Rugmaking. Weaving. A process of sewing in the loose and protruding ends of either **warp** or **filling** yarn that appear on the surface when weaving is completed. In terms of the warp, darning in takes place as a result of a **broken end,** and either the end is simply pulled to the back of the fabric and trimmed, or better it is woven in and out following the same interlacing pattern with the filling that it would have had if the break had not occurred. This is done for two or three **picks,** so that the two broken strands overlap, and then the yarn tips are pulled to the back and trimmed.

For the filling, the same procedure follows, except that the filling is overlapped in the **shed** already, so all that has to be done is to be sure that these yarn tips are on the back side and then trimmed. At the **selvage,** filling yarn can be darned back into the fabric for two or three warp ends following the weave sequence. If the darning in is being done on a **flatweave rug** or a **tapestry,** care must be taken that no unevenness is caused on the surface. Heavy yarn can be tapered by cutting or pulling out loose fibers. The darning in follows the **plain weave** sequence and the yarn tips are tugged to take up any slack before trimming flush with the piece. If more than one yarn is involved in one spot the darning in is staggered, so that the two or more ends do not cause a thickening.

For darning in, a long tapestry **needle** is used, either with a blunt tip or a bent tip. Since most of the yarn tips are quite short, the needle is inserted into the cloth first and then threaded. A fine wire needle threader can be used if the yarn tip refuses to go through the needle eye. Also see **finishing, finishing edge.**

darning needle. Stitchery. See **needle.**

darning on net. Embroidery. (Also called tulle embroidery.) A technique in which the first step is to mark a design on any stiff, shiny blue paper with a permanent felt-tipped pen. When the design has dried, the net is basted to the paper. The lines of the design will show through the net, and the pattern will be darned with cotton **embroidery floss** on the net.

Outline the shapes in **running stitch.** Fill in shape with floss of up to six strands, using **buttonhole stitch, darning stitch,** running stitch, **satin stitch,** or **straight stitch.** The number of strands used depends upon whether a lacy or heavy effect is desired. Care must be taken in starting and ending threads, as all joining will show clearly. Bind off, if necessary, by running a few threads back beside the ones you have just taken on the outlines. Preferably join by making a **lace knot.** This means you can join a new thread to your working one and continue stitching. The tiny knot will disappear invisibly into the embroidery. See ill.

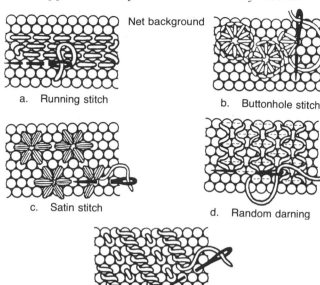

a. Running stitch

Net background

b. Buttonhole stitch

c. Satin stitch

d. Random darning

e. Satin and running stitch

darning stitch. Crewel. Embroidery. A long **running stitch** used for outlines and borders as well as filling shapes. An evenweave fabric is recommended so the threads can be easily counted.

In pattern darning, the size and spacing of the stitches vary to create unlimited variations. Usually done in monochromatic or black thread, this technique is used in **blackwork.** See ill.

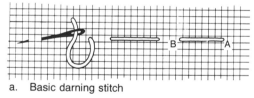

a. Basic darning stitch

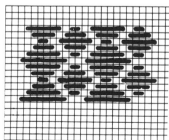

b. Pattern darning

darning stitch. Lacemaking. A continuous stitch made with needle and thread, weaving in and out with the needle, over and under threads running in the opposite direction in an even and continuous manner. Also, crossing perpendicularly, with the same length of stitch, over stitches already laid in. A **filling** stitch.

dart. Toys. A short, pointed, missilelike object, sometimes with feathers at the end opposite the point to offer directional stability, as on arrows or shuttlecocks. Darts are usually weighted for throwing and are used in dart games. Also see **bull's eye, whiplash.**

dart game. Toys. A **game** in which weighted and sharp-pointed **darts** are thrown at a target. The target is usually a **bull's eye.** The player stands at a set distance from the dart board or target to throw the darts.

Daruma doll. Toys. (Also called rocking doll.) A round-bottomed figure, usually weighted, that is a traditional **folk toy** of Japan. It is named for Bodhidharma (Dharma), the sixth-century founder of Zen Buddhism. The figure is made so that it remains upright or returns to an upright position no matter how it is turned or tilted. The **doll** suggests the figure of Dharma, who, according to legend, meditated in the lotus position for nine years; after that he was paralyzed and unable to walk. These **self-righting dolls** are **balance toys**, made with a weighted half-spherical base and a lighter-weight cone-shaped top. When made very small they are called bean dolls. Also see **Toys: Folk Toys.**

Daruma toy. Toys. Any **balance toy** made in a manner similar to the **Daruma doll.**

datolite. Gemcutting. A transparent yellow-white gem **faceting** material with **hardness** of 5½, **specific gravity** of 2.9 to 3, and refractive indices of 1.625 and 1.669. The recommended angle for crown and pavillion facets is 40°; facets are polished on a tin or plastic **lap** with tin oxide. Also see **polishing, refraction.**

dauber. Block Printing. A padded ball used instead of a **brayer** for applying ink to the **printing block.** The dauber can be made by wrapping cloth around a ball of soft fiber, such as cotton, and tying it at the top with string. This pad is dabbed in the **printing ink,** which has been spread with a knife on a sheet of glass, then onto the block. The results are not as even as those obtainable with a brayer.

dauber. Leatherwork. See **Leatherwork: Dyeing and Coloring Leather.**

David and Goliath. Quilts. A **pieced block** made up of 25 small square **patch**es. Many of the patches are formed of two triangles. It is known by various other names, all relating to archery or hunting, such as Bull's Eye, Doe and Darts, Flying Darts, and Four Darts.

daylight measurement. Stained Glass. See **full size.**

day lily. Quilts. See **Quilts: Quilting.**

deairing. Ceramics. The process of removing air from clay bodies by **kneading, wedging,** or pugging. Also see **pug mill.**

deairing pug mill. Ceramics. See **pug mill.**

debubblizer. Jewelry. (Also called wetting agent.) A liquid material used for coating the wax model in **casting** to promote a complete contact by breaking the surface tension between the **wax** and the **investment.** This lessens the possibility of small bubbles adhering to the wax when **investing.** After casting, these air bubbles, which are encased in investment, would be small random balls of metal that would have to be removed. Apply debubblizer with a brush or dip the wax model several times. Allow the solution to dry completely before applying investment. Also see **centrifugal casting.**

debusscope. Toys. A late eighteenth-century **optical toy** that consisted of two mirrors set at 40° angles to one another in a box or frame that could be placed over a design of any kind, reflecting and reproducing it symmetrically. The **kaleidoscope** was based on this device. The polyscope is similar, but has mirrors that can be adjusted anywhere within the 360°. Also see **Toys: Optical Toys.**

decalcomania. Stained Glass. (Also called tonking.) A technique, used in **painting on glass.** The wet layer of paint is blotted with a crushed, folded, or open piece of a variety of papers or plastics, which is then removed. The results are interesting random patterns when the paper is removed.

deckle edge. Bookbinding. The rough or irregular edge produced in the manufacture of paper that is especially characteristic of handmade varieties. Paper that has not been trimmed has a deckle edge; it is sometimes left on fine writing paper.

decomposition. Ceramics. The natural deterioration of unfired **glaze**s with age due to the breaking up of chemical compounds which make up their ingredients. Ware should be fired as soon as possible after **glazing.**

decorating. Candlemaking. Once the candle has hardened the decorating possibilities are almost limitless. Also see **carving, découpage, encaustic, marbelizing, masking, mottling, pinching, texturing, wax bath.**

decorating. Kites. See **Kites: Construction.**

decorative paper. Découpage. Papercrafts. (Also called lining paper.) Art supply stores sell a great variety of patterned papers for use in découpage, such as tea papers, marbelized papers, and tortoiseshell papers. These are sometimes used as a background surface for découpage **cutouts,** but more often as a liner for boxes or other interior surfaces that are not decorated with découpage. Some of these papers have paint that bleeds or runs when moistened with paste or **varnish,** so experimentation is recommended. In most cases the papers can first be coated with **sealer** or sprayed with clear **acrylic** spray to preserve colors.

decorative rivet. Stitchery. See **rivet.**

DÉCOUPAGE

"Découpage" is a twentieth-century term, derived from the French word *couper,* to cut, for the technique of decorating surfaces with paper **cutouts.** Boxes, chests, screens, furniture, and other surfaces are decorated with **glued** cutouts, then coated with layers of **finish** until the surface is glassy smooth.

Throughout the history of découpage, various **lacquers** and **varnish**es have been tried for the finish, and various materials, including **papier mâché,** wood, and tin **(toleware),** have been tried for the background surface. Découpage as we know it today is the technique of gluing cutouts to a suitable surface, then coating them with a **sealer.** The finish is achieved by applying many layers of varnish; the dry varnish is rubbed with **sandpaper** and **steel wool** and given a final polish with **wax.**

The technique has traditionally been used to simulate painted or lacquered surfaces, using motifs cut from **print**s with intricate precision as a substitute for hand-painted designs. The popularity of découpage dates back to late seventeenth-century Italy, when **lacquer ware** imported from the Orient was in such demand that a more accessible and inexpensive substitute was necessary. By the eighteenth century, **prints** were published expressly for the purpose of cutting and pasting. Reproductions of drawings by such artists as Boucher and **Pillement** were widely available. Many of these prints were drawn in a Chinese, or **chinoiserie,** style. The Italian term for this popular craft was *l'arte del uomo povero,* or **arte povero,** the poor man's art, or *lacche povero,* meaning poor man's lacquer.

In France, where it also gained in popularity during the eighteenth-century, the technique was called *l'art scriban,* in reference to the **scriban,** or secretary type of desk, which was often decorated with cutouts.

In England this technique of imitating Chinese and Japanese wares was termed Japan work, or **japanning.** To meet the growing demand for prints for cutting, a collection of reproductions was published in 1760 called **Ladies' Amusement.**

Although the technique was developed to imitate Oriental lacquers, découpage itself has become a unique and elegant art form. Découpage designs can be extremely varied, from reproductions of traditional motifs to more personalized expressions. Découpage also includes three-dimensional techniques such as **shadow-box** and **paper-sculpture** arrangements.

SETTING UP A WORKSHOP   Although the cutting of **prints** can be done in any place that is comfortable, the application of the découpage **finish** should be done at a well-lighted, permanent worktable where cans of **sealer,** finish, and **solvent**s and the wet pieces of découpage can be left. It is important that the work area be free from dust. Because several pieces are often processed at once, a good supply of prints should be sealed, cut, ready to use, and stored in a box in the work area.

Most of the materials for the découpage finish can be purchased at the hardware store. Prints can be collected from various sources or bought at craft or antique shops. The object to be decorated could be an old piece of furniture or a wooden box from the craft store. A complete line of découpage supplies is available at craft stores. The choice between using hardware store **shellac** and **varnish** or craft shop découpage sealer and finish is a personal one that should result from experimentation. The basic techniques described in this section can be done with either hardware or craft store supplies.

Tools and materials should be stored on or near the worktable. Small sharp **scissors** are used to cut out prints. It's helpful to have curved scissors (**a.**) and straight scissors (**b.**). Tweezers are helpful for handling delicate **cutouts.** Although cosmetic tweezers can be used, tweezers purchased from a dental supply house are more flexible (**c.**). A **burnishing tool** is needed for pressing down the edges of cutouts after they are glued down (**d.**). **Color pencils,** a hard gum eraser, and a pencil sharpener are used in tinting prints. **Decorative paper**s are used for backgrounds or **lining.** Various other decorative items, such as **gold-paper trim** or **gold leaf,** may be needed to complete a design. See ill., page 248.

For gluing you will need **glue** and a small glue brush, a bowl of water for cleaning fingers, clean rags, a sponge, and paper towels for removing excess glue and patting down glued cutouts. For finishing you will need sealer, varnish, appropriate solvents, and **brush**es for application. The quantities of materials needed will depend on the size of the surface to be covered. Bear in mind that as many as 20 layers of varnish may be necessary.

The materials needed for final polishing are #280-A, #400, and #600 wet-or-dry **sandpaper,** #0000 **steel wool,** lintless **tack cloth,** and fine furniture **wax. Pumice** or **rottenstone** may be substituted for sandpaper.

Materials needed for preparing and painting the surface to be decorated will vary according to the type of surface used. These techniques are discussed under **Découpage: Preparing the Surface.**

CARE AND MAINTENANCE OF TOOLS An orderly work area is essential to good découpage technique. All tools and materials should be kept clean. You will find on the label of each can of **sealer** and **varnish** a list of the types of **solvent** needed for cleaning and thinning. Since varnish has a tendency to thicken when exposed to air, it should be poured into a small jar so that the varnish comes right to the top of the jar, leaving no room for air inside. Cover with a tight lid. If varnish begins to thicken, mix in a few drops of pure gum turpentine.

Use each **brush** for one purpose only, and always clean brushes carefully. However, when applying layers of varnish day after day, you can leave the varnish brush standing in a jar of solvent rather than cleaning it after each use. To clean, first dip the brush in the appropriate solvent until clean, wiping it on paper toweling or rags. Then wash with lukewarm water and soap. Rinse thoroughly and gently reshape the brush bristles. Dry with bristle end up in an empty can or jar.

SELECTING PRINTS Almost anything printed on paper can be used for découpage. However, there are a few basic considerations to remember. The paper on which it is printed should not be too thick or it will be impossible to completely cover it with layers of **varnish.** Cheaply printed magazines have **bleeding ink.** The printing ink should be permanent when coated with **sealer** and varnish. The print from the wrong side of a magazine page, called verso printing, also should not show through when the print is coated with sealer. Pictures and **prints** should be collected and coated with sealer before cutting. Then only those with permanent ink should be used.

There are several ways of eliminating the bulky backing from a print or thick paper to make it usable for découpage. **Thinning prints** by **razor thinning** involves peeling layers of paper from the back. Another technique is **transferring prints,** accomplished by applying coatings of clear plastic to the front and then removing the backing paper to make a sort of decal.

Prints may be hand colored or given an antique patina before sealing.

Once the technical requirements are met, the only other consideration in selecting printed material is one of style. Although découpage compositions can be as individual as collage or painting, there are several traditional styles associated with the technique. Découpage originated as an imitation of Oriental **lacquer ware,** and the use of **chinoiserie** prints of Oriental scenes is as popular today as it was in the eighteenth century. A variation of this style is the singerie style which is characterized by monkey figures. Découpage done in this style uses **cutouts** from reproduced eighteenth-century prints by such artists as **Pillement,** arranged in a rococo format and often enclosed by **cartouche** borders.

Italian découpage is usually done in the style of eighteenth-century Venetian furniture with ornate decorations of scrolls, birds, and delicate flowers.

French découpage was the most delicate style. This can be imitated with dainty flowers, cherubs, butterflies, birds, and garlands. **Toile de Jouy** is the style of arranging scenes in shades of one color against a plain white background. **Creil** is the style of applying one black-and-white motif to a plain white or yellow background.

Austrian and German découpage is characterized by the **Biedermeier** style, with its massive arrangements of embossed figures, flowers, and birds. Embossed and die-cut pictures were produced in Germany and used extensively in their ornate decorations.

Victorian découpage also used precolored, embossed scrapbook pictures, and **gold-paper trim.** These materials, available from craft shops, can be combined in lavish Victorian designs. Victorian découpage also used other materials, such as **mother-of-pearl,** as accents.

Trompe l'oeil style requires prints of lifelike objects that are cut out and arranged in a realistic manner.

For **millefleurs** style, collect motifs from many different prints, to be arranged in an all-over pattern.

In planning the cutouts to be used, remember that intricate patterns can be cut from plain colored paper and folded for repeated patterns, as described under **Papercrafts: Repeat Patterns.**

Also see **antiquing.**

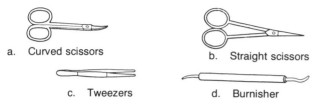

a. Curved scissors   b. Straight scissors

c. Tweezers   d. Burnisher

HAND COLORING Pictures printed in black ink on white paper that is flat rather than glossy can be tinted with **color pencils** before sealing or cutting. **Hand coloring** is generally done with oil-color pencils, using several shades of each color in light to dark tones. The color choice will depend on the **découpage style** being worked on. Traditional prints are colored in various color schemes, or palettes. The **grisaille** palette is based on shades of gray. For **sanguine** palette, colors from dark brown to light red will be needed, plus white for shading.

Chinoiserie and eighteenth-century prints use a broader palette, including more brilliant colors, such as pink, yellow, orange, blue, violet, and bright green.

Toile de Jouy prints are monochromatic.

Keep pencils well sharpened. Apply color with gentle strokes, never pressing down hard on the paper. Continue going over an area until the desired tone is reached. Shade figures and objects, following their forms, making darker shadows where forms recede in space. Remember that the layers of varnish will mute the colors. The white of the paper itself acts as a source of light, which can be left uncolored for highlights. To blend several colors together, overlap them slightly, then blend with a white pencil.

After coloring and before cutting, the print should be coated with a **sealer** to prevent the colors from running when the varnish **finish** is applied.

CUTTING Precolored or hand-tinted **prints** that have been coated with a **sealer** and allowed to dry are ready to be cut. The sealer strengthens the prints, making cutting easier. Cutting is probably the most important step in découpage, as well as the most fascinating. The **scissors** should be held with thumb and third finger in a comfortable, relaxed position. Cutting should be done with scissors slanted away from the print so that a slightly beveled edge will result, with the shorter edge toward the underside. When cutting with a blade, hold it at the same angle, and tape the print to a cardboard backing to prevent slipping. Feed the print into the scissors, moving the print with the free hand. The scissors should open and close steadily while held in more or less the same position. Intricate cutting is manipulated by feeding the print to the scissors in a zigzag rhythm with the free hand. These techniques can be practiced with scrap paper before cutting the print. There is seldom a straight line in découpage cutting. There are four basic cutting techniques. For a serrated edge, the paper is moved back and forth as the scissors cut delicate zigzags. This softened outline will blend into the background far better than a straight line (**a.**). **Feather cutting** is serrated cutting done with deeper zigzags to resemble feathers or dry brush strokes. Variations of feathering can be done in the foreground to suggest tufts of grass (**b.**). Stencil cutting is done with a single-edge razor blade or a knife. Curved openings are cut into the interior of the print (**c.**). Incised

cutting is done in the interior of a large print to open up solid areas for an easier and more binding application of glue and finish. Incised cuts are small, irregular shapes that should blend into the picture without being too obvious (**d.**). See ill.

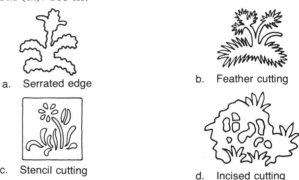

a. Serrated edge   b. Feather cutting

c. Stencil cutting   d. Incised cutting

In cutting prints, the small, inside areas should be cut away first, leaving enough paper around the edges for easy handling. However, when cutting very intricate prints, **bridges** should be drawn with a pencil on the print to connect details such as tendrils and stems. These bridges are left uncut until just before gluing as a protective support for pieces that might otherwise break away. If some lines are too thin to be cut without falling apart, they may be enlarged with a colored pencil.

The cutting technique should be integrated into the style of the print. Simple shapes may require a simple serrated edge, while rococo prints may seem suited to feather cutting. As with many other aspects of découpage, individual preferences for methods result from experimentation.

PREPARING THE SURFACE Découpage can be applied to any clean, dry material except plastic. Decorative objects made of wood, ceramics, metal, pottery or porcelain, glass, marble, stone, and so on should be prepared as follows before **cutout**s are applied. Additional materials and methods needed for specific surfaces are also described.

To prepare the surface, first clean and dry thoroughly, then brush on a coat of **sealer.** If an ivory-smooth surface is desired, apply **acrylic gesso**; a **gesso** surface is recommended as a background for **gilding.** The sealed surface can be used as the background or painted. If painted, a sealer must again be applied over the dry paint. Then the designing and gluing of cutouts can be done.

To prepare new wood, fill the cracks with **filler** and sand with fine **sandpaper** or garnet sandpaper, then with #0000 **steel wool.** Dust away the sand. Apply sealer, and when dry, rub with steel wool. Though any type of paint can be used on wood, enamel paint is recommended. Two coats of paint will make an even surface. Let the paint dry, then coat again with sealer. When dry, it is ready to be decorated with cutouts. Wood may also be treated with **antiquing** or stain before sealing.

To prepare already painted wood, sand with fine sandpaper and dust away the sand. Wash the surface with turpentine and allow it to dry. Apply the sealer and continue as for new wood.

To prepare **varnish**ed wood, first remove the old **finish** with paint and varnish remover, available at the hardware store. Then sand until smooth and proceed as for new wood.

For metal surfaces (tin, steel, iron, lead), sand off any rust with fine sandpaper or steel wool. If the piece is badly rusted, use a commercial rust remover. Then wash with denatured alcohol. Apply a coating of **rust-retarder** metal primer and allow to dry overnight. You can then paint the surface with enamel paint in the desired color, letting it dry overnight between coats.

To prepare old metal pieces, it is advisable to first remove the finish with paint and varnish remover. In order to rust-proof the piece, the bare metal must be treated. Apply a commercial rust remover and rub with steel wool until all rust spots are gone. Wipe with a damp cloth, then wash with denatured alcohol. Once the alcohol has been applied, be careful not to touch the metal or rust spots may form. Apply a coat of rust retarder to the dry metal surface. Dry overnight, then sand lightly if necessary to remove any gritty texture from this prime coat. Apply another coat of sealer. When dry, the surface can be painted with two or three coats of enamel paint.

To prepare glass, proceed with the general technique for preparing the surface, coating with a sealer, then painting if desired with Japan oil-base paint.

To prepare a mirror, first color the back of prints to be used with solid black **color pencil** to prevent reflection. Use shock mirror, which is lightweight and extremely thin, so there will be less reflection on the back of the print. Découpage cutouts can be slightly glued to the mirror and covered with a thin sheet of glass cut the same size as the mirror. Both pieces can be taped together at the edges, then framed in a frame deep enough to accommodate the thickness of both mirror and glass. The glass front provides the protective coating instead of a varnish finish. Also see **antiquing, découpage on ceramics, découpage under glass, stain.**

GLUING   **Prints** that have been sealed and cut are ready to be glued to the surface. Generally, the **glue** is applied to the surface to be decorated rather than to the back of the **cutout.** The glue should be even and thin on the surface, applied with the fingers or a **brush.** Have water, sponge, and toweling ready. Fingers must be kept damp and clean. Pick up the cutouts and place on the glued surface. Gently move the cutout parts into position with **tweezers** or fingers. Rinse and wring out the sponge in clean water. Tap it gently over the cutouts to press them down. Use wet fingers to position delicate parts. Press down edges with a fingernail. When the design has been completely glued down, with no loose edges, remove glue from undecorated background areas with a clean, damp sponge. Glues especially prepared for découpage can be left several hours before cleaning off. This would be the best process, leaving the cutouts to dry and then removing the glue from the background later. Always clean away background glue with care to prevent the cutouts from becoming unglued. When the glue is completely dry, a **burnishing tool** may be used to embed the edges of the cutouts. Check the design for any unglued spots. These can be repaired by slitting the area with a blade and inserting glue with a toothpick or

knife. Press the area down with a damp sponge, dabbing away any excess glue. Allow to dry thoroughly, and then apply the **sealer.**

VARNISHING AND SANDING   The application of the **varnish finish** begins after the completed **cutout** design has been glued and sealed. Rub the dry **sealer** coat with **steel wool** and wipe the surface clean. Varnishing should not be done on damp days. Dip the brush into the varnish and brush it on the surface in one direction only, not back and forth. Overlap strokes slightly so that all strokes blend together. Wipe up excess varnish as it accumulates at the edges. Allow the varnished piece to dry 24 hours. Apply nine more coats of varnish, allowing 24 hours between applications. Then sand the dry varnished surface with #400 wet-or-dry **sandpaper** dipped in water. Clean off the surface with toweling and rub it down with #0000 steel wool.

Apply as many additional coats of varnish as needed to cover the cutouts with a glassy surface. Eighteen coats all together is a minimum; 20 or more would be perfection. Always allow at least 24 hours between coats. To test varnish for dryness, press firmly with a finger. If no mark is left, another coat may be applied.

After the last coat of varnish has thoroughly dried, sand the entire surface with wet-or-dry sandpaper dipped in water, beginning with #280-A, the coarsest abrasive grade. Work with both the surface and the paper wet. Sand in a circular motion, concentrating on one area at a time. Wipe the surface clean occasionally with toweling or tissue, then wet again and continue sanding until there are no shiny spots left. Sand lightly on all edges, being careful not to reach the wood. Next sand the piece with #400 sandpaper to smooth out scratches, sanding in the same way but with a lighter pressure. Finally, use #600 sandpaper and polish lightly until it feels satin-smooth. Clean off the surface with a damp sponge and let it dry. Finish the sanding process with a light rubbing with #0000 steel wool, used dry. When satisfied with the finish, wipe off the surface with a damp sponge and rub with the hand. It should be extremely smooth and free of all gritty particles. Let the piece dry 24 hours before **wax**ing.

WAXING   Use any fine paste furniture **wax** and a soft, damp cloth. Dip the cloth in the wax and apply it to the surface in a circular motion. For large pieces, use small amounts of wax and rub briskly until the surface is covered. Reapply often to prevent the wax from getting gummy. Buff with a dry cloth. If the wax isn't evenly coated, repeat the waxing process. The découpage piece is now completed. Boxes or chests can be given a **lining.**

CARE AND MAINTENANCE   The découpage piece can occasionally be waxed or buffed to preserve the **wax** coating. To remove fingerprints, wipe with a barely damp sponge, then buff with a soft cloth. Spilled material may be wiped off with a sponge; the découpage finish is even alcohol-proof! After wiping with a sponge, the surface may need another coat of wax.

Keep the découpage piece away from direct sunlight and excessive dampness. Although the découpage surface is stain- and alcohol-resistant, it must be treated gently.

Its surface is brittle and will chip if bumped. Since it takes about a year for the varnish to harden completely, don't place extremely heavy objects on it during the first year.

Découpage on other surfaces, such as glass, should be handled with reasonable care. The glass side can be washed.

If the edges of the cutouts on an old découpage piece become slightly unglued, first remove the covering wax by rubbing with **steel wool.** Then reglue the edges and let them dry. Apply several coats of **varnish** until it blends in with the rest of the surface. Then rub it down with steel wool and rewax.

découpage. Candlemaking. Toys. A **decorating** technique that can be adapted most effectively to the surface of a smooth molded candle. Designs can be cut from paper prints and adhered to the candle by painting the back side of the print with hot clear wax and then quickly setting it in a predetermined position on the candle surface. Once the design is securely in place the entire candle can be dipped in hot clear wax, then plunged into cold water to produce a glossy candle surface.

In toys découpage refers to the French cutout sheet-paper toys. The popular cutouts were printed plain or hand tinted and were stiffened and assembled. In the 1850s when lithography made color printing possible découpage sheets reached their peak. **Bilderbage** is the German equivalent of the French découpage.

découpage chinois. Découpage. A style of découpage reminiscent of Oriental **lacquer ware** techniques, in which the background was textured with marbelized and gilt effects and various other rich surfaces. Contemporary materials are used to shorten this process by using patterned Chinese tea-chest papers to cover the entire box, piece of furniture, or surface to be découpaged.

Wet paper cannot be cut, so the paper is cut to fit each side or area while dry. Measure pieces larger than each area to allow for shrinkage when wet with **glue.** Apply glue to the back of the paper and carefully press to the surface, smoothing out wrinkles. Trim off excess paper with small **scissors.** After the paper background has dried, other **cutouts** may be glued down in preparation for the final découpage **finish.**

Because all the colors used in making these **decorative papers** are not fast when damp, experiments with scraps of the paper should first be made.

découpage on ceramics. Découpage. (Also called ceramic découpage, potichomania.) Pottery and porcelain are traditional materials for decorating with découpage. Decorating ceramics in this manner dates back to the eighteenth century, when imitations were made of Oriental wares.

Découpage **cutouts** and **finish** can be applied to any clean, dry, ceramic surface that has been coated with a **sealer.**

Bisque ware is often used as a surface for découpage. The découpage finish protects the unglazed surface just as a ceramic glaze would, eliminating the need for fired glazes. However, unlike ceramics, the découpage surface is not washable. Traditionally, only the outsides of pots were decorated with découpage, leaving the interiors usable. Also see **Découpage: Preparing the Surface.**

découpage on glass. Découpage. See **découpage under glass** and **Découpage: Preparing the Surface.**

découpage styles. Découpage. See **Découpage: Selecting Prints.**

découpage under glass. Découpage. A variation of découpage in which **cutouts** are glued to the inside of glass objects such as lamp bases, vases, or hurricane globes. The **sealer** and background **finish** are then applied behind the cutouts, on the back side. The smooth surface of the glass itself provides the perfect découpage surface over the cutout designs. The glass gives permanent protection and makes unnecessary the application of the many coats of varnish usually required to obtain a glassy-smooth surface.

The glass must first be washed with soap and water and wiped with denatured alcohol. The glass on both sides must be free of dust and fingerprints. The placement of cutouts may be marked on the outside of the glass with a china marking crayon. Then the cutouts are coated with **glue** on their right side, using white glue diluted with water so that it will dry transparent. The cutouts are pressed into place inside the glass, with their right sides visible through the glass. Smooth out any extra glue with the fingers and wipe clean with damp toweling or a sponge. Run a fingernail around all edges to make sure all parts of the print are completely glued down. Let dry overnight. When dry, apply the sealer behind the cutouts, on the inside of the glass, covering all the backs of the cutouts. After this has dried, a final background color of Japan oil-base paint may be painted over the entire inside. A second coat of paint is recommended for smoothness. Instead of painting, foil may be glued inside the glass in small overlapping patches as a background. **Acrylic gesso,** white or tinted, may be applied for a smooth, opaque background after the sealer has dried. The background also may be covered with **gold leaf,** as described under **gilding.**

After the background has dried, finish with two coats of **varnish.** Also see **Découpage: Gluing.**

découpeur. Découpage. A term for a person who practices the art of découpage.

decrease. Crochet. (Abbr. dec.) This is the process of crocheting two **stitch**es together as you ordinarily would crochet just one; it is done to reduce the number of stitches usually as part of a specific crochet **pattern.** It is possible to work the decrease in **double crochet, double triple crochet, half double crochet, single crochet, triple crochet,** and **triple treble crochet.** Also see **Crochet: Decreasing.**

decreasing. Knitting. See **Knitting: Decreasing.**

de Dillmont, Therese. Crewel. Embroidery. Needlepoint. The author of an encyclopedia of needlework published in the nineteenth century in France, and translated into five languages. It remains a widely used book to this day. Also see **D.M.C.**

deep buff. Leatherwork. See **split.**

deerfoot modeler. Leatherwork. See **modeler.**

deer-foot stippler. China and Glass Painting. See **brush.**

deerskin. Leatherwork. Any deer or elk skin with the **top grain** intact.

defect. Woodworking. See **wood.**

deflected warp. Weaving. See **diverted warp.**

deflocculant. Ceramics. A substance, such as sodium silicate or **soda ash,** that is added to a **casting slip** to reduce the amount of water necessary and to maintain a better suspension. Vinegar has a deflocculating effect on clay and is used to repair dry pots. Brush vinegar on the surfaces to be joined and press together. Also see **slip casting.**

deformation. Ceramics. Deformation occurs when a **clay body** can no longer hold its shape at too high a **kiln** temperature and forms molten compounds within the clay.

degumming. Spinning. Weaving. (Also called boiling off.) Removal of the natural gum found in raw **silk** by boiling it in a very strong solution of soap. **Silk** can be spun and woven with the gum in it but the fabric cannot be used unless degummed.

Deka-Type L. Batik and Tie-dye. See **direct dye.**

delamination. Plastics. See **lamination.**

Delany, Mary Granville. Papercrafts. An English artist, born in 1700, who developed a style of cutting out intricate flowers from colored paper and mounting them in arrangements on Chinese paper painted black. The flowers and plants were so lifelike and botanically accurate that they resembled pressed flowers. Delany used real plants as models, cutting the paper details freehand. She described the pictures as **paper mosaics.**

Delectable Mountains. Quilts. A **pieced quilt** design suggesting mountain ranges reaching out to the edge of the **block.** This quilt is **set** in a unique manner. Instead of arranging blocks in alternating patterns or bands, they are placed in rows around a central block so that the mountains always point out. An eight-pointed star is sometimes used as the central block, around which the mountain ranges rise. This quilt was designed in the early 1800s and was inspired by the mountains of Bunyan's *Pilgrim's Progress.* Also see **Kansas Troubles, star patterns.**

Delft ware. Ceramics. A buff-colored **clay body** with a lead-tin glaze. **Overglaze** decorations in cobalt blue are painted on the **unfired** glaze. Delft ware is an imitation of Chinese blue and white **porcelain.** Delft porcelainware is made only at the Porceleyne Fles factory in Delft. Also see **majolica.**

della Robbia ware. Ceramics. Glazed **terra cotta** ceramic sculpture produced in the Luca della Robbia workshop in Florence during the fifteenth century. The glaze used was the tin-lead **majolica** type developed by the Moors in Spain.

delta-wing kite. Kites. A highly successful modern commercial kite, shaped like the Greek delta. See ill. Also See **Kites: Construction.**

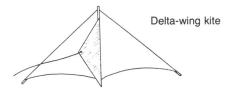
Delta-wing kite

demantoid. Gemcutting. See **garnet.**

demi point. Needlepoint. A description of the scale of the **tent stitch.** The **canvas** used for this is sizes 10–14.

Democrat Rose. Quilts. See **Whig Rose.**

denatured alcohol. Batik and Tie-dye. See **alcohol.**

denatured alcohol. Jewelry. A kind of alcohol that burns smoothly and without leaving carbon deposits used in **alcohol lamps** for heating the tools for working **wax** molds.

denatured alcohol. Woodworking. See **solvent.**

dendritic marking. Gemcutting. Tree or branchlike figures sometimes found on irregularly shaped agates. Also see **quartz.**

denier system. Spinning. Weaving. See **yarn count.**

denim. Quilts. Stitchery. A stiff, durable, smooth **fabric** of **cotton** which has a hard surface that resists snags and tears. The **warp** is colored (usually blue) and the **weft,** or fill threads, are white. The fabric softens in texture and color with use and is a popular fabric (new or used) for quilts, clothing, **appliqué** and stuffed dolls or toys. Also see **bleaching, blue jeans, blue jeans quilt.**

denim art. Stitchery. Any artistic work which is sewn or attached in some way to denims, jeans, or Levi's. The term grew out of the **Levi's Denim Art Show** contest which collected over 10,000 slides from all over the country showing how people had embellished their Levi's with their personal and creative efforts. Almost every known fiberworking method was used. Denim art includes work done on pants, jackets, or skirts.

denims. Stitchery. See **blue jeans.**

density. Weaving. A term used in reference to the feel of a fabric based on its thickness or compactness as determined by its **sett** in the **reed** and how the **filling** is beaten down.

dent. Weaving. See **reed**.

dentage. Weaving. See **reed**.

dental tool. Jewelry. Literally, tools a dentist uses, especially those that resemble spatulas with either scoop or cutting ends. They can be purchased at a jewelry supply house, but a dentist may have some that are no longer needed. They are used primarily for working **wax** in making the model used in **centrifugal casting**. The end of the tool is heated for a few seconds over an **alcohol lamp** and used to cut, scoop up, pierce, or shape the wax. See ill.

a.   Dental tool   b.   Various points used to carve wax

dentelle. Bookbinding. A type of border decoration in **gold leaf** composed of small tooled forms near the edges of a book cover and a lacy pattern near the center.

dentelle à l'oiseau. Bookbinding. A **dentelle** design in which figures of birds are included.

denting. Weaving. See **sett**.

deoxidized copper. Metalworking. See **copper**.

depression. Candlemaking. See **cave-in, cavity** and **Candlemaking: Molding**.

depth gauge. Woodworking. See **gauge**.

derivative weave. Weaving. Any weave developed from a simpler one without unduly changing the basic structural characteristics of the weave. A typical example would be the **basket weave** deriving from the **plain weave**. There are endless modifications that can be made involving the addition or removal of **raisers** (**warp-faced** or **filling-faced** twills derived from a **balanced twill**) and changing the **drawing-in draft**. Also see **crepe weave**.

derm. Leatherwork. A term for the top layer of animal skin used in making leather, which is directly underneath the outer layer of hair and fleshy skin, and which is removed before **tanning**.

deseeding. Spinning. See **flax**.

design. Crewel. Embroidery. Needlepoint. See **Crewel: Preparation and Layout, Needlepoint: Preparation and Layout**.

designer's colors. See **gouache**.

detached. Crewel. Embroidery. (Also called isolated stitches.) Certain stitches are most effective when worked individually and add a dramatic textural quality to the pieces. Almost any stitch can be worked detached; for example, a single **chain stitch** (commonly called a lazy daisy stitch), or a single **buttonhole stitch. Turkey work, French knot,** and **bullion knot** can be very dramatic when isolated. Also see **fly stitch, French knot with stalks, spider's web**.

detached buttonhole stitch. Crewel. Embroidery. A raised **filling stitch** worked on a base of **backstitch**es.

To work this stitch on **fabric**: Work a border in the backstitch. Work **buttonhole stitch**es entirely free of the background. Using a **blunt needle**, come up at A on the right and go under the first backstitch. Keep the thread under the needle, draw through gently, being sure not to pull too tightly. Complete the row, going down into the fabric on the last stitch to secure it (**a.**). Begin the next row, working from right to left and going into each stitch of the previous row for a uniform appearance. Work buttonhole stitches in one direction (**b.**). For variation, a completely different effect can be formed when the first row is worked from right to left, and the second from left to right (**c.**). See ill. Also see **stumpwork**.

Detached buttonhole stitch

a.   b.   c.

detached chain stitch. Crewel. Embroidery. (Also called lazy daisy.) A variation of the basic **chain stitch**. Each chain is worked **detached**; several stitches can be grouped to form any shape other than a straight line. Come up at A, make loop, lay flat, go down at A. Come up at B, go down at C to anchor chain stitch. This stitch may be used as a **filling stitch**, combined with cross bars, or scattered over the ground as a powdering like seeding. See ill.

Detached chain stitch

detached fly stitch. Crewel. Embroidery. See **fly stitch**.

Detached oval cluster. Knitting. See **Knitting: Stitches and Patterns**.

detached twisted chain stitch. Crewel. Embroidery. A variation of the **chain stitch** which forms a twisted loop held down by a small **tacking stitch**. It can only be worked detached. Come up at A, go down at B level with and to the

a.   b.   c.   Detached twisted chain stitch left of A. Holding the thread across and then under the needle as shown, come up at C, in the center below A-B (**a.**). Anchor the stitch down outside the loop at D (**b.**). Finally, the finished effect (**c.**). See ill.

Devcon. Plastics. See **epoxy.**

Devil's Claws. Quilts. A **pieced block** design made up of 64 small **geometric** pieces. These are joined to make **patch**es of four pieces each. The unusual element in this block is that the central part is a **nine-patch,** with half-patches added all the way around. The finished block is the equivalent of 16 patches. When the blocks are **set,** the half-patches join to make new patterns.

"Devil's Claws" is also the name given to a block of an entirely different design—**Gray Goose.**

devitrification. Ceramics. The change which takes place in a **glaze** from a glossy to a **crystalline** state in cooling, giving a frosty look. Also see **matte.**

devitrification. Glasswork. The phenomenon wherein glass appears frosted as a result of the formation of crystals, generally at the surface. Devitrification weakens glass, so procedures are adopted to avoid holding glass at the devitrification range of temperature for very long. Once glass is cooled below the devitrification point, it can be cooled without further problems as long as an **annealing** procedure is followed.

diabolo. Toys. A game played with a wooden spool strung onto a **string.** Each of the string ends is attached to a stick, and the sticks are held one in each hand. The spool is whirled and tossed on the string. The diabolo is sometimes regarded as a somewhat recent (early twentieth-century) **toy,** although other records indicate that it was first brought to France from Peking in the 1700s. How long the toy had been in use in China is unknown. The diabolo is in the same family of toys as the **yo-yo.**

diagonal. Quilts. See **Quilts: Quilting.**

diagonal. Weaving. Area in **tapestry** weaving, where one color is diminished by a specific number of **warp ends** and the adjacent color advances by the same number of ends. A diagonal is low, right-angled, or steep, according to the number of **filling shots** interlaced with a given group of warp ends before the move to the next group of ends is made. A natural closing or locking is formed where the angle is low, because the fillings overlap and no **slit tapestry** is formed, nor is there any need for **interlocking** or **dovetailing** to close spaces between the two colors. A low diagonal is formed by moving over one warp end or more with each filling repeat. The diagonal becomes steeper and, at times, approaches a vertical line, by increasing the number of filling repeats at one juncture of the two colors, before moving on one warp end to the left or right. This is the case where slit tapestry openings could form, or where some weavers use dovetailing or interlocking. When working with diagonals, the area that slopes back or decreases is woven first, thus forming a base for the upper or increas-

ing diagonal area. To outline on a low diagonal, two filling shots are laid in diagonally in alternate **shed**s along the diagonal rim of the lower area. Because of this slant, these **pick**s should be laid in more closely than ordinarily, or the background will pucker when the tapestry is taken off the loom. The upper diagonal area falls in place over the outlining. In a steep diagonal, the **outlining** is woven in progressive steps, such as forward 3, backward 2, etc., so that the slanted picks are kept short and controlled better. Other alternate forms of outlining are akin to **wrapping** and vary according to the slope of the diagonal. Also see **outlining, slit tapestry.**

diagonal basketweave stitch. Needlepoint. See **basketweave stitch.**

diagonal cutter. Basketry. See **side cutter.**

diagonal double half hitch. Macramé. See **chevron pattern, diagonal double half hitch with center closing.**

diagonal double half hitch with center closing. Macramé. This method of working the diagonal double half hitch forms an X-like pattern by working from the outside edges to the center cords, crossing the center cords, and then working out again to the opposite edges.

Work a **chevron pattern** left and right until you reach the center; cross the left and right holding cords. These two holding cords are then tied together with a **double half hitch** forming the "center closing." Extend the holding cords diagonally to the left and right edge; work the diagonal double half hitch from the center to the edges completing the X.

The X can also be performed simply by crossing the holding cords and continuing knotting, eliminating the center closing.

diagonal double half hitch with color. Macramé. This is a very important method of working and should be clearly understood by all who work in color or who blend materials. This method of center crossing is used when two or more colors are being worked. The end result is a very definite dividing of colors.

The #1 cord is the **holding cord** for #2, 3, 4; the #8 cord is the holding cord for #7, 6, 5.

After working **double half hitch**es across these two rows, #8 crosses over #1 but is not tied. The #2 cord is used as holding cord for #3, 4, 8; the #7 cord is the holding cord for #6, 5, and 1. See ill.

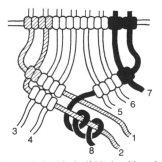

Diagonal double half hitch with color

diagonal in pairs. Weaving. See **slit tapestry.**

diagonal knitting. Knitting. A piece of work knit on the bias, and achieved by continuously **increasing** on one edge of the work and **decreasing** at the opposite edge. Also see **bias knitting** and **Knitting: Stitches and Patterns.**

diagonal plaiting. Basketry. See **twilled plaiting.**

diagonal rib. Knitting. A method of knitting a diagonal rib into the fabric, achieved by moving the strips or **ribbing** pattern one stitch over either left or right every row.

diagonal roll. Batik and Tie-dye. A **tie-dye** method that involves starting at one corner of a **fabric** piece and rolling diagonally before tying. It gives a diagonal pattern when dyed. **Rolling, folding,** or **knotted rope tie-dye** can be done with a diagonal roll.

diagonal scoring. Papercrafts. A paper-construction variation in which **scoring** is used to give added shape and dimension to **accordion pleating.** The pleated paper is folded (**a.**), then folded in half and across to crease the diagonal lines (**b.**). The sheet is opened (**c.**) and diagonal folds creased all in the same direction and vertical folds creased in alternating directions (**d.**), finishing the form. If lightweight paper is used, **scoring** will not be necessary. Many variations can be done with this structure, repeating the folds in rows for a sculpted patterning of light and dark. See ill.

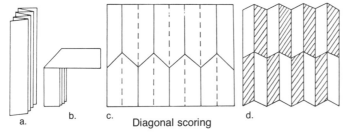

a.   b.   c.   Diagonal scoring   d.

diagonal stripe. Batik and Tie-dye. See **rope-tying.**

diagonal tent stitch. Needlepoint. See **basketweave stitch.**

diagonal thonging chisel. Leatherwork. See **thonging chisel.**

diagonal twining. Weaving. See **Ojibwa weaving.**

diamond. Batik and Tye-dye. A geometric form produced in **tie-dye** fabric.

A diamond can be made using the **tritik** method of tie-and-dye. The fabric is folded in half, and sewing is done next to the fold through the double thickness. Any symmetrical shape can be made in this way. Half of the shape is sewn at the folded edge so that when the thread is pulled tight and fastened off the fabric can be **dye**d, leaving a resist outline of the whole shape. The inside area of the diamond can be treated with another **binding** or the stitching can be repeated to form rows or all-over patterns of diamonds.

A diamond can also be produced by using the **ruching** method. The material is first folded in half. Then half of the diamond shape (obtained by dividing the diamond from one corner to the corner opposite it) is marked or chalked onto the double fabric. The sewing starts at the open or **selvage** edge, goes down to a point, then up at the opening of the opposite side to the other edge of the diamond. A second parallel line is needed to make a channel through which the wood ruching piece can be inserted. When the material is **gather**ed or ruched tightly onto the stick and then **tied** the material is dyed and the finished result yields a diamond shape in the **resist** pattern.

Diamond shapes can also be made in series by forming tucks through the double layer through which the **ruching stick** is inserted. Tucks or channels made in this way can start at the folded edge because the stick does not go between the two layers. Instead, it slides into the tuck formed on one side of the folded fabric.

diamond. Gemcutting. **Crystal** composed of carbon in the isometric system with **hardness** of 10 and **specific gravity** of 3.5. It is singly refracting (isotropic) with a refractive index of 2.43 and occurs in colorless, blue, red, yellow, gray, green, and black varieties due to inclusions. It is transparent (unless black), has strong dispersion of light, and an adamantine luster. It has perfect **cleavage** in all directions parallel to its crystal faces. Its cleavage is used to rough-shape the gem, then it is ground with another diamond in a process called **bruting,** and finally polished with diamond powder of any grit. It is usually **facet**ed in brilliant form. It is slowly combustible at 900° F, transforming to graphite, and is impervious to acids. As a gem, diamond accounts for over 80% of the value of stones imported into the United States.

Borts (also called boarts) and carbonados are diamond crystals that are flawed because of impurities. They are used for drilling points and **wheel dressers,** or they are crushed and used as an **abrasive** carefully graded from coarse to the finest grits. Diamond is the hardest abrasive. Also see **charging, luster, sintering.**

diamond. Quilts. Stitchery. A **geometric** figure used in many **pieced** fabric designs. It consists of 4 equal straight lines connected in such a way as to form two acute angles and two obtuse angles. The diamond is often pieced to form stars or sunbursts in traditional quilts. In **pieced quilt**s, diamond is sometimes used to refer to a square set on one point or on the diagonal.

diamond cement. Diamond cement is useful for cementing pearls or small stones into recesses. Dissolve **isinglass** (pure fish glue) in water until it forms a thick paste, dilute with grain alcohol and set aside. Dissolve mastic resin in grain (ethyl) alcohol to form a second paste. Mix the two pastes in a gently warmed container.

diamond drill. Gemcutting. See **drilling jig.**

diamond engraving. Glasswork. Diamond-point styli or diamond-particle grinding wheels may be used for graphic surface decoration of glass after it has been annealed. It is especially important that glass be annealed properly before surface decoration of this kind because cutting the surface can release internal pressures and lead to fractures. Also see **annealing, engraving.**

diamond eyelet stitch. Needlepoint. See **Algerian eyelet stitch.**

diamond filling. Lacemaking. See **leaf stitch.**

diamond fold. Papercrafts. A **paper sculpture** variation in which **accordion pleating** is accented with diagonal lines to form diamond shapes. Fold a sheet of paper as for accordion pleating, then fold it diagonally from two opposite corners. Press sharply to crease the folds. Open it back to the original accordion fold, and fold it diagonally again, from the remaining two corners. Then open up the sheet all the way. Crease the folds so that the crossing diagonals all face in one direction, carefully forming the diamond shapes. See ill.

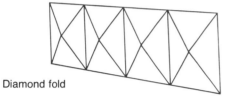

Diamond fold

diamond glass cutter. Stained Glass. The point of this cutter is made of a diamond chip, which should never wear out. Its disadvantages are its clumsiness and lack of maneuverability. It is best for straight lines and is used in the trade for cutting **plate glass** and **cathedral glass.** Also see **glass cutter.**

diamond kite. Kites. (Also called flat kite.) The most familiar kite, it is diamond-shaped and constructed on a two-stick **framework** of various dimensions. It can be flat or bowed, tailed or tailless, and is the simplest kind of kit to build. See ill. Also see **Kites: Construction.**

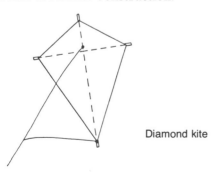

Diamond kite

diamond patchwork. Quilts. **Pieced** work made up of **diamond**-shaped **patch**es of fabric. These are difficult to sew, requiring the most exacting measurements and careful cutting. If any miscalculation occurs in cutting or sewing, the **quilt top** will not lie smooth and flat, but will fold or buckle. Because of the precise skills required to sew this type of **patchwork,** the diamonds are often reserved as **best quilt**s. **Baby Block**s, **Star of Bethlehem,** and **Sunburst** are quilts made from diamond patches.

diamond pattern. Knitting. See **Knitting: Stitches and Patterns.**

diamond-point chisel. Metalworking. See **chisel.**

diamond-point chisel. Woodworking. See **wood-turning tools.**

diamond powder. Gemcutting. See **abrasive, bruting.**

diamond quilt. Quilts. A very simple quilt of Amish design that consists of a large **diamond** set into a square. It is further distinguished by a wide **border** and colored **band**s around the diamond and squares. These quilts are exquisitely sewn with intricate **quilting pattern**s. Also see **Amish quilt.**

diamond quilting. Quilts. See **Quilts: Quilting.**

diamond saw. Stained Glass. See **masonry saw.**

diamond twill. Weaving. A weave effect based on the **twill weave** and composed of diamonds and/or crosses. The diamonds can be of various sizes and types and the weave can be either **warp-face**d, or **filling-face**d, or evenly **balanced.** To get these patterns the **threading** must be a **point draw,** and the **treadling** that for a reversed twill or zigzag twill. Diamond twills are also known as entwining twills. There are many more colloquial names, two of which are **goose-eye** and **rosepath.** See ill.

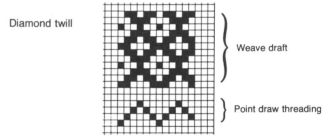

Diamond twill / Weave draft / Point draw threading

diaper design. Bookbinding. A design in which the motif, usually in **lozenge** forms, is repeated at regular intervals.

diaspore clay. Ceramics. See **Ceramics: Clay.**

dibstones. Toys. See **knucklebones.**

dice. Toys. Small cubes that have patterns of dots on each of the six faces, indicating numbers from one to six. They are used in various **games** to determine the number of moves, scores, etc. Craftspeople have made dice from **light wood** and **dark wood,** painted wood, **bisque,** glazed ceramic, plastic, and various other materials. Also see **knucklebones, teetotum.**

diced leather. Bookbinding. Leather (usually calf) that has been ruled with crossing diagonal lines that form a diamond pattern.

dichroism. Gemcutting. See **color.**

dichroite. Gemcutting. See **iolite.**

dichroscope. Gemcutting. An instrument for examination of gems for double **refraction** of light by observing **dichroic** properties when the gem is rotated in direct light in front of the field of view. Also see **color.**

Dick Blick. Batik and Tie-dye. See **direct dye, household dye.**

dicky meadow. Basketry. (Also called red bud.) The smallest available size of **willow** rods, 2' or less in length.

didymium goggles. Glasswork. Goggles fitted with a didymium lens, which tends to filter out yellow-orange colors. They are especially useful for **flamework** where the glare from the **glass fire** makes it difficult to see the glass in the flame.

die. Ceramics. An attachment placed over a wad box or **pug mill** to give a specific shape to the clay that is pressed through; it is used in industry to make ceramic pipes, bricks, and other **extrusion**s.

die. Jewelry. Metalworking. A tool, usually made of steel, but sometimes of brass or bronze, with depressions into which **sheet metal** is forced so that it takes on the shape of the depressions. Often tools that have the same shape as the depressions are used to force the metal into the depressions.

In metalworking "die" refers to a round or square metal block with a hole containing threads for cutting external threads on rods or pipe. It is held in a holder called a die stock. To use, bevel the end of the rod slightly. Insert the correct size die on the rod, pushing down with one hand over the center of the rod. Press and turn the die stock clockwise to start the thread. After the thread has begun, turn the die stock handles one or two complete turns and stop. Reverse the direction and turn about one-quarter turn. Repeat this forward and backward motion until the entire thread is completed. Lubricate with a household oil after every two or three revolutions. See ill. Also see **dapping, dapping die, dapping punch, tap.**

Metalworking die in die stock

Dieppe. Ivory and Bone Carving. In 1364 this town in Normandy established an ivory-carving industry that for centuries—in spite of repeated tragedies, declines in trade, lack of material, competition from China, and other hardships—continued to remain one of the ivory-carving centers of the world.

In the sixteenth century they produced engraved ivory navigational aids. When persecuted by the king's army in the seventeenth century for being Protestants, those who refused to convert to Catholicism fled.

After Dieppe was razed in 1694 by an Anglo-Dutch fleet, it further dispersed the ivory carvers, as well as destroying all the city's records of its ancient ivory-carving history.

The carvers rose once more and filled the churches with ivory holy-water stoups, crucifixes, and other religious articles, all executed with excellence. The French nobles were patrons of numerous Dieppe articles, such as fans, snuff graters, perfume flasks, table ornaments, and navettes (spindles for the silk used in embroidery). When the onset of the Revolution made it dangerous to appear wealthy and the nobles no longer bought their goods, the carvers turned to making utilitarian objects and patriotic plaques, which were generally artistic and commercial failures.

After the fall of the Empire, business began to flourish; **les laboureurs** returned from the British prison camps with their pockets filled with the earnings of their prison crafts. The British army of occupation and the Russians could not buy enough of their ivory carvings. It was not long until tourists from Brighton began ferrying over to Dieppe to obtain their work. Dieppe soon became a fashionable resort itself, and enjoyed immense popularity and good business.

Of the multitudes of objects carved by the Dieppois, their best-known produce was the carved Dieppe rose. Other techniques, such as miniature ivory outline carvings set against a glue glass background, were effective and popular, as were their chess sets and "mosaique," an imitation lace filigree fretwork.

die stock. Metalworking. See **die.**

diffraction grating. See **spectrum.**

diffuse banding. China and Glass Painting. See **banding.**

dihedral angle. Kites. The angle formed by two planes of a kite when they are bent backward along a **spine** or **keel.** This angle, which never exceeds 180°, can be produced by **bowing,** as in the **diamond kite** or **Eddy kite,** or it can be a part of the kite's basic shape, as in the right-angled **box kite** or triangular **Coyne kite.** Its function is to split wind resistance in the same way a ship's bow divides the water, adding to the stability of the kite's flight.

dimensional carving. Woodworking. See **woodcarving** and **Woodworking: Woodcarving and Whittling.**

dimensional stability. Plastics. The ability of a plastic to resist **distortion** under various conditions. When exact shape and measurements are required for a project, ask your plastics distributor to recommend brands with dependable dimensional stability.

dip coating. Plastics. The process of dipping an object into a **dipping resin** to cover or coat it with plastic. Shaped frames may be dipped into resin to create forms, for example, plastic flowers.

dip-dye design. Papercrafts. A technique of folding paper in various ways, then dipping parts of the folded shape into **dye** to give an intricate, repeated patterning when unfolded. Absorbent paper must be used, such as paper toweling or rice paper. A Japanese rice paper, called mulberry paper, is available at art supply stores. The dye can be household liquid dye or food coloring. Add water if paler tints are desired. After the paper is folded, one or more corners are dipped into the dye. Before unfolding, firmly press the folded paper between two pieces of cardboard to remove excess moisture. Unfold the paper and let it dry. Wrinkles may be smoothed with a warm iron.

Several basic folds lend themselves to dip-dyeing. Begin with **accordion pleating** with the paper first folded in half. For a pattern of repeated squares, fold the pleated strip into squares. For repeated rectangles, fold the pleated strip into rectangles, and for triangles, fold the lower left corner up diagonally, repeating to the end of the pleated strip. For all patterns, the paper must be turned over for each new fold. Press in the creases and leave folded until dipped in the dye. See ill.

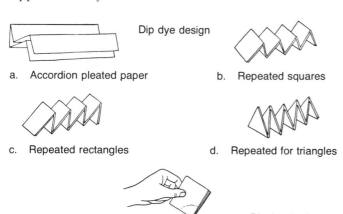

Dip dye design

a. Accordion pleated paper

b. Repeated squares

c. Repeated rectangles

d. Repeated for triangles

e. Dipping in dye

dip dyeing. Batik and Tie-dye. A method of **dye**ing **fabric** in which the material is immersed or dipped into the **dyebath** rather than simmered or soaked.

dip dyeing. Dyeing. Dipping various sections of a **skein** of yarn or a piece of fabric into different **dye bath**s so that the yarn or fabric is multicolored. Also see **skein dyeing.**

dip glazing. Ceramics. See **Ceramics: Glazing.**

dipped candle. Candlemaking. A candle formed by dipping. Also see **Candlemaking: Dipping.**

dipping. Candlemaking. See **Candlemaking: Dipping.**

dipping resin. Plastics. A resin designed specifically for **dip coating** objects.

diptych. Bookbinding. A two-leaved, hinged tablet of wood (although sometimes of ivory or metal) with inner surfaces of wax on which writing is impressed with a stylus.

diopside. Gemcutting. A mineral of the **pyroxene** group which occurs in transparent, green columnar **crystal**s of a monoclinic system. It is a silicate of magnesium and calcium with a **hardness** of 6, and a **specific gravity** of 3.2–3.3, and refractive indices of 1.686 and 1.712 with

slight dichroism and vitreous **luster.** It is often **facet**ed in a step cut and polished with tin oxide on a tin **lap.** Also see **abrasive, faceting, polishing, refraction.**

dioptase. Gemcutting. A mineral composed of hydrous copper silicate **crystal**lized in the hexagonal system. It has **hardness** of 5, **specific gravity** of 3.28, and refractive indices of 1.651 and 1.703. Dioptase has diagonal **cleavage** parallel to the **C axis** and vitreous to pearly luster. It is green and imperfectly transparent. Dioptase is polished with Linde A—on leather for **cabochon**s and on a tin **lap** for **facet**ed gems. Also see **faceting, luster, polishing, refraction.**

diorama. Toys. A variation of the **panorama toy** in which the audience moves around the pictures instead of the reverse. The toy diorama used transparencies inside a cardboard frame that were viewed by reflected and transmitted light. The nineteenth-century preoccupation with geography, historical scenes, and magnificent scenic views was reflected in the subjects chosen for transparencies.

"Diorama" also refers to the specific huge dioramas of the 1820s that were produced by Daguerre, the photographer and inventor of the daguerreotype. He used **protean view**s on the screen in a darkened auditorium to make startling alterations in the images. Also see **Toys: Optical Toys.**

direct casting. Metalworking. (Also called direct-pour casting.) The process of casting without the intermediary stage of burning out a model from a mold. It may be as simple as pouring molten metal into a hollow cavity cut out of **molding sand.** It has been conjectured that ancient peoples may have started direct-pour casting by pouring metal into cavities in rocks. These castings are usually solid and lack a **core.**

direct dye. Batik and Tie-dye. A class of **dyestuff** used in **tie-dye** and **batik,** primarily on cotton, linen, and viscose rayon. The **dye**s are available in a wide range of colors, and some can be used on **animal fiber**s such as silk and wool as well as on **vegetable fiber**s. They do not have the brilliance of the **basic dye**s or **acid dye**s, and the fastness may vary from one color of dye to another. Some are fast to sunlight but will run when washed. Direct dyes are easy to use and are reliable in color consistency.

While these dyes work most efficiently at high temperatures, they can be used lukewarm for batik at about 90–100° F. In **hot dyeing** the **dyebath** is heated nearly to boiling. The **tied** fabric is **wetted-out** and placed in the dyebath for 10–60 minutes. When **cold dyeing,** some craftspeople mix a stronger solution of dyestuff to compensate for the paler colors dyed at these lower temperatures. More intense colors can also be achieved by decreasing the amount of fabric immersed in the dyebath or by keeping the material in the dyebath for a longer period of time. Direct dyes are always **paste**d first, then mixed with hot water.

About 3 tablespoons of **salt** per pound of fabric is added as the **assistant.** Manufacturers' directions vary, so instructions on the dye should be followed.

Some of the common brand names or distributors of direct dyes are: Aljo, Calcomine, Craftool (red label), Deka-Type L, Dick Blick, Fezan, Keco-Direct, Myako, Solamine, and 7-K. These dyes are sometimes called substantive dyes because they do not require a **mordant.** Also see **Batik and Tie-dye: Dyes.**

direct dye. Dyeing. Natural or **synthetic dye**s that are applied "direct" to the fiber without the use of a **mordant.** They are also known as commercial dyes or substantive dyes, and are used on practically all fibers except acetate. They work best on cellulose fibers, such as cotton and viscose rayon. On silk or wool, the color may vary with each fiber. They are rated poor to excellent in lightfastness and not too highly in washfastness due to their being water soluble. There is a wide color range, but no really bright colors.

direct-dye painting. Batik and Tie-dye. Stitchery. A method of applying **dye** to **fabric** in which the dye is thickened, then brushed, printed, or forced from a squeezebottle onto the material. The term is sometimes confused with **direct dye,** which is a **dyestuff.** Direct-dye painting can be done most successfully with direct dye, **fiber-reactive dye, vat dye,** or **leather dye.**

Direct-dye painting has many applications, especially in soft sculpture and stuffed fabric panels. There are various dyes and **textile paint**s made for this purpose that do not require heat to **set** the colors. The direct application is an especially effective method of adding color to stuffed forms as the three-dimensional shape can be finished first. This direct painting method is used on clothing in which the designer prefers to paint on the finished shapes, unifying the painted fabric colors with the structural form of the garment.

Procion dyes and **Versatex** paints are among the most commonly used for direct-dye fabric painting. They can be applied to fabric with paint**brush,** paint roller, plastic squeeze-bottles, sponges, or whatever will hold the dye or ink from container to fabric. India ink or **marking pen**s can also be used in direct-dye painting. When fiber-reactive dyes are to be used as the brush-on dyes they will need to be thickened by adding an **alginate thickener** to achieve a workable consistency. Also see **direct wax painting, Inkodye, steaming.**

direct firing. Ceramics. (Also called open firing.) Firing ware without **saggers, muffle**s, or any kind of protection from direct flame.

direct method. Mosaics. The approach to setting a **mosaic** in which the **tesserae** or mosaic materials are laid directly into an **adhesive** or **mortar** on the final mosaic **backing.** Until the Italian Renaissance, all mosaics, including the great works of Byzantium, were constructed by this method. Its disadvantage, and the factor that led to the development of the simpler **indirect method,** is that all the mosaic material to be used must be within reach of the mosaicist at the installation site. The more practical indi-

rect technique allows the mosaicist to construct his work on a temporary backing in the studio before transporting it to the installation site. Although the indirect method is easier, it should also be pointed out that the direct method is, creatively, far more satisfying for the artist. It is the only method that provides enough flexibility for varying the height and angle of the individual pieces as they are fit into the mosaic. The artist controls the surface. With designs calling for materials of unusual size and height, it is almost mandatory that the direct method be used. Also see **Mosaics: Tools and Materials, Setting the Material.**

direct-pour casting. Metalworking. See **casting, direct casting.**

direct tie-up. Weaving. See **tie-up.**

disappearing filament pyrometer. Ceramics. See **optical pyrometer.**

discharge dyeing. Batik and Tie-dye. A **bleaching** process that reverses the usual procedure of **tie-dye.** It is used to **bleach** out or lighten areas of fabric in a reverse dyeing process sometimes referred to as "bleach dyeing." Previously tie-dyed fabrics can be retied with any of the **binding method**s, then immersed in a solution of household bleach and water. Areas of tie-dye or **batik** can have portions of designs discharged. The bleaching can be done by dipping or immersing the fabric; if only certain areas are to be discharged, the bleach can be applied with a brush or sponge. The bleach is applied only until the color is discharged; then it is rinsed immediately, untied, and rinsed again. For very small areas of discharge the bleach can be poured into a saucer and the ends or tips of the cloth just dipped into it. A lemon juice discharge can be used on fabrics that do not have fast color.

Household dye, basic dye, or **direct dye** that has been used on **cotton, linen,** or viscose rayon (**cellulosic fiber**s) may be **bleached** or discharge dyed. **Fiber-reactive dye**s tend to be resistant to bleaching after being **fix**ed, so if any are used that are to be discharged later, soda or fixer should be omitted from the final **dyebath** and used after discharging. Caledon **vat dye**s also are too permanent to be treated with discharge dyeing.

Household bleaches can be used on many commercially dyed fabrics, but all should be tested. Bleach should be avoided entirely on **silk** because it eats the fibers.

Sizing should always be removed from any new fabric that is to be discharge dyed. Either waxed batik or tie-dyed fabric can be discharged. Vegetable oils such as Crisco can be used as an aid in resisting the bleach. Because bleach does weaken fibers, fabric should not be left in the solution for long. Always work with ample ventilation or outdoors; bleach fumes are toxic. The bleach solution can be saved and reused.

There are two discharge methods—a hot one for tie-dye and a cold one for batik. For the hot method, 10 parts water are used to 1 part bleach. The solution is heated to simmering and the fabric is added and stirred. As soon as the desired color change occurs, the fabric is removed and plunged into a cold bath of vinegar and water. Vinegar is used with 3–5 parts water. Any packaged **color remover** product, such as those by Putnam, Rit, or Tintex, can be used.

In the cold method, 1 part bleach to 6 parts water is an adequately strong solution to start with. Different fibers and dyes respond in varying ways to the bleach, so each should be tested. The discharge solution can be strengthened up to 1 part bleach to 3 parts water. As soon as the color is discharged, plunge the fabric into cold water and rinse thoroughly and repeatedly. If bleach is left in the fabric it may disintegrate the fibers.

discontinuous brocade. Weaving. **Brocade** with the **pattern yarn** not traveling **selvage** to selvage. Also see **laid-in.**

discontinuous pick. Weaving. See **compound weave.**

discontinuous warp. Weaving. See **scaffold weft.**

discontinuous weft. Weaving. A **filling** yarn that does not run **selvage** to selvage, but only in certain areas desired by the weaver for pattern, color, or texture effect. This is most prominently found in **laid-in weaving** and other types of **free weaving.** Also see **compound weave.**

discord. The effect produced when two colors appear in the same field and the **value** of one or both **hues** has been altered so that an inverse relationship exists between them.

If a ground of **primary** blue (a naturally dark color) contains a figure in orange (a naturally light color), and that orange has been darkened by the addition of black so that the resultant **shade** (a dark brown) is of lower value than the blue background, then a dark discord is said to exist.

Similarly, if a violet (a dark color in the normal **spectrum**) is made lighter and brighter by the addition of white and placed next to apple red (a medium-value color in the normal spectrum), the resultant visual disturbance is called a light discord.

If two different hues are altered so that they are of equal value, either by adding white to the darker, or by adding black to the lighter, an enclosed or adjoining color will seem luminous. This effect is the most risky of the discords in that, if overused, luminosity can seem banal; properly controlled, it can lend life to otherwise pedestrian color combinations.

Another kind of color discord can be obtained by adding a light gray to a naturally dark color so that the result is lighter than a naturally brighter color with which it is contrasted (or, conversely, by adding a dark gray to a naturally brighter color). Muted discords of this type are subtle and interesting.

Color discords have been likened to dissonances in music; when used with taste and discretion they can provide excitement. If overused (amateur interior decorators are frequent abusers), the effect tends to cheapen the whole. An example of color discord that would be hard to reconcile is dark red furniture against light green walls. Also see **color clash, color harmony, figure and ground.**

disk punch set. Jewelry. See **circle cutter.**

disk sander. Gemcutting. See **flat, sanding.**

disk sander. Woodworking. See **sanding tools.**

dispersed dye. Batik and Tie-dye. A class of **dye**s designed primarily for use on polyester, nylon, and acetate rayon. Because it requires heat it is suitable for **tie-dye** but not for **batik.** The powdered **dyestuff** must be **paste**d with warm water, using ¼ ounce dispersed dye to 2 or 3 quarts of water. This **dyebath** is heated to 190° F and the **tied** fabrics are immersed for up to 30 minutes. Excess dye is squeezed out and the fabric is rinsed and dried. Further **binding** and dyeing can then be done using additional colors. When all the dyeing is finished the fabric is untied, rinsed, and ironed while damp. Also see **Batik and Tie-Dye: Dyes.**

dispersion. Gemcutting. See **refraction.**

dissected pictures. Toys. Printed picture games made either in book form or as cards. Several pictures, all of the same size, are cut into 3 or 4 horizontal slices each. The object of play is to reassemble the parts belonging to one object or one animal or to create new creatures. Usually a collection consists of all animals, all people, etc.

dissected puzzle. Toys. The original name for the **jigsaw puzzle.**

distaff. Spinning. A stick to which unspun **wool** or **flax** fibers are attached and then drawn off as needed while **spinning.** The first distaffs were either short lengths of a tree branch or forked twigs and were used with **hand spindle**s. As spinning developed, distaffs became ornate and carved and painted, but even today in some primitive areas, spinners still employ a branch or forked twig. With the advent of the **spinning wheel,** distaffs were fixed into stands on the floor and eventually were fitted directly onto the wheel, usually at the back on a bar above the spindle. The wool or flax is usually tied to the distaff; however, if a lantern-shaped distaff or a **tow fork** is used for flax, it is usually prepared or dressed in a specific manner for ease in drawing off. When used with hand spindles, distaffs are either held under the left arm, or tucked into the left side of the apron or skirt of the spinner, with the right hand doing the spinning. In rural areas of some countries, one can still see spinners walking along and spinning with the distaff at hand in one of the two above positions. "Distaff side" has come to mean the left side or the female line or maternal branch of the family. The word originates from the Anglo-Saxon, with *dis* meaning flax, and *staef* meaning stick. Also see **dressing the distaff, German wheel, spinning.**

distaff side. Spinning. See **distaff.**

distorted warp/weft. Weaving. A catch-all term referring to many weaves or techniques that take, or appear to take, the **warp** and the **filling** from their normal right angle relationship to each other. Sometimes both warp and weft are distorted; other times only one or the other. Also see **crossed warp, diverted warp, transposed warp.**

distortion. Ceramics. A condition in which the pottery loses its symmetry and harmony. Also see **pyroplastic deformation, warping.**

distortion. Metalworking. The unplanned change in the shape of a metal due to heat expansion and cooling. When a metal is distorted by heat it is not always possible to correct it, so distortion must be prevented in the design and method of construction of an object before it occurs.

WELDING DISTORTION   To prevent distortion when welding a butt **weld, tack weld** the metal edges at different distances apart at the beginning and end of the seam so that the distortion is compensated for. The surfaces at the beginning end of the seam to be welded should be tacked about 1/16" apart and at the end of the seam about 1/8" apart. The end you start welding on will heat up, expanding the filler metal and edges of the adjacent **base metal** and pushing the seam further open, to about 1/8", which is the gap you have already secured at the end of the seam. Both ends should come out even.

Another welding method is to deliberately set the pieces of metal at an angle so that the heat will put them into proper alignment. A third method is to clamp the joint, using a strong backing material, to a welding table or heavy bars (in the case of long seams) to keep the metal from moving.

A fourth method is to divide the seam into a series of sections and weld each section so that it ends where the previous weld began (called backstep welding).

CASTING DISTORTION   Control this type of distortion by keeping the thickness of the casting walls as uniform as possible and no thicker than 1". Additional cavities in the mold provide attached reservoirs that will supply extra metal to the model section to fill it as the casting shrinks during cooling.

In **sandcasting,** compensate for the overall shrinkage in size by making the **pattern** slightly larger than the size of the desired finished casting. Rulers called shrinkrules are available to compute this shrinkage difference for various metals where precision is necessary. See ill.

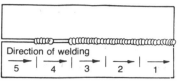

f.   Backstep welding

distortion. Plastics. The change of shape of a plastic under various conditions.

Creep is distortion caused by pressure for an extended period of time. Cold flow is creep at room temperature. Technically, creep is a rapid dimensional change after pressure has been released, while cold flow is the change while under stress directly. Prevent both types by adding **glass fiber** reinforcement to the thermosetting resin or by designing load-bearing areas of unsupported expanses with curved or corrugated sheets.

Warping in a **thermosetting plastic** is caused by unequal heat loss during **curing,** by uneven distribution of reinforcement and/or resin in the **mold,** too much **catalyst,** or by pressure on unsupported or unreinforced areas. To prevent warping keep curing plastic at an even temperature by reducing the amount of catalyst, by putting the mold in a box to protect it from drafts, and by heating it with a **heat lamp.** One may also remove the object from the mold when hard while protecting the surface with an **air shield,** and put weights on it until it is totally cured. Use a **laminating resin** for thin sheet pours and make sure that both **reinforcing material**s and resin are evenly distributed throughout.

Shrinking is contraction of the material toward the center, which occurs during curing of thermosetting resin. It is called crawl when referring to shrinkage of a **thermoplastic** during **heat forming,** and can be controlled by securing the hot object in a holding **jig** until it is cool. Reduce shrinking in **casting** and laminating resins by adding less catalyst and more **filler**s to them.

ditto dye. Batik and Tie-dye. An inexpensive, readily available **dye** made from pink or purple ditto papers. The paper is torn into bits and dropped into one-fourth cup denatured **alcohol,** stirred, and extended with hot water to make about three quarts liquid. The papers will float to the top and can be removed. This mixture can be stored, then some of the dye can be poured off and mixed with cool water for the **dyebath. Salt** is added as the **assistant.**

diverted warp. Weaving. Refers to those **warp end**s that have been turned away from their normal straight-line course in a **fabric.** If this is of a slight nature, it usually is called a deflected warp. The shifting aside that happens in a **mock leno** weave is a good example of a deflected warp. If the turning away has been of a significant nature such as a swerve, curve, or definite slant to one side or the other, then it is called a diverted warp. This can be found in **weft twining, gauze weave**s, and **wrapping.**

divider. Quilts. See **band.**

dividers. Leatherwork. Draftsman's dividers are used for etching circles, spacing stitching and dividing areas

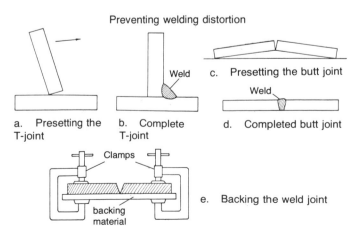

Preventing welding distortion

a.   Presetting the T-joint

b.   Complete T-joint

Weld

c.   Presetting the butt joint

Weld

d.   Completed butt joint

Clamps

backing material

e.   Backing the weld joint

equally on leather. Also see **patent leather compass** and **Leatherwork: Sewing Leather, Tools and Materials.**

dividers. Metalworking. Woodworking. See **measuring tools.**

dividing band. Quilts. See **band.**

division bar. Stained Glass. See **saddle bar.**

division lead. Stained Glass. Used for joining two panels of stained glass together; large stained-glass panels for installation in buildings are often made in sections. A flat (not rounded) piece of **lead came** is used to make a waterproof joint. The came is soldered to the top of one panel, and the leaves are folded into each other. The division lead of ½"- or ⅝"-wide came is abutted over it. Also see **leaf** and **Stained Glass: Glazing.**

division tie. Stained Glass. **Copper tie**s made for use with division bars. They differ from those used for **saddle bars** because, instead of being soldered in the middle of the tie, they are soldered at one end. They are made in 4" lengths, one end of which is bent over itself by ¼". The end is fluxed and a blob of **solder** placed on it. In joining two panels of glass to a division bar, a copper tie is attached to each panel and the ends are twisted together around the division bar. Also see **flux.**

D.M.C. Crewel. Embroidery. Needlepoint. D.M.C. stands for the French company Dollfus-Mieg & Cie., which has been in existence for many years supplying embroidery supplies of all kinds. Their six-strand **cotton embroidery floss** is of such fine quality and is used so universally that very often embroidery floss is simply referred to as D.M.C. In the nineteenth century, **Therese de Dillmont** published an encyclopedia of needlework for D.M.C. that has become a standard work and has been in print ever since.

dobby boy. Weaving. See **dobby loom.**

dobby loom. Weaving. A loom going up to 32 **harness**es whose **shed opening**s operate on the same principle as the **Jacquard loom.** There is a head motion at the top of the loom that is composed of a chain of wooden bars. Each bar has a hole for each harness, into which are fitted metal pegs if the harness is to be raised. From this arrangement came the terms "peg plan" and "chain draft"—indicating a **graph paper** version of how the pegs are fitted into the chain of bars. Originally a dobby loom needed a "dobby boy" who sat at the top of the loom and drew up the **warp end**s that were **raiser**s. Small figures were a feature of dobby patterned fabrics. Now dobby heads are used for a variety of **multiple harness** fabrics and can be hand-operated on a **table loom,** or foot-powered on a **floor loom.** The dobby head is a separate unit that can be purchased and attached to a hand loom. Also see **box loom, draw loom.**

Doe and Dart. Quilts. See **David and Goliath.**

doeskin. Leatherwork. Leather from sheep or lamb which has the top grain removed; a **split** from sheep or lamb.

doffing. Spinning. The removal of **fibers** from both cards after **carding** and from a **comb** after **combing.** The fiber arrangement after carding should not be disturbed while doffing. With combing, correct doffing establishes a better parallel alignment of fibers.

dog. Weaving. See **pawl.**

doily. Lacemaking. Tatting. A small decorative mat, usually round, but sometimes oval. Named for the English draper D'Oyley of the seventeenth century. A draper was a dealer in dry goods. Pattern books of the nineteenth century frequently refer to a tatted D'Oyley or crocheted D'Oyley.

doll. Puppets. Stitchery. Toys. A toy or plaything made in the image of a human being. Dolls are among the oldest toys known, with early examples dating from prehistoric times. The word "doll" did not appear in an English dictionary until about 1700. Before that the playthings were called "babies" or "little ladies." In America, it was not until the middle of the eighteenth century that the word "doll" was known. George Washington reportedly ordered a "wax baby" for his stepdaughter in 1762.

Early dolls were made from **earthenware,** cloth, and wood. As **dollmaking** developed, the range of materials expanded. **Papier mâché, pulp mâché;** and **composition** dolls were commonly available and popular. **Wax doll**s, **china doll**s, **bisque doll**s, and the fragile and prized porcelain dolls were among the early doll types.

In this century the development of molding plastics revolutionized the dollmaking industry. Plastics replaced **rubber** and **celluloid,** allowing for intricate detail and mass production.

Dolls are among the most frequently made of all handcrafted toys. Dollmaking has always been a popular **folk art,** and it has recently become a part of **soft sculpture** processes. Also see **Toys: Dolls.**

doll body. Toys. The body of a **doll,** in most cases made separate from the head. Until 1850 most doll bodies were either peg, wooden, **kid** with wood limbs, or cloth. After 1850, **jointed doll** bodies made of various **composition**s were introduced. **Rivet joint**s were developed for use on kid bodies, and **ball-joint**ed composition bodies were popular for many years. Cloth bodies have always been popular and remain so today. The doll body made of cloth can be given joints by assembling the parts, or the single-piece body can be given **stitched joint**s. In the **single-shape doll,** the body and head are always **stuff**ed as one piece.

doll buggy. Toys. A child-size baby carriage. Early ones were made of iron and leather, and later they were made of wicker in imitation of the buggies popular at the time. The buggy consists of a basketlike bed, protected above by a hood and set on wheels. It was pushed by a wide handle. Because few baby buggies are in use now, there are fewer of them as **toys.** They have been replaced by toy strollers and toy car seats.

doll clothes. Toys. Garments made especially for toy dolls. The commercial manufacture of doll clothes comprises a surprisingly large portion of the clothing industry. Major pattern companies design and sell patterns for almost every type of clothing for dolls. The type of doll determines the kind of clothes needed. A **baby doll** rarely needs more than gowns, buntings, and diapers, whereas the "teen-age" dolls often require more clothes and accessories than their real-life counterparts.

doll club. Toys. Any of several organizations whose members have a common interest in the history of dolls, **dollmaking,** or doll collecting. There are local, national, and international groups. They hold conventions and have publications for the exchange of ideas, information, and dolls or doll parts. Most libraries have a listing of such organizations.

Dolley Madison Star. Quilts. A **block** design made up of small **pieced** squares and triangles that depicts an eight-pointed star within a square. It was named in honor of Dolley Madison, first lady. See ill. Also see **presidents' quilt, star patterns.**

Dolley Madison Star

doll hair. Toys. See **hair.**

doll head. Toys. The head of a doll, especially when it is made separately from the rest of the body. Any time the head is made of a material different from that of the rest of the doll it is made separately. The head includes not only the features and **hair,** but usually the neck and a portion of the chest to allow for some means of attachment. Doll heads made of **bisque** or china often have perforations at the base so that a fabric or **kid** body can be added.

Sock dolls or nylon stocking dolls are made so that the doll head is simply a tied portion of the **stuff**ed whole doll. Most **fabric dolls** are constructed so that the doll head is formed in one piece with the body, as in **arch-shaped dolls** or **single-shaped dolls.** Also see **apple-head, breast-plated dollhead** and **Toys: Dolls.**

doll house. Toys. (Also called baby house.) A small house made as a child's **toy,** often to scale for **dolls.** It is usually a three-sided shell with a fairly elaborate façade and finished roof. The back is open so that dolls and furniture can be set inside, arranged and rearranged. The first such houses were probably architects' models.

Doll houses became popular, especially in France and England, in the 1800s, although there were undoubtedly makeshift or homemade versions long before that. The ear-

liest known one exists, in part, in Nuremberg, Germany; it was made in the fifteenth century.

Many of the nineteenth-century houses became so ornate and so richly furnished that they were essentially **miniature**s or **scale models**—not toys. Today doll houses are made of cardboard or wood and range from simple to elegant. Children often devise their own doll houses from cardboard cartons and boxes. Orange crates are of a good size and proportion, and, when two are stacked, make a good two-story doll house. Also see **Toys: Dolls.**

dollmaker. Toys. See **Dollmaking.**

dollmaking. Toys. The art of making **dolls.** So popular and so universal is this toy that dollmakers are known to have produced them as a principal business as early as the 1400s. While hand-carved wood dolls or fired **earthenware dolls** may have been made by toymakers long before, the first known written records of such a business are from 1413, in Nuremberg.

Because so many toys came to Europe from the Far East, it is reasonable to assume that dollmaking also developed there, especially in China. However, less information is available on the development of dollmakers' activities there. When materials became popular in one country during a particular century, they may have been developed much earlier in some other area. **Wax doll** heads, for example, were highly developed by the German dollmakers in the 1700s. The wax heads, however, were used in Italian religious figures centuries earlier than that.

During the 1600s and 1700s wood and **clay** were the materials most commonly used by European dollmakers, although in some cases a **composition** was used over wood. It added a glossy surface for painting and allowed for more molding of the features. In the late 1700s dollmaking materials were expanded to include a paper pulp, or **pulp máché,** and wax. In the 1800s compositions were varied, including plaster of Paris, and were often painted and waxed. It was also during this century that **Parian** and **bisque,** porcelain, and china were highly developed.

Dollmaking as a trade developed among various families, each having its own specialties and styles. These family businesses thrived during the 1800s when the art of dollmaking was at its peak. Among the well-known dollmaking families are **Montanari, Pierotti,** and **Jumeau.** Their dolls are avidly sought by doll collectors.

During the twentieth century the composition doll was replaced by rubber, **celluloid,** and then plastic. There is now a huge commercial doll industry.

Recently dollmaking has again come to the fore as a revived **folk art** and area for the serious craftsperson. Most dollmakers avoid mass production of any kind, working primarily with one-of-a-kind cloth dolls. Dollmaking has also become an area of personal and expressive work less concerned with toymaking than with soft sculptures. Also see **penny wooden doll.**

dolly. Spinning. See **wheel finger.**

dolomite. Ceramics. A mineral used as a **flux** in **stoneware glaze**s for a smooth surface. Dolomite promotes a longer and lower firing range in clay bodies. Below pyrometric cone 4, add a small amount of a low-firing alkaline flux to the dolomite. Also see **pyrometer.**

domed-head stake. Metalworking. See **anvil.**

domestic oak. Woodworking. See **oak.**

doming. Jewelry. The process of **forming** metal into a dome. A domed shape can be quite high, as in a hemisphere, two of which can be soldered together to form a hollow bead. A dome can also be quite low, used to enrich a flat form.

Making a high dome in preparation for making a bead is done with a **dapping block** and **dapping punch**es. Punch with a **circle cutter** or saw circles out of sheet metal. The disk of sheet metal must fit within the concave circular forms of the dapping block. If the metal is larger than the perimeter of the circle on the dapping block it will ruin the block. Begin with a circle in the dapping block larger than the desired size of the dome. Select the size punch that will fit into the circular depression, less the **gauge** (thickness) of the metal. Place the circular piece of metal in the dapping block, then place the punch on top of it and with a **hammer** strike the punch as many times as necessary to form the first stage of the dome. Then vary the angle of the punch to fully form the hemisphere. As the disk is forced into the concave form of the dome, the perimeter of the disk will become smaller. Remove the partially formed dome and place it in the next-size concave form in the dapping block. It must fit within the circle of the dapping block. Select the correct punch, and proceed as above, progressing to smaller sizes, until you have a full dome.

If you want to construct a hollow bead, make two hemispheres, and file their edges absolutely flat. This can be done on a **bench rub stone,** or with **carborundum paper, emery paper,** or a flat **file,** any of which would be placed flat on the **bench** and the edges of the dome rubbed back and forth over them. Remove any **burr**s. **Flux** the dome and place solder **pallion**s along the edge of one dome, and solder. Drill a hole in at least one-half of the bead to allow gases to escape before **soldering** the two halves together, or they may explode. Sweat solder the two halves together, **pickle,** rinse, dry, and **buff.**

Forming a low dome, which can be a low, curved, noncircular form, is done by placing the flat piece of work over a domed **stake** held in a vise and hammering with a **rawhide mallet** until the desired curve is achieved. See ill. Also see **dapping, quench, sweat soldering.**

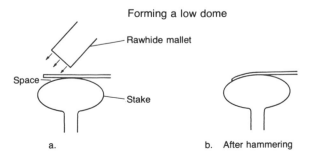

Forming a low dome

Rawhide mallet

Space

Stake

a.

b.   After hammering

Domingan mahogany. Woodworking. See **mahogany.**

doming hammer. Metalworking. See **hammer.**

donkey bead. Beadwork. A type of large **bead** in irregular, round shapes, finished with turquoise glaze. Because of their color, donkey beads were attributed with the same mystical qualities as **turquoise:** protection to the traveler and his horses, camels, or donkeys against mishap or falling. In many countries it was customary to put donkey beads on beasts of burden—hence the name. Today donkey beads are prized for their inherent qualities—a rough shape and vibrant color.

do-nothing machine. Toys. (Also called smoke grinder.) A crank-type **action toy** made from a block of wood into which two dovetail grooves have been milled at right angles. Pistons made of square wooden pegs or blocks are set into the grooves. The pistons are connected to each other by means of a crank arm. When the crank arm is turned, the pistons move from one end of the groove to the other. They never touch, but move in an alternating pattern. The toy, as its name implies, does nothing but is very amusing to see in action. See ill.

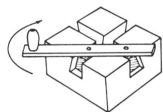

Do-nothing machine

dop. Gemcutting. (Also called dopp.) Wax, resin, cement solder, or plaster of Paris used for temporarily attaching gem material to facilitate handling when grinding, **sanding, faceting,** and **polishing.** Dop is usually applied hot; when it cools, it must bond strongly enough to withstand tugging and pushing without slipping. Ordinarily gemcutters use wax or shellac dops.

Beeswax dop is made by melting together one part (by weight) of beeswax and two, three, or four parts of powdered resin. The stiffness of the cooled dop increases with the addition of resin. It is soluble in benzine.

Shellac dop is made of two parts (by weight) of shellac and one part resin. It is very flammable and soluble in ethyl alcohol. A lower melting point shellac dop is made by adding one part beeswax to the mixture. Carnauba wax is substituted for beeswax for greater stiffness and a higher melting point.

A cold dop is made for stones which are heat sensitive, by mixing one part (by volume) household, quick-drying cement (acetate type) and four parts of cornstarch. This is applied to the stone and **dop stick** and left to dry for 24 hours. Cold dop is soluble in acetone.

Flake shellac mixed with alcohol to a syrupy consistency may be coated onto clean, grease-free gem material. This helps the dop adhere better to the gem and protects the stone if heating is necessary for a strong bond. Also see **cabochon, dopping** and **Gemcutting: Tools and Materials.**

dope dyeing. Dyeing. See **solution dyeing.**

dopping. Gemcutting. The operation of attaching a **preform** or rough stone to a handle for **sanding, faceting,** and **polishing.** Dopping permits more freedom of movement and visibility of the gem.

The stone must be clean, grease-free, and dry. It should be cleaned with alcohol and handled only with tweezers afterward. Difficult stones should be coated with cold shellac **dop.**

An alcohol stove is used to melt the dop and to heat the **dop stick** and the stone (**a.**). Dop will not stick to a cold surface. The dop is flammable and the open flame of the alcohol lamp should be avoided. An electric skillet and commercially available electric dop-heating units are used for the same purpose. Dopping temperatures are about 140° F—not too hot to touch with moistened fingers. Apply the hot dop to the end of the dop stick (warmed first in the flame, if metal) and to the stone. The dop on the stick is shaped on a slab of stone, glass, or metal called a dopping plate. The cold plate does not stick to the dop. Hold the heated stone with tweezers while the dop on the end of the dop stick is redipped into the hot dop or melted above the flame. Position the stone firmly on the dop stick. Trim excess wax with a knife. The dop stick is adhered to the table **facet** of the stone. Do not cover the edges of the stone. Set the dop stick in a holder, container of sand, or shot to cool.

Use metal dop sticks that fit into the handpiece of the faceting unit, and a dopping jig for dopping a preform for a faceted stone. The dopping jig (also called transfer jig and three-way dopping block) is a device that holds two dop sticks exactly lined up end to end and a third holder at right angles, to the other for a centering plate (**b.**).

The metal dop sticks have hollow cone ends and are not more than three-fourths the diameter of the stone. Warm the preformed stone, table down, on the lid of the alcohol stove. Use a wooden handle to manage metal dop sticks while heating; handle the clean, degreased stone with tweezers. Adhere the dopped stick to the table of the stone and place it in the dopping block. Use the centering plate on the opposite side to press the stone firmly into the hot dop. The stone is inserted at right angles to the centering plate and rotated; if the stone shows gaps or pushes the plate away while rotating, it is not centered. Hold the dopping block above the flame to soften the dop while centering. Accurate centering and good contact between the stone and the dop are crucial for faceting.

Remove the dop stick from the dopping jig. To check the contact, lightly oil the exposed part of the stone and look into it to see the dark shadow of dop below. Light and dark shading indicate unevenness of dop and that the stone is not making equal contact. Reheat and press together.

Facet and polish the pavillion of the stone; redop the stone to facet the crown. Affix another dop stick to the dopped stone and place the stick in the opposite holder of the dopping jig. Allow the dop to cool. Remove the first dop stick by heating the dop until pliable; remove the stick from the jig with a pair of pliers. Clean the crown of the dopped stone with a razor blade and a cloth dampened with alcohol.

Avoid overheating to keep the stone from flying off the dop stick, especially when polishing. Use lukewarm water when rinsing the stone between grits; cold water will make the stone loose. Avoid contamination of the dop wax with **abrasive,** as this will lessen its adhesive qualities.

Some gems, such as **opal** or large preforms, are too fragile to be heated on the stove. Place the stones on a pad of steel wool and heat, using a heat lamp held above them at a distance which will provide correct heat to slowly heat stones or to keep several stones warm simultaneously. Place a bit of dop on each stone to serve as a temperature gauge.

To remove the stone from the dop, heat the stem of the dop stick by moving it above the flame of the alcohol lamp, or immerse in ice water until the stone falls off. Another method of removing the stone from the dop stick is to nick the dop with a knife and strike the gem with a knock-off stick while securely holding the dop stick. The excess dop is scraped off with a blade and the stone wiped clean with alcohol. See ill. Also see **Gemcutting: Tools and Materials.**

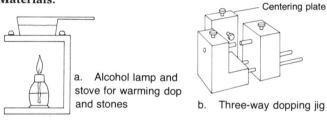

a.   Alcohol lamp and stove for warming dop and stones

Centering plate

b.   Three-way dopping jig

dopping jig. Gemcutting. See **dopping.**

dopping plate. Gemcutting. See **dopping.**

dop stick. Gemcutting. (Also called lap stick.) A wooden dowel or metal tube of different sizes used in **dopping** or **faceting** to temporarily hold the stone. Stones for **cabochon** cutting are **dop**ped on any convenient dop stick, such as a nail, dowel, or metal tube of less than half the diameter of the stone. Metal dops should have wooden handles so they can be handled when hot. Dop sticks for faceting must have shafts the proper diameter for insertion in the handpiece of the **faceting unit.**

The hollow cone dop stick is used to hold a stone at the bottom while faceting the crown (**a.**). The vee dop stick is used in a similar manner as the hollow cone (**b.**). Use a

a.   Hollow cone dop stick
b.   Vee dop stick
c.   Straight dop stick

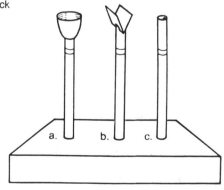

straight dop stick to facilitate cutting a cabochon (**c.**). To facet the pavillion attach the straight dop stick to the table of the stone. See ill. Also see **Gemcutting: Tools and Materials.**

dornik twill. Weaving. See **herringbone.**

dot stitch. Crewel. Embroidery. See **seed stitch.**

dotted swiss. Stitchery. A **plain weave cotton** which is sheer and crisp. Small dots are either woven onto the surface or are added by **flocking.** It is used in **transparent appliqué.** Also see **flocked fabric.**

double appliqué. Quilts. Stitchery. The layering or stacking of one piece of **appliqué** over another. This technique is sometimes used to give the effect of shading. For example, to depict a full-blown rose, petals may be appliquéd over petals, giving a three-dimensional look both through the overlapping of the shapes and the color gradations.

double band plaiting. Weaving. See **chevron plaiting.**

double bobbin shuttle. Weaving. See **boat shuttle.**

double bound seam. Stitchery. A **plain seam** with **raw edge**s trimmed and bound together with **seam binding** or bias tape. See ill.

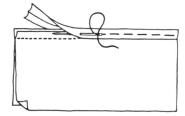

Double bound seam

double buttonhole stitch. Leatherwork. The double buttonhole stitch is a more elaborate version of the **single**

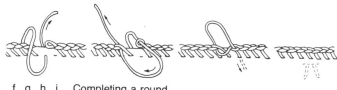

a.–d.   Making a double buttonhole stitch

e.   Double buttonhole stitch

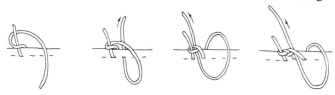

f., g., h., j.   Completing a round

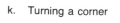

k.   Turning a corner

buttonhole stitch. It is more decorative, covers more completely the edges of the leather being sewn, and uses quite a bit of lace—six to eight times the length being stitched. The stitch is made similar to the single buttonhole stitch except that the lace is being passed through not only the loop being formed, but also under the loop formed by the previous stitch. See ill. Also see **edge stitch.**

double cabochon. Gemcutting. See **cabochon.**

double-card woven. Weaving. See **card weaving.**

double casting on. Knitting. See **Knitting: Casting On.**

double chain knot. Macramé. A **chain knot** worked with four **cord**s rather than the usual two. This knot is also worked in series to form a **chain** or **sennit.** Also see **alternating half hitch.**

double chain stitch. Crewel. Embroidery. A variation of the **chain stitch** in which two chain stitches are looped together to form a lacy band effect. See ill.

a.   b.   c.   d.

Double chain stitch

double cloth. Weaving. (Also called double weave.) A fabric made up of two sets of **warp** threads which are woven simultaneously with two sets of **filling** to form two layers of fabric lying one on top of the other. The simplest double cloth is woven in **plain weave** on four **harness**es. Two harnesses weave the face or top layer and two the back or under layer. Usually the face and back are two different and distinct colors so that the design or cloth structure are apparent. The layers may remain as separate pieces of cloth (although double cloth is rarely woven for this reason) or be joined by having the layers penetrate each other by various means in order to be held together. The penetration can be through **stitching point**s in which threads of one layer interlace with threads of the other to form a very heavy fabric that can be different in weave pattern and/or color on both face and back. It can also be a horizontal and vertical interchange of layers in which all back **end**s are raised and woven as the face and all previous face ends are submerged and woven as the back. Or the penetration can be at the **selvage**s so that either seamless tubing results when both sides are united front layer to back layer or **double width cloth** when only one side edge is joined together.

In planning the warp for a simple double cloth the face and back ends are placed alternately one face, one back or two face, two back. The threading is a **straight draw.** If done one face, one back the face ends would be on harnesses 1–3, back ends on harnesses 2–4. In the case of two face, two back, face ends would be on harnesses 1–2 and back ends on 3−4 (**a.**). In the **reed** everything is **sley**ed double its normal amount. For example: if the separate layers are to each have a **sett** of 10 per inch, the sleying for double cloth would be 20.

The basic steps in weaving double cloth are: (1) weaving the top layer on only the face ends; (2) weaving the bottom layer on the back ends. To achieve this second step the face ends must be lifted up out of the way so that they do not become involved in the back layer. This lifting is accomplished in the **treadling order** and calls for an unequal lifting of harnesses in each **pick**. Double cloth is therefore easier to weave on a **jack-type loom** as opposed to a **counterbalanced loom.**

Although plain weave is most commonly used by handweavers in weaving double cloth, there is no end to the **weave**s that can be used as long as there are enough harnesses to accommodate the weaves. For example, if a weaver wanted to use a **twill weave** (2/2) then 8 harnesses would be required—four for the top layer and four for the back (**b.**). It is also possible to use a different weave on each layer.

Double cloth offers many color, design, and structural possibilities. Even with the simple double cloth on 4-harnesses, seamless **tubular weaving** or double-width fabrics can be had. Complex designs can be achieved by a pick-up design method called **Finnweave.** Or the top layer can be woven in some **finger-manipulated** technique (such as a **gauze weave**) while the back layer weaves plain weave. Interchanging the two layers will form horizontal stripes of, alternately, the front layer color and then the back layer color. Using this principle in conjunction with the tubular weaving can produce completely enclosed pocket areas which many weavers stuff as pillows or as three-dimensional forms. Spaced stitching points can form **quiltweave** patterns that may be padded.

What is possible in 4-harness double cloth can be expanded on 8 harnesses. In addition to having more weave pattern possibilities to choose from it is also possible to interlock and exchange layers vertically. On 4 harnesses the only exchange of layers and colors is a horizontal one. When the vertical exchange is added to the horizontal exchange then it is possible to obtain **block pattern**s in various sizes and colors across the width of the cloth (**c.**). This vertical interlocking is achieved through the alternate **threading** of the various sized block groups of warp ends. One block is threaded on the first 4 harnesses. Its neighboring groups are threaded on the last 4 harnesses. This alternation between first 4 harnesses and last 4 harnesses proceeds as one moves from one block group to the next block group across the warp width. Through the treadling a face block is brought up next to a back block. This interlocks the layers vertically and gives way to a multitude of solid and mixed color effects as well as geometric pattern possibilities.

The double cloth principle and effects may be extended to more layers to become **triple cloth** and multilayered cloth. See ill. Also see **ingrain rug, Peruvian ingrain weave, piqué, quiltweave, triple cloth, tubular weaving.**

double coral stitch. Crewel. Embroidery. See **coral knot.**

double corduroy. Rugmaking. Weaving. See **corduroy.**

double crochet. Crochet. See **Crochet: Basic Stitches, Decreasing.**

double cross bar. Quilts. See **Quilts: Quilting.**

double cross stitch. Needlepoint. See **Smyrna cross stitch.**

double cross stitch. Rugmaking. See **cross stitch.**

double cut. Metalworking. Woodworking. See **file.**

double-cut file. Woodworking. See **file.**

double cutting. Rugmaking. Weaving. See **corduroy.**

double decrease. Knitting. See **Knitting: Decreasing.**

double diamond. Quilts. See **Quilts: Quilting.**

double dovetailing. Weaving. See **dovetailing.**

doubled tool. Bookbinding. A tooled letter or decoration is said to be doubled when it is not placed exactly over the first impression when applied a second or third time.

double-duty thread. Rugmaking. See **carpet thread.**

double dyeing. Dyeing. See **top-dyeing.**

a. Weave draft of simple 4-harness double cloth showing face (A) and back (B) arrangement of warp and filling

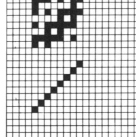

b. 8-harness double cloth for 2/2 twill on both sides

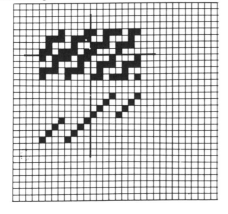

c. Two block pattern (threading and weave draft) for vertical and horizontal interchange of colors

double eyelet stitch. Knitting. See **eyelet stitch.**

double-faced fabric. Stitchery. Those **fabrics** made up of two layers of cloth which are either bonded or woven together. While the two sides are not always identical, either side can be used as the right side of the material. No **facings** are required when it is used for clothing. It is often used in making room dividers, **free-hanging panels**, or **banners**, since no **lining** or **backing** is needed.

double-faced rug. Rugmaking. Weaving. Rugs made with **loom-controlled** weaves that are reversible so that both sides can be used and a different color effect appears on each side. **Flatweave rugs** are reversible by the nature of their technique, but the color and pattern are identical on each side. A double-faced rug appears in different colors, sometimes patterns, on each side.

The simplest reversible rug is a 3-**harness twill** (1/2) which gives more **warp** color on one side and more **filling** color on the other side. In this case, the warp mixes equally with the filling. A double-faced 3/1 twill rug can also be woven in this manner. If it is desired to cover the warp completely, a **pick-and-pick** arrangement is used, and the 3/1 twill is alternated with a 1/3 twill in the **treadling**. More complex double-faced rugs can be woven as **double cloth** arranged in **block pattern**s of two or more contrasting colors. The colors appear in reverse positions on each side of the rug. The weave can be **plain weave** in both layers of the double cloth or twill or any other 4-harness weave in each layer. It is essential to have 8 harnesses for this type of weave and color effect. The warp and filling both show and the colors intermix. Summer and Winter patterns on 8 harnesses also produce a reversible effect, but it is reverse patterns rather than blocks. Many other 4-harness weaves can be adapted in this same way according to the inventiveness and imagination of the weaver. When expanding these weaves for use in rugs, it is essential that durable and heavyweight yarns are used in both warp and filling, so that the desired strength and thickness is achieved.

It is also possible to make double-faced **pile** rugs. In olden times, when **rya rugs** were used as sleigh and bed coverings in Sweden and Finland, **knotted pile** was put in on both sides for extra warmth. Today, this use has been abandoned, and two-sided pile is not necessary unless someone wants an extra lush rug underfoot, or to display a novelty or technical feat. This can be done loom-controlled, as well as hand-knotted, by using **corduroy** weaves. They can be woven as reversible rugs on 4 harnesses if the **threading** and treadling is so arranged. There will be **floats** on both sides of the fabric that can later be cut into pile. The treadling should have enough plain weave to hold the piles firmly in place. Corduroy pile that must be pulled up in order to hide the plain weave is difficult to control in a double-faced rug. The easiest method is to push the floats down from the top surface. Also see **Summer and Winter weave.**

double foundation chain. Crochet. See **Crochet: Basic Stitches.**

double glazing. Stained Glass. (Also called doubling.) A process in which one or two pieces of glass are placed on top of another and together are inserted into an extra-wide **lead came** or are copper foiled. Also see **copper foiling, glazing, plating** and **Stained Glass: Glazing.**

double half hitch. Macramé. (Also called clove hitch.) Two consecutive **half hitch**es worked with one **cord**, over a **holding cord.** The direction can be diagonal, horizontal, or vertical.

Position and secure holding cord. Wrap the next cord around the holding cord twice to complete one knot (**a.**). Continue across, wrapping each cord around the holding cord twice (**b.**). The **cording** can be done right to left as well as left to right (**c.**).

When used as a **mounting knot**, the double half hitch is called a lark's head. Double the macramé cord and lay the loop end downward under the **mounting cord** or bar. Bring the two loose cord ends over the mounting cord and pull them through the loop so that the loop is over the cords. Tighten (**d.**). See ill. Also see **Cavandoli work, chevron pattern, reverse double half hitch, vertical double half hitch.**

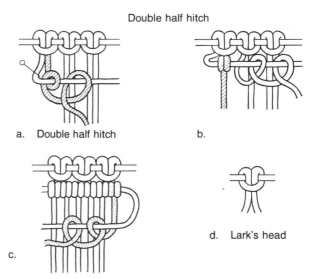

Double half hitch

a. Double half hitch   b.

c.   d. Lark's head

double-headed nail. Woodworking. See **nail.**

Double Hearts. Quilts. (Also called St. Valentine's Patch.) A combination of hearts and arrows in an **appliqué block.** It looks like a cut-out paper design in its pattern and complexity.

double hemstitch. Stitchery. See **hemstitch.**

double herringbone stitch. Crewel. Embroidery. A variation of the **herringbone stitch** using two different colored threads. The stitch must be worked evenly. Begin a row of herringbone taking small stitches on either side (from B to C) (**a.**). After taking each upper stitch (B to C), slide the needle under the stitch just taken (AB), and continue the line of herringbone, spacing the stitches wide apart. One stitch will then always lie completely on top, and one completely underneath (**b.**). With contrasting color thread work another line of herringbone in the same way, weaving the thread over and under to form an interlaced line of stitching. To make the second line a correct weave, the thread must always go under the last stitch (**c.**). See ill.

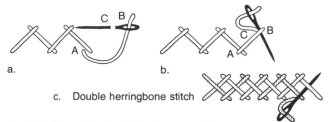

a.   b.

c. Double herringbone stitch

double ikat. Dyeing. Weaving. See **ikat.**

double increase. Knitting. See **Knitting: Increasing.**

double interlocking. Weaving. See **interlocking.**

Double Irish Chain. Quilts. See **Irish Chain.**

double Japanese. Basketry. A **weave** in **woven basketry** using two **weaver**s as one. The **stroke** is made by coming in front of two **stakes** and in back of one. To avoid stacking, the total number of **spokes** should not be divisible by three.

doubleknit fabric. Stitchery. Any material which consists of two knitted layers secured together by occasional binding stitches. These fabrics have a good substantial **body** and are more stable than other knitted materials. Doubleknits have some give or stretch and therefore can be utilized in surface **stuffing.**

double knitting. Knitting. A double fabric knit on only two needles. The **cast-on** edge of the fabric is closed, but the other end can be left open and unconnected when **casting off.**

METHOD:

   Row 1: Cast on an even number of **stitch**es and knit one **row.**
   Row 2: * k 1, yo, sl 1 pw * across the row.
   Repeat from * to * every succeeding row. This will create a **stocking stitch.**

AN ALTERNATIVE METHOD:

   Row 1: * k 1, sl 1 * across the row.
   Repeat * to * every row. This method will create a **garter stitch.**

To cast off with an open end, divide the stitches on two needles, taking the stitches alternately onto each needle, and cast off with a third needle as if the fabric were round.

For a closed fabric, K 2 tog, repeat, pass the knit stitch made by the first K 2 tog over the second. Continue in this manner across the row. See ill.

Double knitting stocking stitch

double knot. Macramé. See **square knot.**

double lacing. Rugmaking. See **lacing.**

double-layer puzzle. Toys. A **jigsaw puzzle** made for very small children. It consists of a wood, Masonite, or stiff cardboard background with a second layer of the same material, cut into the puzzle pieces, placed on top. The pieces at the perimeter are **glue**d permanently in place. The child then can slip the parts in place more easily. This kind of puzzle is popular for very small children who may not yet have the coordination skills to join **interlocking parts.** A picture of the finished puzzle is sometimes applied to the base material so that the puzzle pieces can be matched for placement.

double-line blade. Leatherwork. See **swivel knife.**

double-mesh canvas. Needlepoint. See **canvas.**

double Mexican lace. Weaving. See **Mexican lace.**

double-mirror brilliant. Gemcutting. See **facet, faceting.**

Double Monkey Wrench. Quilts. See **Shoo-fly.**

double moss stitch. Knitting. See **Knitting: Stitches and Patterns.**

double needle stitch. Leatherwork. A **running stitch** done with a needle in each hand with the needles crossing in each hole. Since both hands are in use, a **lacing pony** or **stitching horse** will be needed to hold the work. For a locked double needle stitch, put each needle through the loop of the opposite thread as it passes through. Also see **cross stitch, harness needle, saddle stitch.**

Double Nine-patch. Quilts. A **block** design consisting of nine **patches.** These patches alternate between plain blocks and **pieced** blocks, with the pieced blocks being small **nine-patch**es. It is in effect a nine-patch within a nine-patch. **Set** with alternating blocks of solid color, it becomes the Single Irish Chain.

   Other Double Nine-patch blocks are **Puss-in-the-Corner** and **Burgoyne's Surrender.**

double over. Knitting. (abbr. o2.) A double over (two yarn overs) is used in **faggot** and **faggot lace** stitches. To work, bring the yarn forward and completely around the needle once, then knit the next stitch. On the purl row, **purl** the first over and **knit** the second over.

double over-and-under. Basketry. See **double randing.**

double passage. Weaving. See **tapestry.**

double plaiting. Weaving. A **plaiting** technique similar to **double cloth** in that two layers of cloth (usually in two dissimilar colors) are constructed simultaneously and interpenetrate each other when it is desirable to have the color of one layer show in the other layer. It is also possible to interpenetrate so that the front and back positions are completely reversed—the back plaited layer becomes the front, and the front the back.

double-pointed needles. Knitting. Needles with a point at both ends, used for round or **circular knitting.** Also see **Knitting: Materials.**

double randing. Basketry. (Also called double over-and-under.) A term used in **woven basketry** where two **weavers** are **rand**ed with as one. As in randing, the total number of **spoke**s must be odd. Also see **checked weave, slewing.**

double-rod handle. Basketry. See **handle.**

double rose cut. Gemcutting. See **facet.**

double running stitch. Embroidery. (Also called Molbein stitch.) In **counted thread embroidery** continuous outline designs are worked on **evenweave fabric** with even **running stitch**es. First the geometric design is outlined, working along in one direction, each stitch being equal in length to the spaces between the stitches. These spaces are filled in on the return journey with running stitches to form a continuous line alike on both sides of the fabric. Because the effectiveness of the pattern relies on a strong contrast with the background fabric, the double running stitch is traditionally worked in black silk on white **linen.**

To work stitch, using a blunt needle, come up at A, go over 3 threads and go down at B. Come up at C, 3 threads away and go down at D, over 3 more threads. Continue, making even stitches in a straight line (**a.**). Turn the work completely around and fill the spaces between the running stitches, going into the same holes as the previous ones to make a continuous line of stitching, alike on both sides (**b.**). Double running stitch worked in decorative pattern (**c.**). See ill. Also see **blackwork.**

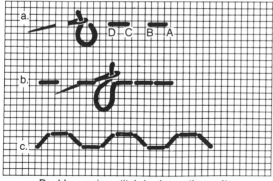
Double running stitch in decorative pattern

double sleying. Weaving. See **sleying.**

double spinning wheel. Spinning. A **treadle wheel** with two **flyers.** They were invented to speed up production and keep up with the weaving innovations of the Industrial Revolution. They could be used by two people at the same time and so became known as friendship, gossip, or lover's wheels. Either flax or wool are spun on it. See ill.

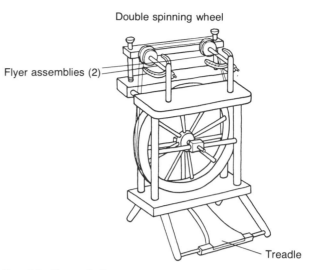
Double spinning wheel
Flyer assemblies (2)
Treadle

Double Star. Quilts. See **Star-within-Star.**

double stitch. Tatting. (abbr. ds.) The tatting stitch. It is composed of two **half hitch**es, reversed. A **left half hitch** is made, followed by a **right half hitch.** Also see **making the double stitch.**

doublet. Gemcutting. A gem made of two units cemented together. Most doublets are **cameo**s or **cabochon**-cut gems. The term also applies to a **loupe** (magnifying glass) with two lenses.

Double T. Quilts. A **pieced geometric block** in which the shapes resemble the letter T.

double thread canvas. Needlepoint. See **canvas.**

double tie-up loom. Weaving. See **countermarch loom.**

double top-stitched seam. Stitchery. A **seam finish** for a **plain seam** in which the **raw edge**s are first **press**ed open, and are then sewn as in the **top-stitched seam.** Each of the two additional lines of **top stitch**ing is placed exactly parallel to the original **seam.** If a contrasting color is used the seam is exaggerated with the decorative lines. See ill.

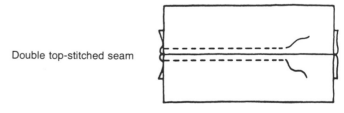
Double top-stitched seam

double topstitching. Leatherwork. A seam-finishing technique in which a plain seam is sewn and the seam allowances turned back as normally. Then, stitching from the right side, topstitch the seam allowance in place by stitching down each side of the seam crease. Also see **Leatherwork: Sewing Leather.**

double triple crochet. Crochet. See **Crochet: Basic Stitches.**

double warp beam. Weaving. See **warp beam.**

double waxing. Batik and Tie-dye. The process of **waxing** a **batik** fabric first on the front and then on the back. Wax at the proper temperature will penetrate the fabric and have a translucent appearance. If it is too cool it will be white and opaque and not penetrate the fabric, resulting in only partial **resist.** If this occurs the fabric must be re-waxed on the other side, or double-waxed.

double weave. Weaving. See **double cloth.**

double weaver. Basketry. The term used to describe a pair of **weaver**s used at the same time. When using double weavers, each weave may be woven alternately as in **chasing** or both weavers may be woven together as one, as in **double randing.** Double weavers are primarily used to speed up the weaving.

Double Wedding Ring. Quilts. A **pieced quilt** pattern, very popular from the early 1900s on, that suggests a series of intertwining circles. It is a difficult pattern to sew because small rectangular pieces must be tapered and joined to form an arc. It is then **pieced** to a solid-color piece of fabric. One of the attractive characteristics of this particular pattern is that it produces a **scallop** at the outside edge of the quilt.

double whirligig. Toys. A toy made like a **whirligig** but with two air outlets in the **blow pipe** instead of one. The outlets, which activate paddle wheels, are arranged so that the paddles stand side by side and rotate in opposite directions.

double-width cloth. Weaving. A **double cloth** woven so that it is connected at one **selvage.** It is then possible to open up, or unfold, the fabric after it is off the **loom,** and have a cloth twice the width it was woven. This makes possible the weaving of wide fabrics on a narrow loom without having to resort to piecing together two separately woven sections. In order to avoid a heavy, vertical streak in the fabric at the fold, the connected selvage should be threaded through the **reed** with single threads in the last three **dents.** It is also possible to weave a fabric 3 times the width using a **triple cloth** weave. Whether double or triple width, two **harness**es are used for each layer of cloth, if it is woven in **plain weave.** This means a four-harness loom could weave double-width fabrics, but a triple width would need six harnesses. Also see **double cloth, triple cloth.**

Double X. Quilts. A **pieced block** design in which **split four-patch**es are combined into a larger **four-patch** design. It is a variation of the **Letter X** block design.

Double Z. Quilts. See **Gray Goose.**

doubling. Spinning. Weaving. The twisting together of two or more yarns. This can be done on a **spinning wheel** for a tight **twist,** or on a **doubling stand** for a loose twist. If the yarns twisted are **single**s this is also called **plying.** Also see **doubling stand, plying, twist.**

doubling. Stained Glass. See **double glazing, plating.**

doubling stand. Weaving. A simple, small wooden piece of equipment for the **plying** or twisting together of two or more yarns. The equipment is used when the weaver wishes to use two or more strands of the same yarn, or of mixed yarns and colors. Instead of merely laying the yarn together in the **shed** while weaving, some control is exercised over how the yarn will fall in the shed by plying it in a loose **twist** in a doubling stand. This is done prior to preparing the **shuttle.** Doubling stands consist usually of two horizontal boards with a sidepiece to which both are attached. The bottom board, which rests on the floor, has pegs for either one or two **spool**s or **cone**s of yarn. Another spool rests on a peg on the top board. This peg is hollow, and through it is fed the yarn from the lower spool or spools. The yarn goes up over a hook in the top of the stand. The yarn from the upper tube wraps around the lower yarn and a **plied yarn** is achieved. A doubling stand can be bought, or constructed at home. See ill.

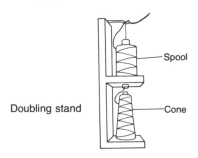

Doubling stand — Spool — Cone

doublure. Bookbinding. The lining of silk, **leather,** or other material applied to the inside of a book cover.

dough art glazes. Toys. See **baker's clay glazes.**

dough mixer. Ceramics. A device originally manufactured for use by small bakeries. They are used by potters to mix powdered clay and water to produce **slip** and have replaced the **blunger.**

doup. Weaving. (Also called doupe, leno heddles, half-heddles.) Special half-**heddle**s or loops used in the making of **loom-controlled gauze weave**s and **leno.** The first meaning of doup is in reference to the long loops on either side of the **heddle eye** in a **string heddle.** It has now come to mean, solely, long loops without a heddle eye which are attached to either the bottom or top frame of a **harness,** that is known as the skeleton harness or doup harness, and is for the use of these doups only. In action, this harness with the doup attachments lifts **warp end**s as a group over the surface of the warp, instead of the individual lifting that is required with a **pick-up stick.** In the lifting, those warp ends threaded through the doups are pulled under their neighboring warp ends to form the twist needed for gauze weaving. Doups can be attached to floor or **table loom**s, that are countermarch or jack-type.

Doups are made of fine, strong cord and cut around a cardboard gauge to insure them all being the same size. The doups must be long enough so that they will not hamper the formation of the **plain weave shed.** The cut length of the doup cord is doubled into a long loop held with a strong knot at one end. This knotted end is slipped around the harness frame or attached to it with a lark's head knot. The loops are threaded through the heddle eyes of a harness either in front or in back of the skeleton harness, which is known as the standard harness. During this process, large safety pins can be attached to the ends of the loops to prevent them from slipping back out. An alternate method is to thread the loops through the heddle eyes at the same time as the warp ends are being threaded through.

In the **threading** arrangement, the warp ends are treated as pairs. One member of the pair is threaded on one harness as normal. The second member is threaded on the harness before the first end and on the harness that comes after the first end. The second threading is through the standard containing the doup in the heddle eye. Between the first and second threading of this warp end, it goes under the first or normal warp end. In the threading, alternate warp ends are threaded on harness #3 as the normal ends. The other ends are threaded on harness #4 first, and then through the doups on the standard. The standard can be either harness #1 or #2. Starting from the right side, the threading arrangement would then be harness #4 first, and then #3, and this order is repeated throughout. Returning to the right, the doups are threaded with the #4 thread going under the #3 thread, before entering the doup. In the **reed,** the pair of warp ends affected by the same doup are threaded through the same **dent.** The threading arrangement mentioned here will give a gauze weave. In order to weave leno, the doup warp end should not go under the #3 end. In treadling then, it is possible to weave plain weave on the two back harnesses (#3 and #4) as long as the standard is also raised.

As the treadling raises the harnesses, it is evident that one yarn in each pair does all the twisting while the other lies stationary. This results in different tension needs for each yarn. Two **warp beam**s are ideal, but if they can not be had, a device known as an easer bar, slackener, or tension release can be constructed at home and can help to ease the strain and avoid breakage of the skeleton or twisting yarns. This movable bar or rod should be set above the warp beam or **back beam,** and over it all, doup warp ends should pass. Its exact position should be dictated by what is easier for the handweaver to construct and manipulate, for in addition to being inserted under all the doup warp ends, the easer bar must have a release cord that will pull the bar down in order to slacken the necessary warp threads when the doup comes into play. As a substitute for this bar, the twisting or doup warp ends can be left as a chain, or divided into small chains, and tensioned by using weights.

A method that is essentially the same as a doup harness is used by Guatemalan Indians weaving on simple **backstrap loom**s. They use a dowel or extra **heddle bar** with the doups attached to it. These doups enclose an alternate set of warp ends and pass under the other set of

warp ends. When the doup heddle bar is raised, the enclosed ends are pulled under and to the left, or right, of the free ends and then raised above the warp to form the shed. See ill. Also see **floor loom, jack-type loom, warp chain.**

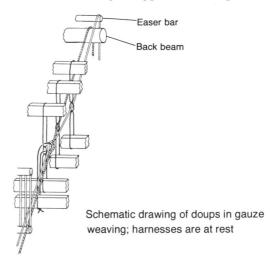

Schematic drawing of doups in gauze weaving; harnesses are at rest

doupe. Weaving. See **doup.**

doup harness. Weaving. See **doup.**

douppioni. Spinning. Weaving. See **silk.**

Dove in the Window. Quilts. Any of several completely different **piece**d **block** patterns, all **geometric** designs within a square. The name came from a time when every barn had a small round window cut in the gable with a tiny ledge beneath for the pigeons. The block has pieced diamonds and triangles that suggest a circular form.

dove of peace. Quilts. See **Quilts: Quilting.**

dovetailing. Weaving. A **tapestry** technique or method of changing colors in adjacent areas without forming a slit. It is a vertical joining of alternate **filling** threads, one from the right and one from the left, both turning around the same or common **warp end.** This creates a serrated line where the colors join, which can prove an interesting design element. The simplest dovetailing is made by alternating one right filling yarn with one from the left. The two fillings should be in the same **shed** of **plain weave.** This is called single dovetailing, comb-dovetailing, or toothing (not to be confused with **teething**), which, when considered as a variety of dovetailing, is called "interpenetrating dovetailing" (**a.**). Two, three, or more filling yarns alternating as groups around a common warp end make for a stronger jagged or saw-toothed pattern between two colors. This is called vertical, multiple, double, or triple dovetailing, or 2/2 dovetailing, 3/3 dovetailing, etc. Because of the build-up of filling yarn at the common warp end, a ridge can be felt and sometimes seen at the joining. There is less of this build-up with the multiple dovetailing than with the single, as the loops of filling around the warp end compress to a point after beating down (**b.**). In irregular dovetailing, alternating groups of filling yarn go around a common warp end as well as adjacent ones in a staggered pattern (**c.**). Dovetailing is done on **diagonals** as well as verticals (**d.**). It is found in Coptic, Swedish, Norwegian, Mexican, **Navajo,** and **Peruvian weaving** as well as Chimayo work from New Mexico. See ill.

Schematic diagrams of dovetailing

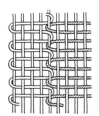
a.   Single dovetailing

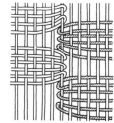
b.   Multiple dovetailing

c.   Irregular dovetailing

d.   Diagonal dovetailing

dovetail joint. Fabric Printing. See **Fabric Printing: Designing.**

dovetail joint. Woodworking. See **joint.**

dowel. Puppets. Stitchery. Toys. A wood rod available in various diameters and lengths. Most hobby shops and hardware stores carry an assortment of sizes. They are made in sizes which correspond to the sizes of drill bits. A ½″ dowel will fit snugly into a hole drilled with a ½″ drill bit.

In stitchery dowel rods provide a good supporting rod on which panels or banners can be hung. They can be stained or painted, and decorative **finial**s or **wood bead**s can be added at the ends.

Toymakers use dowels for the **axle**s of **wheeled toy**s and to make dowel joints. Puppet bodies can be constructed from lengths of dowel.

dowel. Woodworking. The small cylindrical length of wood used as the connecting member in a **dowel joint.** It may also be used to **plug** the hole left by countersinking a screw. Dowels are commonly available in 3′ and 4′ lengths with diameters from ³/₁₆ to ½″; larger sizes are sometimes available.

doweled joint. Woodworking. See **joint** and **Woodworking: Jointing.**

doweling jig. Woodworking. A tool used in making a **doweled joint.** It is clamped onto a piece of wood to aid in positioning and boring perpendicular holes for the dowels. It is adjustable to fit **drill bit**s from ³/₁₆ to ¾″ in diameter. See ill. Also see **Woodworking: Jointing.**

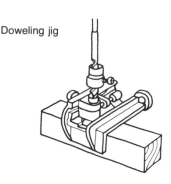
Doweling jig

doweling rod. Kites. See **Kites: Tools and Materials.**

down. Featherwork. The soft, fluffy feathers of young birds, or those that grow at the base of large feathers. Down is often used as insulation in items such as sleeping bags and coats.

down. Weaving. See **sinker.**

downdraft kiln. Ceramics. A **kiln** where hot gases first rise to the roof and then are drawn down through the floor and out the chimney. Heat is more efficiently used and better distributed than in an **updraft kiln.** See ill.

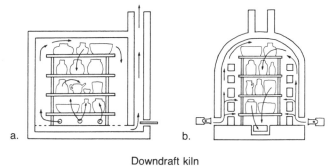
Downdraft kiln

draft. Metalworking. Plastics. The inward slope of the walls of a **mold** to permit easy removal of the **casting.** The **pattern** for **sand casting** an object must have a draft so that it may be removed from the sand mold without disturbing the sand walls around it.

draft. Weaving. Representation on squared **graph paper** to indicate either how to thread or weave a fabric, or how it looks in the final result. The **drawing-in draft** shows the pattern of threading the **warp end**s into the **heddle**s (**a.**). **Chain draft**s show what **harness**es are to be raised on **table loom**s. They can be converted into the **tie-up** and **treadling sequence** for use with a **floor loom** (**b., c.**). The **weave draft** is a literal picture on graph paper of the weave structure as it looks in the cloth (**d.**). Drawing-in drafts can be shortened by changing the draft designation to numbers, although it then ceases to be a graphic representation. These are known as short drafts and are done to save time and money, yet accurately describe what the threading is to be. A weave draft that is large or of great complexity can be condensed graphically into a **profile draft,** which shows the pattern only either in true size or proportionately scaled down.

Within all the drafts there is much variety as to whether one uses a filled-in square, a line, an "x" or some other symbol. They can be read or written left to right, or right to left. The same is true from top to bottom; they can be read or written either from the top down, or the bottom up. Although most books seem to be written for a **rising shed** loom, which would mean that in the weave draft the filled-in squares are **raiser**s and the tie-up is so drafted that it will pull up those raisers, there are other books that operate on the **sinking shed** system, and it is the pulling down of the warp ends that the tie-up affects. It is best to know which system a book is following, before attempting the patterns.

In a complete set of drafts for a weave, the weave draft appears in the center with the drawing-in draft either directly above or directly below. They are aligned end for end. If a chain draft is used it appears to the right of the weave draft. If a tie-up and treadling sequence are used, the tie-up appears to the right or left of the drawing-in draft, aligned by harnesses, and the treadling sequence above or below the tie-up, aligned according to **treadles**. The **warp** and **filling arrangement**s can also be added, appearing above and to the left of the weave draft (**e., f.**). Keeping drafts as records is invaluable to a weaver, especially if a fabric or sample is to be reproduced at some future time. See ill.

a.   Drawing-in draft

b.   Tie-up

c.   Treadling sequence

d.   Weave draft

e.   Warp arrangement

f.   Filling arrangement

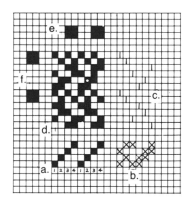

drafting. Basketry. See **Basketry: Preparing the Materials.**

drafting. Spinning. The procedure by which prepared **fiber**s are compressed and drawn out, or extended into a continuous strand. The **spinning** or twisting goes on simultaneously with the drafting. The fibers coming from **sliver** or **roving** have little strength, so a slight twist is added in the drafting to sustain them until they are fully spun. The more the fibers are extended or pulled out, the fewer the fibers in the **twist** and the finer the gauge of the resulting yarn. The less the fibers are pulled, the thicker the fibers in a twist and the heavier the yarn. See ill.

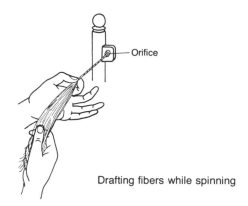

Drafting fibers while spinning

drafting. Weaving. The process of illustrating on **graph paper** what is being woven on the **loom.** Drafting quickly and concisely shows the weaver how a loom is to be threaded, in what sequence the **harness**es are to be raised, and what the weave structure of a fabric looks like. Also see **draft.**

drag. Kites. The frictional resistance of the kite to the wind. According to the principles of **aerodynamics,** the kite's **lift** must be greater than its drag if it is to remain aloft. See **Kites: Construction.**

drag. Metalworking. See **sandcasting molding equipment.**

Drakenfield paints. Stained Glass. See **oil-base paints.**

drape forming. Plastics. A heat-forming process in which a heat-softened **thermoplastic** sheet is shaped between two **mold**s and cooled until hard.

To drape-form, heat the plastic sheet in an oven at 300° F until soft. Remove it from the oven and drape it over the lower mold (**a.**). Use another hollow shape which fits over both the plastic and the lower mold form to press the plastic sheet against the lower mold (**b.**). Wear lint-free cotton gloves to shape plastic by hand. However, the corners may not be as geometrically defined as when a rigid top molding form is used. Remove the molded plastic sheet when the form has become rigid (**c.**). See ill. Also see **Plastics: Thermoforming and Molding.**

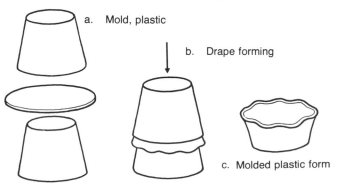

a.   Mold, plastic

b.   Drape forming

c.   Molded plastic form

drape mold. Ceramics. See **hump mold.**

drape mold. Stained Glass. A convex shape over which glass is melted in the kiln to achieve a rounded shape. Also see **lampshade mold.**

drapery glass. Stained Glass. A special type of **cathedral glass** once used to represent folds in clothing or draperies in stained-glass windows. It was made by rolling a special 40-lb. roller over a marver (a steel or marble table top) covered with molten glass. The folds in the glass were determined by the way the roller was moved. Drapery glass was produced at the **Heidt** Glass Factory, Brooklyn, New York, in the early 1900s. Also see **machine-made glass.**

dravite. Gemcutting. See **tourmaline.**

draw boy. Weaving. See **draw loom.**

draw curtain. Puppets. The **curtain** for a **puppet stage** that pulls to the side is called a draw curtain. It operates on a simple pulley. The entire curtain may be drawn to one side, or it may be designed so that half the curtain goes to each side. Also see **proscenium** and **Puppets: Puppet Stage.**

draw-down. Weaving. See **weave draft.**

drawfiling. Jewelry. A filing technique in which the **file** is held sideways on the surface, perpendicular to the direction in which the file will be moved. With a hand on each end of the file, draw the file downward to smooth the metal.

drawfiling. Metalworking. Filing accomplished by pushing a file across the work in order to create a smooth, level surface. A **mill file** may be used for light filing and a **second cut** or **bastard file** may be used to remove greater quantities of metal. Drawfiling is used to smooth away marks from a metal surface. Also see **Metalworking: Filing.**

draw gauge. Leatherwork. (Also called adjustable draw gauge.) A tool used for cutting even straps in heavy leather. Cut one edge of the hide straight with a knife and ruler; adjust the draw gauge for the width of the strap or belt desired; gripping the gauge firmly, start the cut slowly, pulling the gauge toward you. See ill. Also see **Stript-Ease** and **Leatherwork: Cutting and Edging, Tools and Materials.**

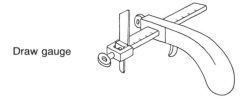

Draw gauge

draw hook. Weaving. See **reed hook.**

draw-in. Weaving. The slight pulling in of the **selvages** during weaving. This compression makes for a **warp** that is narrower at the **fell** than in the **reed.** Draw-in, or pull-in, is natural and varies with the elasticity of the **filling** yarn and the manner of weaving; for example, draw-in often happens because the weaver does not allow the filling to remain slack in the **shed** before **beating.** Draw-in should never be excessive, or the selvage ends will be cut by the **beater,** along with the fabric becoming narrower. Draw-in happens on all types of looms. A **stretcher,** or template, can control it on **harness loom**s, while on a **frame loom** the fabric must be pulled and tied at both selvages to the side supports of the loom. Also see **waist.**

drawing. Glasswork. The thinning of a glass rod or tube by heating and stretching. The ability of glass to retain its shape in cross section while being reduced in size is the operating principle in **latticino** and **millefiori** techniques. It is possible to reduce the thickness of glass to a fiber by drawing it at high speeds and winding the fiber onto a wheel or spool. Historically, glass fiber was made by attaching molten glass to an arrow and firing it from a crossbow. Also see **trailing.**

drawing color. Bookbinding. A term used in **blind tooling** when the color of a **leather** binding is darkened by the heated **tool.**

drawing-in. Weaving. Pulling the **warp end**s through the **heddle eye**s and the **reed** of a **harness loom.** The last procedure of going through the **dent**s in the reed is usually specifically defined as **sleying.** Drawing-in, or threading through the heddles, is done according to a prescribed plan called a **drawing-in draft.** It is usually accomplished with the aid of a **reed hook,** but can be done with the fingers alone. The threading can proceed from left to right or right to left. Prior to this, the number of heddles needed per harness should be determined, so that the correct number are on the harness and more can be added if necessary. Extra heddles on the harnesses can be divided into equal groups and pushed to each side of the harness. Threading can proceed from the back of the loom to the front; that is, the **warp** is at the back of the loom and the heddles are threaded first and then the reed. Or, it can proceed from front to back with the warp wound around the **breast beam,** and then the reed is threaded first, and then the heddles. Some mistakes in threading can be corrected with a **string** or **repair heddle,** but more often an area has to be pulled out and rethreaded. See ill. Also see **slip-knot.**

Drawing-in, or sleying, through the reed

drawing-in draft. Weaving. The graphic representation of the pattern in which the **warp end**s are threaded into the **heddle**s on the **harness**es. On **graph paper**, every vertical row of squares is equal to a warp end; every horizontal row to a harness. The graph is no higher than the number of harnesses being used. Where there is a mark or filled-in square indicates on which harness a warp end is threaded. In every vertical row there can be no more than one mark, since a warp end goes only through one heddle. The harnesses on the loom number from front to back. On the graph paper they number from bottom to top, i.e., harness #1 would be the bottom horizontal row on the graph. In Europe, the harnesses are read from the top of the graph down. There are many variations in the method of recording the threading on the graph paper. Some weavers fill in squares, others "x" in, and still others use either a line or numbers. Drawing-in drafts can be very simple ones, like the **straight draw,** or very complex ones. Sometimes they are designed for a specific weave effect or pattern. They show at least one repeat of the pattern of threading. See ill. Also see **draft.**

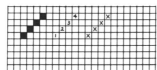

Three methods of indicating a drawing-in draft

drawing out. Jewelry. See **forging down.**

drawing out. Metalworking. See **blacksmithing techniques.**

drawing tubing. Jewelry. (Also called tube drawing.) Drawing **sheet metal** through a **drawplate** to make **tubing.** After the tubing is completed there will be a **seam** along its entire length that will need to be soldered. As tubing can be bought in nearly all sizes that can be made with a drawplate, and with the advantage of being seamless, drawing tubing does not seem worth the time involved.

drawing wire. Jewelry. Pulling wire through a **drawplate,** reducing its gauge and increasing its length. Position the drawplate in a **vise** in a horizontal position. The drawplate is liable to snap in two if held in the vise in a vertical position. File the wire to a long, tapered point. Draw **beeswax** along the length of the wire. This will act as a lubricant during drawing and must be used before each pull. Insert the point of the wire from the rear of the drawplate into the gauge hole which is one size smaller than the wire. The hole in a drawplate is tapered, larger at the back, the accurate gauge in front. Firmly grasp the point of the wire with the **draw tongs** and pull with a smooth, continuous movement until the complete length of wire is pulled through. Stopping or jerking the wire will indent or break it. Pull the wire through each successively smaller gauge hole until the desired gauge is achieved. Do not skip a gauge size to avoid damaging the drawplate.

Caution: when the wire comes out of the gauge hole, the end will snap forward. Wear **goggles** for added safety. The **tensile strength** of the wire increases as it becomes reduced in gauge. Consequently, wire must be annealed after several pulls. This depends entirely on the metal; 24K gold, for example, need never be annealed. Sterling silver may be drawn through 4 or 5 times, perhaps more, before it becomes necessary to anneal it to prevent breakage. Experience helps the jeweler to determine when **annealing** a wire is necessary. Also see **forming, quench.**

drawknife. Woodworking. A tool used for the shaping or rapid **planing** of wood. It consists of a long exposed blade with 2 perpendicular handles.

To use a drawknife, securely clamp the wood to be planed. Place the blade on the edge to be cut, and tilt the handles up to adjust the angle and depth of the cut. Holding it with both hands, draw the knife toward you, making successive cuts until the desired depth or shape is reached. See ill.

Drawknife

draw loom. Weaving. A **multiharness** loom with an extra set of pattern harnesses behind the regular or front counterbalanced harnesses which control the **ground weave.** In a simple version, the pattern harnesses are controlled by separate sets of hand levers or pulleys hanging in front of the **loom,** while the ground harnesses are controlled by **treadle**s. In a more complex version, and the one that was used before **power loom**s came on the scene, two persons operated the loom—one of them a "draw boy" who stood at the side of the loom and raised the pattern harnesses in accordance with the designer's plan. The draw loom goes back in the Middle East to shortly after the time of Christ. Individually operated **heddle**s replaced the pattern harnesses in the seventeenth century. They were weighted and strung up through a perforated board (comber board). This same sort of arrangement led to the invention of the **Jacquard loom** in France about 1804, which replaced the draw loom. However, the simple draw loom with the front pulleys is still occasionally found in some handweaving schools, and in the Finnish and Swedish countryside, where handwoven patterned **damask**s are still made.

drawn-thread border. Embroidery. A decorative border used in **whitework** and **counted-thread embroidery.** It must be worked on linen, and is the basis for other drawn-thread borders, **hemstitching,** and **needleweaving.**

Work a band of **buttonhole stitch**es (loops facing in) the width of the border. Work another band at the other end. Next, carefully cut each horizontal thread in a straight line (at arrows), close to the band of buttonhole stitches. Repeat this on the other end. Draw out the threads, one by one, until the border is composed of only vertical threads.

The horizontal threads are secured at the base with hemstitching. Work **chain stitch,** buttonhole stitch, and needleweaving on threads, forming a pattern. See ill., next page. Also see **knotted ground and drawn thread border.**

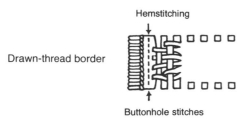

Drawn-thread border

Hemstitching

Buttonhole stitches

drawn-thread work. Embroidery. See **whitework.**

drawplate. Jewelry. A flat, generally hardened steel plate perforated with graduated openings through which wire is drawn (pulled) with **draw tongs** to reduce its dimension. Drawplates are available with round, square, oblong, triangular, half-round, or elliptical holes. Some have holes of several different shapes. See ill. Also see **annealing, drawing wire.**

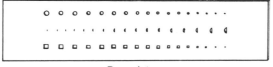

Drawplate

draw spike. Metalworking. See **sandcasting molding equipment.**

draw tongs. Jewelry. Heavy, square-jawed steel **tongs,** or **pliers,** with one end of the handle curved toward the jaws to give the hand added leverage when **drawing wire** through a **drawplate.** See ill.

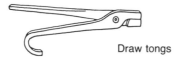

Draw tongs

draw trial. Ceramics. The process of gauging the **firing** temperature when it is unknown. Draw trials enable the potter to know the exact condition of the ware in the **kiln** at any time. Test pieces, identical in body and **glaze** to the **ware** being fired, are placed in the kiln in line with the sight hole. The test pieces have holes in the top to facilitate removal from the kiln with a long metal hook. Remove test pieces to check **shrinkage** and glaze conditions.

Dresden Plate. Quilts. (Also called Aster, Friendship Ring.) An ever-popular **quilt block** design made by a combination of **piecing** and **appliqué.** It originally took its

Dresden Plate

name from the custom of tracing around a plate to get the basic circle. The circle is then sliced into twenty radiating sections, and a smaller circle is cut out of the center. The pieces of assorted prints are joined, and the completed wheel design shape is appliquéd to a **background block.** See ill.

dress. Metalworking. See **dressing.**

dress cut. Leatherwork. See **ornamental cut.**

dressed length. Weaving. The length of the **warp** as it runs from the back **apron bar** to the front apron bar after **dressing the loom.** Also see **yarn calculation.**

dressed pillow. Lacemaking. A **pillow** is "dressed" when everything is in place, ready for the lacework: the **pattern** on the pillow, the **bobbin**s wound and hanging from **pin**s, the **cover cloth**s in place. See ill.

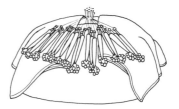

Dressed pillow

dressed size. Woodworking. See **wood.**

dresser. Metalworking. Woodworking. A cutting and sharpening tool used for **dressing** the grinding wheel on a bench grinder. It has a star-shaped wheel at one end and a handle on the other. Sticks with abrasive ends are also used in the same way. Also see **grinding tools.**

dress form. Stitchery. An adjustable torso-shaped form on a stand. The proportions can be changed and adjusted to correspond to the size of the person for whom a **garment** is being made so that the garment can be hung and fitted on the dress form.

dressing. Fabric Printing. See **size.**

dressing. Leatherwork. Woodworking. The process of finishing or rounding beveled strap and belt edges to prevent fraying.

In woodworking, dressing refers to the process of cutting or planing a clean edge, end, or surface on a rough piece of wood. Also see **bissonette edge tool, burnisher, edge cutter, wood** and **Leatherwork: Cutting and Edging Leather.**

dressing. Metalworking. The process of sharpening and shaping the edges of a **grinding wheel** on a **bench grinder** with a **dresser.** When the wheel becomes worn smooth and loses its grinding ability, dress the wheel by turning on the power and holding the dresser against the turning wheel. Move the dresser from side to side across the wheel edge while steadying it against the grinder tool rest. Press more firmly if there are many sparks. This process also straightens and balances the wheel. Wear goggles or a face shield while dressing. Also see **grinding tools.**

dressing doll. Toys. See **paper doll.**

dressing the distaff. Spinning. A preparation in **flax** spinning to permit the easy pulling out of the long flax fibers from the **distaff** without tangling. An ordinary distaff, or a lantern-shaped one, can be used. A small portion of the flax bundle, or strick, is attached to the waist of a seated spinner who has a cloth spread over her lap. In a series of fanlike motions with the hand, back and forth to the bundle of fibers and across the lap, the layers of flax fibers are spread out and crisscrossed gauzelike on the lap. This crisscrossing is important to permit the proper and easy drawing out of fibers from the distaff during spinning. The distaff is laid in the center of this fan shape of fibers and they are then rolled onto it and tied around with a crisscrossing ribbon. See ill.

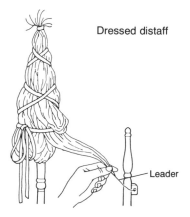

Dressed distaff

Leader

dressing the loom. Weaving. Preparation of the **warp** and the **loom** for weaving. This includes on a **harness loom** the following steps:

Getting the **warp specification**s through **yarn calculation**s.
Warping
Chaining
Spreading the warp
Beaming
Checking the **heddle**s on the **harness**es to see if there are a sufficient number on each harness and to place those heddles to be used in the center of each harness with the excess number evenly distributed on each side
Drawing-in
Sleying
Tying on or **lacing on** to the front **apron bar**
Doing the **tie-up** of the **treadles**
Gating
Checking the loom by opening the **plainweave shed**s for any quickly apparent errors in **threading** or sleying
Bobbin winding or winding on **filling** yarn onto **stick shuttle**s
Weaving in the **heading** and again checking for errors

The order of the above steps may differ according to which type of beaming procedure is being followed, but basically these are the steps that must be followed if one is to weave on any type of floor or table harness loom. The tie-up is of course omitted on **table looms.** The term "dressing the loom" is not usually applied to a **primitive loom.** However, in the case of a **frame, Navajo,** or **tapestry loom** dressing the loom would include warping the **continuous warp,** inserting the **shed stick,** preparing the **heddle cords** and **heddle bar,** and putting in a **chain spacer** or **twining** at the beginning point of the weaving. See ill.

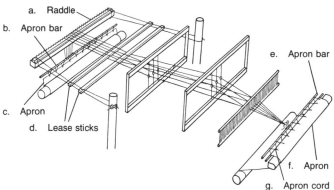

a. Raddle
b. Apron bar
c. Apron
d. Lease sticks
e. Apron bar
f. Apron
g. Apron cord

A loom dressed and ready for weaving the heading

dressing the wheel. Gemcutting. See **grinding wheel, wheel dresser.**

dressmakers' carbon. Batik and Tie-dye. Quilts. Stitchery. Toys. See **embroidery carbon paper.**

dressmakers' carbon paper. Crewel. Embroidery. A paper faced with a carbon preparation which makes it possible to transfer a design to a **fabric.** Most importantly, a design transferred in this manner will completely wash out of the fabric. Ordinary carbon paper will ruin a piece because it cannot be washed out and will run into the yarns. It is available in a variety of colors and can be purchased in almost any sewing or notions shop. Also see **Crewel: Transferring a Design.**

dressmakers' chalk. Crewel. Embroidery. A chalk that comes in a variety of colors, used to draw a design freehand on the **background fabric.** The chalk is easily removed by washing the finished piece. Also see **Crewel: Transferring a Design.**

dressmakers' pin. Stitchery. A needlelike metal shaft having no eye, but a head instead. It is used to temporarily fasten pieces of **fabric**s together. Pins are available in different sizes.

dress the figure. Puppets. To dress or clothe the **marionette.** This sometimes involves making special openings in the garments so that the **strings** can move freely. The figure must be dressed before the final stringing of the marionette can proceed. Also see **framework** and **Puppets: Dressing the Marionette.**

driers. See **vehicle.**

drift. Metalworking. See **blacksmithing tools.**

drift. Woodworking. When drilling a hole, the natural tendency for the drill bit to wander unless a starting or centering hole is **punch**ed first. This is particularly noticeable when drilling **hardwood**s.

drifting. Metalworking. See **blacksmithing techniques.**

drill. Beadwork. For drilling holes for stringing in beadmaking, a Yankee-type ratchet drill or an Archimedian fretwork drill is recommended.

drill. Jewelry. See **hand drill** and **Jewelry: Tools and Materials.**

drill. Plastics. Woodworking. See **drilling tools.**

drill bit. Woodworking. Drill bits used in woodworking are of two types: those for use in a **brace,** and those for use in other **drilling tools** such as a **hand drill,** a **portable electric drill,** or a **drill press.** Brace bits have a tapered, squared tip on the shank designed to be held in the brace **chuck** and are turned at slow speeds; the others have plain cylindrical shanks and are used at high speeds.

SQUARED-SHANK BITS   Auger bit. A spiraled tool used exclusively on woods. It has a spur on the cutting end that pulls the bit into the wood; a thin layer of wood is sliced away on each turn. It is used with a brace to bore holes ¼–2″ in diameter; bit sizes indicate diameter in sixteenths of an inch (e.g., number 7 indicates a bit diameter of 7/16″). Standard lengths range from 7 to 10″, but for heavy construction they come up to 24″ long (**a.**).

To sharpen the auger bit, with the bit clamped in a vertical position, take a small square **file** and, from behind one of the cutting edges, lightly file the inside edge of the nib until a fine **burr** develops on its outer edge (**b.**). File the inside cutting edge from behind in the same manner. In both procedures, be careful to maintain the original angles or **bevel.** Do the outside cutting edge of the bit in the same way. Finish sharpening by removing all burrs with a light pass of the file or the sharp edge of an **oilstone.**

Expansion bit. Used with a brace, it has a feed screw like the auger bit but has an adjustable cutter and gauge for boring holes of various diameters from ⅞ to 3″ (**c.**).

Forstner bit. Used to bore holes in wood that might be splintered by an auger bit. Because it does not have a feed screw, it is possible to drill almost through wood without breaking through to the other side (**d.**).

Screwdriver bits are also available.

SQUARED- OR ROUND-SHANK BITS   **Countersink** bits come with both shank types. There are several kinds, all designed to produce the conical hole needed for **countersinking** the screw head; the most common is the rose countersink, a fluted cone (**e.**).

ROUND-SHANK BITS   *Twist bit.* Similar to a metal-drilling twist bit in shape and size, but with a cutting angle of 40–45° for wood. Ideal cutting speeds vary with size—the larger the bit, the slower the speed. Run a 1″ bit at 700 rpm, ½″ at 2300 rpm, and ¼″ at 3800 rpm in **softwoods;** run all bits faster in **hardwoods.**

Spade bit (also called speed bore or flat power bit). Used for boring holes ⅜–1½″ with a power drill; it is good for fast, rough construction work (**f.**).

Hole saw. Used for high-speed boring of very large holes; it is best used in a drill press for accuracy. Basically it is a cylindrical saw clamped to a centering twist bit; it comes in various sizes for holes from ½ to 2½″ in diameter (**g.**).

Pilot bit. A single bit that drills the lead hole, shank hole, and countersink hole in one operation; numbered sizes fit corresponding wood screws (**h.**). See ill. Also see **Woodworking: Screwing, Boring, and Drilling.**

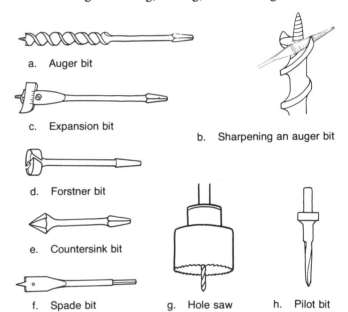

a. Auger bit

b. Sharpening an auger bit

c. Expansion bit

d. Forstner bit

e. Countersink bit

f. Spade bit

g. Hole saw

h. Pilot bit

drilling. Amber Carving. See **needle drill** and **Amber Carving: Carving.**

drilling. Glasswork. Small holes can be drilled in glass, albeit with some difficulty. Ordinarily this requires the use of a drill press, the chuck of which is filled with a piece of copper tubing of the size of hole desired. The end of the tubing is sawed off perfectly square and then sanded or polished while the tubing is turning in the chuck. The area of the glass where the hole is to be drilled is surrounded with a doughnut-shaped dam of wax or modeling clay and filled with a pool of abrasive **slurry** (diamond dust or silicon carbide grit in kerosene or light oil being most often used). The pool of slurry and the glass are placed on the bed of the drill press, and the copper tubing is lowered onto the required point while turning at medium speed. Periodically it is necessary to raise the spindle of the drill press to allow fresh abrasive to come between the copper-tubing tool and the glass, and then the tube is again lowered into the work. Proceeding in this fashion, in time, the hole will be worn into the glass. It is important to use minimum pressure as the tool reaches the end of its cut to avoid breaking the glass away on the opposite face.

drilling. Jet Carving. See **bowdrill** and **Jet Carving: Cutting.**

drilling. Jewelry. The piercing of metal with a drill. There are several tools with which holes can be drilled. A **hand drill** is the least expensive and the most awkward to use. A **flexible shaft machine** can be used easily and efficiently. A **drill press** can handle a wide variety of sizes of drill bits and perform with absolute precision.

The metal must always be **center punch**ed prior to drilling or the drill will slip and skid over the surface of the metal, causing deep scratching. Support the metal on a wood surface, preferably on a plank of scrap wood. If you drilled directly on your **bench,** the top of it would soon be badly marred.

The tip of the drill should be lubricated with **beeswax.** Touch the tip of the drill against the wax when the drill is turning. The heat from drilling will melt the wax and lubricate the metal and the drill. If the metal is a heavy gauge you may need to lubricate the drill more than once to prevent it from burning out. If using a flexible shaft machine, make sure the drill is straight up and down and not canted. Use a firm steady pressure. Hold on to the metal tightly with your free hand. The drill can get hold of the metal and spin it around frantically, which can be dangerous. If it does get loose, simply get your hand quickly away, and take your foot from the rheostat. Also see **automatic center punch.**

drilling. Metalworking. Plastics. See **Metalworking: Drilling; Plastics: Drilling.**

drilling. Shell Carving. See **needle drill** and **Shell Carving: Tools and Preparation.**

drilling. Woodworking. The process of making a hole ¼″ or smaller. (Drilling larger holes is called **boring,** although the process is the same.) Holes of this size are made to accept small **screws, dowels,** and other fastening devices, or **plugs.** Drilling is done with the aid of a **drill bit** turned with a **drilling tool.** Also see **Woodworking: Boring and Drilling.**

drilling jig. Gemcutting. (Also called sphere jig.) A device for holding round gem material so that a hole can be pierced in it. The gem rests on the V groove of the drilling jig which is placed on the drilling table of a drill press. The hole is bored into the gem with a drill bit and **abrasive.** After the stone is drilled halfway through, it is turned around, so that the hole fits over a guide pin, and the drilling is completed from the other side. This method prevents chipping caused by the bit breaking through the gem material.

Before the hole is drilled the stone is spotted; a shallow concavity is ground with a ball-shaped **carving point** slightly larger than the bit to be used at the spot where the hole is desired. Spotting prevents chipping when starting a hole.

Bits are usually solid metal, although very small gauge

tube drills can be used. For soft materials hardened steel or tungsten carbide-tipped bits are effective. Holes may be drilled in most materials by using a finishing nail and silicon abrasive (100 grit) with oil. A slight bend is given to the end of the nail to impart a wobble when it rotates for the bit's clearance into the hole.

Diamond drills are the best. Some have one or two whole **crystals,** attached to the end of a metal rod. The diamonds used for drilling are flawed crystals called borts or carbonados. Smaller diamond drills have bits made by **sintering** or **charging** needles with diamond powder.

Drilling with diamond bits should be done under water at a speed of 3000 rpm for holes 3 mm in diameter. Holes ½ mm to 1 mm should be be bored with speeds up to 5000 rpm. The drill is raised and lowered as it runs to allow fresh grit and coolant to get into the hole and to keep the bit from overheating the gem. See ill. Also see **sphere** and **Gemcutting: Tools and Materials.**

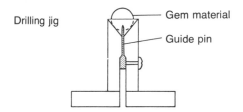

Drilling jig — Gem material — Guide pin

drilling tools. Metalworking. Plastics. Woodworking. Devices or machines used to produce holes in metal, wood, or plastics and similar materials, usually by turning a **drill bit** or boring attachment. The simpler ones are hand-powered and are widely used in woodworking; electric drilling tools, often used for wood, are necessary for metalworking and most plastics applications.

HAND-POWERED DRILLING TOOLS *Bradawl.* An **awl**-type tool with a chisel point used to make lead holes for small **screws** and for larger drills. It is used like an awl with the chisel edge in the direction of the grain.

Gimlet. A T-shaped tool with a spiraled bit used like a corkscrew for hand-turning small holes.

Push drill. A **screwdriver**-shaped tool with a spiraled shank that converts a pushing motion to the rotation needed to drill with the **gouge**-shaped bit. It may be a separate tool, but often an **automatic screwdriver** has interchangeable screwdriver and drill bits.

Hand drill. The most common hand-powered wood drill (also usable on plastics). It works like an old-fashioned eggbeater; the hand crank is turned, and the gears turn the **chuck.** The end handle is used to adjust the drilling pressure and angle. The standard chuck will accept **twist drill bits** up to ¼″ in diameter.

Brace. The tool to turn squared-shank drill bits for boring larger holes in wood. The hand-tightened chuck often has a built-in ratchet that permits boring in tight corners with only a partial sweep of the U-shaped handle. Pressure and angle are contolled by pressing on the doorknoblike handle with one hand while cranking with the other. Besides **auger, Forstner, expansion,** and **countersink** bits, other bits are available with the special shank needed for the brace—screwdriver bits and, infrequently, twist drill bits.

ELECTRIC DRILLING TOOLS *Portable electric drill.* A versatile hand-held tool available in a range of sizes: a quarter-inch drill accepts only drill bits ¼″ or smaller; more powerful drills will accept 3″ or ½″ bits. The motor may be single-speed or variable-speed. Various attachments are available for **sanding, grinding, polishing,** etc.

Drill press. A motor-driven stationary tool mounted on a column above an adjustable table. It is especially useful where precision drilling is necessary; it accepts twist bits, countersinks, **circle cutters, router**ing bits, and attachments for sanding, etc. The speed of the tool is usually adjustable, either through a variable-speed motor or a system of pulleys and belts. The drill press is a potentially dangerous tool and should not be used without expert instruction. See ill. Also see **Metalworking: Drilling, Woodworking: Boring and Drilling.**

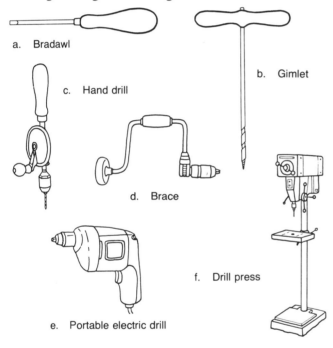

a. Bradawl
b. Gimlet
c. Hand drill
d. Brace
e. Portable electric drill
f. Drill press

drill press. Jewelry. An electrically powered machine used for **drilling, tapping,** reaming, boring, and countersinking metal. Available in both floor and bench models,

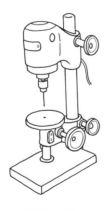

Drill press

the size is determined by the largest diameter of material through which the press will drill. See ill.

drill press. Metalworking. Plastics. Woodworking. See **drilling tools.**

drill stop. Woodworking. See **gauge.**

D-ring. Leatherwork. See **belt findings.**

drip-dry. Batik and Tie-dye. Quilts. Stitchery. A **fabric finish** that enables a wet fabric to dry smoothly. The fabric must be hung while it is wet, without wringing, so that the water runs and drips out of it. Most **wash-and-wear** garments specify a drip-dry method. This finish usually makes a fabric resistant to dye and therefore unsuitable for **batik** or **tie-dye.** Drip-dry fabrics are preferred by some stitchers for banners, panels, and **appliqué quilts** as they require no ironing when washed or dampened.

drip-feed. Ceramics. See **oil-fired kiln.**

dripping. Candlemaking. If the **wick** is unable to produce a flame large enough to consume all the melted wax, the excess overflows and drips down the sides. Dripping can be caused by either an inferior grade of wax or too small a wick. Also see **Candlemaking: Selecting the Wax, Selecting the Wick.**

drive punch. Leatherwork. (Also called hand punch.) Any of various punching tools used to punch out different sized and shaped holes. The **punch**es are held vertically on the spot to be punched, then struck firmly with a mallet. A drive punch is especially useful for areas where a **revolving punch** won't reach.

TYPES OF DRIVE PUNCHES Four-in-one round-hole drive punch. An especially good tool for punching evenly spaced lacing holes. As you punch along a marked sewing or lacing line, the first hole of the punch is placed in the last hole of the previous series of holes to assure even spacing.

Oval drive punch. For oval holes and oblong slots of various sizes for attaching bag straps and buckles.

Round drive punch (also called single drive punch). For round holes of various sizes ¹/₁₆−1″) in heavy leather. See ill. Also see **arch punch, nailhead punch, oblong punch, strap end punch,** and **Leatherwork: Care and Maintenance, Sewing Leather, Tools and Materials.**

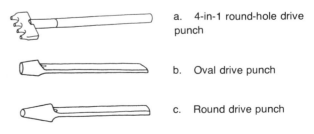

a. 4-in-1 round-hole drive punch
b. Oval drive punch
c. Round drive punch

drive wheel. Spinning. See **driving wheel.**

driving band. Spinning. A cord running from the **wheel** of a **spinning wheel** to the **spindle pulley** and **bobbin pulley.** It is found on all types of spinning wheels. It sets the pulleys in motion when the wheel is turning. Also see **flyer assembly, treadle wheel, wool wheel.**

driving pulley. Spinning. See **spindle pulley.**

driving wheel. Spinning. (Also called drive wheel.) The large wheel mounted on **upright** supports on a **spinning wheel.** A **driving band** goes around it and to the pulleys. When the wheel is rotated by hand, as in a **wool wheel,** the driving band turns the **spindle pulley** which then turns the **spindle.** In a **treadle wheel,** the wheel is turned by foot **treadle,** and the driving band revolves both the spindle pulley and the **bobbin pulley,** so that the **flyer** and **bobbin** rotate.

drop. Puppets. A part of the scenery, including the **backdrop** and the **topdrop,** which may be lowered or hung from above the stage.

dropped stitch. Knitting. A stitch that has inadvertently slipped off the knitting needle. It usually takes only a row or two to discover the small gap left behind by a dropped stitch. To pick up the stitch, knit to the point of the dropped stitch in the row you are working on. Then use a small crochet hook to work the dropped stitch up to the present row, catching the stitch one row at a time. When you reach the top row, slip the recovered stitch back onto the left-hand needle.

A dropped **knit** stitch is picked up by inserting the crochet hook into the loose stitch front to back, catching the strand above, and pulling it through (**a.**).

A dropped **purl** stitch is picked up by reinserting the crochet hook through the loose stitch front to back after each stitch has been reworked (**b.**). See ill.

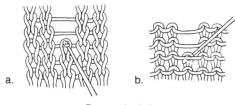

a.   b.

Dropped stitch

dropped stitch pattern. Knitting. See **Knitting: Stitches and Patterns.**

drop spindle. Spinning. See **spindle** and **Spinning: Using a Drop Spindle.**

dross. Jewelry. Metalworking. The metal oxides that form on, or are present in, molten metal.

dross. Stained Glass. A sulphurlike layer, that develops on molten lead. The dross is skimmed off the top and discarded when the lead is being melted to make **lead came** before it is poured into molds. Also see **casting lead came.**

druggist's lead plaster. Metalworking. See **wax.**

drum. Toys. A hollow cylinder with skin or parchment stretched over the ends that when struck produces a sound. It is primarily a rhythm instrument. It is a **musical toy** that in some cases can be regarded as a **noisemaker.** Simple drums can be made for children from oatmeal boxes or from wood, as in the **drum box.**

drum box. Toys. A homemade toy **drum** based on the same principles as some old hollow log drums or box drums from Africa or India. Four boards of identical size are used for the sides of the box. There are no top and bottom boards. Lines are sawed into each of the four sides to form a letter H, a letter Z, a half-circle, or some similar shape. The drum is beat with any makeshift drumstick. Tones are controlled by the density of the drumstick and by the shapes and sizes of the cuts. If a hollow log is available, it can be used similarly.

Drummer. Batik and Tie-dye. See **household dye.**

drum sander. Gemcutting. See **flat, sanding.**

Drunkard's Path. Quilts. A **quilt block** consisting of a **square** with a quarter-circle **pieced** into one corner. Usually, two contrasting colors are used and the color placement is alternated in sewing. This block can be put together to form numerous different **block patterns.** Among the most common are: Algonquin Trail, Around the World, Country Husband, **Falling Timbers, Fans, Fool's Puzzle, Lone Ring, Robbing Peter to Pay Paul, Rocky Road to California, Rocky Road to Dublin, Trip around the World, Vine of Friendship,** and **Wonder of the World.**

The name "Drunkard's Path" is sometimes also used to refer to any of the numerous Robbing Peter to Pay Paul arrangements. See ill.

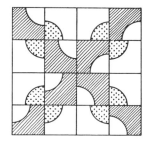

Drunkard's Path

dry brush texture. Papercrafts. A painting technique used for finishing **paper sculpture, papier mâché,** or other surfaces to produce a textured, grained effect. A coarse, dry brush is touched in thick paint and drawn lightly across the surface, leaving an irregular, linear texture similar to wood graining or an antiqued wooden surface.

dry cleaning. Batik and Tie-dye. Quilts. Stitchery. A cleaning process for removing stains and dirt from fabric in which naphtha or benzine are the **solvent**s usually substituted for water in commercial use. Carbon tetrachloride is used in some home dry cleaning. It is used on nonwashable fabrics or on those fabrics in which shrinking or fading may be problems. It is sometimes used to remove the final traces of **wax** from **batik** fabrics. Unless very strong special batik **dye**s have been used it may be unwise to wash the finished batik or **tie-dye** articles; therefore, dry cleaning is recommended. Most dry cleaning is done commercially, although various home **dry-cleaning** agents and dry cleaning sprays are available. Directions must always be carefully read and followed in using any cleaning solvents.

dry dusting. China and Glass Painting. See **dusting.**

dry foot. Ceramics. The clean, unglazed bottom of glazed ware that enables the piece to sit directly on the kiln shelf. Stilts or other supports are not needed. Also see **kiln furniture.**

dry fresco. See **fresco.**

drying. Woodworking. See **wood.**

dry point. Plastics. See **intaglio process.**

dry strength. Ceramics. The degree of strength in a **clay body** when it is air-dry. All clays vary in amount of dry strength. Clays used in children's classes, such as new clay (which is not to be fired) is high in dry strength. **Porcelain** has low or weak dry strength, and secondary clay can be as hard when air-dry as it is after **bisque firing,** i.e., high in dry strength.

Ducali binding. Bookbinding. The Venetian bindings of the decrees of the Doges, which are decorated with a combination of Oriental and Western motifs.

duck. Quilts. Stitchery. Any of several durable, closely woven, **plain-weave fabric**s which are strong and somewhat lighter weight than **canvas.** They are usually **cotton,** or a combination of cotton with other **fibers,** and have a good **body** or stiffness. Because of its weight it makes a good **background** fabric for **machine appliqué** or for large-scale **appliqué** work. Duck may be extremely heavy and firm (used in tents and awnings) or it may be soft and pliable. While the term is sometimes used interchangeably with canvas, duck rarely is as stiff or as heavy.

Duck Puddle. Quilts. See **Bear's Paw.**

Duck's-Foot-in-the-Mud. Quilts. See **Bear's Paw.**

Duco cement. Toys. A brand name of a transparent household **glue** made especially for use on china and glass, but that also works well for bonding wood, paper, and leather. It dries clear, is waterproof, and remains flexible, not brittle, when dry. It sets in five minutes or less, taking longer for a thicker application. Care should be taken in using it, as it cannot be removed from the hands by washing in water; **acetone** or nail polish remover is required. Duco cement cannot be used on Styrofoam because it eats or melts it away. The cement is flammable. Caution must be exercised to avoid breathing the fumes and getting any of the cement in the eyes, where it can cause extreme irritation. Duco cement is available in squeeze tubes so that it can be applied directly without handling. Testor's and

Elmer's are other commonly known brand names for this hobby glue. **Airplane glue** is a similar **adhesive.**

ductility. Jewelry. Metalworking. The ability of a metal to be hammered very thin or to be drawn into fine wire. Also see **drawing wire.**

dukagang. Weaving. (Also written dukagång.) A **laid-in** pattern **weave** most prominently found in Sweden whose characteristic is long, vertical bars. The weave is also used in many other countries, but has been developed most by the Swedish weavers. The word *dukagång,* translated literally in Swedish, means paths in the cloth, and refers to the straight bars. It comes in two versions. There is half dukagång, in which just the design is in the vertical bar pattern, and there is whole dukagång, in which both the design and the background are in vertical bars, with the difference between the two distinguished by color. Traditionally, dukagång is woven on the wrong side with the back facing the weaver, and the weaver checking the design on the right side with the use of a hand mirror. Working on the back side allows for a neater insertion of the **pattern yarn.** Half dukagång on the face, or right side, has the pattern **filling** yarn over three **warp end**s and under one in only the sections where the design is to be placed. The vertical bar develops because in every **pick** of pattern it is the same three over, one under that the pattern filling interlaces. Weaving it wrong side up, the pattern thread goes under three, over one. After every pattern shot, there are **binder** picks in **plain weave** that hold the pattern together. Whole dukagång is woven with the background as well as the pattern in a three down, one up vertical rib. Between each row is the plainweave binder thread. Since the whole fabric is made of the thicker pattern yarn plus the finer plainweave yarn, the end result is a heavier fabric than that achieved by half dukagång. The vertical bars lend themselves to stylized versions of trees, buildings, flowers, birds, or animals and to abstract or geometric patterns. Dukagång is used in wall hangings, pillows, towels, tablecloths, purses, and bags, aprons, and as border trim in apparel wear such as blouses, jackets, and skirts. Sometimes dukagång is referred to as a **pickup weave,** because on a two-shed or **frame loom** the warp threads are picked up by hand to obtain the pattern **shed.**

dulling. Stained Glass. After a piece of **glass** is cut, the edge is extremely sharp. To dull this edge, scrape a piece of scrap glass at right angles along the sharp edge. Also see **lamination, vitrified silicone stone** and **Stained Glass: Cutting Glass.**

dullness. Candlemaking. The lack of sheen on the surface of a molded candle. Waxed carton container molds tend to impart a relatively dull surface because the coating of the container is itself partially transferred or melted onto the candle by the heat of the hot poured wax. **Buffing** with a nylon stocking should help to reduce the dullness and increase the sheen.

dummy warp. Weaving. See **tying-on.**

dungaree. Stitchery. A coarse weave **cotton fabric** of blue, used for sailor's work uniforms. It is similar to **denim.**

dunting. Ceramics. The cracking of fired ware while cooling in the **kiln.** It is the result of opening the flues too quickly. Dunting is common in **bisque** ware and dense clay bodies. Also see **clay body,** firing, and **Ceramics: Firing.**

Dunton's Tinner's Fluid. Metalworking. A mild solution of **hydrochloric acid** used to clean **tin.**

duo-canvas. Needlepoint. See **canvas.**

duplicate stitch. Knitting. See **Swiss darning.**

durable press. Batik and Tie-dye. Stitchery. A process for treating fabrics to make them **wrinkle resistant,** stable to shrinkage, and to aid in retaining desired creases and shaping. The materials are chemically treated, then the finished garments or articles are heat cured. When sold as yardage, a durable press material is precured. Since durable press weakens **cotton fibers** it is almost always applied to a **blend** of cotton and **polyester** or to polyester and acrylic. Articles made from fabric treated by durable press need no ironing and **seam**s stay flat.

Durable press fabrics are not suitable for tie-dye or **batik** since this finish prohibits the absorption of dye. To remove the **finish,** the procedure used is the same as that described under **wash-and-wear.**

Durand, Victor. Stained Glass. See **Stained Glass.**

dusting. China and Glass Painting. A technique used in china painting to deepen colors and add to the luster of the surface by rubbing dry powder on **glaze color** over a still-damp painted surface.

Paint the background color and let the piece stand for several hours until just moist enough to hold the powdered color. Rub the powdered color onto the tacky surface with cotton. When there are several colors, use a different piece of cotton for each, beginning with the lightest color and blending the colors with light strokes. Blow or shake to remove all loose powdered color and set aside to dry. The piece is then ready for **firing.** If after firing the color is not deep enough, repeat the process.

If desired, dust powdered paint over a dry, painted surface so that only a small amount of color will adhere, to tint the background slightly. This method is called dry dusting.

Metallic color may also be used for dusting. For a rich **gold,** paint the surface with liquid bright gold, then dust with a finely powdered gold. For **silver,** paint the background with liquid bright silver, then dust with powdered platinum. Other metallic colors in powdered form can be dusted over gold or silver paint for various metallic effects.

dusting. Enameling. See **Enameling: Basic Operations.**

dust mask. Plastics. A mask covering the nose and mouth, used to filter out small particles. Use it when dry sanding or grinding plastics. To filter out chemicals or organic compounds, use a chemical mask.

dust ruffle. Quilts. A ruffle used around the bottom edge of a bed to cover the space between a coverlet or quilt and the floor. The dust ruffle is often attached to a piece of **muslin** the same size as the mattress. The muslin is then placed under the mattress, and the ruffle drops over the springs or frame to the floor. A quilt or bedspread then covers the top of the mattress and the sides of the bed down to the dust ruffle. Because the head of the bed is ordinarily against the wall, the dust ruffle is usually used only at the sides and foot of the bed.

Dusty Miller. Quilts. A **pieced block** design reminiscent of the waterwheel or mill wheel, after which it takes its name. The millstones ground the grains into flour, accounting for the miller's being dusty!

Dutch doll. Toys. See **penny wooden doll.**

Dutch knitting. Knitting. Old Dutch knitting patterns that were influenced by traditional quilting designs. These patterns are simple, based on squares and diamonds, and produce an **embossed knitting** effect.

Dutch leaf. Metalworking. See **brass.**

Dutchman's Puzzle. Quilts. A variation of the basic **pieced four-patch** design. See ill. Also see **Windmill.**

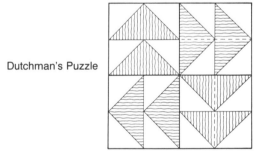

Dutchman's Puzzle

Dutch raising. Metalworking. See **raising technique.**

Dutch Rose. Quilts. (Also called Broken Star, Carpenter's Wheel, Double Star.) A **pieced** eight-pointed star that spreads out to become a sixteen-pointed star. It fits into an **octagon**al **block.** It may also be worked large so that what would ordinarily be a block design becomes the single **over-all** design of a **quilt top.** In this case the octagon is pieced at the corners to produce a square. It is a variation of **Star-within-Star.** Also see **eight-pointed Star, star patterns.**

Dutch tile. Quilts. (Also called Arabian Star.) A **pieced** six-pointed star joined to fit into a **hexagon**al block. Also see **star patterns.**

dye. A colorant used to stain or impart a particular color to fabric, wood, etc. Dyes generally differ from **pigments** in that the coloring material soaks into the object to be dyed rather than remaining on the surface.

dye. Batik and Tie-dye. Dyeing. Fabric Printing. Soluble substances that penetrate into the fiber and color it by a chemical reaction or heat. A dye substance must be reduced to very small particles from whatever its original source, so that it can be thoroughly dissolved in water, or some other carrier, in order to penetrate the fiber. Undissolved particles, though microscopic, stay on the outside of the fiber, and the color then has poor **colorfast**ness and tends toward **crocking**. Fibers have affinity for certain dyes, but will not absorb others. Some are absorbed directly into the fiber on contact and are called **direct dyes** or substantive dyes. **Adjective dye**s need a **mordant** that has an affinity for both the **dyestuff** and the fibers. In synthetic fibers, dyes are often developed chemically in the fiber. Dyes are classified first into whether they are **natural dye**s or **synthetic dye**s, and then according to their chemical composition and method of application. Some categories familiar to home dyers, in addition to direct and adjective dyes, are **acid dye**s, **vat dye**s, **aniline dye**s, and **procion dye**s.

Dye (also called dyestuff) is mixed with a **thickener** or an **emulsion** binder to make a **dye paste** for fabric printing. Well-known brand names of dyes are Helizarin, **Procion**, and Tinolite. Dyes are available from crafts stores or dye supply houses. Instructions for use are obtainable with the dyes. Fabrics printed with dye paste must be given a heat treatment to be colorfast. Also see **dyebath, fixation,** and **Batik and Tie-dye: Dyes; Dyeing: Synthetic Dyes, Natural Dyes; Fabric Printing: Finishing.**

dye. Beadwork. Papercrafts. Powdered or liquid household dye is used to color beads and papercraft designs. Also see **dip-dye design** and **Beadmaking: Coloring and Finishing.**

dye. Egg Decorating. Any type of dye, such as household fabric dye or even diluted paint, may be used to decorate eggshells that have been emptied of their contents. However, eggs that are to be eaten should be decorated with nontoxic vegetable dyes such as food coloring (commercial vegetable dyes available for decorating Easter eggs) or carefully chosen **natural dyes** (some may be poisonous) obtained by boiling natural materials with water.

dye. Featherwork. See **Featherwork: Dyeing Feathers.**

dye. Leatherwork. Liquid leather dyes, which penetrate fibers to permanently color leather, are available as water-soluble or as oil or spirit solvent dyes. Many colors are available and they may be mixed to produce new colors. Paler shades may be made by mixing with a dye reducer. Also see **Leatherwork: Dyeing and Coloring Leather, Tools and Materials.**

dye. Plastics. See **colorant.**

dyebath. Batik and Tie-dye. Dyeing. Fabric Printing. The mixture of **dye, assistant,** and **dye liquor** or water into

which fabric is immersed for the dyeing process. If the water evaporates during heating, more must be added to the dyebath so that there is always enough water for the **fleece** yarn or fabric to stay covered and not be crowded. An enamel pan is used to hold the dyebath for fabric printing.

dyed binding thread. Batik and Tie-dye. Strings, cords, or threads that have been precolored by **dyes** and that are then used as tying or **binding materials** in the **tie-dye** process. The threads or cords must be capable of absorbing dye, so cotton strings and strips of fabric will work well. They are immersed in a **dyebath** and dried without rinsing. When used for binding, color will transfer from the strings to the **tied fabric** in the dyeing process. Also see **clump tying.**

dyed-in-the-wool. Dyeing. Stitchery. Also known as dyed-in-the-fleece or fleece dyeing and is synonymous with **stock dyeing.** It is the dyeing of unspun wool after shearing and scouring but before blending, oiling, mixing, or carding. The unspun wool should be placed in a laundry net bag or cheesecloth bag that is large enough so as not to cramp the fleece and retard penetration. The bag will facilitate lifting the fleece in and out of the **dyebath.** Heather or tweed mixtures are obtained by dyeing various colors in-the-wool and then carding and spinning together. Also see **piece-dyed, yarn, yarn-dyed.**

dyed style. Fabric Printing. A term used to describe an ancient technique in which fabric was dyed after a pattern was applied to **fabric** with a thickened solution of **mordant.** Where the **dye** and mordant combined, a colorfast print was formed in the fiber. When the fabric was rinsed, the dye came away from areas to which the mordant had not been applied, leaving them uncolored. **Madder** is the traditional dye used in dyed style. Also see **mordant dye printing.**

DYEING

Dyeing is the process of coloring fibers, yarns, fabrics, or other substances so that the coloring matter becomes an integral part of what is being dyed rather than a surface coating applied to it. As a craft it is usually practiced by people involved in other fiber crafts who dye their yarns and fabrics because of expediency, or a desire to obtain certain unique colors, or who, as a normal course of events, spin and dye all their own yarn. It would be rare to find a dye craftsperson whose sole purpose in dyeing was to become a good dyer. In most cases, it is a step in producing an article of crochet, knitting, hooking, braiding, macramé, appliqué, or quilting or weaving.

However, in the days of pre-**synthetic dye**s, a dyer was considered a fine craftsman solely for his ability to get good colors and, as such, belonged to guilds as important as other craft guilds. The dyer's talent and worth was recognized even after synthetic dyes became an established fact and, today, the availability of so many different and perfect colors is due to the constant experimentation and upgrading within the commercial dye profession.

If substances are available in so many colors, why do craftspeople dye their own? One reason—although oversimplified—is that to a fiber craftsperson, there are never enough colors or the right ones. Also, there is the need to redye (**top-dyeing**) left-over yarns or fabrics. There are also certain effects such as **dip dyeing** and **spot dyeing** that can be best obtained by home methods. When it comes to dyeing with natural substances there is a softness and subtlety of color that can never be achieved in a commercial dyehouse. Further, there is the main joy of dyeing which allows for the working with colors and seeing it emerge before one's eyes; texture is important in the finished textile, although it is often color that has the greater and final appeal.

There are two types of **dye**s and dyeing, natural and synthetic—both are home dyeing procedures because they are easy to practice in a kitchen. The chemical properties of a **dyestuff** should be considered because these properties determine the dye's penetration into the fiber and **colorfast** qualities. The desire for the best penetration possible will dictate which procedure of dyeing is followed. In using natural dyestuffs, these chemical properties also determine the **mordant** that is used and thereby the resulting color. With **natural dye**s, the chemistry is affected by climatic and geographic differences as well as the time of year that the natural substance was picked, general handling procedures, and storage.

The emphasis in home dyeing is definitely on natural dyestuffs that are not used in the commercial dyeing industry; these natural dyestuffs are decidedly unreliable when compared with synthetic dyes as no two batches of a natural dye will give the same results. This is so since natural substances cannot have a standardized chemistry as is the case with synthetic dyes. This variability in natural dyestuffs has added to the appeal for its use and has given rise to books of **dye recipe**s which give the natural dyestuffs an individual stamp not found in their man-made counterparts.

Dyeing is an ancient art without a definite history as to what was the first **dye plant,** and where it was first used. However, it is known that dyeing was practiced in Persia, China, and India thousands of years before the birth of Christ. In all likelihood, dyes were brought to Egypt—from the East—by Phoenician traders. The Egyptian tombs at Thebes have revealed the earliest dyed textiles; they date back to 3500 B.C. and show traces of blue **indigo** dye. Further, it is thought that **mordanting** was practiced in India around 2000 B.C.—perhaps possibly earlier in Egypt.

Indigo was an important dye in the ancient world; the Romans had it imported at great expense from India, naming it Indicum (after the location of its source). Its name went through a number of changes, being known as indican and then indigo. The plant, *Indigoferae*, has a yellow juice that oxidizes to a permanent blue upon exposure to air. Centuries later, **woad** would be used as a substitute for indigo in Western Europe. The blue color produced by woad was much like that of indigo, but not as brilliant.

For yellow, the Greeks and Romans used **saffron,** which was obtained from the dried pistils of the saffron crocus. Bulbs of the plant were supposedly introduced into Western Europe by returning Crusaders, although today, this

crocus is very rare, even in the Middle East where it had first originated.

A rich carmine red called kermes was considered to be the best red in ancient times; it was prepared from dried insects (**cochineal**) which fed on the Kermes oak. **Madder** was the other important red dye; this was made from the ground-up root of dyer's madder or dyer's weed. Other important natural dyes included **weld** and safflower. However, the most famous and most prized color was Tyrian purple. This was produced in Phoenicia where it was obtained from the secretions of a Mediterranean mollusk. Cloth colored with this valuable dye was worth its weight in gold. The Phoenicians ruled the dye industry from the fifteenth century B.C. until 638 A.D. when conquering armies destroyed the dyeworks. The Phoenician and Alexandrian merchants were instrumental in bringing many dyestuffs into Greece. From there the dyestuffs, their cultivation, preparation, and dyeing methods slowly found their way into Western Europe via Italy.

By the fourteenth century A.D., dyeing was greatly stimulated in Western Europe by the introduction of a purple dye called orchil. It was a **lichen dye** made from several varieties of the Rocella lichens gathered from rocks along the Mediterranean coast. Orchil had been used by the Phoenicians as an underdye for fabric to be dyed with tyrian. The knowledge of using orchil as a dye found its way to Northern Italy, which had become the dyeing center of Europe.

In 1540, Giovanni Ventur Rosetti of Venice published the first edition of his *Plictho del Arti de Tentori*, a book that contained 217 dye recipes and the techniques used for dyeing cloth and leather in Europe and the Near East. It remained the best source of information and instruction on dyeing for 200 years.

During the sixteenth century, dyeing experienced a great change in Europe. Spanish explorers brought back a number of dyestuffs such as cochineal, **logwood,** and **fustic** from the Americas. Cochineal became the first product to be exported from the New World to the Old. As it was much cheaper and a more brilliant red dye than kermes, cochineal soon replaced kermes as a source for a red dye. Some years later, **tin** was used as a mordant with cochineal; the result was an extremely bright scarlet. This color was to be used at the Gobelins tapestry dyehouse in Paris in 1630.

Logwood was brought to Europe from Mexico, Central America, and the West Indies. It produced shades of gray, brown, black, blue, and purple. Fustic, another tree-derived dye, came from Brazil and parts of Central America; it produced a deep yellow.

In an attempt to maintain high standards, the countries of Europe enacted rather severe laws with regard to the "proper" use of dyes. In France, legislation was enacted establishing a distinction between dyers using fast dyes (called greater dyes) and **fugitive dye**s (called lesser dyes). The fast dyers were prohibited to have in their possession dyestuffs used by the fugitive dyers. Other countries were quick to follow the example of France. Between the sixteenth and eighteenth centuries, France and the Netherlands were reputed to have the best dyers. Many books and papers were written on the subject of dyeing. However, very few secrets—if any—were ever revealed; the books often contained rather vague instructions as to weights and measures, etc.,—one such treatise instructs the dyer to "use as much water as will fill a hat."

The home dyer in the colonies had to rely on whatever dyestuffs were available from peddlers or such stores as existed. Most of these dyestuffs were imported from London and were quite expensive. Native American dyestuffs were first shipped off to England and then "reimported" back to America at exorbitant prices. Indigo, the most popular dyestuff, was for a time grown on Southern plantations. However, the planters soon turned their attention to the cultivation of rice and cotton, which proved to be more profitable. Due to the expense and the unpredictable availability of European dyestuffs, the home dyer looked to what was available on her homestead and found plants, trees, nuts, and berries that served as substitutes. Through experimentation, dye recipes were formulated that yielded many browns, yellows, and olives. Good reds and blues were still dependent on imported dyestuff.

Professional colonial dyers were usually apprenticed to European-trained dyers or trained in Europe. Consequently, the professional dyer depended solely on imported dyestuffs. Although there were constant efforts at improvement and much research, there were no discoveries of any import until the nineteenth century. Then, in 1856, in England, Sir William Henry Perkin accidentally developed the first synthetic dye, mauve, from an organic compound derived from coal tar.

From that time on, discovery followed discovery in quick succession so that eventually the art of natural dyeing came to an end except for areas in Africa, Central and South America, isolated pockets in Europe, and in the mountain and rural areas of the southeastern United States.

The new mauve and other synthetic dyes did not reach the United States for several years; eventually America became dependent on Germany for synthetic dyes. During World War I this supply was cut off and temporarily there was a demand for natural dyes. The synthetic dyes that were manufactured in the United States during World War I were not washfast. Experimentation and the use of German dye patents improved dye quality; American firms were able to supply 60% of the dye used for home dyeing. Protective tariffs were levied on imported dyes to aid the fledgling American dye industry. During World War II, German dye patents were confiscated and distributed to leading American dye firms. In time, the United States became an independent producer of versatile household dyes that are available in a wide variety of colors and that are used to dye both natural and synthetic fibers. During the 1960s, a revival of natural dyeing began and old colonial recipes were resurrected and improved upon. Although many natural dyers prefer to pick their dyestuff in the fields and woods themselves, natural dyestuffs are available in select craft stores.

CLASSIFICATION **Dye**s or **dyestuff**s are classified in a number of ways. Within a category, the dyes are neither equally **colorfast,** nor fast under the same conditions. Fibers have affinity for certain dyes but will not absorb others, so that successful dyeing depends upon the selection of the right dye for a particular fiber used.

Perhaps the broadest classification is according to source or origin. Dyestuffs are either natural or synthetic. Under **natural dye**s there are animal, vegetable, lichen, and mineral categories. **Synthetic dye**s are those made from aniline (coal tar) or other sources. Artificial, chemical, commercial, and **household dye**s are common names for synthetic dyes, although natural dyes are also available commercially.

Another method of classification is according to chemical, commercial, and **household dye**s are common names for synthetic dyes, although natural dyes are also available mordant. Mordant dyes (also called **adjective dye,** chrome dye, or indirect dye) need preliminary or subsequent treatment of the fiber with a **mordant** to render the color fast. **Direct dye**s (also called substantive dye or **non-mordant dye**) color fibers placed directly in the **dyebath.** The chemical category has many other dye classifications—some that are more complex structures and are for dyeing both natural and synthetic fibers and others that are exclusively for special synthetic fibers.

The degree of colorfastness is another classifying method; a dye is broadly considered as either a fast or **fugitive dye.** Other dye classification systems categorize according to affinity for certain fibers (for example, **procion dye**s), methods of application (**cold-water dye**s), dependence upon auxiliary agents (**acid dye**s), and reactions with mordants. Many categories overlap and a dye can fit into more than one category.

Dye categories illustrate the various methods of dyeing; some are absorbed directly by the fiber, some require a **mordant** or assistant which has an affinity for both the dye and the fiber, and some are developed in the fiber by chemical treatments usually through the use of some acid agent. There are thousands of dye recipes as well as types of dyes available, and based on both of these a number of dyeing procedures have been developed. The dye and procedure used depends on the color and the colorfast quality desired. The procedure can usually be reduced to three steps: 1) preparing the fibers so that the dye will penetrate them; 2) impregnating the fibers with the dye; 3) fixing the dye, which is an optional step depending on the type of dyestuff used. There are variables within these steps due to the chemical properties of the dyestuff.

Color loss such as through **bleeding** or **crocking** occurs when the dye is not combined chemically with the fiber. Salt and vinegar are used in the **exhaust bath** for home dyes, but there is no available research to conclusively support the theory that they will absolutely set color. If a color is not fast in a yarn or fabric when the dye process is finished it may not be possible to make it fast. When dyeing, the dyestuff must be in small particles which can be thoroughly dissolved in water. Undissolved particles stay on the outside of the fiber and the color then has poor fastness.

When attempting color matching or a particular shade it should be remembered that most colors dry lighter than the shade they are when wet. Only deep values will show little difference between wet and dry. To test for the right shade, a small piece of fabric or yarn should be dipped into the dye bath, remain there for a short period, and then be blotted out between paper towels or an old cloth towel until dry. The test piece can also be cut off from the larger amount still in the dyebath. The resulting blotted color should be the color of the material when thoroughly dyed and dried. Also see **vat dye.**

SYNTHETIC DYES **Synthetic dyes** in the form of **commercial** or **household dyes** can be purchased at any store. They all come with specific directions and are easy to handle, but the success of the project depends on following the directions carefully and in having selected the proper dye for a particular fiber. Prepackaged household dyes usually contain an amount sufficient to color one pound of white cloth or yarn to the intensity of the color indicated.

Equipment needed for various steps in dyeing

Soft water. A few drops of **acetic acid** or vinegar will sometimes soften hard water.

A large pan to be used as the dyepot. It can be enamel, stainless steel, or copper and should be deep enough to hold the material covered by water.

Wooden or glass rods, sticks, or spoons for lifting and stirring the **dyebath.** Home items like wooden chopsticks or metal egg tongs can also be used.

Plastic or enamel buckets or pans to use if a sink is not handy for **wetting-out** the material before dyeing and for rinsing after dyeing.

A 2–4 cup glass measuring pitcher in which to mix the dye concentrate before adding it to the water in the dyebath.

Soap flakes for the wetting-out process that takes place before the material is dyed. This helps the dye to penetrate further into the fiber.

Table salt to be used at the end of the dyeing time to exhaust the dyebath.

Glass jars with lids to save the remaining dyebath or dye concentrate for another time.

Cloth-lined rubber gloves as a protection against hot water and the dye.

Scale to weigh the dry materials to be dyed and the dyestuff.

Thermometer to test water temperature.

In preparing the fibers so the dye will penetrate them, the material—yarn or fabric—is first submerged in a wetting-out bath of warm water and soap flakes and soaked in this bath for about ten minutes or until saturated. The wetting-out bath will also clean the material so that yarn oil or fabric sizing and surface dirt will be removed. The yarn should be in loosely tied skeins to prevent tangling, but not tight enough to prevent dye penetration. The material is rinsed to remove most of the soap.

While the material is soaking the dye solution is prepared in a measuring cup and the water for the dyebath is simmering on the stove. There should be enough water in the bath to completely cover the fabric. The dye is dissolved in the measuring cup with hot water. This can be a paste mixture or a watery solution depending on the dye and dye recipe used. Directions on dye packages should be followed carefully.

Some of the dye concentrate is poured into the bath and a test is made. If the color does not come out dark enough, pour in more dye concentrate or redye the material several times until the desired shade is achieved. At this point, remove the material from the wetting-out bath, wring out excess water, and put into the dyebath. Stir the dyebath to ensure even penetration. Keep the dyebath at a simmering point until the desired shade is achieved or until the bath is exhausted. Follow the timing and temperature instructions packaged with each dye.

Add a tablespoon of common salt to the dyebath (synthetic dyes only) at the end of the dyeing period to exhaust whatever dye is left in the bath. Adding salt to a fresh dyebath may cause uneven dyeing.

When the desired color is achieved the material is lifted from the dyebath, drained, and transferred to the rinsing bath where it is rinsed until the water runs clear. The first rinse bath should be only slightly cooler than the dyebath; subsequent baths are going to be cooler in degrees; the last rinse can be quite cool. After the final rinsing, the material is squeezed (not wrung) dry and then hung in a shaded airy place to dry completely. The dyed material can also be spun dry in an automatic washer and then hung out to dry.

Any leftover dye is saved by storing in large covered containers. The concentrate goes into small, labeled containers. For future dyeings, records should be noted as to amounts of dyestuff, water, etc., with attached pieces of the material before and after dyeing.

NATURAL DYES With certain additions and modifications the preceding instructions can be followed when dyeing with natural substances such as roots, lichens, buds, flowers, leaves, fruits, berries, seeds, skins, nuts, twigs, branches, and tree bark (It is important to remember that although these are natural elements they also have chemical properties and, with almost all of them, it is the function of the **mordant** to work with these properties in uniting color to fiber.) Many **natural dyes** change color according to the mordant used. **Mordanting** controls the colors of dyes and makes them permanent and can be done before, during, or after dyeing. Some of the more common mordants are **alum, acetic acid, caustic soda, chrome, copperas, tannin,** and **tin.** They can be purchased in drugstores, chemical supply houses, and dye supply stores.

Natural Dye Sources

Dye Plant	Color	Mordant
alder (bark)	brown	alum
bayberry (leaves)	grayish olive	alum
blackberry (shoots)	gray to black	copperas
black walnut (hulls)	dark brown	no mordant
bloodroot (roots)	reddish orange	alum
coreopsis (flowers)	burnt orange	chrome
dahlia (flowers)	rusty red	chrome
elderberry (berries)	violet to purple	chrome
fig (leaves)	yellow	tin
goldenrod (flowers)	yellowish tan	alum
grapes (leaves)	lavender to purple	alum
larkspur (petals)	blue	alum

(continued)

Natural Dye Sources (*continued*)

lily-of-the-valley		
(spring leaves)	yellowish green	chrome
marigold (flowers)	yellow	alum
nettle (whole plant)	greenish yellow	alum
onion (dried skins)	burnt orange	alum
privet (clippings)	yellow	alum
sassafras (bark)	rosy tan	alum
scotch broom		
(flowering branches)	yellowish gold	chrome
sumac (berries)	yellowish tan	alum

Most natural dyes give their best result in either a neutral (soft) or slightly acid bath—as opposed to an alkaline one. Litmus paper is used to test the acidity or alkalinity of the water; the paper turns red for acids and blue for alkalines. A slightly acid bath is preferred for wool. Adding a little vinegar to the dyebath ensures the acid quality.

There is more uncertainty with natural dyes than with synthetic ones. It is not easy to repeat the same color at another dyeing and it is also a game of chance to arrive at the exact color desired in the first place. There are many environmental variables that determine the strength and quality of the resulting color from a **dye plant.** Dye materials should be gathered when the part of the plant to be used as the dyestuff has just about reached its maturity. Dig roots in late summer or early autumn; pick flowers either as they are about to come into full bloom, or after long exposure to sunlight; gather berries and fruit when fully ripened, and collect nuts after they have fallen to the ground. Leaves and bark are best collected in the spring, although bark will give good color if cut off in the late fall and winter. Dye plants that are not used fresh should be cleaned of foreign matter, air dried, and crushed. Air dry the substance either by hanging in a dry barn, garage, or basement, or by placing on a wire mesh in the sunlight. Elevate the mesh to insure complete air circulation. Store completely dry dye plants in a paper bag or any porous sack. Berries can be quick-frozen after they are washed and stored in plastic bags or containers. Some flowers and leaves can also be frozen. Dye materials such as onion skins, coffee, tea, and cinnamon bark can be found in the kitchen, while dried **cochineal, indigo,** and **madder** are available from botanical supply houses and some yarn supply stores.

Steep the **dyestuff** in a small amount of water in an enamel bowl from two hours to overnight. Boil the **dye liquor** for half an hour to two hours depending on the particular dyestuff. Strain the liquid through cheesecloth; save the remaining pulp, wrap in several layers of cheesecloth, cover with water and boil again for about an hour. Add about four gallons of water to the liquid dyestuff and heat until lukewarm. This **dyebath** is sufficient for the dyeing of one pound of material and it requires about one pound of dry natural dye plant to make the dyestuff.

The material to be dyed is put into the dyebath. If mordanting occurs prior to the dyebath, the last rinse should be in water the same temperature as the dyebath. If mordanting follows dyeing, the material is placed in the **wetting-out** bath prior to immersion in the dyebath; the last rinse of the wetting-out bath is in lukewarm water the

same temperature as the dyebath. The dyebath is brought to a simmer and maintained for the time indicated in the **dye recipe.** The material is removed from the dyebath when dyeing is complete and rinsed first in a hot bath. Subsequent rinse baths are cooler by degrees until the water runs clear. The material is dried in the shade after squeezing out the excess water.

MORDANTING Almost all **natural dye**s require that the fiber to be dyed is mordanted either before, during, or after dyeing. **Mordanting** before dyeing is probably the most popular method as this allows for fibers to be prepared in different **mordant**s and yet put in the same **dyebath** so that it is possible for a variety of colors and shades to come from one dyebath.

Different fibers, because of their individual properties, are mordanted in different ways and with different mordants. Wool and silk both hold chemicals in the fiber while cotton and linen do not absorb mordants as easily. These vegetable fibers do, however, combine well with tannic acid (see **tannin**) which can be used either as a mordant or as an agent for fixing mordants in the fiber.

For mordanting wool before dyeing, it should first be thoroughly washed of its grease using a mild soap. It will perhaps take several washes to remove the natural grease and dirt. Wool should be treated gently in all phases of the mordanting and dyeing. The water temperature must remain constant to prevent matting and shrinkage. Simmer wool gently rather than boiling vigorously and avoid undue agitation—only that which is necessary to open up the fiber so that the mordant and dye penetration is even. Never wring or twist wool.

Mordant the wool after washing; should the wool dry between these baths, it must be wetted-out before immersion in the mordant. The mordant bath is a solution of 4 ounces of **alum** (less for lighter shades) and one ounce of cream of tartar to 4–4½ gallons of soft water at a warm temperature. The alum and cream of tartar are first dissolved in a small amount of hot water and then added to the warm water. Place the wool in the warm mordant, bring to a simmer slowly and maintain for an hour, stirring occasionally. Thoroughly rinse the wool after mordanting; immerse in the dyebath or dry for future use. Other mordants can be used as well as alum; the mordant used will have an effect on the color obtained from the dyestuff. (See chart in **Dyeing: Natural Dyes.**)

Raw silk is mordanted similarly to wool except that a waxy gum is present on silk fibers and should be boiled off in strong soap suds. Wash spun silk in a warm, soapy bath in order to remove the gum.

Cotton, linen, and rayon are mordanted in three solutions. Prior to mordanting, boil or wash vegetable fibers in a hot, soapy bath using soft water for at least a half hour. Rinse at the same temperature as the wash bath; subsequent rinses are cooler; squeeze out excess water.

The first solution for mordanting contains 4 ounces of alum and 1 ounce of washing soda in 4 gallons of water; boil the fiber for one hour and keep overnight in the mordant. Squeeze out mordant and put in a bath of one ounce tannic acid and 4½ gallons of water (second mordant solution). Simmer slightly for one hour; cool and let stand overnight. Remove the fiber, rinse slightly, and repeat the first mordant solution. Rinse on the third day, squeeze out the excess water, and immerse in the dyebath.

There are many mordant recipe variations—especially if mordanting occurs during or after the dyebath. Certain varieties of lichens do not require a mordant, but a little **acetic acid** will help to induce dyeing.

METHODS OF DYEING   A fabric can be dyed at any stage of production: when the yarn is still in fiber form up until when the fabric is a completed piece. At which stage the dyeing is done will not affect the **colorfast**ness as it will penetration of the **dye** into the fiber. The most thorough dye penetration occurs in yarn that is **dyed-in-the-wool** or "in-the-fleece" (the commercial name being **stock dyeing,** i.e., the dyeing of the basic stock of which a yarn is composed). This type of dyeing colors the individual fibers before blending, carding, or spinning. **Stock dyeing** is done for all fibers, whereas fiber dyeing in the home is most commonly done to wool only. **Solution dyeing** is a somewhat comparable method used only for man-made fibers.

The next level of dye penetration is yarn or **skein dyeing,** which is the dyeing of the already spun yarn wound in skein form. This is the usual method of dyeing since yarn is easier to handle than fiber or a large finished piece of fabric. **Warp dyeing** is an extended form of skein dyeing; the warp chain is larger, heavier, and more compact than the skein. Therefore, more care must be taken that dye penetration is as thorough as possible.

The last level of dye penetration is **piece dyeing,** the dyeing of fabrics "in-the-piece," i.e., after weaving, knitting, or some other manner of construction. It is not uncommon to find undyed spots caused by the closeness of the yarns and insufficient agitation.

In addition to the above methods, there is **top-dyeing,** used when certain colors or a degree of colorfastness is desired, and **simultaneous dyeing,** which is required with some types of natural dyes. Top-dyeing can also relate many different colors by dyeing them in a single dyebath together. Although a relationship between the various colors will exist, there may or may not be a substantial change to the colors.

If the desired effect is to remove color rather than add it, **bleaching** is required. Soaking and washing the dyed fiber in a detergent or a household bleach is the simplest method of lightening the color of a dyed yarn. Simmer the bleaching bath on the stove to enhance the action of some detergents.

While the above methods deal with dyeing the total fiber, yarn, or cloth, there are other types of dyeing that produce patterns and mottled or multicolored effects. **Ikat** or tie-dyeing is noted for its planned and sometimes elaborate patterns in warp and weft. Tie-dyeing can also be quite random so that no definite pattern exists. **Spot dyeing** also produces irregular mottled or spotted effects which can be obtained by either applying the dye to a wetted-out surface or by sprinkling a concentrated dye solution on the yarn or fabric at various intervals when immersed in a dyebath. Not stirring yarn or fabric in a crowded dyebath will produce soft shadings of one color.

Dip dyeing renders a multicolored effect that can be composed of either shades of one color or several different colors depending on how many various dyebaths the yarn or cloth is dipped into.

dyeing. Basketry. See **Basketry: Dyeing and Coloring.**

dyeing. Candlemaking. See **coloring.**

dyeing. Leatherwork. See **Leatherwork: Dyeing and Coloring Leather.**

dye liquor. Batik and Tie-dye. The liquid—usually water—to which the **pasted** dyestuff is added. The **assistants** are added to the dye liquor before the dyestuff is stirred in. The resultant mixture is the **dyebath.** Sometimes the term dye liquor is used interchangeably with dyebath.

dye liquor. Dyeing. (Also called dye ooze.) A concentrated dye solution made by boiling or dissolving the **dyestuff** in water.

dye ooze. Dyeing. See **dye liquor.**

dye paste. Fabric Printing. (Also called printing paste.) A paste mixture in which **dye,** chemicals (**assistant** or **mordant**), and **thickener** or emulsion binder are combined in order to be applied to definite design areas of the **fabric.** Thus, the dye is contained within desired design areas and doesn't bleed into the background areas. There are various recipes for pastes, available with the dyes from craft stores or dye supply houses. Recipes vary with the printing technique, type of fabric, type of dye, and so on. Experiments must be made on scrap fabric to find the best consistency for the printing to be done. The paste should be as thin as possible but shouldn't run beyond the edges of the design. If the paste is too thick, excess dye may collect on the surface and then run into background areas during **fixation.** Generally, thin fabrics need a slightly thinner paste than thick fabrics. In traditional recipes, all the dry ingredients are weighed or measured in dry form and prepared individually, and the thickener is mixed to a paste. Then the powdered dye is dissolved in water in a glass bowl and stirred until the mixture is the consistency of cream. Finally, all the ingredients are combined until the desired thickness is obtained. In an **emulsion,** the dye is mixed with the emulsion binder and kept in airtight jars. Fabrics printed with dye paste must receive a fixation treatment for **fastness.**

dye penetration. Batik and Tie-dye. The degree to which a **dye** penetrates the individual **fibers** of a **fabric** in the dyeing process. Also, the degree to which dye penetrates areas of the fabric, especially in **tie-dye.** In the latter, **mordants** used on the tied fabric increase the receptivity of fibers for dye, thereby increasing penetration. In tie-dye the dye penetration should be thorough in the loose or untied areas and minimal or absent in the tied portions. In **batik** the dye penetration should be absent in the **wax-resist** areas, although there is penetration of the **fractures** that creates the **crackle** pattern.

Several factors will affect the degree of dye penetration:

the type of fiber being dyed, the weight or bulk of the fabric, the thoroughness of the **waxing** or tying, and the length of time the material is left in the **dyebath.**

Starching, **sizing,** and water-repellent or stain-repellent **finish**es will affect the fabric's ability to take dye. To prepare these fabrics for better penetration, use a **finish removal** technique.

dye plant. Dyeing. The natural growing substance that yields a dye that will color a fiber. In some cases the whole plant is used, but usually only some part of it will yield a color. It can be the root, flowers, branches, stigmas, leaves, stalks, bark, seeds, berries, or nuts. The dye plants vary in their dyeing ability according to different areas, different seasons, climate, and growing conditions. It is, therefore, wiser to dye the full amount of fiber necessary with the **dyestuff** from dye plants gathered at the same time, in the same locale, than attempt to match the color at some future dyeing. Most dye plants can be dried and stored, but there are some dye plants that give brighter colors when fresh. **Mordant**s are used with almost all the dye plants.

dye printing. Fabric Printing. (Also called local dyeing, pattern dyeing.) Any printing process that uses a **dye paste** as the color. Also see **mordant dye printing** and **Fabric Printing: Printing Techniques.**

dye recipes. Dyeing. Instructions on how to **mordant** and dye a fiber with a specific **natural dye.** Also included are directions on how to prepare the **dyestuff** from the natural source and, where necessary, tips on when to pick the **dye plant.** There are many books, old and new, that contain dye recipes—some of the more interesting ones coming down to us from colonial times when natural dyes were a part of most homemakers' lives. Following a recipe exactly does not assure that the specified color will ensue, since it is in the nature of natural dyes to be fickle. **Syn**thetic dye**s do not have recipes but are accompanied by manufacturer's instructions with each package.

dyer's weed. Dyeing. See **woad.**

dyestuff. Batik and Tie-dye. Dyeing. Any vegetable, animal, mineral, or chemical in liquid or powder form that will color a fiber. Before **synthetic dyes** were discovered in 1850, most dyestuffs were either animal or vegetable in origin. Today many dyestuffs are made from coal-tar preparations. Also see **dye, dyebath, paste.**

dyestuff. Fabric Printing. See **dye.**

dye vessel. Batik and Tie-dye. The container in which the **dyebath** is held for **fabric** dyeing. For hot or cold dyes any enamel, stainless steel, or galvanized ware can be used. If only cold dyes are being used any rustproof container other than aluminum is satisfactory. A washing machine or boiler is ideal for bulk dyeing. The dye vessel must be large enough to accommodate the **tied** or **wax**ed material easily so that it can move freely in the dyebath. Saucepans, bowls, basins, and buckets can be used as containers for hot or cold dyes. Plastic and glass can also be used for cold dyes.

dye wood. Batik and Tie-dye. Any wood that yields a coloring matter from which **dye**s can be made. The extracts from **logwood** and **fustic** are among the most commonly known.

Dylite. Plastics. See **foam.**

Dylon. Batik and Tie-dye. See **fiber-reactive dye, household dye** and **Batik and Tie-dye: Dyes.**

Dyplast. Plastics. See **foam.**

ear. Ceramics. See **Ceramics: Form.**

earth colors. Any color paint that uses pigments that occur naturally in the earth's crust. These pigments consist mainly in oxides of iron, such as sienna or umber. Earth color has come to mean any color from yellows to reds at medium **saturation** and medium **brightness**, regardless of the derivation of the pigment.

earthenware. Ceramics. Toys. Pottery that is made from coarse, porous, and low-firing clay. It is red or tan in color. Also see **all-bisque, bisque.**

earthenware clay. Ceramics. See **Ceramics: Clay.**

earthenware doll. Toys. One of the oldest kinds of dolls made. Before knowledge of making china reached Europe, the lower-fire **earthenware** was used. It was less durable than china but more easily produced. Some of the earliest dolls known were of earthenware, and one existing Greek doll from the fifth century B.C. is **joint**ed and has strings. Earthenware dolls were common during the 1800s. Also see **bisque doll, burnt clay.**

earthenware glaze. Ceramics. A **soft glaze** that matures below 1150° C. It is used to cover a porous body in order to prevent running of glaze during firing. **Soaking** is recommended in firing to improve body fit and quality of the glaze. These glazes are shiny and smooth, usually with a lead oxide base. This base gives a good white background for bright and clear colors. Also see **white lead.**

eastern oak. Woodworking. See **oak.**

ebony. Jewelry. A black hardwood with such a tight grain that it appears almost grainless. The very best, and blackest, is from Ceylon and Madagascar and is becoming difficult to find. Other ebonies have areas of light gray in them, which can sometimes be desirable. Ebony is slightly toxic. If any itching or rash appears when you're working with it you are probably sensitive to it. Because it is grainless and takes a high polish, ebony is a marvelous wood for making jewelry. It can be used just as is for **inlay** and **piqué work.**

ebony. Woodworking. An exotic, dense, durable **hardwood** used for **woodcarving,** fine **inlay,** and **marquetry.** Its color ranges from dark brown to the prized jet black. It is used in making piano keys and stringed-instrument parts.

eccentric axle. Toys. See **axle.**

Eccentric Star. Quilts. A **pieced block** of a square within a square within a square, surrounded by four eccentric blade shapes. It is an **all-over pattern.** The **set** of these blocks and the color arrangement are what distinguish Eccentric Star from **Churn Dash** and **Windmill.** This pattern is sometimes made using a single square in the center. When blocks of this pattern are set, an off-center star is formed.

eccentric weft. Weaving. A **tapestry** technique in which the **weft** or **filling** is not woven at a right angle to the **warp.** It can lie in curves or be put in obliquely. When beaten down firmly, as in **tapestry weave,** and used in quantity, a textured or bubbly three-dimensional surface results. It is found in the tapestry weaving from all countries in all eras, but never so much as in the Coptic tapestries from Egypt. Because the horizontal/vertical relationship between warp and filling has been deviated from, the pull on the warp threads may cause them to be "eccentric" also—a condition that is not apparent until the tapestry is taken off the loom. This, in turn, can result in an eccentric **selvage** that looks scalloped, as in a **wedge weave. Lazy lines** and **outlining** of diagonal or curved shapes belong to the eccentric weft category. Areas of eccentric weft can be woven in over areas of horizontal/vertical interlacing as long as the latter is built up so that the former can lie on a curve.

An eccentric warp, other than one that is pulled that way by the filling, is possible on a **frame loom** with nails, a **cardboard loom,** a **branch loom,** or a **hoop loom.** On all these looms it is possible to have the warp lie in diagonal lines.

ecclesiastical needlework. Stitchery. The use of stitchery, **appliqué,** and embroidery on the **fabric** articles used in religious services. While these have been predominantly traditional in design, some have been exceptionally modern, of which **vestment**s designed by the painter Henri Matisse are well known. Among the articles most likely to be embellished by stitchery for religious services are altarpieces, **banner**s, copes, Torah covers, and vestments.

economy stitch. Crewel. Embroidery. See **Roumanian stitch.**

EDC. Plastics. See **acrylic cement.**

Eddy kite. Kites. A variation of the **diamond kite**, invented by an American, William Eddy, in the late nineteenth century, in which the bowed cross **spar** is equal in length to the vertical **mast**. Also see **Kites: Construction.**

edge. Knitting. The beginning or ending of a row of knitting. Some methods for edges are: 1) work every edge stitch following the specific pattern; 2) slip the first stitch of every row; 3) slip the first and last stitch of every other row; 4) yo, k2tog, repeat at beginning of every row, continue pattern every row as indicated in directions. Also see **selvage.**

edge beveler. Leatherwork. See **common edge beveler, edge cutter,** and **Leatherwork: Tools and Materials.**

edge coloring. Bookbinding. The coloring of the edges of the leaves of a book for decorative purposes.

After clamping the book to prevent penetration or bleeding of the color onto the face of the leaves, powdered paint or poster color mixed with **paste** is applied to the edges with absorbent cotton. A speckled effect called **jaspering** is achieved through brushing the color on with a stiff brush through a screen.

edge creaser. Leatherwork. A finishing tool used to recess a line for decoration or stitching along the edge of moistened leather. Place the creaser along the edge with the creasing point in position. Push or pull it along, using the leather edge as a guide, sliding the creaser back and forth until the crease is deep enough. The creaser is available in several sizes; each creases a line a different distance from the edge. See ill. Also see **creasing, patent leather compass, stitching groover** and **Leatherwork: Creasing, Scoring and Folding Leather, Sewing Leather, Tools and Materials.**

Edge creaser

edge cutter. Leatherwork. (Also called edge beveler.) A tool with a U-shaped blade used for **dressing** and rounding off sharp edges of belts and straps on heavier leathers. The cutting is usually done on the **grain** side. The edge cutter is available in various sizes, usually numbered 1 to 5. The larger the size, the larger the size of bevel peeled off. Hold the edge cutter at about a 45° angle to the edge of the leather and push along the edge; maintain even tension, as a slice is pared off from the top edge. Also see **common edge beveler** and **Leatherwork: Cutting and Edging Leather.**

edge dye. Leatherwork. See **Leatherwork: Dyeing and Coloring Leather.**

edge glow. Plastics. See **light piping.**

edge lighting. Plastics. See **light piping.**

edger. Leatherwork. See **common edge beveler, edge cutter.**

edge slicker. Leatherwork. See **circle edge slicker.**

edge stitch. Leatherwork. Any stitch motif where the thread or lacing loops over the edges of the leather, as opposed to a line stitch. The effect is both functional (protecting the edges of the leather) and decorative. Also see **cross stitch, double buttonhole stitch, Florentine lacing, single buttonhole stitch, whipstitch.**

edge thickening. Jewelry. (Also called swaging, upsetting.) A forging process that thickens the edge of metal. Support the work on its edge at right angles to the surface of a **steel block.** Tap along the upper edge of the metal in light overlapping blows with the slightly curved surface of a **planishing hammer.** The metal will begin to flare out along the top and bottom edge simultaneously, although slightly more so along the top edge. If the work is a square or rectangle, turn to the next edge and continue working. If a circle, progress around the entire rim.

Do not use heavy pressure when hammering because it may cause the work to bend, especially if the metal is thin or pierced. Edge thickening requires a minimum of at least three complete passes with the hammer to have any visual effect. It can, however, be repeated many times to produce a larger flare. Thickening an edge not only produces a visual feeling of weight, but as the metal flares it is being compressed, strengthening the rim. If a great deal of hammering is done, **annealing** may become necessary, in which case remember to lighten the pressure of the hammer blows, as the metal will be soft again.

If opposite edges of a piece are not identical, the piece can be worked on a **sandbag.** Only the edge being struck will thicken. Also see **heading.**

edge thickening. Metalworking. See **raising technique.**

edge weld. Metalworking. See **weld.**

edging. Crochet. A series of crochet stitches worked in a pattern, along the edges of a completed item of crochet (or a noncrocheted item, such as a pillowcase, tablecloth, or cape) to form a border trim. **Shell stitch, cluster stitch, filet crochet,** and **picot** crochet can all be used as edgings. Also see **Crochet: Basic Stitches.**

edging. Stitchery. A material used in **binding** or **finishing** a **fabric.** Common edgings are **bias tape** or **woven binding.** Sometimes an edging may be purely decorative, as a **fringe** or **ball fringe.**

edging. Tatting. A narrow tatted strip of **lace,** one side of which is straight, the other scalloped, with motifs of **rings, chains,** or **scallops** decorated with **picots.** Sometimes a crocheted chain stitch is added to form the sewing edge, the straight edge of the edging. See ill. Also see **lace edging.**

Edging

a.   Rings   b.   Scallops

edging stitch. Rugmaking. A **stitch** providing a finished edge to an **embroidered rug.** Also see **blanket stitch, braid stitch.**

edible dough. Toys. Any batter used in **baker's art** to produce dough art that can be eaten. Most **cookie art** is edible, including gingerbread and other **dark doughs. Cookie boards** and cookie molds are used with edible doughs, including **spingerle, lebkuchen,** and **marzipan. Bread dough sculpture**s made from regular homemade bread dough are edible, but **baker's clay** varieties are not. Also see **inedible dough** and **Toys: Ephemeral Toys.**

edible toy. Toys. A toy that is made to be eaten, therefore an **ephemeral toy** and a temporary toy. The toy horse made of cheese from Poland, **chocolate rabbits** molded for Easter, and **gingerbread boy**s are all edible toys. Many products of the **baker's art** are made of **edible dough.**

educational toy. Toys. A toy in which learning is the goal or aim rather than a byproduct of the activity. The addition of letters and pictures to building **blocks** offers a good example of an attempt to make an educational toy of one that is already a **learning toy.** Toy sewing machines and typewriters are considered educational toys.

Both educational toys and **scientific toy**s are basically learning toys meant to involve mental exercise, in contrast to **action toy**s, which involve physical exercise. Educational toys do not necessarily involve learning on the part of the child, although they usually provide an incentive and always a potential to learn. Also see **alphabet blocks, crystal garden.**

efflorescence. Ceramics. A white surface scum due to excessive modeling or overhandling of red clay. The direct cause is due to the appearance of sulfates and carbonates of calcium, magnesium, and sodium in the body.

egg. Toys. A form used in toys throughout the world. It is part of the **chicken-and-egg** toy and the **nested egg.** Eggshells are also used in making **peep egg**s, similar to small **peep show**s. The insides are removed to make the **hollow egg. Sugar egg**s are formed in molds and used for traditional Easter decorations.

eggbeater hook. Rugmaking. See **speed hook.**

egg carton sculpture. Papercrafts. See **found objects.**

EGG DECORATING

Chicken eggs are generally used for decorating because they are so available. For best results the eggs should be emptied of their contents by blowing, then rinsed and dried before dyeing or decorating.

Allow eggs to reach room temperature before emptying them. Pierce a small hole at each end of the egg with a needle, rotating the needle to enlarge the holes slightly. The hole at one end should be a little larger than the other. Practice will help determine the size of hole necessary for

the operation. Ideally, the holes should be mere pin-pricks—hardly visible. Hold the egg over a bowl and blow into the smaller hole. It may be necessary to insert a long needle into the hole to break up the yolk sac; if it still does not empty out the other hole, make the holes slightly larger. Blow the contents of the egg into the bowl. Rinse the egg inside by sucking water into one hole of the shell from a saucer of water and rinsing the egg under running water. Blow out excess water and let the egg dry overnight. If the egg is spotted, soak it in a bowl of water with a few drops of bleach; then empty and dry overnight.

Egg decorating has a long tradition in just about every country, embracing many different techniques. Perhaps the best-known decorated eggs are the Ukrainian **Pysanky** eggs, which are done with a variation of the batik process, using wax lines and **dye** to apply intricate, multicolored patterns. Eggs may be painted or dyed If eggs are hard boiled, rather than blown and emptied, and to be eaten, only vegetable or **natural dye** should be used. To dye eggs, immerse them in a pan of hot dye until the desired shade is reached. Remove from the dye pan with a slotted spoon and allow them to dry on a wire rack. A glossy surface can be given to decorated eggs by rubbing on a bit of vegetable oil with paper towels.

To hang hollow decorated eggshells, thread a long length of thread through the holes of a button. Then thread a long needle with both thread ends and draw the needle through the egg, bringing both thread ends out at top. Put a dab of glue between the button and the egg and pull the button snugly up to the bottom of the egg. Tie a knot with the threads extending at the top of the egg to form a loop for hanging.

eggs. Découpage. Real eggs, blown first, or artificial eggs can be decorated with découpage. Real eggshells should be soaked in bleach and then dried before using. Also see **Découpage: Preparing the Surface.**

eggshell candle. Candlemaking. A candle formed by **molding** using a blown eggshell as the **mold.** The eggshell, with roughly a ½" opening at the wider end, should be rinsed with vinegar and water and then allowed to dry. **Wick** the shell before pouring by threading the wick through the blowing hole at the smaller end and then securing it with a stick across the wider open end. Place the egg in a small glass, wide end up, for **casting.** Allow the wax to harden, and then peel away the shell. See ill.

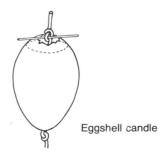

Eggshell candle

eggshell inlay. Découpage. Bits of broken eggshell may be adhered to the découpage surface as an embellishment, similar to **mother-of-pearl** work. The eggshells should be soaked in bleach and dried before using. After gluing to the surface in a mosaiclike design, clean off excess **glue** with vinegar. The eggshell pattern is then buried under layers of **varnish**.

egg-yolk painting. Toys. A decorative method used primarily in **cookie art** and other forms of the **baker's art.** As it is edible, it can be used on **edible doughs**. It consists of a small amount of egg yolk mixed with a few drops of water to which liquid **food coloring** is added. It can be painted by brush onto baked or unbaked dough and then set by heating or baking it in the oven. The colors are **glossy** and brilliant.

egote. Ceramics. See **throwing stick.**

Egyptian card weaving. Weaving. See **card weaving.**

Egyptian cotton. Quilts. Stitchery. A fine **cotton fabric** woven from the long-fibered Egyptian or **pima cotton.** The **cotton** plant is grown along the Nile Delta and is naturally a tan or brown color, so must be **bleached.**

Egyptian knot. Weaving. A **weft looping** or **wrapping** around a **warp end,** resulting in a knotted-weave effect in which only the **filling** is visible. Simple Egyptian knotting starts with the filling yarn going under and over the first warp end. Working from either direction, the filling yarn then goes under two warp ends, the one being wrapped and the next one to be wrapped. Egyptian knotting can be done in specific design areas, in rows running **selvage** to selvage, or as the entire woven piece. In any case, when the time comes to reverse direction and return to the opposite end, the outside warp end is wrapped twice, and then the filling goes under and to the next warp end. Tension should be regulated on the filling yarn if traditional Egyptian knotting is desired—this makes every knot or loop look like a little bead of yarn. The loops can also be pulled higher or made around a rod used as a **gauge** for a **pile** effect. When several rows of the tight loops follow one another, they produce warpwise ribs. This type of Egyptian knotting is done with a closed **shed,** but it can be done also with an open shed, and then every other end is wrapped in each row. With the closed shed there can be rows of **plain weave** between each row of knotting, or the fabric can be total knotting, depending on the height of the loops. The name Egyptian Knot is said to go back to the use of this wrapped loop in Egypt about 2000 years ago when it was used to make a woolen looped pile fabric. See ill.

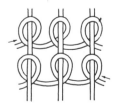

Egyptian knot

Egyptian paste. Ceramics. A self-glazing clay made by adding a soluble copper salt to the **clay body.** This soluble copper comes to the surface as a scum and produces an intense blue glaze upon firing. Also see **bead, efflorescence.**

Egyptian plaitwork. Weaving. See **sprang.**

Egyptian top. Toys. Any of several excavated spinning tops dated from 1250 B.C. made from wood, **composition,** or stone. These tops were highly decorated and glazed. Any **spin top** made similarly may be referred to as an Egyptian top.

Eight Hands Round. Quilts. A **block** for a **pieced quilt** consisting of 16 **patches.** Each patch is made up of smaller **two-patch** or **four-patch** designs. This is one of the few quilts named for a dance step: it derived its name from a popular square dance of colonial times.

eight-harness weaving. Weaving. See **multiharness.**

Eight-pointed Star. Quilts. A **pieced** star made up in a great variety of ways. In some, the star design is based on **diamond** shapes, and these patterns are known as **Broken Star, Carpenter's Wheel, Dutch Rose, LeMoyne Star,** and **Star of Bethlehem.** Other eight-pointed stars are made with triangles joined in **blocks,** as in Ohio Star, **Texas Lone Star,** and **Variable Star.** See ill. Also see **star patterns.**

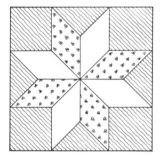

Eight-pointed Star

ejector head. Ceramics. A separate disk mounted in a shallow dish in the center of the **wheel head** which can be raised or ejected to remove a pot.

elastic. Toys. An expandable stretchy material usually woven in bands or strips and composed of **rubber** or rubberlike strands. It is used in various ways in toymaking, particularly to **join** parts where flexibility and movement are essential. It is also used to gather fabric by sewing it (in an extended, or stretched, state) directly to the material or by threading it through a channel. **Composition dolls** were sometimes strung or **joint**ed with elastic. Elastic is available in various widths by the yard in fabric and notions shops.

elastic memory. Plastics. See **plastic memory.**

elastolin. Toys. A molding material made of brown flour, water, and water-soluble **glue** developed in the eighteenth century for molding toy animals. Dried, the material resembles **bisque.** Its disadvantages are its susceptibility to moisture and its attraction for insects and vermin. **Papier-mâché** and **pulp mâché** proved more durable.

elastomer. Plastics. Any plastic material that returns to its original shape after being stretched may be a natural **polymer,** such as rubber, or a synthetic **thermoplastic,** such as **silicone** rubber. Elastomers can be used as **flexible mold-making** materials.

elbow string. Puppets. The **string** attached to the middle arm **joint** on a **marionette.** Much of the movement of the arm may be directed through this string, with the wrist tending to follow. A more common arrangement is to simply run a string to the hands, eliminating the elbow string. Only the most complex marionette has strings that run to both the elbows and wrists. Also see **arm string, hand string** and **Puppets: Stringing the Marionette.**

electrical porcelain. Ceramics. A variety of **porcelain** used for switches and insulators.

electric-arc welding. Metalworking. See **arc-welding equipment, welding.**

electric drill. Woodworking. See **drilling tools.**

electric engraving tool. Jewelry. (Also called automatic engraving tool.) A hand-held electric tool used to produce patterns, designs, and textures on metal. Although the metal is cut into, it is not truly "engraved." The action of an electric engraving tool is reciprocal, somewhat like that of a jackhammer. It can be adjusted, usually through a spring device, for either deep or shallow cuts. The lighter the cut, the straighter the line appears. The deeper cuts tend to be slightly more wiggly, due to the action of the tool. It takes some practice before good control is acquired. Most have a hardened steel tip, but diamond tips are usually available and these make deep cuts more smoothly. The vibrating quality of the machine can be put to use in a number of fashions. One way is to run the machine quickly over the surface of the metal to produce a dash pattern. Also see **graver, liner, scribe.**

electric kiln. Ceramics. A **kiln** that is heated by electric wires or rods. Also see **kiln furniture, kaolwool blanket.**

electric kiln. Stained Glass. See **kiln.**

electric pickler. Jewelry. An acid-proof pickler (made by Ferris), for use with **Spanex #2,** with an on-off cord switch and power indicator light. It maintains the **pickling** solution at 160–175° F, so that the solution cannot boil. Also see **pickling tongs.**

electric train. Toys. See **toy train.**

electrode. Metalworking. See **arc-welding equipment.**

electroetching. Enameling. A process similar to **electroforming** but with the poles of the electric charge reversed so that metal is removed from the work. Areas to be protected are coated with a stop-out such as **asphaltum,** which will resist the etching action. The work is attached to the **anode,** and a piece of **metal,** usually copper, is at-

tached to the cathode to receive the accumulation. Also see **camel's hair brush, electrolyte, electroplating, etching, resist.**

electroforming. Enameling. A process similar to **electroplating,** in which the deposits of **metal** are built up in bumpy nodules on the exposed metal areas of the enameled piece. Electroforming is used to add strength, emphasis, and texture. The **anode** of an electrical source is attached to a piece of copper to supply the metal. The work to be electroformed is attached to the **cathode** to receive the copper deposits. The electrodes are then suspended in **electrolyte.** A higher amperage gives a heavier, more granular deposit; lower amperage produces a smoother surface. Also see **electroetching.**

electrolyte. Ceramics. A substance added to **slip** which causes deflocculation.

electrolyte. Enameling. (Also called electrolytic solution.) A solution of sulfuric acid, metal salts, and water used as a medium to conduct the electric current between the **anode** and the **cathode** to aid in the transfer of metal in **electroetching, electroforming,** and **electroplating.** Electrolyte is stored in a glass, plastic, or ceramic container. The electrolyte should be agitated and kept at 70–80° F. Sediment should be strained and purity of ingredients maintained.

An electrolytic solution for copper is composed of 1 part copper sulfate dissolved in 4 parts distilled water, to which 4 parts of concentrated sulfuric acid are added.

electrolytic solution. Enameling. See **electrolyte.**

electroplating. Enameling. The process of depositing a thin coating of **metal** onto a metal surface using **electrolyte** and electric current. The article to be electroplated is attached to the **cathode** of a direct current; the metal used for plating is attached to the **anode.** These are then suspended in a container filled with electrolyte.

Current can be supplied by batteries, or by a rectifier such as a battery charger, which transforms alternating current to direct. A rheostat for varying the strength of the current and an ammeter for measuring the strength of the current are connected to the anode for control of the electroplating action. A condition called polarization, caused by the accumulation of gas bubbles on one or both electrodes, will slow down electrolytic action. To correct this, remove the pieces supplying and receiving the metal particles, rinse them with distilled water, and replace them.

Exposed **cloisonné** wires, the metal edges of bowls, and raised areas of **champlevé** work are often plated with gold or silver to enhance color and prevent tarnishing. This work is usually sent to a commercial plating company, with the desired color of gold specified. Enameled surfaces are not affected by electroplating unless they are pitted or broken, when the acid can penetrate. Metal surfaces should be polished before plating, as the tiniest scratches will show even after plating.

The deposit of metal is heaviest on the closest surfaces; that is, those facing the anode. The deposits will be smaller on depressed areas and greater on raised ones. The shape of the anode can be altered to provide the coverage desired; for example, a three-dimensional piece may be surrounded by a cylindrical anode or several anodes may be connected around the piece. Also see **camel's hair brush, electroetching, electroforming, mercury gilding, resist.**

electrostatic charge. Plastics. (Also called static electricity.) Electrification resulting from the contact of two dissimilar substances. Plastics become electrically charged by friction as in applying and removing **masking paper.** This electrostatic charge attracts dust to the plastic and will return after washing it with soap and water. Use a special antistatic coating to dissipate it. Also see **antistatic treatment** and **Plastics: Care, Cleaning, and Maintenance.**

electrum. Jewelry. A pale-yellow gold and silver **alloy** used by the ancient Greeks and Romans.

element. Basketry. The **rod** or **weaver** in a given weaving procedure. The weaver is the weaving or **active element;** the rod is the structural passive element.

element. Knitting. The material—yarn, thread, or cord—that is interlooped to form a knit fabric. Also see **Knitting: Materials.**

elephant ivory. Ivory and Bone Carving. Elephant ivory is obtained from the tusks, the two incisor teeth that protrude from the elephant's mouth. They are made up of concentric lozenge-shaped fibers. Average African tusks weigh about 60 pounds, but tusks weighing as much as 200 pounds have been recorded; the largest tusk recorded was over 12' long. Small tusks of 18 pounds or less are called scrivelloes. Elephant ivory has an internal hollow space that starts at the base of the tusk and extends roughly ⅓ the length of the tusk, but this and many other general descriptions of the nature of ivory vary with its provenance. Live ivory or ivory from a freshly killed animal is called green ivory; aged ivory is called seasoned ivory.

African elephants feed on tree roots and boughs and tend to use their left tusks for gathering them, thus making the left tusk shorter. Seldom if ever are a pair the same size.

Ivory from West Africa turns whiter with ages; after a time veins appear and slowly broaden until the ivory appears milky white all over. African ivory is among the most prized because it is straightest and longest. It was West African ivory that was used most commonly in the Middle Ages, and by the ivory carvers of **Dieppe.**

The Indian elephant is a smaller animal than the African, with smaller tusks; the longest tusk recorded was 9' long, and most of the large tusks weigh in the vicinity of 80—90 lbs. Indians believed elephants to be sacred and spared them, but burnt their tusks as offerings to the gods. Often female Indian elephants are tuskless. The Ceylonese elephant is believed to have been transplanted from India, and therefore is similar in characteristics. The ivory turns pink with age. Ivory from Thailand turns yellow with age. Also see **fossil ivory, Hornbill ivory, vegetable ivory.**

Elizabethan embroidery. Embroidery. (Also called Tudor embroidery.) The Elizabethan era (1558—1603) was one of the greatest periods for embroidery in England. Embroidery was practiced by men and women and by all classes of society. Among the most popular forms were embroidery in silk and gold (used extensively on costumes and often incorporated with jewels), black-and-gold embroidery (used for men's shirts, collars, cuffs, ruffs, and bed pillows), needlepoint (used for valances, hangings for four-poster beds, coverlets, and table carpets), and raised worked (later known as **stumpwork** and used for bodies, small bags, gauntlets for gloves, caps, and coifs).

In needlepoint, designs were often representational, as in tapestries adapted from well-known paintings, frequently with religious themes. In other forms of embroidery, designs were often geometric or an all-over tracery of trailing vines, reminiscent of wrought-iron patterns, interspersed with beautifully stylized flowers, animals, and birds. Also see **blackwork, counted thread embroidery, metallic thread embroidery.**

Elizabeth of Hardwick. Embroidery. Born in 1520, Bess of Hardwick's great interests were designing, building, and furnishing her houses, and planning and working embroideries for them. She and her husband, George Talbot, became the "custodians" of Mary, Queen of Scots at Queen Elizabeth's behest. And between 1574 and 1586 the two ladies produced several pieces of needlework together, the most notable being the "Oxburgh Hangings." They were worked in needlepoint and incorporated emblems and coats of arms.

It was customary to send Queen Elizabeth gifts of embroidery, especially as New Year's gifts, and those given by Bess of Hardwick or her family always found special favor with the queen.

elm. Woodworking. An extremely tough wood that is difficult to split but bends easily. It has good resistance to shock and fair resistance to decay, but shrinks excessively. Its color is light brown with traces of reddish-brown. It is used for boxes, barrels, kegs, bent parts of furniture, and posts. The bark of the elm was traditionally used for rope and chair bottoms. The American elm has become scarce because of Dutch elm disease.

Elmer's Glue All. Plastics. See **polyvinyl alcohol.**

embedment. Plastics. (Also called encapsulating, potting.) A process of enclosing an object in a **casting resin** or **acrylic lamination.** Embedment or encapsulating occur when a colorless transparent plastic is used to enhance visual display, whereas in potting protection and preservation, not transparency, are the main purposes. Also see **Plastics: Embedment.**

embossed knitting. Knitting. A knitting pattern that creates raised or embossed surfaces on the knit fabric. Embossed motifs are either "detached" or "attached," depending on the way they are knit. Detached motifs are knots, tufts, and **bobble**s. Attached embossed motifs are based on **increasing** and **decreasing** within a confined area. The embossed exchange principle is based on solid increasing and decreasing clusters. Also see **clustering** and **Knitting: Stitches and Patterns.**

embosser. Jewelry. A **punch** used in **repoussé** to emboss metal. Also see **pitch bowl, repoussé tool.**

embossing. Jewelry. (Also called bossing.) A form of **repoussé** that produces a design in metal, generally done from the back with round **punch**es. The work must be supported on a piece of hardwood or in a **pitch bowl,** but the area being struck must be able to "give." The design appears on the front of the work as a raised shape or boss, from which the term *embossing* is derived. Also see **ball-peen hammer, embosser, punch.**

embossing. Leatherwork. A process done mostly commercially, of stamping or impressing simulated **grain** patterns, usually of exotic skins, such as alligator, with a **stamp** or **embossing wheel.** This process is also used for producing repoussé designs, that is, designs raised above the surface of the leather.

Also embossing refers to a **tooling** technique in which after **outline tooling,** the design is raised by pressing the leather from the back, or flesh side, with a ball end **modeler,** then pressing the background down from the grain side, repeating the process until the desired relief is obtained. The raised areas can be filled from the back with a papier-mâchélike mixture of flour, water, and shredded newspaper. When the mixture dries, a **lining leather** can be glued across the back. Also see **calfskin, carton-cuir work, finish, modeler.**

embossing. Plastics. The process of making a relief design by pressing a sheet of heated **thermoplastic** between a male and female **mold.**

embossing dough. Toys. In early **dollmaking,** a mixture that was added to the surface of the wooden **doll head** or **doll body** to give it shape. The dough was probably a mixture of rye flour with lime water and glue. Other **compositions** were also used over wood to emboss or shape it.

embossing hammer. Metalworking. See **hammer.**

embossing wheel. Leatherwork. A **tooling** instrument, available in many patterns, for decorating leather. The wheel is run along the cased leather to produce continuous stamped patterns. It can be used freehand; straight lines can be premarked or can be guided with a lightly held ruler; be careful not to let the ruler mark the damp leather. See ill. Also see **casing, embossing, stamp, stamping.**

Embossing wheel and carriage

embroidered knitting. Knitting. The surface embellishment of a piece of knitting with hand embroidery, often in geometric or floral patterns. **Swiss darning, cross stitch,**

standard embroidery stitches, or **smocking** are used. Also see **Austrian knitting, Tyrolean knitting.**

embroidered rug. Rugmaking. A rug made by means of decorative needlework stitches sewn through a background. Most embroidered rugs are made on **rug backing**s and the stitches cover the entire backing. However, it is possible that the embroidery is only an embellishment on another fabric that composes the rug proper. An embroidered rug requires the easiest tool with which to make a rug—a large blunt needle. Most embroidery stitches will produce a flat-looking rug, but it is possible to get different textures and raised effects by combining a variety of stitches, **padding** underneath the stitches, or putting in areas of **pile.** A fairly rigid backing and heavy yarn can make a rug as sturdy and stable as a **flatwoven** one. In addition, the design can be very free and can range from the smallest and most intricate to the boldest, simplest motifs. Embroidered rugs have been part of the American home since the mid-eighteenth century, when New England colonials stitched fanciful representations of their everyday scenery and activities. Also see **needleworked rug**s, **stitch.**

EMBROIDERY

Embroidery is a generic term for all forms of decorating cloth with needlework, including **crewel, needlepoint, counted-thread embroidery, stumpwork, blackwork, whitework,** and **metallic thread embroidery.** Embroidery presupposes a **background fabric;** macramé, bobbin lace, weaving, knitting, and crochet are distinct from embroidery because they are formed from twisted, woven, or knotted threads and are not an embellishment of already woven cloth.

Needlepoint is often distinguished from embroidery, perhaps because of its close relationship to woven tapestry. However, the word "needlepoint" was given to show that this type of work was stitched with a needle instead of being woven, and is therefore a form of embroidery.

Although technically incorrect, over the years the word "embroidery" has come to mean only the kind of decoration of cloth that leaves the background open. Work, such as needlepoint and **bargello,** that closely and completely covers the canvas mesh with stitches is generally considered separately.

embroidery beads. Beadwork. (Also called rocailles.) Slender, cylindrical **glass bead**s for bead embroidery are made in Austria, Czechoslovakia, West Germany, and Italy and are available in many colors. They may be purchased loose or in strings. They come in three basic types: round rocailles or **seed beads,** with round outsides and round holes; toscas or round rocailles, with round outsides and square holes; and charlottes, with faceted outsides.

embroidery carbon paper. Batik and Tie-dye. Quilts. Stitchery. (Also called dressmakers' carbon.) A paper used to transfer designs, available in needlework or fabric shops in a variety of colors. The carbon is placed, colored side down, on the fabric. Then designs can be drawn or traced by using a blunt needle or a **tracing wheel.** Care must be taken to avoid getting too much of the carbon on the fabric.

embroidery cotton. Stitchery. See **embroidery floss.**

embroidery floss. Stitchery. (Also called embroidery thread, floss.) A **silk, rayon,** or **cotton** thread, either plain or twisted, used for embroidery. There are 6 strands lightly twisted together, and the strands may be used individually or together. The number of strands desired for the finished embroidery work are threaded through the embroidery **needle** at one time, then they are knotted at one end. The strands are never doubled and knotted. When threaded singly, any twisting can be worked out as the embroidery progresses. Also see **Stitchery: Hand Appliqué.**

embroidery frame. Crewel. Embroidery. Needlepoint. A structure of wood, metal, or plastic over which **background fabric** can be stretched for ease in working. When worked in the hand, fabric tends to draw together and pucker; a frame helps prevent this. Many types of embroidery, such as crewelwork, **silk embroidery,** and goldwork, are best worked on a frame. Even **canvaswork** is easier to stitch on a frame.

An embroidery hoop, ring hoop, or tambour frame is made of two rings that fit together concentrically, with or without an adjustable tension screw (**a.**). The adjustable screw hoop allows for the variation in thickness of worked and unworked areas. It is available in a variety of sizes, the most commonly used size being 10″. If the piece being worked is smaller than 10″ it can be basted onto a larger piece of cloth for use in the hoop.

To place the background fabric into an embroidery hoop, place the fabric between the two rings. Adjust the screw before putting the fabric in, never while it is in the hoop, as it could damage the fabric. Gently alternate pulling the fabric and pushing the top ring until the two rings are flush and the fabric is taut (**b.**).

The main advantage of the square frame is that the worked areas of the fabric can be rolled on one of the end dowels (**c., d.**). The disadvantages of this frame are that the width of the piece is limited by the size of the frame, and the frame can be awkward to handle.

Stretcher strips are pieces of wood in various lengths, used in two pairs, that fit together to form a rectangular or square frame over which canvas can be stretched (**e.**).

Freestanding frames leave both hands free to work. The lap or fanny frame is an adjustable ring attached to a stand that can rest on a table, stand in the lap, or be steadied by being sat upon by the needleworker (**f.**). Two frames used for larger pieces, especially rugs, are the oval rug frame and the standing frame. A 36″ oval ring with adjustable supports on either side, enabling it to be tilted toward the worker. The standing frame has a single post and an adjustable hoop that can be easily changed to any height or angle to suit the worker. See ill.

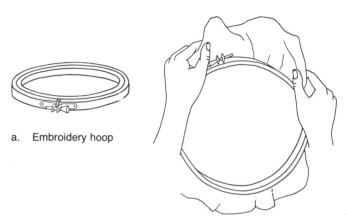

a.   Embroidery hoop

b.   Fabric on embroidery hoop

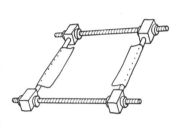

c.   Square frame

d.   Fabric on square frame

e.   Stretcher strip frame

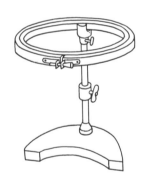

f.   Lap frame

embroidery hoop. Crewel. Embroidery. See **embroidery frame.**

embroidery loop. Beadwork. See **Beadwork: Basic Operations.**

embroidery needle. Crewel. Embroidery. See crewel needle.

embroidery needle. Stitchery. See **needle.**

embroidery paint. Crewel. Embroidery. Permanent paints available in tubes in a large assortment of colors, used to put a design on a **background fabric** by drawing it freehand. They can also be used to paint some areas of the fabric to contrast with the texture of the stitches.

embroidery scissors. Crewel. Embroidery. Needlepoint. Small scissors with narrow blades useful for getting into small areas and between threads. Varieties of embroidery scissors are **curved scissors,** stork scissors, and surgical scissors.

embroidery scissors. Stitchery. Small **scissors** with both blades pointed, used in **snip**ping threads or in very fine trimming and cutting. A 4″ or 5″ size works easily.

embroidery stitch. Crewel. Embroidery. See **satin stitch.**

embroidery stitch. Rugmaking. See **stitch.**

embroidery weave. Weaving. A weave bearing such a strong resemblance to an embroidery stitch that it is difficult, at first glance, to distinguish whether it was embroidered or woven. The best examples are the weaves in the **laid-in** category.

emerald. Gemcutting. See **beryl.**

emerald cut. Gemcutting. See **facet.**

emergent toy. Toys. Any of those seemingly **universal toys** that appear in totally unrelated cultures; or, **toys** that disappear, then reappear or emerge years later in a different part of the world. The **pestle doll,** the **yo-yo,** and the **rattle** are examples. Also see **archetypal toy.**

emery. Gemcutting. See **abrasive.**

emery. Jewelry. A black, natural **abrasive** used to remove fine scratches from metal surfaces. It is a mixture of corundum and iron oxide (in the form of hematite or magnetite), and is available in paste form or bonded to paper, cloth, and tools such as an **emery stick** for **hand polishing.** Also see **buffing compound.**

emery. Metalworking. See **abrasives.**

emery bag. Stitchery. A **pincushion**like bag filled with an abrasive powder to remove rust from pins and **needles.** It is especially helpful to any stitcher living in an area of high humidity.

emery cloth. Jewelry. Cloth coated on one side with **emery.** It is more flexible than **emery paper.** Emery is used more as a **polishing** than as a cutting agent. Also see abrasive, carborundum cloth, crocus cloth.

emery paper. Jewelry. Paper coated on one side with **emery** that is used for **polishing** rather than for cutting. It is available in numbered grades from extra fine to extra coarse. Also see **abrasive.**

emery paste. Jewelry. See **buffing compound.**

emery stick. Jewelry. A commercially available, disposable flat piece of wood with **emery paper** glued around it. It

is used to reach crannies that machine **polishing** would miss. It is economical to purchase a plastic emery stick on which only the strips of emery paper need to be replaced when worn. When replacing the paper, trim any overhang that might scratch other parts of the metal. See ill. Also see **abrasive, hand polishing.**

Plastic emery stick

emigrette. Toys. See **yo-yo.**

emulsifier. Fabric Printing. See **emulsion binder.**

emulsion. Fabric Printing. A liquid suspension of **dye** and **mordant** in a **dye paste** for fabric printing. Printing with emulsions is a recent development in dye printing in which the traditional **thickener,** such as gum tragacanth, is replaced by an **emulsion binder.** There are numerous advantages to this method. The emulsion binder is easier to prepare than the tragacanth mixture and it can be kept indefinitely without deterioration. The printed fabric will have brighter colors and a softer surface.

emulsion binder. Fabric Printing. An agent, or emulsifier, that stabilizes the suspension of **dye** and **mordant** in a **dye paste.** In **emulsion** printing the emulsion binder replaces the traditional **thickener.**

enamel. China and Glass Painting. A colored, vitreous **glaze** available as a powder for decorating pottery, glass, or metal, and fused by **firing** in a **kiln** to produce a smooth, hard surface. The base of enamel is **flux** (clear glass), to which various ingredients are added for desired color and consistency. The depth of the color is controlled by the amount of lead oxide added. Lead, potash, and soda in various quantities are added for brilliance. Tin oxide is used for making transparent enamels opaque. In china painting enamel is often used as a raised decoration that projects from the background, often in imitation of jewels.

enamel. Enameling. Glass composed of clear **flux** or **frit,** with **metal oxide** for color, in either powder or liquid form. It is fused to the surface of **metal** by **firing** at high temperatures. Enamels are classified as opaque, allowing no light to penetrate; transparent, allowing light to pass easily; and opalescent, combining transparency and opacity. Commercially ground enamels are 80 mesh—the powder will pass through a sieve that has 80 holes per square inch. Enamels are also available in large chunks that retain their intense color. They must be ground with a porcelain mortar and pestle to the desired degree of fineness.

Soft or low-firing enamels melt at about 1300–1360° F. Medium-fusing enamels melt at 1360–1420° F, and hard or hard-firing enamels mature at temperatures of 1420–1510° F.

Enamel threads (strands of enamel drawn while molten), beads, chunks, and **millefiore** are used for special effects. Slush or crackle enamels are liquids that produce cracking and crazing when they are applied over a base coat of enamel and fired at a high temperature. Contaminated enamels and cheaper grades are used for **counterenameling** surfaces that will not be visible. Also see **atomizer, basse-taille, binder, champlevé, cloisonné, color testing, firescale, frit, grisaille, guilloche, overfiring, overglaze, plique-á-jour, raku, repoussé, sgraffito, stencil, torch firing, washing enamel, wet inlay, wisteria line.**

enamel. Mosaics. See **smalti.**

enameled cane. Basketry. See **cane.**

ENAMELING

The process of fusing enamel to a prepared metal surface by melting it at a high temperature.

Enameling was originated in the sixth century B.C. by Greek artisans who covered gold with blue and white vitreous substances in floral or figurative designs. Small gold wires were often embedded in the borders of the enamel in the style called **cloisonné.** Celtic peoples decorated their shields and swords with enamels as early as the fifth century B.C. Molten glass was poured into openings in the bronze implements in the style called **champlevé.** This style was copied by the Romans and used by the Anglo-Saxons during the sixth through ninth centuries A.D. Japanese enameling in the cloisonné style, depicting flowers, dragons, and clouds, has been found dating from the third to sixth centuries A.D. Indian enamelists from the sixth century A.D. strove for perfection of color. The achievement of a ruby-red color was their goal. They often used enamel work in combination with precious gems. Cloisonné was popular and **repoussé** is also represented.

Byzantine enamels from the late ninth to eleventh centuries A.D. show the strong influence of the Eastern Orthodox Church. The pieces are generally in the cloisonné style with wires as fine as 1/100″. Splendid collections of Byzantine enamels are in the Cathedral of St. Sophia in Istanbul, St. Marks in Venice, and the Metropolitan Museum of Art in New York.

Enameling was introduced into Germany by Theophano, a Byzantine princess who married King Otto II. The art spread through the monasteries along the Rhine and Meuse rivers. A fantastic collection of gold and enamel pieces known as the Guelph treasure accumulated in Brunswick in lower Saxony during the eleventh through fifteenth centuries. Much of the collection is now in the Cleveland Museum of Art. German enameling contributed cloisonné and champlevé pieces with Christian themes, represented by the work of the Mosan school in the eleventh and twelfth centuries.

Although luxury and finery were not widely popular during the Middle Ages, there was a small market for such items among religious officials and the nobility. During this period metalworking and enameling were used for heraldic decorations.

Enameling flourished in the sixteenth century in the French town of Limoges. The technique developed was an imitation of oil painting in which translucent enamels were layered on a copper plate, often over an opaque white enamel. Leonard Penicaud would apply an opaque white ground, draw the design in black oxide, fire several coats of transparent enamels, then apply opaque white enamel in careful gradation for a modeled effect, complete with violet transparents for sharp details. He called this style "Nardon." Leonard Limousin and Pierre Raimond were enamel portraitists of the Limoges school. An excellent collection of enamel portraiture is found in the Taft Museum in Cincinnati, Ohio.

The Renaissance in Italy produced an enameling technique called **basse-taille,** in which the metal form is prepared by hammering, punching, stamping, **etching,** and engraving to provide a brilliant textured surface that is then covered with transparent enamels.

Russian enamelists are credited with development of the **plique-à-jour** technique, in which the wires embedded in the enamel are not backed by metal so that light can shine through, like a miniature stained-glass window. Plique-à-jour was used for earrings, necklaces, and spoon handles, often over braided filigreed wire, for extra strength.

English enameling began in the eighteenth century at Battersea, where the Jansen factories manufactured boxes and dishes in pink and white enamels, usually with sylvan themes. In 1864 the art was revived by Alexander Fisher, Harold Stabler, and H. H. Cunyngham, who made fine enamel portraits that combined the Limoges methods with precious metals and jewels.

Peter Carl Fabergé, who was born in Russia in 1846 and died in Switzerland in 1920, was one of the finest enamelists of the past. His work was done on precious metals with a highly reflective, patterned surface called **guilloche.** Some of his work was in a style called en plein, a smooth covering of enamel over a large, sometimes textured surface. His workshops produced many snuff, cigarette, powder, and jewel boxes, and picture frames, bottles, clocks, and brooches with art nouveau decoration in enamel, as well as his well-known Easter eggs.

In the modern era, the Vienna School of Fine Arts has internationally encouraged enameling since 1929. American interest in enameling emerged in the 1930s and is celebrated annually at the National Ceramic Exhibition sponsored by the Syracuse Museum of Fine Arts in Syracuse, New York, and the May Show at the Cleveland Museum of Art.

SETTING UP A WORKSHOP   Although the space required for an enameling workshop is moderate, separate areas are needed for working **metal**; for planning, washing, and applying enamel; for **firing** and cooling the work; and for rinsing, cleaning, and **stoning.** If possible, it's useful to have buffing and **polishing** equipment.

Shaping metal for enameling requires a sturdy, well-lit bench with tools conveniently placed. A cut-out bay in the top of the bench with a leather apron suspended below the vise or bench pin is useful for catching bits of precious metal when sawing, snipping, and filing. Good ventilation is needed in this area to remove dust and fumes. Working metal produces most of the mess involved in enameling.

A clean, brightly lit surface is needed for designing and for applying enamels.

The firing and cooling area should be free from drafts

that might cause rapid lowering temperature and possible damage to enamel. A thick slab of stone or metal on a counter near the **kiln** is useful for cooling pieces.

A sink facilitates rinsing and stoning finished work.

Polishing materials must be kept uncontaminated and dust-free; buffing wheels should be hooded or covered when not in use.

Workshop space must be sufficient to allow materials and tools to be kept clean, neat, and orderly without crowding.

Also see **washing enamel.**

TOOLS AND MATERIALS Tools for working metal preparatory to enameling include a **jeweler's saw** frame with a # 3/0 or # 4/0 blade and beeswax for lubrication; metal shears and duckbill snips are also used for cutting out shapes.

A dogwood or rawhide mallet is used for shaping metal forms over a sandbag or pitch bowl to support the work. Modeling and finer shaping is done with dapping and chasing chisels, as in the **repoussé** and **basse-taille** techniques.

Several pairs of pliers with different-shaped jaws such as flat-nosed, half-round, and round-nose are needed for bending and manipulating metal shapes. Assorted files are used for cleaning and smoothing metal edges. Tweezers with a cross-locking device are used to hold small pieces of metal while working them.

Cleaning metal surfaces requires acids or ferric chloride and pyrex containers with covers. Copper tongs or wooden sticks are used for handling and lifting pieces in pickle or an **etching** bath. Rubber gloves should be worn to protect your hands when working with acid.

Metals are also cleaned manually with steel wool, pumice, or emery cloth.

Grind enamels with a mortar and pestle, rinse with water, and allow to dry. Grade by sieving through wire screens with particularly sized openings, and store in small jars with labeled covers.

Working on sheets of white typing paper makes handling dry enamels when sifting and pouring easier. Wire screens tied or rubber-banded over the mouths of small jars are used for dusting enamels onto the metal surface.

A **camel's hair brush** is used for covering relatively large areas, as in applying stopout for etching or **electroplating**; applying coats of **flux** enamel; or treating bare metal for **firescale.**

Enamels are held in place prior to firing with binders that burn cleanly away in the kiln. The **binder** may be brushed onto the bare metal, but not over unfired enamels; it may be sprayed with an **atomizer** or aerosol spray unit; or it may be mixed with the enamel and applied with a **spatula** and **spreader** or with a **sable brush.** The binder must be dried thoroughly before firing. A sable brush is also used for work with **metal foil**, delicate **wet inlay** technique, and **overglaze** shading. A small, sharp scissors is used for cutting metal foil and a small tweezers is used for handling these **pallions.** A **scriber** is used to mark out lines of a design on the metal.

Pliers with the jaws filed so that one is round and the other rectangular is used for bending **cloisons.**

A soldering **torch** or blowpipe is handy, although the enamel will discolor and possibly deform if it covers the solder. Yellow **ochre** is used to protect soldered joints from melting during firing.

An electric **kiln** or torch set-up is necessary to achieve the high temperatures required for fusing enamel. A **pyrometer** is used to show kiln temperature, although the color of the interior is a sufficient guide for the experienced.

A firing rack or **trivet** is used to support the piece when firing. A **firing fork** is used to handle the support when inserting and removing it from the kiln. Asbestos gloves should be worn to protect the hands.

A flatiron or other convenient weight is placed on cooling enamel pieces to prevent warping.

A scraper is used to clean spilled enamel from the floor and walls of the kiln. **Kiln wash** is painted on the inside of the kiln to prevent spills from penetrating and to make scraping easier.

Cleaning the finished work is done with a **glass brush** or small carborundum stone. Greater luster may be achieved by polishing the work with a polishing buff and ultrafine abrasive.

BASIC PROCEDURES Dry powdered enamel is applied by sifting it over a metal surface premoistened with **binder.** If the binder is brushed on evenly before sifting the coating of dry enamel, the binder for the application of a second coat prior to **firing** must be sprayed on with an atomizer.

The dusting technique is fast and effective and is done with small sieves or jars with screens attached over their mouths. The edges of a piece should be dusted more heavily, as the heat burns out there first. The binder burns cleanly away when the piece is placed in the kiln.

Another common technique for applying enamel uses liquid enamel premixed with binder and painted on, as in the Limoges technique, or placed on the surface with other instruments, as in the **wet inlay** technique. Enamel threads are sometimes applied with a few drops of binder.

Pieces are sometimes dipped in liquid enamel and set on a **trivet** to dry.

Areas that flake off may be touched up with moist enamel and a finger or delicate tool.

Liquid enamel may be dripped, thrown spattered, and, like dry enamels, used with stencils. With proper equipment, enamel may even be sprayed on.

Unless special lead-free enamels are used, food containers should not be enameled. Rings, bracelets, or other pieces that will receive heavy wear should be well reinforced with metal. Also see **basse-taille, champlevé, cloisonné, color testing, firescale, fuming, grisaille, guilloche, plique-à-jour, raku, repoussé, sgraffito, torch firing, wet inlay, wisteria line.**

REPAIR OF FLAWS Pinholes appearing in fired work may be due to air bubbles, dust, or other contamination of the enamel. Careful washing and testing will avoid this problem. To remove pinholes, pierce them with a sharp point either manually or mechanically, scrub the piece well with carborundum or a glass brush, and rinse thoroughly.

Reapply the enamel and fire; multiple firing may be necessary to cover the flaws.

Cracking around the edges may be caused by hasty cooling after firing. Shallow surface cracks may be caused by underfiring. These may be repaired by heating to a higher temperature and cooling carefully.

Enamel flaking off, bubbling, or crawling is caused by metal that has not been properly cleaned before enameling.

If the enamel pops off when cool, this indicates that the piece should have been **counterenamel**ed.

Blistering may be caused by impure copper, air bubbles, or dust. Cloudiness may be caused by impure enamel or by underfiring transparent enamel.

SAFETY PRECAUTIONS   The tools and materials of this craft must be handled with care because many of them are potentially dangerous.

Sharp metal edges may cause laceration or incision. Clean, disinfect, and cover the injury to promote healing. Consult a doctor if the wound is anything but very minor.

Burns can be caused by touching the **kiln** or anything that comes out of it with unprotected hands. Acids used for **etching** and **cleaning metal** can also cause burns. Rinse acid burns under running water and neutralize with baking soda. Rubber gloves should be worn when working with acid, and asbestos gloves when using a kiln or other heat source. Always pour acid into water, **never** vice-versa.

Fumes from chemical and thermal reactions are harmful, and good ventilation should be provided. A respirator can be worn to filter the air.

Goggles to protect the eyes and face are sometimes worn when metalworking or looking into the kiln.

enameling. Stained Glass. The technique of applying low-temperature colored frits to the surface of a piece of **stained glass** and **firing** the piece at a temperature lower than that used for paint so that the frits fuse with the surface of the glass. Enameling was especially popular during the seventeenth and eighteenth centuries when intricate pictures and copies of paintings were the style. In modern adaptation, it provides an occasional dash of color but its use is limited. Finely ground enamel can be thinned with oil of spike for **painting on glass.** Very soft **brush**es are used for applying the enamel. Enamel is hard to control and tends to dissolve paint already applied to the glass.

enameling glass. Glasswork. A method of decorating glass that involves the application of a glass with a low softening point in powder form to a glass surface and then firing to melt the enamel and fuse it to the "harder" glass. There are several methods of applying the enamel to the glass. Commercial methods include stenciling or printing a **slurry** of enamel in an oil base. The slurry can be applied with a pen or brush, or **squeegee**d onto a previously etched surface. Another method is to print a sticky oil on the glass with a rubber stamp and then dust on the enamel powder. This method can result in especially clear, sharp lines.

After the enamel and vehicle are applied, the glass is first brought to a temperature sufficient to evaporate the oil, and then the oven temperature is raised to the melting point of the enamel material. Following enameling, an **annealing** procedure must be carried out. Also see **hardness.**

enamel paint. Puppets. Toys. A smooth, hard, glossy nontoxic paint that gives a surface similar to enamelware. It is available in a wide range of colors at hardware and paint stores in aerosol **spray paint** or by the gallon, quart, pint, or half-pint. While fast-drying paints and enamels are available, most take 4–6 hours before they are dry to the touch. Enamels are permanent, waterproof oil-base paints; excess paint on brushes must be cleaned with a **solvent** such as paint thinner or **mineral spirits.** Oil-base enamels are among the more durable paints. Some paints now on the market are advertised as latex enamels or water-base enamels, meaning that they have a shiny or glossy finish.

enamel paint. Woodworking. See **paint.**

enamel thread. Enameling. See **enamel** and **Enameling: Basic Operations.**

encapsulation. Plastics. See **embedment.**

encaustic. Candlemaking. The process of painting candles with hot wax. Molded candles can be effectively decorated by the application of designs with hot wax and a brush or hot melted **crayons.** For best results, short, quick strokes are recommended.

enclosing the pin. Lacemaking. See **pin enclosed.**

encroaching gobelin. Needlepoint. (Also called interlocking gobelin.) A variation of the vertical **gobelin stitch** worked over any number of meshes. It creates a smooth surface with a substantial backing, uses a great deal of yarn, can be worked up quickly, and is an excellent technique for shading. However, it should be worked on an **embroidery frame** to avoid pulling the **canvas** out of shape. See ill.

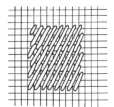

Encroaching gobelin stitch

encrustation. Jewelry. The addition of metal pieces or units onto a base metal, either by **inlay** technique or by soldering. Also see **appliqué, married metal, mokume.**

end. Macramé. The **cord** used in the working of a macramé knot may also be called an "end."

end. Weaving. The term used to refer to the individual lengths of **warp** threads.

end-and-end. Weaving. A color repeat in the **warp** made up of two alternating colors. Color A would be followed by color B throughout the entire **warp arrangement.**

end bar. Quilts. See **stretcher.**

end frame. Quilts. See **stretcher.**

end grain. Woodworking. See **wood.**

end-lap joint. Woodworking. See **joint.**

Endless Chain. Quilts. See **Job's Tears.**

endpaper. Bookbinding. Leaf of plain or decorated paper which links the body of the book to its **board**s and protects the first and last **sections** of the book.

The endpapers of casebound books are usually folded sheets of various constructions that are tipped with paste. The endpapers of **bound books** require more strength than those of cased books and are made of multiple sheets sewn to the first and last sections of the book with the outside sheet glued to the boards. The outside sheet is sometimes a **waste** that is glued to the **super** and **tapes** of the **back,** trimmed to 1½", and inserted into a **split board,** attaching the book to the boards.

Sawing-in is usually done before attaching endpapers, as they tear easily. Before sewing on the endpapers be certain the waste leaf is on the outside. The waste leaf is often covered with a single sheet of **board paper.**

A very simple way to make endpapers is to fold two single sheets (one for the front and one for the back). Use plain colored paper, cut to size if the book will not be trimmed, or roughly the same size if it will; insert each between the board and the section and tip. Also see **casing-in, tipping, trimming.**

ends-per-inch. Weaving. See **sett.**

English antique glass. Stained Glass. Considered to be the best-tempered glass. The best colors are greens and reds. It can be purchased at glass supply houses. The English also **flashed glass** and most of the beautiful **streaky glass.** The size of their glass sheets are 24″ × 18″. Also see **antique glass** and **Stained Glass: Tools and Materials.**

English crewel yarn. Crewel. Embroidery. Needlepoint. See **Appleton Crewel wool.**

English pink. Ceramics. See **chrome-tin pink.**

English punch. Leatherwork. See **strap end punch.**

English quilting. Quilts. Stitchery. See **English trapunto.**

English rug. Rugmaking. Weaving. See **ingrain rug.**

English T-box. Quilts. See **Baby Blocks.**

English trapunto. Quilts. Stitchery. (Also called English quilting.) A decorative **quilting** technique in which two large layers of fabric, placed one on another, provide the **quilt top** and **backing** for a quilt. The design is made entirely with the quilting—that is, no piecing or appliqué is used. A design is outlined in the **quilting stitch.** Traditionally, this design was a central motif of some kind, usually fruit or flowers. The quilting design was completely finished, then small openings were cut through the backing layer of fabric. **Padding** or **stuffing** was inserted from the back to raise areas of the design. This made a bas-relief on the quilt. English trapunto was regarded as the "ultimate" for quilters because it required so much of the needleworker's skill.

Traditionally the stuffing was **cotton batting.** In contemporary work, **Dacron polyester batting** is used. Many of today's quiltmakers use **trapunto** in an **overall** design, making sculptured surfaces of the quilts. Also see **Italian trapunto, trapunto.**

engobe. Ceramics. A prepared **slip** containing **feldspar,** flint (**silica**), and **flux** that is used as a **glaze** on **bisque** ware. Also see **slip glaze.**

engraver's block. Jewelry. (Also called ball vise.) A metal device weighing about 15 lbs. used for holding small work during engraving. The standard model is 5″ in diameter and 2½″ deep. The adjustable jaws open to 3″ maximum. The engraver's block rests in a **ring pad** and can be moved easily and smoothly with slight pressure. Attachments such as pins and holders are placed in the holes of the jaw face to hold any object the jaws can accommodate. Adjust the jaws with the key provided. See ill. Also see **clamp, graver.**

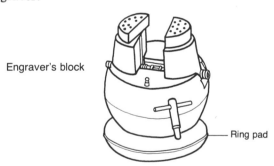

Engraver's block

Ring pad

engraver's cement. See **stone setter's cement.**

engraver's sharpener. Jewelry. A tool into which a **graver** is placed and held at precisely the correct angle— 45° for normal engraving—during sharpening. Also see **Arkansas oilstone, clamp, India oilstone.**

engraving. Ceramics. The cutting of a design in clay at any point up to the **leather hard** state. The dryer the pot, the sharper and tighter the design and line quality. A variety of tools can be used for this process but usually a pointed wooden or bamboo tool is used. Also see **fluting.**

engraving. Glasswork. The process whereby glass is abraded or scratched for decorative purposes.

Diamond-point engraving is done with a hand-held stylus with a point of diamond or silicon carbide. Designs are more or less freely traced, most often in **lead-crystal glass,** which is softer than most kinds of glass.

Intaglio cutting and copper-wheel engraving both utilize spinning wheels of small diameter rotated by a variable-speed lathelike spindle. Intaglio cutting uses carborundum abrasive wheels kept wet by a stream of water to reduce airborne glass dust, which is harmful to the lungs.

Copper-wheel engraving is very old and in many ways still the most satisfactory method of decoration, as the cuts are very smooth, although matte and translucent. The method uses an abrasive **slurry** of emery powder and oil (to reduce dust), which is fed onto a rotating copper disk. The work is held against the underside of the rotating wheel so that the operator can see the line of the wheel cut.

engraving. Jewelry. The process of cutting lines and textures into metal with tools such as **gravers, electric engraving tool,** and **machinist's scriber.** Also see **engraver's block, peg clamp.**

engraving. Plastics. See **intaglio process.**

engraving tool. Jewelry. See **electric engraving tool, engraver's block, graver, machinist's scriber, scriber.**

enlarging and reducing a design. Crewel. Embroidery. Needlepoint. There are three principal methods of changing the size of a design:

The simplest method of enlarging or reducing a design is to get a photostat of it; most cities and towns offer this service. With any given design, determine how large or small the finished work is to be. It is necessary to give the photostat service only one dimension; the other will be enlarged or reduced proportionately, although there may be a slight distortion when enlarging to a size many times that of the original. In the photostating process a negative is made first, then a positive "stat." It is a good idea to always request the negative as well as the positive, as frequently the negative is the clearer.

The squaring method is an old-fashioned method of enlarging or reducing a design that is still useful and simple to do at home. Begin by squaring the design into a grid using a ruler or **clear plastic grid overlay (a.).** Take a sheet of paper the size the finished design is to be and fold or measure it into the same number of squares. Draw the design to fit within the squares, working one square at a time **(b.).**

Using a **pantograph** or opaque projector is an easy but impractical method of enlarging or reducing a design because the equipment is not easily accessible. With the pantograph, an outline can be traced with a scribe attached to the machine, and the outline is mechanically transformed to the desired size. The opaque projector allows great versatility in enlarging and reducing because it projects the design onto a screen or wall to almost any size.

Squaring method

 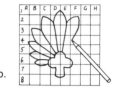

a.   b.

enlarging design. Rugmaking. See **transferring design.**

en plein. Enameling. See **Enameling.**

en resille. Enameling. A technique in which **enamels** are fired on a base of glass or quartz crystal. The design is scratched on the crystal and lined with gold, then soft, transparent enamels are inlaid and fired carefully.

entering. Weaving. See **drawing-in.**

entering hook. Weaving. See **reed hook.**

entwined laid-in. Weaving. See **laid-in.**

entwining twill. Weaving. See **diamond twill.**

ephemeral figure. Toys. Any of those images of human figures, or **simulacrum,** made for certain occasions or for a short duration. Some familiar ephemeral figures are snowmen, scarecrows, effigies, and Halloween ghosts.

ephemeral toy. Toys. (Also called perishable toy.) A momentary, transient, or temporary toy that, by nature of the material from which it is fashioned, disappears after a short life. **Gingerbread men,** sugar babies, **soap bubbles,** jack-o'lanterns, sand castles, and **flower dolls** are among some of the best known. Many are made to be consumed, such as the chocolate rabbits given to children at Easter. All are made with the knowledge that they will eventually be eaten or will wilt or disintegrate. Many ephemeral toys are also **edible toys,** others are **ephemeral figures.** Also see **Toys: Ephemeral Toys.**

epi. Weaving. See **sett.**

epidote. Gemcutting. A mineral composed of hydrous silicate of aluminum and calcium with a **hardness** of 6½ and a **specific gravity** of 3.25−3.5; **crystals** are of the monoclinic system with **cleavage** in two directions parallel to the crystal faces. Epidote occurs translucent to transparent, colorless, pale yellow, red, and green with vitreous **luster.** Its refractive indices are 1.733 and 1.768 with mild dichroism often resembling the colors of a pistachio nutmeat. Main crown **facets** are cut at 37° and main pavillion angles are cut at 42°. It is polished on a tin **lap** with tin oxide. Also see **abrasive, faceting, polishing, refraction.**

epoxide. Plastics. See **epoxy.**

epoxy. Jewelry. See **cement.**

epoxy. Plastics. A **thermosetting** plastic available commercially in many forms: **resin**s, solid blocks, **foams, adhesive**s, coatings, **sealant**s, paints, and **body putty.** Epoxy is derived from epoxide, the basic molecular unit of the plastic. Epoxy technology started in 1945. Epoxy resin does not deteriorate as quickly as **polyester** resin and is more stable. It shrinks less in **curing** but is more brittle when cured. Epoxy will adhere to metal, whereas polyester will not. Amine hardeners or **catalysts** for liquid epoxy are toxic and corrosive, causing skin irritation. The acid anhydrite hardeners can cause skin burns. Safety hardeners, such as amide catalysts (Araldite, for example) should be used when possible; they are nontoxic and act also as **plasticizers.** Never mix an epoxy catalyst with a polyester catalyst, or an explosion may result. Epoxy adhesives, such as Devcon and Five-Minute Epoxy, are popular for bonding dissimilar materials. Also see **Plastics: Casting.**

epoxy glue. Toys. A two-part **adhesive** made from epoxy resins. When the two parts are mixed a chemical reaction occurs that heats and then sets the **glue.** It is extremely strong and hard and dries clear.

epoxy-metal casting. Plastics. See **resin-metal casting.**

epoxy paint. Toys. A smooth, hard paint made for a wide variety of surfaces, including ceramic, metal, and enamel, but not to be used on plastic. It has pigment in a modified epoxy base. The vapors are extremely flammable and care must be taken to avoid breathing the vapors. It is a durable material available as a brush-on paint or **spray coating.**

epoxy resin. Mosaics. (Also called synthetic resin.) A clear resin that, when mixed with a catalyst or diphenyl, polymerizes spontaneously to form a strong **adhesive.** Several types are sold in hardware stores in packages containing a tube of resin and a tube of catalyst. Care should be taken in working with epoxy resin, because prolonged inhalation of the fumes can be injurious to one's health. Also see **Mosaics: Tools and Materials, Setting the Material.**

epoxy resin. Stained Glass. Epoxy resin is a clear bonding agent. It is available with colored **ballasts** added, which extend the resin and make it opaque. Epoxy resin is usually white, gray, black, or brown for stained glass, although it can be any color. It can be used with **slab glass** or crushed glass, and in **lamination** and **mosaics.** Epoxy comes in two parts, a monomer and a polymer. They are sold together, with explicit mixing instructions enclosed. Rubber gloves should always be worn and the room should be free of dust and have good ventilation. Fumes from the resin are toxic. Also see **dalle-de-verre, lamp black, micro-balloons** and **Stained Glass: Safety Precautions.**

epoxy resin glue. Tincrafting. See **Tincrafting: Joining the Tin.**

eraser. China and Glass Painting. See **china eraser.**

Erector set. Toys. A **constructional toy** made up of metal strips, nuts, and bolts for erecting girders, etc. It is similar to **Meccano,** but the latter is available with gears, pinions, and an electric motor.

ermine stitch. Crewel. Embroidery. A filling stitch worked with a long straight vertical stitch with a **cross stitch** of slightly shorter length over it. It is effective as a **blackwork** stitch when worked in patterns.

escapement file. Jewelry. Similar to **needle file**s but with square handles.

Eskimo style. Amber Carving. Ivory and Bone Carving. Jet Carving. Shell Carving. A primitive engraving tool, still employed to carve materials softer than steel, most commonly **ivory.**

Whittle a rounded head on one end of a wood dowel 7⅞″ × 3″ long; cut a deep notch behind it to aid in gripping it. Insert into the vise a thick nail. Saw off the head and then file it to a point. Drill a hole the diameter of the nail into the rounded end of the dowel and insert the blunt end of the nail into this hole with a little glue. Push it all the way in with pliers, and allow it to dry.

Make a few styles, with nails of varying thicknesses, and file the points into different shapes (notched, broad, and narrow). The points must be sharpened frequently while working.

Eskimo yo-yo. Toys. See **mountain bolo.**

~~**essonite.**~~ Gemcutting. See **garnet.**

estimating amount of thread needed. Tatting. Wind a given amount of **thread** on the **shuttle.** Make a sample, either of one unit of the **design** or, as in an **edging,** of a few inches of tatting. Subtract the amount of thread left on the shuttle from the total amount wound; this will give you an estimate. Figure a generous allowance. Also, in using two shuttles, remember that the **knot bearer** doesn't get used up as quickly as the **loop thread,** which makes the knots.

Estonian sun lace. Lacemaking. See **sol lace.**

etching. China and Glass Painting. See **acid etching.**

etching. Enameling. The use of acid to erode a design in **metal** or **enamel.** Areas to be protected from the action of the etch are coated with a **resist.** Most metals are etched with a solution of 1 part nitric acid to 3 parts water in a Pyrex dish. Wear rubber gloves and handle the piece with copper tongs or a wooden stick. Immerse the piece, clearing bubbles with a feather. The etch may be mixed with 1 part nitric acid and up to 7 parts water for a slower but straighter bite.

Ferric chloride etching crystals are used on copper. Mixed 13 ounces to 1 pint of water, ferric chloride cuts slowly but gives a very even depression. It must be stored in an opaque container to preserve its strength. After etching, soak and scrub the piece with a strong ammonia solution to remove greenish deposits of copper chloride, which would release deadly chlorine gas if fired.

Enamel and glass are etched with hydrofluoric acid, a volatile and dangerous material. Beeswax is used as a resist.

Etching is a preparatory step for many enameling techniques, including **basse-taille, champlevé,** and **plique à jour.** Also see **Camel's hair brush, electroetching.**

etching. Glasswork. Finished glass pieces can be decorated by chemically incising the surface, using combinations of acids in which glass is soluble.

Acid polishing, a method of producing a uniformly glossy surface, can be performed by immersing the glass piece in a solution of 6 parts concentrated hydrofluoric acid (HF), 7 parts concentrated sulfuric acid (H_2SO_4), and 1 to 4 parts water. *Always* add acid to water slowly. Never add water to acid, because the mixture could boil and spatter acid.

If a translucent matte etch is required, the proportion of hydrofluoric acid is increased. **Lead-crystal glass** requires a higher concentration of hydrofluoric acid for polishing, and **frosting** requires a still higher.

Decorative etching can be carried out by applying wax to the glass surface and then scratching away the parts where the glass is intended to be cut away. This method is commonly used for **enameling.** The incised areas are filled with enamel and then fired to the melting point of the enamel.

Deep cutting using acid etching may also be done, but care must be taken that the stencil is not undercut by the acid. Also, it is necessary to wash the acid and dissolved glass from the surface occasionally.

etching. Jewelry. Metalworking. The process of removing portions of metal with the use of acid solutions. Areas of metal which are not to be removed must be covered with some form of stop-out (acid-resisting material) such as **asphaltum varnish** or **beeswax.** There are two basic types of etching, intaglio, and relief. In **intaglio** the metal is completely covered with a stop-out (also referred to as a **resist**). After the resist has thoroughly dried, a sharp tool, such as an **etching needle,** is used to scratch designs through the resist. The exposed metal is eaten away by the acid, rendering a design that is lower than the protected metal. In **relief,** the design is applied to the metal with the resist material. The acid eats away the exposed metal, leaving the design in relief, or higher than the background metal.

Following are some acid solutions. Different metals require different formulas. When mixing an acid solution the acid must be poured into the water, never the reverse. Do not attempt to use these or any formula containing acid until reading **Jewelry: Safety Precautions.** For gold 18K or lower use 8 parts hydrochloric acid, 4 parts **nitric acid,** 1 part perchloride of iron, and 40−50 parts water. For silver use 1 part nitric acid to 3−4 parts water. For **copper** and **brass** use 1 part nitric acid to 2 parts water. For steel or iron use 2 parts hydrochloric acid to 1 part water. Acid etches in two ways, depending on the strength of the solution. Strong solutions will etch quickly with an undercutting action and will lift the resist if applied thinly. Weaker

acid solutions will etch slower and straight down. The resist will begin to break down if left in the acid solution too long. The acid solution will cause the surface of the metal to bubble. These gas bubbles are caused by the etching action and can be used as an indicator of the strength of the solution. The faster the bubbling action the stronger the acid solution. Do not breathe the fumes. During etching a sludge is formed on the surface of the exposed metal which slows the etching process if not removed. Wipe the etching surface lightly with the end of a feather to remove sludge. If the resist should begin to lift, it will be necessary to remove the work from the acid solution and rinse it thoroughly under running water. Dry it thoroughly and reapply the resist where necessary.

Metal placed into the acid solution, especially flat pieces, should be immersed slowly to avoid splashing. Copper **pickling tongs** can be used to handle the work. To provide a good etch, the acid solution should cover the metal by at least 1″. Also see **mordant.**

etching. Stained Glass. Cutting away areas of glass with acid. Also see **aciding.**

etching needle. Jewelry. A lightweight steel tool, roughly the diameter of a pencil, that comes to a needle point on one or both ends, and sometimes has wood or cork surrounding the center section to make it easier to handle. It is used to scratch designs through a **resist** in preparation for etching. A **scribe** may also be used for this purpose. Also see **machinist's scribe.**

Eternal Flame. Quilts. See **presidents' quilts.**

eternal toy. Toys. Any toy that survives changes in taste, popularity, and toymaking methods. The carved wooden horse is an example of an eternal toy. No matter how beautifully made or elaborate mechanical toys may be, simply carved wooden animals will always be among the favorites of children. Eternal toys often utilize some basic law of physics, and therefore the appeal is less altered by style, fad, or culture than are many more elaborate toys. Many **folk toys** have this kind of perpetual appeal, as do building **blocks, balls,** and **tops.**

ethyl alcohol. Batik and tie-dye. Toys. See **alcohol.**

ethylene dichloride. Plastics. See **acrylic cement.**

Etruscan style. Bookbinding. A **binding** style originated in the eighteenth century characterized by a calfskin cover that is stained with acid and decorated classical designs.

euclase. Gemcutting. A mineral composed of hydrated **beryl** with **hardness** of 7½ and **specific gravity** of 3; **crystals** are of the monoclinic system with perfect **cleavage** parallel to the **C axis** in one direction. It has refractive indices of 1.658 and 1.677 with mild dichroism and a vitreous **luster.** Euclase is transparent and occurs in colorless, blue, and yellow-green varieties. Main crown **facets** are cut at 43° and main pavillion facets at 39°; polish with tin oxide on a tin **lap.** Also see **abrasive, faceting, polishing, refraction.**

European oak. Woodworking. See **oak.**

eutectic. Jewelry. Metalworking. Any **alloy** formed at the lowest solidification temperature of any of the components, to insure a uniform melting temperature.

Evening Star. Quilts. Either of two **pieced block** designs that suggest stars. The six-pointed Evening Star is made up of **diamonds**; the eight-pointed one is formed from squares and triangles. Also see **star patterns.**

even point draw. Weaving. See **point draw.**

even-sided weave. Weaving. See **balanced weave.**

exhaust a dyebath. Dyeing. See **exhaust bath.**

exhaust bath. Dyeing. A **dyebath** that has already been used but that still contains color potency and will color fresh fibers. As a rule, the term "exhaust bath" is mainly used in conjunction with **synthetic dyes**, where salt is added as the exhausting agent that forces the rest of the dye out of the water and into the yarn or fabric. To exhaust a dyebath means to draw out the fullest dye possible from it.

exhausted dye. Batik and Tie-dye. A **dye** is said to be "exhausted" when most of the coloring matter has been absorbed by or soaked into the fabric. In **tie-dye** a fabric may be placed in the **dyebath** for only a short period of time, which means there is still coloring matter that can be used for a second, usually paler, color.

exotherm. Plastics. The heat given off during the **curing** of **resins.** Exotherm should be controlled when **casting,** or the following undesirable results may occur: milky surface, **brittleness,** discoloration, **cracking,** or igniting. To reduce the exotherm, lessen the amount of **promotor** and **catalyst in thick pours, cast** in a series of pours rather than in one large pour, use **fillers** in the resin, or use a **mold** material that conducts the heat away from the plastic.

expanded plastic. Plastics. See **foam.**

expanded polystyrene. Plastics. See **foam.**

expanded polyurethane. Plastics. See **foam.**

expanding. Papercrafts. Any of various techniques by which a piece of paper is enlarged in volume by cutting. For example, by folding a rectangle in **accordion pleating,** then cutting slits into the folded sides in alternating rows, the shape, when unfolded, expands to form an open meshwork pattern much larger than the original sheet of paper. Other shapes, such as a circle, can be folded and cut similarly to expand. See ill.

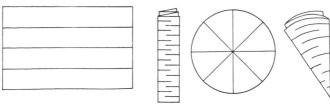

a. Expanding a rectangle b. Expanding a circle

expansion. Metalworking. See **coefficient of linear expansion, distortion.**

expansion bit. Woodworking. See **drill bit.**

exposed warp tapestry. Weaving. (Also called open warp tapestry.) **Tapestry** techniques in combination with the **warp** entirely unwoven and exposed. It is usually the so-called background that is left exposed or open, and the design covering the warp appears to float in front of the open warp. The tapestry woven design should be solidly in the warp so that it will not shift out of position. The warp yarn should have inherent beauty so that exposing it will add to the overall aesthetic quality. It should also be strong, as it will be holding together the heavier tapestry areas. This technique of leaving open warp has become popular during the last fifteen years and is thought to be very contemporary; but it was done by the early Peruvians and the ancient Chinese.

extender. Fabric printing. (Also called reduction paste.) A clear paste of **thickener** made to the same consistency as the **dye paste** but without color, used to dilute the color of dye paste or **textile color.**

extension arm. Jewelry. A metal form bolted down to a work bench or a heavy upright log about a foot high. It has a square hole for housing the **tang** of a **stake.**

exterior spar varnish. Woodworking. See **varnish.**

extra binding. Bookbinding. A flawlessly executed hand binding.

extrusion. Ceramics. Clay forced through a die on a **pug mill** or wad box to form bricks and pipes.

eye beads. Beadwork. An ancient type of **bead** with a spot or ring, suggesting an eye. Early eye designs were painted on clay beads. Later, techniques were developed in glass **beadmaking** for many variations of eye beads. The eye was considered a potent protection against evil or harm, or "the evil eye." Strings of eye beads were cherished and handed down from one generation to the next as insurance against the ills of life.

eyelet. Kites. A small metal ring that can be punched into the **covering** of a cloth kite with a machine called an eyeleter. The eyelet, like a **grommet,** reinforces an opening in the cloth against tearing.

eyelet. Leatherwork. A **finding**, shaped as a one-piece metal tube with a rim which, when placed in a pre-punched hole in leather and struck with a **mallet,** is spread to form an overlapping rim around the hole. The eyelet is used to reinforce and finish many leather articles with punched holes, such as belt holes, drawstring holes, etc. To set an eyelet, a hole is first punched with a **revolving punch** or a small round **drive punch.** Place the eyelet in the hole with the rim on the grain side of the leather; with the leather grain side down over a hard surface, place the eyelet setter in the open end of the eyelet (on flesh side); hold the eyelet setter vertically and strike firmly with a mallet. The eyelet will be spread outward, forming a second rim on the flesh side which holds the eyelet in place. See ill. Also see **eyelet punch, grommet** and **Leatherwork: Tools and Materials.**

Eyelet and setter

eyelet. Weaving. See **openwork technique.**

eyelet buttonhole. Knitting. See **Bébé buttonhole.**

eyeleteer. Rugmaking. Weaving. See **bodkin.**

eyelet embroidery. Embroidery. See **white work.**

eyelet punch. Leatherwork. A tool similar to a paper punch, for setting small **eyelet**s for decoration and **lacing.** It is available in sewing and notions shops.

eyelet setter. Leatherwork. See **eyelet.**

eyelet stitch. Knitting. The term "eyelet" encompasses a number of stitch patterns. The eyelet stitch is a unit composed of two knitting actions—an over increase and a decrease—and can vary in size or be doubled.
Method:

Row 1: yo, k 2 tog, or yo, s 1, K 1, psso.
Row 2: P across row.
Double eyelet:
Row 1: K 2 tog, yo 2, s 1, K 1, psso.
Row 2: P across row, P first over, knit second over.
Chain eyelet:
yo, k 2 tog.
Open eyelet:
yo, s 1, K 1, psso.

eyelet stitch. Needlepoint. See **Algerian eyelet stitch.**

eye loupe. Jewelry. (Also called jeweler's loupe.) A magnifying lens used to examine small detail. It is used in the manner of a monocle. There are also spectacle loupes, which fit onto eyeglasses, visor units with lenses that flip down and up, adjustable stand magnifiers, and diamond loupes, which fold into a pocket-sized case.

eye protector. Metalworking. Plastics. Woodworking. Wear goggles or a face shield when **grinding,** sanding, or **cutting** metals with any power tools. Full face shields should be used when pouring molten metal for **casting.** Use specially designed and ventilated goggles for gas **welding,** and full **arc welding** helmets when using any form of arc- or electric-welding equipment. Also see **arc-welding equipment, oxyacetylene welding equipment.**

eye shields. Jewelry. Shatterproof plastic glasses or **goggles** worn to protect the eyes during operations such as **grinding** and **buffing.** Also see **Jewelry: Safety Precautions.**